A DOMINANT CHURCH

Liam Swords

A
DOMINANT
CHURCH

The Diocese of Achonry 1818–1960

the columba press

First published in 2004 by

the columba press

55A Spruce Avenue, Stillorgan Industrial Park, Blackrock, Co Dublin

Designed by Bill Bolger
Printed in Ireland by ColourBooks Ltd, Dublin

ISBN 1-85607-395-5

CONTENTS

LIST OF ABBREVIATIONS

ADA	Achonry Diocesan Archives
Adm.	Administrator
AD UCD	Archives Department University College Dublin
Adj.	Adjutant
A/G	Adjutant-General
APCK	Association for Discountenancing Vice and promoting the Knowledge and Practice of the Christian Religion
APF	Archives of the Congregation 'de Propaganda Fide', Rome
Arch. Hib.	*Archivium Hibernicum*
ASU	Active Service Unit
ASV	Archivio Segreto Vaticano, Vatican City, Rome
Batt.	Battalion
CDB	Congested Districts Board
CID	Criminal Investigation Department
C-in-C	Commander-in-Chief
Coll. Hib.	*Collectanea Hibernica*
Comdt	Commandant
C/S	Chief-of-Staff
CSORP	Chief Secretary's Office Registered Papers
C.T.	*Connaught Telegraph*
DC	District Councillor
DCA	Dublin City Archives
DDA	Dublin Diocesan Archives
DI	District Inspector
D/I	Director of Intelligence
Dil. P.	Dillon Papers
DP	Distress Papers
ED	Education papers in National Archives
F.J.	*Freeman's Journal*
FP	Fenian Prisoners
GHQ	General headquarters
GPO	General Post Office, O'Connell Street, Dublin
GS & W Rly	Great Southern & Western Railway
HCSA	Habeas Corpus Suspension Act
ICP	Irish College, Paris
ICR	Irish College, Rome
INF	Irish National Federation
INL	Irish National League
IRA	Irish Republican Army
IRB	Irish Revolutionary Brotherhood
I.T.	*Irish Times*
KPS	Kildare Place Society

LHS	London Hibernian Society
L.W.	*Labour World*
MGW Rly	Midlands Great Western Railway
Nat Arch	National Archives, Dublin
NCO	Non Commissioned Officer
NLI	National Library, Dublin
NS	National School
O/C	Commanding Officer
OP	Outrage Papers
OPW	Office of Public Works
PLG	Poor Law Guardian
QM	Quartermaster
RDC	Rural District Council
R.H.	*Roscommon Herald*
RIC	Royal Irish Constabulary
RLFC	Relief Commission Papers
RM	Resident Magistrate
RSCG	Religious Sisters of Charity Generalate Archives, Sandymount, Dublin
SC Irlanda	Scritture riferite nei Congressi, APF
S.C.	*Sligo Champion*
SFFP	Society of Friends' Famine Papers
SL & NC Rly	Sligo, Leitrim and Northern Counties Railway
SOCG	Scritture originali riferite nelli Congregazioni Generali APF
TCD OL	Trinity College, Dublin, Old Library
UCD	University College, Dublin.
UIL	United Irish League
W.P.	*Western People*

LIST OF ILLUSTRATIONS

Preface

It is just five years since I wrote a short preface to Liam Swords' history of the Famine in North Connacht, *In Their Own Words*. This was the second volume in his history of the Diocese of Achonry. And now we have the third volume which brings that history into the twentieth century. Here we read accounts of many historical events of which we have heard and of people whose names are familiar to us. This, of course, brings with it an element of risk as the historian writes about people who are still remembered and members of whose families are still with us. What is seen as objective reporting by a historian may be interpreted as unfair by family relations. And yet historical integrity does not allow the historian to ignore or omit historical facts even when these may offend family friends or relations.

In this period in our history – 1818 to the 1960s – our ancestors experienced two devastating famines. After three hundred years of religious persecution Catholics were beginning to emerge, slowly at first and then more confidently, from that religious slavery but with an undaunted determination to live and die for their faith if called upon to do so. Most dioceses already had their calendar of martyrs. And now, as the opportunity arose, Irish Catholics embarked upon two great undertakings – education and the building of churches. They did these things despite the poverty and hardships which most of them endured. The devotional revolution quickly followed and this reached out to most people in the land.

The Land War had its origin in Achonry and quickly spread to the rest of Ireland. It could be seen as the first, if not the only war which the Irish people won. Here we read about the 'War of Independence' and the Civil War in the diocese, and we read through the names of those people who fought with the British army in Europe in the First World War. There is much to read about and reflect on – and this volume gives an insight into our relatively recent past. We may not like it all but it is part of what we are.

✠ Thomas Flynn
Bishop of Achonry

Introduction

The church portrayed in this volume is radically different from that described in *A Hidden Church*. There, religion was predominantly rural and home-based, steeped in long-standing customs and folk traditions preserved in the oral Irish of the people. With the various Catholic Relief Acts culminating in Catholic Emancipation, church practice emerged from the underground and followed the Tridentine norms found elsewhere in the Catholic world. Besides, the Great Famine had decimated the cottier and labourer classes who had formed the backbone of the rural church. The result was a new church-centred religion based in the growing towns and nourished by new devotional practices imported largely from continental Europe and adopted by an increasingly English-speaking population. The priest played a dominant role, not only in religion but in the new and expanding communities of shopkeepers, merchants, teachers and professional classes, while small farmers and labourers were consigned to the parish hinterland.

Chapters are divided into four sections, two thematic and two chronological. The book opens with a thematic section of four chapters, beginning with an account of bishops and priests which will hopefully make the reader familiar with the names of the *dramatis personae* who feature throughout the work. This is followed by chapters on education and social life. The next section is chronological, detailing local involvement in the major national movements beginning with Catholic Emancipation and the Tithe War and ending with the Land War and the Parnell Split. Remote and insignificant as Achonry may be, it sometimes played a surprisingly important role in some of these movements, particularly the Land League, where the dominant figures, Michael Davitt, John Dillon, Anne Deane and Denis O'Hara were all natives or had close associations with the diocese, while the bishop, F. J. MacCormack enjoyed a popularity among Land Leaguers second only to that of Archbishop Croke of Cashel.

Another thematic section follows, again comprising four chapters dealing with church-building, the foundation of convents which radically altered the religious landscape, and parish missions which contributed to a 'devotional revolution', the growth of towns and the development of secondary education. The final section, 1914-1925, is chronological and covers the war years, including the First World War, the 'war' of Independence and the Civil War. The book concludes with a short aftermath giving a broad outline of later developments up to the sixties and seventies.

Certain editorial decisions were made at the outset. No ecclesiastical titles are attributed to bishops or priests in this volume for a number of reasons, not least the practical consideration that they would greatly enlarge what is already a substantial volume. As it happens the five bishops who figure largely in this work present almost no identification problem as three of them, MacCormack, Lyster and Morrisroe, have surnames which do not occur elsewhere among the diocesan priests, while Patrick McNicholas and Patrick Durcan are given the title of 'Bishop' to distinguish them from other priests with similar surnames. With the exception of 'Canon', there is no very convincing historical precedence for the use of other titles. 'Reverend', 'Very Reverend' and 'Most Reverend' were apparently adopted from the Established Church. Even the more cherished 'Father' is of relatively recent vintage. For much of the nineteenth century Achonry was Irish-speaking and priests were referred to as *An Sagart* which was translated in official documents as 'the Priest' followed by his surname. 'Father' was originally used to designate religious order priests, such as Franciscans, Dominicans etc, and later adopted by diocesan priests. These were frequently addressed as 'Mr', certainly in the first half of the nineteenth century. Even in the later decades of that century, female religious were commonly referred to as 'Mrs' before they began to adopt religious names with the titles of 'Mother' and 'Sister'. Parish priests here are identified as 'of' the parish where they ministered, such as 'John Coleman of Swinford', 'Denis Tighe of Ballymote' etc.

This work is not intended as a mere ecclesiastical history of the diocese but as a social and political history describing the life and times of its inhabitants. Nor is it intended to give a detailed history of each of its parishes. Ideally the writing of such histories should have preceded this work and if some parishes, like Kiltimagh, receive greater prominence than others in these pages it may well be because the author could draw upon a reservoir of information from its own published local history. Others, like Foxford, had part of their history well chronicled in the convent archives. As in the earlier volumes, extensive use is made here of *marginalia* and footnotes. Histories such as these are rarely read from cover to cover. Most readers tend to dip in from time to time, usually in search of some item of local interest and the *marginalia* should greatly facilitate such searches. This volume is the result of extensive researches over many years in numerous archives in several countries and the copious footnotes provided here are intended to help and perhaps inspire local historians to revisit these sources in compiling their own histories. Experience has shown from the two previous volumes that amateur genealogists scour these histories for clues to their ancestors and the several appendices in this volume with numerous family names should be of special interest to them.

The history of Achonry now comprises three volumes, *A Hidden Church, In Their Own Words* (devoted to the Great Famine in the north-west) and the present volume. This whole project, which was a labour of love for me, was the brainchild of the bishop, Thomas Flynn. Future generations doubtlessly will applaud his initiative and these volumes will represent a significant part of his legacy to the diocese. I wish also to show my appreciation to the priests of the diocese for their co-operation, particularly in the compilation of the list of missionaries from each parish. The extent of many of these lists are indicative of the enthusiasm of the priests in accepting this challenging undertaking. A special word of thanks is due to Paddy Kilcoyne, Jim Finan, Joe Spelman, Eugene Duffy, Joe Caulfield and the late Dudley Filan, whose other contributions are duly acknowledged elsewhere in the book. Above all, Martin Jennings and John Doherty deserve a very special mention.

My thanks are also due to Mary Ann Bolger, Dublin, Dan Bray CSSR, Dundalk, Mary Eugenia Brennan SJG, 14B Connolly St, Wembley, Western Australia, Mícheál Campbell, Swinford, Castlebar County Library, Phyl Clancy RSM, Swinford, Mary Clarke, archivist, and staff of Dublin City Archives, Vincent Coleman, Carracastle, Michael Collins, Benada, Mary Convey, Swinford, Prof. John Coolahan, Maynooth, Thomas Davitt CM, Dublin, Luke Dempsey OP, Rome, Michael Farry, Trim, Ivor Hamrock, County Library, Castlebar, Thomas Hennigan, Killasser, Michael Hughes OMI, Inchicore, Alvarez Kelly SM, Charlestown, Kevin Laheen SJ, Dublin, Mark Leonard of W.H. Byrne & Son, architects, Suffolk St, Dublin, Brian MacAongusa, Dublin, Frank McCarrick, Maynooth, Pius McCarthy FLG, Dublin, Brigid M. McGuinness SM, Tubbercurry, Denis MacManus CSSP, San Francisco, Máirtín McNicholas, Dublin, J. C. McTiernan, Sligo, Joe Mellet, Swinford, Michael Murphy, Killasser, Emer O Boyle, Dublin,

Maurice O'Connell, Swinford, Marie Bernadette O'Leary RSC, Dublin, Andy O'Loughlin, Dublin, Raymond Refaussé, Representative Church Body Library, Dublin, Pat Rodgers CP, Dublin, Bernard Share, James Shryane, Barnsley, U.K., Betty Solon, Kiltimagh, Drs Tom and Ursula Staunton, Castlebar, Rita Tully, Ballaghaderreen, Brendan Woods SJ & Trish Quigley, Milltown Park Library, Dublin and Dr C. J. Woods, Dublin. I wish also to acknowledge the assistance of the director and staff of the National Archives and of the National Library, the staff of Trinity College Archives, of the Archive Department of University College Dublin and of the Architectural Archives, Dublin, of the Vatican Archives and the Archives of Propaganda Fide, Rome, as well as John Fleming, former rector of the Irish College, Rome. The actual production of this book was the work of two old friends, the designer, Bill Bolger and the publisher, Seán O Boyle, for whom no words could adequately express my appreciation.

CHAPTER ONE

'Rome's Anointed'

When Patrick McNicholas became bishop in March 1818 he found numerous
abuses prevalent in the diocese which he attributed to the fact that his immediate predecessor, John Flynn, had been paralysed for several years before his
death and Flynn's two predecessors, Charles Lynagh and Thomas O'Connor,
were non-resident and only 'visited the diocese hastily in summertime'.[1]
During these thirty years clerical discipline was seriously weakened. 'Very
many evils sprang up among the clergy, whose deadly fruit religion now
laments and will lament for some time to come.' *Patrick McNicholas*

McNicholas also inherited a deeply divided clergy arising from the bruis-
ing campaign which resulted in his own election. James Filan, his main rival
and former vicar-general, continued for a number of years 'to foment dissent
among the clergy' and McNicholas complained about him to Rome in 1822
and was advised to suspend him.[2] Six months later at the beginning of 1823
Filan repented and McNicholas asked Rome for permission to lift the
suspension and absolve him 'from the irregularities contracted by having
exercised the parochial office while under censure' and Rome somewhat
reluctantly agreed. *James Filan*

There were other parish priests, notably John Doddy, James Dalton
and Roger MacDermot, who remained unco-operative rather than openly
hostile to McNicholas. The parish priest of Kiltimagh, Patrick Grady, a clerical eccentric and now a septuagenarian, had already been suspended for
eight years by Bishop Flynn. His parishioners in Kiltimagh complained to
McNicholas several times about 'his greed, his harsh and bitter manner and
the neglect of his duties'.[3] McNicholas admonished him frequently to mend
his ways but to no avail and matters came to a head when during Sunday
Mass Grady cursed the people unless within a few days they paid him money
to which he was in no way entitled. After Grady shut the chapel door against *Patrick Grady*

1 SC Irlanda, vol 23, ff 211r-214rv
2 Sc Irlanda, vol 23, ff 633rv, 635v, 661rv, 662v; vol 24, ff 11rv, 12v, Lettere, vol 303, ff 317v, 318r,
413v-417r, 493v, 494r, 506r, 795rv, vol 304, ff 138v, 139r, Udiense, vol 61, ff 153v, 185r; see also
Swords, *A Hidden Church*, pp 369-70
3 SC Irlanda, vol 24, ff 595r, 596r, 597rv, 602rv, 603rv, 605rv, 606rv, 685rv, 686rv; see also
Swords, *A Hidden Church*, pp 371-2

McNicholas and refused to open it, the bishop publicly suspended him in front of the people and appointed James McNicholas to replace him.

Drunkenness

'Wherever the pastor is endowed with piety, doctrine and good morals,' McNicholas stated in his 1822 report to Rome, 'the people advance in piety and in their Christian lives bear abundant fruit. Alas rare are the priests endowed with these virtues!'[4] Some priests were addicted to drink. Patrick Sweeney, 'who by drunkenness and bad behaviour inflicted great wounds on religion, but at length repented, went to America and there behaves himself well.' McNicholas suspended two others, John Doddy, a parish priest and his curate, Michael Fitzmaurice. Doddy was later restored when he showed signs of reform but Fitzmaurice was irreformable. One of the Augustinians in Benada was also addicted to drink while his two colleagues were 'not particularly commendable for their morals'. McNicholas painted a very bleak picture of the quality of his clergy. 'Other priests are liable to censures on strict points of law but taking into account this region I am not sure whether it would be in the interests of religion to impose them and therefore I have abstained from so doing. By persuasion and opportune threats, I hope to bring some of them back to proper norms of behaviour.'

Maynooth

McNicholas inherited another problem with some priests ordained by his predecessor without any formal training or spiritual formation. 'Would that bishops be rigidly restrained from ordaining such candidates unless they had previously undergone a period of spiritual formation in Maynooth College where they are carried out in an orderly manner and at least a two year course in theology in some recognised seminary.' Rome agreed whole-heartedly with him and the Congregation of Propaganda stated that in future no one should be ordained not only without completing at least a two-year course in theology but also without having shown definite signs of integrity and good morals, and doing a ten-day retreat.[5] There were already some students from the diocese in Maynooth at their own expense and McNicholas had performed the ordinations there twice in his first four years at the invitation of Archbishop Troy of Dublin. As a former professor and president of the lay college, Maynooth offered the only prospect for an optimistic future. 'There are many junior clerics trained in Maynooth College who by their probity of morals and ardent zeal, give great hope that in a few years the ancient discipline will revive and evils now flourishing will be rooted out.'

Conferences

A conference of parish priests and curates was held in the month of September each year where moral theology questions and discipline were

4 SC Irlanda, vol 23, f 614rv
5 Lettere, 18 May 1822, vol 303 ff 413v-417r

discussed and each priest was obliged to prepare two short sermons in Irish adapted to the ordinary people. McNicholas told Rome that because of the lack of a suitable place it was not possible to hold a diocesan synod, but the authorities there showed little awareness of the material conditions of the church in Achonry when they suggested that he could use the 'diocesan cathedral or his episcopal residence' to house the synod. McNicholas was then living in Collooney where he may have been sharing a house with the parish priest, James Henry, and in fact he remained there for the first thirteen years of his episcopacy.

From the River, Collooney.

Collooney

James Henry had led the campaign for the election of McNicholas as bishop and it was not long before he reaped his reward. In May 1821 McNicholas recommended three names to Rome for the post of apostolic notary, i.e. the person whose duty it was to authenticate official church documents in the diocese.[6] The first of the three listed was James Henry, followed by Patrick Durcan, a 'theological expert' and then administrator in Ballaghaderreen, and Patrick McDonnell, prefect of the recently established seminary in the diocese. Rome nominated Henry for the post the following August and one of his first official acts was to sign McNicholas' report to Rome (*Relatio Status*) on the state of the diocese on 9 January 1822.

James Henry

McNicholas sent three names to Rome in July 1836 to fill the vacant deanship, with James Henry top of the list, followed by Patrick Durcan, parish priest of Ballymote and Richard Fitzmaurice, parish priest of Keash. Rome appointed Henry as dean.[7] Five years later Henry suffered a stroke which left him paralysed and in July 1831 McNicholas once more proposed three names

Deans

6   SC Irlanda, vol 23, ff 354rv, 355rv; Lettere, vol 302, ff 348v, 349r
7   Udiense, vol 67, ff 183r, 957rv; Lettere, vol 307 f 480r, vol 308, f 8v

to Rome to replace him, Patrick Durcan, Bernard O'Kane and another James Henry.[8] Before nominating Durcan as his replacement, Rome insisted on first receiving Henry's letter of resignation which was signed for him by Durcan's brother, Bernard.[9] Patrick Durcan also replaced Henry in Collooney while he himself was replaced in Ballymote by Bernard O'Kane.

Ballaghaderreen   McNicholas had taken up residency in Ballaghaderreen by the summer of 1831 and probably moved there when James Henry suffered a stroke.[10] Shortly after he became bishop in 1818 he asked Rome for the parish of Ballaghaderreen as a mensal together with Tourlestrane because of the poverty of the diocese.[11] He was the first commoner bishop of the diocese with no family money to support him and therefore needed an income from the diocese. Of his two mensal parishes Ballaghaderreen was easily the more prosperous, which probably accounted for his decision to establish his episcopal seat there. Geographically it was a strange choice as it was the only parish in the diocese situated in County Roscommon.

Apart from periodic requests for the renewal of faculties or specific dispensations he carried on very little correspondence with Rome and, surprisingly, made no other report on the state of the diocese, though bishops were required to submit such reports every five years. Six such reports in Latin, which could scarcely have posed a problem to a former professor of that language, should have been made during the remaining thirty years of his episcopacy. Among his last communications with Rome were acknowledgements of the contributions sent in 1847 and 1848 for the relief of the famine victims in the diocese.[12] He was inactive for the last few years of his life and suffered periodically from bouts of insanity. He did not attend the Synod of Thurles in 1850, sending instead Bernard Durcan of Swinford to represent the diocese. Cardinal Cullen was the first to inform Rome when he died in February 1852. 'He was fairly old and could not do anything for many years.'[13]

Election   Archbishop John MacHale informed Rome on 24 February of the death of McNicholas and the election of Patrick Durcan as the vicar-capitular. A new set of rules for the selection of bishops had been drawn up by the Congregation of Propaganda Fide on 1 June 1829 and subsequently published on 17 October of that year. All parish priests were to meet and elect by

8   SC Irlanda, vol 25, f 458r; Lettere, vol 312, ff 601v, 602r, vol 313, ff 37v, 661r, 691v, 858rv; Udienze, vol 79, f 49rv
9   Udiense, vol 79, f 49rv
10 Lettere, vol 312, ff 601v, 602r
11 Udiense, vol 56, f 607v
12 SC Irlanda, vol 29, ff 200rv, 271r, 272v, 335r, 336v
13 SC Irlanda, vol 31, ff 96r, 97rv, 98rv, 99v

secret vote three candidates who would be designated *dignissimus* (most worthy), *dignior* (very worthy) and *dignus* (worthy), a three-some referred to as a *terna*. The bishops of the province subsequently met to give their opinion of those designated candidates and all information was sent to Rome where the cardinals of Propaganda studied the qualities of the proposed candidates and made a recommendation to the Pope. His final choice need not necessarily have been one of the three recommended.

John MacHale

MacHale convened on 15 March a meeting in the chapel in Ballaghaderreen of all the parish priests for the election of a new bishop.[14] The administrator in Ballaghaderreen, John Howley, acted as secretary while Bernard Durcan and Peter Brennan of Gurteen were appointed scrutineers (*scrutatores*). Nineteen votes were cast of which Patrick Durcan received fifteen and was thus judged *dignissimus*, Bartholomew Costello, parish priest of Crossmolina, and vicar-general of Killala received three, while Bernard Durcan got one. It is tempting to conjecture that his solitary vote was cast by his older brother, Patrick. The results were signed by the archbishop, the secretary and the two scrutineers, sealed and despatched to Rome on the same day.

The bishops of the province met in Tuam on 24 March to give their opinions on the three candidates proposed by the priests of Achonry.[15] Bernard Durcan, who was fifty years old, suffered from a foot ailment which as he grew older caused him to limp. Thus he lacked 'both the dignity and physical vigour that the episcopal status required' though he was in no way inferior to the other two 'in zeal, piety and other spiritual talents'. Bartholomew Costello was also fifty years old and about seventeen years previously had been among those recommended as bishop of the diocese of Killala. If it had been a question of some diocese other than Achonry the bishops would have favoured Costello as his age made him more suitable for carrying out the duties of a bishop. Patrick Durcan was sixty years old and, while he had all the necessary qualities, the bishops expressed some reservations. They could not decide between Costello and Durcan.

Provincial meeting

Given the inconclusiveness of the provincial bishops, Rome decided to consult Archbishop Paul Cullen on 7 April. Cullen had been appointed Archbishop of Armagh just over two years previously and from then Rome was to rely heavily on his advice in Irish episcopal appointments and other

Paul Cullen

14 Udiense, vol 115, ff 489v, 518rv, 519rv; Acta, vol 214 (1852), f 361r
15 Acta, vol 214 (1852) ff 361v, 362r

church affairs.[16] The fact that Durcan had got the vast majority of the votes of the clergy, Propaganda suggested, should not be taken as evidence of his outstanding merit. 'Daily experience shows how much it is necessary to proceed always with greater caution in these choices.' Rome decided to defer its decision until Cullen had furnished them with more information on the three candidates and had expressed his own opinion. He consulted a 'trustworthy' parish priest and a bishop from the western province. The priest assured him that while Durcan had an excellent reputation as a good and pious parish priest and a man of prudence, Costello had more talent for governing and reforming the diocese. With the defect in Bernard Durcan's leg, he could not walk without difficulty but as McNicholas' representative at the Synod of Thurles had shown prudence and judgement, according to Cullen.

Propaganda Meeting

Meanwhile, a letter had arrived in Rome from Edward Murray, a priest of Killala diocese, making a number of accusations against Costello, mainly that he never recited his breviary. The Congregation of Propaganda Fide, comprising nine cardinals with their prefect, Cardinal Fransoni, met on 22 June to discuss the appointment to Achonry.[17] A summary of all the relevant documents had been prepared by the secretary, including the report of the priests meeting in Ballaghaderreen, 15 March, of the meeting in Tuam on 24 March of the provincial bishops, the letter from the Killala priest, 15 April, and Paul Cullen's letter from Drogheda, 14 May 1852. The secretary had also retrieved from the archives the comments made by the provincial bishops in November 1834 on Costello, who was then one of the three candidates proposed for the diocese of Killala. He was then judged too young for the post. It also emerged from the archives that Patrick Durcan was one of three candidates proposed in 1839 for Killala which was then once more vacant.

The cardinals felt that the information provided by the Western bishops 'appeared to leave much uncertainty' and decided that the secretary should write to Cullen and MacHale seeking more information. Letters were despatched on 14 July.[18] The cardinals wished to know what was Durcan's responsibility as vicar-general for the lax regime which began among the clergy during the prolonged illness of McNicholas. Was this the reason he gained so many votes? If so, his appointment would not be for the future good of the diocese. With regard to Costello, they wanted more information on the charges made against him and on the credibility of his accuser.

16 Lettere, vol 341 (1852), ff 425v, 416v, 417r
17 Acta, vol 214 (1852), ff 354r, 355rv, 356r, 357r, 359r
18 Lettere, vol 342 (1852), f 725rv

The first to reply was John MacHale on 30 July.[19] Durcan ought not to be held responsible for the alleged state of laxity among the clergy during the deceased bishop's illness because even then McNicholas never delegated full authority to his vicar-general. He gained so many votes because of his merits and because the scarcity of outstanding priests in the diocese rarely gave the diocesan clergy an opportunity of voting for one of their own. The charges made against Costello by the priest Murray were without foundation. Murray, who had been expelled from Maynooth suffering from a mental infirmity 'scarcely dissimilar from insanity', had been subsequently ordained by his bishop without taking 'sufficient precautions'. MacHale followed with a second letter on 10 August after he had spoken to the Bishop of Killala who assured him that there was not even the slightest rumour in the diocese that Costello was guilty of the charges made against him by Murray and that he was 'completely above suspicion'.

Cullen's reply, dated 21 August, came from Dublin where he had recently moved from Armagh.[20] He made some inquiries 'but on account of the distance of those places from Dublin and the difficulty of communications', he had not been able to learn anything decisive. He believed that what Costello's accuser, Murray, had written was 'crazy or at least high on fantasy' and should not be given much credence. The charge against Durcan that, while he was vicar-general, he had not corrected the abuses prevalent in the diocese was not worth much consideration because he thought McNicholas 'did not give much power to his vicar and managed things himself or at least did not want anyone else interfering.' A few days before, Durcan's brother had written to him saying that Costello would be badly received in Achonry and that if his brother was not nominated, it would be better to seek someone else outside the *terna*. An Achonry priest had promised to visit Cullen in a few days and he promised to write again. He did write again, this time on 30 August after he had interrogated the Achonry priest on the state of the diocese and was assured that there were no 'perversions or proslytism' there, that Durcan was a good parish priest and 'still fairly active'.[21] The priests were generally opposed to Costello and it would be better to go outside the *terna* if Durcan was not chosen. His informant was even more blunt about Costello's accuser, Murray, describing him as 'completely mad'. Cullen repeated again that 'it was fairly difficult to get news from the western province of Ireland because it is remote from Dublin and communications are fairly rare.'

19 SOCG, vol 975 (1852), ff 569r, 570v
20 SOCG, vol 975 (1852), ff 571v, 572r
21 SOCG, vol 975 (1852), ff 573v, 574r

Letter from Achonry

A letter signed by fifteen parish priests pointed out that all Achonry parish priests but three had voted for Durcan.[22] 'It is not without sorrow, therefore, and surprise that we have heard that representation had been made to the Sacred Congregation, that he (Durcan) was less suitable for episcopal duties, because of his advanced age and poor health. With all sincerity we declare this allegation, particularly regarding his health, to be untrue: on the contrary that he enjoys the best of health. We also declare him suitable in every way to fulfil successfully the office of bishop in this diocese.'

Patrick Durcan

The cardinals of Propaganda Fide met for the second time on 28 September and were presented with a new report comprising all the correspondence, including the petition from fifteen Achonry priests, received since their last meeting on 22 June.[23] They decided to recommend Patrick Durcan to the pope to be the new Bishop of Achonry and his brief was issued on 4 October and sent to John MacHale to be transmitted to Durcan. Significantly, Paul Cullen was also informed about Durcan's appointment on the same day, 6 October.[24] Durcan was consecrated by MacHale, assisted by George Browne of Elphin and Thomas Feeney of Killala, in the presence of John Duggan of Clonfert on 13 November, the feast of St Andrew, in his own new church in Collooney.

Mensals

Conveying this information to Rome on 15 December, Durcan availed of the opportunity to request the parishes of Kilmactigue (Tourlestrane) and

Patrick Durcan
(courtesy Thomas Flynn)

Kilcolman and Castlemore (Ballaghaderreen) as mensals as his predecessor had.[25] Rome appeared to be under the impression that there were three parishes involved and in January 1853 consulted with MacHale whether 'all these parishes' should be granted to the Bishop of Achonry. MacHale enlightened them on this point and they were eventually granted to Durcan on 13 March 1853. Later in December 1854 he wrote to Rome seeking to exchange a part of Ballaghaderreen parish for part of Gurteen to make it more convenient for parishioners to attend Mass on Sundays.[26]

At the same time he requested permission to appoint Terence O'Rorke as his successor in Collooney. As Durcan had been appointed dean by Rome, it reserved to itself the right to appoint to the parish he had held. O'Rorke, then a professor in the Irish College, Paris

22 SOCG, vol 975 (1852) f 577rv: Acta, vol 214 (1852), ff 498v, 499r
23 Acta, vol 214 (1852), ff 496v-499r
24 Lettere, vol 342 (1852), ff 971rv, 972v
25 Udiense, vol 117, ff 43rv,44rv; see also SC Irlanda, vol 32, f 260rv; Lettere, vol 343 (1853), ff 22rv, 23r, 24v
26 Udiense, vol 120, ff 2721r, 2758r

was about thirty-five years old and Collooney, which was his first and only appointment in the diocese, was his native parish. Durcan recommended his brother, Bernard, to succeed himself as dean and Rome duly complied with his request.[27] Durcan took part in August 1853 with Killala, Clonfert, Kilfenora and Kilmacduagh in the Synod of Tuam presided over by MacHale and five years later he attended another synod there, this time accompanied by Bernard, who attended as an expert.

Monsignor Kirby of the Irish College Rome presented Durcan's first report on the state of Achonry diocese to Propaganda on 1 June 1862. Durcan, who was then about seventy years old, asked to be dispensed from making his *ad limina* visit on his doctor's advise.[28] This first such report for forty years was very brief and short on detail. There were now thirty-four churches in the diocese (including a cathedral) as against twenty-three in 1822. Durcan had held three diocesan synods during his ten years in office and had carried out a visitation of the diocese every three years. The priests held conferences in the months of May, June, July and August and there was also a priests' retreat each year. Durcan, who was a native of Tourlestrane, solemnly dedicated the church there in 1865 to St Attracta on her feastday, 11 August, and Rome granted a plenary indulgence to all who attended the dedication and in perpetuity to those who go to confessions and communion in the church on her feastday.[29]

Relatio Status

Durcan wrote to Cardinal Barnabo at the end of October 1869 requesting to be exempted because of his age and poor health from attending the Vatican Council which had been summoned by Pope Pius IX.[30] He was then seventy-nine years old. A month later the pope duly dispensed him and thus Achonry, in the persons of their bishops, was to miss the two great church events of the nineteenth century, the Synod of Thurles in 1850 and the First Vatican Council in 1870. The decree on papal infallibility was the council's major contribution and a victory for ultramontanists like Cullen. It was opposed by John MacHale who had gallican sympathies. He left the council early to avoid having to accept publicly the new decree.

First Vatican Council

One of the Irish bishops at the Vatican Council presented an unsigned memorandum to Cardinal Barnabo on 22 April 1870 on the necessity of appointing coadjutors in both Killala and Achonry because of the great age and poor health of the incumbents.[31] The memorandum was written in

Gilloolys Memorandum

27 Udiense, vol 120, ff 2721r, 2758r; Lettere, vol 346 (1855) f 807v
28 Udiense, vol 141, f 1823
29 Udienze, vol 149, ff 303r, 313r
30 SC Irlanda, vol 36, f 593rv
31 SC Irlanda, vol 36, ff 692v, 693r; Udiense, vol 164, ff 549v, 582rv

French and the anonymous author was undoubtedly Gillooly of Elphin who almost always communicated with Rome in that language. Durcan was almost eighty years old and though he occasionally visited parishes to administer confirmation and regularly attended priests' conferences, he did not know what was going on in the diocese and had no influence over the clergy, who did as they pleased. All the parish priests were young and inexperienced and a majority of them sympathised with Fenianism. Some were addicted to drink and the sudden deaths of priests were attributed to this vice. No priest in the diocese was qualified for the episcopacy and the writer suggested as a possible coadjutor, a Passionist, Pius Devine, a native of the diocese and a nephew or cousin of Bishop Durcan.

Laurence Gillooly

Coadjutor for Durcan

He also suggested that the two dioceses might be united. 'It would seem therefore advantageous, in so far as the local situation allowed, to unite them under the same bishop or administrater. If, however, the clergy or people of one or other diocese, especially of Killala, were opposed to this arrangement, it should not be attempted. The question could be submitted to the bishops of the province and then to the clergy of the dioceses in question, provided the Holy See judged the suggested unification prudent.'

Barnabo discussed the memorandum with Paul Cullen who agreed with its contents and it was decided that the two bishops, Durcan of Achonry and Feeney of Killala should be asked to request coadjutors. Propaganda's letter to Durcan was a masterpiece of tact, scrupulously careful not to ruffle any episcopal feathers: 'It is reported to the Sacred Congregation that Your Lordship, on account of advanced age after so many heroic labours in the Lord's vineyard, is less equal to fulfilling all the duties of the pastoral ministry and thus it might not perhaps be inopportune if the Supreme Pontiff in his kindness were to grant you the assistance of a coadjutor bishop.'[32] Following the custom prevailing in Ireland, the bishop was encouraged to summon a meeting of parish priests to elect three candidates for coadjutor bishop. Accepting Rome's decision, Durcan insisted that he carried out all his episcopal duties despite his age and pointed out that diocesan funds were limited and 'not sufficient for the decent support of two bishops'.[33]

The same procedure was being followed in Killala where shortly afterwards

32 Lettere, vol 363 (1870), ff 381rv, 382r
33 SOCG, vol 998 (1871), f 248rv; Acta, vol 237 (1871), f 87r

three names were put forward, Thomas MacHale, Hugh Conway and Peter Nolan. Durcan wrote to Cardinal Barnabo in July expressing his opinion in favour of Thomas MacHale for Killala whom he described as 'eminently qualified in every respect both by great learning, zeal and piety and by his general excellent character.'[34] MacHale, then professor of moral theology and canon law in the Irish College, Paris where he had spent the last eighteen years, was, more importantly, the nephew of the Archbishop of Tuam. The latter was then, perhaps conveniently, 'not at home' just then and could not summon the usual meeting of the provincial bishops to express their views on the three proposed candidates and had asked Durcan to send Rome his own choice.

The Terna

Acknowledging his letter a week later, Rome told Durcan bluntly to get on with his own election as Propaganda intended to make the two appointments at one and the same general meeting of the Congregation.[35] In fact, the very next day, 21 July, before he received that letter from Rome, Durcan presided at a meeting of parish priests in the cathedral in Ballaghaderreen.[36] Matthew Finn of Kilmovee acted as secretary while Roger Brennan of Gurteen and Bernard Durcan acted as scrutineers. Terence O'Rorke of Ballysadare topped the poll with nine votes, while Matthew Finn and John McDermott of Tubbercurry were joint seconds and a single vote each was cast for the Passionist, Pius Devine, a Sligo Dominican, Bernard Goodman and Bernard Durcan. The names of the first three (the *terna*) were despatched to Rome on that same day.

Episcopal Split

Normally this should have been followed by a meeting of the bishops of the province to express their opinions on the three proposed candidates but only MacHale and Durcan attended the meeting in Tuam on 25 August and they complained about the absence of their colleagues from Elphin and Galway.[37] 'We do not know the motives which led these two bishops to act against the explicit prescriptions of the 1829 decree to the obvious detriment of ecclesiastical discipline.' Gillooly of Elphin and John McEvilly of Galway, while in Rome attending Vatican I, had expressed reservations about the present system of the provincial bishops meeting together to discuss the merits of candidates. 'When the bishops were assembled together, it happened very often in spite of the different opinions they had of the merits of the candidates, only one view was presented to the Holy See, which was the opinion

34 SOCG, vol 998 (1871), ff 262rv, 263rv
35 Lettere, vol 364 (1870), ff 578v, 579r
36 SOCG, vol 998 (1871) f 250rv; Acta, vol. 237, f. 87rv
37 SOCG, vol 998 (1871), ff 257rv, 258r; Acta, vol 237 (1971), ff 89v, 92r

of one or other bishop who enjoyed a greater influence in the province.' They obviously had MacHale in their sights and the dominant role he exercised in these matters in the province, declaring that the situation was particularly exacerbated when one of the candidates was related to a bishop or archbishop. Propaganda was reluctant to tamper with the 1829 decree which ordered that the provincial bishops would meet together to discuss the merits of the candidates, thus assuring greater transparency, but given the present particular circumstances in Killala and Achonry it was agreed to permit Elphin and Galway communicate separately with Rome.

Terence O'Rorke   In reality there was a remarkable convergence of views among the western bishops on the proposed candidates for Achonry. Terence O'Rorke was now the archdeacon but apparently no longer enjoyed the favour of his bishop, as both he and MacHale declared that 'for the honour and good name of the episcopacy he should be excluded.' Gillooly, while accepting that O'Rorke was eminent amongst the candidates for theology, eloquence and intelligence, (*ingenii ubertate*) stated that 'in the opinion of bishops and priests who had known him since his youth he was wanting in veracity, moral rectitude and ecclesiastical spirit, and such is his character that nobody could be certain about his future behaviour.'[38]

McEvilly thought O'Rorke 'completely unworthy to be promoted to the episcopal dignity.' In Maynooth he was not numbered among those who had a reputation for piety and McEvilly did not believe that he had improved in this respect since he became a parish priest. Patrick Moran, Bishop of Dunedin in New Zealand (subsequently Cardinal Moran of Melbourne), a classmate of O'Rorke's in Maynooth told McEvilly in Rome: 'For the honour of God, don't recommend O'Rorke.' McEvilly's only explanation why he got so many votes was that he was a very warm-hearted character (*est indolis valde callidae*). He also mentioned that O'Rorke did not know Irish which was a prerequisite for a bishop in Achonry. 'For these and other reasons in my opinion, it would be dangerous to the cause of religion and the salvation of souls if O'Rorke was promoted to the episcopacy.'

Paul Cullen informed Barnabo on 7 October that O'Rorke was reputed to be very talented but there were reasons to believe he was a 'turbulent man' and the rector of the Irish College in Paris was never happy with him. Bishop Moran told Cullen that it would be 'a calamity for Ireland' if O'Rorke became a bishop and Cullen also believed that O'Rorke would probably be a follower of MacHale.[39]

38 SOCG, vol 998 (1971), ff 251rv, 252rv, 253rv, 255rv
39 SOCG, vol 998 (1871) ff 297rv, 298rv; Acta, vol 237 (1971) f 103r

There was complete unanimity about O'Rorke's unsuitability but another much more serious charge was made against him. 'Confidential revelations regarding his morals have been made to me,' Gillooly informed Rome, 'which shows him to be completely unsuitable for the episcopacy.' MacHale and Durcan were somewhat more explicit, pointing to a pervasive rumour in the diocese that O'Rorke had fathered a child. A similar rumour was circulating about Hugh Conway, one of the candidates for Killala diocese but given that his own nephew was a candidate there, MacHale's motives for introducing it in a letter about the Achonry candidates is highly suspect. In this case Rome seemingly was not swayed by the allegation as they selected Conway for Killala.

The bishops were also unanimous in their opinion on the unsuitability of John McDermott. According to Gilhooly, he came from an excellent family, probably related to the Coolavin branch of the MacDermots. He had spent some time as a professor of theology in All Hallows College, Dublin and the Irish College, Paris. However, according to Gillooly, he was a fickle character, shy of work and fond of travelling. (*Laboris impatiens et vagandi cupidus.*) 'In my opinion he is and will be not only incapable of running a diocese but even a parish. It is a wonder to me and to others that he was recommended by four parish priests.' (In fact he was only recommended by three.) McDermott's fondness for travelling was also mentioned by McEvilly. 'He scarcely seems to be happy to remain for any space of time in one place or job. If he was made a bishop it is feared he would wander excessively outside the diocese.' McEvilly also mentioned that McDermott did not know Irish. MacHale and Durcan said that McDermott spent most of his time travelling and visiting his friends. 'Above all he lacked the gravity and prudence required in a bishop.'

John MacDermott

Like John McDermott, Matthew Finn, parish priest of Kilmovee, had also received three votes. McEvilly commended his theology and piety but questioned his fitness for the job as he had recently broken his leg, which was mentioned also by Gillooly. MacHale and Durcan. also mentioned Finn's broken leg from which he suffered a lot. Gillooly described Finn as 'a fairly satisfactory parish priest but lacked the eminent qualities, both natural and supernatural, required in a bishop.' MacHale and Durcan said that Finn carried out his priestly duties in a praiseworthy manner but had nothing to offer which would enhance the honour of the episcopacy.

Matthew Finn

Of the three others who received a single vote each, the Sligo Dominican, Bernard Goodman, and Bernard Durcan of Swinford were dismissed as unacceptable on the grounds of old age and poor health. It was altogether

Pius Devine

otherwise with regard to the third, the Passionist, Pius Devine whose single vote may well have been cast by his uncle, James Devine of Carracastle. He was rector of the Passionist college in Harold's Cross, Dublin, where according to Gillooly, he had fulfilled his duties there for many years with zeal and prudence. 'He is the only one among the candidates whom I believe worthy of the episcopacy and the only one who could restore ecclesiastical discipline in that diocese.'

Pius Devine

McEvilly also came out strongly in favour of Devine, believing he would have received many more votes if he had not denounced the Fenians so bitterly in missions he had given in the diocese which prejudiced the younger parish priests against him. 'These younger parish priests in that diocese close to the diocese of Tuam are highly infected with principles and a false spirit of independence which they brought with them into the mission from Maynooth College.' Among the candidates, Devine alone would promote the good of religion and the salvation of souls and was the only one McEvilly could recommend to Rome. 'Besides, he understands the Irish language and knows clearly the diocese of Achonry and its needs.' MacHale and Durcan also supported Devine who according to them was fluent in Greek, Latin, French, English and Irish and preached both in English and Irish. Surprisingly, even though he had been a professor of theology in the Passionist college for some years, and was now the superior, he was only thirty years of age. 'He has written some works', Cullen informed Barnabo on 7 October, 'and has a reputation of being quite learned.' Devine was at the time in America visiting some of the houses of his order there and was expected to return shortly. His appointment to Achonry seemed a certainty.

Bombshell

Then came the bombshell. Cullen dashed off a note on 14 October to Mgr Kirby of the Irish College.[40] 'Today I received information regarding the same (Devine) which obliges me to request the Sacred Congregation to do nothing until I have time to investigate the matter and make a report on it.' He urged Kirby to speak immediately with Propaganda and persuade the cardinals to postpone their deliberations and if they had already made their nomination to suspend it. Cullen wrote another letter at the end of October, this time to Cardinal Barnabo. A nun had informed him that Devine had acted or spoken to her in confession in a manner which merited him being denounced. 'I believe after having examined the matter that there was nothing very serious, but the priest himself confessed that he had behaved frivolously with the nun (*che aveva fatto delle ragazzate colla monacha*) and that he had acted imprudently and without thinking.' Cullen thought it would not

40 SOCG, vol 998 (1871), ff 300r, 306rv, 313r; Acta, vol 237 (1871), ff 103v, 104v

be a good idea to promote Devine to the episcopacy 'at least for the present' but he was still young and would have time to show signs of greater prudence and caution in the future.

Cullen had informed both Gillooly and McEvilly and they wrote in haste to Rome to withdraw their support for Devine.[41] 'Though this crime does not appear to be excessively serious,' Gillooly wrote, 'it inspires the fear that given the opportunity the delinquent might offend more gravely.' McEvilly had a similar view and both of them now reluctantly and with great reservations recommended Matthew Finn.

Later in December both bishops sent a joint letter recommending a new candidate for Achonry, Patrick Duggan, the parish priest of Cummer, near Tuam.[42] Propaganda wrote in February 1871 to Cullen seeking his opinion on Duggan for Achonry and Hugh Conway for Killala and to MacHale asking him about Duggan.[43] MacHale replied that Duggan was often absent from his parish without permission and, more seriously, that his uncle and predecessor, Dominick, had suffered from a mental disease implying that it was hereditary in his family.[44] Cullen had spoken with Gillooly and McEvilly who told him that Duggan's uncle had indeed become mad and had died in that state. 'But that had happened in 1848 when because of the terrible famine and extreme poverty many others suffered in the same way.' In no case was the disease passed on to other members of the family and besides Duggan was now fifty-seven or fifty-eight and had never given any signs of this ailment. He was also a friend of Dublin's vicar-general who spoke very highly of him.

Patrick Duggan

In a postscript to their joint letter in December 1870 Gillooly and McEvilly gave the name of another priest, Francis MacCormack, the curate in Westport, as a possible candidate for Achonry but added 'perhaps not mature enough for episcopal office.' During spring and summer of 1871 MacCormack began to emerge as the front-runner. Cullen told Mgr Simeoni, secretary of Propaganda, that MacCormack was the more suitable person for Achonry as Durcan would not be happy with the choice of Duggan and McEvilly described MacCormack as 'one of the best priests in the Irish church, learned, pious, zealous and prudent.'[45]

Francis J. MacCormack

July passed and there were still no appointments not only to Achonry but also to Killala and Clonfert. Gillooly was becoming worried about the delay

Elphin's Intervention

41 SOCG, vol 998 (1871), ff 302r, 304rv; Acta, vol 237 (1871), ff 103v, 104r
42 SOCG, vol 998 (1871), f 314r; Acta, vol 237 (1871), ff 104v, 104r
43 Lettere, vol 365 (1871), ff 134rv, 135rv, 136rv, 142rv
44 SOCG, vol 998 (1871), ff 941v, 942r, 956rv
45 SOCG, vol 998 (1871), ff 943v, 949rv, 952v

and wrote on 1 August to Barnabo expressing his fears.[46] 'Disorders in the diocese of Achonry and Killala are on the increase ... Divisions and intrigues

are becoming more and more public, encouraged by your delays and the uncertainty attributed to your decisions.' 'The Reverend Fathers Duggan, Conway and MacCormack which we finally recommended respectively for the dioceses of Clonfert, Killala and Achonry are zealous, edifying and learned priests devoted to the Holy See and share the same thinking as the body of bishops. If their nomination is opposed by our venerable metropolitan, M. MacHale, it is because they are *ultramontanists* and would not join with him in opposition to our worthy cardinal. Two of them are priests of his own diocese and he wished, as it seemed, to substitute for them two others, on whom he could count as *aides de camp*. To surrender to his intrigues (*desseins*) would be to perpetuate the disorders amongst us and also to weaken for a long time to come the authority of the Holy See.'

Francis MacCormack
(*photo Vincent Sherlock*)

He urged Propaganda not to allow the opposition to be reinforced and perpetuated by nominating adherents of MacHale. 'If MacHale was to succeed in his plans it would be one of the greatest misfortunes for the Irish church.' For several years, directly through his own acts or indirectly through some of his priests, he had contested the authority of the Holy See. McEvilly informed Rome that a rumour was circulating in Galway that some ecclesiastics had proposed for Clonfert a priest who for several years was notorious for his Fenian sympathies. He again strongly recommended Duggan, among whose many virtues was devotion to the Holy See and who was more suitable for Clonfert as he was a native of the Galway portion of Tuam, while MacCormack, born in Mayo, would be best acquainted with conditions in Achonry.[47]

Bishop MacCormack

The cardinals of the Sacred Congregation of Propaganda held their general meeting on 5 September to discuss the selection of a Bishop of Clonfert and coadjutors for Achonry and Killala. Patrick Duggan was chosen for Clonfert, while the cardinals favoured Hugh Conway as coadjutor in Killala and Francis MacCormack for Achonry. A week later Propaganda wrote via McEvilly to Durcan informing them of their preference for MacCormack and asking him whether he was willing to accept him. McEvilly replied on

46 SOCG, vol 998 (1871), ff 934rv, 935r; Acta, vol 237 (1871), f 384r
47 SOCG, vol 998 (1871), f 938rv; Acta, vol 237 (1871), f 385rv

29 September, enclosing a letter which Durcan had asked him to write, indicating his willingness to accept MacCormack.[48] He was appointed on 21 November 1871 coadjutor Bishop of Achonry with the right of succession and with the title of Bishop of Claudiopolitano and the Apostolic Letters containing the briefs of appointment were sent to MacHale on 9 December to be forwarded to MacCormack and Hugh Conway of Killala.

He was consecrated in the cathedral in Ballina on 4 February 1872 by McEvilly of Galway as Durcan was too old and feeble to assist.[49] Then just one month short of his thirty-ninth birthday, he was born in Gatestreet, Ballintubber and after studying in St Jarlath's College, Tuam and Maynooth College was ordained on 14 June 1862. He served as a curate in Islandeady where he spent five years and from there was moved to Westport for a further five years before his appointment as bishop. The old bishop appointed MacCormack administrator of Ballaghaderreen and when Killasser became vacant in December 1872 with the death of John Finn, Durcan asked Rome for permission to confer it on MacCormack as a further source of income. MacCormack undertook to pay a curate £50 pounds sterling a year to look after the parish.[50]

MacCormack informed Barnabo at the end of September 1873 that the last report on the diocese (*relatio status*) had been presented in June 1862 by Mgr Kirby of the Irish College.[51] Eleven years had elapsed since and another report was overdue. Durcan was too old and infirm to make an *ad limina* visit but MacCormack was prepared to make such a visit if the cardinal would cover part of the costs. Propaganda wrote to Durcan on 18 November to persuade him to pay at least a portion of MacCormack's expenses for the journey.

Relatio Status

MacCormack presented his report in Rome on 18 January 1874. He had been not quite two years in the diocese and the report in places reflected this. There were then thirty-nine churches, 'four of them built within the last three years', and during his two years in the diocese no diocesan or provincial synod had been held. The chapter consisted of a dean, archdeacon and seven canons, all parish priests who 'take no part in the ruling of the church and in no way impede the free exercise of jurisdiction by the bishop.' There were forty-two priests in the diocese, forty native priests and two 'outsiders', 'all of good morals'. Almost all parish priests had curates. (The exceptions were Attymass, Bonniconlon, Coolaney and Straide.)

48 Lettere, vol 366 (1871), ff 792v, 793r; SC Irlanda, vol 36, f 975
49 Lettere, vol 366 (1871), ff 947rv, 1042v, 1043rv, 1090v, 1091r; SC Irlanda, vol 36, ff 1243r, 1244rv
50 Udiense, vol 174 (1873), ff 62r, 69r
51 Udiense, vol 175, ff 1027v, 1044rv; Lettere, vol 369 (1873), f 556rv

MacCormack had an equally good opinion of the laity. 'They are almost all good Catholics, some, however, are addicted to drink and a few stay away from the sacraments of confession and communion, but with God's help, these abuses can be eradicated.' Rome found his report '*vite exaratam*' and made an observation on only one item, some non-Catholic schools in the diocese 'which were attended by very few Catholics.' 'Nothing should be left undone', Rome insisted, 'so that all Catholic children should avoid or be withdrawn from non-Catholic schools.'[52]

Durcan's Death

Patrick Durcan, died on 1 May 1875 in his eighty-sixth year.[53] MacCormack presided at the Solemn Requiem Mass on 4 May attended by MacHale as well as the Bishops of Galway and Ardagh, all the priests of the diocese and some others from Tuam, Killala and Elphin. He was buried in the same tomb as his predecessor whose remains had been re-interred in the cathedral after Durcan had it built. At his Month's Mind on 2 June Terence O'Rorke was invited to preach the sermon. Bernard Durcan died in 1881 and Bishop MacCormack proposed three names to succeed him as dean, Matthew Finn of Swinford, John McDermott of Ballymote and Michael Staunton of Tubbercurry.[54] Finn was far ahead of the others in 'learning, piety and zeal', with a long record of erecting churches and establishing schools and exemplary to clergy and laity everywhere in the diocese. Finn was duly nominated.

Relatio Status 1882

MacCormack presented another report to Rome on the state of the diocese (*relatio status*) in November 1882, this time in his own right.[55] Again he painted a complimentary picture of the diocese describing the laity as 'almost all well-disposed, orthodox in faith and of good morals.' Those who did not frequent the sacraments were rare and abuses such as drunkenness and quarrelling were gradually diminishing among them. Thirty-nine native priests and four outsiders now worked in the diocese and 'almost all are of good morals and many labour zealously in the Lord's vineyard.' There were about 90,000 Catholics in the diocese (with about 3,000 others mostly Protestants) and Propaganda commented that thirty-nine priests were insufficient for such a population. In fact, there was a shortage of priests, as MacCormack himself had already informed Rome in 1876 when he sought a dispensation for Edward Connington to be ordained even though he was just over twenty-two years of age.[56] A number of years before that Michael Staunton, who had been appointed a professor in the Irish College, Paris, was recalled to the diocese before taking up this appointment because of the shortage.

52 Lettere, vol 370 (1874), ff 53v, 54r.
53 Udiense, vol 180. f 525rv; O'Rorke, *Ballysadare and Kilvarnet*, pp 512-15
54 Udienze, vol 198, ff 1665rv, 1679r
55 SC Irlanda, vol 39, ff 699r-705r
56 Udienze, vol 183, ff 853, 861rv

Almost everyone who met MacCormack were deeply impressed by him. *MacCormack's*
An Englishman, William Scawen Blunt, stopped in Sligo in April 1886 to *Popularity*
meet Laurence Gillooly who was out, 'which I don't much regret as he is a
lukewarm patriot.' From there he took the train to Ballaghaderreen and, following Michael Davitt's instructions, called at Anne Deane's. There he found
MacCormack, his chaplain and Denis O'Hara at dinner. 'The terms on which
the bishop stands with Father O'Hara and the chaplains are worthy of notice.
It is pleasant to see clergy of this kind.'[57]

The conversation turned to a frequently discussed topic of that time,
whether Catholic priests should be paid by the State. 'But they one and all
scouted it, saying they were far stronger as they are with the people. The people supply them with all they want, in some parts of the south with more
than is good for them.' Blunt commented that the unendowed Catholic
churches were flourishing in every village in Ireland, while the until recently
endowed Protestant churches were 'moulding in decay'. 'The Bishop is an
admirable little man, a man of the people, who speaks Irish and is quite without pretension, lives in a poor way and is full of the milk of human kindness.'

MacCormack was often invited to preach charity sermons, as in Castlebar
on St Patrick's Day 1884 in aid of the new presbytery, and in Knockcroghery
in 1885 in aid of St Patrick's Church there.[58] He even went as far as Dundalk
in 1881 to preach at the opening of the Redemptorist Mission House.[59] He
also enjoyed widespread popularity among clergy even outside the western
province. He came second with nine votes in 1878 in the *terna* in Longford
to chose a bishop for the diocese of Ardagh.[60]

Thomas Carr, Bishop of Galway, was appointed Archbishop of Melbourne *Transfer to Galway*
in 1886 and on 31 January 1887 the Galway priests meeting in Craughwell elected MacCormack in first place to succeed him with thirteen out of twenty-
three votes. When the provincial bishops met to express their opinions on the
candidates, four of them, including McEvilly, Gillooly, Duggan of Clonfert
and Conway of Killala, voted for MacCormack. 'We can truly assert that in
all of Ireland there is no other bishop who is held in higher esteem both
among the clergy and the people than Francis Joseph MacCormack.'[61] It was
an extraordinary tribute from his fellow bishops. His predecessor in Galway

57 William Scawen Blunt, *The Land War in Ireland*, pp 58-9
58 *C.T.* 22 Mar 1884 & 24 Oct 1885
59 I am grateful to Dan Bray CSSR for this information
60 10 Sept 1878, McGettigan of Armagh to Croke of Cashel, 'Calendar of Croke Papers',
    Collectanea Hibernica, vol 13 (1970), pp 116-7
61 SOCG, vol 1026 (1887), ff 1166rv, 1167r, 1168rv, 1169rv, 1172rv, 1173r; Acta, vol 257 (1887),
    ff 255rv, 256rv, 257rv

said MacCormack possessed 'in an eminent manner all the qualifications requisite to rule with success the united dioceses of Galway and Kilmacduagh.' Much later, at the end of December 1902, the Tuam clergy put MacCormack first with a massive thirty-two votes when they met to chose a successor to McEvilly.[62] MacCormack was then sixty-nine and John Healy, who was second with a mere nine votes, was eventually chosen by Rome.

A Formidable
Foursome

During MacCormack's time in Achonry four remarkable people came together in Ballaghaderreen: MacCormack himself, Anne Deane, Denis O'Hara and Agnes Morrogh Bernard. All four of them made their own individual mark on their time and place and though separated later all remained close friends for the rest of their lives. Anne Deane was the only one who was a native of Ballaghaderreen. 'Mrs Deane is a very clever woman of about fifty-five,' Blunt wrote in 1886, 'she is a thoroughly good person without pretense or nonsense … I have enjoyed my talks with Mrs Deane more than anything yet and they have been more instructive.' She was a woman of considerable business acumen and created a virtual emporium with almost thirty employees out of Monica Duff's which she inherited from her mother.

Her entreprenerial skills were only equalled if not surpassed by her friend Agnes Morrogh Bernard who arrived in Ballaghaderreen in 1877 as foundress

Bishop MacCormack
with niece and
husband in Waterford.
Daily Sketch,
Mon 16 Aug 1909

there of the convent of the Sisters of Charity. She moved from there to Foxford in 1891 to found another convent and later the celebrated Providence Woollen Mills. Denis O'Hara was also to prove himself an entrepreneur of considerable stature. After Durcan's death in 1875 MacCormack had taken Denis from his curacy in Kiltimagh and appointed him administrator in Ballaghaderreen and this marked the beginning of an extraordinary relationship between the two men. Both MacCormack and O'Hara were strong Home Rulers and Land Leaguers, a passion they shared with Anne Deane who became the first president of the Ladies' Land League. They also shared a deep admiration for Michael Davitt, described by MacCormack as 'Achonry's most distinguished son.' Anne Deane had Davitt's portrait hanging on a wall in her house beside that of her nephew, John Dillon.[63] All of them were deeply concerned with the plight of the poor. Agnes, the daughter of a County Cork landlord, spent her life as a religious in the service of the poor, though she was in no way involved in the political movements of the time.

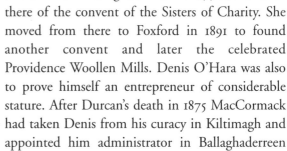

62 N.S. vol 259 (1903), ff 319r-322r
63 'From the moment she saw him she was converted to a blind idolatry.' Blunt, p 59

MacCormack earned a huge reputation in Achonry for kindness to the poor and crowds of them flocked daily to his house. His reputation followed him to Galway. 'Dr MacCormack is just the right man here', Anne Deane wrote from Galway, 'he is always surrounded by the poor and trying to help them.'[64] One of MacCormack's last official acts in Achonry was to instal Denis O'Hara as parish priest of Kiltimagh where he was to remain for the rest of his life. Both he and Anne Deane were regular visitors to MacCormack in Galway. 'The Bishop is one of the best hosts in the world,' Anne Deane wrote in 1890, 'he makes me feel as if the house were my own.' She stayed there again in the summer of 1899. 'Father Denis was with us for two days and it was like old times to us all.'[65]

Priests meeting in Swinford on 13 June 1887 to chose a successor to MacCormack elected a *terna* with Denis O'Hara in first place.[66] Ten days later the bishops of the western province met in Maynooth to give their opinions on the candidates and four of them, Tuam, Clonfert, Killala and Galway (MacCormack) came out strongly for O'Hara. Both Gillooly of Elphin and Healy, coadjutor of Clonfert, rejected O'Hara because of his political activism, particularly in the Land League and the Plan of Campaign. All the bishops rejected the other two candidates, Michael Staunton and Thomas Gilmartin. Rome, possibly influenced by the intervention of the Duke of Norfolk, rejected O'Hara and called for a new *terna* and this time Thomas Loftus of Charlestown came first followed by an Elphin priest, John Lyster. The provincial bishops unanimously recommended Lyster who was subsequently nominated by Rome on 21 February 1888.

First Terna

John Lyster was consecrated by Archbishop McEvilly, assisted by Gillooly and Healy of Clonfert on Low Sunday, 8 April 1888 in the cathedral in Sligo. MacCormack preached the sermon and made a powerful plea on behalf of the poor, for whom a bishop should have special concern. Commenting on the sermon, the *Freeman's Journal* wrote that if Lyster was looking for a model 'it would commend that set by the prelate who preceded him.' [67] Five days later Lyster was received in the cathedral in Ballaghaderreen by the clergy and people.

John Lyster

A native of Athlone, the thirty-eight year old Lyster was educated in Summerhill, the diocesan college, (where he later became a professor and president), and went on to study in Maynooth College where he achieved

64 Anne Deane to John Dillon, 22-26 Jan 1890, Dil. P. 6885
65 Anne Deane to John Dillon, 22-26 Jan 1890; same to same, 20 July 1899, Dil. P. 6889
66 For detailed account see Chapter Ten
67 *S.C* & *C.T.* 14 April 1888

first place in his class. Later he was conferred with an honorary doctorate in theology by Leo XIII. When informing Rome of the details of his consecration and reception, he asked for Tourlestrane as well as Ballaghaderreen as mensal parishes. [68]

Coadjutor for Elphin

John Lyster
(*photo Vincent Sherlock*)

Three names were submitted by the priests of Elphin to Rome in January 1891 as candidates for coadjutor to the now aging Gillooly and Lyster was joint third with Healy of Clonfert.[69] Tuam, Elphin and Galway thought it might be inopportune to transfer Lyster from Achonry as the dissensions, which preceded his appointment and which Lyster had done much to diminish, might re-emerge. The same bishops were scathing in their remarks on Healy. 'Among the ordinary people he is universally given the odious nickname of "landlord's bishop".' His appointment would be generally attributed to the intervention of the English government with the Holy See.

Gillooly, who was terrified of getting Healy as his coadjutor, wrote himself directly to Rome and left no doubt as to what he thought of Healy: 'As a priest on the mission in this diocese his conduct was passable but no more. In him piety, zeal, priestly spirit always appeared weak … Proud, stubborn, brusque, given to extreme opinions, seeking to attach himself to the rich and powerful, fond of the good life and glittering social events, he showed no sign, in my opinion, of a divine vocation to the episcopacy.' He reiterated what had been said by the provincial bishops about Healy taking the side of the government and landlords against the people who would attribute his appointment to the influence of a 'hostile government'. The only bishop who voted for him was Duggan of Clonfert who was eager to rid himself of his coadjutor. In the end Gillooly avoided the worst by dying on 15 January 1895 a few days after John Clancy was appointed as his coadjutor. After Matthew Finn's death in 1891 Lyster proposed three names to succeed him as dean, Michael Staunton, who followed him in Swinford, Roger O'Hara of Kilmovee and Thomas Loftus of Charlestown and Rome nominated Staunton on 28 December 1891.

Relationes Status

Lyster made his first *ad limina* visit to Rome in October 1890 where he had an audience with Pope Leo XIII.[70] There is no record of a report (*relatio status*) presented by him on that occasion though he may well have reported

68 Udienze, vol 227, f 1027rv
69 ICR, Kirby Papers (1891) 49; SC Irlanda, vol 45? (1891), ff 74v, 75rv, 76rv, 77r, 78v, 79rv
70 N.S. vol 69 (1895), ff 164r, 165r

verbally on the state of the diocese. It was now eight years since the last report had been made by his predecessor. His first recorded report was in October 1895, followed by two others, one in November 1900 and the other in December 1904.[71]

While bishops were expected to carry out an official visitation of every parish in the diocese every three years, Lyster in fact visited each parish 'once, twice or three times every year to preach, receive men or women into sodalities and visit schools.' By 1900 he was carrying out official visitations 'with due solemnities' every two years. MacCormack reported in 1882 that there had been no provincial synod in the previous seven years and Lyster stated in 1895 that there had been no diocesan or provincial synod since he had become a bishop. By 1900 there still had been no provincial synod but in July 1897 Lyster held a diocesan synod with full formalities while each year he held informal synods or meetings of all the clergy where he preached the sermon.

Lyster painted a glowing picture of the faith of the laity in his reports. His 1895 report attributed the improvement in religion in the previous twenty years to education of children in more and better schools with trained teachers, to the establishment of sodalities and confraternities in all the parishes, to the long hours priests spent in the confessionals and the more frequent reception of the sacraments. To the above he added in 1900 the custom of reciting the family rosary. 'This region with regard to morals was the best in the whole world.'

Rome

Wooden scaffolding for erection of spire on cathedral c. 1909 *(courtesy Thomas Flynn)*

71 N.S. vol 69 (1895), 15277, ff 140rv, 141rv, 142r; vol 1899 (1900), ff 818rv, 819rv, 820r, 821v; vol 323 (1905), ff 813rv, 814rv, 815rv, 816rv, 817rv, 818rv

Patrick Morrisroe
*(courtesy
Thomas Flynn)*

*Patrick Morrisroe
(1911-1946)*

Lyster travelled considerably both in the country and abroad. He carried out the ordinations in the Irish College, Paris and presided at the annual prize-giving in the college in June 1891, and on that occasion attended at the consecration of Basilique de Sacré Coeur in Montmartre. He was much in demand as a preacher, particularly in Scotland.[72] He preached in Glasgow at the opening of St Agnes' Church, Lambhill on 24 June 1894 and the following year gave the St Vincent de Paul appeal in St Andrew's Cathedral there. He also preached several times in St Mary's Cathedral in Edinburgh. In Ireland he preached in Loughrea in October 1897 at the laying of the foundation stone of St Brendan's Cathedral and in Belfast in 1905 at the opening of a boys' home, Nazareth House. He died abroad at the age of seventy-one on 17 January 1911 in a nursing home, Nazareth House in Hammersmith in London, where he had gone in his final illness. His remains were brought back to Ballaghaderreen and buried in St Nathy's Cathedral.

The parish priests presided over by the Archbishop of Tuam met in Swinford church on Monday 18 February to elect a successor to Lyster.[73] Patrick Morrisroe topped the poll with sixteen votes with Dean Connington and Michael Keveney of Charlestown receiving one each. Morrisroe was nominated bishop on 12 June and was consecrated on 3 September in the cathedral in Ballaghaderreen (the first bishop of the diocese to be so), with his cousin, Michael O'Doherty, who was consecrated as Bishop of Zamboanga in the Philippines. Both were natives of Charlestown. Morrisroe was educated in the diocesan college and later in Maynooth and was ordained in the cathedral in Ballaghaderreen on 2 February 1893. After a brief period as chaplain to the Sisters of Charity in Benada, he was appointed to the staff of the diocesan college and in 1896 third dean in St Patrick's College, Maynooth where he remained for fifteen years until he became a bishop.

Relationes Status

In all Morrisroe made six official reports to Rome (*relationes status*) but only two of them are available to researchers in the Vatican Archives. His first official report to Rome was dated 1917 but probably not presented until later because of the First World War, and second was made in 1922. His sixth and last report was made in 1937 just before the outbreak of the Second World War.[74]

72 Bernard T. Canning, *Bishops of Ireland 1870-1987*
73 *W.P.* 18 Feb 1911
74 Congregazio Consistoriale, Relationes Diocesium, 5. ASV 1917

CHAPTER TWO

'Maynooth Men'

The Catholic Church in Ireland in the nineteenth and twentieth centuries was remarkable in at least one important feature. For the first time since the sixteenth century the vast majority of priests in the country were educated in Ireland. Most of the priests and all of the bishops in Achonry studied in Maynooth College or in the case of a tiny fraction elsewhere in Ireland. At least two in the early part of the twentieth century studied in St Patrick's College, Carlow and one, John Horan of Keash, in St John's Waterford. St Jarlath's College in Tuam was a fully fledged major seminary in the early decades of the nineteenth century and of the ninety-five seminarians there in 1839-40, two of them were from Achonry.[1] Patrick McNicholas, who became bishop in 1818, was not only trained in Maynooth but was also a professor there for a number of years, and Patrick Morrisroe was a dean in that college for fifteen years before he was consecrated in 1911.

As bishops and priests increasingly assumed a more dominant role not only in the church but also in Irish society Maynooth tended to become a far more influential institution than just a mere seminary. 'Maynooth men', as the new breed of priests were sometimes described, were not always as highly regarded by others as they seemingly were by themselves. One English traveller described the Maynooth-trained priest as 'a coarse vulgar man or a stiff, close and very conceited man ... fully impressed with or professing to be impressed with a sense of his consequence and influence.'[2] He was often adversely compared with his predecessor, the continentally trained priest. 'No subsequent generation of Irish priests has left so good a reputation as the better class of these educated in France.' According to the historian, William Lecky, 'they had at least the manners and feelings of cultivated gentlemen and a high sense of clerical decorum.' This was the generation who had inspired the legend of the 'Soggarth Aroon', a title their home-trained successors tried unconvincingly to assume.

---

1 John Cunningham, *St Jarlath's College, Tuam, 1800-2000*, p 38
2 Henry Inglis, *Ireland in 1834*, p 392

Comparing generations of any profession is at best a hazardous undertaking. Society changes and priests like others adapt to the prevalent *mores*, often aping the admired virtues of their age. If they seemed brash, loquacious, pompous, even authoritarian and arrogant, with a fondness for titles, respect and honour, these were as much part of the 'manly' accoutrements of the Victorian period as were top-hats and riding whips. Even their critics admitted that they were 'charitable and heedful of the poor ... and grudged no privations in the exercise of their religious duties.' [3] This was especially true during periods of great hardship, such as the great famine (1845-9) or the lesser famine (1879-80) when their over-riding concern for their starving parishioners insured that they left a larger legacy of correspondence to aid agencies, government departments and newspapers than any previous or subsequent generation of priests.

A number of Achonry priests had distinguished academic careers. Terence O'Rorke, ordained in 1848, was later appointed a professor in the Irish College, Paris where he spent five years. They were turbulent years in the

college and among his colleagues there was the later notorious Patrick Lavelle who was already showing signs of the formidable agitator he was later to become. Michael Staunton, ordained in 1866, spent some time on the Dunboyne and then was appointed professor of theology in the Paris college, but before he could take up his appointment he was recalled to the diocese because of the shortage of priests there. John McDermott, who ended his days as parish priest of Tubbercurry, was also a professor in the Paris college and previously in All Hallows College in Dublin.

Thomas Gilmartin was appointed dean in Maynooth on 1 October 1884 and two years later became professor of ecclesiastical history. He died of consumption in 1892 but in his short life published two volumes of *A Manual of Church History*, a very successful textbook,

Thomas Gilmartin
from a portrait in
Maynooth

and the copyright provided Maynooth with funds to establish an annual prize named after him. Thomas Judge, ordained in 1887, was appointed professor of philosophy in Maynooth the same year but resigned in 1893 and returned to the diocese as curate in Kiltimagh. Shortly afterwards he went to the United States where he became a professor in St Paul, Minnesota. Perhaps the most academically distinguished Achonry priest, Michael Louis Henry, did not study in Maynooth at all but in the Irish College, Salamanca, where he gained in quick succession not one but two doctorates. 'Doc' Henry as he was

3   Inglis, op. cit., p 392

generally known in the diocese was ordained in Salamanca in 1906 and died at the end of 1947 as parish priest of Straide.

Up to the very end of the nineteenth century no degrees were awarded in Maynooth but the Dunboyne establishment existed from almost the very beginning and exceptional students who had completed the ordinary course of theology were invited to spend one or more years of further study there. Some Achonry priests were awarded honorary doctorates by Rome, mostly during the episcopacy of Lyster (1888-1911) who had himself received such a doctorate while he was president of Summerhill College. He recommended John McDermott to be given a doctorate of divinity by the pope citing his academic achievements as well as 'his ancestry, his people, having been the mainstay of the Faith in the district and all through the persecution, managed to have a priest to minister to the people.'[4] The following year Lyster sought a similar doctorate for Michael Staunton, then fifty years old, and in 1904 for Edward Connington whom he described as taking 'first honours' in Maynooth and had recently taken part in a concursus for a vacant professorship in that college.[5]

Honorary Doctorates

Michael Louis Henry

Maynooth was granted a pontifical charter by Rome in 1896 with power to award pontifical university degrees and the BD was awarded for the first time in June 1897, the first licentiate in theology in 1898 and the first doctorate shortly afterwards. The National University of Ireland was established in 1908 with colleges in Dublin, Cork and Galway and Maynooth, a 'recognised' college, was granted the power to award university degrees. The first conferring of degrees took place there in December 1911 and Martin McCarrick from Cloonacool, who gained an MA in classics, was probably the first Achonry priest to gain a secular degree. From now on matriculation was required of all entrants into Maynooth and all students had to have a National University degree before being admitted to theology. For about the next sixty years Irish diocesan priests were probably the most academically accomplished in the Catholic world, when even the most humble country curate had a primary university degree and a sizeable number of priests had also a degree in theology. For much of the century it became the norm for priests with honours degrees to be assigned to teaching posts in St Nathy's College and later in Coláiste Pádraig, Swinford.

University Degrees

Martin McCarrick

A small but significant number of students from Achonry went to the Irish colleges in Salamanca, Paris and Rome in the nineteenth and twentieth

Irish College, Paris

---

4 7 Mar 1889, Bishop Lyster to Tobias Kirby, ICR, Kirby Papers (1889) 84; 29 Mar 1889, Kirby to Propaganda, SC Irlanda, vol 44, f 98
5 Udiense, vol 241; N.S. vol 323 (1905), ff 813rv-818rv

Patsy Travers CM
(courtesy John Doherty)

Irish College,
Salamanca

Spanish Civil War

John Francis O'Hara

centuries.[6] Of the forty-five who studied in Paris, twelve were there in the 1930s, five of whom entered in the last year of the college's existence. It closed in 1939 with the outbreak of the Second World War and the last rector was Patrick (Patsy) Travers CM, a native of Gurteen, whose younger brother, Thomas, was ordained for Achonry but served permanently in Southwark. Patrick, who was posted to Paris in 1933, stayed on with Louis, the French *concierge*, to protect the college and they survived by raising rabbits and growing vegetables in the courtyard until the end of the war. The college then became home to a Polish seminary many of whose members had spent the war years in Dachau concentration camp and the seminary continued to be housed there until the last decade of the twentieth century.

Achonry diocese also played a major role during the final years of the Irish College, Salamanca. Michael O'Doherty from Kiltimagh was appointed rector of the college in June 1904 and one of his first official acts after his arrival in Salamanca was to welcome the King of Spain, Alfonso XIII, to the college in September of that year.[7] O'Doherty remained in Salamanca until 1911 when he was nominated Bishop of Zamboango in the Philippines and was consecrated in Ballaghadereen on the same day as his cousin, Patrick Morrisroe. He was succeeded as rector by his brother, Denis, who, though a native of Achonry, was a priest of the diocese of Elphin. Denis remained in Salamanca until his death and is buried in the cemetery in Salamanca beneath a large celtic cross erected by his brother, then Archbishop of Manila. Francis Stenson was vice-rector from 1925 to 1930 when both rector and vice-rector were natives of Achonry.

John Francis O'Hara who had been a student in Salamanca from 1925 to 1931, became the last vice-rector in 1935 and remained in the college until 1945. When the Spanish Civil War began in 1936 O'Hara was in charge of the Irish students, then on vacation in their summer villa in Santander on the Atlantic coast where they spent two months each summer when classes finished. The house, which had been bought by Denis O'Doherty in 1926, was on the main road running along the northern coast of Spain, about a ten minute walk from the sea-front. Lorries loaded with soldiers of the International Brigade passed along this road from Bilbao to Oviedo where the miners from Asturias were besieging the town which was held by one of Franco's generals. They gave the clenched fist salute to the Irish seminarians as they went to and from the beach. The salute was not returned by them though it was by the local militia who escorted the students back to their villa.

6 See Appendix 9
7 M. J. Noone, *Michael O'Doherty, Archbishop of Manila, His Life and Times*, qtd in *Kiltimagh*, pp 128-9

There was no communication with Ireland as postal services had ceased. *Rescue*
As stories of the war in Spain filtered back to Ireland the families of the students became anxious about their safety and approaches were made to the government seeking to have them returned to Ireland. Eamon de Valera, who was then prime minister, approached the English government and as a result the Admiralty sent a destroyer to Spain. On arrival the Captain sent a message to O'Hara asking him did he wish to have the students evacuated. O'Hara, who had no idea why the destroyer had come, told the Captain to pass on the message that that they were safe and well and did not wish to be evacuated at present. The Captain told him to get in touch with Bates, the British Consul in Santander. Bates sent him a peremptory message to make up his mind quickly as 'His Majesty's government could not be keeping destroyers indefinitely at the disposal of people who were undecided.' With no time or means to get confirmation from Ireland O'Hara decided to avail of the opportunity and brought the students immediately to Santander for embarkation. Thus the Irish students of Salamanca left Spain never to return again. This whole incident did not escape the sardonic eye of *Dublin Opinion*, bemused at the sight of a Spanish named Irish prime minister requesting the help of the English navy to rescue Irish students from Spain. For much of its early history Irish students had considerable difficulty in evading capture by the English fleet as they made their way to and from Salamanca.[8]

**Nelson: 'Gosh for a moment I thought I was losin'
the sight of me sound eye!'**

Dublin Opinion, December 1936

8   From an interview given by John Francis O'Hara to the author for Radharc / RTÉ documentary 'Spanish Ale', 1984; see also *Dublin Opinion*, Dec 1936, p 337

O'Hara himself remained behind to make some provision for the domestic staff which he had brought from Salamanca to the summer house and then left for Ireland in October 1936. The following February he set out again for Salamanca, travelling by way of Lisbon where he hoped to get a pass from the Spanish embassy. At an hotel in Lisbon he had a chance encounter with Tom Gunning from Ballaghaderreen who had been a student with him in St Nathy's and was now a captain in General O'Duffy's Irish Battalion fighting for Franco. O'Hara accepted Gunning's invitation to travel with him.

Final Years   Salamanca was now Franco's headquarters and the Irish College was used to house the German embassy, some of whose personnel were Nazis. There were a lot of English-speaking visitors to the college during this period including Kim Philby and General O'Duffy. The German embassy transferred to Madrid when Franco moved there. Life was more difficult during the Second World War when supplies were short and food was strictly rationed. O'Hara returned to Ireland in 1945 and when he learned that the bishops did not wish to re-open the college he submitted his resignation and was appointed curate in Bohola. In 1951 Browne of Galway and Kyne of Meath went to Spain to arrange for the disposal of the college. During their visit the bishops had an interview with General Franco and informed him of their intentions, to which the General replied 'If ever Ireland is again in need, Spain will be ready.'

Clerical Numbers   The number of priests in the diocese in the nineteenth century remained static, hovering around forty. In 1816-17 there were about forty-one, twenty-two parish priests and nineteen curates.[9] The figure remained the same in 1841 and 1851, before and after the Famine. MacCormack reported to Rome in 1882 that there was a total of forty-three, thirty-nine native priests as well as four 'externals'. The population of the diocese was then about 90,000 and Propaganda commented that 'it seems that thirty-nine priests are not sufficient to meet the needs of about 90,000 Catholics'. There was also then a number of students destined for the diocese in Maynooth.

The first increase in the number of priests was recorded in 1895 when Lyster reported that there were then forty-eight priests, all natives. All except four parishes had curates, numbering from four to one and from now on there is no mention of priests from outside working in the diocese. Indeed some Achonry priests were serving elsewhere. Felix Gallagher, ordained in Ballaghaderreen in September 1889, spent his first two years in Galway

---

9   See Swords, *A Hidden Church*, Appendix 23-24, pp 388-93

diocese, first as curate in Kilfenora and later in Ennistymon.[10] In 1895 Thomas Judge was a professor of theology in St Paul in USA, while Thomas Coen was in Los Angeles and Patrick Filan 'was following the life of a monk' in St Bernard's Cistercian monastery in Leicester. By 1904 two Achonry priests, Mark Dempsy and John Hurst, had gone to the US where they worked as chaplains to nuns, Dempsy in Denver and Hurst in Scranton. There were also seminarians from the diocese studying for the priesthood in other dioceses. Three of them, Denis O'Doherty, D. Tighe and D. Devine were all destined for Elphin while Joseph Henry was studying in the American College, Rome for the archdiocese of Chicago and Michael Wynne in St Mary's College, Cincinnati for that diocese.

The number of vocations grew rapidly at the beginning of the twentieth century. In 1917 there were fifty-six priests working in the diocese with a population of about 78,000 Catholics, twenty Achonry priests working elsewhere and eighteen clerical students.[11] (In 1922 exactly the same number of priests and seminarians.) By 1930 there were thirty priests ordained for the diocese working temporarily elsewhere and this flourishing state of vocations was to continue for almost fifty years.

The increase in the number of diocesan priests was probably largely due to the establishment or more probably the transformation of a diocesan 'seminary' in the last decades of the nineteenth century. Many of the diocesan priests from the middle of the century on were said to have been educated in the 'diocesan college' before going on to Maynooth.[12] A small number were educated in Summerhill College, Sligo, St Mel's College, Longford and St Muredach's, Ballina.[13] Morrisroe was responsible from 1914 to 1916 for the building of St Nathy's College which was no longer reserved exclusively for students destined for the priesthood. Vocations, however, abounded as the century advanced, with often as many as half the final year students in St Nathy's College choosing to become priests for the home or foreign mission.

Diocesan Seminary

In the early nineteenth century the number of curates reached about twenty and remained more or less static for the rest of the century. At first they were employed by ailing or aging parish priests who paid them for their services but when Patrick McNicholas became bishop he immediately took control

Curates

10 *S.C.* 26 Aug 1893
11 Congregazio Consistoriale, Relationes Diocesium, 5. ASV 1917
12 John Doherty, *Achonry Priests in the Twentieth Century*, (unpublished typescript)
13 Summerhill College: T.H. Quinn (ordained 1895), Thomas M. Gallagher (ordained
   1903). St Mel's College: Thomas E. Judge (ordained 1887), Patrick Cuniffe (died 1891).
   St Muredach's College: M.D. Staunton (ordained 1866)

of their appointments. There was a remarkably high turnover of curates in each parish. In the eighty years between 1840 and 1920, almost two hundred curates were changed after only one year in a parish. (Twenty-two such changes in Tourlestrane and seventeen in Ballymote.) Almost another hundred curates were changed after two years and a further hundred after four years and only seventy-five curates lasted five years or longer.

The reason for such frequent changes is not clear. The pattern was so widespread throughout the diocese it could hardly have been due to personality clashes between curates and parish priests. It may have been in some way linked to their accommodation. For most of the century there were no church-owned presbyteries in the diocese and curates had to find their own lodgings which must have presented a problem in some of the more rural parishes. Later on in the century when parish missions began, one of the great difficulties was finding suitable accommodation for the missioners. Very often they stayed in the homes of Catholic landlords like the Mullarkeys of Drumartin during the Jesuit mission in Tourlestrane in 1867. One Jesuit stayed with the administrator in his house which was called the 'friary' as it was acquired by the parish from the Augustinian friars when they left earlier in the century. The young curate in Straide, Francis Hannon from Keash, died after a short illness early in 1888 in Redhill, Ballyvary, in the house of John Vahey, a Poor Law Guardian.[14]

Priests' Houses

Parish priests acquired houses for themselves either from their own resources or with help from their families to whom they were always

Ballymote presbytery (courtesy W. H. Byrne)

bequeathed. Strangely, there was no parochial house in Swinford, the largest parish in the diocese, until Edward Connington became parish priest. Following the death in 1910 of his predecessor, Michael Staunton, his house in Main Street became the property of his family and still retains after nearly a hundred years, the word 'Deanery' inscribed over the door. Terence O'Rorke lived his long life until his death in 1907 in his family home in Collooney.

The first church-owned presbyteries or parochial houses were built in the last decades of the century. The presbytery in Ballaghaderreen was built in 1882 through the exertions of the administrator, Denis O'Hara who was also responsible for the building of the parochial house in Kiltimagh. The parochial house in Attymass was built

14 *C.T.* 4 Feb 1888

PAROCHIAL HOUSE, KEASH.

about 1880 while John O'Grady was appointed administrator rather than parish priest so that the money saved could be devoted to that purpose. The parochial house in Charlestown was built probably in the 1880s while Thomas Loftus was parish priest, and Patrick Scully was responsible about the same time for having built both the parochial house and the curate's house in Keash. The curate's house in Mullaghroe (Gurteen) was built while Patrick Hunt was curate (1884-88) and the one in Killasser was built shortly afterwards when Andrew Callaghan was curate. In fact, Callaghan's predecessor, John Horan died at the age of forty-two from consumption, said to be the 'evil result of overwork and defective lodgings' which may well have prompted Callaghan to have a curate's house built.[15]

Parochial House, Keash, with Fr Scully on right

John Horan CC

Early Deaths

A sizeable number of priests died young, often from tuberculosis or other infections which they picked up during one of their frequent sick calls. Francis Hannon, the curate in Straide, was only twenty-seven when he died early in 1888 after a week's illness 'from congestion of the lungs.'[16] He had only been ordained for four years. Patrick Cuniffe, a native of Swinford, was about five years ordained and a curate in Ballaghaderreen when he died in January 1891.

15 *S.C.* 7 April 1888
16 *C.T.* 4 Feb 1888

'During the influenza epidemic he was almost always on horseback going about from house to house anointing and consoling. The fact that he caught the disease himself did not prevent him continuing his labours, and he took to his bed only when he was no longer able to walk and then it was too late.'[17] Felix Gallagher had spent only two years as curate in Keash when he died of TB in August 1893 at the age of twenty-seven.[18] Some parish priests also died at an early age. Mark Cooke of Keash was only forty-four years old when he died in 1880 from 'an attack of bronchitis contracted in the discharge of his sacred duties', while Thomas Conlon, who became parish priest of Curry in May 1881, was only forty-eight years old when he died in 1889.[19]

Clerical Incomes

'The priest of this parish may with due attention to his own interest, receive £300 yearly, between the accustomed fees or dues payable to him, and the voluntary offerings made at Easter and Christmas.'[20] The priest in question was parish priest of Tourlestrane in 1814. There appears to have been very little inflation in priests' income during the nineteeth century. From the very beginning of the century there was simmering discontent with the level of clerical fees. The Thresher movement in 1806 was directed against not only the tithes but also the fees charged by priests.[21] An anonymous notice was posted in Swinford in 1822 demanding that both Protestant and Catholic clergy 'dispense with the one-half of their charge on us poor worms and footstools.'[22]

The Penny Boys

The last major agitation against clerical fees took place in the winter of 1842-3 and was largely confined to the diocese of Achonry, particularly to the baronies of Costello and Gallen in east Mayo and Lyney in County Sligo. The movement was said to have originated in Carracastle with those involved called the Penny Boys because a penny was their recommended fee for baptism and spilled over the Ox Mountains into the Sligo end of Killala.[23] Unlike earlier movements it was confined almost entirely to the question of the charges by priests for their various ministries and relied mainly on peaceful demonstrations. Usually a large body of men came to a parish, held meetings and administered an oath to the inhabitants binding them to pay no more than certain sums to the priests. 'The most respectable Roman

17 *W.P.* 24 Jan 1891
18 *S.C.* 26 Aug 1893
19 *S.C.* 23 Oct 1880, 28 May 1881 & 9 Feb 1889
20 James Neligan, *Statistical Account of Kilmactigue*, p 377
21 See Swords, *A Hidden Church*, pp 77-80
22 SOC 2362 / 18, J. D. Ellard, Swinford, 18 Mar 1822
23 T. O'Rorke, *Ballysadare and Kilvarnet*, pp 266-270; S. J. Connolly, *Priests and People in Pre-Famine Ireland*, pp 250-52

Catholics', one magistrate reported from County Sligo, 'attended these meetings and the feeling appears very general that priests' dues are excessive.'

Charges were fixed at ten shillings for marriages, one shilling for Masses for the dead while the dues were two shillings annually. No oats, money or potatoes were to be given to curates, and priests who employed servants were to pay them themselves. There was also a demand that confessions and baptisms take place in the chapel thus doing away with the stations in private houses which caused much resentment. 'The Carracastle Penny Boys, after summoning the inhabitants of the next parish to meet them on a certain day, on the mearing of the two parishes proceeded on that day to the rendezvous, with a form of oath in the left hand and a blackthorn stick in the right and swore those they met to two things – first to observe the new tariff in all dealings with the clergy; and secondly to administer in due time the oath of confederation to the inhabitants of the adjoining parish. In this way the league was extended from parish to parish, and from diocese to diocese, till it took in considerable portions of the dioceses of Achonry and Killala.'[24] In most cases the oath regarding priests' fees appears to have been willingly taken and enthusiastically carried from one parish to another.

A party of four to five hundred men who assembled in Coolcarney informed a constable 'that they did not come to do anything contrary to the Queen nor the laws of the land, but if possible to quit themselves of the enormous charge their priest was imposing on them.' Generally the emphasis was on voluntary compacts and mass demonstrations of popular disapproval rather than threats or intimidation but there were occasional instances of violence. Those who refused to abide by the new fees sometimes had their turf-stacks set alight, one man's house was burned and another man had a shot fired into his house.

O'Rorke gives a highly colourful and partisan account of a pitch battle which took place on 7 February 1843 on the strand in Ballysadare between the Penny Boys and their opponents. Patrick Durcan was then the parish priest and O'Rorke's predecessor. 'The people of this parish have been always remarkable for attachment to their clergy.' When they heard that a large contingent of Penny Boys was approaching Ballysadare from the direction of Dromard they decided to confront them.

Clash on Ballysadare Strand

All classes were there – mill men from Camphill bleach and corn mills; masons, carpenters, stonecutters, poolers from Collooney and Ballysadare, which were then flourishing little colonies of tradesmen; shopkeepers and dealers, who had shut up their concerns in order to have a share in the

24 O'Rorke, pp 266-7

danger and glories of the day; agricultural labourers from all parts of the parish, determined on doing as good a day's work with the shillelagh as they had ever put in with the loy; and farmers and sons of farmers, after suspending the pressing labours of spring, to show that they felt the same interest as their neighbours in the events about to happen.

Needless to say, the Penny Boys were quickly put to flight and were being pursued across the strand when Dominick O'Connor, the curate in Collooney, persuaded the victors to desist and retire quietly to their homes. 'Such was the "rise and fall" of the Penny Boys.'

Collections   Priests' income was made up of station dues, Christmas and Easter offerings and stole fees or charges for baptisms and marriages. It was estimated in 1892 that an ordinary or comfortable family in the congested districts paid from one pound to ten shillings a year to the church while a poor family paid five shillings. An annual ten shilling payment included one shilling at each of the two stations, one shilling and sixpence at Christmas and at Easter and five shillings for one baptism.[25] In the post-Famine period it became customary to have the list of contributors at Christmas and Easter read from the altar on the occasion of Sunday Mass and this custom continued well into the following century. In some instances the names were read out 'including those who paid and those who did not pay.' In Mountbellew in the diocese of Clonfert in 1879 a large two-feet high poster was placed in front of the church naming a parishioner who had attended Mass in the parish for the previous five years and never paid dues or the Christmas or Easter offerings.[26] This obligation, according to the poster, was 'cheerfully discharged by the most humble and poorest of every flock'. The defaulter in this case was a magistrate.

Two-thirds of the dues were paid to the parish priest while the remaining third went to the curate or was divided between them where there was more than one. The curate in Killasser received £50 per annum in 1872 and almost twenty years later the salary of the chaplain in Benada was raised from £50 to £60. Bishop MacCormack and Denis O'Hara told William Scawen Blunt in Ballaghaderreen in 1886 that 'the people supply them with all they want', adding that 'in some parts of the south with more than is good for them.' The parish revenue in Collooney in 1905 amounted to 575 guineas of which the parish priest received 425 and the curate 150, while the neighbouring parish of Coolaney had an income of 265 guineas.[27]

25 James Morrissey, *On the Verge of Want*, pp 11, 36, 47, 63, 83, 95, 102, 136, 155, 161, 185
26 SC Irlanda, vol 38, ff 1027r, 1034r-1046r
27 Lyster to Cardinal Gotti, 26 Oct 1905, N.S. vol 323 (1905), ff 460r, 461v

Priests were often supplied with turf, probably by the poorer classes in the country who could not afford to make offerings in cash. Thirty carts of turf were delivered to the parish priest's house in Straide at the end of July 1915 and 'a magnificent pile of turf' was built there.[28] Father Higgins thanked the people the following Sunday for their generous act which was 'unexpected as provision had been made hitherto for a supply of fuel'. In Carracastle a row developed between political opponents when supporters of the republican parish priest, Philip Mulligan, were bringing him turf in carts bedecked with tricolours.

The bishop's income which was made up from a portion of the revenues from the two mensal parishes, Ballaghaderreen and Tourlestrane, the cathedratics, and a small subvention paid by the parish priests from their marriage offerings, was estimated at £800 in 1917. The cathedratics were annual subscriptions made by parish priests and were estimated at about £70 in 1922. Morrisroe reported to Rome then that each priest had 'sufficient and more to live decently' from Mass stipends, offerings of the faithful and stole fees charged mainly for baptisms and marriages.

Bishops' Income

P. J. O'Grady and Martin Henry outside Curry Church c. 1906 *(courtesy Christina Murphy)*

28 *W.P.* 31 July 1915

Priests' lifestyle reflected their growing wealth. Parochial houses were large and lavishly furnished and, like Roger O'Hara's house in Kilmovee, were modelled on those of the gentry. Roger lived with his sister on the upper floor while his housekeeper occupied the lower floor where the kitchen, pantry and scullery were situated and it was said that he had never seen these servant quarters. Parish priests also often kept carriages and horses that were the envy even of the Protestant gentry.

Priests, like their wealthier parishioners, were among the first to take regular summer holidays. Within the country Kingstown or modern Dún Laoghaire was a favourite destination and accommodation was not always

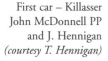

First car – Killasser
John McDonnell PP
and J. Hennigan
(courtesy T. Hennigan)

available. 'Father Denis telegraphed from Kingstown that there was not a bed to be had for love or money.'[29] As a result Denis O'Hara and Tom Loftus of Charlestown were put up by John Dillon MP in his North Great George's Street home in Dublin. Later Denis went further afield to the continent for his summer holidays. Together with his niece, Michael Keveney of Charlestown and Sir Henry Doran and his wife, he went to the spa, Bad Neuenhar. 'We stopped a few days at Ostend and a couple of days at Brussels. We remain here for about twelve days more and after that a week somewhere else and then we make our way home.'[30] In July 1888 Michael Staunton, then

29 John Dillon to Anne Deane, 25 Aug 1892, Dil. P. 6886
30 Denis O'Hara to John Dillon, 6 Aug 1912, Dil. P. 6769

in Tubbercurry, spent his summer holidays in Harrowgate in England. More modestly, Peter O'Harte of Bonniconlon spent his that year in the Aran Islands.[31]

Priests were often accorded the status of minor aristocracy. When Michael Staunton was installed by Bishop Lyster as parish priest of his native Swinford he was presented with a number of addresses by the leading bodies in the town, each of which was preceded by a lengthy speech by the town's most accomplished orators. The town was 'magnificently illuminated' for the occasion. 'The windows of all the private and business residences displayed innumerable lights, immense tar-barrels blazed in the principal streets, while paraffin oil ran like a river of fire through the lanes and alleys, the whole forming a brilliant *coup d'oeil*, and presenting a scene of rejoicing in honour of the Rev. Canon's appointment surpassing anything hitherto witnessed in Swinford.'[32]

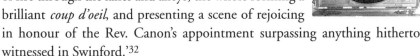

Clerical Status

Michael D. Staunton
(courtesy Dr Tom Staunton)

Staunton had been transferred from Tubbercurry to Swinford and a lavish presentation 'regardless of expense',was made to him by his former parish.[33] However, such lavish presentations to departing priests were not typical and this one may have something to do with the fact that Michael was replaced in Tubbercurry by his brother, Patrick. Michael was presented with a 'splendid carriage by Windover of London which took first prize at the late Horse Show, a spanking pair of chestnuts and a silver-mounted set of harness' with the motto *En Dieu est ma foi,* as well as a beautifully illuminated address.

The lettering is surrounded by wreaths of shamrock, interlaced with Celtic ornamentations; the upper corners are occupied by religious emblems, chalice, ciborium, monstrance etc. On either side are photographs of the parish churches of Tubbercurry and Cloonacool. Here and there are interspersed the wolf-dog, sunburst, Round Tower, and the family arms. Below two typical pikemen stand guard over the surrounding splendour, while a life-like portrait of Dr Staunton surmounts the whole. The address stands over four feet high and is enclosed in the heaviest and richest framework we have ever seen.

Staunton entertained his visitors to Swinford with 'a sumptious banquet'.

Clerical scandals were few but of considerable notoriety nonetheless. Matthew Healy, a curate in Ballymote, was accused in 1833 of fathering a child

Patrick Staunton
(courtesy Dr Tom Staunton)

Matthew Healy

31 *S.C.* 28 July 1888
32 *W.P.* 1 Aug 1891
33 *S.C.* 24 Oct & *C.T.* 31 Oct 1891

with the daughter of the man in whose house he was lodging.[34] The girl's father, Charles McManus, 'a man of respectable birth', went to the bishop and accused Healy who was summoned to an ecclesiastical trial in the presence of the parish priests of the deanery. From the evidence of sworn witnesses it was clear to McNicholas and the others present that Healy was guilty. The trial ended on 20 November 1833 and about a week later McNicholas ordered Healy to go to the Irish College, Paris, where he hoped he would improve his knowlege and 'change his morals for the better'. Healy was among a number of young priests ordained by McNicholas' predecessor without any formal training. He entered the college at the end of January 1834 probably about the time an 'outrage' was reported to the police in Ballymote.[35] Four stacks of oats belonging to McManus, the girl's father, were 'maliciously thrown down and scattered by persons unknown.' McManus told the police that he believed that this 'outrage committed on him must have been through the influence of Priest Healy and the country people' because following his complaint the bishop had 'discarded' Healy. Healy left Paris early in April 1835 and returned home without the bishop's permission but, meanwhile, word of his fall from grace had spread throughout the whole diocese and there was nowhere the bishop could send him as he was regarded by the people everywhere 'with horror'.

Still unemployed thirteen years later, Healy wrote in May 1848 to Pope Pius IX seeking redress and claiming that he had been falsely accused and that the girl's brother was the father of the child. He had been given no appointment in the diocese since 1833 and for fourteen years had lived in the greatest poverty and need. He had appealed to Archbishop MacHale but believed it was to no avail. 'Now, Holy Father, in advanced age, I appeal to the Holy See for justice, nothing else but justice.' He ended his very long letter, written in very quaint Latin, with the strikingly misplaced quotation: 'Into your hands, Most Holy Father, I commend my spirit.' McNicholas wrote in July giving Rome his very different version of the case. 'The diocese of Achonry is numbered amongst the poorest and there was no place of refuge for fallen priests', and while the laity would subsidise sick and poor priests 'they shun and detest unworthy priests especially those who sin against chastity.' MacHale also made that point that there was no such asylum provided in

---

34 Ballymote, 23 May 1848, Matthew Healy to Pope Pius IX; Ballaghaderreen, 18 July 1848, Bishop McNicholas to Cardinal Fransoni; Irish College, 3 Sept 1848, Archbishop MacHale to Cardinal Fransoni, SC Irlanda, vol 29, ff 777rv, 778rv, 824rv, 825v, 908r, 909v

35 Chief Constable John Whittaker, Ballymote to Major Warburton, Inspector General, 3 Mar 1834, Outrage Papers, 12, Sligo 1834

Achonry or in almost any of the other dioceses for such priests and believed that if some charitable fund was made available the Bishop of Achonry would not be found wanting in helping the 'unfortunate' priest. What eventually happened to Healy is unknown as his name does not appear in the recorded lists of priests working in the diocese before or after 1848.[36]

Later in the century the diocese was rocked by a much more serious clerical scandal. Dominick O'Grady was ordained a priest in the convent in Ballaghaderreen just before Christmas in 1888, one of the first ordinations performed by John Lyster who had become bishop a few months earlier. O'Grady had impeccable priestly credentials. His older brother, John, was already parish priest of Bohola, another brother, James, was a Jesuit in Gardiner Street, Dublin, while a third brother, Patrick J., was a Salesian in Argentina. His only sister, Ann, had joined the Sisters of Charity taking Bernardine as her religious name, and was attached to St Vincent's in Fairview, Dublin. Dominick had two other brothers, one who was in business in the United States and Michael, who stayed with his elderly father on the family farm in Stonepark, Aclare. The patriarch of this levitical family, eighty-one year old Michael senior, died on 6 September 1889, about nine months after Dominick's ordination and, not surprisingly, there was a large clerical attendance at his funeral.[37] When his mother died in the parochial house in Bohola in July 1893 her funeral cortege passing through Aclare 'extended over an Irish mile in length' and was 'the largest ever witnessed in the parish.'[38]

O'Grady Murder

Dominick's first appointment in February 1889 was as chaplain to the convent in Benada where he remained for about eighteen months, moving in July 1890 to the curate's house in Mullinabreena where he served 'with efficiency and zeal' for the next three and a half years. 'During this period he gave no cause of complaint and was regular and attentive to his sacred duties.'[39] Suddenly, on Wednesday 8 November 1893 he disappeared leaving a note with Patrick Lowry, his parish priest, saying that he 'was urgently summoned to Dublin to his dying brother.' As a result there was no Mass in his chapel on the next two Sundays and by now it was assumed by the bishop and others that he had gone to America 'under suspicious circumstances'.

O'Grady's Disappearance

36 One is tempted to identify him with Mark Healy who was listed as curate in Collooney from 1845 to 1848 but these were among the fourteen years Matthew stated in his letter to Rome that he was unemployed. M. Healy was a curate in Kilmovee in 1849 and Mark was curate in Carracastle in 1850. See Appendix 5
37 *W.P.* 14 Sept & *C.T.* 21 Sept 1889
38 *S.C.* 22 July 1893
39 ADA De Clero Diocesano, Dr Lyster's Book G

Mollie Gilmartin

He had indeed gone to America and under circumstances which were to emerge later.[40] A short time previously O'Grady had attended a Mrs Gilmartin on her death-bed and before she died she asked the priest to look after her daughter. Mary, better known as Mollie, and described as 'beautiful, aimable and well-liked', had graduated from the Ursuline convent in Sligo, an 'accomplished linguist, musician and vocalist and excellent cross-country rider.' 'Several of the most wealthy young men in Sligo were paying her addresses but she did not seem to reciprocate their affections.' Now nineteen years old she was deeply affected by her mother's death but 'consoled by the love of the priest.' One of her brothers, Thomas, professor of ecclesiastical history in Maynooth, had died young from consumption in May 1892 and Dominick O'Grady was one of thirteen priests from the diocese who attended his funeral.[41] Another brother, Michael, was a priest in Chicago and Mollie decided to go and visit him. She set out in October 1893 and O'Grady accompanied her as far as Liverpool where she was to board a ship bound for America.

Mollie Gilmartin
Evening Herald
12 May 1894

In Liverpool Mollie begged the thirty-year-old O'Grady to come with her to America which he refused 'pleading duty', but eventually agreed to follow her some time afterwards. This he did about six weeks later on 8 November rejoining Mollie in Springfield, Massachussets, and afterwards they set out for Chicago to visit Mollie's brother, Michael, stopping for a few days in Buffalo NY and were thought to be travelling together as man and wife. Michael was 'indignant' at their conduct 'saying that it would create talk' and tried to persuade Mollie to return home, but in the meantime kept her under strict surveillance in his house.

O'Grady's Return

O'Grady, however, decided to return to Ireland. He left New York on the *SS Etruria* on Saturday 16 December, sending a telegram to inform his brother John in Bohola, who told Lyster the following day. When Dominick reached Ireland he found that 'the story had gained credence that he had eloped with the girl.' He called on Lyster in Ballaghaderreen on 23 December, five years exactly to the day he was ordained there by him but the bishop refused to see him. O'Grady tried again on the last day of the year when Lyster saw him and gave him permission to say Mass in Achonry and Mullinabreena the following day, New Year's Day. O'Grady addressed the congregation 'for which he had no leave', presumably to explain his conduct. He spent the following

40 *Sligo Independent*, 12 May 1894 culled from *New York Herald*, 26 April 1894; *Evening Herald*, 12 May 1894 from *Commercial Gazette of Cincinnati*
41 *FJ.* 11 May 1892

week in Collooney with the curate, another Dominick O'Grady, who may have been a cousin. He had a final interview with Lyster on 10 January 1894 and the bishop gave him his *'exeat'* i.e. in this case, a somewhat less than honourable discharge from the diocese in which Lyster testified in Latin that O'Grady was 'under no censure or canonical impediment' thus allowing him to be employed as a priest in another diocese.

Armed with this and a strong recommendation from Patrick Lowry of Mullinabreena for his 'good character, sobriety and truthfulness', Dominick returned to America. Towards the end of the month he was staying with a priest, Gerald P. Coghlan, in Philadelphia, who was a 'townsman' of his and said to have 'beguiled him with a lot of false promises'. He received a *celebret* from the Archbishop of Philadelphia on 27 January and 13 February which allowed him celebrate Mass for ten days on each occasion. On 2 February Lyster gave his brother, John, a letter of commendation for Dominick 'giving him a good character up to his sudden disappearance.' Apparently, Dominick was not happy with it as he sent Lyster an 'impudent' letter in March and the bishop sent him another recommendation this time 'with no reference to his escapade.' Dominick made several attempts to find a curacy in New York and received a reply from the vicar-general informing him that the archbishop had been consulted and that there was a possibility for him there. Thomas Taafe, pastor of St Patrick's in Brooklyn, also told him that there was an opportunity there for him.

Back to America

What happened to Mollie Gilmartin in Chestnut Street, Cincinnati at seven o'clock on Saturday morning 25 April was best described by the *New York Herald* on the following day:

Street Shooting

Pedestrians noticed her hurrying along, as though fearful of a short dark-complexioned man, with clean shaven face, who was following her. Almost opposite No. 35 Chestnut Street, and directly across from the house in which the girl boarded, a man caught up with her. The man suddenly grasped her by the hair with his left hand and, placing a revolver against her left temple, fired. He then released his hold and with a stifled sound, half scream, half sob, the girl fell to the pavement.

MURDERED BY HER PRIEST LOVER.

—

KICKED HER AS SHE LAY DEAD.

—

CAST OFF BY HIS BISHOP.

—

THE PRIEST'S CONFESSION.

We cull the following from the *New York Herald* of 26th April:—

In rapid succession the man fired four more shots at the prostrate body, none of which took effect, and then, administering a savage kick to his victim, he turned and fled towards John Street.

Sligo Independent
12 May 1894

O'Grady was pursued by a gang of street workers who had stood open-mouthed while he committed his crime. They caught him at the corner and managed to wrest the revolver from him and were threatening to lynch him when Officer Jinks Kelly arrived on the scene. Kelly drew his revolver and kept the crowd at bay until a police wagon arrived. O'Grady was taken to the Central Police Station where he was questioned and searched by Lieutenant Casey who found a small vial containing a light coloured fluid. O'Grady declared it was a cough medicine and succeeded in snatching it from the desk where Casey had placed it and swallowed some of it. He was placed in a cell where he began to to pace up and down excitedly and call repeatedly for a Catholic priest. He then admitted to Casey that he had swallowed poison and was taken to City Hospital where the vial was found to contain arsenic.

When O'Grady recovered he was brought back to the police station where he recounted to Casey the history from the very beginning of his relationship with his victim, Mollie Gilmartin. Revenge, he said, was the motive for his crime as Mollie refused to deny the stories about them that were circulating in Ireland and thus exonerate him in the eyes of the public. When brought before a magistrate he made a similar statement and added that 'he had given up all thoughts about the girl and wanted to straighten out his affairs with his superiors and go to Cleveland and devote himself to the duties of the priesthood.' He wanted Mollie to write a letter to Bishop Lyster to clear up the matter.

Mollie's Letter   Among a bundle of letters found with his effects in Grand Central Station was in fact such a letter written by Mollie and addressed to Lyster.

My Lord, Having heard since I came to this country that it was reported in Ireland that Father O'Grady came with me, I wish to have this contradicted. I am sorry that Father O'Grady has got into trouble on my account, and if you require any proofs I am prepared to give them and to swear to all I have said. I am sorry that such a thing has happened and I shall not feel content until I hear he is re-instated in his old place again.

O'Grady, apparently, was not satisfied with this letter, perhaps, because it stated what was already well known, that he had not accompanied Mollie to America. He asked her for another letter but she refused saying she would rather be dead. 'He had decided then to kill her and himself and when he broached the subject to her she acquiesced.'

The coroner stated at Mollie's inquest that 'there were no positive evidences of the murdered girl's not having been chaste, as the physical imperfections noted in the examination might have been due to other causes than illicit love.' Thus there was seemingly no basis to the allegation that they had spent time together as man and wife.

O'Grady's trial opened on 4 June but was deferred due to his inability to plead. The trial re-started on 2 July but again without success as the state of O'Grady's health continued to cause concern. There may have been other attempts at suicide, as on 26 November he was removed from prison to a hospital. At length around March 1896 he was finally brought to trial and committed to an asylum. The earliest suggestion that O'Grady was insane came from his cousin, Anthony G. Gavigan, 'an author and journalist' living on Long Island who came to Cincinnati on 25 April 1893 to look after O'Grady's interest. O'Grady escaped from the asylum in the autumn of 1899.

Trial

His subsequent movements are shrouded in mystery. Lyster received a letter on 23 April 1900 (?) from the Bishop of San José in Costa Rica who was approached by O'Grady looking for employment in his diocese but Lyster's reply detailing the whole story scuppered that possibility. He may have then continued southwards to Agentina where his brother Patrick was a Salesian. However, towards the end of 1902 a young man who returned home to Tubbercurry from Boston told Patrick Staunton that O'Grady was a time-keeper in the same place where he himself worked in Boston. He had revealed his identity to the Tubbercurry man, telling him the whole story but placing the blame on his victim.

Shrouded in Mystery

Some years later when Ambrose Blaine was touring Argentina to raise funds for the building of St Nathy's College, he stayed with the Irish Salesians in their house in Buenos Aires where O'Grady's brother was a member of the community. In the course of a conversation when Blaine dropped O'Grady's name the superior putting his finger to his lips, hushed him to silence. 'The walls have ears', he whispered, which might have suggested that O'Grady was then in the house.[42] If he was there he would only have been in his mid-forties and nothing further was ever heard of him.

Ambrose Blaine

A small number quit the priesthood, mostly at the turn of the century. Patrick Conlon, the curate in Foxford, died in July 1896 and three weeks later was replaced by James Taaffe Finn. After about eighteen months in Foxford Finn told Agnes Morrogh Bernard, the superioress in the convent, that he intended to become a Protestant.[43] He had been stationed in Collooney for a number of years and, according to the convent diary, 'being a gentlemanly presentable young man he was taken up by the principal Protestants in the locality.' From Dublin he wrote twice to Agnes telling her that he had become a Protestant and he enclosed in his second communication a letter

James Taaffe Finn

42 Recounted to the author by Bishop Flynn who was informed by Ambrose Blaine
43 RSCG / H 26 / 449

for Bishop Lyster. Finn was replaced in Foxford by Peter Cawley who was in-strumental shortly afterwards in the conversion on his death-bed of Ogilvy Evans, a local Protestant. 'This conversion coming so soon after the unhappy departure of Father Finn,' the nuns recorded, 'put a damper on a good deal of the Protestants' crowing over their conquest and they could not throw much abuse at us.' Protestants stayed away from Evan's funeral and the nuns had to send out men to dig his grave.

At least two left the priesthood early in the twentieth century long before it became if not fashionable at least acceptable. One of them was mentioned, though not named, by Morrisroe in his 1917 report to Rome.[44]. He had been ordained in 1910 and left the priesthood in July 1915 and, when Morrisroe compiled his report, was engaged on the front in the First World War. It caused little or no scandal in the diocese as he had spent his short priestly life on the English mission. It was similar with Joseph Higgins who was ordained in 1914 and worked in Scotland and the United States before leaving to get married. His brother, Patrick, ended his days as parish priest of Swinford.

Patrick Morrisroe outside Maynooth c. 1900 (*courtesy Thomas Flynn*)

44 ASV Congregazio Consistoriale, Relationes Diocesium 5, 1917

CHAPTER THREE

Educating The Masses

At the beginning of the nineteenth century an attempt was made by Protestant societies to proselytise Irish Catholics.[1] The cumbersomely named Association for Discountenancing Vice and Promoting the Knowledge and Practice of the Christian Religion (APCK) was founded in 1792 and by 1800 was in receipt of a parliamentary grant which it spent in the establishment of schools and the payment of teachers. Two other evangelical societies, the London Hibernian Society for Diffusing Religious Knowledge in Ireland (LHS), founded in 1906, and the Baptist Society for Promoting the Gospel in Ireland by Establishing Schools for Teaching the Native Irish, founded in 1814, became active in setting up schools in the diocese. The latter had a school in Tubbercurry by 1816. Albert Blest of Coolaney was the principal agent in the west of Ireland of the London Hibernian Society and in 1815 there were two LHS schools in Tourlestrane with an average of sixty pupils in each.

Protestant Societies

The Society for Promoting the Education of the Poor in Ireland, generally referred to as the Kildare Place Society (KPS), was established in 1811 and its grant-aided schools, at least in the early years, were widely acceptable to Catholics. In these schools the Bible was to be read without comment and no doctrinal matters were to be raised. Bishop McNicholas was at first strongly opposed to the KPS schools. He was under the impression that the New Testament was a textbook which was used indescriminately 'without note or comment' allowing the reader the right of private interpretation. One of the KPS inspectors, Matthew Donnelan, a Catholic, went to meet him at Strickland's house in Loughglynn and explained to him that the patron of the school had the right to make selections from the New Testament. As a result McNicholas withdrew his opposition and in fact applied to the Society for 'a considerable grant'.[2]

Kildare Place Society

KPS inspectors were sent throughout the country to report on the state of schools seeking their grants. Richard Fitzmaurice of Keash applied in 1823 for a grant of £50 towards the building of a school in Templevanny but his application was rejected in June 1825 'as it appeared from the inspector's

1 Swords, *A Hidden Church,* pp 181-85
2 Parliamentary Papers, (1825), vol 12, p 488

report that the principles of the Society were not acted on in the school.' [3] Fitzmaurice made another application in August, this time for help to furnish the school and was promised £10 'on assurance being given that the rules of the Society will in future be complied with.' The problem may well have been that the catechism was being taught by Francis Soden in the school, a practice which the Society informed John Coleman in Swinford in 1818 was totally precluded by the regulations during school hours.[4]

KPS also provided a training course in Dublin for teachers which usually lasted only a few weeks. Patrick McManus, aged nineteen, who started teaching in 1816, was recomended by the vicar, James Neligan, to be trained by KPS for a school in Kilmactigue. John Hart, aged thirty, walked from Ballina to Dublin in 1817 'without purse or scrip etc. and was nearly starved since he came to Dublin.' John Coleman of Swinford recommended John Mullaney in 1817 as Richard Fitzmaurice of Keash did Francis Soden in 1824.

1825 Report

The Kildare Place Society began in 1820 to allocate part of its own income to the schools of the various Protestant proselytising societies such as the London Hibernian Society and the Baptist Society. Daniel O'Connell, who was a member of the board of governors, resigned in 1819 and led an agitation against the Society with the support of the Catholic bishops, notably John MacHale of Tuam. A petition signed by the leading Catholic bishops led to the establishment by the government in 1824 of an official inquiry into Irish education. The resulting report divided the existing schools into 'free' and 'pay' schools, those which were grant-aided described as 'free' while the other hedge schools where the pupils paid a fee to the teacher were called 'pay schools'. Many of the teachers in the pay schools were also subsidised by the bishop or parish priest for teaching catechism. In Ballymote, the parish priest paid Pat O'Gara £6 a year in addition to the 1s 3d paid quarterly by each of his pupils, while John Ormsby, who got £6 per annum from his pupils in his little school in Tumgesh, also received 'a trifling gratuity' from the parish priest, John Coleman.

Pay Schools

Most of the schools in the diocese in 1824 were pay schools where pupils paid the teacher a quarterly fee and in many of them a range of fees were paid by pupils, most probably determined by their parents' ability to pay. John Nangle gave no rates for his twenty-two pupils in a school held in a cow-house in Sragh, Gurteen because it 'depends on the parents.' In Bunninadden Patrick Davey charged his pupils in his Ballyfahy school at rates varying from 1s 8d to 3s 4d. John May's quarterly fees in Derroon, Ballymote ranged from 1d

3   Parliamentary Papers, XII, part 2, p 2131
4   Pádraig de Brún, *The Irish Society's Teachers 1818-1827*, p 257 (to be published)

to 2s 6d while Ellen Gallagher in Swinford charged from a penny to a penny-halfpenny a week.

The two poorest teachers in the diocese were both in Charlestown parish (which then included Carracastle), Michael Kelly in Baroe who earned £1 10s and Charles Shrihane in Rooskey who earned £1 15s a year from their pupils who paid about 3s a year each or about 9d a quarter. Salaries at the bottom of the scale varied from £4 to £10 and about half of all teachers were in this class. A sizeable number had salaries ranging from £11 to £20 while a small number, like the six in Ballaghaderreen parish, earned over £20.[5] The top salary, £78 13s 9d, was earned by a Protestant couple in Ballymote, Jackson and Anne Hawkesley.

The Hawkesley-run school was a free school, one of about twenty-nine in *Free Schools* the diocese which received grants from one or more of the societies, usually in the form of the teacher's salary. The Protestant parish school in Ballymote was grant-aided, not only by the London Hibernian Society and the KPS but also got a grant from the Protestant Bishop of Killala and the vicar in Ballymote, as well as receiving private subscriptions. Half of the 116 students in this school were Catholics.[6] Of the free schools, twenty-four got a grant from the London Hibernian Society, sixteen from the Baptist Society and seven from the Kildare Place Society while some schools got grants from more than one society.[7] In fact all seven schools grant-aided by the Kildare Place Society also received grants from another society. Two other schools, one in Ballysadare and the other in Collooney, were described as pay and free because the teachers' salaries were paid partly by grants and partly by pupils' fees.[8]

The smallest schools in the diocese had only ten pupils, Baroe, with eight *Pupils* boys and two girls, and Malachy Dowd's school in a dwelling-house in Ballaghaderreen with seven boys and three girls. Rooskey school where Charles Shrihane taught in 'a small hut' had twelve pupils, nine boys and three girls while Patrick Diffely's 'wretched thatched cabin' in Currower, Attymass, housed

5   Edward Duffy in the town of Ballaghaderreen, who was assisted by Bishop McNicholas and J. C. Strickland, earned £24 as did his namesake, John, in Derranacarta. Another teacher in Ballaghaderreen, John Neilan, earned £26 while Martin O'Hara who taught in the chapel in Cragaghduff got £30.
6   In Drumfin in the same parish, John Kivlaghan, a Catholic, was paid 9d a quarter by the LHS for for each of his 95 pupils, which gave him a modest salary of £14 5s.
7   In Killasser Edward Hart, a Protestant, received grants from the Baptist Society and the Kildare Place Society as well as from his patron, Colonel Jackson. In Swinford, the Mullaneys, father and daughter, received each £5 a year from the Kildare Place Society and one shilling per quarter for each of up to sixty pupils who pass inspection, and sixpence for each further pupil from the London Hibernian Society.
8   In Ballysadare, Hugh Gilmer, a Protestant, got a grant from the LHS while in Collooney, John O'Brien, also a Protestant, received a gratuity from the Cooper family.

thirteen pupils, nine boys and four girls. In four of the six schools in Gurteen parish, three of them had twenty-two pupils and another twenty-four. One of the largest schools was held in the market-house in Swinford with between 120 and 140 pupils, while Ballymote chapel housed about 100 pupils, sixty-six boys and thirty-four girls.

Boys far out-numbered girls in most schools and of the total number of about 5,000 pupils in the diocese about one-third were girls. Only in one school were girls slightly more numerous and two others where girls and boys were exactly the same and significantly two out of these three were Protestant schools. The girls' school in Ballymote had sixty-four pupils while the boys' school had fifty-eight, both run by the Hawkesley couple. Mrs Frazier's school in Collooney had thirty-five boys and the same number of girls. The school in Swinford, run by John Mullaney and his daughter Sarah, had sixty boys and sixty girls while in Kiltimagh there were seventy boys and only ten girls.

There were 640 Protestant pupils in the diocese, about 12% of the total, the vast majority of them in County Sligo and the single greatest number of them, fifty-eight, in Ballymote parish school. There were less than eighty of them in the Mayo half of the diocese, twenty-two in the Protestant parish school in Foxford and ten in another, ten also in Swinford and five in Owen Reilly's school in Kiltimagh, twelve scattered among the three schools in Ballaghaderreen, ten in two schools in Killasser and four in Attymass.

Teachers

Presbyterians were the only other denomination in the diocese and all twenty pupils attended school in the Presbyterian meeting-house in Graniamore in Keash where John Moore was the teacher.[9] Patrick Brennan from Kilmactigue who became a Protestant and an itinerant Irish reader of the

Graniamore Presbyterian Church, Keash

9   This may well have been the school 'taught by J. M. near Ball(y)mote' referred to by Patrick Brennan in 1830-31. de Brun, op. cit., pp *76-7;* on Brennan see also Swords, *A Hidden Church*, p 162

Scriptures under the Baptist Society 'visited a good part of the counties of Sligo and Leitrim'. About John Moore's school in Keash he wrote that there 'were only two Protestant families living here when the school commenced, and they only differed from the Roman Catholics in name, for, when they had a child to baptize they took it to the priest and got it done, and if any of their cattle were ill, they would get a charm from the priest also; now I am rejoiced to be able to say that they have not only been weaned from their superstition, but some of them have been brought to a saving knowledge of the truth, and are living ornaments of their profession.'

Of the 110 teachers in the diocese, seventeen were Protestants, of whom all except three, John Barden in Foxford, Charles Taafe, Tullynahoe, Swinford and Edward Hart in Croghan school in Killasser, taught in the Sligo section. Of the eight women teachers, three were Catholics, Sarah Mullaney and Ellen Gallagher in Swinford and Mary Fitzgerald in Lismirane, Bohola. The five others were Protestants and taught in County Sligo.[10]

Apart from their names little is known about the teachers or their qualific- *Qualifications* ations for that profession. Schools in receipt of grants were often dependant on favourable inspector's reports. John Barden, the Protestant teacher in Foxford was described in 1830 by the vicar, Rev George Giles, as 'a person quite calculated for his office, combining unremitted attention and perfect capability with an unexceptional character', which was not corroborated by the KPS inspector who reported in 1825 'a total absence of order, discipline and improved methods' in his school.[11]

There were two Durkans, father and son, both called James, teaching in two different schools in Killasser.[12] James Neligan, vicar of Kilmactigue, described James senior at the beginning of 1821 as 'weak and feeble and upwards of 70 years of age', and when summoned to Dublin to be examined by the KPS Committee Neligan wrote to explain why he was unable to undertake such an arduous journey. James Durkan junior, who taught in an LHS school in Cartron, was described in 1824 as 'a young man, who, by read-ing the word of life in Irish and English, made considerable progress in a short time' and Rev Charles Seymour believed that in time he would become 'an efficient instrument of much good among the peasants of C(onnaught)'.

Thomas Durkin, a Catholic, who taught a pay school in connection with the Baptist Society at Lugnadeffa in Ballysadare, was fifty-six years old in

---

10 Anne Hawkesley in Ballymote, Mrs Frazier in Collooney, Jane Ellis in Templehouse, Elizabeth Davis in Coolaney and Mary Anne Ellis in Lugawarry, Ballysadare
11 de Brún, op. cit., p 63
12 de Brún, op. cit., pp 133-34

March 1825 when he petitioned KPS in English and Irish for assistance to repair his schoolhouse and for books, paper etc., and recommended the Society 'to encourage the instructing of the Irish in the Native letter meerly for the better edifying of the rising generation and not to suffer them to walk after their own evil ways for want (of) timely instruction and in particular in their own language which would be most exceptable (*sic*) to those who dont know english.'[13]

Pat Fe(h)eley, a Catholic, who taught a pay school in 1824 in Tubbercurry, was employed as a Scripture reader by Rev Joseph Ivimey and Rev Christopher Anderson on their tour through Connacht, the first and apparently the only

The Little Scholars of the Foxford School (*Lady of the House*, 15 June 1895)

Catholic so employed by the Irish Baptist Society. Feeley was in the habit of reading the Scriptures in Irish to his neighbours as they went to Mass. 'Last winter, the poor people came to his house from two miles around, bringing their own candles. "When I read," said he, "the account of the rich man and Lazarus, they were so pleased, that they called out, "Read it again! read it again!" '[14]

John Mullaney of Swinford, was trained in Dublin early in 1818 by KPS on the recommendation of the parish priest, John Coleman who described Mullaney as 'a very proper man', and had been teaching in the neighbourhood for nearly twenty years. His daughter, Sarah, 'was well qualified for the education of females'.[15] The KPS Committee believed that the joint exertions of Coleman and the Presbyterian minister, James Burrowes, 'would be productive of the best consequences' for Mullaney's school and informed

13 de Brún, op. cit., p 135
14 de Brún, op. cit., p 148
15 de Brún, op. cit., pp 256-57

Coleman that the regulations totally precluded the use of catechisms during school hours. Mullaney had spent ten days on the road to Dublin because of sickness and returned again to Swinford after completing the three week-training course. [16]

Bishop McNicholas suppressed Mullaney's school on 1 January 1820 and Mullaney petitioned KPS for assistance until his school was re-established which happened early in 1821 as an LHS school under Sir William Brabazon. The best boy and girl in each of the six classes was to be given a new jacket or frock or gown. Mullaney informed KPS in 1824 that he was the first to teach under a religious society 'in this dark region' and had to endure the insults of priests and rabble, but persevered even though his salary was 'too slender to support a weak family.' He succeeded in increasing the number of pupils to nearly 200, and employed a boy, Timothy Carrabine, to instruct the lower classes, and he supplanted him in November 1823.

School-houses varied enormously. Two schools in Kilmovee were housed *School-houses* in 'miserable cabins', the three in Attymass were described as 'a bad thatched cabin', 'a wretched thatched cabin', and 'a most miserable thatched hovel' and two in Bonniconlon were held in 'a tolerable cabin' and 'a poor cabin.' Most schools were thatched cabins built of stone and lime at an estimated cost of £2-£10. Eight schools were held in 'barns' and one in Gurteen parish in a cow-house. Nineteen chapels in the diocese served as schools.[17] A school in Coolaney parish was held in a mill. Two schools were held in the Sessions House, the Protestant school in Ballymote and the Catholic school in Swinford. The latter was held in the upper rooms of the market house, given by Sir William Brabazon, which were also used for the Sessions. Many teachers sometimes like John Hart, a Protestant, and Pat Feheley, a Catholic, both in Tubbercurry, taught their schools in their own dwelling houses.[18]

The Ballaghaderreen school run by Edward Duffy was a slated house valued at about £100, built jointly by Bishop McNicholas and J. C. Strickland while the Templehouse school-house also slated was built by the Perceval

16 The woman with whom he lodged claimed that he owed her money but Mullaney told KPS that the woman was in fact the wife of his brother, Michael, a tailor at 23 Stafford St, Dublin who had promised that he would be kept *gratis*

17 Ballaghaderreen (Cragaghduff), Ballymote, Bohola, Bonniconlon, Bunninadden (Bunninadden & Trianvillan), Carracastle, Charlestown, Collooney, Coolaney (Carrownacly? Carrownacleigha), Gurteen (Cloonloo), Keash (Keash & Longwood), Kilmovee (Glentavraun & Kilmore), Meelick, Mullinabreena, Straide & Tourlestrane (Baratogher)

18 John Hart, Pat Feheley (Tubbercurry), John Gibson, Morgan Finn, John Battle and Francis McDonough (Coolaney), John McGettrick (Knockadalteen, Ballymote), Charles Shryhane, John Neilan and Malachy Dowd (Ballaghaderreen), Ellen Gallagher (Swinford), James Durkan senior (Killaser), James Egan (Kiltimagh) and John Barden (Foxford)

family for about 100 guineas. Two schools in Collooney were built by the Coopers of Markrea Castle at an estimated cost of £100 and £150. The school-house in Templevanny, Keash was built at a cost of £80 or £90, while Thomas Brennan kept his school at Branchfield, Ballymote 'in a large house lately occupied by a gentleman'.

1835 Report
Hedge Schools

There were seventy-one hedge schools in the diocese in 1835 and fees varied considerably from school to school with both the highest and lowest pupils' contributions recorded in the parish of Gurteen. James Brennan received £25 from sixty-one pupils while Terence MacDermottroe received £4 from twenty-one. The number of pupils was not always the determinant factor in the amount received. Martin O'Hara with seventy-nine pupils in his school in the Ballaghaderreen parish only had an income of £5. Student fees ranged from 6d to 4s per quarter but most of them ranged from 1s to 2s. In two of the three schools in Attymass, the students paid weekly from a penny to sixpence in Margaret McDonnell's school and from a penny to twopence in Edward Mc Nulty's. In Meelick, where Patrick Ryan and Mary Fogarty (Haguerty?) taught in 1843, pupils paid sixpence a quarter for reading, spelling and writing on slates and ninepence a quarter for the same on paper. Getting suitable writing paper could be difficult as the parish priest of Foxford, John Corley, pointed out to the National Board: 'The children would feel much convenienced by getting a supply of paper at reduced prices as they are constrained to buy at present at a high price in these country shops and the quality is very bad.'[19]

LHS and Baptist
Society Schools

Forty-one schools in the diocese received grants in 1835 from the National Board, local Protestant landlord or Protestant society and were called 'day schools'. London Hibernian Society made grants to eleven schools, all in the Sligo portion of the diocese except John Barden's in Foxford and Mary Matthew's in Clogher, Ballaghaderreen. Of the LHS grant-aided schools, two were in the civil parish of Achonry, two in Ballysadare, two in Coolaney and one each in Ballymote and Keash. Seven schools received annual grants from the Baptist Society, all in County Sligo, two in the civil parish of Achonry, two in Collooney (Kilvarnet), and one each in Coolaney (Killoran), Bunninadden (Cloonoghill) and Gurteen (Killaraght). Scriptural instruction was given daily in all these and in one of them, Bridget Tiernan's in Ballysadare parish, the Roman Catholic catechism was also taught on Fridays.

Landlord's
Patronage.

Some twenty-one schools received patronage from local landlords, often in the form of a rent-free house and land to the teacher. Patrick Disney got a house from Captain Irwin in the civil parish of Achonry, while Mr and Mrs Bartly got a house and land worth £10 per annum from John Armstrong, and

19 ED 1/61 nos 8 & 52

Major O'Hara of Annaghmore gave a house and land worth £3 annually to John McAlvee. The Coopers of Markrea Castle paid James Whiteside in Ballysadare £25 a year as well as giving him a house and land and £20 a year to Hannah Palmer in the same parish. Mary Matthews of Clogher was provided with a house by Mr Holmes, and Col. Perceval paid Robert McAuley £14 a year. In these schools, as in those receiving grants from Protestant societies, the scriptures had to be taught daily except in four, two in Ballaghaderreen with grants from Lord Dillon, Keash where Francis Soden received a house and one acre of land from Lord Kingston, and in Tourlestrane where John Jordan received one acre of land from Jones of Benada Abbey, and a

INFANT SCHOOL HAND SPINNERS

'Irish Industrial Revival – The New Movement – what has been done in Foxford 1905'

school in Kiltimagh which received a grant from Thomas Ormsby. One school in the diocese run by Sarah McGuinness in Ballymote, received a grant of £3 from the parish priest.

The 1835 Report did not give the religious denomination of either the school or the teacher but it may be reasonably supposed that those schools – twenty-one in all – where there was daily scriptural instruction were Protestant and presumably also, those seventy-four schools where the Catholic catechism was taught daily were Catholic. Another fifteen schools provided religious instruction on only one day a week, usually Saturday; these may have been mixed religiously or though predominantly of one religion had a substantial minority of another.

Teachers   Edward Duffy of Ballaghaderreen was one of about fifteen teachers whose names had been listed in the 1825 Report.[20] In 1825 Andrew Collins had been teaching in Lognahaha in Killasser but later replaced Timothy Carrabine in Swinford between 1826 and 1828. An inspector reported in 1827 that he was competent but not sufficiently respected by the scholars. In the 1835 Report Andrew and Mary Collins were named as the teachers in Kiltimagh school. A man of that name was a national teacher in Attymachugh in Killasser in 1837 and in Foxford 1839-41. Charges were made against him and after a full investigation Foxford was struck off the rolls by the Board in December 1841. Andrew was forty-seven years of age in 1843. Foxford national school was restored about a year later when John Cooke was appointed the teacher.[21] There were three couples teaching in the diocese in 1835, Mr and Mrs Bartly in the parish of Achonry, Stewart and Catherine Woodland in Ballymote, as well as Andrew and Mary Collins in Kiltimagh. Of the total number of teachers, twenty-two were women.

Pupils   Of over 8,339 pupils in the diocese in 1835 only 2,793, or a little over one-third were girls as was the case in 1825. Ballaghaderreen parish had the largest total number of pupils with 759 on rolls, closely followed by Ballymote with

Some Oireachtas Prize Winners. Aggie Sherry, Teresa Coghlan, Bridie Gaughan and Sadie Coghlan in *Morning and Evening Telegraph*, Saturday 13 August 1904

20 John Gallagher (Ballysadare), John Bree (Collooney), Edward Duffy, Martin O'Hara (Ballaghaderreen), John Casey (Monasteraden), John May (Ballymote), Francis Soden, John Moore (Keash), James Minane, Elizabeth Davis, Morgan Finn (Coolaney), John Jordan (Tourlestrane), Andrew Collins (Kiltimagh), Patrick Langan (Bonniconlon), John Barden, Pat Swift (Foxford) & Nicholas Hughes (Straide). Pat Swift is wrongly named James and Nicholas Hughes, Michael in the report. A similar error occurred with Michael Anderson who is called James
21 ED 1/61 no 52; ED 2/32, folios 37, 146, 204; de Brún, op. cit., p 95

slightly over 500 pupils, while Bonniconlon had the least with 136. Ballymote parish had the highest number of girls on rolls with 319 while Bonniconlon had only twenty-two. The largest school in the diocese was in Bunninadden (Kilshalvy) where Michael Anderson had 314 pupils on his rolls, 203 boys and 111 girls, although his average daily attendance was only 120.[22] There were about fifteen single-sex schools in the diocese, seven boys' and eight girls' schools. The largest single-sex school was Edward Duffy's boys' school in Ballaghaderreen with 170 pupils on rolls and an average daily attendance of 110.[23] The largest girls' school was in Collooney where Biddy McKinn taught 109 pupils, though her average daily attendance was only forty-eight. The smallest school in the diocese was in the parish of Achonry where John Wynne had eighteen pupils on rolls, twelve boys and six girls, with an average daily attendance of twelve.[24]

All schools taught the three R's, reading, writing and arithmetic as well as religious instruction, the catechism to Catholics and the scriptures to Protestants. Thirty-six schools taught one or more additional subjects. Needlework was a subject in a small number of girls' schools.[25] English grammar was taught in fifteen schools. While Irish was the spoken language of the vast majority of the pupils and teachers it did not become part of the school curriculum until the early years of the twentieth century and in 1835 it was taught in only one school in the diocese, by James Minane in the parish of Coolaney. This was probably a Protestant school as there was daily scriptural instruction and Minane got an annual grant of £16 from Major O'Hara. Oral Irish was probably taught which would help the pupils later in life to communicate with their Catholic tenants and labourers. Minane also taught book-keeping, geometry and mensuration, knowledge of which would be valuable for the land-owning class. Book-keeping was taught in thirteen schools. With the growth of towns there was a greater demand for shop assistants. Edward

Subjects

22 Other large schools included James McManus' in Bohola with 181 pupils, Patrick Flaherty's in Kiltimagh parish with 178, and Michael Brennan's in Swinford parish with 160. Brennan had the largest average daily attendance of any school in the diocese with 140 pupils.

23 Another boys' school in the same parish had 131 pupils on rolls. There were two large girls' schools also in the parish run by Mary O'Donnell and Honor Giblin, with over a hundred pupils in each.

24 Another school in the same parish, that of Bryan Kennedy, had only twenty pupils on rolls and an average daily attendance also of twelve. There were three schools of a similar size in Gurteen parish, taught by James Scanlon, John Gildee and Terence McDermottroe and one in the parish of Ballysadare where Patrick Moore was the teacher.

25 Taught by Hannah Palmer and Bridget Tiernan in Ballysadare, Mary O'Donnell and Honor Giblin in Ballaghaderreen, Catherine Woodland, Sarah McGuinness, and Catherine Ellis in Ballymote, Mary Collins and Jane Robinson in Kiltimagh, Jane Mulherin in Coolaney, Jane Gunning in Collooney and Bridget Leyden in Tourlestrane.

Duffy, the Fenian, who learnt book-keeping from his father in Ballaghader-reen, later became a shop-assistant in Castlerea. Geography was taught in seven schools, in two schools in Ballysadare and in one school in each of the parishes of Bohola, Bunninadden, Foxford, Killasser and Swinford. Latin was taught in only one school in the diocese, by Martin Canovan in the parish of Achonry. This was probably to older boys destined for the priesthood for which they paid a special fee of 10s per quarter which was the highest quar-terly fee of any school in the diocese.

National Schools   As a result of the 1824 inquiry, the government decided to establish a national system of popular education which would be neutral between religious denom-inations and superintended by a state board. Edward Stanley, the Chief Secretary, established a board of national education in 1831 to distribute an annual parliamentary grant for organising and maintaining primary schools. The Board made grants covering much of the building costs of schools, paid most of the teacher's salary and appointed inspectors to insure that uniform standards were maintained. It published an excellent set of school texts, a series which was not only used in Ireland but later throughout Great Britain and the empire. In particular, six reading books were produced which brought a child from elementary literacy to fairly sophisticated lessons in geography, science and literacy. The Irish national system of education was a great success and became a model for many countries in the English-speaking world. In Ireland there was a dramatic fall in the national illiteracy rate to 53 per cent of those aged five and over by 1841, and ten years later to 47 per cent, which were impressive figures by contemporary European standards.

Timetable   Each school was under the control of a local manager which in Catholic schools was almost always the parish priest and in Protestant schools, the rec-tor, minister or landlord. The manager had the power to hire and fire teachers, to chose which of the several approved textbooks the school would use and within limits arrange the school's timetable. The length of the schoolday varied from school to school and from winter to summer, usually one hour longer in summer. In Bonniconlon, school lasted from 10 a.m. to 4 p.m. in summer and to 3 p.m. in winter. The longest schoolday, from 9 a.m. to 5 p.m., was in Bellaghy where Michael and Margaret Brennan taught.[26] The day began with spelling, reading and repetitions from 9 a.m. to 11 a.m., fol-lowed by writing for an hour up to midday, while the afternoon up to 4 p.m. was taken up with spelling, reading, arithmetic and English grammar.

Religious Instruction   The last hour, which was outside the official schoolday, was spent teaching catechism as national schools were strictly non-denominational. When the

26 ED 1/61 nos 2, 20, 68; ED 1/79 no 52

inspector reported in August 1851 that Rockfield school in Coolaney had moved into the chapel while the school-house was being repaired, the Board stated that it was contrary to the rules to have a national school in a place of public worship and that the teacher would not be paid a salary while the school was held in the chapel.[27] However, school buildings could be used for the teaching of religion and in fact the Board encouraged teachers to do so but only outside school hours or on Saturdays. Thus the practice arose of devoting the last hour or half an hour from Monday to Friday or some time on Saturdays to the teaching of religion. In Knockroe school in Bonniconlon pupils who could read were obliged each day to commit to memory a small portion of the catechism on which they were examined on Saturdays, which were set apart for religious instruction.[28]

(courtesy Vincent Coleman)

Diocese of Achonry.

REPORT OF RELIGIOUS EXAMINATION.

Name of Parish _Carracastle_   No. on Rolls _77_

Name of School _Cloonfane Male_   Average for year _52_

Date of Exam. _20th Sept 1915_   No. examined _55_

MARKS:—
"EXCELLENT" (90—100 per cent.). "VERY GOOD" (75—90 per cent.). "GOOD" (60—75 per cent.). "FAIR" (45—60 per cent.) "MIDDLING" (30—45 per cent.) "BAD" (less than 30 per cent.).

MARK ASSIGNED _Good (60%)._

OBSERVATIONS:—

Both teachers are doing the work of Religious Instruction successfully

The annual promotion of pupils was highly satisfactory

P. Higgins Examiner.

This copy is taken verbatim from the Report submitted to his Lordship Most Rev. Dr. MORRISROE, Bishop of Achonry.

Edward Duffy in Ballaghaderreen was one of the best paid teachers in the diocese, receiving £10 from the Board, another £10 from Lord Dillon, as well as £10 in children's contributions and £1 from the vicar. Usually the teacher received two-thirds of his salary from the Board and one-third from pupils' fees which were regulated by the manager who was generally the parish priest. A memorial was sent to the Board from Foxford in 1836 complaining about the exorbitant fees charged by Patrick Swift and the parish priest was asked to actively supervise the school and reduce the fees to within the means of the parents.[29] Poor children were often accepted free, for which the teacher was sometimes remunerated by the parish priest. Terence Rodgers and Sarah (Sally) McGuinness in Ballymote were paid by the parents of the children in

Pupils' Fees

27 ED 2/41 folio 146
28 ED 1/61 no 169
29 ED 2/32 folio 37

1832 with the exception of a small gratuity paid by Patrick Durcan for a limited number of poor children and this was continued by his successor. The pupils of John Gallagher in Clooncarha school in Kilmovee paid him a penny per quarter in 1845 but twenty pupils were admitted gratuitously 'on the authority' of Bishop McNicholas. Pupils in Tubbercurry in 1840 paid from a halfpenny to a penny a week 'paupers excepted'. Constantine Cosgrave admitted a quarter of the pupils free in 1846 to the school in Killaraght and a similar number got free admission in Ballysadare school in 1850.

Early National Schools

From the very beginning several parish priests applied to the Board for grants.[30] The earliest applications came in March 1832 from Patrick Durcan of Ballymote for a salary grant for Terence Rodgers and Sarah McGuinness teaching in Ballymote chapel and for John McGettrick in Kilmorgan chapel, as well as a building grant for the Kilmorgan school. Bernard O'Kane of Bunninadden applied in July 1832 for a salary grant for Michael Anderson in Killavil and when O'Kane replaced Durcan in Ballymote later that year he applied for grants for teachers in Emlanaughton and Drumfin. Other early

Swinford convent with national school at back left

applicants included James O'Hara of Keash, Bernard Durcan and Thaddeus Mullaney of Ballaghaderreen and James Gallagher of Achonry. A school was established in Foxford in the upper part of the courthouse in front of the church in 1826 and James Henry applied in 1833 for a teacher's grant and in 1834 for a building grant for a school in Attymachugh. Daniel Mullarkey applied in 1833 for salary grants for John Jordan and Bridget Leyden who taught in Kilmactigue chapel which he described as 'at least 88 feet long and 24 feet wide with four large windows and a gallery sufficiently spacious to

30 see Appendix 19

accommodate 200 scholars.' He also applied for a grant for building a school-house and a building grant for a school at Largy as well as a salary grant for Thomas O'Gara.

Of a total of 112 schools listed in the diocese in 1835 thirteen (probably fourteen) were grant-aided by the National Board of Education, four in the parish of Ballaghaderreen, three in Ballymote, two (probably three) in Tourlestrane, and one each in Foxford, Keash, Bunninadden and Killasser.[31] An application was made in 1835 for a building grant for a boys' and girls' school at Doocastle.

When Patrick Durcan arrived in Collooney in 1832 there were four schools *Collooney* in Collooney, two Protestant, a boys' and girls' school under the patronage of Cooper, and two Catholic in the town, also a boys' and a girls' which were badly housed. 'One respectable schoolhouse would accommodate the children at all four schools.' He applied in 1834-5 for building grants for schools at Camphill and Lissaneena.

When his brother, Bernard, moved to Kiltimagh in 1836 there were *Kiltimagh* two pay schools there and two or three hedge schools in different parts of the parish. He applied for building grants for a girls' and a boys' school in Kiltimagh as well as for schools at Canbrack and Oxford. His last application was in April 1844 for a building grant for Bushfield school. He was transferred to Swinford in 1846.

The population of Tubbercurry was estimated in 1838 at about 5,000 with three schools, two under the Baptist Society and one pay school, when James McHugh signed a petition for a building grant. Thaddeus Mullaney of Bonniconlon applied in 1839 for a building grant for a school on a site leased from Thaddeus O'Dowda. There were then two other schools in the parish, one at Carra and the other at Carrowcrum. John Coleman and his curate, Michael Muldowney, applied in 1839 for a building grant for a large two-room school in Swinford and for a boys' and girls' school in Meelick on a site given by John Bolingbroke of Newcastle, which began in November 1842. An application for a building grant for a school in Cully was signed in 1841 by John Flynn, parish priest of Curry, Daniel Jones of Benada Abbey, one Protestant and forty Catholics, among whom was Luke Colleran.

The Dominican, Patrick Sharkey, applied in November 1840 for a teacher's *Kilmovee* salary in a school not long established in Tavrane, Kilmovee. A building grant was also received. The girls' school in Tavrane opened on 1 June 1842. An

31 On the status of Thomas O'Gara's school in Largy the Report commented: 'Could not be ascertained as the Board have not yet paid him his salary.' Second Report of the Commissioners on Public Instruction, pp 82d, 92d-99d

application was made in 1844 for a building grant for a school at Clooncarha, Kilmovee on a site provided by Viscount Dillon at an annual rent of one shilling. The school had been held for many years previously in the chapel. The application stated that 'there were a great many in this neighbourhood who have never been to any school.' The only schools in the neighbourhood were Brusna and Kilmovee and 'and some cabin schools' which were open only during the winter. The superintendant reported that the population of the parish was about 4,500, all of whom, with the exception of four or five families, belonged to the poorer classes.

Charlestown   The parish priest of what was soon to become known as Charlestown, William McHugh, made an application in 1841 for salary grants for Michael and Margaret Brennan whose school in a house erected by Brennan in Bellaghy was described as 'slated, glazed and lofted' with two large windows to the front and one to the rear. McHugh applied in October 1845 for a building grant for a school in Lowpark, informing the Board that there was 'a rapidly increasing new town' in that townland. There were then 250 pupils in the Bellaghy school, as well as two cabin schools in the immediate neighbourhood with about 100 pupils. The Brennans and the Bellaghy school transferred to Lowpark in 1848. McHugh applied in 1844 for building grants for schools in Barnacuaige, 'a poor wild thickly populated district' with 'a wretched school in a cabin', and Cloonfane, both on sites given by Viscount Dillon at an annual rent of one shilling. Dillon also gave £50 or one-third of whatever the Board granted. Up to then school was held in Carracastle chapel with about 100 pupils.

Gurteen   Constantine Cosgrave of Killaraght applied in 1840 for a salary for Peter Scanlon in Cloonloo who had built at his own expense a schoolroom annexed to his own dwelling house and used the schoolroom as his kitchen with another room set apart entirely for his own use. Peter Brennan of Kilfree (Gurteen) applied in 1844 for salary grants for John Tansey, Mullaghroe, Hugh Devine, Ballynaclassa and James Brennan, Cloonenure. Tansey had a small farm of four acres rent free in return for private tuition and the thatched schoolhouse, built by himself of stone and lime, was in good repair. All three were granted salaries in September and each sent a supply of books for 100 children. Michael McGauran paid rent for the thatched schoolhouse in Kilfree which was built by a farmer of stone and lime. There was an estimated 6,000 in the parish, nine-tenths of whom were very poor, described by the inspector, William Robinson, as 'an immense population of poor ignorant creatures.'

Patrick Henry of Coolaney applied in May 1845 for salaries for James Mi- *Coolaney*
nane who taught in Coolaney and Richard McCally in Dynode. Minane had
built the thatched school himself of stone and lime attached to his appart-
ments and in pretty good repair when Robinson inspected it in July. He estimated the population of the parish at about 3,000, most of whom were very
poor. Dynode school had also been built by the teacher. In August both
teachers were granted salaries and were sent each a supply of books for 100
children.

Luke Brennan of Cloonacool was among a group of seven laymen who *Cloonacool*
signed an application in December 1845 for a building grant for a school-
house in the village. 'At present the nearest place where many of the inhabitants of the district can procure the means of education for their children is
the village of Tubbercurry, distant some four or five miles, and to get to which
the children are actually obliged to wade across shallow parts of the river Moy
during the greater parts of the winter months.' Robinson visited Cloonacool
in April 1846 and reported that there were in the area 'a few hedge schools
which do more harm than good.' The school was up and running on 1
December 1847 when John Balfe and Ellen Nenoe were appointed teachers
but only on trial as 'their literary acquirements were reported very low.'

John McHugh, parish priest of Straide, with a population of about 3,500, *Straide*
applied in 1840 for a building grant as well as a salary for James McNulty who
taught seventy-eight boys and fifty girls in the school. The survival of this
school, as of others in the diocese, was severely threatened during the Great
Famine. Charles Strickland wrote in January 1847: 'But the attendance at all
schools in this country has decreased considerably since the failure of the
potato crop. Many from want are not able to come the usual distance to
school.' A number of widows and home-owners in Straide, who between
them had over a hundred children in the school and 'no means for their support or to pay the teacher for his attentive instruction', sent a signed petition
at the end of February to the Lord Lieutenant.[32] 'The regret on our hearts at
present for not being able to afford sending our children to the Straide national school is incomparably grievous.' They asked that relief be given to
those 'who do deplore the idea of not having the youth educated' but there
was no relief forthcoming from the Lord Lieutenant.

Nevertheless, the school continued to survive at least until the middle of
October 1848 when James McNulty himself wrote to the Lord Lieutenant.
'This school is in constant operation for the last nine years during which time

32 ED 1/61 nos 18 & 19; ED 2/32 folio 145; CSORP Z.2219, O.9887; see Swords, *In Their Own Words*, pp 142, 352, 415-6

the attendance of the pupils has been pretty fair and also paid the trifling salary charged to them during this present time.' By now the attendance had declined dramatically and McNulty feared he might have to shut down his school. 'The poor of this parish are almost starved from hunger which renders them incapable of sending their children or paying the salary or schooling.' He suggested that the only way to save his school was for the commissioners of national education to pay the teacher's salary in full and thus exempt the poor from paying any fees.

Workmistresses   Workmistresses were usually employed for about two hours a day to teach the girls needlework. Peter Brennan applied in 1845 for salaries for work-mistresses for three schools in Gurteen parish and William Robinson visited the schools in July to make a report. 'The mothers of children here cannot teach their daughters almost any useful needlework.' In Mullaghroe Jane Ward, the wife of a local constable, had resigned as she was unwilling to provide a work table or incur other expenses, and was replaced by nineteen-year-old Winifrid Finn, who according to Robinson was 'recommended by Royalty itself', the wife of the Prince of Coolavin. Twenty-one year old Anne Flanagan, the workmistress in Ballynaclassa, whom Robinson described as 'a very proper person', also had testimonials from the 'princess of Coolavin'. In Cloonenure the workmistress was nineteen-year-old Anne Coleman. All three were granted salaries in September 1845. Robinson strongly recommended in 1846 a salary for a workmistress in Kilfree school, nineteen-year-old Margaret Coyne, whom he found to be very competent. 'This school is in a very wild mountainous district. The children are very numerous and their mothers are not competent to teach the female children to sew.' Robinson visited Keash school in 1846 and reported that Catherine Taaffe, the teacher's wife, was very competent. 'This school has been long in a very flourishing state – it is attended by a large number of females who are in great want of instruction in needlework – a small sum would be well employed in teaching so many little girls to sew.'

National School Teachers   Most of the early national teachers were quite young, many of them in their early twenties. Out of forty teachers and workmistresses whose ages were given in the first twenty-five years of the operation of the system only six were over forty. The oldest at fifty was Patrick Ryan who taught in Meelick. John Jordan, who was forty-seven in 1842, was teaching in Mullaney's Cross. His name had been listed in the 1825 Report as indeed was that of James Minane of Coolaney, who was forty-two years old, and John May of Ballymote, who was forty years old, when both were given salaries by the Board. James Brennan, Cloonenure, and Patrick McCarrick, Ballysadare, were forty and forty-three years respectively. Four others, Edward Duffy, Ballaghaderreen, John Casey, Monasteraden, Francis Soden, Templevanny, and Patrick Swift, Foxford, who were mentioned in the 1825 Report, were obviously in the same age bracket. The two youngest teachers, Honor Boyle, Cloonfane, and Michael Loftus, Bofield, were both only eighteen years old, and in the other three schools in Bonniconlon, Carra and Knockroe and Bonniconlon itself, Patrick Corcoran was twenty-seven, Catherine Dockry twenty-two and Anthony Touhy twenty-five. Michael and Margaret Brennan in Bellaghy were twenty-nine and twenty-one respectively.

Very few of them had received any formal training before they were accept- *Training* ed by the Board. Francis Soden in Templevanny had got some training in the KPS model school in Dublin. Thomas and Hannah Fenton of Achonry were also trained there. Teachers receiving salaries from the Board were required to spend a number of weeks in training at the Marlboro Model School. Michael O'Brien, who taught in Tubbercurry in 1840, had been trained there as were Anthony Touhy of Bonniconlon and Edward Duffy of Ballaghaderreen in 1840. Jane McGawley was one of the first teachers who was already trained before she started teaching as she was sent from the Dublin Model School to take up her appointment in Ballaghaderreen in April 1846.[33]

Some, who had not been to a model school, were themselves educated in a national school. Hugh Donoghue of Lissaneena school spent some time in Sligo National School 'to learn the method of instruction to be adopted' and Mary Woods, Tavrane, and Margarert Dogherty, Kilmovee, were both educated in Loughglynn National School while Honor Boyle, Cloonfane, Carracastle, was educated at Ballaghaderreen National School.

Though many of the early teachers were untrained they were well qualified *Qualifications* for their jobs. The inspector reported in 1845 that eighteen-year-old Michael Loftus in Bofield, Bonniconlon 'reads and writes well and has read some geometry.' John Dalton in Carrowmore in 1833, had been teaching in the parish of Achonry for ten years. 'He is well known to possess a sufficient knowledge of reading writing, arithmetic – in which science he is eminent – bookkeeping, geography and practical measurement.' Thomas O'Gara in Largy, Tourlestrane, was 'able to teach reading, writing, arithmetic, bookkeeping, elements of geometry, theory and practice of surveying, mensuration, gauging etc.' Michael O'Hara in Kilmactigue school was 'an experienced teacher of a public pay school and a private tutor in respectable families.' A

33 Others who spent time in Marlboro Street were Thomas Healy, Oxford school, Kiltimagh, Michael Brennan, Bellaghy, Patrick McCarrick, Ballysadare, John Gallagher, Clooncarha, Kilmovee, and Patrick Tarpey, Cloonfane, Carracastle

few days before Christmas 1836 the Revenue Police discovered in the school a quantity of barley malt in process for the purpose of illicit distillation. When Daniel Mullarkey was informed he stated that he did not consider Michael O'Hara to be at all implicated. The inspector reported in 1845 that the work-mistress in Kilmactigue, Bridget Feely, who had served four years to a dress-maker, was 'very well qualified in plain and fancy needlework, dress-making, knitting etc.' 'The character of this school stands very high with all denominations. All parties are anxious to send their children to this school. The population is very dense and great numbers receive instruction at this school.'

Twenty-year-old Michael McGauren in Kilfree in 1846 was 'pretty well qualified' though he required training, as was James Minane in Coolaney as well as his neighbour in Dynode, Richard McCally, who was 'young and busily employed improving himself' and 'a good subject for training.' Mary Anne May *alias* Moffett, who taught in Tubbercurry in 1840, had been educated in a boarding school in Sligo and certainly impressed James McHugh. 'As Mrs Moffett is such a superior person beyond the rank of those generally employed by the Board in country schools I apprehend she will not remain with us for the small sum allowed for probationary teachers unless the commissioners allow her £6 for needlework which she is most eminently qualified to teach.'

Inspection   From the very beginning the Board of Education established a regular inspection of schools. The country was divided into districts with a certain number of schools in each district and inspectors responsible for supervising these schools. The diocese was covered by two district inspectors, one of whom resided in Swinford and the other in Boyle in the 1850s. Once an application was received for a building or salary grant the inspector visited the school and reported back to the Board and if his report was favourable the grant was generally accorded.

Thereafter he made regular unheralded inspections which sometimes led to the dismissal of the teacher. When an inspector visited Drumfin school in Ballymote in November 1836 he found the schoolroom filled with straw which had been thrashed there and only five pupils present. He recommended that the salary be withdrawn from the teacher, John Farrell, and the Board ordered that the school be struck off the rolls in December. Bernard O'Kane immediately protested against the order which was rescinded in January 1837 but the school was again inspected in August and the inspector found that a large part of the free supply of books had been destroyed.

An inspector visited Foxford school at the end of November 1836 and reported that the 'master was indolent and careless' but in fact Patrick Swift was suffering from a medical condition and in less than a fortnight became paralysed and died about three months later. He was replaced by Michael O'Brien from Attymachugh who was so highly thought of by parents that when he sought and was granted leave in 1839 to go for a month to take the salt waters, they were unwilling to intrust their children to another teacher. When the new school opened in Tubbercurry he moved there in 1841 and continued to enjoy a very high reputation.

When the inspector visited the boys' school in Benada in December 1836   *Dismissals*
he found the house 'in a most filthy and disorderly state' and the school neglected by both teacher and manager. He found the girls' school there also neglected and the teacher, Bridget Leydon, absent when he called. She was admonished several times over the next few years. The Board ordered her dismissal in 1845 but she was given a further trial period and eventually dismissed in 1851. The inspector reported in December 1843 that the girls' school in Doocastle was very bad and suspected that Mary Moffett, the teacher, sometimes resided in it. The school closed in November 1845 when Moffett resigned. Bridget Toolan was appointed almost a year afterwards but was dismissed sixteen months later having been admonished and continuously reported as incompetent.

Eugene McGuire in Swinford was dismissed in December 1845 for 'improper use of schoolroom' and for making a false entry in his account books, having entered an attendance on a day the school was closed. Furthermore, the manager stated that he did not give satisfaction.[34] Mary Logan was dismissed from the girls' school in November 1847 for incompetency but refused to leave until a year later when Anne Duffy replaced her. An inspector called to Meelick school at 11.30 in the morning in October 1850 only to find the teacher absent and only thirteen children present and when he examined the roll books he found the attendances listed for the three preceding days given as forty, thirty-eight and forty. When an inspector recommended in 1853 that Mary Doyle (*née* Bolingbroke) be dismissed for inefficiency, the manager rejected the inspector's report and called for an inquiry. An investigation was carried out and found that the school was 'in a declining and inefficient state' and that Mary Doyle was 'wanting in zeal and energy'.[35]

Whenever complaints about a school were made to the Board, an inspector was sent to carry out an investigation *in situ*. A petition was sent to the

34 He was still in possession of the school in April 1846 when he was told that his salary arrears would not be paid until he quit the school.
35 Given her maiden name she may have been related to the local landlords in Newcastle who had given the site for the school. She was allowed to continue on trial for another six months when she would be removed if the school had not improved.

Board from Ballymote in February 1837 accusing the teacher, Anthony Gallagher, with neglect and after investigation the inspector deemed Gallagher incompetent and recommended his dismissal. Subsequently Gallagher appealed to the Board offering an explanation which it accepted as satisfactory. Eight Protestants signed a petition that year complaining about the state of Killavil school and accusing the parish priest, Thomas Healy, of taking away books. Healy insisted that the petition was 'got up from malicious motives' and the Board accepted his explanation. A petition signed by parishioners in Straide was sent to the Board in 1843 making accusations against James Mc-Nulty. The Board informed the manager, John McHugh, who carried out a full investigation and found that there was 'nothing in the conduct of the teacher to call for his dismissal.' Peter Scanlon in Cloonloo was accused in 1848 of keeping a 'sheebeen house which is frequented by bad characters' but his accuser failed to appear at the investigation and the inspector reported that the charges were not proven. Complaints were made in July 1848 against John Cooke in Foxford school, that he was neglecting the school while acting as a steward on the public works but the manager claimed that he only acted as steward before and after school hours.

Francis Soden   A petition complained to the Board in September 1843 that Francis Soden of Templevanny 'does not give proper attention to the school having too many other situations' and, on investigating, some of the charges were proved against Soden. The manager was informed in November that Soden was 'very improperly too frequently absent from school', that he held other situations such as driver and cess collector and used the schoolhouse as a barn and stable. Unless he gave up these situations his salary would be withdrawn. The manager wrote in December that Soden denied ever having used the school as a barn or stable, that he was temporary agent of Lord Lorton and that the writers of the petition were of a 'very questionable character.' A second memorial was sent in May 1844 stating that Soden continued to act as driver for Lord Lorton and also that he was connected with the Ribbon Society.

A second investigation was carried out and the inspector reported in July that Soden had resigned as driver but continued to get a salary from Lord Lorton as his duties were performed by his son and his servant. The inspector dismissed the charge that he was connected with Ribbonism by the very fact that he was employed by Lord Lorton. The accusations made against Soden were out of personal malice as twenty-five families had been ejected by Lord Lorton last year and Soden had acted as driver, taking away their livestock. Since then he had been subjected to many annoyances, among them having his horse poisoned. The previous driver had been murdered.

In October the manager was informed that Soden's salary would be suspended until a letter was received from Lord Lorton's agent stating that Soden had resigned as driver. The Board withdrew his salary in July 1845 because he continued to act as driver and the manager was requested to appoint a new teacher. However, Soden remained in possession of the school and was still refusing to give up possession in December 1846, and finally on 15 April 1847 the school in Templevanny was struck off the rolls.

A row developed in Keash between the teacher, Martin Carney, and the workmistress, Anne Noon and in January 1852 an inspector arrived at the school to carry out an investigation into accusations made by Carney against Noon. On the evening before the investigation the inspector was presented with a petition by some of the inhabitants containing allegations about the character and efficiency of Carney himself. Following the inspector's report the Board ordered that Carney's salary be withdrawn and that Anne Noon be admonished for using 'exciting language', but later that year she too was dismissed.

Fines were also imposed on teachers. D. Mullarkey in Castlerock school, Tourlestrane, was fined £1 for his 'indifference to the improvement of his pupils', and being absent without leave when the inspector called. The manager, Daniel Mullarkey, (possibly his uncle), protested against the fine stating that the teacher was obliged to attend a fair on that day and that he, the manager, was away. The Board stood its ground and refused to remit the fine, adding that the teacher had been previously admonished. The workmistress, Catherine Gilmartin, was also fined for being absent, the lesser sum of five shillings. Thomas Matthews, who taught in Lughome in Gurteen, was fined £1 after having been admonished several times for his neglect of the accounts but he failed to mend his ways and the school was struck off the rolls in 1851 as he was 'unfit for his office having wilfully falsified the accounts.' Ellen Nenoe in Cloonacool was fined £1 10s in August 1854 'for the retrograde state of the school and the neglect of accounts.' The inspector reported 'her unpopularity on account of levity of conduct' and recommended that she be dismissed if the next report was unfavourable.

Fines

Dean Hoare and the parish priest, James Gallagher, applied in 1844 for a grant for building a school in Achonry on a site given by John Armstrong of Chaffpool. Towards the end of 1850 Hoare was moving to Waterford and the new parish priest, Patrick Spelman, asked to replace him as manager. The Board consulted Hoare who stated that the site for the school which adjoins the Deanery, was given by Armstrong on the understanding that the manager of the school should be the Dean of Achonry and the management was duly

Protestant Opposition

Vere Foster

granted to Hoare's successor, Dean Lord Mountmorres. Hoare's participation in national schools was quite exceptional as from the very beginning the clergy of the Established Church had been consistently opposed to the national system of education. His predecessor, Theophilus Blakely, who was an absentee Dean, authorised in 1833 Henry Brett of Tubbercurry to sign on his behalf an application for Carrowmore school and similarly in 1838 an application for Tubbercurry school.

The Protestant clergyman refused to sign an application by the parish priest of Ballymote in 1832 for a grant for Emlanaughton even though fifteen of his parishioners had signed. Daniel Mullarkey had a similar experience the following year with James Neligan, vicar of Kilmactigue. 'We applied to the Protestant clergyman of the parish to join us in this application but he refused to comply from which it may be inferred that the fault rests not with the Catholics.' That year the Protestant clergyman refused to sign an application for Monasteraden school 'tho' he said at the same time that he approved of the system.' Patrick Durcan asked Rev Mr Potter of Collooney in 1835 to sign an application for Lissaneena school but he refused though Durcan did manage to get no less than fourteen Protestant signatures. In Ballysadare Rev George French refused his signature on the application for Camphill school but told Durcan that 'he had no objection that we would establish the school.'

When James O'Hara of Keash applied in 1840 for a building grant, he stated: 'The Rector informed me that he does not approve of the System of National Education and therefore would have nothing to do with this school.' That same year the Rev Mr Seymour 'made his objection but readily admitted the necessity of establishing the school' in Tavrane, Kilmovee. The Protestant clergyman refused to sign the Meelick application in 1841 'on the grounds that his bishop did not approve of the system', and John Corley of Foxford did not even bother to approach his Protestant counterpart in 1843 as he knew he was 'opposed to the system'.

Superintendant M. Hickey visited the school in Ballysadare in 1850 following an application from Patrick Durcan for a teacher's salary and while there had an interesting experience which he thought important enough to include in his report: 'I have called upon the Revd McGuinness, the Protestant Rector of the parish, and he expressed his entire opposition to the national school system, though he made a distinct admission, which appeared to me peculiar and important. He said he was convinced that in any national school he could obtain every opportunity desirable to instruct all the Protestant pupils in religion according to his own wishes and particular views but he claimed a right to interfere in the religious instruction of the entire people.' How representative that view was of the Established Church would be difficult to determine. Dean Hoare took a much more moderate position in his application for the Achonry school: 'A portion of one day at least in each week shall be set apart for the religious instruction of the children, under the superintendance of their respective Pastors or other persons approved by the parents of the children.'

The philanthropist, Vere Foster, who had already gained a huge reputation *Vere Foster* for his work in assisting female emigrants in the years immediately after the Famine, now turned his considerable energy and fortune to remedying the plight of impoverished national schools. He sent circulars to needy schools asking for particulars of their requirements which found their way to every corner of the west of Ireland and the response was immediate. In 1859 he spent over £2,000 on materials for over 785 schools, causing one inspector to report: 'With princely but discriminating generosity, he has given sums of money, often very considerable, for effecting the most useful improvements in the school-houses.'[36] He also travelled extensively all over the country, even to the most remote places, like Belmullet, to see for himself at first hand the condition of the schools and within fifteen months he had improvements carried out on almost one thousand school buildings. Between 1859 and 1863 fourteen hundred school-houses had their clay floors replaced by timber and by 1870 Vere had spent £13,000 on re-roofing, re-flooring school-houses and supplying them with other necessary materials.

Many schools were poorly supplied with writing materials as one inspector *Copy-Books* reported in 1856: 'In a school in the County Donegal which I inspected last year I found each child carrying a huge slate, four or five times the weight of an ordinary slate, with him every day from home, moving about from place to place in the school during the day, the slate all the while suspended from his neck, and returning home again with it in the evening.'[37] The inspector had observed a similar practice in Dublin which was probably widely prevalent throughout the country. Good handwriting, which was almost impossible to attain in these conditions, was an obligatory qualification for any boy

36 Mary McNeill, *Vere Foster 1819-1900, An Irish Benefactor,* p 118
37 *National Education Report, 1856,* p 157

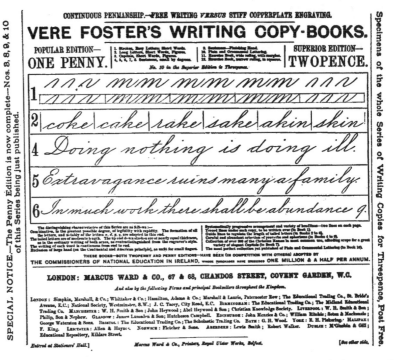

seeking to become an apprentice, clerk, or shop-assistant and also very important in every country home to maintain vital communication with family emigrants in America. Otherwise a scribe, often the village teacher, had to be employed thus becoming 'the depository of little family secrets, which people, no matter how poor, are always anxious to hide from the eye of a stranger.'[38]

Vere Foster commissioned in 1865 a series of thirteen copy-books with a printed headline on the top of each page to be copied several times on the lines below. The series began with 'Strokes, Easy Letters and Words' working up to Nos 8 and 9 which contained sentences in the form of proverbs which were to become familiar to hundreds of thousands of school children. 'The good is the enemy of the best', 'He that cannot bear a jest should not make one', 'Property has its Duties as well as its Rights', etc. The writing paper was specially made, of excellent quality, smooth and firm, with stiff paper covers decorated with a border of shamrocks, roses and thistles, incorporating two medallions depicting children playing, and a crowned harp surrounded by the motto 'A Nation's Greatness Depends upon the Education of its People'. The copy-books were circulated in 1865 with incredible speed. 'There is

38 *National Education Report, 1866*, p 169

scarcely a school in this district (Westport) in which these copy books have not come into use during the year, and the teachers one and all appreciate them highly.'[39]

The copy-books were supplied to the Board of National Education at £6 4s per thousand and the Board sold them to teachers at one penny each. 'Vere Foster Copy Books' were greatly acclaimed not only in Ireland but were also an instant success in Britain and used widely throughout the English-speaking world. Orders poured in from America and their use remained virtually unchallenged in its field for more than fifty years. Annual sales were counted in millions and made great profits, every penny of which was ploughed back for the benefit of pupils.

In 1870 he established a competition in writing, lettering, drawing and painting open to all schools throughout the British Empire with entries from India, Australia, New Zealand etc. From Ireland alone in 1872 there were over two thousand competitors divided into classes with prizes from £5 to 2s 6d and books for children under eleven. Over 9,000 prizes amounting to £3,356 were awarded before the end of the century. Vere Foster also produced a series of drawing books featuring trees, animals, landscapes, buildings etc.

39 *National Education Report 1866*, p 225

Good Service
Supplements

He also played a large role in helping to improve the salaries and status of teachers and in the early years presided at the annual congress of the Irish National Teachers Association, the forerunner of the modern INTO. Teachers' salaries were very poor, averaging less than £30 a year, of which the Board of Education paid just over £20 but talented teachers could supplement this by winning premiums and earning what were called 'good service salaries' based on inspectors' reports. Michael O'Brien, Tubbercurry, Patrick Stenson, Benada and Michael Anderson, Killavil, earned good service supplements, ranging from £6 to £8 in 1858, as did Anne Duffy from Ballaghaderreen, a sister of the Fenian, Edward, for her work in Loughglynn school. O'Brien and Anderson also got the supplements in 1860 as well as Terence McDermott of Swinford and Eugene Hynes of Foxford. In 1858 and 1860 twelve teachers in the diocese were awarded premiums, graded from first to fourth class. The only first class premium awarded in the diocese in 1858 was to Honoria Walsh in Kilmovee girls' school.[40]

1868 Report

It was decided to carry out an inspection of every primary school in the country on 25 June 1868 and record the number of pupils in attendance on that day. There were then 122 schools in the diocese, 103 national schools and nineteen others, seven of which were described as private, four in Ballymote parish, and one each in Bonniconlon, Mullinabreena and Tourlestrane. Another ten were under the patronage of the Established Church, six of them in Ballysadare and Collooney parishes and one each in Ballymote, Coolaney, Tourlestrane and Tubbercurry. The remaining two schools were in Coolaney and Ballysadare and were grant-aided by the Irish Church Mission and the Irish Ref. Society respectively. There were two convent schools, one run by the Sisters of Charity in Benada and a national school run by the Mercy Sisters in Swinford.

No figures were recorded for some schools which were closed on 25 June 1868.[41] Three national schools in Coolaney parish were closed because the children were attending games provided by the landlord and two schools in

40 1858: J. Donovan, Knocknamonal (Killasser?), A. Touhy, Bonninconlon, M. O'Boyle, Tonroe, Honoria Walsh, Kilmovee, David O'Dowd, Doocastle, F. M. Causland, Ballaghaderreen, J. Egan, Culleens, John Tansey, Mullaghroe, M. McGauran, Kilfree, John. Dodd, Achonry, H. Donoghue, Camphill, M. O'Brien, Tubbercurry. 1860: John McDonald, Ballaghaderreen, David O'Dowd, Doocastle, Honoria Walsh, Kilmovee, Kate Duffy, Lowpark, Edward Cunningham, Callow, Arthur Gough, Cross, Thomas Caffrey, Rooskey, Thomas J. Little, Keash, John Dodd, Achonry, Dominick Heney, Cloonacool, William McCally, Clogher
41 Boys' and Girls' N.S. Foxford (Fair Day), Cloongee N.S. Straide (Fair Day), Callow N.S. Killasser (measles), Largan N.S. Tourlestrane, Clooneagh Girls' N.S. Gurteen, private school at Graffy, Bonniconlon, private school in Branchfield, Ballymote, ('for want of attendance')

the parish of Ballysadare 'for want of a teacher', but local constables sensibly recorded the average weekly attendance in these. The total number of pupils in 114 out of 122 schools in the diocese amounted to 6,238. Boys still outnumbered girls but the gender gap was narrowing with girls now representing over 46% of the total and, in fact, on 25 June girls outnumbered boys in Ballymote, Mullaghroe, Kilmovee, Swinford, Lowpark and in a number of other schools. The largest attendance was recorded in the convent national school in Swinford where the 152 pupils comprised seventy-four girls and seventy-eight infants.

The 1871 Census revealed that illiteracy rates of persons over five years of age continued to drop. The rates varied from parish to parish and showed a fairly wide discrepancy between parishes in Mayo and those in Sligo. Sligo had less illiteracy, with the lowest rate, 36%, recorded in Collooney, Ballysadare and Coolaney, 40% in Ballymote and Gurteen and 47% in Keash. Of the Sligo parishes Tourlestrane had the highest illiteracy rate at over 60% which was closer to many of the rates recorded in the Mayo parishes, such as Bohola, Swinford and Kilmovee. Ballaghaderreen and Kiltimagh had the lowest rates in Mayo with about 48%. Straide and Killasser had just over 55% and Charlestown and Foxford just over 57%. One of the worst was Meelick with 69%, but the worst in fact was Attymass where a staggering 79% of people over five years of age could neither read or write. John O' Grady described his parish in 1879 as 'exceptionally illiterate' which made it almost impossible for him to set up a relief committee. Attymass was closely followed by neighbouring Bonniconlon with 76% illiteracy. As might be expected from the lower female school attendance, illiteracy among women was everywhere a few points higher. Again the worst was Attymass where almost 85% of women were illiterate, followed by Bonniconlon with over 82%. Best were Collooney and Ballysadare with about 36% and Coolaney with 39%.

Illiteracy

Lyster reported to Rome in October 1895 that there were 200 schools in the diocese catering for 21,601 pupils.[41] The pupil population in the diocese had more than tripled in less than thirty years and was still growing, and five years later there were 22,500 pupils in 208 schools. The number of pupils probably reached a peak that year (1900) as Lyster's final report in December 1904 revealed that the number had fallen back to 22,000 and during that decade the Catholic population of the diocese had fallen from 89,545 to 85,400. The number of schools in each parish varied from twenty in Ballaghaderreen to three in Straide and Coolaney.

Lyster Reports 1895-1904

41 N.S. 69 (1895), ff 140rv, 141rv, 142r; vol 189 (1900), ff 818rv, 819rv, 820r, 821v; vol 323 (1905), ff 813rv, 814rv, 815rv, 816rv, 817rv, 818rv

The largest school in the diocese was the convent school in Swinford with 254 pupils, followed by the convent schools in Ballaghaderreen and Kiltimagh with 243 and 242 respectively in each. As well as their girls' school, convents also had mixed infants' schools which accounted for their large size. The largest mixed school was Curryane (Cashel) in Swinford parish with 199 pupils, followed by Lismirane in Bohola with 182 and Kinaffe (Swinford) with 177 pupils. The largest single sex schools for boys and girls were both in the village of Curry with 191 boys and 171 girls. The smallest mixed school was Derrykinlogh in Carracastle with twenty-six pupils and the smallest single sex school was Lackagh with seventeen boys. By now the gender gap in the pupil population had not only disappeared but had actually swung in favour of girls. Taking only the single sex schools in each parish into account, the average attendance of girls outnumbered boys in all except six while in one other parish, Curry, the attendance of both sexes was almost equal.

In 1904 two primary schools were run by Religious Brothers, the Marists in Swinford and the De La Salle in Ballaghaderreen. Two schools were reserved exclusively for Protestants while a third school in the parish of Ballysadare with a Protestant manager and teacher had twelve Catholic pupils in attendance in 1895 and fourteen in 1900. Here, according to Lyster, the landlord was 'so nasty and proud that when asked by us time and again for a site to build a school he vehemently refused'. Another problem in Ballysadare was that the parish priest, Terence O'Rorke, was almost ninety and mentally unstable but by 1904 when Edward Connington succeeded him, Lyster hoped that a Catholic school would soon be built. The number of primary schools declined during the twentieth century, a decline which accelerated from the middle of the century and by the end almost three-quarters of them had disappeared

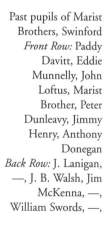

Past pupils of Marist Brothers, Swinford *Front Row:* Paddy Davitt, Eddie Munnelly, John Loftus, Marist Brother, Peter Dunleavy, Jimmy Henry, Anthony Donegan *Back Row:* J. Lanigan, —, J. B. Walsh, Jim McKenna, —, William Swords, —,

CHAPTER FOUR

The Struggle to Survive

The standard of living of poor tenants and farmers declined from the beginning to the middle of the ninetenth century. 'About forty years ago', John Coleman of Swinford stated before the Devon Commission in 1844, 'land was set at half the price that it is now and they (tenants) had double the means to pay it to what they have at present; they got £6 for a cwt of butter and they will not get £4 now. They have no yarn to employ them and their sole trade is rearing a pig and going to England.'[1] Not only had tenants to pay exorbitant rents, but also they had no fixity of tenure as Coleman pointed out to the commissioners. 'There is another evil and a great evil it is, their not getting leases or compensation for their improvements.' They were tenants at will and could be ejected at any time and their holding given to the highest bidder, a completely demoralising system as there was no incentive for the tenant to improve his holding. Bernard Durcan of Kiltimagh believed that if the small-holders were given fixity of tenure their condition would be enormously improved. 'I am convinced, that if the people have sufficient tenure, and if on the termination of their tenure they were entitled to compensation for all the valuable improvements they would have made, labour would be enhanced, the waste lands would be brought into cultivation, the necessity of going to seek wages in England would be removed, and the general condition of the people, both physical and moral, would be improved beyond calculation.'

Life on the Land

1 Devon Commission – Evidence taken before the Commissioners appointed to inquire into the occupation of Land in Ireland, 1844: evidence of John Coleman PP Swinford at Swinford, Wednesday 24 July 1844, part 2, pp 390-92; others who gave evidence in Swinford were Bernard Durcan PP Kiltimagh, pp 380-84, Thomas Dillon, merchant, Ballaghaderreen, pp 384-87, Luke Colleran, farmer, Curry, pp 387-90, James Harkan, farmer & shop-keeper, Swinford, p 390, Michael Howley, land surveyor, Swinford, pp 392-3, John Durcan, Gurtarslin near Tubbercurry, p 393, Ulick Burke MD Swinford, pp 393-4, Michael Millet (Mellet?), bailiff, Swinford, pp 394-95. Among those who gave evidence at Sligo on 12 & 13 July were Andrew Baker, cess collector, Coolavin, John Brett, Tubbercurry, pp 180-90, Thomas Fibbs, farmer, Cloonamahon, John Armstrong, Chaffpool, John Finn CC Kilturra, Cloonoghil & Kilshalvy, pp 233-35, Charles King O'Hara, Annaghmore, pp 190-95, Rev Lewis Potter, rector, Dromard, pp 199-202, William Christian, deputy weighmaster, Sligo town, pp 219-221. John Davis, barrister, Frenchpark gave evidence at Castlerea, 23 July, p 366 and Edward Deane, farmer, Carragowan near Swinford, at Castlebar, 31 July

Country dress at
Killedan. *Left to
right:* Pat Sweeney,
Nancy O'Brien (Mrs
Shaun Brennan), Mrs
Nicholas McDonagh
(Bid Jordan),
Mrs Groake
(Biddy Cosgary) –
Killedan, 1903
(courtesy Betty Solon)

Holdings

In general the holdings were too small to support a family. The general size of farms in Upper Leyny were six to ten acres and John Brett in Tubbercurry estimated that the smallest size that could support a family was ten to twelve acres. In Bunninadden where the curate, John Finn, stated that 1,150 families were 'in very low circumstances', farms varied from six to twelve acres in the Sligo portion of the parish and two to five in the Mayo portion. In general farm holdings were smaller generally in Mayo, from three to fifteen acres in Kiltimagh parish where the rundale system was widespread with farmers jointly occupying land.

Sub-Division

One of the main causes of the progressive impoverishment of tenants was the practice of sub-dividing their holdings among their children, described in 1844 by John Armstrong of Chaffpool: 'The poorer order of occupants divide their ground very much; those who have not fortunes to give their daughters gave them small holdings. If a man has 10 acres and four daughters, he will give 2 acres to each as a marriage portion and keep 2 acres himself. They regard the son very little; he is expected to make the same bargaining with some other man's daughter and get the same portion.' Sub-division was rampant according to Andrew Baker in Coolavin. 'Where I have known one man residing there are four, five or six now.' On the eve of the Great Famine over-population was the single greatest problem facing the country: 'We are not able to sustain the human stock upon it', Coleman said of the extremely populous district of Swinford. Hindsight lends a certain poignancy to the remark made by John Brett on the eve of the Great Famine: 'I do not see how you can get rid of the surplus population; it is in that the great difficulty is.'

Labourers, who occupied the lowest rung, had a cabin and a potato patch for which they paid about two pounds a year in the form of duty-work, computed at sixpence to eight pence a day without food. Coleman complained about the harsh regime of duty-work imposed by one sub-agent in Swinford parish: 'They must go six or seven miles to plant his potatoes and reap his oats and do his work for him.' Labourers on the Ormsby estate in Kiltimagh were obliged to work at any period of the year at sixpence a day without food and anyone who refused was fined one shilling or have his crops taken. *Labourers*

Living conditions showed very little improvement in the course of the nineteenth century. The cabins which John Barrow described and illustrated on his journey from Ballaghaderreen to Swinford in 1835 were not dissimilar from those described by travellers at the end of the eighteenth century or those still widely inhabited at the end of the nineteenth. By 1844, when Coleman had been twenty-eight years parish priest of Swinford, the landless poor still had no bedding. Lord Dillon asked Coleman at the beginning of the *Cabins*

Typical Foxford
cottage from
The Gentleman,
14 Sept 1895

century to show him a cabin in the barony of Castlereagh. 'I brought him into a house; he did not see a bed in it; he saw a very interesting woman with three or four children. He said, "What covering have you at night?" and she pointed to the covering on the cradle – that was all that they had. In the night they lay in their clothes. "Why" I said, "You would not let your dog lie there." They have not a pound of straw in it; they lay upon the floor.'

Bedding

People with two or three acres were 'more comfortable.' Ulic Burke, who by then had been the dispensary doctor in Swinford for seventeen years, described their 'species of bedsteads':

They have a small recess built in the side of the house merely perhaps little more than the length of a man; outside of this a stick or two are laid, and from that to the wall some cross sticks, and over that some straw, and under it in general they keep the potatoes ... The younger part of the family sleep with their parents, and two or three others sleep upon the floor or perhaps there may be another bed in the wall ... Some of them have blankets of their own manufacture; but generally they are of a very scanty description. There are very few houses with the luxury of a sheet.

Thatched Cottages

There was a some improvement, albeit slight, from the beginning to the end of the nineteenth century in the living conditions of the great mass of the people, particularly of the poor cottiers. The thatched cottages then were about thirty feet long and twelve feet wide with walls eight feet high, made of stone

Typical peasant's cottage, Foxford. *Daily Graphic,* 9 Jan 1897

without mortar and plastered on the outside. The floors were composed of 'flags' of schist or foliated granite. The poorest class had only one general living room with the fire-place against one end wall which animals continued to share. 'After dark the family and their friends sit round the fire, and the cow, heifer, calf and pig, get as near as they can. The poultry are also under the roof wherever they can perch. The customs of daily life are simple and natural: and the sense and manner of the dwellers in these rude homes are such that one can never enter or quit one without paying a mental tribute of respect to its owner.'[2]

2 Morrissey, *On the Verge of Want,* p 170

Henry Doran, a Congested Districts Board inspector living in Kilmovee, described a better class cottage in Kiltimagh in 1892:[3]

Two-Room Cottages

> The interior is divided into two apartments, one used as a living room, and at one end the cattle are usually kept. In it, also, there is a recess in the side wall near the fire place, in which a rude bedstead is fixed which is occupied by the husband and wife. The children of both sexes sleep in the second apartment, and the milk and butter are kept there.

The kitchen or living room was about eighteen feet long and the sleeping room twelve feet long. The furniture was basic but often included a dresser 'usually furnished with clean and ornamental crockery or china.'

There is a description of the accomodation division between animals and humans in the neighbourhood of Pontoon:[4]

Sharing with Animals

> Cattle share the living room of the family, their part of the floor space being separated from the rest by an open drain cut and built almost entirely across the width of the room, so as to leave a bridge for the cattle, and passing out under the foot of the wall to the manure heap or pit which I regret to say will always be found close under the window of the house. The cattle are thus confined strictly to the end of the room furthest from the fire and stand or lie in due order.

Doran was surprised at how moral the people were.

> Reflecting on the habits of the people of this and neighbouring districts, who are born and reared in the same room as their cattle; where brothers and sisters occupy the same sleeping apartment, insensible of any violation of human decency; living in such foul surroundings, in such close association with the brutes of the field, I have often marvelled how they are so moral, so well disposed, and so good in many ways as they generally are.

Sir Henry Doran

3   TCD OL microfilm 395 The Congested Districts Board commissioned base line reports on the living conditions in the various congested districts. Doran submitted reports in 1892 on Swinford (2 May), Foxford (5 May), Kiltimagh (6 May), Tubbercurry (21 May), Ardnaree, including the electoral divisions of Kilgarvan and Attymass East and West, (31 May) and Ballaghaderreen (2 July). Each district comprised a number of electoral divisions: *Tubbercurry:* (Sligo) Glendarragh, Tubbercurry, Kilmactigue, Aclare, Benada, Achonry East, Achonry West, Breencorragh & Cloonacool, (Mayo) Cloonmore & Doocastle. *Ballaghaderreen:* (Sligo) Cuilmore, Kilfree, Coolavin, (Mayo) Kilmovee, Ballaghaderreen, Edmondstown. (Roscommon) Buckhill, Artagh North, Kilcolagh, Loughglynn. *Foxford:* Shraheen, Toomore, Callow, Cuildoo. *Swinford:* Tumgesh, Meelick, Swinford, Sonnagh, Kilbeagh, Brackloon, Toocananagh, Killedan, Urlaur, Kilkelly. *Kiltimagh:* Kiltimagh, Knock North, Murneen. (Kiltimagh is reproduced in James Morrissey, *On the Verge of Want*, pp 104-109. Doran also submitted on 30 March 1893 a general report on the counties of Galway, Mayo, Roscommon and Sligo.)
4   Report of Major Gaskell, 1 Dec 1892. TCD OL microfilm 395

Visitors Shocked   The twin evils of humans sharing their cabins with farm animals and the consequent manure heaps in front of the cabins continued to shock visitors to the west of Ireland. When an English priest, Charles Rothwell, accompanied by two members of the Manchester Committee, visited Foxford, Ballaghaderreen and Kiltimagh in 1898, the first thing that struck them was the appalling condition of the houses. 'They are really little more than shelters ... In most cases the pigs and other animals owned by the peasants share with them these miserable dwellings. The unpleasantness from a sanitary point of view, which one would expect from this joint occupation, is to a large extent deadened by the pungent smoke from the turf fire. There is almost an entire absence of windows.'[5] Living conditions seemed somewhat better in the more prosperous Sligo portion of the diocese. 'Mud cabins so common formerly in the county, and not uncommon even in the town, have nearly disappeared. Stone houses, consisting of one apartment for the family and the cattle of the family, are hardly to be found – animals being now kept in some kind of separate steading.'[6]

Country people,
Foxford, 1890s

Manure Heaps   Each morning the manure deposited by animals the previous night was shovelled out the door and left in a heap close by. People in Kiltimagh parish put down large quantities of turf-mould on the cabin floor as bedding for the cattle and this increased the size of the manure-heaps and some thought that this explained why fever epidemics were not more frequent.[7] Doran recommended that the police be obliged to enforce the sanitary laws. 'No person should be allowed to keep cattle, pigs or fowl in their dwellings; a manure

5   *Manchester Guardian*, 3 May 1898
6   O'Rorke, *Sligo*, vol II, p 586
7   Henry Doran to the Congested Districts Board, 6 May 1892 qtd in James Morrissey, *On the Verge of Want*, p 108

heap should not be kept within twenty yards of a dwelling; the houses should
be whitewashed inside and out at least once a year.' The campaign launched
by the Congested Districts Board to remove animals from homes and manure heaps from close proximity to them was to take the best part of a generation to achieve.

The Sisters of Charity in Benada, Ballaghaderreen and Foxford were ad-   *Foxford Scheme*
mirably placed to observe the living conditions of the people as twice weekly
they visited the sick in the surrounding districts within a five-mile radius of
their convent. In her memoirs, Agnes Morrogh Bernard later recalled the role
her Sisters played in Foxford:[8]

> Our Missioners visited the various townlands and many little villages,
> some of very few scattered cabins and others more pretentious of perhaps a
> dozen houses or so. To reach these the Sisters had to leave the road and
> cross fields and almost always had to pick their way as best they could past
> very unpleasant manure heaps, lucky if they found a stone or two to step
> on; often there was the narrowest little causeway between two of these
> abominations. If your foot slipped – tragedy! The doors of the cabins
> opened on to these. We decided in the face of all discouragement, that we
> would wage war against these unhealthy manure pits. For a moment we
> did not condemn the people for the sordidness of their surroundings – the
> blame lay elsewhere. For long generations no one had taken any interest in
> the lives or well-being of these poor souls.

The Sisters organised a competition among the cottiers, awarding prizes
for replacing the manure pits in front of their cabins with gardens, clean
streets or part street with the manure heap walled off and, in the three years
1896 to 1899, over 600 cottiers took part. 'A marked improvement is to be
seen all over the country in this respect, the manure pits being removed and
cattle and pigs put out of the dwellings into newly erected sheds and stables.'
It took many years to complete the removal of all the manure pits. By 1908
the total had reached 752 cottiers and the last removal of a pit was recorded in
1912.[9] By then Foxford was probably one of the more advanced districts as
CDB reported in 1919 that elsewhere 'a great improvement in the houses and
home-management is still most urgently required' with cattle, pigs and poultry still kept within many dwelling houses.[10]

8 RSCG / H 26 / 449, p 51
9 RSCG / H 26 / 105 Names and addresses of all cottiers given.
10 CDB Twenty-seventh Report, p 10

Food   People remained largely vegetarians as they had been in the previous century. 'They go out in the fields and there is a kind of wild rape and they take them and boil them; and if a beggar asks you for a halfpenny to buy a halfpenny worth of salt, it is for the wild things they get in the fields.'[11] By mid century all were living on potatoes. 'Those that have no lands have rarely milk and it is a luxury to get a red herring', and according to Ulic Burke MD, Swinford: 'Their diet is principally potatoes; they very seldom indulge in meat.' Their diet was 'as low in the scale of humanity as possible.'

Improvements   Later on in the century there was a marked improvement in their diet according to Terence O'Rorke, whose long life spanned much of the nineteenth and the early years of the twentieth century:[12]

> No one would put up in these days with the potatoes and salt, which not unfrequently formed the poor man's meal in the first years of the current century; nor with the potatoes and salt herring, or potatoes and butter-milk, which, more commonly, served about the same time for the dinner and the breakfast of labourers and their families ... If the potato forms still the chief article, the *piece de resistance*, of the poor man' dinner, the sweet milk, the bit of butter, the occasional egg, or the slice of American bacon which accompanies it, gives it a palatableness and nutritiousness which it lacked in the past; while the breakfast of bread, butter and tea, and the supper of stirabout, or of bread and milk, give the diet of the day the variety so conducive to health and enjoyment.

Bread and Tea   By now bread and tea were added to the normal diet of potatoes and a considerable amount of tea was consumed with even children of five or six drinking tea strong enough for any adult.[13] Potatoes were generally available from August to the following May and together with milk were consumed for breakfast, dinner and supper, occasionally flavoured with salted fish or a little fat American bacon. In a good year potatoes would last nine to ten months when a family of six in fairly ordinary circumstances would normally consume about five tons. When potatoes ran out in April or May they were replaced by Indian meal stirabout or porridge, frequently without milk, followed by bread and tea for breakfast, and bread and tea for dinner and supper with occasionally an egg for the man of the house. Bread was made from oatmeal or a mixture of oatmeal and flour. Eggs and milk were more available during the summer but people who had no cows or no cows giving milk ate their food without it as milk was never bought.

11 John Coleman to Devon Commission, Swinford, 1844, part 2, pp 390-92
12 O'Rorke, *Sligo*, vol II, pp 586-7
13 TCD OL microfilm 395, Report of Henry Doran on Kiltimagh district to the Congested Districts Board, 6 May 1892, p 403; qtd in Morrissey, p 107

Thomas McNicholas
doing his bakery
round in Kiltimagh
c. 1900
(courtesy Betty Solon)

Clothes

Clothing had improved by the middle of the century, mainly, according to
John Coleman, because calico was so cheap. People had looms and wove their
own flannels and manufactured their own frieze. 'The humblest countrymen
are now clad in fair suits of frieze or tweed.'[14] Women wore petticoats and
shawls. Boots were generally worn by adults, particularly by men but not frequently by children while women wore them going to Mass or fairs and markets. Flannels, socks, stockings and underclothes were made up at home and
all other clothes were bought either in shops or second-hand from travelling
pedlars at markets and fairs. Sunday clothes were almost always bought either
readymade from the 'clothes men' at fairs or made by tailors from bought
cloth. The check and fancy shirts worn by men on Sundays, as well as the
Sunday dresses particularly of younger women, were always bought. Both men
and women wore hats in public and younger boys wore caps. It was estimated
that a family of six living on a holding of the lowest valuation in Kiltimagh in
1892 spent five pounds a year on clothes, almost one-fifth of its total annual
expenditure.

Markets

Weekly markets were held in Swinford, Tubbercurry and most of the other
towns in the diocese where country people sold eggs, butter, poultry and
other produce and at the same time bought bread and tea and other supplies
in the shops. Usually local dealers travelled round the countryside and
bought up all the eggs which they brought to the weekly markets in Tubbercurry and Swinford and sold them to an egg exporter who packed them in

14 O'Rorke, op. cit., p 588

the market place as fast as he got them and then had them despatched for their ultimate destination that same evening. A northern dealer, who traded with Liverpool, went from village to village in the Foxford area with a horse

The Tansey family,
Carrowcrory, Keash
c. 1920

and cart buying eggs from the cottiers.[15] Eggs were seldom more than a week or ten days old before they reached the consumer, except in harvest time when they were sometimes stored for six or eight weeks in anticipation of a rise in price, leading English and Scottish dealers to complain of Irish eggs being frequently stale. The 'egg-money' was the property of the woman of the house who decided how best to dispose of it.

Market Day,
Charlestown
(courtesy Thomas
Hennigan)

15 RSCG / H 26 / 449

Systematic fraud was practised in the market and William Christian, a *Market Fraud*
deputy weighmaster in Sligo town, described some fraudulent practices there
in 1844. A great deal of oats was brought to the market by carmen, men who
owned a horse and cart and earned their living transporting goods for others.
Most poor farmers could not bring in their oats themselves and sent it in
with the carmen who very often were in collusion with merchants who
bribed them to avoid the official weighmasters, under-weighed the oats and
under-paid the poor farmer.

Farmers who sold butter at markets were often victims of fraud. The butter
was inspected by the public officer who gave it a quality mark and then
weighed by the weighmaster who gave the seller a ticket. The merchant who
bought the butter asked the farmer to deliver it to his store where he insisted
that it be re-examined by his own inspector who marked it with a lower grade
and demanded a reduction in price. The disappointed farmer took his butter
and tried unsuccessfully to sell it for the original price to other merchants because it now bore an inferior mark and was thus obliged to return to the first
buyer and sell his butter at a loss. Merchants also frequently changed the
qualities marked by the official inspector and often changed second, third
and even fourth quality into first and exported them as such. 'Scarcely a cask
of butter leaves this port with the original market brands upon it.'

Fair Day, Kiltimagh
(courtesy Betty Solon)

Credit dealing was quite common especially during the 'hungry months' *Credit*
of May, June and July in ordinary years but sometimes much earlier in a year
when the potato crop was bad. Anne Deane, proprietor of Monica Duff's in
Ballaghaderreen, one of the largest shops in the diocese, told John Dillon that

Ploughing with donkeys on a farm near Carracastle in the early 1950s *(courtesy William Winter)*

'the people around here are so steeped in debt they have little money to spend.'[16] All goods which could be bought in comparatively large quantities such as oatmeal and flour, were got on credit. Doran estimated that a poorer landholding family in Kiltimagh in 1892 bought four bags of flour and six pounds worth of Indian meal for the family, pigs and poultry, most likely on credit at 6%-10% interest. Most people were in debt to the shopkeepers, who usually gave a year's credit and expected their accounts to be paid or at least a substantial payment made when the migratory labourer returned in November from England.

> Regular customers have a running account; they seldom clear off the debt. While the debt remains within safe limits, if he pays two or three pounds on account he can get goods to that amount before making another payment. If the shopkeeper suspects a customer is distributing his patronage with others, he presses for payment and in this way keeps his customer and charges them his own prices.

Credit Prices

Very often, instead of interest shopkeepers charged credit prices which were 15%-20% higher. For instance, where the cash price for a bag of meal was twelve shillings the credit price was 13s 6d. Credit might be extended for twelve months, but if a bad year followed, unless last year's bills were paid up, credit was stopped. Usually the credit lasted on average about five months for a fairly well-off farmer and about half that for a poorer farmer. Eggs and sometimes butter, were nearly always exchanged at market prices for tea, sugar, tobacco, snuff and retailed foodstuffs. Shopkeepers preferred to give tea rather than any other commodity in exchange for eggs because they had 100% mark-up on tea and people would not consume as much tea as they did if they had to pay cash for it.

There was some criticism of shopkeepers' treatment of the poor. One letter writer to a local newspaper had Monica Duff's in Ballaghaderreen in mind when he castigated 'those merchants who pose as honest and unflinching patriots and at the same time shower bills throughout the country for miles at an unseasonable time.'[17] Shop debts were a particularly sensitive issue for priests and when John McDermott of Kilmovee told a public meeting during

16 Anne Deane to John Dillon, 25 Sept 1889, Dil. P. 6885
17 John Hunt, Ballaghadereen, to the Editor of the *Connaught Telegraph,* 5 May 1886 *C.T.* 15 May 1886

the famine of 1879 that shopkeepers should remit the debts of the poor, one of his parishioners, a Kilkelly shopkeeper, incensed at the suggestion, criticised McDermott's 'diatribes on merchants, shopkeepers and bankers, the generosity of whom he was never yet known to spurn.'[18]

Each town had moneylenders or usurers, called 'gombeen men' (*fear gaimbín*), one of whom operating in Swinford was described by John Coleman in 1844. His name was McEvoy and was underagent for Francis Blake Knox, an absentee landlord whose agent also did not reside in the neighbourhood. When the tenants had no money to pay the rent, McEvoy lent them money and charged them, according to Coleman, 'whatever his avarice pleases'. McEvoy's father who was 'of the class of "gombeens" or extraordinary usurers' lent the money to the son. Michael Mellet, a landlord's bailiff, stated that there were many local usurers around Swinford who were a 'great cause of distress in the neighbourhood; but the poor creature must get his rent whatever usury he is charged.'

'Gombeen Men'

Gombeen men were not licensed moneylenders and had to resort to certain devices to escape the attention of the law as Edward Deane described to the commissioners in 1844:

Swinford

> I know a poor man residing three miles from Swineford, who bought a bag of oats for 30s; the man had occasion to get the money to go to England, and the party bought back the same bag of oats from him for 12s., and the poor man took his 12s. with him, having passed his IOU for 30s. This is not a rare instance. Another man came in then and bought the same bag of oats at the same price, and sold it back to the same person for 12s. again, so that the bag of oats was sold fifteen or twenty times.

John Davis, a barrister in Frenchpark, gave an almost identical description of the operation of the gombeen man, a large farmer who brought a bag of corn in his horse and cart to the market and what appeared to be the sale of corn was in fact a cover for moneylending. According to Luke Colleran, a farmer in Curry, very few gave out money but generally meal or oats usually in March or April with payment demanded at Christmas when they sent out 'one or two of the neighbouring farmers to raise the markets in order to claim a higher price from their debtors.'

Some individuals were both moneylenders and pawnbrokers, like the moneylender in Kiltimagh who had a drapery shop and pawnshop as well. That town was 'accommodated with a few of those notorious concerns' in 1870.[19]

Kiltimagh

18 Kilkelly shop-keeper to the Editor of the *Connaught Telegraph*, 28 Oct 1879 *C.T.* 8 Nov 1879
19 J. O'Regan, *Articles Worldwide and Local*, pp 56-58

'There were also private money-lenders known by the name of gombeen men, who had no shops or signs over their doors to indicate their nefarious trafficking, which was a very remunerative business for them. This class of moneylender would carry on his business at all hours of the day or night to suit the unfortunate borrowers for the purpose of privacy.'

Tubbercurry   Some shopkeepers in Tubbercurry were moneylenders and a strongly-worded resolution was passed in 1886 by the Achonry branch of the Irish National League against 'the usurers of Tubbercurry' who 'seem to be more dreaded by the people than the rack-renters.' [20] 'It is our conviction that the men who charge 'gombeen' at the rate of 70% to 80% p.a. on their guano and from 50% to 60% on their provisions, are as great a curse to the country and as effective a cause of the people's poverty as the most grinding land-lords.'

Migratory Labourers   Bernard Durcan told the Devon Commission that a large proportion of the labouring classes in the parish of Kiltimagh go every year to England.[21] 'In some districts of this parish at an average, I believe, nine-tenths of the male adult population go there every year. There is scarcely a house which there are not some gone from it, the younger men particularly.' It was the same in Swinford according to John Coleman. 'The population being so great and the holdings so small, they have no opportunity of paying their rent but by running off to England. They contrive to keep a cabin by that means; and the wife and children till the land.' John Armstrong of Chaffpool de-scribed how undertakers formed parties of labourers in Ireland and took them over to England. From Coolavin they invariably went to the fen coun-tries and those who went early in time for the hay harvest brought home about £5 while those who went later for the corn harvest only brought home about £3.

The same pattern of migration continued after the Famine and right into the next century. An area extending from Ballaghaderreen to Ballina and Tubbercurry to Claremorris, with a population in 1891 of 135,521, the most thickly populated in the country, supplied the greatest number of migratory labourers on English farms every year. In fact such migration was almost pe-culiar to this area as there were no migratory labourers from the other con-gested districts from Donegal to Kerry, even from impoverished places such as Glencolumbkill or Connemara. Both MacCormack and Lyster mentioned this seasonal migration in their reports to Rome as one of the peculiarites of the diocese of Achonry.

20 *S.C.* 17 April 1886
21 Part 2, pp 380-84

'Bridge of Sighs', Swinford Station

An estimated 20,000 to 22,000 went every year from the west of Ireland in the last decades of the century, about 14,000 leaving between March and June from Ballaghaderreen railway station and the other stations along the line from Ballina to Castlerea, on the first leg of their journey to England. On one Friday in June 1888 over 500 'harvest men' left from Ballaghaderreen railway station for England and 2,463 from Foxford station in the month of June 1892.[22]

Numbers

Two-thirds of all the migrants left on Mid-Summers Day or 24 June or as near as possible to it and their chief destination was Cheshire or Lancashire while some went to the midland counties. They remained there from three to nine months, more often the latter, and earned on average fifteen to twenty-five shillings a week, out of which they saved ten to twelve shillings bringing home on average £8 a head, which amounted to almost one-third of their annual income. The number declined during the First World War because of the fear of conscription with 13,000 travelling to England and Scotland in 1915, three-quarters of them from Connacht, the largest number of whom were from Swinford Poor Law Union

Earnings

Much of the work on their own holdings was completed during the spring before they departed. 'The cultivation of land for crops is seldom begun until Spring sets in and when that season turns out wet the crops are late and more precarious.' While away, all farm work was carried out by their womenfolk and children as in the district around Ballaghaderreen:

22 *C.T.* 7 July 1888. The number who left from Foxford station each month in 1892 from information provided by the manager of the Midland Great Western Railway: Feb, 42: Mar, 392: April, 496: May, 440: June, 2,443: July, 98. TCD OL Microfilm 395

Womens' Labour

When the men are absent in England the women work very hard. They generally assist in the digging of the soil for the potato and oat crops and attend to the after cultivation of the potatoes. They carry manure in baskets on their backs, often long distances, to fields that are inconveniently located. They also work hard cutting and saving the turf and they carry it on their backs from the bog to the nearest road.

After the migrants returned home, usually in October, they virtually hibernated, doing little or no work from November to February. 'They remain winter after winter lounging idly about awaiting the time to return again to England.' There was little or no motivation for them to work at home as they had no prospect of remuneration but when employed in England 'better unskilled labourers could not be found.'[23]

Tuberculosis

Tuberculosis was to the nineteenth and the early decades of the next century what cancer was to the following period, the dreaded terminal disease. It was by no means peculiar to Ireland and when the young nun Thérèse fell victim to it in her convent in Lisieux, the extraordinary rapidity with which the cult of the Little Flower swept accross Europe was at least partially due to the numbers of families who could identify with her. Though later very much associated with the squalor of city slums, TB was no respecter of classes. Two daughters of John Blake Dillon died of consumption at the ages of eighteen and twenty respectively as also did his wife, Adelaide, and a son, William, threatened with TB, went to Colorada in his mid-twenties and made America his permanent home. Another son, John, lived in fear of it all through his long and turbulent political career and his health was closely monitored by the authorities during his frequent spells in prison. The Fenian, Edward Duffy from Ballaghaderreen, also suffered from TB and died from the disease in Millbank prison as his father did also years before in Ballaghaderreen. Priests sometimes were also victims. John Horan from Keash, who contracted consumption while he was a curate in Killasser, returned to his family home where he died in spring 1888 at the age of forty-two.[24] Thomas Gilmartin, professor of ecclesiastical history in Maynooth, was only thirty-five when he died of consumption in May 1892.

It was a horrible way to die:

There is shortness of breath, pains in the breast, profuse sweats during sleep, spitting of blood and matter. Shivers succeeded by hot fits, with flushing of the face and burning of the hands and feet, and, in the last

23 Henry Doran to CDB, on Foxford, 5 May & on Ballaghaderreen, 2 July 1892
24 *S.C.* 7 April 1888

stages of the illness, a diarrhoea that helps to waste what remains of flesh and strength.[25]

The hacking cough and expectoration created perfect conditions for the contagion which is carried by droplets in the air. Tuberculosis accounted for 14% of all deaths in 1909 and in 1921 there were more than 7,000 deaths from the dreaded consumption, almost twice as many as from cancer that year. With the discovery of pennicillen and an energetic programme of building sanatoria, the disease was virtually eradicated in the forties and fifties.

Swinford market in snow
(Photo Fr Browne SJ Collection)

25 *Irish Times*, 25 Aug 2001

CHAPTER FIVE

The Religious Divide

Catholic Association

Throughout the nineteenth century there was a steady erosion of the influence and prestige of the Established Church, leading to its disestablishment in the last quarter of the century. What was called the 'Protestant ascendancy' in the previous century was gradually dismantled and Irish Protestants felt threatened by the renewed campaign for Catholic emancipation and were increasingly on the defensive because of the growing support for emancipation in British political circles. The launching of the Catholic Association of Ireland in May 1823 and the subsequent campaign by Irish Catholics, spearheaded by Daniel O'Connell, was on a scale never before witnessed by Protestants. By introducing what came to be called the 'Catholic rent' which could be as little as a penny a month, O'Connell opened up the Association to mass membership and throughout the country thousands of associate members became involved by their regular subscriptions. The collection of the rent made necessary the creation of local committees in parishes everywhere which quickly expanded their roles, organising meetings, drawing up petitions and corresponding with the central committee on a variety of local issues and grievances.

Priests' Involvement

In 1828 the Association introduced a new system of local organisation by selecting two churchwardens, one chosen by the parish priest and the other by the local people, whose function was to act as links between their area and the national leadership, sending regular monthly reports and publicising information from headquarters. Priests played a pivotal role as local agents and organisers of the Association, announcing the rent scheme from the altar, helping to set up the committees to organise the collection, and carrying on much of the correspondence with the central body in Dublin. They played a prominent part in the general elections of 1826 and 1828, speaking in support of the candidates favoured by the Association and even leading processions of their parishioners to the polling booths on election day.

Forty-Shilling Freeholders

In the Catholic Relief Act of 1793 the vote was given to forty-shilling freeholders, i.e. to those who held a lease for life of a house or land in which the lessee had an interest worth forty shillings. This placed Catholics and Protestants on equal terms as far as voting was concerned. However, these tenants were placed under enormous pressure by their landlords to vote for his candidate and thus increase the landlord's political influence and, while freeholders could not be evicted at will, landlords could make life very difficult for those who disobeyed his wishes in times of elections. He could threaten that the lease would not be renewed or insist on the strict performance of all the conditions of the lease and on the immediate payment of rents which in practice were always paid six months in arrears. The Catholic rent was used to help financially tenants who suffered because of how they voted.

Following the general election of 1826 liberal clubs were set up in various counties as the localised political organs of the Catholic Association. Sligo Liberal and Independent Club was set up in October 1828 and its stated purpose was 'to watch over and protect the Forty-Shilling Freeholders of the County should they suffer persecution on account of their conscientious discharge of their duty towards their Religion and country.'[1] The inaugural meeting of the club was held in the Catholic schoolhouse in Chapel Lane in Sligo and attended by the leading Catholic gentlemen of the county, six of whom were magistrates. Charles MacDermot of Coolavin was elected president and Joseph 'Mór' McDonnell of Doocastle, vice-president. The three bishops, Burke of Elphin, MacHale of Killala and McNicholas of Achonry were members of the committee which also included from the diocese Daniel Jones of Benada, Thomas Phillips of Cloonmore and Andrew Kelly of Camphill. Commitees were also formed in each barony which were to form a register of Catholic freeholders and report on the activities and numbers of the Protestant freeholders.

Liberal Clubs

Joseph 'Mór' McDonnell

Catholic emancipation, when it finally arrived, came in a surprising and spectacular fashion. A by-election took place in Clare in July 1828 and O'Connell was put forward as a candidate which was perfectly legal. Catholics were not prohibited from seeking election but were prevented from taking their seats by the nature of the oath they were required to swear which contained a declaration against the Catholic doctrine of transubstantiation. The Clare by-election was not only a massive victory for O'Connell but it gave a dramatic demonstration of the control the Catholic Association exercised over its followers. Thousands marched into Ennis on polling day, marshalled by members of the Association and led by their priests. O'Connell's election left the government with no alternative but to grant Catholic emancipation. His victory could be repeated all over the country.

Clare By-Election

1 John C. McTernan, *In Sligo Long Ago*, pp 172-3

Catholic
Emancipation

A Catholic Relief Act became law on 13 April 1829 which permitted Catholics to sit in parliament and to hold any civil or military office, other than those of monarch, Lord Chancellor of either Great Britain or Ireland and Lord Lieutenant of Ireland. A new oath was drawn up by which Catholics bound themselves to accept the Protestant succession to the throne and to deny the Pope's power to depose temporal rulers. Other clauses in the act forbade the holding of Catholic religious services anywhere except in churches or in private houses and prohibited members of Catholic religious orders coming into the country. The downside to emancipation came in a separate bill which was passed at the same time, which disenfranchised the fory-shilling freeholders. Henceforward, the freehold qualification for an elector was raised from forty shillings to ten pounds and, as a result, the number of electors in County Sligo dropped from 5,036 to 610.

Tithe War

After Emancipation was achieved, Catholic agitation turned to the payment of tithes and the 'tithe war' which began in 1830 was intense, widespread and bitter. The income of Protestant clergymen was largely derived from tithes which consisted in the payment of the farmers of the parish of one-tenth of the annual yield of their farms. Such was the practice everywhere, in Catholic countries such as France and Spain, as well as Protestant countries like England and Germany, and everywhere people paid their tithes unwillingly. What made the custom uniquely iniquitous in Ireland was that the people were compelled to pay for the support of the clergy of another religion. As the Frenchman De Latocnaye observed, tithes were paid to the Protestant minister, who was often the only Protestant in the parish, which was certainly the case in a number of parishes in Achonry.[2] Nothing was more resented by the people than the payment of tithes.

Tithe-Proctors

Protestant vicars were only too well aware of this deep resentment and to avoid unpleasantness often employed tithe-proctors or agents to collect the tithes, which only compounded the problem for tenants. Often an agent agreed a fixed sum which he paid the vicar and then extorted exorbitant amounts from the unfortunate tenants. They also applied a double standard, as Arthur Young had noted in County Leitrim, where the proctors were 'very civil to gentlemen but exceedingly cruel to the poor'.[3] Such apparently was the case in Coolaney and Collooney (Killoran and Kilvarnet) whose vicar, Josiah Hern, sent Charles O'Hara his tithes' account book for 1813, detailing the townlands and tenants who pay tithes. He noted in passing that the estate of Templehouse, the seat of the Perceval family, was 'not subject to tithes' and

2   *Rambles through Ireland*, vol 1, p 92
3   *Tour of Ireland*, vol 1, p 275

that the O'Hara estate itself had 'not paid tithes since I was Incumbent of this union.'[4] In this instance poor Catholics were obliged to pay tithes to the Protestant vicar while rich Protestants were exempt.

James Neligan, vicar of Kilmactigue, was entitled to tithes on corn of every kind, flax and meadow, as well as 'small dues, but these were never demanded.' The 'small dues' consisted of among other things, a tithe on wool and lambs which were paid to his predecessor but the number of sheep was so small and the collection of other sundry tithes so difficult that Neligan decided to relinquish them after establishing his right to them by citing some of the farmers to the ecclesiastical court to acknowledge that right. Thus his main income came from tithes on oats and flax as there was very little meadow in the parish. Oats and flax were paid by the acre at the rate of a tenth for the best crops and proportionately less for lower quantity. Typically, an acre of oats produced four barrels, two of which had to be sold by the tenant to pay the rent as well as the tithes.

Kilmactigue Tithes

Killasser was the scene of violent opposition to the collection of tithes in 1832, scenes which were repeated in early February 1834.[5] On Monday 10 February Chief Constable David J. Barry in Swinford sent two of his constables, Horan and Barrett, to the village of Boleyboy in Killasser where they were stationed in the house of Patrick Gaughan. Their mission was to post up the tithe notices. In the early afternoon a large number of people gathered outside the house and eight of them rushed the house, seized one of the notices from the policemen, which they trampled underfoot. The policemen held one of their attackers but he was soon rescued and they were told to quit the village 'on pain of death' but continued to take refuge in the house until their attackers had retired.

Killasser Attack

When word of the attack reached Barry in Swinford that evening he dispatched three more constables to reinforce the party and they all remained in Gaughan's house for the night.

R.I.C Reinforcements

On the following day about the hour of two o'clock an infuriated and ferocious mob, in number about three-hundred, armed with stones and bludgeons advanced from the neighbouring villages to the house where the police were stationed and immediately commenced tearing down the tithe notices which had been posted in front of the door; and while the

4 O'Hara Papers, Ms, 20, 280 (30)
5 Chief Constable David J. Barry, Swinford, to acting Sub-Inspector William Lewis, Castlebar, 10 & 11 Feb & 11 Mar 1834; same to Inspector General, 24 Feb 1834; Capt Ireland, sub-inspector, Castlebar, to Inspector General, 18 Feb 1834, Outrage Papers, 6, 9 & 11, Mayo 1834

police were engaged endeavouring to preserve the notices, upwards of twenty men entered the house, closed and barricaded the doors, and took possession of all the papers which they flung to the mob outside who trampled upon same. The Schedule however after a great struggle was recovered by the police and saved from destruction.

Police report on Tithe
War in Killasser

On the following day about the hour of two oclock and infuriated and ferocious mob in number about three hundred, armed with Stones and bludgeus advanced from the neighbouring Villages to the House Where the Police were Stationed, and immediately Commenced tearing down the Tithe notices which had been Posted in front of the door;

Police Retreat

The crowd threatened the police that if they attempted to fire their guns 'they would sacrifice each and every one of the policemen's lives and if the Light Horse and all the military from Castlebar was brought to Bolabee (sic) that they would beat them out of it and deprive them of their arms.' They also threatened to kill Gaughan if he allowed the police to stay another night in his house thus forcing them to leave. Magistrates at the Swinford Sessions praised them 'for their sturdy conduct in retreating to Swinford' and advised the chief constable not to send out his small party on the following day as it was Ash Wednesday and there would be a large number of people congregated in Boleyboy chapel.

Reinforcements

He reported the incident to his superior in Castlebar who immediately ordered sixteen men to march to the relief of the Swinford constabulary, and

Barry with fourteen men arrived in the village of Boleyboy on Thursday and began to post up the tithe notices. Several individuals approached and were allowed to read the notices and copy extracts from them and the same was repeated on Friday when 'matters began to assume a very tranquil appearance'. However, when Barry and his escort arrived on Saturday, 15 February he was informed that Gaughan had been threatened with death the previous day for admitting the police into his house.

Then matters began to turn nasty:

Parish Priest's Intervention

When about the hour of twelve o'clock the surrounding hills were covered with men. The chief constable feeling alarmed at so unexpected a sight, posted sentries at the doors and took the precaution to order that only two men at a time should be allowed to enter the house where the tithe Schedule was exhibiting. In a few moments after the Parish Priest[6] made his appearance and informed Mr Barry that he feared an attack on the Police party was meditated and advised him to be prepared, and on the look out, while he would advance to the hills for the purpose of reasoning with the people, which fortunately had the desired effect; and about three o'clock the crowd began to disperse and return to their homes.

On Sunday the scene changed to the parish chapel where Captain Ireland, the sub-inspector from Castlebar, and two local magistrates, Ellard and Deane, explained to the congregation what the government's purpose was in posting up the tithe schedule. On Monday and Tuesday Captain Ireland was present in the village all day when numerous people came to view the schedule while 'at the same time protesting against the returns, which they considered exorbitant and unjust and declared their determination to defend themselves legally if afforded the opportunity.' There was no further violence on that occasion.

Magistrates in Chapel

Captain Ireland left no doubt about the seriousness of the incident in his report to Major Warburton, the Inspector General in Dublin Castle.

I am bound however to state that I observed on the part of the peasantry a desperate determination to oppose the collection of Tithes: and I very much doubt that if such had been our object, we could (not) have succeeded without an imposing force and then only by sacrificing many lives.

It was not, however, the end of tithe-related violence in Killasser. Five days later three houses were attacked at night by an armed party and guns were taken and in one of them, in Carrowmoremoy, Michael Geraghty was badly beaten and his kitchen garden was trampled over by a large number of men. Geraghty was the proctor of Walter Burke who was the lay proprietor of the

House-Attacks

6 John McNulty

tithes in the parish. Tithes themselves were a marketable commodity and were sometimes sold to what were called 'lay impropriators' who themselves employed proctors or agents to collect them. Those who broke into the houses were strangers and 'quite undisguised'. Geraghty, however, was convinced that people from Boleyboy were in the attacking party and later gave a sworn statement to the police, naming three of them, Patrick Niland, Luke Browne and James Diamond, who were taken into custody to await their trial. Two other houses were attacked that night, Martin Devit(t)'s in Carrowbeg where a gun was taken, and that of Thomas Bartley who lived nearby and made his escape through a back window. Chief Constable Barry described the parish of Killasser as the 'very worst place in this district for committing crime and violating the law.'

Gurteen Tithe
Defaulters

Incidents occurred elsewhere in the diocese. Fourteen hundred people from Gurteen were summoned before magistrates in Ballymote at the end of February 1834 for failing to pay the tithes due to James Elwood, vicar of Kilfree but the two magistrates, Armstrong and West, 'did not think themselves justifiable in going into the inquiry.' [7] When they were making their way home from Ballymote they began shouting 'O'Connell forever!' and 'Down with the Brunswickers!'[8] An onlooker, William Ross, who was standing in front of his door, told the crowd to go home quitely but his intervention was

RIC group with
Andy Casey,
Swinford, at back left
(courtesy Ann Phelan)

7   Chief Constable John Whittaker, Ballymote, to Major Warburton, Inspector General, 6 Mar 1834, Outrage Papers, 14 Sligo 1834
8   Brunswick clubs were set up among militant Protestants to resist Catholic emancipation

not well received. The crowd began to pelt him and his house with stones and some of his windows were broken and his son got a gun and fired shots over the heads of the crowd. A neighbour, Charles Sands, who was also armed, fired into the crowd and hit one of them, John Gaffney, wounding him in the face and hand. Chief Constable John Whittaker in the barracks nearby heard the gunshots and arrived on the scene. He ordered the Rosses back into their house and remonstrated with the crowd whom he eventually persuaded to leave town. Gaffney's wounds were dressed by a medical attendant.

Later all the parties involved in the fracas were summoned to an inquiry. When the Gurteen people failed to show up, Whittaker approached their parish priest who was with them at the tithe sessions in Ballymote on that day, to give him a list of persons who could provide information to the inquiry. 'After some persuasion on my part and much reluctance on his, he gave me a list of persons.' As a result of the inquiry the two Rosses and Sands were committed for trial.

Ballymote also had its tithe defaulters. John Garrett, vicar of Emlaghfad, took out decrees in the summer of 1836 against those who defaulted in the payment of his tithes.[9] William Moore and Peter O'Brien, who were executing the decrees, were severely beaten by a party of seven people but Moore managed to escape and informed the police. When they were making their way to the scene they met O'Brien on the road, scarcely able to walk. No arrests were made. Those who executed decrees against tithe defaulters had the legal power to seize crops or animals and have them impounded. Three cattle were impounded in Aclare for tithes due to James Neligan, vicar of Kilmactigue but the pound was forcibly entered on a January night in 1835 and the cattle taken away.[10]

Ballymote Defaulters

Executing decrees on tithe defaulters was a dangerous occupation. A large party of men with blackened faces broke into the house of Thomas Gallagher of Lisbrogan in Meelick in October 1836 and dragged out Denis Murray, a driver for Thomas Ormsby of Knockmore, who had been serving decrees on the tenants.[11] He was so severely beaten that it was later reported that he was not likely to recover. The attackers also cut off the ears of his mule. The chief constable from Swinford could get no information in Lisbrogan on the guilty

Meelick Incident

9 Chief Constable John Whittaker, Ballymote, to Inspector General, 5 July 1836, Outrage Papers, Sligo 1836

10 Chief Constable John Whittaker, Ballymote, to Inspector General, 7 Jan 1835, Outrage Papers, 2, Sligo 1835

11 Chief Constable David J. Barry, Swinford, to Inspector General, 26 Oct & 4 Nov 1836, Outrage Papers, 103, Mayo 1836

party and summoned several of the neighbours to appear before magistrates but here again the investigation proved fruitless. However, probably because of Murray's precarious condition, the tenants must have felt the heat was on them as they paid up their tithes.

Kiltimagh Intimidation

Organised intimidation was used to insure that people did not pay tithes. At midnight on Sunday 16 October 1836 'a party of Rockites or night marauders' visited houses in the village of Bane in Kiltimagh and swore the inhabitants not to pay tithes to Mr Ormsby or to any other persons.[12] No information was provided to the police as the visitors were disguised. A similar incident occurred in the same parish at Derryvohy early in December when five men, Thomas Cassidy, Daniel Creighton, Edward Gilgin, John Gill and Anthony Walsh were compelled to take an oath, not only not to pay tithes but also to meet their visitors next night on Rathslevin hill in Bohola parish. The reason for this rendezvous was probably to employ the Kiltimagh group to intimidate people in Bohola where they were less likely to be recognised, an established practice in this form of intimidation.

Tourlestrane

A threatening notice, signed by Captain Rock, Captain Steel and Captain Fear-not, was posted in 1836 on the chapel of Kilmactigue as well as on the gate leading to the Glebe House, now occupied by William Tyndall who had recently replaced James Neligan as vicar of the parish.[13] Tyndall apparently intended to block access to a path which was used as a short-cut in the parish. Not only was Tyndall threatened with death but so were his parishioners in very lurid language. 'If you live under the Rule of Kilmactigue Church, you will be massacred, quartered and nailed to the gate and your Blood will not be staneful (sic) to that false Church.'

Intimidation

Later Tyndall complained to Sub-Inspector William P. Tracy in Sligo about intimidation in Tourlestrane.[14] 'This immediate neighbourhood is in the greatest state of excitement and alarm as scarcely a night passes that there is not an armed mob parading the country and swearing the people not to have any dealings with Protestants, not to work for, nor take con-acre from them.' His own labourer, Luke Leonard, together with his wife, had been beaten up the previous night. Tracy went to Tourlestrane and interviewed several people including the vicar whom he thought was unduly alarmist basing his information largely on rumour. The sub-inspector had his own explanation for the

---

12 Chief Constable David J. Barry, Swinford, to Inspector General, 18 Oct & 6 Dec 1836, Outrage Papers, 92 & 114, Mayo 1836

13 Chief Constable John Whittaker, Ballymote, to Inspector General, 20 Jan 1836, Outrage Papers, 3, Sligo 1836

14 William Tyndall, Vicar of Kilmactigue, to Sub-Inspector William P. Tracy, Sligo. 3 Mar 1837, Outrage Papers, 117, Sligo 1837

state of Tourlestrane – poteen: 'Every second or third cabin is a whiskey shop – the welcome rendezvous of night walkers – and the mass of the population are smugglers and idlers, ready for the commission of any offence and being at present under a considerable degree of excitement, they are more easily led into combinations and opposition to the laws.'

Whatever the explanation, incidents continued to be reported to the police. An armed party came to the house in Lislea of John Conway, a blacksmith, pointed a pistol at him and compelled him to swear not to work for Samuel Robinson, a Protestant, and then entered his forge and destroyed his bellows.[15] Another large well-armed party visited the village of Carrowreagh and some neighbouring villages and ordered the inhabitants to go on the following morning and repair the road from Kilmactigue chapel to Gurtlas which they duly did. Possibly this was to insure that they did not work for any Protestant.

Other Incidents

The police reported from Ballymote that a 'system of exclusive dealing has lately manifested itself in this town and neighbourhood.'[16] The struggle was entering a new phase, with widespread attempts to boycott Protestants. Threatening notices signed by Captain Rock, Captain Moonlight and John Right, had been posted up in the neighbourhood warning people not to take conacre or have any other dealings with Protestants, especially Mrs Motherwell.

Ballymote Boycott

A petition, signed by Bernard O'Kane, his curate, Bernard Egan, and fifty-five inhabitants of Ballymote, was sent to the Lord Lieutenant complaining about the justice they received from the 'Tory magistrate' and asking that a chief constable 'of well known liberal and unbiassed principles' be sent to Ballymote.[17] They also alleged that a certain Lewis Clerke and his sons, who lived next door to the police barracks, fired on and terrorised the inhabitants of the town 'whom they designated with the opprobrious epithets of Popish dogs.' The 'Tory magistrate', James Little, reported on 6 September that 'a party composed of about 100 people dressed in white shirts and carrying lighted torches was seen parading the country last night. Intimidation and night parading of parties, prevail to a frightful extent.' [18] He thought a military detachment should be stationed in the town 'to restore this neighbourhood to its former tranquillity'.

15 Chief Constable John Whittaker, Ballymote, to Inspector General 20 Jan & 23 Mar 1837, Outrage Papers, 17 & 51, Sligo 1837
16 Chief Constable Whittaker, Ballymote to Inspector General, 12 Jan & 3 April 1837, Outrage Papers, 4 & 5, Sligo 1837
17 Memorial to Lord Lieutenant, 24 Aug 1837, Outrage Papers, Sligo 1837
18 Outrage Papers, 151, Sligo 1837

Mullinabreena Boycott

Mrs Motherwell had already been chosen as a boycott target in Achonry parish. A party of about dozen of what the chief constable liked to call 'midnight legislaters' visited some houses in the townland of Cloonderahur (Cloonarahur?) and swore the occupants not to take conacre from Mrs Motherwell 'on pain of having their heads cut off'. One of them, Bryan McGuire, had to take an oath to go to the the chapel of Mullinabreena on the following Sunday and to proclaim aloud to the people not to take conacre from Motherwell. There McGuire 'made himself so conspicuous in fulfilling the mandate of this lawless Bandetta' that magistrates had him committed for trial. The chief constable summoned the parties to an inquiry in Carrowmore school but failed to get the slightest information about the members of the midnight party. Victims of intimidation never disclosed the names of their visitors.

Cloonacool Police Attacked

Police themselves were sometimes attacked like the patrol passing through the village of Cloonacool one night in February who were confronted by a group of men and disarmed.[19] Later, the magistrate, Daniel Jones, sent a message that a policeman should call on the parish priest, James McHugh. McHugh returned the stolen carabine with its stock and hammer broken, refusing, however, to give any information about how he got it but said he thought he could also retrieve the ramrod and bayonet which were also seized during the attack.

1838 Tithe Act

The tithe 'war' came to an end in August 1838 when parliament passed a new Act giving a minor reduction in tithes but, more importantly, exempting altogether from paying tithes yearly tenants and tenants-at-will, who formed one of the more active parties in the campaign. The government paid the bulk of the arrears which had accumulated over the previous eight years and Protestant clergymen were no longer targets as the tithe became part of the rent paid to the landlord which placed that class firmly in the front line of future agrarian agitation.

Repeal Movement

After gaining emancipation, O'Connell turned his attention and his considerably enhanced political stature to campaigning for the repeal of the Act of Union. He attempted to form a party from among Irish Liberals by insisting that candidates for election took the repeal pledge. By 1832 some forty of the new MPs were clear 'repealers' and several of the leading Irish Liberals who had refused to take the pledge were defeated. When O'Connell proposed in April 1834 in parliament his motion for the repeal of the Act of Union it was defeated by the crushing margin of 523 votes to 38 with even the majority of Irish members voting against it.

19 Chief Constable Henry B. Warburton, Tubbercurry, to Inspector General, 17 Feb 1837, Outrage Papers, 37, Sligo 1837

Before the 1837 general election there was a lot of political excitement surrounding the registration of free-holders who would comprise the franchise. Quarrels developed between opposing parties leading even to duels being fought.[20] One was fought on the strand in Sligo where three shots were exchanged by each party without causing any injuries and another 'affair of honour' took place near Collooney between Captain Fawsett and Patrick Somers of Achonry who narrowly escaped, 'his antagonist's ball having lodged in his clothes.'

Registration of Voters

Eighteen Liberals and seven Conservatives were registered in Ballymote in December 1836.[21] Another registry of free-holders was held there at the Quarter Sessions on 27 March 1837 which was also a fair day. Five Conservatives came from Sligo 'for the purpose of invalidating the qualification of some persons who served notices to the Register'.[22] They stayed overnight and while at dinner stones were thrown and windows broken in the house where they were staying and they drew their pistols and fired shots into the street. The police arrived and took away their pistols but when they protested that they were being left without protection two policemen were stationed at the house for the rest of the night. The sub-inspector in Sligo reported that 'a very considerable degree of political animosity has been created in it by the recent contests at the Registry of Freeholders.'[23]

Ballymote Incident

£20 REWARD.

I HEREBY Offer a REWARD of

TWENTY POUNDS

To any Person who shall, within Six Months from the date hereof, give me such information as may enable me to discover and bring to justice all or any of the Armed Party, who, on the Night of the 29th of last Month, entered *Manus Snee's* House, at *Lissalough*, in the Parish of *Killoran*, and County of *Sligo*, administered an unlawful Oath to him, left a threatening Notice in the House, and fired a Shot.

T. L. RAYMOND, *Chief Constable.*

TUBBERCURRY, *14th November, 1838.*

20 Sub-Inspector William P. Tracy, Sligo to Inspector General, 10 & 11 Jan 1837, Outrage Papers, 2, Sligo 1837
21 *Sligo Journal,* 6 Jan 1837
22 Chief Constable John Whittaker to Inspector General, 28 Mar 1837, Outrage Papers, 53, Sligo 1837
23 Sub-Inspector William P. Tracy, Sligo to Inspector General, 27 Mar 1837; Outrage Papers, 117, Sligo 1837

O'Connell in Sligo

As part of the general election campaign a visit to Sligo by Daniel O'Connell was planned for 24 January 1837 which, according to Edward Cooper of Markrea Castle, one of the Conservative candidates, caused great apprehension among the 'respectable inhabitants of that town'.[24] He warned the Chief Secretary 'of the danger to life and property upon this occasion should not

Alexander Perceval MP

the strongest precautionary measures be adopted forthwith.' On the day a large procession 'with music, banners, sashes and other badges', marched out through the town to greet O'Connell and escort him back. The Provost of Sligo, John Ormsby, wanted to have some of the more prominent participants arrested but the police sub-inspector advised against such a proceeding and instead ordered his constables to take down their names.

O'Connell addressed the crowd from the window of the house of a prominent local Liberal and that evening a public banquet was held in his honour. Many windows in the town were illuminated for the occasion and those which were not, belonging to local Protestant shopkeepers, became patently obvious targets and some were broken. The police were called out but discovered that little damage had been done and decided to put out 'a strong force to patrol the town during the night, which had a very salutary effect.' As no serious offence had been committed the sub-inspector recommended that no further notice be taken of the affair.[25]

General Election

There were three candidates in County Sligo in the general election in August 1837, Edward Joshua Cooper of Markrea Castle and Colonel Alexander Perceval of Templehouse, both Tories, and Daniel Jones, junior, of Benada Abbey, a Liberal and the first Catholic to contest a parliamentary election in County Sligo. Considerable tension arose between Catholics and Protestants in the county. Bonfires were lit on the mountains of Geevagh on the night of 22 August with large numbers of people gathered round them shouting and Protestants in the neighbourhood were so alarmed that they left their homes and went elsewhere for protection. All the excitement, according to the police, was due to a rumour circulating that Colonel Perceval had been struck dead as a result of a curse placed upon him by priests at the election.

Kidnapping

It was a bitterly fought election and a close contest was anticipated with every vote important. The morning of the election, 12 August, two Perceval

24 Edward Cooper to Thomas Drummond, 18 Jan 1837, Outrage Papers, 5, Sligo 1837
25 Sub-Inspector William P. Tracy, Sligo to Inspector General, 25 Jan 1837, Outrage Papers, 5, Sligo 1837

employees, Thomas McKenzie of Carrowntober and his father-in-law, Thomas Allen, set out in a jaunting car from Tubbercurry to pick up an elector, Edward Gouldrick of Sessuegarry and bring him to Sligo to cast his vote for Perceval.[26] Gouldrick had already set out on foot for the election. When McKenzie and Allen were returning through Cloonacool they were attacked by a mob who beat them severely and imprisoned them in a barn where they found Gouldrick who had been kidnapped earlier.

Allen's Death

McKenzie and Allen were taken from there to the Ox Mountains where they were tied up. They tried to escape on the second night but were caught, beaten with blackthorn sticks, brought back and imprisoned in a byre. When they escaped a second time they were helped by Bartley O'Hara who took them to his home, bandaged their wounds and gave them food and shelter for the night. The following day, after O'Hara had gone to a fair in Tubbercurry, a group came to the house and dragged them once again back to the mountain, where they were blindfolded, tied up and thrown into a cave. They were found here the following morning by a local farmer, Dominick Wynne, who managed to carry them, one at a time, to his home and gave them food. Later, with the help of Luke Brennan, he brought them on a mule to McKenzie's home outside Tubbercurry where two days later Allen died. The subsequent inquest revealed that he had several head wounds as well as five broken ribs.

Priest Arrested

A reward of £50 was offered by the Lord Lieutenant for information leading to the conviction of the persons responsible for his death. McKenzie made a sworn statement identifying some people whom he alleged were involved in the affair, including Patrick Spelman, the curate in Tubbercurry, who McKenzie claimed was present in Cloonacool when he and Allen were attacked and condoned the barbarous treatment they received on the mountain. Spelman was arrested by Sub-Inspector Tracy from Sligo and the resident magistrate, James Little, who arrived from Boyle with a miltiary detachment. He was detained in Tubbercurry barracks with five others who were also arrested.[27]

Rescue

Word spread quickly about the arrest of the priest and a large crowd gathered outside the barracks. Three Catholic magistrates, Daniel Jones, senior, of Benada Abbey, Charles MacDermot of Coolavin and Joseph 'Mór' McDonnell of Doocastle heard about the situation. McDonnell, who was holidaying on Coney Island, arrived in Tubbercurry on his famous grey mare and together

26 John C. McTernan, 'Kidnapping & Death' in *Olde Sligoe*, pp 289-292
27 Report of Sub-Inspector William P. Tracy to Inspector General, 18 Sept 1837, Outrage Papers, 176, Sligo 1837

with MacDermot went to the barracks and demanded that Spelman be released on bail. When this was refused McDonnell got a sledge hammer from Cawley's forge and broke down the door of the cell. Spelman was led out and paraded in triumph through the streets by the magistrates. Later the other prisoners were taken to Sligo by a strong military escort.

Special Inquiry   A special inquiry by seven magistrates into the charges against Spelman was held in Tubbercurry on 14 and 15 September. Five of the magistrates wanted to commit Spelman for trial while two others, both Catholics, Charles MacDermot and Joseph 'Mór' McDonnell, were for admitting him to bail. A heightened atmosphere surrounded the inquiry which 'required such delicate management'.

> There were some slight attempts at intimidation and hints thrown out as to an intended rescue but a proper determination to vindicate legitimate authority and the presence of a respectable body of military and police had the desired effects as not the slightest breach of good order occurred during or subsequent to the investigation although the interest and excitement produced by it were unusually great.

Sub-Inspector Tracy who reported the inquiry admitted: 'I was never more anxiously employed in my whole life.'

McKenzie made a long statement repeating his allegations against the priest which were challenged by a number of witnesses who testified that Spelman was not present when Allen and McKenzie were attacked. He visited the prisoners later for the sole purpose of preventing their ill-treatment and persuaded the attackers to allow Dr Twomey to treat their wounds, but after he was forced to leave the prisoners were moved and he lost track of them. McKenzie's statements both at the inquest and the inquiry were riddled with inconsistencies and his evidence was regarded by the majority of the magistrates as unreliable. The *Freeman's Journal* described the charge against Spelman as 'an improbable story which has evidently been got up by deeper and more designing men than the ostensible prosecutor in the case ...' [28]

Not Guilty   When the case came up at the Sligo Assizes in March 1838 the bills against Spelman were ignored by the unanimous consent of the grand jury. Of three others indicted the jury found two of them not guilty and the third, O'Connor, was returned for trial at the next Assizes, where he and a second man, Durkan, were tried for Allen's death. The evidence was not sufficient to convict them and they were released. Those responsible for the death of Thomas Allen were never caught.

28 *FJ.* 25 Sept 1837, qtd in McTernan, op. cit., p 292

Wolfe Tone St
Ballymote c. 1900
(courtesy Bob Flynn)

A dispute in Sligo on election day led to a duel which caused considerable   *Doocastle Duel*
excitement. The chief constable in Ballaghaderreen reported on 20 August
that on the previous Friday night 'upwards of 20,000 peasants from counties
Sligo and Mayo, numbers of whom were armed with guns, pistols, pikes,
bayonets, grapes, reaping hooks and various other destructive weapons' had
assembled at Doocastle. When they got there they met a number of people
returning home who told them that a duel had been expected to take place
there between a Tory, Griffith from Sligo, and a Liberal, Kelly from Galway.
Dublin Castle was so alarmed by the report that they called for an immediate
inquiry into the incident and as a result two further reports followed, one
from the chief constable in Tubbercurry and another from the sub-inspector
in Sligo.[29] Chief Constable Henry B. Warburton of Tubbercurry was given
three different estimates of the crowd present, 1,500, 1,000 and 500-700. It
emerged that a rumour had been circulated by Joseph McDonnell's stable-
boy that a great duel was to take place between Kelly and Griffith who was to
bring with him a large Orange mob from Sligo. It was to confront that mob
that the armed crowd assembled.

A dispute had arisen between Griffith and Kelly on the last day of the election in Sligo as a result of which the duel was arranged. Kelly, who was given
the option of deciding the time and place, left Sligo without informing Griffith

29 Chief Constable John S. Kelly, Ballaghaderreen to Inspector General, 20 Aug; Chief Constable Henry B. Warburton, Tubbercurry to Inspector General, 24 Aug; Sub-Inspector
   William P. Tracy, Sligo to Inspector General, 25 Aug 1837. Outrage Papers, 137, Sligo 1837

of the arrangements and the latter followed him to Doocastle where he had stopped off at Joseph McDonnell's residence on his way home to County Galway. A huge crowd had gathered there in expectation of the duel. Griffith was accompanied by only a few friends. 'Were it not for the exertions of McDonnell Mr Griffith would have been murdered, the ferocity of the mob was such.' McDonnell persuaded the duelling parties to steer clear of the mob and settle their quarrel elsewhere, which they did. The chief constable in Tubbercurry heard four or five carriages driving very fast past the barracks there at 7.30 a.m. and the police followed them to somewhere near Achonry. But when they reached the spot the duellists had already exchanged a few shots without inflicting any injuries and had returned to their respective homes.

Constable Attacked in Bunninadden

In the election itself, Daniel Jones was narrowly defeated by Colonel Perceval while the seat for Sligo borough went to a repealer, John Patrick Somers, the son of Patrick Somers of Achonry. Feelings continued to run high after the election and several outrages were reported. At the fair in Coolaney at the end of August five or six strangers entered a public house and beat up John Powell of Gurteen and John Armstrong of Coolaney because they voted for E. J. Cooper and Colonel Perceval.[30] Chief Constable Henry B. Warburton was travelling from Ballymote to Tubbercurry on 5 September when he was accosted by a party of about twenty men near Bunninadden.[31] 'I got out of my gig and told them how wrong they were acting. I had a pistol in my hand and cautioned them to take care. I was instantly surrounded, my pistol was wrenched from me and fired, I received one or two blows on the back and my hat was knocked off but afterwards returned to me by a man who came up and said "Shout 'Jones forever' and no one will harm you." I said "I have nothing to do with any but 'Jones forever' if you like. Some said "Give him back his pistol" but it was not returned. I was allowed then to drive on.'

Established Clergy

Even without the tithe war and the mounting political confrontations, there was little to endear the majority population to the clergy of the Established Church in Achonry, almost none of whom were natives of the diocese. Names like Seymour, Verschoyle, Townsend etc. were alien to a largely Irish-speaking country people who continued to refer to them as *Sasanaigh*. The only native clergymen were sons who succeeded their fathers like John Garrett who followed William as vicar of Emlaghfad in Ballymote in 1806, and when John himself died in 1855, father and son had held that vicarage for ninety years. In Ballaghaderreen Joseph Seymour became vicar of Castlemore

30 Outrage Papers, 140, Sligo 1837
31 Outrage Papers, Sligo 1837

in 1811 when his father, Charles, resigned in his favour, though Joseph was probably not born in Ballaghaderreen. Many clergymen were natives of Dublin like James Verschoyle who succeeded Joseph Stock in 1810 as bishop of the united dioceses of Killala and Achonry and was Dean of St Patrick's when he was elected bishop. When he died in 1834 the the diocese was united to Tuam. The Verschoyle family, of Dutch extraction, provided a number of clergymen in the diocese, among them the bishop's son, Joseph junior, also born in Dublin, who was Provost of Achonry from 1818 until his death in 1867, and Joseph senior, probably a cousin, Archdeacon of Achonry during almost the same period. He was vicar of Killoran from 1818 until his death in 1862. His predecessor, Sir James Hutchinson, son of Samuel, Bishop of Achonry and Killala, was born in County Antrim and his successor, Hamilton Townsend, in County Down.

With so many of the clergy born in Dublin or in the north of Ireland probably very few of them spoke Irish, the language of the majority of the population of the diocese for much of the nineteenth century. One of the few exceptions was Charles Seymour, who was fluent in Irish which he learned as a child growing up in County Galway and later ministered in Connemara. James Neligan, vicar of Kilmactigue, was also probably proficient in Irish and in his statistical survey of the parish provided a glossary of Irish placenames. Neligan's successor, William Tyndall, probably had little or no Irish, as he was born in Dublin.

Families like the Garretts, Seymours and Verschoyles were virtually clerical dynasties. William Garrett who became vicar of Emlaghfad in 1765 was the son of John, Rector of Crossboyne, and William's own son, John, had three sons who became clergyman. Charles Seymour was the son of a vicar and his son, Joseph, who was married three times, had two sons who took orders, one who became Dean of Tuam and another who himself was the father of a rector in Limerick. A great-grand nephew became Archdeacon of Cashel.

Clerical Dynasties

Edward Newenham Hoare, son of the chancellor of Limerick, who became Dean of Achonry in 1839, spent eleven years in Achonry before moving on to Waterford where he remained as dean until 1877. While he was in Achonry he was active as a clergyman and magistrate, playing a leading role in providing relief during the Famine. The indications are that Hoare's predecessor, Theophilus Blakely, who became dean in 1824, was an absentee until he resigned to become Dean of Down, and his aristocratic successor, Hervey de Montmorency, 4th Viscount Mountmorres, was probably also an absentee. The remaining deans were all actively engaged in the ministry in the diocese. William Jackson who became dean in 1872 had spent sixteen years as

Deans

vicar of Straide and in fact his first wife, Julia, died in Foxford in 1863 and his successor, Arthur Moore, was vicar of Emlaghfad and remained so until his death in 1882, while another dean, Thomas Gordon Walker, was also vicar in the same parish. Two others, Hamilton Townsend and Thomas Allen were rectors of Killoran. When Allen died in 1927, killed by the accidental discharge of his gun, the office of dean was united to that of bishop of the diocese.

'The Second Reformation'

Irish Protestantism experienced what was called the 'second reformation' in the second decade of the nineteenth century, which was characterised by large-scale attempts at evangelism among Catholics by Protestant societies. For the first time in over a century, Protestants were making serious efforts to win converts among the Catholic population and claimed several conversions in Achonry diocese.[32] The activities of the Protestant evangelical societies, such as the London Hibernian Society and the Baptist Society, particularly in the field of education caused alarm among priests. Schools grant-aided by the Kildare Place Society, at first acceptable to Catholics, were later rejected when they accused the KPS of indulging in naked proslytism.

Proselytism

Priests were especially fearful of proselytism where Catholic children were attending Protestant schools. Daniel O'Connor forbade his parishioners in Coolaney to send their children to a school where the master was a Protestant and Charles O'Hara of Annaghmore wrote to him in 1819 seeking an explanation for his action.[33] O'Connor replied that he was obliged in conscience 'to watch over the faith and morals of his flock' and that he objected to the use in the school of extracts from the New Testament translated by the Protestant Church. A school, where the master attempted to proselytise his pupils and who, according to O'Connor, had on many occasions in front of the pupils 'bestowed the vilest epithets on the Catholic religion' 'could never under any circumstances meet with his approbation or concurrence'.

Clogher Bible School

Another proselytising school in the diocese was later to cause bitter recriminations. It was situated at Clogher, a few miles from Ballaghaderreen in the half-barony of Coolavin and its patron was the local landlord and magistrate, Joseph Arthur Holmes. His father Richard, who had acquired the estate of over 1,000 acres in 1824, was said to have been the first Protestant to have settled in the half parish of Monasteraden since the Reformation. Clogher school had an average daily attendance in 1835 of thirty, almost all of them Catholics, the children of tenants on the Holmes' estate.

The Famine

During the Famine the numbers attending the Clogher school increased spectacularly, rising to 150 in June 1847, to 220 by the end of July and 300 by

32 Swords, *A Hidden Church*, pp 157-164
33 Swords, op. cit., pp 184-85

February 1848. The reason for this spectacular growth was that Elizabeth Holmes provided each child in the school with a meal of cooked rice every day for six days a week, paid for by the Society of Friends.[34] A similar school run by Emily and Rebecca Irwin in the neighbouring parish of Boyle engaged in unashamed 'souperism'. 'He, who has in righteous judgement sent this calamity,' Emily wrote to the Society of Friends, 'can in mercy cause it to work for His own glory and the salvation of souls. Many now send their children to our school and would gladly have the gospel preached, who before could not be persuaded to do so.'[35]

J. A. Holmes himself was very active in relieving distress during the Famine and sent many letters to the Lord Lieutenant and the Chief Secretary drawing their attention to the plight of the inhabitants in the district. In 1846 he was a member of the Ballaghaderreen Relief Committee which was chaired by Charles Strickland and among its members were Denis Tighe, the administrator in Ballaghaderreen, as well as the parish priests of Carracastle and Bunninadden. With the help of the Society of Friends he set up a soup kitchen early in 1847 to feed the starving and by May he was providing a meal of soup and cooked rice to 146 families daily.

Soup Kitchen

The Clogher school angered local priests, particularly Denis Tighe, who believed it was being used as an instrument for blatant proselytism and his dispute with Holmes was due to what he sarcastically called 'his Bible school for the accommodation of his Catholic neighbours.'[36] Catholic opposition to the school mounted and Holmes, feeling his life threatened by Tighe's 'inflammatory harangues' against him from the altar in Ballaghaderreen left his home in Clogher early in December 1847.

'Inflammatory Harangues'

The affair took a dramatic turn on Thursday 6 January 1848.[37] It was the feast of the Epiphany and the chapel in Ballaghaderreen was packed. A visitor arrived at the chapel just as Mass was about to begin and demanded permission to address the congregation from the altar. Alexander Erskine Holmes, Joseph's younger brother, had come directly from London for this purpose and when Tighe agreed to his extraordinary request, Holmes insisted that the priest and his curate stand one each side of him while he spoke.

Drama in Chapel

He then began to speak about his brother:

34 Swords, *In Their Own Words*, pp 191, 213-14, 226-7, 288-89, 323, 333-34
35 Swords, op. cit., p 156
36 Denis Tighe to the Editor, *Dublin Evening Post*, 20 Jan 1848
37 *Sligo Journal*, 14 Jan 1848 qtd in J. C. McTernan, *In Sligo Long Ago*, pp 414-17 & in Swords, *In Their Own Words*, pp 268-71

Is there amongst you a man who can say that my brother has ever done an unkind or unjust act by him? Is there, I say? If there is, let him hold up his hand. Is there amongst you a man who can deny that for the last two years my brother has been your slave? If there is, let him speak. – (A pause) – During the last two years, my brother has expended £20,000 in provisions to keep down the markets here so that you and your children do not starve! [38] He has daily for the last sixteen months fed 150 of your children at his school-house. He has turned his house and offices into a provision store for your accommodation. Is there a man amongst you who can deny this? If there is let him speak.

'Assassins'

Holmes then referred to the 'assassins' who came to Ballaghaderreen to murder his brother. Dramatically pointing to Tighe he accused him of inspiring the would-be assassins by his inflammatory remarks about his brother. At this point uproar broke out in the chapel. At length when silence was restored, Tighe denied that he had ever made attacks on Holmes' brother but Holmes would have none of it:

'I know that you did, and I tell you at this altar to your face and in the presence of your congregation, that it is your attacks on my brother from this spot that have brought these murderers into this parish.' (Here the uproar re-commenced and some of the more violent of the congregation appeared disposed to pass over the rails to the altar, the priests endeavouring to restrain them.)

Letter from London

At this point Alexander Erskine left the chapel surrounded by the people 'who refrained from any act of personal violence, but saluted him with groans and execrations on his driving away.' When he returned to London he published a handbill addressed 'to the Roman Catholic inhabitants of Ballaghaderreen and its neighbourhood' where he reiterated the charges he had made against Tighe. Tighe himself wrote to the editor of the *Sligo Journal,* which had published an account of the chapel incident, admitting that it was 'substantially correct' but vehemently rejecting the charges made against him by Holmes. Joseph A. Holmes did not return to Clogher until the summer of 1854 and then only for a brief visit. His estate in Clogher was later sold and acquired by MacDermot, Prince of Coolavin.

Proslytism in Killasser

A tentative move was made in December 1847 towards proslytising school-children in Killasser.[39] The curate in Foxford, Geoffrey Huston Mostyn, complained to the Society of Friends that in Killasser 'there is no school

38 He later explained in a letter to the Editor of the *Times* (15 Jan 1848) that his brother had imported into the district provisions for that amount which he sold to the inhabitants at cost price.
39 Swords, *In Their Own Words,* pp 250-1

TO THE

ROMAN CATHOLIC
INHABITANTS OF BALLAGHADERREEN,
And its Neighbourhood.

My Friends,

You remember that on the 6th of this Month, in the Chapel of Ballaghaderreen, I charged the Priest of your Parish, Mr. Tigue, with conduct abhorrent to his Office as a Christian Minister.

I gave Mr. Tigue notice on the morning of that day that I would address you, and I refused to open my lips until he stood at my side at the Altar. This you will allow, was fair, and open, and straightforward

I now hear that no sooner had I left the Country than he made an attack upon me at the Chapel, heaping upon me all kind of abuse, and, amongst other things, said, that I had called you Assassins and Murderers.

Some of you perhaps do not know the meaning of the word " Assassin!" It means a man who will stab you as soon as your back is turned.

But base as an Assassin is, there is even a more degraded character than that,—a man who, without he courage to be an Assassin, will incite others to deeds of blood.

I never charged you with being Assassins. I said that strangers had come into the Parish to commit murder ; and we all know that the murders which now disgrace our Country are committed by strangers to the Districts where they are perpetrated.

That is what I said, and Mr. Tigue knows it is what I said ; but it suits his purpose to put into my mouth words that I never uttered, that he may make dissession between you and me. I have walked through the Parish alone at all hours and seasons, without even a switch in my hand. Does that look as if I thought you Assassins ?

If I thought you were Assassins, I should have asked for a guard of Policemen to attend me at the Chapel on the 6th of January. Did I do so ? No. And the orderly and peaceful conduct of most of you on that day, and generally, proves how little you have suffered by the bad example you have so long had before you.

One word more, and I have done. The interruption I met with when I addressed you prevented my telling you that he who assumes the privilege of deciding who shall live and who shall die in his Parish, cannot evade the responsibility that attaches to it. Let it be borne in mind, that when murder is committed, the Law makes no distinction between the head that counsels and the hand that is raised for the shedding of blood.

I remain,

Your sincere Friend,

A. E. HOLMES.

London, January, 1848.

where the child must (as all teaching must be compulsory) read and commit to memory the Word of God' and he asked the Society for a grant to build such a school, pay a schoolmaster and provide food for fifty pupils. 'My only desire is to teach the Word of God.' The Society replied that none of their funds were 'applicable for such an object.'

Sectarianism, often bitter, characterised the relationship between Catholic and Protestant clergies for most of the first half of the nineteenth century and it took the greatest catastrophe in recent Irish history, the Great Famine, to bring out a more ecumenical spirit among them. Relief committees were set

The Great Famine

up throughout the diocese to alleviate the distress among the poor and Protestant clergymen and Catholic priests worked side by side in their efforts to avert the worst, bombarding the Chief Secretary's office with jointly signed petitions seeking government help for the starving people. As the great majority of these were Catholics the heroic efforts of many of the Protestant clergymen were particularly commendable. A similar ecumenical spirit was displayed during the lesser famine of 1879-80.

Edward Hoare

Dean Edward Hoare of Achonry, chairman of the Upper Leyny Relief Committee, played a leading role in alleviating distress, operating together with his committee nine soup kitchens in February 1847 in an area with about 20,000 in a state of destitution. One of the soup kitchens was in one of his outhouses where sixty gallons of soup were made daily and as a result his own house was continually surrounded by a multitude of starving people. Hoare was also chairman of the Tubbercurry Relief Committee and the parish priest of Achonry, James Gallagher, proposed in 1847 a motion of thanks to the Dean for 'his unwearied and very efficient exertions'.

Threatening Letter

Notwithstanding these exertions, Hoare received on 24 November 1847 a threatening letter from somebody signing himself Molly Maguire.[40] 'You are, Mr Dean, one of the chosen few in Sligo whose days are numbered.' A few hours later his steward found a warning note stuck in one of the dean's hayricks. 'Your Riverance would need to have the Polis to watch when driving the Roads.' The following day George Knox, the resident magistrate in Tubbercurry, made an official report recommending that the dean's house be given police protection. The author of the threatening letter was said to be a Tubbercurry man called McDermott, recently sacked from his post as relieving officer because he was a publican in the town and he blamed the dean for his dismissal.

Hoare was already aware of McDermott's feeling about him, having been advised by a 'respectable person', who overheard a conversation between Mc Dermott and others in the public house, to return home early and with protection from a meeting in Tubbercurry. 'I did return early and by another road, but without protection.' He wrote to the parish priest of Tubbercurry, to speak to McDermott and assure him that he had nothing to do with his dismissal but McDermott denied to the priest that he ever wrote the letter.

Police Protection

Hoare continued to be alarmed. 'Every one fears to come forward but many give dark hints and warn me not to be without the protection of the police.' The threatening letter had specifically referred to the fate of Major Mahon of Strokestown House who had been murdered, allegedly by members of the Molly Maguires, and Hoare feared that the 'fatal word may have

40 Swords, *In Their Own Words*, pp 243-47

already be given' to murder him. He appealed to the Under Secretary to grant him police protection as he considered it unbecoming to his office to carry firearms. Two policemen were assigned to live at the deanery, providing protection for him there and 'to accompany him on his lawful business' as Hoare also exercised the functions of a magistrate. A reward of £20 was offered by George Knox for information leading to the arrest of the writer of the threatening letter but there were no further developments in the affair.

John Garrett, vicar of Emlaghfad, also played a prominent role during the Famine as secretary of the Corran Relief Committee. He endorsed in August 1846 a petition to the Lord Lieutenant signed by James O'Hara, the parish priest of Keash and 173 of his parishioners with the comment: 'I do believe every word in this memorial verified as it is by the signature of Priest O'Hara, a most respectable man.' Later he confided to the Under Secretary: 'It has for years been my desire to earn as far as I humbly could the confidence of my parishioners of every religious persuasion.' [41]

John Garrett

Garrett intervened on behalf of a young priest whose 'seditious speech' brought him to the attention of the authorities when the police reported to Dublin Castle an incident which occurred in Ballymote in July 1848.[42] A crowd of over fifty people collected outside the lodgings of the curate, Patrick McNicholas, who addressed them from the window, speaking against the government 'in an inflammatory manner'. When Sub-Constable Jackson arrived on the scene, McNicholas pointed him out as a government spy, a blackguard and a ruffian and encouraged the people to remove him by force. Constable Patrick Curley later reported 'that the Revd gentleman was under the influence of liquor and that not much heed was paid to his discourse' but the incident could have been deeply embarrassing to Bishop McNicholas, the priest's uncle. Garrett wrote to the Under Secretary asking him to refrain from taking steps to punish McNicholas for his seditious speech. 'The speech was made when the young priest was after dinner and excited by too free indulgence.' He pointed out that he was a nephew of the Bishop of Achonry 'and I have no doubt he will exercise his episcopal authority to silence this youthful agitator upon political subjects in future.'

The McNicholas Affair

The decline in the power and prestige of the Established Church accelerated in the second half of the nineteenth century, accounting in 1871 for only twelve per cent of the population of Ireland, sixty per cent of which was concentrated in the province of Ulster. Catholics made up over three-quarters of the population. That the religion of such a small minority was the established

Church Disestablishment

41 ibid, pp 51,54
42 OP 26 / 226, 228 qtd in Swords, *In Their Own Words*, pp 341-42

one with all the privileges that entailed was a glaring injustice which was ac-knowledged by more and more English politicians and was to lead eventually to its disestablishment. William Gladstone, who made the solution of Irish problems one of the central planks of Liberal policy, moved resolutions in parliament early in 1868 in favour of the disestablishment of the Irish Church. Nothing was better calculated to secure Irish Catholic support in the general election called in November of that year. Catholic priests were particularly active in the election campaign, turning it almost into a crusade in favour of Gladstone and his Liberal Party. Terence O'Rorke of Collooney used the oc-casion of the dedication of the new church in Killasser to launch a tirade on the 'pampered clergy' of the Established Church which was 'toppling fast and soon to be numbered with all its baneful and cursed memories among the very worst things of the past.'[43]

The Liberal Party won sixty-six seats in Ireland, contributing considerably to Gladstone's handsome majority and he moved quickly to fulfil his pledge on Irish disestablishment, introducing the bill in March 1869. 'So long as es-tablishment lives, painful and bitter memories can never be effaced.' Before the end of July the Irish Church Act was passed. From 1 January 1871 the church's corporate property was to be transferred to commissioners who were to compensate the clergy and others such as sextons and parish clerks. Protes-tant bishops were no longer members of the House of Lords and ecclesiastical law, except where it related to matrimony, no longer existed as law. The church was to be incorporated and arrangements were made for the disposal of churchyards and other church ruins, with those considered national mon-uments like the Rock of Cashel taken over by the Board of Works. A grant was also made to the Presbyterians and to Maynooth College.

Church of Ireland   The former Established Church adopted the title, 'Church of Ireland' which rankled with many Catholics at the time. Bishop MacCormack referred to what he described as 'the standing insult of designating their disestablished body the Church of Ireland' and accused Protestants of continuing 'to assume airs of superiority and supremacy in the days of their decline'.[44] Whatever airs they assumed the era of the Protestant ascendancy was over and the era of Catholic ascendancy was advancing rapidly, with its own peculiar airs and graces. The number of Protestants in the diocese continued to decline, from 2,734 in 1881 to 1,316 in 1911 and to 400 in 1980 though the overall population also declined during that period from 104, 490 to 39,000.

43 *C.T.* 18 Nov 1868
44 *C.T.* 1 Mar 1884

CHAPTER SIX

The Great Famine

A disease which attacked the leaves of the stalks and then spread to the pota-toes underneath was first reported in Ireland early in September 1845. The blight, as it came to be known, was described as having the appearance of soot as the plant rapidly decomposed, turning black and rotting, producing a putrid smell. One source of the disease was thought to have been South America, particularly Peru, but it was more likely to have originated in the eastern United States where it largely destroyed the potato crops of 1843 and 1844 and vessels from New York and Philadelphia could easily have brought diseased potatoes to European ports. By the late summer and early autumn the disease had spread throughout the greater part of central and northern Europe.

Blight

There was still no sign of disease in the potato crop anywhere in the dio-cese by the end of September and police reports indicated that a bumper crop was expected. In Ballymote it gave 'every appearance of a most abundant re-turn in this part of the country' while Sub-Inspector J. S. Stewart reported from Tubbercurry 'that the general opinion in the country is that there has not been so good a crop of potatoes for some years', a view shared by the Mayo county inspector, 'there never was to all appearances a finer crop of potatoes in this county.' [1]

One month later there was a dramatic change. 'The potatoes in this district are universally afflicted with the rot', Sub-Inspector Edward Hunt reported from Swinford on 22 October, and by then the disease was universal through-out all County Sligo and the part of Mayo adjoining Ballaghaderreen. The blight struck rapidly so that what one day appeared to be a very healthy crop was a few days later in what the curate in Gurteen described as 'a state of melancholy putrefaction'. George Vaughan Jackson of Carramore exhibited a diseased potato at a Board of Guardians' meeting in Ballina on 21 October which he discovered 'in one of his best fields only the day prior, and which to all external appearances was a most healthy crop.'

First Signs of Rot

---

1 RLFC. 2/Z.13210 qtd in Swords, *In Their Own Words*, p 18. Unless otherwise stated all quotations in this chapter can be sourced from that work

Potato Failure

The general digging of the main crop of potatoes in the diocese began early in November. Unusually heavy rains caused the Moy to burst its banks near Foxford and the bridge at Ballylahan gave way under the force of the flood waters. Jackson, on his way to Foxford on 8 November, observed acres of potatoes entirely covered with water and ruined. 'We also saw poor creatures up to nearly their knees digging potatoes to save them.' By now the first alarm bells were being sounded. The curate in Gurteen wrote on 25 October to the *Sligo Champion* that many of the eleven hundred families in the parish had lost all their potato crop. 'My heart bleeds to contemplate the dark future that appears before the suffering people. They have neither oats, nor money, nor potatoes, nor the hope of relief from a kind and indulgent landlord.' James Henry of Bunninadden confirmed in the same paper in mid-November the general failure of the potato crop in County Sligo. 'All this is very distressing but we must only hope that Providence will not desert the people in their extremity.'

Appeals for Help

He called on the government to provide employment to enable poor people to earn something to ward off starvation. 'This can be readily done as there are many localities entirely shut out from the public roads for the want of anything in the shape of a public pass to their villages and the people are at present obliged to carry the produce of their own land on their backs to the high road.' Peter Brennan of Gurteen made a similar appeal warning that 'famine with all its accompanying horrors is rapidly approaching' and Swinford Board of Guardians warned the government of the 'gloomy and alarming prospects' unless it took prompt and efficacious steps. John Garrett of Bally-mote was probably the first in the diocese to propose practical measures to alleviate their condition when he suggested to the Lord Lieutenant on 24 November that food depots providing rice and oatmeal should be established in each union and that public works be set up to provide employment.

Relief Committees

The prime minister, Sir Robert Peel, had already secretly arranged in November 1845 for the purchase and importation into Ireland of £100,000 worth of Indian meal (maize) and had established a temporary Relief Commission whose duties were to advise the government and to supervise and co-ordinate local relief committees. Local committees were originally based on the barony as a unit and were comprised of local notables, including landlords, clergymen, magistrates and large farmers. One relief committee looked after the baronies of Gallen and Costello, the Mayo portion of the diocese, while there were four, Corran, Upper and Lower Leyny and Coolavin, for the Sligo portion.

George Vaughan Jackson, of Carramore, Ballina, chairman of the Swinford Board of Guardians, was chairman of the Gallen and Costello Relief Committee and other members included magistrates, Charles Strickland,

Edward Deane and Francis R. O'Grady and Poor Law Guardians, John Bolingbroke, Luke Colleran, Patrick Durkan and Daniel Keane. All parish priests and curates were members as were Protestant ministers, Geoffrey Mostyn of Foxford, B. W. Eames of Swinford and Joseph Seymour of Ballaghaderreen. Corran Relief Committee was chaired by Richard Gethin while the vicar of Emlaghfad, John Garrett, was secretary and other members included the parish priests of Ballymote, Bunninadden and Keash and James Fleming, a Presbyterian minister. John Armstrong of Chaffpool was chairman of the Upper Leyny Relief Committee but was later replaced by Dean Edward Hoare of Achonry. John Hamilton, perpetual curate of Tubbercurry, the parish priests of Tourlestrane, Curry, Tubbercurry and Achonry, Frederick G. Jones of Benada Abbey and the Poor Law Guardians, John Brett of Tubbercurry, Luke Colleran of Curry and John Durkan of Kilmactigue were also members. Lower Leyny was chaired by Charles King O'Hara of Annaghmore and Coolavin by Joseph A. Holmes. The parish of Ballysadare came under the care of the Tirerrill Relief Committee whose chairman was Edward J. Cooper of Markrea Castle with the parish priest, Patrick Durcan, and the vicar members of this committee. As the famine worsened the relief committees became centred on parishes rather than baronies.

The Indian meal purchased by Peel was stored in government depots in ports such as Sligo and Westport and sold to local committees to re-sell to the needy at or under cost price. Meal depots were set up in some of the larger centres such as Swinford and Ballymote, obliging some people to travel up to ten miles to buy a stone and a half of meal. The parish priest of Tubbercurry suggested that depots should be set up in every police barracks. Dean Hoare established a depot at his glebe house at his own cost where he sold about two tons of meal a week at one penny a stone above the price he paid for it, which saved the poor going four or five miles to the the nearest town where they would have to pay more. *Meal Depots*

Meal depots were financed by raising local subscriptions which were matched by a government grant of up to 100%. The list of subscribers was quite small, often less than twenty individuals and many of them members of relief committees whose resources were often limited. Parish priests usually subscribed £3 and curates £1, although Peter Brennan of Gurteen gave £10, probably to match the local vicar who also subscribed £10. Protestant clergymen were also landowners and sometimes contributed more. Archdeacon Verschoyle of Killoran contributed £30 but, surprisingly, Dean Hoare only contributed £3, though it must be admitted that as a landowner he was also subject to Poor Law rates. A small number of subscriptions were received *Subscriptions* from elsewhere, particularly from individuals in Dublin and in several places in England, most likely relatives or friends of Protestant members on the committee who had approached them for help. Rev John Garrett of Hull contributed £10 to the Corran committee and Alexander E. Holmes and his wife, sent £5 each from London to his brother Joseph, chairman of the Coolavin committee.

Resident Landlords

Resident landlords made large contributions often for specified public works carried out on their own lands. Lord Lorton gave the Corran relief committee £150 for a specified road from Ballymote to Boyle where he had his seat, and Charles K. O'Hara gave £100 to the Lower Leyny committee for a similar purpose. Very few non-resident landlords made contributions though Viscount Dillon contributed £100 to the Gallen and Costello committee, probably through the influence of his agent, Charles Strickland, who was very active on the committee. Dean Hoare stated that after circularising them several times, only £68 was received by February 1847 from thirty-six landlords in Upper Leyny who had estates yielding £20,000 per annum.

Absentees

Attempts to name and shame the non-subscribing absentees produced little effect. Local committees were required to send in their list of subscribers before they were given a grant and were encouraged to include a list of those who refused to subscribe. Upper Leyny Committee named eighteen non-subscribers in July and in August Lower Leyny Committee named eight absentee landlords from whom they had received no reply in August. No replies were received from Sir Alexander Crichton, Lord Palmerston or Thomas Jones who held extensive properties in the barony of Corran. However, some non-subscribers undertook to look after their own tenants such as E. J. Cooper, Colonel Perceval and Lord Lorton in Lower Leyny. Sir Robert Gore Booth, who had an extensive estate in the neighbourhood of Ballymote, the rents from which amounted to £2,000 a year, undertook to employ and support the people on that estate which, according to John Garrett, 'greatly lightened the labours' of the local relief committee.

Public Works

Peter Brennan watched anxiously as his parishioners in Gurteen faced the prospect of starvation in March 1846. 'Many of my people having for many weeks continued to subsist on diseased potatoes, have not now even that description of food on which to subsist ... Unless the people get employment, the result will, I dread, be most melancholy.' Legislation had been introduced in March paving the way for the establishment of public works by constructing and repairing roads with money provided by a Treasury grant, half of which was to be repaid by the locality, the other half beng a free grant.

A time-consuming bureaucratic system was devised for allocating grants to needy localities. Firstly, the distressed area had to send a petition to the Lord Lieutenant requesting assistance which was then forwarded in turn to the Relief Commissioners and the Board of Works for their comments and then sent to the local surveyor for his inspection. When the Board of Works received his report it made its decision and if accepted it made a recommendation to the Lord Lieutenant, who then asked for the sanction of the Treasury. Only after this cumbersome procedure was completed could the works commence.

Delays caused great hardship for the poor as well as considerable frustration to their priests who tried to help them. James Henry of Bunninadden complained in the middle of June that no works had started there though they had long since applied for them while James McHugh of Tubbercurry complained at the beginning of July 'that week after week passed in vain expectation of getting some employment.' The people were 'every other day running to me crying for redress and it is not in my power to relieve them.' *Delays*

Where works were undertaken the local relief committees were responsible for selecting the labourers among the destitute to whom they issued work tickets and who were paid a daily rate of 9d or 10d. The total number employed daily was approximately 21,000 in June which increased to 71,000 in July and peaked in the second week at almost 98,000, and five-sixths of all employed in the country were confined to seven counties which included Galway, Mayo and Sligo. The Treasury announced on 21 July 1846 that all the public measures introduced to meet the emergency were to be brought to a close as soon as possible in the expectation that the impending early potato harvest would render them unnecessary. *Number Employed*

It was a vain expectation. The early potato crop was usually harvested in July and in the middle of that month, after touring the northern part of the barony of Gallen, George Vaughan Jackson reported that 'the new potato crop is everywhere attacked by the disease of last year or one like it.' There was great distress in Attymass, Bonniconlon, Foxford and Killasser and other parts of the barony where no works had been undertaken and Gallen and Costello Relief Committee requested Bernard Durcan of Swinford, Bernard Egan of Bonniconlon and Denis Tighe of Ballaghaderreen or John Coghlan of Kilmovee to go to Dublin and inform the Relief Commission there about the condition of the population in their localities. *Total Potato Loss*

Conditions worsened dramatically when blight struck the main potato crop. There were so few sound potatoes in Tubbercurry at the end of August that, according to the sub-inspector, it would take a man a whole day to dig enough to feed his family, which would have taken him only a half an hour in normal circumstances. Eating diseased potatoes endangered peoples' health and the smell of them after being boiled was 'so bad as to prove they are not fit for any creature.' The report from Swinford was equally bad. 'Both early and late crops are a total failure.' The 'great' famine had begun.

Meal Shortages   Soon Dublin Castle was being inundated with appeals for help from various parts of the diocese. Peter Brennan wrote from Gurteen about the misery he encountered in the course of his pastoral duties, asking the Lord Lieutenant to 'make allowance for the feelings of a pastor who sees starvation and death impending over his people.' James McHugh sent a petition signed by parishioners in Tubbercurry. 'I assert without fear of contradiction that one-third of the population in the district are without a four-footed beast or a grain of corn in the world, as they depended on daily labour and conacre potatoes, which are all lost by this awful visitation of Providence.'

Petitions from Swinford underlined the absolute necessity of keeping the meal depot there constantly supplied. 'The supply to Swinford depot is totally inadequate to the wants of the people, some of whom have to come a distance of more than 10 miles for a miserable half stone of meal and have sometimes to wait an entire day before they obtain it.' The situation in Foxford was even worse. The police constable there told G. V. Jackson that there was no meal there except two bags sent on Friday by Jackson in his own horse and cart. One bag was sold on Saturday and the other bag did not last a half an hour on Monday morning. Jackson tried to buy two tons for Foxford from a merchant in Westport. 'He could not give it, the demand was too great.'

The reason for the shortage in September was that the government had not anticipated another failure of the potato crop and when the failure was confirmed fresh supplies of Indian meal were ordered from America but were not expected to arrive in Ireland before the end of October or sometime during November. The government believed that local merchants should be encouraged to import grain to meet the demand but G. V. Jackson told the Under Secretary that no merchants in Ballina or Killala were willing to do so. The Relief Commission was disappointed and told the vicar in Swinford, 'The want of local exertion for promoting importations of food is much to be lamented.' The government also believed that the home-grown oats should be sold at the local markets to meet the present need. 'Gentlemen of local influence should therefore unite their exertions to have the produce of the home harvest brought largely into the markets for the subsistence of the population.'

Famine Prices   An excellent grain harvest both in quantity and quality was indeed being sold at the markets but at exorbitant prices. There was no meal in the food depot in Ballymote in the middle of September and Garrett complained that the poor people were 'left at the mercy of hucksters who charge enormous profit.' The Swinford depot was also empty and Bernard Durcan complained that as a result 'private vendors have raised the price of meal beyond the reach of the poor.' The only way to keep the market price down was to keep the food depot supplied. Two priests, John Coghlan and Michael Muldowney, proposed a resolution to Gallen and Costello Relief Committee strongly condemning the 'speculation of heartless selfish merchants' who 'have taken advantage of the poverty of the people and have raised food even beyond famine prices. They have and are exacting the pound of flesh.'

Exports

In port towns like Ballina and Westport the poor were frightened and angered at the sight of grain being exported, and the carts carrying oats from a local merchant in Westport to the quay to be shipped the following morning were forced to return to the store by a crowd of about 700 people. A large crowd 'of wretched-looking people' collected outside a magistrates' meeting in Ballina and handed in a note complaining that a merchant in the town was shipping oats while the poor of Ballina were starving. The chairman addressed them, pointing out the 'illegality of attempting to prevent the exportation of grain and the bad consequences likely to result from such an imprudent course' and persuaded them to disperse quietly when he assured them that there would be a large quantity of Indian meal arriving soon in Ballina. In fact the meeting raised a large subscription to buy a cargo of Indian meal to sell at cost price to the poor.

Bernard Durcan

John Garrett believed that it was 'clear to every thinking man' that prohibiting the export of the home produce 'would be the ruin of Ireland' and argued that as Ireland had no industries it would face bankruptcy if it did not continue to export grain, beef, pork and butter, a view shared by almost all landowners, including smallholders. In normal circumstances oats was grown not for consumption but as a cash crop to pay the rent. The potato was the sole diet of the poorer classes who had no oats and were the first victims of the potato failure. As the famine worsened, it moved up the social scale with smalholders now threatened and obliged to use their oats to feed themselves and their families.

Public Works Suspended

A petition from Swinford signed by Bernard Durcan and his two curates, as well as the vicar, B. W. Eames, and almost 100 inhabitants complained that the suspension of the public works had reduced great numbers in the parish to a state of the 'most utter destitution'. The public works had been suspended on 15 August. A letter was also sent by Dr Ulic Burke: 'No official report, no public memorials, no even private accounts can convey or give an adequate idea of the misery our people are still patiently enduring.'

Wages Delayed   From Ballymote John Garrett sent a stream of letters complaining bitterly that the county surveyor had been ordered to stop all the works which had only just commenced. 'The cup has been held to the lip of the most patient peasantry in Ireland and is dashed suddenly from their grasp without slaking their hunger or thirst.' There were also complaints from G. V. Jackson and others about delays in the payment of labourers. 'Intense suffering is entailed on the labourers and their families not being regularly and promptly paid their wages.' John Corley pointed out to the Lord Lieutenant the dire consequences on the labourers in Foxford from the delay in the payment of their wages:

Foxford   Such as are employed are fast sinking under the weight of labour, owing to their having no nourishment. When they first commenced persons gave them some meal on credit, until they would receive their pay, but when that was delayed as it has been for the last fortnight, they would get no credit and were obliged to live on cabbage, without any other species of diet. It would, I think, be more merciful to treat them as Bonaparte did his wounded soldiers, than thus leave them a prey to famine and victims to all those diseases and afflictions which accompany it. I hope, my Lord, you will attend to this appeal and see justice done to the most indigent and wretched people on earth.

Geoffrey Mostyn had already described their plight to the Under-Secretary:
Many must perish from hunger, specially some of those who were employed as stone breakers on a projected road near this village. I have seen the poor things come in day after day, week after week, for their few shillings hard-earned indeed and they were told by the paymaster that they could get no money as the pay sheets were not forwarded to him. There is gross negligence somewhere. Such cruelty to those starving creatures! Their tears of complaint are truly heart-rending and in my opinion many of them will perish.

Mostyn's complaint produced a rapid reaction from the Board of Works who sent word to the paymaster 'urging the immediate discharge of monies due to the labourers in the district of Foxford'. However, delays in the payment of wages continued to occur and John Garrett reported at the end of October the death of a labourer whose wages of eight pence a day had been unpaid for ten days. The Upper Leyny relief committee complained in December that labourers in their area did not receive their wages for several weeks.

Works Recommended   Magistrates meeting in Swinford in the middle of September under the chairmanship of G. V. Jackson passed a resolution that 'national works are indispensable for the safety of the country in its present melancholy position.'

The government itself was becoming increasingly convinced that public works would have to be undertaken on a massive scale to meet the impending calamity. On 3 October the Office of Public Works recommended that over £12,500 be spent on sixty-three specified works in the barony of Gallen and a few days later almost £22,000 for eighty public works in the barony of Costello with smaller sums for the Sligo baronies of Corran and Leyny and the half barony of Coolavin.

By the end of December there were over 7,000 employed in the Mayo baronies and over 5,000 in the Sligo baronies of the diocese, over 1,500 of them women and 1,100 boys. The numbers continued to rise week after week until they reached a peak in the middle of March 1847 with about 10,500 employed in Gallen and Costello and about 9,500 in Leyny, Corran and Coolavin, making a total of approximately 20,000 employed on public works in the diocese, of whom almost 7,000 were women and almost 4,000 were boys. For the following few months the numbers began to decrease, falling to a total of about 5,000 by the beginning of June.

Women Labourers

An eyewitness left an account of women working on roads near Tubbercurry:

> It was melancholy in the extreme to see the women and girls labouring in mixed gangs on public roads. They were employed not only in digging with the spade and pick, but also in carrying loads of earth and turf on their backs and wheeling barrows like men and breaking stones, while the poor neglected children were crouched in groups, about the bits of lighted turf in the various sheltered corners along the line.

Complaints

Complaints continued to be made about the public works. A petition from Bohola in the middle of November 1846, signed by the parish priest and curate and a number of other prominent inhabitants, complained that out of a population of 4,800, three-quarters of whom were in a state of 'the most frightful destitution', only 230 were employed which was about one in every sixteen who required it. In the parishes of Swinford, Kiltimagh and Bohola with a combined population of almost 22,000 not more than one in ten of those requiring relief were employed and Denis Tighe complained that only one-fifth of those in Ballaghaderreen who needed it were given employment.

Abuses

Only the destitute selected by the members of the local relief committee were to be given employment on the public works but undoubtedly some of those employed were not destitute but small landholders. Some committees and individual members were criticised for choosing people to enable them to pay the arrears of rent due to their landlord. Garrett alleged that many of the workers in the barony of Corran had been 'smuggled on the lists by some of the priests in proportion to the liberality with which they paid their Christmas dues'. This allegation was made at the end of January 1847 when many who were once in comfortable circumstances were now numbered among the destitute and priests whose ministry to the sick and dying brought them into many homes were far more likely to know the real conditions of their parishioners than a Protestant minister.

Lord Lucan told the Lord Lieutenant at the end of February that the Foxford relief committee had placed on their public works' list forty-nine persons who had between them 'upwards of 200 cows, 50 horses and asses, several sheep and a quantity of oats' but Lucan, however, was not a disinterested party but a substantial ratepayer who was liable for the funding of public works. Nevertheless, the Board of Works issued a special warning: 'Lists of persons who are to be employed to be prepared by the Board's engineer to prevent the jobbing and irregularities which were committed last season in the issue of tickets, a safeguard that gross injustice and impartiality are not practised in the selection.' Only the 'labouring poor' were to be chosen.

Jobbery

Allegations were also made about the appointments of officials. Pay-clerks in Sligo included the sons of a clergyman, a magistrate and grand juror. In Lower Leyny Pilsworth Whelan was the son of a stipendiary magistrate and in Coolavin James Elwood was the son of a clergyman. It was argued that pay-clerks had to be chosen from the well-off as not only did they require to have a knowledge of accounts but also they were required to provide two securities, each of £400, and their salary of £2 a week was regarded as comparatively small.

There is some evidence that some national school teachers were double-jobbing during the Famine. Edward Duffy in Ballaghaderreen, who was put in charge of the distribution of government rations by the relief committee there, was accused of neglecting his school. Complaints were made against John Cooke that he was neglecting his school in Foxford while acting as a steward on the public works in 1847 but his manager claimed that he did so outside school hours. John Tansey in Mullaghroe acted as a clerk on the public works in 1847 but a substitute teacher was appointed to replace him.

Patronage

Patronage was also rampant particularly in the appointment of overseers. It was a deeply entrenched practice in Irish society long before the famine began and continued to thrive not only in the public works but elsewhere during the course of that calamity. The master of Swinford workhouse was the brother of the matron, and the medical officer a brother-in-law of both, while all of them were either cousins or connected with three or four of the Guardians. On a surprise visit to the workhouse, the inspecting officer found the master drunk and demanded that the Board dismiss him but because of his connexions he thought the Board might reject his demand. 'The tendency of these connexionships is adverse to the proper working of the system.'

The number employed on public works was diminished in March 1847 not as a result of improved conditions but of a change in government policy. By now the government recognised that public works were failing disastrously to prevent starvation, and decided to put into place a system of relief designed to deliver cheap food directly and gratuitously to the destitute. But a delay between the partial suspension of public works and the introduction of the new system caused huge anger and hardship. John Coghlan complained that 523 people dismissed in Kilmovee 'will be found among the dead before many days', and Denis Tighe thought the same in Ballaghaderreen. 'Oh! 'tis a cruel thing to strike off at once 860 poor starving fellow creatures and to sign one morning their dismissal, I may say, their death warrants.' He was particularly angered that the government official who decided those to be dismissed had not consulted the local relief committee who knew their real condition. Over a thousand were dismissed in Swinford parish.

Many complained about bureaucratic delays or what Swinford Relief Committee called 'the most frivolous and vexatious delays and impediments'. When a head of a family was sick and unable to work, no other member of his family could take his place, until it was referred to the inspecting officer in Castlebar which frequently took up to a fortnight, and overseers prevented any member of his family replacing a sick labourer. Heavy snow in November and December 1846 caused works to be suspended and loss of wages to workers and brought a complaint from Upper Leyny Relief Committee. 'Thousands of human beings, thrown out of employment and exposed to inevitable starvation and certain death, presents a spectacle so appalling that we can find no language to describe our feelings on the subject.'

Denis Tighe

Wages were calculated on the basis of task work, on the amount of earth removed or stones broken and, according to John Garrett, a boy could not earn more than sixpence a week at breaking stones and a woman at most two shillings. He suggested that they should be allowed to avail themselves of a brother or a child to help them and thus increase their earnings but the Board of Works rejected the proposal. An ordinary labourer could earn between ten pence and a shilling a day which would provide one daily meal for himself and a family of six, but in reality most were paid eight pence a day and, as they became more and more weakened by malnutrition, considerably less.

Task Work

Deaths from Starvation

The earliest reports of deaths resulting from destitution came from Attymass in the middle of November 1846 when the parish priest informed G. V. Jackson that four people had died there recently from that cause. Denis Tighe told the Lord Lieutenant on 15 January 1847 that 'the hand of death is rapidly doing its work of destruction' among his parishioners in Ballaghaderreen, five of whom had died from want within the last three days. Two people died from starvation four days later, one of whom, Mark McCaen, declared a few hours before his death that he had not eaten a full meal for twelve days previously. Tighe claimed that there was an average of twenty deaths from starvation every week from the first of January to the middle of February when the number was 'frightfully increased' due to a heavy fall of snow, and Bernard Durcan thought that in Swinford 'deaths from starvation are much more numerous than can be imagined even from the number recorded by coroners' inquests'. Four inquests were held in Foxford at the end of January and verdicts of death from starvation were returned in each case. By early February in Kilkelly 'every day several are dying of starvation', and a month later Charlestown parish was averaging two to three deaths a day.

Nancy Kelly

The first detailed account of such a death came from Tourlestrane on 9 February, written by Sub-Inspector J. S. Stewart of Tubbercurry who attended an inquest at Annagh which returned a verdict of death by starvation on Nancy Kelly, a beggar woman.

> I found the body lying in Patrick Kelly's, her brother's house, on a wisp of straw over a few boards and a creel. The brother himself was sitting without a coat nursing a child which was quite evidently rapidly hastening to the grave, as the doctor said, from want of food, and he has three other children from eight to three years old, mere skeletons, hunger painted on their shrunken cheeks, the mother being gone to work on the Benada and Cully public works in order that she might earn something for her famishing children and there was nothing in the miserable cabin but some old bed clothes, a box and two plates.

> It was proved in evidence that this wretched man, hearing that his sister was unable to go about begging as usual, and that the storm had rendered her little hut totally uninhabitable, had borrowed an ass and brought her a distance of nearly two miles to his own place and gave her a division of his own miserable supply of food. This amounted to one pound of meal and one quart of sowings during a period of six days, and death mercifully closed her eyes and put an end to her sufferings.

Beggars, like Nancy Kelly, who represented a comparatively large class of people at the bottom of the social ladder, were among the earliest casualties of the famine as Denis Tighe was only too aware by the middle of February. 'That unfortunate class is completely gone. They are found in every direction lying on the roads either dead or breathing their last.' Two of them had recently died near his house 'as they were crawling to it to get relief.' In Bally-mote attitudes towards them hardened. 'Beggars at length are driven from door to door without alms, quite a new feature in the Irish peasant's character. Even the gentry are forced to deny what formerly they freely gave.'

Stewart had persuaded the coroner to give 7s 6d to provide a coffin and *No Coffins* funeral for Nancy Kelly, but many of the dead had to be buried without coffins. He complained that the few members of the relief committee were constantly obliged to contribute towards the purchase of coffins. The relief committee in Collooney asked the Lord Lieutenant to provide a fund for coffins to 'prevent the spread of pestilence, which otherwise inevitably will take place, as bodies have been a week in some cases unburied', but they were informed that 'his Excellency has no funds to provide coffins.' The dead were carried out at night and buried without coffins in Ballymote. 'Funerals even when coffins are obtained seldom appear attended by any number and deaths have become so common that the natural feelings have become quite blunted among the population.'

With the increasing reports of deaths from starvation, the government, *Soup Kitchens* realising that its public works schemes were not sufficient to prevent widespread deaths, passed at the end of February what was popularly known as the Soup Kitchen Act, providing direct relief in the form of cooked food or soup. New administrative measures were required, forms and documents had to be prepared, printed and distributed, including no less than three million ration tickets, and detailed regulations were issued to inspecting officers, finance committees and district relief committees. All this required time while the condition of the people deteriorated and, though the actual distribution of food was authorised to begin on 15 March, weeks elapsed in many areas before the new scheme was introduced.[2]

The idea of soup kitchens was borrowed from the successful operation of *Quakers* soup kitchens since the previous November in Cork city by the Society of Friends, better known as Quakers. The Quakers met in Dublin in November 1846 and set up the Central Relief Committee of the Society of Friends with Joseph Bewley and Jonathan Pim as joint secretaries. They published an

2 Inspecting officers were nominated by the Relief Commissioners on 1 March, including Capt Broughton in the Swinford Union, Capt Gilbert in Sligo, Capt Farren in Castlebar, Capt Burmester in Boyle, Lieut William Hamilton in Ballina and James Auchmuty in Castlerea

Soup kitchen

address which they sent to England and America and particularly to the Quakers in Philadelphia and funds began to pour in, first from the Friends in Ireland itself, then from those in England and later from those in America.

They began their relief operations in December and before the end of that month Dean Hoare and William Tyndall of Kilmactigue had already received £20 each from them to set up soup kitchens. At the beginning of February 1847 they granted one ton of rice to Charles Strickland for immediate distribution in the barony of Costello, and £20 to J. A. Holmes to establish a soup kitchen in Coolavin, suggesting that he purchase one ton of rice in Sligo to be paid for by the Quakers. By now William Tyndall had set up a sixty gallon boiler in Tourlestrane and was giving out soup four times a week to about 100 of the most destitute families. The Quakers were very insistent, as they told Ulic Burke in Swinford, that cooked rice be given as dysentery and diarrhoea were causing many deaths. 'We would suggest that immediate arrangements be made for distributing rice in a cooked state amongst the most destitute of the poor, especially those afflicted or threatened with dysentery.'

The Quakers spent approximately £200,000 in 1847 mostly in the west of Ireland and for over two years they continued to make grants of money, boilers, food and clothes to numerous parishes, including almost 120 donations to individuals and committees in some twenty-three different towns and parishes in Achonry.[3] While strictly non-sectarian, making their grants to Protestants and Catholics, ministers and priests alike, they showed a certain preference for Protestant ministers for practical reasons only, the ministers being better agents as they usually had the help of wives and daughters, while priests were already overstretched ministering to the dying. When Archdeacon Verschoyle asked for a grant for his Protestant school in Coolaney, Bewley and Pim informed him that they could not make a grant to a school which is 'evidently sectarian' and that their 'funds have been contributed by persons of all persuasions, with injunctions in very many cases to distribute them without reference to sect or party'. They rejected a similar request from Geoffrey Mostyn who wished to establish a Protestant school in Killasser.

Many of the poor had to pawn all their possessions, including clothes, to provide food for themselves and their families and were virtually reduced to nakedness as James Higgins witnessed in Charlestown in March 1848.

No Clothes

> They are now in a state of perfect and absolute nakedness, so much so that two-thirds of the poor creatures must decline coming into public for want of more covering and that in a village the same cloak or coat is used by ten or twelve persons on the same day to bring home a few quarts of meal from the market for their sustenance.

Pawnshops sprang up everywhere and quickly flourished in towns like Ballaghaderreen.

> The best proof of the wretchedness of this town is that a pawnbroker's shop not more than a few month's established contains £700 worth of property, principally bedding and wearing apparel sacrificed to ward off the approach of hunger by tradesmen always remarkable for sobriety and who have hitherto been able to support their families in decent independence.

The Quakers set up a sub-committee to oversee the distribution of clothes and they circulated a query form, seeking information on the clothes most needed. Mrs Jones of Benada Abbey was one of the first to return the filled-in query form in the middle of May. 'Nothing short of starvation would induce the peasantry of this neigbourhood to sell or pawn their clothes, many consider it a disgrace to do so. However, within the last winter many have done so in every family.' Men gave their coats to their wives on the public works to wear over their tattered petticoats leaving themselves 'somewhat indecent in their torn garments'.

In Tourlestrane 'shoemakers and tailors are in very great distress not getting any work since this famine has set in' and these were now employed to

3   For those who received grants from the Quakers see Appendix 29

Jonathan Pim of the
Society of Friends

make clothes and shoes from cloth and leather provided by the Quakers. Denis Tighe employed also a number of women in Ballaghaderreen making clothes from materials provided by the Quakers who always took pains to maximise the use of local amenities and labour. When they granted a ton of rice the local relief committee was encouraged to buy it at the nearest port, Sligo, Ballina or Westport, for which Quakers undertook to pay the bill and thus provided employment for local carriers who brought the meal in their horses and carts to local centres.

The help provided by the Quakers was credited by people at that time, like Ulic Burke in 1848, with saving large numbers from almost certain death. 'The active and unobstentatious benevolence of the Society of Friends has been under Providence the means of saving hundreds from a premature grave during the past calamitous season and I assure you that gratitude is but a poor expression of our feelings with regard to them.'

John Garrett expressed similar sentiments: 'Your Society have done much in relieving the destitute, clothing the naked, healing the sick, and rescuing multitudes from death.'

British Association   The British Association also made a significant contribution towards alleviating famine conditions in Ireland. Established in London in January 1847 by wealthy merchants and businessmen, including the Baron de Rothschild, it raised approximately £470,000, of which Queen Victoria subscribed £2,000, for the relief of famine victims in Ireland. Its agent, the Polish Count Strzelecki, decided in November 1847 to use the remaining funds to help schoolchildren in the west of Ireland and wrote to the Poor Law Inspectors in Swinford, Sligo, Ballina, Castlebar and elsewhere to procure a list of schools in their Unions. Capt Gilbert informed Patrick Durcan of Collooney that destitute school children would be given one meal a day and clothing and asked him to provide the number of those in each of the schools in his parish, and schoolchildren in Sligo Union, a sizeable section of the diocese, were being fed daily before the end of November.

Capt Broughton was still trying to organise the system in Swinford Union in the middle of December with the number of schools growing dramatically once the scheme was announced. 'They seem to have sprung up like mushrooms under the shower of relief to be afforded.' Killedan electoral district had three schools with fifty-six, seventy-nine and forty-one pupils respectively on 18 November and a month later Broughton was given a list of seventeen schools with a total of 2,138 children. These schools were aptly described by a school inspector visiting Coolaney early in 1848 as 'temporary bread or relief schools'.

The British Association scheme was operating extensively by January 1848 when 3,297 were receiving daily rations in Castlebar Union, 12,000 in Ballina, 7,400 in Castlerea and similar numbers were fed daily in Swinford, Sligo and Boyle Unions. Swinford Board of Guardians commented in May on the 'cheerfulness' with which rates were being paid, 'the ratepayers expressing their anxiety to pay, as their children are being fed by the British Association'. When the British Association wound up its activities that July it had expended over £78,000, feeding and clothing 200,000 schoolchildren, insuring that many of them survived Ireland's greatest calamity.

Help from Rome

At the end of January 1847 Archbishop Murray of Dublin received £730 sterling, donated by the people and clergy of Rome from Cardinal Fransoni who informed him that Pius IX was sending a personal contribution of £1,000 and the cardinals of the Congregation of Propaganda Fide £500. Murray was to distribute the money throughout the country, 'giving most where there was the greatest need, and seeing that the suffragan bishops in districts badly affected receive a just allocation.' Two months later, on 25 March, the pope issued an encyclical addressed to bishops worldwide appealing to them on behalf of famine victims in Ireland. Three days of public prayer were to be held in all churches and collections taken up for the relief of the Irish poor. Soon money began to pour into Rome, particularly from Italian and Swiss dioceses and a donation was received even from the nuncio in Bogota, Columbia, while other dioceses worldwide sent their contributions directly to the Archbishop of Dublin. By July Bishop McNicholas had received two separate contributions of £50 each, another £50 in August and £100 in September.

Government Rations

However, the food provided in soup kitchens by the Quakers and other benevolent agencies was supplementary to rations provided by the government, which rose from over 800,000 in early May to over two and a half million by the beginning of July, distributed to over three million people a day. The highest proportion of the population receiving rations was in the west of Ireland and as high as 84% in Swinford Union which the inspecting officer described as 'a Union of paupers for there are very few who will not require gratuitous relief'. Rations consisted of either one pound of meal or flour or one pound of biscuit or a pound and a half of bread for all persons over nine years, with those under nine receiving a half ration. In practice, a ration consisted usually of two-thirds Indian meal and one-third rice, cooked in water as a form of 'stirabout' or porridge.

Many believed that one pound of Indian meal was quite insufficient. A family of seven in Straide had to survive from Friday to the following Tuesday on three and a half pounds of Indian meal, and the curate in Bohola complained that rations 'doled to the poor are both inadequate and unsatisfactory'. The quality of the meal in Tubbercurry was described as 'of the very worst description' and 'near rotten' and the treasurer of the local relief committee was accused of buying it from friends in Sligo.

Those receiving rations were drastically reduced at the end of August from 1,000 to 134 in Kilshalvy electoral division and from 1,087 to 173 in Kilturra electoral division in Bunninadden. John Garrett, chairman of the local relief committee, complained bitterly that the reduction would 'multiply deaths by starvation'. The rations ceased completely early in September. By then the relief committee in Tubbercurry had distributed since 15 May 367,640 rations at less than twopence per ration, the total cost amounting to £2,690 of which only £160 was spent on salaries and other incidental running costs.

For all its shortcomings the soup kitchen scheme must be judged more than a qualified success as was acknowledged by the Swinford committee: 'We feel there cannot be any second opinion as to the motives by which these measures were dictated, the object at which they were aimed and their surpassing magnitude by which thousands of lives were saved in this Union alone.' The appearance of people in Mayo that September told its own story: 'The condition of the people since April and May is much improved. Then an immense number appeared to be starved; now altho' generally the peasantry and working people look thin and careworn, they do not appear to be suffering from want of food to such an extent as they did before.'

Poor Law   The potato crop of 1847 was largely free from blight but people were no better off because very few potatoes had been sown, only about one-seventh of the previous year, because those who had seed potatoes in the spring were forced to eat them. From now on the government resorted to the Poor Law system as the principal means of providing relief for the destitute. The Poor Law, introduced into Ireland in July 1838, divided the country into 130 new administrative units known as 'unions' consisting of a group of electoral divisions which in turn were made up of a number of townlands. Swinford

Union comprised twelve electoral divisions while other parts of the diocese belonged to five other unions, Sligo with twenty-three electoral divisions, Ballina, seventeen, Boyle, sixteen, Castlebar, ten, and Castlerea, eighteen.

Workhouses

A workhouse was built in the principal market town of each union with the only one in the diocese in Swinford, which was opened in March 1846. A large section of the Sligo end of the diocese was served by the workhouse in Sligo while the destitute in Ballymote, Keash and Gurteen were accommodated in Boyle, those from Ballaghaderreen in Castlerea, those from Attymass and Bonniconlon in Ballina and those from Straide in Castlebar. Each workhouse was administered by a Board of Guardians who were a mixture of elected and *ex-officio* local men, usually chosen from the wealthy and propertied classes. Swinford had twenty-one elected Guardians, Sligo thirty-nine, Ballina thirty-three, Castlebar twenty-one and Castlerea twenty-seven. The workhouses were financed locally by the poor rates on the principle that 'property should pay for poverty' and, to force landlords take a greater interest in the management of their estates, an act was passed making them liable to pay poor rates on land valued at under £4 per annum.

Paupers could not enter the workhouse as individuals but only as whole family units and, once inside, families were strictly segregated on the basis of sex. Male children over the age of three years were separated from their mothers, as happened to Michael Davitt who was over four years old when his family entered Swinford workhouse after the family were evicted in Straide. His mother, Catherine, refused to accept such a harsh regulation and left with her family after a stay of only one hour. Nobody was to be idle in the workhouse, as the name suggests, and breaking stones in the workhouse yard for gravelling roads or other such work was mandatory for men and women and used as a deterrent to any pauper remaining too long. For the same reason, food was inferior and monotonous.

Swinford Workhouse

Popular Aversion

The workhouse or poorhouse was universally despised and for a family to be assigned there was the ultimate in degradation. In Sligo such was 'the deep-rooted aversion of the peasantry to the workhouse, causing them almost to starve before they will enter it', and Michael Muldowney said of his parishioners in Achonry that 'they abhor the workhouse as a place of immediate dissolution.' In Swinford Union 'the prejudices of the population to the poorhouse were so deep and inveterate that the house was a long time open before one pauper could be induced to enter it.' But famine changed all that so that on 10 November 1846 there were 'upwards of 100 persons in the workhouse over the number the house is calculated to contain (700) and the Board of Guardians decline to admit anymore altho' there were 200 persons at the door seeking relief.' Of 200 applicants a month later, 113 were admitted, 'such was the awful state of the applicants that the Board could not reject them.'

Gregory Clause

Destitution was the only criterion for admission to the workhouse and no one occupying more than a quarter of an acre of land could be relieved out of the poor rates. This infamous quarter acre or Gregory clause was proposed by a Galway landowner, Sir William Gregory, later the husband of Lady Gregory of Abbey Theatre fame, to enable landlords to clear their estates of impoverished smallholders who were paying little or no rent. It was a draconian

Workhouse interior

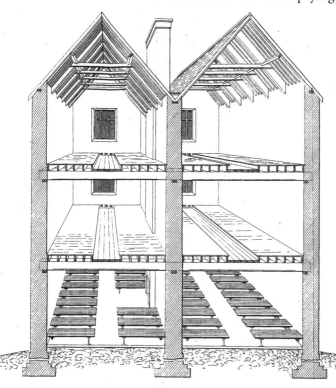

measure that condemned countless occupiers of small patches to starvation as henceforth, any person who occupied more than a quarter acre who applied for a place in a workhouse or for food in outdoor relief for his family had to give up his patch of land or face starvation. There were 2,000 families in Swinford parish, most small occupiers of three to six acres of inferior land and Bernard Durcan estimated that three-quarters of the entire population were reduced to utter destitution in the summer of 1848 because they were excluded from relief by the Gregory clause. G. V. Jackson stated that there was great suffering among this class in Killedan electoral division. Charles Durkan of Bonniconlon, who applied for relief in February 1849, was refused until he showed a certificate that he had given up his land, which he did on 28 February, was given 14lbs of meal and died the following day. Pat Roache of Knocknakillew in Straide, a tenant of Colonel McAlpine, refused an offer of ten shillings to give up his land and later died of starvation. Those who surrendered their lands saw their cabins demolished and were thus reduced to permanent homelessness.

Even those lucky enough to gain admission were also in danger of starving as whatever rates were collected were quite inadequate to meet the expenditure of the workhouse, which cost £60 for food and fuel for a week in Swinford. Those who had contracted to provide food refused to do so on credit for which they could hardly be blamed as they were small operators who needed the money to feed their own families. Turf was purchased in ass-loads from at least fifty poor persons and milk from over eighty 'who dispose of these necessaries to purchase meal for themselves, several of whom have solemnly declared that they had no means to procure a morsel for their families, until paid for what they had delivered to the workhouse.' The baker who was owed £68 in January 1847 refused to provide bread in future as he would not accept cheques. That January the clerk of the Union, Richard Kyle, had to approach on two different occasions William Fleming, a shopkeeper in the town, for money to buy some meal which he 'kindly advanced' while at the same time 'droves of beggars are to be met with in every quarter, pining from cold and starvation' and surrounding the workhouse 'crying and bawling, craving admission'.

Financial Problems

The greatest benefactor of Swinford workhouse, however, was the chairman of the Board, G. V. Jackson himself, who made several donations out of his own pocket to buy supplies. He gave £50 in the middle of November 1846 and was guarantor for three tons of Indian meal early in December but he was feeling the pinch. 'I cannot individually further assist the Board in funding the food of the paupers as I have not received anything like the amount of rent hitherto paid at this period nor any prospect of ever receiving it.' However, he continued providing supplies on his own security in the early part of 1847, assisted by his vice-chairman and deputy vice-chairman, but matters were exacerbated by the enormous hike in food prices during this period. When he received an urgent message from the master of the workhouse on the night of 7 February that the inmates had to stay in bed for want of fuel and that 'there is not a shilling's worth of food in the house for their support tomorrow', he immediately sent £20 to avert the crisis. But by now he had reached the end of his tether. 'It is my own conviction that the government in each department has done and is doing all that any government can do to

G. V. Jackson

mitigate the horrors of the calamity we suffer under; but my own experience satisfies me that it is beyond the reach of human means to meet.'

Government Loan

The manager of the Provincial Bank in Ballina had been approached for a loan with the rates as security but the London directors refused and the manager informed the Board of Guardians that 'if no other security of a business like character be offered, it is useless to repeat any application.' Finally they turned for a loan to the government who had already decided to make money available for three workhouses, including Swinford, which from the end of February received a weekly loan of £60.

Number of Inmates

The average number of inmates in workhouses fluctuated constantly, with over 100 more in Swinford workhouse in November 1846 than it was designed to accommodate and it continued to be over-populated until the end of December. The house was full, hovering around 700, for the early weeks in 1847 and, surprisingly, for much of 'Black '47' it housed comparatively few. The number was about 550 at the end of February where it remained until the beginning of April when it began to decline from 480 on 3 April to just over 300 in the middle of May and it remained between 300 and 400 until the end of October when it began to rise again to 730 by December.

It continued to be overpopulated during the early months of 1848 reaching over 1,000 in early March but there was a dramatic decline at the end of that month when the figure stood at just over 400 and remained at 400-500 in

Workhouse bed

April and 500-600 in May. (The numbers in the other workhouses in Ballina, Castlerea and Sligo showed no such similar decline.) In June it began to rise steeply from about 700 at the beginning of that month to over 1,100 at the middle. A decline set in at the end of that month until the beginning of August when it stood at just over 700 but began to rise steeply at the end of that month when it was over 900 and almost 1,000 at the end of September. It peaked at the end of November when it stood at a staggering 2,327 and remained hovering around the 2,000 mark to the end of 1848.

Children

By far the largest single group in the workhouse were children under the age of fifteen. Of just over 2,000 inmates on 11 November 1848, 1,155 were children, the rest were made up of 540 women and 237 men, proportions that remained more or less constant. At one of its lowest points with only 300 inmates, at the beginning of October 1847, over 170 were children and only twenty-two men and forty-three women. In fact, there may have been even more children in the workhouse than the weekly statistics recorded. When Capt Broughton investigated eighty-four men in Swinford workhouse on 11 December 1847 he discovered that forty-five of them were 'in fact, only children, who, by calling themselves fifteen, thought to avoid school, and as the weather had been dreadfully severe, and very little outdoor work capable of being done, preferred roasting themselves over the fire in the mens' wards to going to school.' He promptly ordered them back to school.

The Poor Law Act of June 1847 authorised the provision of outdoor relief to the destitute if there was no accommodation for them in the workhouse. Weekly rations in Swinford Union consisted of 7lbs of Indian meal for adults over fifteen years, 6lbs for children from nine to fifteen years, 5lbs for children from five to nine years and 3½ lbs for children under five years. By the end of June over 800,000 countrywide were receiving outdoor relief. Over 2,400 were on outdoor relief in March 1848 in the seven electoral divisions of Sligo Union in the diocese and two months later almost 11,000 in Swinford Union illustrating the stark difference in the conditions in the Mayo and Sligo parts of the diocese.

Out-Door Relief

Malnutrition inevitably led to an outbreak of disease which was reported from various places like Coolavin from early 1847. 'Fever and dysentry are raging to a frightful extent in the district … carrying off our population in great numbers.' Fever and other contagious diseases appeared in Sligo 'to an alarming extent' and the county fever hospital was unable to accommodate the victims. Deaths from disease in Tourlestrane were 'of almost daily occurrence' early in February, and Denis Tighe reported from Ballaghaderreen where fever and dysentery were rampant that '"deaths from starvation" is the awful news that reaches me from every quarter.' Fever and dysentry were 'committing frightful ravages' in Charlestown with an average of two to three deaths a day. Over 330 inmates in Sligo workouse were then diseased, half with fever and the other with dysentry. A Dublin doctor sent to examine the situation there reported that dysentery had 'always a tendency to end in chronic diarrhoea, which is most obstinate and will wear out the patient from one to nine months' and could not be cured without proper nourishment 'as medicine cannot supply the place of food'.

Disease

By summer dysentry had disappeared from Keash but fever was increasing 'to an alarming extent' and spreading 'fearfully' in Ballaghaderreen. Troops moving from Boyle to Castlebar infected with fever, who sought to be billeted in Ballaghaderreen, were refused accommodation by some and one man who took in one of the sick soldiers died himself of fever four days later. It was so prevalent in Castlebar that nobody would attend the assizes there and already one doctor had died from fever, as well as the matron of the jail.

Fever

'Fever' was in fact typhus, a highly contagious disease transmitted by body lice with an incubation period of seven to ten days, and characterised by headaches, fever, skin rash and intense thirst. It lasted two weeks with a 50%-70% death rate. 'Once these hapless people are struck down by this strange malady they lose all mental and physical powers, and die in the most acute agony.' It could only be prevented by the elimination of lice which, given the insanitary and crowded conditions in which the poor lived, was an impossible task.

The number of workhouse inmates suffering from fever fluctuated constantly. Swinford workhouse had 9 cases in January 1847, eighteen a month later, and over twenty in March until the end of April. By October the numbers had fallen back again to single figures but began to rise again in November and reached eighteen in December. They remained in the early or mid teens for the first four months of 1848 but from May fell back to single figures, falling as low as three in early August. For the rest of that year they rose but that rise coincided with a dramatic rise in the total number of inmates, thirty-two cases out of a total over 2,000 inmates in November.

Fever was no respecter of persons. Some of the more comfortable classes fell victim to it and while some recovered, others like William Tyndall of Kilmactigue died and John Garrett lost a son and a daughter in Ballymote, while another son struck down with fever recovered. One priest, Dominick O'Connor, the curate in Collooney, is known to have died from it and considering that priests were constantly administering the last rites to the dying in fever-infected cabins, it is truly amazing that he was the only one who succumbed to it. Bernard McGauran, the Ballysadare-born chaplain in the quarantine island of Grosse Isle had his own explanation. 'The Master Whom I serve holds me in his all powerful Hand.' In fact, McGauran did fall victim to fever but later recovered and even returned to work among the fever-stricken Irish emigrants in Grosse Isle. Of the forty-two priests of the diocese of Quebec who ministered there, nineteen contracted fever and four died as well as two Protestant ministers. Relieving officers like Francis Soden in Keash and the Mallee brothers in Straide and workhouse functionaries were particularly exposed to it and while they recovered, Kelly, a teacher in Swinford workhouse died from fever as did the inspecting officer, Capt Broughton.

Cholera   Other diseases like measles and smallpox were also taking their toll. Keash reported in July 1848 an outbreak of measles together with smallpox which were 'taking their rounds through each family.' Cholera made its appearance in the western Unions in March 1849 reaching Ireland from Britain and first detected in seaports such as Westport. By early July the workhouse there reported eighty deaths during the previous week, over half of them from cholera, while Castlerea workhouse reported nine deaths from cholera out of a total of fifteen. Sligo had fifty-five cholera deaths out of a total of fifty-seven early in August while Tubbercurry national school was closed for a fortnight in September, 'cholera having made its appearance in the neighbourhead'.

The highest weekly number of deaths in Swinford workhouse was thirty-six during the week ending 1 May 1847, almost 10% of the total number of inmates. The previous week there were thirty-two deaths but for most of the earlier months of that year the weekly number of deaths was in the single figures, rising to ten early in March and twenty a month later. Deaths were back in the single figures by October, with one death for each of three weeks and none at all in the last week of that month and that remained the pattern until the end of 1847. The figure rose to a weekly average of about twenty during the month of April 1848 but slipped back to the low single figures for the rest of that year. Deaths outside the workhouse are more difficult to count. Mortality in 1849 reached a new peak with more deaths in Connacht that year than in either 1847 or 1848. An estimated 45,000 deaths occurred in 1849, 2,000 more than was estimated for 1847.

Deaths

Some deaths were recorded in reports and inquest accounts.

Farrell McGloin left Sligo workhouse on Good Friday, 6 April (1849), travelled about five miles when he reached the place of his death. His legs and feet were much swollen and he appeared in ill-health and much debilitated. He was placed in the chapel on the wayside on some straw. He received no food and from his weakness, want of nourishment and the cold of the chapel, he was discovered dead the following morning. He had applied to a person near the chapel to give him shelter in his house, but having stated that he came from the workhouse and appearing so seriously ill, he was refused admittance, fearing he might introduce fever amongst a numerous family of children. He died in the chapel of Currhowna.

Farrell McGloin

Dominick Hughes of Belgarrow, Foxford and his family had spent over a fortnight in Swinford workhouse in the spring of 1849 as he had also done the previous year, according to his son, James, at his inquest on 20 April:

Dominick Hughes

They left the workhouse on each of the occasions of their own free will, they being in bad health while in the workhouse, as being exhausted from hunger and weakness before they went into it. Their bad state of health in the workhouse was the cause of their leaving it ... He was three days the week before his death without a morsel of food to eat except about a pint of barley meal gruel ... The want of food was the cause of his death. He was everyday crying out for food and that he was dying with hunger. My mother is now lying in her bed, and got the last rites of the church on yesterday, from hunger and starvation, and the rest of the family are nearly as bad as she is, as the jury may see by myself and my two brothers now present at this inquest.

Thomas Hopkins

Thomas Hopkins, Cloonieron, Kilmovee, his wife, Bridget, and five children, also spent a fortnight in Swinford workhouse about the same time. He died in March and Bridget stated at the inquest that in her opinion the want of sufficient food was the cause of his death.

The Wednesday week before deceased's death, he, deceased, left his own house about dinner-time, to go to the market of Bellaghy to buy half a stone of meal, that he had got the price of from Hugh Regan of Uggool. He, deceased, went only forty or fifty perches from his house when he returned in a weaker state than when he left the house and he told me that he met something strange, having some appearance of a human being, which he believed to be Death, and which desired him to return home and that he had not long to live.

Emigration

Jonathan Pim described in February 1847 how many people were fleeing the country to escape the famine. 'Inclement as is this season, they are going already. A ship left Sligo just before Christmas and instead of the sorrow usual on leaving their native country, there was nothing but joy at their escape, as from a doomed land. The country in many places is becoming depopulated. The people are deserting their families, crowding into towns and cities; spreading themselves over our eastern counties, where destitution is less because the people have been accustomed to rely on wages for their support; and when they can beg their passage, crossing over to England and Scotland.'

Sligo Port

A total of 11,200 emigrated from Sligo port in 1847. The great majority went to Canada and landed at a tiny island, Grosse Isle, in the St Laurence River about thirty miles downstream from the city of Quebec. In all twenty-five ships sailed there from Sligo in 1847 and a further five from Killala with a total of just over 7,000 passengers. The length of the voyage varied from fifty-three days which it took the *Royal Adelaide* from Killala to twenty-seven days for the *Transit* from Sligo. The first ship, the *Jessie*, arrived from Sligo on 24 May with 243 immigrants, and no less than eleven ships arrived from there in June, four of them on the same day, 10 June. Eight ships from Sligo arrived in New York in 1847 with a total of just over 700 passengers, three in 1848 with almost 500 passengers and nine in 1849 with just over 1,000 passengers.

Passengers

Passenger numbers varied greatly, with most ships carrying from about 130 to 300 passengers. The *Sarah-Brown* sailed to New York in July 1847 with only twenty-six passengers, while the *Larch* arrived at Grosse Isle on 20

FOR

NEW YORK.

Direct from Limerick,
ON OR ABOUT 20th OCTOBER, NEXT,

WIND AND WEATHER PERMITTING,

THE SPLENDID FIRST CLASS FAST SAILING FULL RIGGED UNITED STATES SHIP,

"JOSEPH MEIGS,"

DANIEL H. WOOD, COMMANDER.

355 TONS REGISTER, 600 TONS BURTHEN.

This truly magnificent American Ship is now at the Quay discharging grain from New York, (which Port she belongs to,) and is engaged to leave here for home at the advertized time. She will be found on inspection one of the finest Vessels that ever conveyed Passengers from this port ; and the accommodation she offers is of a superior style, such as, a well arranged First Cabin, for select Parties, an excellent intermediate one, and extensive decks, permanently laid, giving considerably more height than required by law, 70lbs. of Bread Stuffs and 10lbs. of Beef will be put on Board for each Passenger, and Capt. WOOD, who is well experienced in the trade will have every comfort afforded those sailing with him during the voyage. Early application to secure berths is absolutely necessary to the Agents,

RYAN, BROTHERS & CO.

Ship, Insurance & General Agents, Howley's-quay, Limerick.

J.W. HOGAN, Printer, Town-hall, Limerick

August with 440, the largest complement. Out of a total of almost 36,000 emigrants who arrived at Quebec and Montreal, all but about 1,200 were described as labourers or farmers as well as about 600 of those who travelled to New York from Sligo in 1847, 1848 and 1849. Most of the other passengers who made up the total of 2,200 were women and children. Twenty ships bound for New York in 1847, 1848 and 1849 carried about 660 women and about 850 children and other young people under the age of twenty. A small number of the better-off also emigrated and, according to John Garrett, his 'best conditioned parishioners' in Ballymote were leaving the country at the end of 1848.

Very few deaths were recorded on ships bound for New York and, in fact, on twenty ships which sailed there in 1847, 1848 and 1849 there were only

Ship Deaths

four deaths, two one-year-old children, Mary Faiver and Michael Tighe, and Hugh Haran, an infant. The only adult, Rose Gillooly, was twenty-three and married when she died on the *Sarah-Maria* which sailed in October 1849. These vessels hardly merited the term 'coffin ships' nor did those which sailed to Grosse Isle where the death rate on most of the ships during the voyage ranged from four to ten. The thirty ships which sailed from Sligo and Killala carried over 7,000 passengers of whom about 500 died during these crossings although almost 120 of these were lost at sea following the shipwreck of the *Carricks* off Cape Rozier. Thirty-six survivors were brought to Quebec.

Quarantine   Almost 360 other emigrants died while in quarantine in Grosse Isle bringing the total number of deaths to 858. When a ship arrived it was detained in quarantine where it was examined and the sick removed and hospitalised and, after the ship was cleansed, it was certified to continue to its port of landing. The period of quarantine varied from one day spent by the *Ellen* and the *Wonder* on 10 and 15 July and seventeen days spent by the *Wolfeville* which arrived on 10 June. Most periods in quarantine varied from three to six days. Sixteen on board the *Wolfeville* died while in quarantine while thirty-two others died in the quarantine hospital. Having already lost thirty-seven at sea, its total number of deaths came to eighty-five out of a passenger list of 311. The *Larch* lost 110 at sea and a further eighty-six in quarantine, making a total of 196 deaths out of 440 passengers. But these two ships were not at all *Bernard McGauran*   representative of the majority of ships from Sligo, where quarantine casualties were in single figures and six ships suffered no casualties at all.

When the first ship from Sligo, the *Jessie*, arrived at Grosse Isle on 24 May, there were thirty-two ships there, which were like 'floating hospitals', according to Bernard McGauran, first chaplain on the island in 1847, 'where death makes the most frightful inroads'. Born in Ballysadare in 1821, the son of George, a merchant, and his wife, Bridget Colleary, he came to Quebec as a young man and studied for the priesthood. He had only been ordained a year when his bishop sent him to Grosse Isle in May.

McGauran described 'the very sad state of Grosse Isle' and the ships waiting there on 24 May.

'There are usually four or five hundred aboard. Today I spent five hours in the hold of one of these where I administered the sacraments to a hundred people ... It would be better to spend one's entire life in a hospital than to spend a few hours in the hold of one of these vessels where there are so many people and so many

Bernard McGauran

sick among them ... I have not taken off my surplice today; we meet people everywhere in need of the sacraments; they are dying on the rocks and on the beach where they have been left by the sailors who could not carry them to the hospitals. We buried twenty-eight yesterday, twenty-eight today, and now (two hours past midnight) there are thirty dead whom we will bury tomorrow. I have not gone to bed for five nights ... Night and day we are in the midst of the sick where there are so many sudden deaths. We can hardly stop to take a rest, but someone comes in haste to summon us ... my legs are beginning to bother me, because I am always on my feet.'

Though struck down by typhus during his first tour of duty, McGauran recovered and returned again to Grosse Isle where he was among the last priests when the navigation season ended in October 1847.

A scheme was inaugurated in 1848 to send female orphans, aged between fourteen and eighteen, selected from the various workhouses, to Australia. The voyage lasted from ninety to 100 days and their passage was paid by the Colonial Lands and Emigration Commissioners, while their outfits and conveyance to the port of embarkation was funded by their own Union. They were taken by steamboat from Dublin and Cork to London and Plymouth where they were identified, subjected to a medical examination and they and their clothes cleaned before embarcation.

Female Orphan Emigrants

By the beginning of September, twenty-five such orphans had been sent from Ballina and forty from Sligo, and by December thirty from Boyle and twenty from Castlerea. Another 200 from ten Unions were selected for the next ship due to sail on 1 March 1849 and from then on vessels were to sail once a month with such passengers. In Australia they were employed as domestic servants and Bishop T. Murphy, chairman of the Children Apprenticeship Board in Adelaide which organised their employment, described them as 'as useful a class as could have been sent to this colony.' By late 1849 the total number sent was 4,175 of which eighty-seven were from Ballina Union, fifty-one from Boyle, fifteen from Castlebar, twenty from Castlerea and sixty-eight from Sligo.

Adelaide Dillon, who visited Ballaghaderreen in June 1849, described the famine-ravaged countryside to her husband, John Blake, then in exile in New York. 'It would make you sorrowful, dear love, if you could see the country now ... it is very sad to be among them and see their suffering ... There is some mysterious fate over poor Ireland I think. It seems to me the end of it will be that all the people will either die, emigrate or be transported (they are transporting them now from the poorhouses to Australia). All the land will then be taken possession of by the English Government (for all the different Unions in course of time must become insolvent) ... And the end of it will be a new plantation.' [4]

Population Decline   Emigration proved to be the most lasting legacy of the Famine for the next hundred years and more. Over one million people emigrated in the five years 1845-51 and just under another million in the following five years. The population of the diocese in 1841 stood at about 136,000 and ten years later it was 101,516, showing a decline of 34,477, or of about a quarter, for the famine decade. It was probably somewhat in excess of that figure as the population would have continued to grow rapidly for the five years between 1845 and 1851. Mayo and Sligo had the highest excess mortality rates in the country at 58.4 and 52.1 respectively and, taking 55 per thousand as the average for the diocese, somewhere in the region of 8,000 died and about 27,000 emigrated.

The population decline varied from parish to parish. Ballysadare, which lost over two-thirds of its population, was completely exceptional and can only be explained by massive emigration from the port of Sligo to which the population had very easy access. Elsewhere in the diocese, Foxford and Tourlestrane had the highest decline with 37%, closely followed by Coolaney, 36.9%, and Swinford, 34.5%. Other parishes, like Attymass, Killasser, Meelick, Straide, Keash and Bunninadden, hovered round the 30%. Surprisingly, Kiltimagh and Bonniconlon were at the lower end of the scale with 21.9% and 23.5% respectively. Gurteen and Ballymote were 25% and 27% respectively. Ballaghaderreen and Charlestown had very slight decreases while Kilmovee actually recorded an increase and the only thing they had in common is that most of their inhabitants were tenants of Viscount Dillon, whose agent, Charles Strickland played an active role in providing relief during the Famine.

These percentages represent the rural portions of these parishes but it was quite a different story in towns, some of which like Ballymote, Kiltimagh, Kilkelly and Bellaghy actually recorded a growth in population during the Famine decade, while others like Gurteen and Aclare remained almost unchanged. Small decreases were recorded in Swinford and Tubbercurry while 10%-15% decreases occurred in Ballaghaderreen, Foxford, Collooney and Coolaney. Ballysadare town had the largest decrease, almost 30%, which again was probably explained by its proximity to Sligo port.

4   Adelaide Dillon to J.B. Dillon, 9 & 23 June 1849, Dil. P. 6455

CHAPTER SEVEN

A Forgotten Fenian

The *Nation* newspaper, founded in 1842, and the movement it gave rise to, known as Young Ireland, was to have an immense influence on the formation of Irish nationalism for its own and later generations. The *Nation* was the brainchild of a remarkable trio, Thomas Davis, Charles Gavan Duffy and John Blake Dillon, from Ballaghaderreen.[1] His father, Luke, had moved there from the family holding at Lisyne, Co Roscommon because he was unable to renew the lease and died in Ballaghaderreen in 1823. John Blake Dillon's mother, who gave her son his middle name, was Anne Blake from Dunmacrena, Co Galway. Another of her sons, Thomas, started a small shop in the town which he later handed over to his widowed sister, Monica Duff, which she in turn passed on to her widowed daughter, Anne Deane. 'Monica Duff's' expanded and prospered and was to dominate the economic life of Ballaghaderreen from the later decades of the nineteenth century to the middle of the following.

John Blake Dillon

John Blake Dillon was born in 1814 and received his early education from classical masters in Ballaghaderreen. He grew up in a house 'where the rosary was said every night and no person ever allowed to pass the door without assistance.'[2] He went to Maynooth in 1830 with the intention of becoming a priest for the diocese of Achonry, 'not that he felt any vocation to the priesthood but that his mother wished him "to try" seeing that he loved books and was of a serious disposition.' Finding after two years that he had no vocation, he left but retained an 'affectionate remembrance' of the college. He entered Trinity College on 17 October 1834 where he read ethics and mathematics and there he met and befriended Thomas Davis, a friendship which profoundly affected his life. Both were deeply interested in politics and active members of the College Historical Society. Dillon took up the study of law and was called to the Bar in 1841. In later years Charles Gavan Duffy drew a pen picture of Dillon:

Maynooth

---

1 The following account of John Blake Dillon draws heavily on F. S. L. Lyon's, *John Dillon*, pp 1-6 and Brendan Ó Cathaoir, *John Blake Dillon*
2 Memoir of Adelaide Dillon, Dil. P.

John Blake Dillon

In person he was tall and strikingly handsome, with eyes like a thoughtful woman's, and the clear olive complexion and stately bearing of a Spanish noble. His generous nature made him more of a philanthropist than a politician. He was born and reared in Connaught amongst the most abject and oppressed population in Europe and all his studies and projects had direct relation to the condition of the people ... and he saw with burning impatience the wrongs inflicted on the industrious poor by an aristocracy practically irresponsible ... Dillon desired a national existence primarily to get rid of social degradation and suffering which it wrung his heart to witness without being able to relieve. He was neither morose nor cynical but he had one instinct in common with Swift, the villanies of mankind made his blood boil ... [3]

Marriage   Dillon's health took an ominous turn in 1845 and, while recuperating in Ballaghaderreen, he learnt of Thomas Davis's death after what had seemed only a mild attack of scarlet fever. His condition deteriorated rapidly and he began to spit blood. To save his life he was sent to Madeira for the winter from where he returned in the summer of 1846. The following year he married Adelaide Hart of Fitzwilliam Place. Her father, Simon Hart, was a solicitor, whose firm, Hart and O'Hara, is said to have been one of the first, if not the first, Catholic law partnerships to begin practice after the relaxation of the penal laws. The name of the firm suggests that both families originated in Achonry diocese.

Young Ireland   When William Smith O'Brien, a Protestant and a landlord, founded the
'Rising'   Irish Confederation, in January 1847, Dillon speedily identified himself with it and under the influence of another member, John Mitchel, a more militant note began to predominate. 1848 was the fiftieth anniversary of the Rising of 1798 and its spirit was again abroad in the land, while in Europe it was the year of revolutions and the news from the continent encouraged Mitchel and

3   Charles Gavan Duffy, *Young Ireland*, I, pp 60-61

others to believe that a successful rising might be possible in Ireland. The government was well-informed of the conspiracy and arrested Mitchel in May. The 'rising' in late July, led by Smith O'Brien, consisted of a brief encounter with the police in Widow McCormack's cabbage garden in Ballingarry, County Tipperary.

O'Brien and Thomas Francis Meagher were taken prisoners but Dillon, *On the Run* who also took part in the rising, avoided capture and and went on the run for a few weeks, mostly in the counties of Clare and Galway, even taking refuge at one point in the Aran Islands where he was believed to be a priest. Most of the time he was passed from one priest's house to another. He spent his last days in Ireland in St Jarlath's College in the care of the president, Anthony O'Regan. O'Regan arranged a passage for him on a ship leaving from Galway for America and accompanied him to the ship. Dillon wrote from America to Adelaide, now pregnant with their first child and told her that 'but for the devoted and heroic conduct of O'Regan he would be on his way to Van Diemen's Land.' [4]

The fiasco of Ballingarry had long-lasting political effects as many Young *America* Ireland rebels, like Dillon, escaped to America where they nurtured anti-English sentiments among the famine emigrants. Later Irish nationalists were to find Irish Americans an important source of financial as well as moral support. A small number of rebels like James Stephens and John O'Mahony, who later co-founded the Fenian movement, escaped to Paris. Four of the captured ring-leaders, Smith O'Brien, Meagher, Terence Bellew McManus and Patrick O'Donoghue were convicted of high treason and sentenced to death but later commuted to transportation to Van Diemen's Land. Their courage during and after the trial captured the popular imagination at home and abroad. Adelaide Dillon visited them in Richmond prison before their transportation: 'I saw them all on Saturday evening and bid them goodbye. It went to my very heart – above all poor O'Brien and as I shook hands with him he looked so noble and true – such a perfect gentleman as he always does – to send him out as a convict with 250 common English convicts! And poor Meagher that I love so – Such a glorious noble spirit. Well the bloody old British Empire has triumphed this time.' [5]

Adelaide Dillon visited Ballaghaderreen in June 1849, probably to show *Ballaghaderreen* her new-born daughter to John Blake's mother. She had assured her husband *Visit* in New York that there was no cholera outside the workhouses and none at all in Ballaghaderreen. People in Ballaghaderreen were curious to see the wife

4 O'Regan later became Bishop of Chicago
5 Adelaide Dillon to J. B. Dillon, 31 May 1849, Dil. P. 6455

of their famous son: 'By the way I forgot to tell you that my arrival here caused considerable excitement in this celebrated town. Nothing could equal the anxiety of the people to get a sight of "Councillor Dillon's wife". I can't say whether they were satisfied or not – very likely not, for they have a far higher idea of your desserts than you have yourself.'[6] Their admiration of Dillon was not reciprocated by him:

> You will find little or nothing to attract you in that country. The aspect of the country is monstrous and poor, the peasantry degraded in mind and body and the gentry (as they call themselves) most base and beggarly. If the few who are dear to me there were out of it, I would most willingly lay aside forever the remembrance of the place of my birth. This is a very old opinion of mine viz., 'that Ireland is the most degraded country in the world, Mayo the most degraded county in Ireland, and the barony of Costello (in which Ballaghaderrin is situated), the most degraded district in Mayo.' Now you may congratulate yourself on having seen the lowest point to which humanity can be reduced. I have often wondered how such decent people as my own family are, could grow up in the midst of such influences.

His own family was the only exception to his general condemnation:

> They have not as you will perceive much refinement about them but they have many solid virtues. They have always been very strictly honest and very charitable. I cannot call to mind any act of any one of them in their dealing with the world, which I would be ashamed to have mentioned. As for public spirit, they were, I believe, the only people in that region who ever exhibited any. These solid and substantial virtues are more than sufficient with me to cover such oddities from which some of them are not free and on the whole I not only love them but I am proud of them.

He went on to warn Adelaide about his mother's 'little foibles': 'She is so very shy and so distrustful of herself that unless you insist on her being with you she will be sure to think that you want to get rid of her ... She will shut herself up in her little bedroom and console herself by reflecting that she will be soon out of people's way etc., etc.'[7]

Young Italy Movement

In the summer of 1849 the eyes of the world were turned on Italy which was in the throes of a popular movement leading to the unification of the country. It also led to a confrontation between the papacy and the Young Italy movement as the Papal States separated the north of the country from

---

6   Adelaide Dillon to J. B. Dillon, 9 June 1849, Dil. P. 6455
7   John Blake Dillon to Adelaide Dillon, 26 June 1849, Dil. P. 6455

the south. In February 1849 a republic had been proclaimed in Rome and Pius IX had been driven out. Catholics world wide were divided on the issue, as Adelaide discovered in Ballaghaderreen. 'By the way, I have battles royal with the priests here (including your friend, Mr Durcan) about Rome and the Pope. Not one of them will take the true honest view of it.'[8] Her husband held even stronger views on the question:

> ... I never could understand why the happiness and freedom of millions should be made secondary and dependant upon the interests and intrigues of that petty Italian state ... If the church (that is to say, the Pope, the bishops and the priests) must be leagued, as it is now, with the despots and murderers, Catholicity is gone out of it and we must seek for it elsewhere. Christ did not come into this world to put fetters on men's limbs or thoughts nor was it his custom to ally himself with powerful oppressors and to trample the weak and humble in the dust.[9]

Dillon's Return

Soon afterwards Adelaide joined her husband in America with the daughter he had never seen and they settled on Long Island and John began to practise law in New York. Their eldest son was born in 1850 and another son, John, was born not in America but in Blackrock, Co Dublin when his mother was home visiting her family, but she returned with the child to New York. The government declared an amnesty in 1855 and the Dillon family came back to Dublin and John Blake Dillon began yet another legal career. They lived in Fitzwilliam Square where the children were taught by a succession of tutors, including James Stephens who by 1858 had returned from Paris, and was later to become the leader of Fenianism.

Death

Dillon was elected MP for Tipperary in 1865 as an independent oppositionist and shortly afterwards called a meeting in Dublin of the independent oppositionists in the hope of creating a coherent parliamentary group to support the liberals. Within little more than twelve months he was stricken by cholera and died on 15 September 1866 after only a few days illness. He was only fifty years of age. During a parliamentary career of just one year he had persuaded the independent opposition party to reconstitute itself as a parliamentary force, a strategy that was to prove spectacularly successful within a few years of his death.

Fenianism

On St Patrick's Day 1858, James Stephens founded in Dublin a secret, oath-bound society, the Irish Revolutionary Brotherhood. Later that year Stephens went to America and early the following year, together with John

8   Adelaide Dillon to J. B. Dillon, 23 June 1849, Dil. P. 6455
9   John Blake Dillon to Adelaide Dillon, 16 July 1849, Dil. P. 6455

O'Mahony and Michael Doheny, founded an organisation which was named the Fenian Brotherhood and, as a result, the IRB became known to history as the Fenians. The movement flourished in the 1860s, largely among young artisans and shop assistants in the fast-growing towns. Shop assistants were the new rising class of educated young men in small and large towns which by the middle of the century were beginning to dominate the economic, social and political life of the country

Edward Duffy

Edward Duffy

Edward Duffy from Ballaghaderreen was a young shop assistant destined to play a leading role in the Fenian movement.[10] He was born in 1840 in Barrack Street, where his father, also called Edward, a national school teacher, died of consumption when his son was only nine years old. A few years later Edward became an apprentice in a dry goods store in Castlerea and after serving his time went to Dublin where he got a situation in Pim's and later in Cannock's. After taking the Fenian oath in Dublin at the end of 1859, he advanced quickly through the ranks and soon became acquainted with Stephens. 'After the interview with the "Captain" he (Duffy) gave his whole being to the movement and was the medium by which Connaught was organized.'[11] Duffy was among the inner circle who were invited to meet John O'Mahony at his lodgings when he visited Dublin from America before Christmas 1860.

McManus Funeral

Terence Bellew McManus died in San Francisco on 15 January 1861 and was buried there, but a few months later it was decided to disinter his remains and send them to Ireland as their final resting place. News of this plan did not reach Ireland until after the middle of May 1861 and early in June a McManus funeral committee was formed. Smith O'Brien, John Blake Dillon and other former comrades of Young Ireland days expressed their approval, assuming they would play a leading role in the funeral. But James Stephens had other ideas and, with the help of Duffy and other young Fenians, took charge of the arrangements.

The remains were brought ashore in Cobh and from there arrived by train in Dublin on 4 November where they lay in state in the Mechanics' Institute. A dispute with Archbishop Cullen resulted in no formal religious rites being provided. The funeral procession to Glasnevin took place on 10 November. The remains, followed by a number of carriages carrying Smith O'Brien, John Blake Dillon and other noteworthies, were followed by seven or eight thousand marchers, marshalled by men on horseback, including many of the

10 This account of Duffy's life is based on an article by his sister, Annie, published in *The Irishman*, 14 Mar 1868. See also Pádraig G. Ó Laighin, *Eadbhard Ó Dufaigh, 1840-1868*
11 Joseph Denieffe, *A Personal Narrative of the Irish Revolutionary Brotherhood*, p 58

Dublin trades in full regalia. Vast numbers of people lined the streets to see the procession. Edward Duffy led the Connacht representation at the funeral and his mother was later to take with her to America the scarf he wore on that occasion.[12]

Duffy remained in Dublin at Cannock's until after the McManus funeral and returned then to Castlerea to become foreman in Gannon's drapery where he had served his time. Someone who first met him when he was behind the counter there described him as 'an agile fellow, with dark flashing eyes, dark hair and palish face.'[13] From there he began to organise Fenianism in the province. In 1861, according to his sister Annie, 'he sowed the first seeds in his native town (Ballaghaderreen); but had great difficulty in the surrounding districts, as Ribbonism was rampant, and the men, thinking that the Fenians did not mean to fight, would not join Fenianism on any account.'[14] One of the leaders of Ribbonism retired (or died) at this time which resulted in a split, one party calling themselves the 'Pride of Erinn Boys' and the others the 'Sons of Hibernia'. Edward visited the neighbouring towns, meeting with both sides.

Fenianism in Connacht

Finally, he succeeded in swearing in James Hyland, a schoolteacher at Cross, outside Ballaghaderreen, who had considerable influence with both sides. Hyland was born in Monasteraden, the son of John Hyland, described as 'a poor man.'[15] 'The County Sligo was a quarter deeply tainted with this foolish business (Ribbonism) and by the help of a friend (Hyland) he got amongst "the boys".'[16] After this considerable progress was made and soon the Fenians were established in Mayo, Sligo, Roscommon and Leitrim. 'He was the first who made much impression', John O'Leary later recalled, 'on those intractable and ignorant Ribbonmen, who have, I hear, been much come-at-able for political purposes ever since.'[17]

James Hyland

However, bad feeling continued to exist between the Fenians and those who remained Ribbonmen. Faction fights broke out at fairs and markets where Hyland's men were weak in numbers. Gradually Hyland's faction became stronger and wanted to beat the remaining Ribbonmen into the Fenian organisation but Hyland would have none of it. When O'Donovan Rossa visited the West in 1864-65 he and Duffy met Tom Ward, Dominick Kilcullen and Paddy Marren, reputed to be some of the chiefs of the Ribbonmen

12 Annie Duffy, *The Irishman*, 14 Mar 1868
13 *The Irishman*, 5 Dec 1868
14 *The Irishman*, 14 Mar 1868
15 HCSA, vol 3 pp 509-11
16 *The Irishman*, 5 Dec 1868
17 John O'Leary, *Fenians and Fenianism*, I, p 132n

in Sligo. 'We spoke to them about the unfriendly feeling between their men and ours, a feeling that should not exist, as the English enemy was the enemy of all of us. They promised to do their best to do away with that unfriendliness.'[18]

Duffy's Activities

Duffy followed a punishing routine.

From the first hour he joined the organisation until that of his arrest, he worked night and day, in sickness and in health, through good repute and evil repute, with all the energy of his active mind, all the passion and enthusiasm of his earnest nature ... All his intimates still speak with wonder of his long and fatiguing journeys – they marvel how the strong fiery spirit supported the weak delicate frame and forced it to endure such hardship.

He enrolled members in the Brotherhood in Loughglynn, Ballaghaderreen, Swinford, Ballymote, Boyle and Balla. 'Many a wet cold Saturday night he left after eleven o'clock and walked, delicate as he was, fifteen or sixteen miles in order to meet some of those men the following Sunday.'[19]

Punishing Routine

His huge exertions proved damaging to his health and in 1862 he became prey to consumption which would finally cost him his life as it did that of his father. One night in March 1865 O'Donovan Rossa and Duffy were passing Duffy's mother's house in Loughglynn when they saw a light in the window.[20] They went in. 'His mother kissed him, saying, "Eddie, won't you stay over? You'll kill yourself." "Not yet, mother," he answered.' They kissed again and mounting their jaunting car continued their journey. On one occasion he left the house in Loughglynn early in the morning without eating and rode on horseback to the shores of Lough Gara, between Ballaghaderreen and Boyle, where he left his horse and rowed across the lake to a meeting.[21] His business finished he returned across the lake that evening, still without having taken any food. He recovered his horse but on his way home he was inundated by a sudden heavy shower so common in that area and was drenched to the skin. Wet, hungry and tired, he fainted and fell off his horse. Some time later he was found by a neighbour, who took him home but the result was a heavy cold from which he contracted consumption.

Duffy's mother

Church Opposition

Though deeply religious, Duffy's activities brought him into conflict with the church, which also took its toll. An organisation called the National Brotherhood of St Patrick was launched in Dublin in March 1861 for the purpose of holding St Patrick's Day banquets in Dublin, Cork and Belfast and in

18 *United Irishman*, 11 Feb 1899.
19 *The Irishman*, 5 & 26 Dec 1868
20 O'Donovan Rossa, *Irish Rebels in English Prisons*, p 188.
21 Ó Laighin, p 17

centres of Irish population in Britain. It was soon infiltrated by young Fenians in Dublin and it was at one of these meetings in Dublin in 1861 that Duffy first met the Dublin Fenian, Joseph Denieffe and told him 'that he was willing to join us and devote his life to the cause'.[22] The Brotherhood administered an oath of support for an Irish republic and as a result membership of the Brotherhood was made a reserved sin in Dublin and condemned by name at a meeting of the bishops in August 1863. Duffy was spreading Fenianism under the guise of the St Patrick's Brotherhood. 'Rumours of a secret society were now mooted. The priests commenced of course to warn their flocks. Duffy was marked; his visits through the country watched and one Sligo priest actually denounced him by name from the altar.'[23] The denunciation, however, was counter-productive and drove a lot of the young men to join Duffy.[24]

A journalist writing for the Fenian newspaper, *The Irish People*, (8 April 1865) named three parish priests, Joseph McTucker of Boyle, Roger Brennan of Gurteen and Matthew Finn, then administrator in Ballaghaderreen, who denounced Fenianism from the altar. 'The priests in that neighbourhood and all about Ballaghaderreen seem to know you all intimately, at least to know all your characters well and with perfect unconcern they speak the strangest things regarding you.' He singled out Matthew Finn who had come out against the Fenians for special mention.

Matthew Finn

> Father Finn, I dare say, understood that he was speaking from an altar dedicated to the God of Truth and that he is a minister of that God. I therefore believe that Father Matt Finn believed he was speaking truth, while calumniating and slandering you ... The pro-English priests are not tongue-tied and the hands of good priests are so tied that they cannot lift them over the heads of anyone holding your principles.

Not all Achonry priests were anti-Fenian. Bishop Durcan, then in his late seventies, was not capable of exercising much control over his priests, according to a report by an anonymous bishop to Rome a few years later.[25] The bishop, probably Gillooly of Elphin, claimed that many of the priests, 'even the majority,' encouraged Fenianism.

Duffy made periodic progress reports to Stephens at meetings held in Denieffe's tailor's shop in Anne Street and attended by the heads of the other provinces. It was becoming increasingly clear that the movement could not

Connacht Progress

22 Denieffe, p 58
23 Parish priest of Breedogue. *The Irishman*, 5 Dec 1868
24 Ó Laighin, p 16
25 SC Irlanda, vol 36 f 692v, 693r

continue to progress in Connacht while Duffy continued in full time employment in Castlerea. Therefore, Stephens ordered Duffy in the autumn of 1863 to give up his job in Gannon's and devote himself to promoting the Fenian Brotherhood full-time. It was a costly decision for Duffy and Denieffe later recalled that Duffy 'had given up lucrative positions to spread the light'. [26] At the end of 1863 and the beginning of 1864 the movement advanced rapidly. 'Our success in Connaught was largely due to Edward Duffy, in whom an all-absorbing and overpowering fervour of devotion to the cause', O'Leary later recalled, 'seems to have more than made up the absence of any special knowledge or even, as far as I could see, any mental capacity above the ordinary.' He was greatly impressed by Duffy's success. 'The West was certainly wide awake at last.' Duffy 'left Connaught in probably as good a state of preparation as Munster and most likely somewhat in advance of either Leinster or Ulster.' And all this progress was made at Duffy's personal expense with possibly some local contributions. 'Anyway, there could not be anything drawn from the central exchequer, for there was seldom or ever anything in it.' [27]

Fenian Numbers

When Stephens visited Connacht in December 1864 there were 3,764 members in the Brotherhood.[28] Accurate figures are difficult to come by but the government claimed that there were almost 8,000 members in Connacht.[29] These ranged from 2,000 in Sligo town and 1,000 in Ballina to thirty in Oughterard. In the diocese there were 300 in Ballaghaderreen, 150 in Swinford, 100 in Foxford and fifty in Bohola. No figures are given for the Sligo portion of the diocese where it is known that there were sizeable contingents especially in Tubbercurry and Ballymote.

O'Donovan Rossa

Jeremiah O'Donovan Rossa toured the province in 1864 and 1865.[30] His visit began in Galway where he was told there were over 600 men devoted to the cause and from there he went to Athenry, Ballinasloe, Athlone and Roscommon. Then in Castlerea he met Duffy, in the drapery shop of the Gannon brothers. 'I met those three brothers of the Gannons – and good, decent, patriotic men they were.' From there Rossa and Duffy together went through the rest of Connacht. In Loughglynn Rossa met Duffy's mother whom he described as 'a tall, straight, handsome woman' who must have been 'very handsome in her younger days.' She was very concerned about her

Jeremiah
O'Donovan Rossa

26 Denieffe, p 88
27 O'Leary, i, p 193, ii, pp 27-28n, 86 & 235-6
28 Stephens to O'Mahony?, 11 Dec 1864, in S. Pender, 'Survey of Rossa's Papers', in *Journal of the Cork Archeological and Historical Society*, lxxviii, (May-Meitheamh), 1973, pp 14-26
29 State Papers, A. 124
30 O'Donovan Rossa, *United Irishman*, 11 Feb 1899

son's health. 'Bidding good bye to him she wept, saying she feared he would ruin his health travelling about so much as he was doing late and early.'

From Loughglynn they went to Ballaghaderreen where they stayed in the house of Thomas Spelman 'who was Ned's right-hand man there'. They also met James Hyland who lived there and used to write to the *Irish People* under the pen-name 'Shemus Andy'. The following day Duffy and Rossa went by side-car to meet two farmers called Neary, one on the road to Ballymote and the other on the road to Frenchpark. The Nearys were 'tall strapping men, over six feet high'. The next night Hyland brought them to meet a large body of men somewhere in Keash. 'The meeting place was on a hill within view of rocky eminences that were full of caves.' They left their side-car and driver at a house on the roadside and tramped through the heather. 'We had to cross streams on trees of logwood that were laid over them as bridges.' Due to a mistake in the rendezvous, they only met half of the men, the other half having assembled on another hill about two miles away. The meeting finished about midnight. 'When we got back through bog and heather to the roadside where our jarvey was, our shoes were wet, our stockings were wet.'

Keash Meeting

In Boyle they met Patrick Connolly who later settled in Tubbercurry. [31] From there they passed the caves in Keash on the right hand side of the road on their way to Ballymote where the two most important Fenians were Dyer and May 'who had charge of the district.' They stayed in a hotel on the bridge run by another man called May and his sister. 'From this bridge we could see the standing walls of the grand old castle of Ballymote – a castle that must have been a grand one in its day of glory. I went through it; I walked around it – within the walls of it – for, within the standing walls today is a passage way that you can walk through all round.' From there Duffy and Rossa went to Sligo.

Ballymote

They returned from Sligo to Tubbercurry where Patrick O'Brien, a schoolteacher, was head centre.[32] Like so many other Fenians, O'Brien later emigrated to America where Rossa occasionally met him in New York and where he had 'sorrowful seanachie with him about the faded hope and glory of the olden time.' From Tubbercurry they went to Swinford where they met Pat O'Dowd who with his mother and three sisters kept a large general store. O'Dowd also kept a store in Westport.

Tubbercurry & Swinford

---

31 Was this Michael Connolly, a tailor, whose son, James, was a leading Fenian in Tubbercurry in 1868? See p 184

32 Patrick O'Brien had been appointed monitor in 1853 in Tubbercurry NS where his father, Michael, was a prize-winning teacher. ED 2/41, folios 35 & 246, see Appendix 19

From Swinford they went via Foxford to Ballina and Killala and returned via Pontoon to Castlebar. They put up at Gibbons' Hotel in Castlebar. Mrs Gibbons was a sister of the Daly brothers who owned an hotel in Tuam and, as Rossa had initiated her brother, John, into the Fenians, she was able to provide them with a lot of information about people in Castlebar. From there they went to Westport where Pat O'Dowd from Swinford had formed a Fenian circle and was there himself at the time. They travelled sitting on the top of a four-horse Bianconi coach. A landlord's agent, who carried out many evictions in Mayo, sat alongside Duffy, 'and going down that long hill from Castlebar to Westport I feared Ned would throw him off the coach, as they got into an angry conversation about landlordism.' They returned to Castlebar and from there to Balla, where the Nally brothers were prominent Fenians.

George Henry Moore

While Duffy continued his Fenian business, Rossa went to meet George Henry Moore at Moore Hall, 'a hall, a mansion, a castle, the largest I saw in Ireland; acres of green lawn in front, the end of the lawn being the brink of the silvery lake of Lough Carra.' It was a Friday and Moore told Rossa there was no meat for dinner but he could provide some refreshments. 'He rang the bell and the butler was soon at hand with some bottles of wine, bread and biscuit.' They talked about the Fenian organisation and Moore queried the necessity of the Fenian oath, believing it to be a hindrance to the propagation of the movement among the mass of the people as the priests were opposed to it. He thought a simple pledge would be sufficient and could be taken at fairs and markets and at the chapel gates on Sundays. Rossa arranged for Moore to meet Stephens in Dublin where the two did meet later and Rossa believed that Stephens wanted Moore to do a lecture tour of the United States. From Castlebar they took the Bianconi car to Dublin, going via Tuam, Longford and Mullingar. Westmeath, Longford and Cavan formed part of Duffy's Connacht.

Police Surveillance

Duffy's movements were closely watched by the police. Rossa received a letter from Duffy a month after his visit to Connacht stating how 'he had to run from Ballymote to Ballyshannon as he was only two minutes out of the hotel when an inspector of police came looking for him. This, I believe, is partly the work of the Bishop of Sligo, who the Sunday after we were there spoke of us.'[33] Gillooly of Elphin was strongly anti-Fenian. Edward's sister, Annie, who said that he was posing as a commercial traveller seeking orders when he was sought by the police, gave a slightly different account. 'They searched the house where they heard he was and read every letter they got in

33 Denieffe, p 196

the place. They thought he had gone to Ballymote; but he went to Co Donegal where I was at the time.'[34]

Government spies like Pierce Nagle, who kept Dublin Castle informed on the movements of all the prominent Fenians in the provinces, told the authorities in October 1864 that Donal Carey (Ó Ciardha) and Patrick McDonnell from Ballaghaderreen were members of the Fenian Brotherhood. Constabulary reports in 1865 referred frequently to the activities of Fenians. The sub-inspector at Clogher, Ballaghaderreen, saw Edward Duffy and James Hyland passing in a car in July to a meeting on the islands of Lough Gara. It was later alleged that Hyland, together with John Duffy and Thomas Gallagher from Ballaghaderreen, was drilling 300 or 400 men at Carrigeens at 3 a.m. on Sunday 3 September. Hyland was arrested on 26 September 1865, charged with illegal drilling and admitted to bail on 16 October to stand trial in Castlebar.[35] He was dismissed from his teaching post but the police in Ballaghaderreen reported that he appeared to have plenty of money and 'living very comfortably'. He travelled around the country collecting money for the Fenians making regular visits to Dublin and the police believed he was 'a paid and active organiser'.

Illegal Drilling

Thomas Gallagher, a cousin of Edward Duffy's, was also arrested and charged with illegal drilling.[36] He was born in Loughglynn and educated in Ballaghaderreen from where he went to Queen's College, Galway to study engineering. The sub-inspector in Ballaghaderreen reported in February 1866 that he was out on bail. He was re-arrested and a letter was written on his behalf at the end of May by a Patrick Gordon who claimed to have known him from his infancy. 'The opinion of every honest industrious man in the district is that Gallagher had nothing to do with Fenianism.' Gallagher's own petition asking to be released on bail denied any complicity with Fenianism and claimed that Charles J. MacDermot JP of Coolavin offered to be one of his sureties.

Thomas Gallagher

An order was issued for his discharge in September and the sub-inspector reported from Ballaghaderreen in December that Gallagher since his release 'appears to be actively organising the Fenian conspiracy and is the most active agent in the sub-inspector's locality'. He was then trying to dissuade the tenants on the Power estate from paying their rents, 'alleging that in a few days an outbreak would occur which would render the payments of these rents unnecessary.'

34 *The Irishman*, 14 Mar 1868
35 HCSA vol 3, pp 509-11; Fenian Briefs, 6 (E)
36 HCSA vol 2, pp 377-8; FP 139; CSORP. 10566, 10914, 11078, 11817, 14401, 15143, 15721, 16009, 16525

It was feared that the coasts of Galway and North Mayo would be used for landing arms from America. The police reported on 8 September that 'a man called Duffy was in Tuam on a certain day last week to arrange matters and organise drill courses'. and Duffy was expected to bring plenty of arms with him. The police believed that the Fenians planned to use the railroad to mount attacks on their barracks.'[37]

Arrests

The *Irish People* was seized on 15 September 1865 and John O'Leary, Thomas Clarke Luby and O'Donovan Rossa were arrested while a wanted poster was circulated for James Stephens. The newspaper, founded by Stephens as an organ for Fenianism, first appeared on 18 November 1863. Pierce Nagle, the government spy who worked in the newspaper's offices, later alleged that Duffy was a frequent visitor there and that he, Nagle, used to send weekly a packet of the newspapers to Duffy in Castlerea. Duffy had told him that the profits he and Denis O'Riordan made by way of commission 'were to be expended for rifles for the use of the Movement'. O'Riordan, also an assistant in Patrick Gannon's drapery shop in Castlerea, was long suspected by the sub-inspector there 'of being an active member of the Fenian conspiracy'.[38]

James Stephens

After the seizure of the newspaper and the arrests of the journalists, Stephens took Charles Kickham, Brophy, and Duffy into his home in Fairfield House. Probably from fear of arrest, Stephens used Duffy as his medium of communication with the organisation and during this time Duffy interviewed people in the back parlour of a house across the Grand Canal at Baggot St Bridge. It was here that he met John Devoy one evening in the company of other Irish-Americans, General Halpin, Colonel Kelly and others.[39] 'After a preliminary lecture about stories of dissatisfaction among the men over lack of preparation, and a rather extravagant expression of his personal confidence in "The Captain", Duffy handed me a letter with "Dev" on the envelope.' The letter, dated 26 October 1865, was from Stephens appointing Devoy 'chief organiser of the British troops in Ireland'.

Duffy and
Stephens Arrested

Stephens, Duffy, Brophy and Kickham were arrested on the night of 11 November in Fairfield House. Stephens and his wife occupied one room while in an adjoining room Duffy and Brophy were in one bed while Kickham slept in a bed on the floor.[40] Duffy's clothes were searched and a small

37 Constabulary Reports, 72 (7), 14 Oct 1864; 258 (1)-258 (3), 15 Sept 1865; 243 (1-2), 8 Sept 1865; 212 (3), 31 Aug 1865; 285 (1-2), 4 Sept 1865; 293, 22 Sept 1865
38 Crown Briefs, 6 (d); 13 Dec 1866, Sub-Inspector John Hutchinson, Castlerea to Inspector-General. CSORP 13269, F. 1982
39 Devoy, *Recollections of an Irish Rebel*, p 145
40 Statement by John Smollen, 15 Nov 1865. Crown Briefs, 6 (D)

leather purse containing a bill of exchange for over £1500 was found in the pocket of his trousers. Some keys were also found, one of which opened a portmanteau in Rathmines where a prayer-book was found with the name of Edward Duffy written on the fly-leaf. At the time of the arrest 'Duffy was pale and ill, yet cheerful-looking'.[41] The prisoners were returned for trial.

Stephen's Escape

Two weeks later, on 24 November 1865, Stephens was spectacularly rescued from jail. An impression of the prison keys had been taken and a counterfeit set made in the premises of Patrick Durkin, a Mayoman in Dublin.[42]. Rossa was told of Stephen's projected rescue by Duffy who was housed in the same part of the prison and Rossa in turn told O'Leary. They were then having a consultation with their solicitor in Luby's cell. Surprisingly, in view of his poor health, Duffy was not included in the rescue. Duffy's health had deteriorated rapidly in prison and he was now in an advanced stage of consumption. However, his counsel succeeded in getting him released on bail at the end of January 1866. 'He returned to Connacht to see his mother and friends. There was a great welcome for him in his native place. All his old friends ... thronged round him. He believed it was his last visit, as he expected to be called for trial and expected transportation.' Charles Strickland reported that Duffy spent all the time he was out on bail 'visiting all the small towns and doing a great deal of mischief'. The sub-inspector reported from Castlerea that Edward Duffy had left there for Dublin on 18 February.[43] He stayed at the European Hotel in Bolton Street.

John Devoy

John Devoy insisted to Stephens that the Fenians should fight or disband. and Stephens invited him to a meeting of a number of the top Fenians.[44] At the meeting Stephens said: 'I wish Ned Duffy were here.' Thinking that the decision on whether to fight in the near future or to postpone it depended on how Duffy would vote, Devoy, convinced that Duffy would vote for immediate action, offered to go for him at his hotel in Bolton Street. The hotel was closely watched during the day but not at night, because Duffy being in an advanced stage of consumption was not expected to go out at night. Devoy was convinced that he could succeed in bringing Duffy to the meeting. 'Besides, I was dressed like a countryman, with a heavy brown frieze coat, and, as the house was frequented by farmers and country shopkeepers, I could probably pass in or out unnoticed.' Stephens would not hear of it, however and

41 *The Irishman*, 12 Dec 1868
42 Denieffe, p 123
43 HCSA, vol 2, pp 301-2
44 Devoy, *Recollections*, pp 103-4

Devoy knew why. 'I have been convinced ever since that had Duffy been there that night or the next ... an immediate fight would have been decided on.'

Habeas corpus was suspended in February, permitting detention without trial of suspected Fenians and hundreds of arrests were made all over the country, seriously discapacitating the movement. Constable Philip Clarke arrested James Connolly, a tailor, and twelve others at a suspected Fenian meeting on 12 February in Tubbercurry.[45] Very early in the morning of 21 February Sub-Inspector Lennon of Swinford with a party of police went to the house of Patrick J. O'Connor a shopkeeper in Bohola. O'Connor, a former member of the Pope's Brigade had returned from Italy in 1860 and became involved in the Fenian movement, acting as a head-centre in Swinford and Tubbercurry. The police found him in the attic of his shop in Bohola concealed in a bag of feathers and arrested him on a charge of Fenian membership. He was detained in Castlebar jail with other suspected Fenians and after his release a fresh warrant was issued for him which he evaded by emigrating to America, where he was later elected sheriff of Richmond County, Augusta, Georgia.[46]

Also arrested with O'Connor was Charles O'Hara, a farmer, also from Bohola, Thomas Colleran, a labourer from Swinford and James Benson, a draper's assistant from Ballaghaderreen.[47] Benson was arrested on 27 February and the sub-inspector reported from Ballaghaderreen that he was an active member of the Fenians and 'a disseminator of Fenian practices.'[48] 'Because of his position, which gives him the opportunity of meeting country people', Benson could do a great deal of harm. James Hyland, the schoolteacher from Cross, was arrested in Ballaghaderreen and confined in Sligo jail.

Edward Duffy's younger brother, John, was arrested in Ballaghaderreen on 15 March, charged with illegal drilling and detained in Castlebar jail. The sub-inspector reported to Dublin Castle on 24 February that John was 'an active agent travelling about a great deal ... and has not been in Ballaghaderreen for the past month.'[49] Michael Kielty was arrested in Ballymote in the middle of March and held in Roscommon jail and Thomas Gannon of Ballaghaderreen was arrested about the same time.[50] Charles Strickland JP reported to Dublin Castle on 1 March that Edward Duffy had returned to Castlerea and

45 Fenian Files, 44R
46 *W.P.* 15 June 1889
47 *Mayo Constitution*, 27 Feb & 6 Mar 1866
48 HCSA, vol 1
49 HCSA, vol 1, pp 303ff
50 Nat Arch, Fenian arrests and discharges, 1866-69

was 'incessantly travelling about the country by days and night ... forwarding the Fenian conspiracy in everyway in his power'. As Strickland's statements were based on hearsay, the attorney-general thought there was not sufficient evidence to arrest him.[51]

Stephens in America

Stephens escaped to Paris in disguise in March 1866 and that evening Duffy called on Joseph Denieffe 'in great glee'.[52] '"I have great news for you", said he. "The Captain is on his way to France." "Well," said I, "Ed, I firmly believe you will never see him again." "Don't say that," said he, "'tis treason." I did not tempt to shake Duffy's faith in him, but he afterwards came to share my view ...' From France Stephens went to America, arriving in New York early in May. After a failed Fenian invasion of Canada, John O'Mahony became discredited and Stephens took over the O'Mahony wing. He raised $60,000 during the summer and autumn declaring that 1866 would be the year of action and telling a rally in New York at the end of October that his next public appearance would be in Ireland at the head of a rising.

Duffy in Charge

Before leaving Ireland, Stephen had appointed Duffy in his place as head of the organisation in Ireland and promised to send him money. 'Poor Ed was stopping quietly in the European Hotel and had not a pound in his possession ... No financial assistance came from Stephens ... not a shilling for poor Duffy and the cause. Were it not for the kindness of Mrs Moloney, the lady of the hotel, he could not have existed.'[53] Annie Duffy told the same story [54] 'For several months Stephens never wrote a line, nor sent him a dollar ... He had to borrow money from personal friends in the country ...' A correspondent to *The Irishman* (24 Oct 1868) described Stephen's treatment of Duffy as 'treachery and black deceit', and repeated what Duffy had told him a short time before Christmas 1866. 'I know but very little of his (Stephen's) movements in America. It is scandalous the way he treats me; three months without a letter, as if I were a child.' When Duffy learnt in November that he could get O'Leary and the other prisoners released, if he could raise £300, he sent another sister to the West and she returned with 'a large sum'. The money was needed to pay counsel to defend the prisoners.[55] The funds of the Ladies' Committee, intended for that purpose, were exhausted and Richard Pigott, the proprietor of *The Irishman*, had stolen large sums of money collected by that paper for the Fenian movement. 'It is a wonder that the organisation survived,' Devoy commented, 'But it did.'

51 HCSA, vol 2, pp 301-2
52 Denieffe, p 128
53 Denieffe, p 130
54 *The Irishman,* 14 Mar 1868
55 Devoy, p 160

Bad Health

Meanwhile in America, when Stephens at a gathering of New York Fenians in mid-December advocated another postponement he was immediately deposed and replaced by Colonel Thomas J. Kelly. Kelly and his associates came to England in January 1867 and Duffy joined them there. His health was causing concern. 'He had been failing in health for a considerable time and his friends were about to establish him in some quiet nook in one of the Channel Islands (Jersey, I think), where they fondly hoped his health would be restored.'[56] His sister, Annie, said that because of his bad health, Duffy intended going to America and resigned in favour of one who later abandoned his post. Duffy got as far as London where he met Colonel Kelly.[57]

The Rising

The rising was decided for early March but Duffy was opposed to it because of the lack of preparation. 'Before God, I would sooner that Ireland remained another half century, even as she is, than that the people should rise in arms and fail.'[58] But once the decision was taken he did not hesitate. 'Duffy opposed the March rising with might and main; but when he was overruled, he would not shrink from his post ...' [59] 'When Edward could not stop the fatal and miserable rising in March he returned to Connaught, to the men he brought into danger and ordered the men to keep quiet.'[60] A notice appeared in the newspapers at the beginning of March stating that Duffy had died in Rathmines, probably deliberately placed there by Duffy himself to throw the police off his trail.[61] The rising on 5 March, no more than a few incidents in Dublin and the South, quickly fizzled out.

Castlerea

That day the parish priest of Boyle, Joseph McTucker, sent his curate to Dr O'Farrell JP to inform him that he had 'undoubted information' that the Fenians planned an attack on the town. The plan was 'to assemble in large numbers here under cover of the fair and make a rush on the military and police barracks.' The resident magistrate in Boyle, James T. Butler, immediately reported this to Dublin Castle.[62] Duffy, James McDermott, a draper in Boyle, and two suspended priests, Lavelle and Maxwell, had already met all the sympathisers in Boyle on Wednesday 27 February. Patrick Lavelle was parish priest of Partry and well-known for his nationalist sympathies. Police from outlying stations were ordered into Boyle as Butler feared they would make soft targets and the town was patrolled by the military. Two days later he informed Dublin that 'everything has passed off quietly ... If we had not

56 Dick, Cork to 'Cairn Thierna of "the Factions", *The Irishman*, 24 Oct 1868
57 *The Irishman*, 14 Mar 1868
58 *The Irishman*, 24 Oct 1868
59 An ex-IRB to the Editor, *The Irishman*, 26 Dec 1868
60 *The Irishman*, 14 Mar 1868
61 James Butler RM, Boyle to Under-Secretary, 10 Mar 1867, CSORP no 3960
62 James Butler RM, Boyle to Under Secretary, 5 Mar 1867, CSORP 3734

been prepared something would have been attempted as large numbers of suspected persons assembled under cover of the fair.' [63]

Duffy Captured

While out with a patrol at 1 a.m. on the night of 9 March, Butler saw lights in O'Leary's Hotel, one of the principal hotels in Boyle.[64]. There he found and arrested three strangers without luggage (one of them a woman). Duffy fainted after he and his companions were accosted in the hotel. It was snowing that night and bitterly cold and Duffy, a sick man, had just travelled fourteen miles from Castlerea. They gave their names as John Moran, Thomas Egan and Mary Egan and said that they were employed by Murtagh Bros but the following day John Moran was identified by a gentleman from Castlerea as Edward Duffy 'There is no doubt that Duffy (if not the principal leader) is one of the chief leaders in the country.' Butler also warned the government about the priest, Lavelle, 'a most dangerous person', and strongly recommended that a warrant be issued for his arrest. 'Mr Lavelle is frequently in the habit of coming here in disguise for Fenian purposes'.[65]

Thomas Egan of Phibsboro, Dublin, said to be acting as Duffy's secretary, later wrote from Kilmainham where he was detained, that he was employed by Murtagh Bros & Co, North City Mills, Dublin, which tallied with what he had told the magistrate in Boyle.[66] Another account of the arrest said that Duffy 'was kneeling at his prayers in the hotel' when he was arrested.[67]. According to Annie the only document found on Duffy was a prayer-book and a single pound note in one of his pockets.[68] After being held for three days in Boyle, Duffy was taken by train to Dublin on 12 March and detained in Mountjoy. On 9 April he was moved to Kilmainham.

Swinford

Following Duffy's arrest, a detachment of the 59th Regiment was sent from Athlone to Castlerea and arrests were made there and in Castlebar. Two magistrates of Swinford Petty Sessions district petitioned the Lord Lieutenant on 10 March to send a fifty-strong military detachment to Swinford because 'the Fenian conspiracy is widespread in the town of Swinford and its neighbourhood' with only fifteen police including the sub-inspector which was 'quite inadequate.' They wanted military quartered in Swinford 'until the presence of evil-disposed persons be subdued.'[69]

63 James T. Butler RM to Chief Secretary or Under Secretary, 7 Mar 1867, CSORP 3678
64 James Thomas Butler gave details of Duffy's arrest at his trial in May 1867. County of Dublin Special Commission 15 May 1867, The Queen v. John Flood, Edward Duffy and James Cody. Fenian Briefs, 19-21, 6 (E)
65 James Butler RM, Boyle to Chief Secretary, 10 Mar 1867, CSORP 3960
66 HCSA, vol 2, p 320. CSORP 5771, 27 Mar 1867
67 *The Irishman*, 19 Dec 1867
68 *The Irishman*, 8 Feb 1868
69 George J. O'Malley JP & Myles H. Jordan, Newcastle & Swinford to the Lord Lieutenant, 13 Mar 1867, CSORP 4324

John Kilmurry   A young baker, John Kilmurry, employed by Patrick Corley, was strongly suspected by the police of being 'an active member of the Fenian conspiracy.'[70] Sub-Inspector John S. Lennon received information on 12 March that a Swinford woman, Ann Durkan, could give 'material evidence' about Kilmurry's Fenianism. Accompanied by the resident magistrate, Mr Hill, Lennon went to Durkan's house and took down what she had to say though she refused to take an oath. She told him that the previous Friday Kilmurry and a number of others armed with guns had come to her house and asked for her husband, John. Lennon issued a warrant for Kilmurry who fled but was later arrested on 27 March in a widow's house in Frenchpark and detained in Castlebar jail to await his trial. Shortly afterwards, Ann Durkan and her husband left for England fearing she would be compelled to give evidence.

Swinford Arrests   In the meantime, on Tuesday morning, 18 March, Lennon and a police party went to different houses in the town and arrested six men on charges of complicity with the Fenian Brotherhood, and brought them before Capt Plunkett RM who committed them to jail in Castlebar.[71] Shortly afterwards, Lennon shot himself and at the coroner's inquest a jury of 'twenty-three of the most respectable men of Swinford' returned a verdict of suicide 'while labouring under a fit of insanity'. Probably as a result, the six Swinford detainees were released on 25 March after only a week in jail.

Fenian Prisoners   Of the ninety-five prisoners in Castlebar jail on that day, twenty of them were Fenians. Besides the six Swinford men, there were also six from Castlebar, four from Ballinrobe and one each from Westport, Ballina, Balla and Ballaghaderreen. The latter, Michael Fogarty, was a twenty-year-old house carpenter who had recently come to Ireland from New York where he was born and was resident in Ballaghaderreen at the time of his arrest on 12 March.[72] Desmond Blythe from Ballaghaderreen was arrested in Roscommon together with Thomas Harmon, a teacher from Castlerea, and John Keegan Casey, a friend of Duffy's. Casey, a clerk in Murtagh's corn stores in Castlerea, was regarded by the police as 'a most active leader of the Fenian conspiracy' and was transferred immediately to Mountjoy where he was detained until November.[73]

70 Head Constable John Foster, Swinford, to inspector-general, 13 April 1867; Memorial of James Kilmurry to Lord Lieutenant, 7 April & 13 July 1867, CSORP 9101; Myles Jordan, crown solicitor, to Sir Thomas Larcom, 4 July 1867
71 Stephen Walsh, nailor, Michael Thompson, shoemaker, James O'Malley, saddler, John Collins, baker, Anthony Convey, carpenter, and James Campbell, grocer, CSORP 5049, 25 Mar 1867; *Irish American*, 13 April 1867
72 F.P. 171
73 HCSA, vol I, pp 118-19; W. D'Arcy, *The Fenian Movement*, pp 243-4

John Kilmurray, however, remained in jail, charged with being an active member of the Fenians and carrying arms in a proclaimed district. His father, James, also a baker in Corley's, stated that 'young Master Corley', who had a gun licence, came to the bakehouse on 7 March and asked John Kilmurry to clean his gun. Kilmurry brought the gun to his lodgings for safe-keeping and there it was discovered by the police. Corley later told the police that he did give the gun to Kilmurry to clean. The police claimed that Sub-Inspector Lennon was perfectly sane when he issued his warrant for Kilmurry's arrest. The attorney general directed that Kilmurry be prosecuted if evidence could be obtained but this was difficult as Lennon was dead and 'the woman Durkan if produced as a witness will be reluctant and unwilling to give such evidence'. The crown solicitor, Myles Jordan, did not feel justified in incurring the expenses of sending a constable to England to bring her back. Kilmurry was still in jail in the middle of July when his father again appealed to the government to let his son out on bail 'that he may thereby have an opportunity of earning as much as will enable him to fee a lawyer to defend him.'

Kilmurry in Jail

The police continued to be jittery, over-reacting on the flimsiest of pretexts. They seized a quantity of powder and shot in a shop in Tubbercurry on 11 April and charged the owner, Mary McDonnell, with having ammunition without a licence.[74] It appears that her husband, who died a little over four months previously, had a licence and the powder and shot had remained unsold in the shop ever since, something which was attested to by a number of prominent Tubbercurry citizens, including the parish priest and curate. The widow was totally unaware of the necessity of having a licence and appealed to the Lord Lieutenant to prevent the case going to court.

Tubbercurry Widow

Four men, three shoemakers and a baker, were arrested in Ballaghaderreen on 14 July 1867 charged with illegal drilling.[75] At midnight on 12 July a patrol consisting of four constables, Daniel Donovan, Richard Geoghegan, Felix McDonald and Charles Healy, encountered a party of between six and eight men congregated near the Market House, 'having come out of some theatrical entertainment'. One of the constables ordered the men to go home as he saw they were under the influence of drink but when he turned his back, one of the men gave orders 'Right, Left', and they began to march two deep.

Ballaghaderreen Prank

74 Memorial of Mary McDonnell, Tubbercurry, to the Lord Lieutenant, 11 May 1867, CSORP 8472
75 Thomas Bourke, shoemaker, Patrick McGee, shoemaker, (Westport) James Mannion, shoemaker and Anthony Bourke, baker (lately returned from Manchester). Report of F. McCarthy RM & Michael Kelly, 2nd Head Constable, Ballaghaderreen, to inspector-general, 14, 17, & 26 July 1867, CSORP 13155; F 4058, F 4073

When the police pursued them they dispersed, running away in different directions. Two of the policemen lodged statements against them the following day and the four were arrested and remanded to Castlerea bridewell. Two days later they were tried at Ballyhaunis Petty Sessions where the presiding magistrates, Felix McCarthy and Charles Strickland, dismissed the case with a caution to the parties. Both believed the incident to have been a prank 'for the purpose of annoying one of the policemen', adding that 'it was a most unlikely thing that they, being known to the constable, would attempt to drill so publicly under his notice.'

Duffy's Family

Duffy's family was also singled out for special punishment. 'Certainly, they have visited the brother's patriotism on his sisters.' Annie and Margaret, teachers in Loughglynn, were dismissed in June 1866 by Charles Strickland, 'who happened to be a magistrate, a descendant of the Saxon race, and, it is needless to add, a loyal Catholic.'[76] Annie had been teaching for eighteen years, for twelve of which she held the highest rank teachers could attain. There were then seven grades of classification, through which teachers progressed after successive oral and written examinations and taking into account evidence of their students' progress. Annie had reached the summit of her profession, which out of 3,000 female teachers in Ireland was attained by only fifty-four.

She applied several times to the Board of Education, 'foolishly imagining that I had a claim on them', but she was turned down each time. A third sister, after eleven years service, was forced to retire through failing sight and though entitled to one-to-three years' salary, she was refused any remuneration by the Board 'though she has become blind in their service.' A correspondent to *The Irishman* suggested that the newspaper open a fund to help the sisters. 'I trust the public will take some steps in the matter to convince those parties that their petty acts of vengeance has not had the desired effect.' Annie declined any subscription. '... The noble mind of these ladies in declining a subscription ... (was) in keeping with that of their noble-minded brother.'[77]

Trial

Duffy's trial began before a Special Commission on Wednesday, 15 May 1867 where himself and two others, John Flood and James Cody, were defended by Isaac Butt.[78] Butt asked the court to appoint a doctor to examine

76 Annie Duffy to the editor, Dublin, 3 July 1867, *The Irishman*, 6 July 1867 For correspondence on the sisters' dimissal see also, *The Irishman*, 22 & 29 June, 20 & 27 July 1867
77 F.K. to the Editor, Dublin, 15 June & 22 July 1867, *The Irishman*, 22 June & 27 July 1867
78 County of Dublin Special Commission 15 May 1867, The Queen v. John Flood, Edward Duffy and James Cody. Fenian Briefs, 19-21, 6 (E)

Duffy, 'sickly and haggard in appearance', whose health was such that it would be 'perfectly dangerous to him to remain in court during his trial' but his request was refused. 'He coughed with a short consumptive cough, expectorated a good deal in the dock and frequently had to recline his head on the back of the chair with which he was accommodated.'[79] One of the first witnesses called by the Crown was John Joseph Corydon, an officer in the American army who joined the Fenians in 1862. He first met Duffy, together with Stephens and Charles Kickham, in the house of the tailor, Joseph Denieffe, in Anne Street when he was sent to Ireland in August 1865 by John O'Mahony. Soon afterwards he became a government spy.

On the second day of the trial Thomas Kelly from Ballaghaderreen took the witness stand. A member of the North Mayo Militia for six years, he claimed that he had been sworn into the Fenians by Duffy in June 1865 in Moloney's public house in Castlebar. He was present at 4 a.m. on Sunday 3 September at Carrigeens, Co Mayo where James Hyland with John Duffy and Thomas Gallagher from Ballaghaderreen, was drilling 300 or 400 men, among whom he recognised Frank Grady, Patrick Farrell and John Finn. Kelly also claimed that in August he saw Duffy in Enniscrone. Cross-examined by Isaac Butt, he stated that after he heard that Duffy had been arrested, he informed Constable Maginn in Ballaghaderreen that Duffy had sworn him into the Fenians and made a statement to Sub-Inspector Maguire. He was then employed by Mr Dillon of Ballaghaderreen. In due course Kelly's betrayal was rewarded with 'thirty pieces of silver' as he was paid £30 on 15 July 1867 for his services as a crown witness to enable him to go to Australia.[80]

Thomas Kelly

The trial ended on Friday 17 May when the jury found all the accused guilty and the court adjourned until Monday 20 May for sentencing. Before sentence was passed Duffy made a speech from the dock in which he made no apologies for his politics:[81]

Speech from the Dock

There is no political act of mine that I in the least regret. I have laboured earnestly and sincerely in my country's cause, and I have been actuated throughout by a strong sense of duty. I believe that a man's duty to his country is part of his duty to God, for it is He who implants the feeling of patriotism in the human breast. He, the great searcher of hearts, knows

79 *Irish American,* 15 June 1867
80 CSORP 11891
81 Duffy's speech was later included in an anthology of such speeches by A. M. Sullivan of the *Nation,* to make amends, it was said, for having once referred to Duffy as a 'bogtrotter from Ballaghaderreen'. A. M. Sullivan, *Speeches from the Dock,* pp 204-5

that I have been actuated by no mean or paltry ambition – that I never worked for any selfish end.

Duffy stated that he was not responsible for the recent rising. 'I did everything in my power to prevent it for I knew that, circumstanced as we were, it would be a failure.' He was scathing about Stephens: 'It is but too well known in Ireland that he sent numbers of men over here to fight, promising to be with them when the time would come. The time did come, but not Mr Stephens. He remained in France to visit the Paris Exhibition. It may be a very pleasant sight, but I would not be in his place now. He is a lost man – lost to honour, lost to country.'

He repudiated the evidence given by Thomas Kelly of Ballaghaderreen. While admitting he saw him in Enniscrone, he never spoke to him. 'I knew him from a child in that little town, herding with the lowest and vilest. Is it to be supposed that I would put my liberty in the hands of such a character?' Constable John Ryan from Castlerea had given evidence at the trial that he knew Duffy for about ten or twelve years when he worked there as a shopboy. Having often seen Duffy fill out orders in McDonagh's and Gannon's shop, Ryan claimed he could recognise his signature on the prayer book found in Rathmines. Duffy told the court that it was not his handwriting but that of another shop assistant in McDonagh's and also pointed out that the book in question was not a prayer book but the *Imitation of Christ*, a gift from Mrs McDonagh.

'I am proud to be thought worthy of suffering for my country; when I am lying in my lonely cell I will not forget Ireland, and my last prayer will be that the God of liberty may give her strength to shake off her chains.' He spoke in a feeble voice with an evident effort and seemed to be quite exhausted when he resumed his seat. 'But hardly had he done so when he stood up again and begged it would be understood that the agitation under which he laboured was not owing to the position in which he found himself but was due altogether to his ill-health.'[82]

Sentenced   He was sentenced to fifteen years penal servitude which began in Mountjoy with the intention that he be moved later to a prison in England but this was delayed due to his health. Seventeen other prisoners were transported to England on 5 July but Duffy, who had been confined to the hospital there, was not fit to be sent with them. He was visited in Mountjoy in August by his mother and his sisters before they emigrated to America and according to

82 *The Irishman*, 15 June 1867

Annie, Edward regretted staying so long in Ireland.[83] He was transferred to Pentonville prison on 28 September and from there to Millbank on 4 October.

He was an intensely religious person. 'I was alarmed on learning that there was no chaplain here,' he wrote from Pentonville, 'but the governor has kindly sent for a priest, so that I may go to my duty. I will be lonely on Sundays and to one in my state of health the loss of Mass is a great thing.'[84]. Even before he was arrested he turned more and more to religion as his health deteriorated. He found it very difficult under police surveillance to attend Mass on Sundays and on one occasion he went to confession on Saturday but was in danger of missing Mass the following day as he believed members of the G Division police attended the church. 'Still he put his trust in God and boldly waited, passing to his place of hiding in the open day without any discovery.' John O'Leary said of him: 'He was very much of a saint and altogether a martyr.'[85]

Religious Convictions

He suffered intensely as his tuberculosis advanced, growing weaker every day with violent pains in his head. 'It is swelled in two or three places and the pain from one of them particularly drives me almost crazy at times' but 'it has not enfeebled my mind.'[86] O'Donovan Rossa, also a prisoner in Millbank, saw Duffy once in the prison chapel.

Suffering

> I saw him one Sunday morning going to communion. I would give any-thing to have his eye catch mine but he never raised his eye going to the altar or coming from it. He had somewhat of a stoop in his carriage and looked as if the treatment was bending him to the ground. When his last days were approaching an officer of the prison told me that Duffy would like very much to have a talk with me.

Rossa asked the governor for permission to visit Duffy but was refused.[87]

Death

Edward Duffy died in his cell on Monday 17 January 1868 at the age of twenty-eight. Shortly afterwards Rossa heard the news.[88] 'I lay on my bed-board one morning, when prisoners were coming from chapel, one of them put his lips to the ventilator and whispered. "Duffy is dead! Duffy is dead!"' Rossa was devastated. 'Ned Duffy's death ... threw me into a melancholy mood and for days I lay stretched on the flat of my back travelling, with my eyes closed, through the ups and downs of life and the queer ways of the world. I got my bed at night and when I could not sleep I turned my thoughts to rhyming.' The result was his *Lament for Edward Duffy*:

83 *The Irishman*, 14 Mar 1868.
84 *The Irishman*, 14 Mar 1868
85 O'Leary, *Fenians and Fenianism*, ii, pp 27-28n
86 *The Irishman*, 11 Mar 1868
87 *United Irishman*, 11 Feb 1899
88 O'Donovan Rossa, *My Years in English Jails*, pp 182, 184

But sad and lone was your death Ned, mid the jailors of your race,
With no one by to touch the hand, with none to smooth the face;
With none to take the dying wish to homeland, friend or brother.
To kindred mind, to promised bride, or to the sorrowing mother.

Mary O'Leary   The 'promised bride' was John O'Leary's sister, Mary. Edward had been on his way back to Dublin with the intention of marrying Mary when he was arrested in Boyle. They first met when Edward was let out on bail in January 1866 and 'loved each other almost at first sight.' Edward was reputed to have 'one strange peculiarity – he never cared much for female society'. 'I will never marry a woman', he used to say, 'unless she loves God first, her country next, and then, of course, loves me.' Mary was that woman. Shortly after he was detained in Mounjoy, Mary wrote on 28 March to the Chief Secretary, Lord Naas, seeking permission as his fiancée to visit him but prison rules only permitted visits from relatives. 'I think it very hard if such rules excluded me as I am engaged to be his wife.' Her request was refused. Later from Pentonville Duffy wrote to Ellen O'Leary to prepare her sister Mary to hear the worst.[89]

John O'Leary

'I dare not write to her on such a subject ... I often repent our ever having met ... You know my love for her. Would to God hers for me was less. Somehow, the lives of all good, quiet, amiable women like her's are shrouded with sorrow. It might be well for me too that I could forget her; but the thought of her possesses me now more strongly than when I was sentenced.'

Mary never forgot Edward, according to her brother John: 'Up to the hour of her death she held Duffy in the highest esteem.' [90]

Duffy's Mother   His 'sorrowing mother' did not survive him long in America. 'Have you heard from my family?' Edward asked Ellen O'Leary in his letter from prison, 'I am most anxious to hear about them, particularly my poor mother ...' [91] The Duffy sisters with their mother had settled in Peoria in the vicinity of Chicago. A Tubbercurry correspondent to *The Irishman* (24 January 1871), calling himself a 'Duffyite' informed the editor that Duffy's mother 'scarcely settled in America, she became tired of living and sank beneath her load of sorrows and her glad spirit fled to join that of her son.'

John Duffy   Edward's younger brother, John, had been arrested in the middle of March 1866 and was detained in Castlebar jail. He was then twenty years old and described as having a fresh complexion, blue eyes and brown hair and five foot

89 *The Irishman*, 14 Mar & 5 Dec 1868; Mary O'Leary to Lord Naas, 28 Mar 1867, CSORP 5738
90 O'Leary, *Fenians and Fenianism*, I, p. 132n
91 *The Irishman*, 14 Mar 1868

ten of slight build. From there he petitioned to be released offering to emigrate to the United States.[92] Other petitions followed in July, October, and November 1866 and January 1867. Finally, he was discharged on 22 February 1867 on condition of going to America and he sailed from Queenstown on 19 April 1867. Apparently, he returned shortly afterwards as he was arrested in Ballina on 6 July 1868. Later that month he was discharged and a month later left once more for America where he remained. He died in April 1914 and was buried in Maryland.

One of Edward's sister, Eliza, remained in Ireland, married to Edward McGough, a school-teacher in Castleknock. McGough requested that Edward's remains be returned to Ireland and they duly arrived at the North Wall on 24 January 1868 and were interred that day in Glasnevin. 'And now in the vaults of Glasnevin all that is earthly of this noble fellow now rests ... one of Ireland's truest, bravest and most devoted sons.' [93] Another correspondent described him as 'one of the truest and noblest patriots who ever trod the soil of Erin.'[94] 'A purer or nobler type of man I have never met' was the extraordinary admission of John O'Leary, who saw Duffy frequently in the office of the *Irish People*. 'To see him was to like him; and I now regret that I did not see him oftener and come to know him better.' 'Ireland never forgets those who die for her,' O'Leary commented, 'though she often forgets and neglects those who merely live for her.' [95] Not only did Ireland very much forget Edward Duffy but so did his native Connacht and Ballaghaderreen, the town where he was born.

Glasnevin

At the time of Duffy's death, his first collaborator, the schoolteacher James Hyland, was back in prison. From there he sent a petition in May 1866 denying all connection with the Fenians and asserting that he was the only support of his 'old and decrepit' father and gave as character referees Charles MacDermot of Coolavin and the priest, Matthew Finn. Let out on bail in the middle of July, he continued his work as a Fenian organiser and the police reported that he lived and dressed well. Back in prison early in 1867 he sent another petition with numerous signatures, stating that he had not violated the terms of his release and that his father had died since his arrest. He was discharged on 7 February 1867 and soon afterwards emigrated to America. Years later O'Donovan Rossa met him at Hyde Park near Scranton, Pennsylvania where he had continued his profession as a school-teacher.[96]

James Hyland

92 HCSA, vol I, pp 303-4; FP 139
93 *The Irishman*, 19 Dec 1868.
94 *The Irishman*, 24 Oct 1868
95 O'Leary, *Fenians and Fenianism*, i, p 132n; ii, pp 27-28n
96 *United Irishman*, 11 Feb 1899

Duffys Legacy

Duffy's legacy in the West, the Fenian organisation he had established there, continued to be active if not indeed to thrive after the failed rebellion and his own death. At least they continued to cause the police some anxiety. Popular sympathy for the Fenians continued to be expressed and when O'-Donovan Rossa, still languishing in Millbank Prison, was returned as MP for Tipperary towards the end of 1868, the inhabitants of Swinford celebrated the victory by illuminating their houses. A similar manifestation 'of dissaffection and disloyalty' occurred in Kilkelly but there was no disturbance in either place. [97] Fenianism continued to thrive in Castlerea where Duffy had spent so much of his time, and when Jesuits began a mission there in September 1873, the parish priest informed them that one of the local vices was Fenianism 'which prevailed throughout the parish.'[98]

Sligo Arrests

Fifteen people, including James Connolly, a tailor from Tubbercurry, were arrested on the night of 29 December 1867 in the public house of Mrs James Rea in Pound Street in Sligo. Connolly had been under police surveillance since his previous arrest with twelve others at a Fenian meeting in Tubbercurry on 12 February 1866. The police in Sligo were warned on Sunday morning by their colleagues in Tubbercurry, who believed Connolly to be a head centre, that he was about to visit Sligo. At 10 p.m. that night the police swooped on the public house and arrested fifteen young men all from different parts.[99] Five of them were shop assistants, two from Ballina, two from Sligo and one from Boyle. Besides James Connolly from Tubbercurry, there were two others from the diocese, Denis Hunt from Bunninadden and James McGovern from Ballaghaderreen who was employed as a draper's assistant in Sligo. They were searched, arrested and the following morning brought before magistrates who discharged all but two with a severe caution. The police requested a warrant for the continued detention of Connolly as 'an active and dangerous member of the Fenian body'. Another was detained because the police had found in his possession 'four verses of a seditious character.' [100]

97 County Inspector to Constabulary Office, Dublin Castle, 29 Nov 1869, Fenian Files, 5092R
98 *Collectanea Hibernica*, vol 42, p 137
99 William Taylor & William Mooney, shop assistants, Ballina, James Armstrong, shop assistant, Boyle, Michael J. Hand, Dublin, draper's assistant, Sligo, Denis Hunt, Bunninadden, James McGovern, Ballaghaderreen, draper's assistant, Sligo, Henry McNiff, James & Michael McGoldrick, & Ino Hopper, Sligo, James Ward & Charles Harrison, Aughamore, James Jordan, Newtownholmes, Michael Gillan, Kiltycahil (all three miles from Sligo. Head Constable Philip Clarke to County Inspector Thomas MacMahon, 31 Dec 1867, Fenian Files, 163R
100 Head Constable Clarke to Co Inspector MacMahon, 31 Dec 1867, Fenian Files 163R

A few days later Connolly's father, Michael, also a tailor, petitioned the
Lord Lieutenant for his son's release, claiming that he had nothing whatever
to do with any illegal society and that his visit to Sligo was entirely connected
with his trade as a tailor.[101] The petition was certified by a number of prominent Tubbercurry citizens, including the parish priest, John Brennan.[102]
Michael himself was 'a struggling poor tradesman about sixty years old, in
delicate health and entirely dependent on his son for support.' 'All my life I
have been a peaceable loyal subject.'

James Connolly

On the same day Head Constable Clarke received an anonymous note:
'... It is better for you to let out them fenians that is in Sligo Jail for if you
dont let them out I will come and let them out. To Hell with the Queen and
her subjects.' Connolly and his companion were brought before magistrates
again on 6 January 1868 but were discharged for want of proof. 'Every effort
has been made since 31 December to procure information against James
Connolly but except corroborative evidence and strong suspicion nothing
could be found.' Dublin Castle was assured that the men in question would
be closely watched and the police in Tubbercurry were contacted about Connolly.[103]

Early in 1868 four suspected Fenians from Ballaghaderreen, John and
Thomas Sheran and Anthony and Francis Grady who were detained in
Castlebar jail, 'were escorted by eight policemen, one jailer and a large crowd'
to the house of the resident magistrate, A. R. Stritch. After a brief examination, lasting three or four minutes, they were discharged on their own recog-
nissances.[104]

An amnesty meeting was held in Tubbercurry on 17 October 1869 calling
for the release of the Fenian prisoners. One of those who marched in the procession wearing a green sash and carrying a banner was Michael Brennan
from Chapelfield in the Easkey district, an ex-policeman who had been
dismissed from his post in Creggan, Co Galway for singing Fenian songs. He
had relations living at Dereens near Cloonacool with whom he stayed when in
the district and he also had connexions in Tubbercurry. Parties from several
parishes brought all the arms they could collect to a meeting early in December in a field in North Leitrim in Cloonacool to be inspected by Brennan.
People in Achonry and Chaffpool along to Ballymote had 'carefully

Michael Brennan

101 Fenian Files 44R
102 Others included John Brett, vice-chairman of the Tubbercurry Union, Abraham Powell of
    Powellsboro and Nicholas H. Devine
103 County Inspector MacMahon to inspector-general, 7 Jan 1868; E. Neymoe to inspector
    general, 10 Jan 1868, Fenian Files 226R
104 *Irish American*, 29 Feb 1868

concealed' revolvers. A second meeting attended by about sixty people was held at Tullinavilla and the government was kept informed about these meetings.[105] Recent well-organised outrages connected with Fenianism were reported in the district. 'People of this part of the country are ripe for any acts of violence and sedition.' Dublin Castle was assured that the police hoped 'by constant patrols day and night to check the movements of the ill-disposed.'

Mullaghroe

Constable Peter Lyons of Mullaghroe received information early in December 1869 from Charles Costello JP that Fenianism 'is about to establish itself in this part of the country with more energy than ever' and that head centres had lately been appointed in Tubbercurry and Ballymote. The information was passed on to the police in Ballymote who had already been informed from Clogher, Ballaghaderreen 'that there was a widespread and deep-rooted conspiracy in this neighbourhood'.[106] Meetings had been held in Knocknaskeagh, Moygara, Coagh and Everlawn near Bunninadden and money collected at night, 'enforced at the muzzle of a revolver,' to purchase arms. A great change had come over the people and police found it impossible to get anyone to give information. 'Those who used to communicate information to the police are afraid to be seen speaking to them.'

Kilfree Incident

Towards midnight on 26 November two pistol shots were fired into the back door of the house of Terence Finn in Cloonlaheen, Kilfree and two hundred men marched from Finn's house to the public road.[107] Finn, a tenant of Richard Caddell, was father-in-law of Barrett, Cadell's bailiff, from whom all the Cadell tenants had received a letter warning them to come to Boyle on an appointed day and pay an advance of rent or they would be served with ejectments. The morning after the shots had been fired Finn found a threatening note signed 'Men of Tipperary'[108] pinned to his front door accusing him of being the first to pay the advance.

> Some persons who can sit down to a good tea breakfast with plenty of ham and eggs walked into the rent table and laid down the advance ... The rest of the poor tenants had to walk there and back without as much as a pennyworth of bread to refresh themselves while O'Reilly (agent) and Barrett (bailiff) can sit down and gorge themselves with plenty of beef and claret and ride home by rail or in an easy carriage.

105 Thomas Reeves to inspector-general 14 & 19 December 1869, Fenian Files 5318R
106 Constable Peter Lyons, Mullaghroe to Constable John Connors, Ballymote, 7 Dec 1869, Constable Willliam Doherty, Clogher to Constable John Connors, Ballymote, 2 Dec 1869, Fenian Files, 5188R
107 Report of Constable John Connors, Ballymote, 29 Nov 1869, Constable William Doherty, Clogher, to Constable John Connors, Ballymote, 2 Dec 1869, Fenian Files 5188R
108 Reference to Tipperary which had recently elected imprisoned Fenian, O'Donovan Rossa

A similar note was found on Mrs Mulrenan's door in Gurteen which cautioned the accused parties against paying the next time or they would receive a second visit. The notes were passed on to the police in Mullaghroe and Ballymote and orders were issued to keep a close watch on all suspicious characters. The Fenians now appeared to have reverted to their old role as Ribbonmen, more concerned about local agrarian issues rather than the big national question. Not surprisingly, when the Land League began a decade later the Fenians would be found in the forefront of that movement.

Keshcorran Cave
(Photo Fr Browne SJ Collection)

CHAPTER EIGHT

Spectre of Famine 1879-80

Blighted Potatoes
There had been a poor potato crop in 1878. Excessive rainfall in the summer of 1879 resulted in a blighted potato crop and a deficient grain harvest. The problem was compounded by a depression throughout western Europe which continued for a number of years and as a result there was a greatly reduced demand in England for the seasonal migratory workers from the west of Ireland, and those who found employment returned home in 1879 with greatly reduced earnings. Mathias Leonard called a public meeting in Kiltimagh in July to raise funds to alleviate the great distress prevailing throughout his parish.[1] An appeal was made to fifteen landlords but only one of them, an English lady, subscribed. £30 was raised at the meeting itself which relieved no less than 400 families for a week. In the autumn of that year the Swinford Board of Guardians warned the Lord Lieutenant of a possible 're-occurrence of the awful visitation of '47.' With successive bad harvests and the depreciation in all kinds of farm produce 'the tenant farmers are in extreme poverty and hopelessly in debt to the shopkeepers, the banks and the landlords, the labourers are without employment and in almost starving condition'.[2]

Fundraising
Because of the very wet summer, very little turf was saved. A relief fund was opened in Tubbercurry 'to enable the poor have the comfort of a fire in their cabins during the severe weather'. Amateur theatricals and a concert were organised to raise further funds and four hundred persons were helped from local resources on Christmas Eve. [3] That very same day about three hundred clustered round MacCormack's door in Ballaghaderreen looking for help, and he gave a little to every one of them.

> This little town is in the centre of a dense rural population, most of whom are small landholders. They will cling with persevering tenacity to their holdings and houses and consequently are not duly qualified to share in even the cold and repulsive comforts of the workhouse ... We, Irish bishops and priests, are custodians of morality and order. It is our duty to counsel

1 *C. T.* 19 & 26 July 1879
2 *C.T.* 18 Oct 1879
3 10 Jan 1880, DCA CH 1/39/1

peace and preach loyalty. But it is hard to instil loyalty and promote peace when there is a question of empty stomachs and an unsympathetic government.[4]

MacCormack used his Lenten pastoral in 1880 to highlight the plight of the people. 'Let us leave nothing untried to serve our poor people ... to appeal on their behalf to every source of well-known public and private charity in and out of Ireland.'[5] He had created his own relief fund with early subscriptions of £50 each from Archbishop Croke, St Nicholas' Church, Dublin, and the Bishop of Liverpool.[6] He received a cheque early in January for £150 collected in the archdiocese of Dublin. 'This munificent sum enables me to allocate to several distressed parishes, according to their respective population and the prevalence of actual want.'[7]

MacCormack Relief Fund

By the end of that month he had received £1,254, over half of which had come from the archdiocese of Dublin. By early August 1880 Dublin had donated £2,517 to MacCormack's fund. Only a fraction of this was collected within the archdiocese of Dublin, most coming from monies sent to Archbishop MacCabe from abroad to be distributed amongst the most distressed areas in Ireland. Pope Leo XIII sent £400 and MacCabe also received donations from the Archbishops of Paris and Bordeaux as well as from the editor of *Le Monde*. A Bordeaux wine producer sent him two cases of vintage Haut Medoc with instructions that one case be raffled to raise money for the relief of distress and the other case for his own personal use.[8]

Dublin Contributions

Most sent their contributions directly to MacCormack, including the Archbishop of Armagh and the Bishops of Ferns, Kildare and Down and Connor. The diocese of Liverpool sent £100 and Salford £150 and numerous donations came from many American dioceses whose bishops were of Irish origin. These contributions totalled over £4,000 from some twenty-three dioceses, with Philadelphia topping the list with £500. Individuals in America, such as Fanny Parnell in New Jersey, the Mayor of Charleston and the wife of General Sherman, Washington, also sent donations. Some American cities like Philadelphia, Baltimore and St Louis established Irish relief committees to raise funds.

American Donations

Parnell and Dillon had gone to America just before Christmas 1879 to raise funds for the Land League. Parnell later claimed that wherever they went throughout the length and breadth of America, they advised relief

Parnell's Help

4 Bishop MacCormack to Patrick Egan, sec., Land League *C.T.* 10 Jan 1880
5 *S.C.* 14 Feb 1880
6 ADA 'Relief Fund of Dr MacCormack 1879-1885'. See Appendix 30
7 *C.T.* 20 Jan 1880
8 DDA 346/1

committees to send their contributions to MacCormack and Bishop Conway of Killala. 'We selected these two bishops out from all the rest, because we knew that they were true-hearted above all others and secondly, because we knew they were in the midst of the most famished districts in Ireland.'[9] This would explain how MacCormack managed to assemble so quickly such a wide group of contributors across the United States. However, Parnell revealed this information in Castlebar just prior to the election and just after he had been strongly criticised by MacCormack for imposing his own candidature on the Mayo electorate and wanted to show that there was no real differences between himself and a popular and influential bishop.

Irish-Americans   Priests in America and elsewhere held collections in their parishes and Michael O'Brien sent £40 from Lowell, Massachusetts. Some priests were natives of Achonry as were H. Dudley and Patrick Filan of Philadelphia, members of the Killasser family who provided a number of priests to the diocese. Some even specified the parishes to which the money was to be allocated. A grant from Pottsville was to be shared between Kilmovee and Lisacull and G. P. Coghlan of St Aloysius' Church, Pottstown sent £20 to be divided equally between Swinford and Foxford. The Philadelphia relief committee specified the parish of Ballaghaderreen to receive their £100 grant and a portion of the Rochester grant was designated for Charlestown. John M. Higgins, a leading member of the relief committee of Richmond Va. sent a subscription for the relief of the starving people in Curry of which he was a native.[10]

Other Countries   Monies also came from other countries. John O'Brien sent two donations of £100 each from Port Elizabeth, South Africa and contributions also came from the Archbishop of Toronto as well as the Bishops of Autun and Angers in France. M. Veiullot, editor of the French Catholic paper, *L'Univers*, opened a subscription list among his readers and sent several contributions to MacCormack. Other notables who subscribed included the Nun of Kenmare (£150) and Michael Davitt (£100) from the National Land League. By early September MacCormack had received a total of £10,420.

Grants   The first grant from this fund was made to Kilmovee on 2 January and between that and the end of the month every parish had received at least one grant and some of them two, three or even four grants.[11] Charlestown made its first distribution of relief to 450 families with its £20 grant. Gurteen and Tubbercurry also received grants and according to John O'Grady of Attymass

9   *S.C.* 17 April 1880
10   An acknowledgement was inserted in the *Daily Despatch* of Richmond by James Kennedy, secretary of the Curry Relief Committee. *S.C.* 14 Aug 1880
11   Ballaghaderreen, £50, Foxford, £10, Keash, £10, Straide, £12 and Curry, £20. DCA CH 1/39/219, 190, 416

'but for the aid our good bishop has sent us many would have died.'[12] Within the diocese between January and July numerous grants were made to each parish with Swinford receiving the largest amount, totalling over £500, due to its size and poverty.

Office IRISH FAMINE RELIEF FUND,

Room 59, No. 32 Park Place,

From the Devoy Papers
(NLI MS 18041)

New York, January 30th, 1880.

Sir:

We beg to enclose you copy of an Appeal which we have issued to the American People   The circumstances of the case are of so pressing and so terrible a nature, that we trust they will form a sufficient excuse for addressing you.

We would venture to suggest the immediate formation of a Relief Committee in your city, composed of gentlemen of all Nationalities, so that an opportunity may be afforded every citizen of assisting us to keep our people alive until the Government of England comes to their relief.

All money sent to Drexel, Morgan & Co., will be cabled promptly to Ireland, and used within a week, in saving the Peasantry of the West of Ireland from death by starvation.

Yours, truly,

CHARLES S. PARNELL,
JOHN DILLON.

Sisters' Appeal

MacCormack also made grants to the Sisters of Charity in Ballaghaderreen, and Benada Abbey and to the Sisters of Mercy in Swinford who were ideally placed to provide aid in cases of great urgency. 'We visit their

12 ibid 303, 130, 199

dwellings, know them by name.' The Sisters launched their own appeal for funds for their school children in Ballaghaderreen.

> We have three to five hundred children coming to our schools, and want money to give them one good meal of stirabout every day and to put a fire in the school-room to dry their wet clothes, as many of them have to sleep in them, having pawned their beds to get food.

Grants were also used to employ poor labourers in the towns.[13] MacCormack made some grants to people outside the diocese such as the parish priest of Loughglynn, the Presentation Convent, Lixnaw, Co Kerry and James Keane, parish priest of Rosmuck, Co Galway, following the wishes of the donor. Lixnaw convent was specified by the rector of the Seminary of St Francis de Sales, Milwaukee, who sent a grant to be divided between it and the convent in Ballaghaderreen.

Relief Funds   The Mansion House Fund was established on 2 January 1880 under the presidency of the Lord Mayor of Dublin, and proprietor of the *Freeman's Journal*, Edmund Dwyer Gray MP, and by the beginning of March had raised almost £85,000. Over £55,000 was subscribed in Australia and New Zealand, with Sydney and Melbourne donating almost £20,000 each. The Fund eventually raised in excess of £180,000.[14] The Duchess of Marlborough, wife of the Lord Lieutenant, had already set up a fund for the relief of distress in the previous mid-December and she raised £135,000. The owner of the *New York Herald*, James Gordon Bennet, created his own Irish relief fund, to which he himself subscribed $100,000.

Relief Committees   To apply for and administer subscriptions from all the various funds now set up, and particularly the Mansion House Fund, local relief committees were established in every parish, consisting of the wealthier and more prominent parishioners, usually under the chairmanship of the parish priest. The Mansion House Committee insisted that Protestant ministers be members of local committees which caused a certain frustration to some like Thomas Judge in Bohola: 'I have searched *Thom's Directory* in vain to find the rector or curate for Bohola and failed to find one. Perhaps you could tell us yourself who the aggrieved gentleman is ... If there was such a being we have no objection that he would join our committee and administer to the one and only Protestant family in the parish.'[15]

Members   Charlestown relief committee, chaired by Thomas Loftus, had thirty-five members including nineteen merchants or shopkeepers, six national school

---

13 ibid 219
14 *Proceedings of the Mansion House Committee*
15 8 Mar 1880, Thomas Judge to Mansion House Committee, DCA Ch 1 / 39 / 266

teachers, eight farmers, as well as a Poor Law Guardian and the relieving officer.[16] Tubbercurry's committee had sixteen members, eight of whom were
described as merchants and the others included the Protestant rector, the
Catholic curate, two doctors and two gentlemen.[17] Swinford's committee
was also dominated by merchants, accounting for twelve of the twenty-three
members while the others included Dean Durcan and his two curates, the
Protestant rector, a pawnbroker, a butcher, three farmers and one Poor Law
Guardian.[18] The treasurer was almost always the manager of the nearest Hibernian or Ulster Bank. Killasser relief committee was more typical of a rural
parish, consisting of landed proprietors or farmers, five national school teachers and two doctors, one from Swinford and one from Foxford.[19] Most committees were set up before the end of January 1880, though Ballymote and
Tubbercurry had its committees operational at the end of December 1879
and the one in Straide was not formed until 4 February at a meeting in
Straide chapel.

Families Relieved

When a grant was received from the Mansion House Fund or one of the
other relief funds, tickets were issued to the heads of families on the relief list
which entitled them, depending on the size of the family, to one to four stone
of meal weekly, which they could procure from the nearest or a designated
meal merchant. Usually the custom was farmed out between the local merchants. In Bunninadden early in February, Matthew Hunt supplied Indian
meal to fifty-nine with tickets, John O'Dowd to ninety-seven, and P. Graham
to sixty.[20]

Tubbercurry

A list of 179 families who received relief in the parish of Tubbercurry the
week ending 24 January has survived, the only such list for any parish in the
whole diocese [21] It gives the name of the head of family, his age, occupation,
number in family (from 1-10), townland, amount and value of relief. No less
than 106 of these families were resident in the town of Tubbercurry and their
occupations included labourers, thirty-three, householders, eighteen, lodgings, three, tailors, one, shoemakers, four, carpenters, three, servants, five,
blacksmiths, three, milk-sellers, three, and cottiers, two. There was also a
painter, a weaver, a nailor and a tanner. Six were described as farmers amd
one a farmer's widow. The youngest, twenty-eight year old Mary Gaffney,
was single and a servant, and the oldest, also a woman, Susan Brennan, was

16 ibid 130: see Appendix 31
17 ibid 1
18 ibid 37
19 ibid 319
20 ibid 25
21 See Appendix 32

seventy-five. The remaining seventy-three families were scattered over a number of townlands and were generally described as farmers with one to seven acres, though four had ten acres and one, John Walshe of Carrowreagh Knox, had twelve acres. This solitary list of 179 families represented only a fraction of those who received relief in Tubbercurry which peaked in early June at 649 families, totalling 4,110 persons.

Numbers   An estimated 9,894 families or approximately 60,000 individuals in the diocese were either in need or actually receiving relief in January 1880. The lowest number of distressed families was in the parishes of Achonry and Ballymote, with two hundred each, though the number in Ballymote had risen to 459 families by early February out of a total of 900. Swinford had the highest number with a thousand families or two-thirds of the population in need, which increased dramatically over the early months of 1880.

> Exaggerated rumours of the amount of relief sent to us gathered the people from all parts of the country, and for the past four weeks the town is besieged from Monday till Saturday with crowds of starving people, men, women and children, in whose countenances the gaunt spectre of famine has already set its mark.

Swinford had 1,750 families or a staggering 8,750 individuals on its relief list on 20 March out of a total of 1,800 families in the parish, which meant that only fifty families or 250 persons were not receiving relief. [22]

Pawned   Charlestown was providing weekly relief at the end of January to 450 families, one of whom, Thomas Carroll of Carn, with nine in his family, the eldest of them twelve years old, had no cattle and no provision. The two beds in the house had been pawned, as was one of the blankets for three shillings, a quilt for six shillings and his own suit pledged for twelve shillings (which cost £2 two years ago), a week before St Patrick's Day last, and he had not attended Mass since then. He was given two stones of meal weekly.[23] Attymass had a similar story to tell. 'They have pawned their clothes, not only their best wearing, but in most cases their bed clothes, and are not able to redeem them. Many are not able to pay their interest to the broker. I know of persons who have to use their wearing clothes as a night covering.'[24]

350 families in Curry were 'without a cow, without a stack of corn, without a bad potato ... and hundreds of young children from two to ten years old, little scraps of half naked humanity, made to the image of God, trying to subsist upon Indian meal stirabout without a drop of milk.'[25] A landlord in

22 11 Feb 1880, Bernard Durcan to Mansion House Committee, DCA CH 1/39/37
23 ibid 130
24 22 Feb 1880, John O'Grady to Mansion House Commitee, ibid 303
25 29 Jan 1880, Peter O'Donoghue to Mansion House Committee, ibid 416

Bonniconlon, Charles Downing, gave a few shillings weekly to fifteen families (or seventy-five persons on average) to ward off starvation but could not continue 'for I am myself literally living on borrowed money'.[26]

The correspondence of parish priests with the Mansion House Committee reads like a re-run of the Great Famine over thirty years earlier. Patrick Durkan wrote from Carracastle on 8 March:

Letters from Priests

> As I was attending a "sick call" in a distant part of this parish on yesterday, a poor woman came up to me and begged of me to give her something to buy a little meal, for said she, "My children are all day screeching with hunger", and true enough, on going into the house, I found her sad story, but too true ... I know for a fact that many mothers have fasted here on one meal for the entire week in order to give to their dear little ones as much as would keep them from crying with hunger.[27]

Thomas Judge had a similar experience in Bohola. 'While I write I am beset on all sides with the cry, "Give us a pound of meal for the children tonight. They had not a bite since yesterday".'[28] Priests' houses, like Michael O'Donnell's in Foxford, were surrounded by hungry crowds begging for food. 'I have been besieged all day here at my residence.' 'I had this evening to address five-hundred starving creatures from my window, as I could not open the door. It was only after night closed when those creatures were induced to leave with empty stomachs.'[29] John McDermott had an almost identical experience in Kilmovee. 'They come daily about my house craving food.' 'Hundreds are now at my door and were there up to a late hour last night begging even a quarter stone of Indian meal to prevent starvation during the night.'[30] From Tubbercurry Michael Staunton wrote at the end of February:

> I visited a family today. There was literally nothing in the house, except the naked starving children. No clothes, no bed clothes, no provision. The half cwt of meal got last week was devoured. The half crown sent by the parish priest for groceries was gone. I never saw anything so bad. The youngest child is five months and I scarcely ever saw an infant as small as it is this moment. The withered pinched appearance of the poor child frightened me. The mother said that as she had no nourishment herself, except Indian meal, the child could not be nourished.[31]

26 23 Jan 1880, Charles Downing to Lord Mayor, ibid 63
27 ibid 42
28 18 Feb 1880, ibid 266
29 22 Jan 1880, ibid 190
30 27 Jan 1880, ibid 267
31 25 Feb 1880, ibid 1

Distribution of Seed   Numbers needing relief rose sharply, peaking early in March when almost 65,000 persons in the diocese were receiving food.[32] By now Charlestown's relief list had risen from 440 families to 840 or 4,337 persons and Swinford's from 1,000 families to 1,750 or a staggering 8,750 persons.[33] This was partially due to the fact that many of the labouring classes were then engaged in sowing their own crops and consequently were not able to sell their labour locally.

As most tenants were now destitute there was a serious problem obtaining the necessary seed, and the bishop used his funds to purchase large quantities of seed potatoes and manure which he provided to each parish.[34] Much of the seed potato was purchased in Monica Duff's to whom the bishop paid over £650, but some may have been imported direct from Glasgow as he paid a company there £354 on 15 March. Swinford and Ballaghaderreen were given eight tons of seed potatoes and seven tons of manure each and, at the other end of the scale, Straide and Attymass got three tons of seed potatoes and two tons of manure while others got six, five, four or three tons depending on their size. In order to interfere as little as possible with sowing crops, most relief committees made their food distributions fortnightly instead of weekly.

No Migration   In normal times after the spring sowing, most of the labourers and tenants migrated to England to work as agricultural labourers. Now with most of them destitute they had not the wherewithal to pay for the crossing and some in Carracastle were even without clothes. 'Many of them would have gone to England as has been usual with them at this time of year had they possessed the means. In former years they were obliged to pawn their clothes to get money to bear their expenses, but this year the alternative is not left them, as many of them have scarcely clothes to cover their nakedness.'[35] Charlestown, which had similar problems, requested a case of shoes 'much needed for those preparing to go to England'. 'There are hundreds of stalwart men trespassing on our resources who, if they had the means of making the journey to England, would by this time be affording their families very substantial relief.'[36]

Abuses   Inevitably, abuses occurred as had happened thirty years earlier during the Great Famine. When £400 was voted in the middle of June for road-making in the parish of Achonry, it proved of very little benefit to the poor, because no conditions were laid down with the contractors about the men they

32 *Proceedings of the Mansion House Committee*, pp 33-35
33 DCA. CH 1/39/130 & 37
34 ADA 'Relief Fund of Dr MacCormack'
35 6 April 1880, Patrick Durkan to the Mansion House Committee, DCA CH 1/39/42
36 3 & 17 May 1880, Thomas Loftus to the Mansion House Committee, ibid 130

should employ. 'They are employing friends, customers and members of their own families and refusing work to those who are getting relief.'[37] John McDermott described other abuses in Kilmovee:

I carry the lists out to the suppliants and tell them publicly I have only a small sum to distribute. Therefore, the man having food at home is, in trying to get it from us, trying to take it out of the starving one's mouth. I advised at the same time the poor to see for their own sake that the queries I put are answered truly. The worst feature on the whole is its demoralising character. Yesterday (3 February) was a beautiful spring day, worth gold to the labourer and still a crowd, which I could only compare to a Ballaghaderreen fair – men and women – was round my door the whole day. Men too I thought would sooner die than beg. Some too of them not requiring it … They are losing all shame too, even those who are not destressed …. I myself am near dead from over work and over persecution.[38]

Certain people in Bohola complained to the Mansion House Committee against the parish priest and his relief committee, for discriminating against them. The matter was referred to the bishop for his comments.

Bohola

Such complaints very often emanate from certain discontented men, who think they should get a share "of what's going" … I have received complaints of the same description. My feeling is to look upon them with suspicion, while at the same time to enquire into the matter … No one seems grateful. Those who receive think they should get more. Those who are refused are malcontent … I would give the committee the benefit of the doubt … I think Father Judge incapable of lending himself to any such proceeding as the one complained of.[39]

Three families in Carracastle complained at the end of April that they were in great need but were refused by the local relief committee 'as it all goes by favour and faction and unless you bribe and ransom those committee men you have but a small chance of getting any portion of the relief.' The committee replied that 'there was not a particle of truth in the whole statement … They have not received relief because each and every one of them is in very good circumstances, each of them possessed about six head of cattle and very good means besides.' Later in June five other families, all of Coppulcarragh in the same parish made similar complaints, describing the members of the committee as 'the greatest knaves in the country.'[40]

Carracastle

37 14 June 1880, Michael Keveney to Mansion House Committee, ibid 426.
38 ibid 267
39 16 Mar 1880, Bishop MacCormack to V. B. Dillon, ibid 266
40 21 & 27 April & 16 June 1880, ibid 42

Bonniconlon   From Bonniconlon, seven heads of families, 'all from a little mountainy village called Glenree', complained that they were starving but were refused relief by their parish priest. A row flared up between the priest and Charles Downing, a Church of Ireland landlord and member of the local committee. Downing resigned from the committee, claiming that Peter Harte had struck off his tenants from the relief list because 'they failed to make their usual Easter gift to the priest,' a remark which Harte 'treated with contempt'. Downing further alleged that Harte had replaced his tenants with those that Downing had previously struck off because one of them was a 'gombeen' man who had £60 or £70 out on loan and another was earning eighteen or twenty shillings a week selling turf.[41]

Charlestown   Charlestown relief committee had 924 families on their list early in June but were only able to provide relief to 732 families. Naturally, the other 192 families felt aggrieved and eleven of them appended their names to a complaint to the Mansion House Committee. The Charlestown committee had very good reasons for dropping them from the list. One of them, Augustine Duffy, was a labourer who had employment. His daughter was at service in the home of a member of the committee, one son was an employed labourer and another engaged as a car-driver, 'in all five persons able to work and at work.' Dominick Morrisroe, a labourer in the town in constant employment, earning tenpence a day, had a daughter at service and a son working in a baker's shop, and his wife a 'walking dealer'.

Another woman described as 'a sad case' had a husband and son engaged as bakers. Yet another, Pat Kain, was a cobbler with only a wife and daughter to support. The author of the complaint was James Leo Leonard, a young man, who belonged to a family which had been struck off and had thus his own axe to grind. His father, a baker, was obliged to go to England for a time and in his absence his family applied for and was given relief, but after his return he re-opened his bakery and the family was struck off the relief list.[42]

Coolaney Deaths   As the summer approached the crisis deepened. Deaths were reported in Coolaney at the end of April.

We had three coroners' inquests in this parish ... The first was held on Matthew Murphy, Moymlough, Coolaney. He died suddenly and before the priest had arrived to administer the last rites of the church, though he had hastened as quickly as possible to attend him. When the priest reached the cabin where the poor man had lived and died, he found him lying on the floor on a little straw with a scanty covering ... The priest gave two

41 ibid 63
42 ibid 130

shillings and sixpence to purchase candles for the wake but afterwards the neighbours of the deceased made so strong an appeal that he found it necessary to contribute seven shillings and sixpence more to defray the funeral expenses ... An inquest was also held on James Fury?, Rockfield. This poor man had served in the navy in her Majesty's service. Having received sunstroke and paralysis, he was sent home on a small pension. On the night of 2 April he took suddenly ill. The priest was called upon between two and three o'clock at night to administer the last sacraments. The night was extremely wet – the rain fell in torrents – and the priest upon entering the poor man's cabin found it almost flooded, the deceased sitting on a seat by a fire of sticks, and his wife trying to support his head. He died next morning, leaving a wife and three children after him – the youngest being only about two years of age. The widow has no land or any means whatsoever for support ... Another inquest was held on Michael Moffat, Carrowgavneen. He was receiving relief from our committee ...[43]

When funds ran out relief committees had to reduce those on their lists, an unenviable task for priests like Michael O'Donnell of Foxford. He wrote from Foxford early in May: *Foxford*

We gave to the most urgent from two stone to half a stone, but under heaven, I don't know what will become of the 274 yet about my house. 'Tis 8 p.m. They refuse to leave. They say they are not able to go home. They have no business there. They have nothing to eat. They will, as they say, prefer to die round my house where they will have the benefits of the rites of the church, rather than die on the way to a miserable home ... While I write my eyes are filled with tears ...[44]

A month later the situation had worsened:

The distress here now is fearful ... Several families are this moment living on cabbages, nettles and water-cresses. I was an eye-witness, where I had with considerable difficulty to quell a quarrel over the carcass of an old cow found dead in a field not far from this town. Disagreeable as my position was, I had to be present till the old bones were divided, a few pounds to each ...[45]

With the arrival of the 'hungry months', the dreaded famine fever made its appearance in the Swinford and Tubbercurry Unions. Because of the danger of bringing people together in large numbers, Charlestown relief committee changed its method of dispensing relief. Instead of giving each recipient a *Fever in Charlestown*

43 30 April 1880, P. J. MacDonald to Mansion House Committee, ibid 421
44 7 May 1880, Michael O'Donnell to Mansion House Committee, ibid 190
45 4 June 1880, ibid

ticket with the name and quantity of meal marked on it, lists of recipients were sent to each shopkeeper who supplied meal on relief tickets. Fever was then rampant in Charlestown.

Tom Loftus PP
Charlestown

The state of this poor parish is daily becoming more alarming, the famine fever and a most dangerous type, is now prevalent and making such progress that I fear there will not be ere long a village in all the parish free of it. Of course, the destitute were the first to be visited by this awful disease, but like death itself it respects not persons, and very shortly makes its unwelcome visit to the well-to-do and independent. I have seen three pass by me this week to the workhouse from the little village in which I reside: only the week before I saw the widow borne to the grave from her orphans, and only the wall separates me from the room where the wife of a respected member of our committee lies dangerously ill. Only a fortnight since on the same day and forth from the same house went the corpses of the grandmother and the grandchild, and the son now lies dangerously ill in the workhouse ... a fear of this dreadful disease has given rise to a mutual distrust and fear of having intercourse with each other ...[46]

A week later Charlestown was panic-stricken:

The people are flying from this place as fast as they can get ready; the schools are all closed; and all are terribly frightened ... We have lived to see terrible times. When none could be got to attend the sick with drink, Fr Loftus has nobly acted the priest, physician and nurse and I have now seen him bear out the entire family and all sick, put them into a cart – the only mode of conveyance to be had – and send them to hospital. Things have come to a terrible pass ...

Tom Loftus

The *Freeman* called him 'the big, brave and generous Father Tom Loftus' and MacCormack told Archbishop Croke that in 'plague-stricken Charlestown there was no one to nurse them but the parish priest, who is the chief and almost only nurse, at all hours of the day and night, going from pest-house to pest-house.' Croke had sent £200 for fever-victims. Twenty persons suffering from fever were removed from Charlestown to Swinford workhouse at the end of June.

Sisters of Charity

People were still haunted by the fear of fever since the Great Famine and as the only way of bringing fever-victims to the workouse was by farm carts it was almost impossible to find men at any price to drive them. Burying the

46 18 June 1880, Michael J. Doherty, sec. to Mansion House Committee, ibid 130

dead was a problem in Ballaghaderreen. 'Had it not been for some Sisters of Charity the dead might have been left without burial. Two of these ladies had undressed, washed and coffined a destitute woman the day of my arrival (25 June), carrying her remains into the street.'[47] It was only then that a few men, less panic-stricken than the others, ventured to lend a hand. Priests, like the curate in Killasser, found themselves in the front line. 'The famine fever, I fear, is beginning to spread in this parish. Within the last week I have administered the last sacraments to five fever patients.' [48]

J. A. Fox, who made a tour of inspection for the Manion House Commit- *Carracastle Hovels*
tee during the summer, was accompanied by the parish priest when he visited some of the hovels in Carracastle.

> Men, women and children sleep under a roof and within walls, dripping with wet, while the floor is saturated with damp, not uncommonly oozing out of it in little pools. In one case I asked a gaunt starved looking man, whom I found literally endeavouring to sleep away the hunger, where his little children slept in the moist room, in which I could see no sign of bedding. "Do they wear clothes at night?" "No." "How do they keep warm?" "There is" he replied with the most simplicity and composure, "a deal of warmth in children", signifying that they obtained warmth by huddling together like little animals.[49]

He made a house to house inspection in Attymass 'through a very wretched mountainous district, where the destitution was in several cases so urgent I had to relieve them then and there with my own hands.'

In Foxford he found thirty-five cases of fever. *Foxford Scenes*

> We visited more than thirty hovels of the poor, principally in the townlands of Culmore and Cashel, in which I beheld scenes of wretchedness wholly indescribable. In some of these hovels evicted families had recently taken refuge, so that overcrowding added to the horrors of the situation. In one hovel in the townland of Cashel, we found a little child, three years old, one of six, apparently very ill, with no one more competent to watch it than an idiot sister, eighteen years old, while the mother was absent begging the committee for relief, the father being in England ... In another in the townland of Culmore, there were four young children, one of whom was in a desperate condition for want of milk without which it was no longer able to eat the Indian meal stirabout. I took off my glove to feel its little emaciated face, calm and livid as in death, which I found to be stone

47 3 July 1880, J. A. Fox to Mansion House Committee qtd in *C.T.* 7 Aug 1880
48 27 July 1880, Thomas Bowler to Mansion House Committee, DCA CH 1/ 39/319
49 *Reports on the condition of the peasantry of County Mayo to the Mansion House Committee* pp 11

cold. My companion gently stirred its limbs and after a while, it opened its eyes, though only for a moment, again relapsing into a state of coma, apparently. It lay on a wallet of dirty straw, with shreds and tatters and other things covering it. The mother was in Foxford begging for relief, the father being in England. In no Christian country in the world would so barbarous a spectacle be tolerated.[50]

Pessimistic Prospects   By late June there were all the signs of a bumper harvest. 'The whole country is sown with potatoes and corn to an extent never before remembered.' Fox attributed this 'to the splendid gifts of seed and manure bestowed on the people by the Catholic Bishop of Achonry, Dr MacCormack.' But as the time for digging the new potatoes approached the prospects became more pessimistic.

> The happy and long-expected "Garland Sunday" seems still faraway, and the golden expectations of the poor creatures have turned into gloomy anticipations, for we have in those parts for the last eight or nine days, no sunshine, nothing but one continual downpour of rain. Consequently, the crop which promised food to the starving about the middle of July, shows no prospect at all presently.[51]

Heavy rains and thunderstorms which continued for most of July were expected to 'retard the ripening of potatoes which are already showing signs of the blight.'[52] That dreaded word was also spoken in Straide: 'The blight is very severe here and a great amount of the tubers affected. The weather has continued bad here those fourteen days back and if it continues wet for fourteen more days, the potatoes will be worse than last year.'[53] Fortunately, these predictions did not come true. The new potatoes were generally healthy and plentiful.

Lack of Clothes   However, lack of clothes remained a serious problem throughout the diocese and local committees continued to seek funds to alleviate this problem.[54] A large house in Bellaghy was 'filled from floor to ceiling with the pawned goods of the poor' and Charlestown relief committee made a very practical suggestion: 'If you could vote us a sum to redeem some of their clothes now in pawn, we would have them at less cost and better to fit them than if new clothes were sent us.'[55]

50 *C.T.* 7 Aug 1880
51 2 July 1880, Peter Harte, Bonniconlon, to Mansion House Committee, DCA CH 1/39/63
52 24 July 1880, Michael Keveney to Mansion House Committee, ibid 426
53 6 Aug 1880, P. White, sec., Straide to Mansion House Committee, ibid 519
54 21 July 1880, Keash Relief Committee to Mansion House Committee, ibid 199; 8 Aug 1880, John Gunning to Mansion House Committee, ibid 416
55 *C.T.* 7 Aug 1880; 7 July 1880, M. J. O'Doherty to Mansion House Committee, ibid 130

The plight among schoolchildren was particularly severe in Coolaney. 'A *Schoolchildren* great many children in the parish cannot attend either school or prayers on Sunday for want of clothes.' The same applied to many adults and he asked that the clothing be specifically for children, 'otherwise adults will besiege our committee for the clothes.' [56] Fox had noted a marked difference in the appearance of the children in convent schools and those in country schools: 'At Ballaghaderreen and Swinford something like vitality is maintained amongst the convent school children by the indefatigable exertions of the nuns in supplying them with food and clothing, in contrast to the sad appearance of those in roadside schools.'

Carracastle Relief Committee gave a detailed explanation of how the *Carracastle* clothes crisis had arisen came from Carracastle where people 'fear and justly being exposed almost naked to the (in)clemency of the weather.'

Some years ago when our people had a supply of food, they bought clothing whenever required for the younger portion of their children from the profit of their hens, but for the last three years, owing to the failure of the potato crop, these people were obliged to buy food for the money got from the same source from the beginning of March to the middle of August, after which time they bought article after article until their children were provided with warm clothing for the winter. All the hens have died, both parents and children are naked … Most of them have not attended their place of worship for the last twelve months and their children are unable to attend school for want of clothing.[57]

In Attymass too 'their fowl which was a large source of means to them is swept off by some strange disease, and in Charlestown hens were said to be 'as rare as pheasants'.[58]

Even though the immediate crisis had passed with the healthy potato har- *Continuing Famines* vest of 1880, distress continued to be experienced in subsequent years in the west. MacCormack joined a delegation consisting of the Archbishop of Tuam and the Bishops of Killala and Clonfert to discuss distress in their dioceses with the Lord Lieutenant at Dublin Castle in January 1883. They informed him that people in many districts were 'short of food, destitute of money and hopeless of credit' and requested loans from the Board of Works for drainage and farm improvements. The same message was enshrined in a resolution of the Swinford deanery early in March.[59]

56 23 May 1880, P. J. MacDonald to Mansion House Committee, ibid 421
57 29 July 1880, Thomas Davey and Michael Casey to Mansion House committee, ibid 42
58 25 June 1880, John O'Grady to Mansion House Committee, ibid 303, 130
59 *C.T.* 9 Jan & 12 Mar 1883

Female Emigration   J. A. Fox had noted in July 1880 a rapid increase in the rate of emigration, particularly among single young females. 'From the parish of Charlestown alone more than eighty had gone up to mid-June.' Vere Foster, the batchelor philanthropist, spent £30,000 (mostly his own money) between 1880 and 1884 helping single girls in the west of Ireland to emigrate to Canada, United States, Australia and New Zealand. He made an extensive tour of Canada and a portion of the United States where he found 'the demand for servants appears to be illimitable'. The wages of female domestic servants varied from five, six or seven dollars a month to ten, eleven or twelve in Quebec, Montreal or Toronto, from eight to thirteen in Detroit, ten to twenty dollars in St Paul, rising to twelve to twenty-five in Winnipeg. 'Girls will meet with a kind reception from Bishop Ireland and the nuns at St Paul and the archbishop and nuns at Winnipeg.'[60]

Vere Foster's   Foster assisted 20,250 unmarried girls between the ages of eighteen and
Assistance   thirty with subventions. He issued vouchers, usually to the value of £2, available within three months of issue for embarkation from Liverpool or from any Irish port. He did not approve of shipping young girls in large batches but gave them the utmost freedom of choice of ship, port and time of embarkation, to enable them to travel in the company of friends and neighbours, 'such company and protection being far more satisfactory than any that I could possibly provide.' Foster received 34,000 applications signed by 900 Catholic priests and 300 Protestant ministers who certified the girls. 4,104 successful applications were made from the diocese, 2,858 from the Mayo portion and 1,246 from the Sligo portion, signed by twenty-three parish priests and fourteen curates, as well as eleven ministers.[61]

Denis O'Hara   Denis O'Hara, then administrator in Ballaghaderreen, signed no less than 723 successful applications:

> I am glad to be able to tell you that all (723) or nearly all of them appear to be doing well. I took frequent opportunities of enquiring from their parents how they were getting on. In almost every case I was told they had received a good letter on such a day, meaning that the good affectionate daughter sent them some money to keep them at home from starving. Many a family in this parish would be in sore distress this year but for the faithful daughter on the other side of the Atlantic. Notwithstanding the number who left us in the last few years, there are many others anxious to emigrate, if they only had the means.

60 29 Oct 1882, Vere Foster to P. J. Mellet, Swinford, *S.C.* 25 Nov 1882
61 See Appendix 33

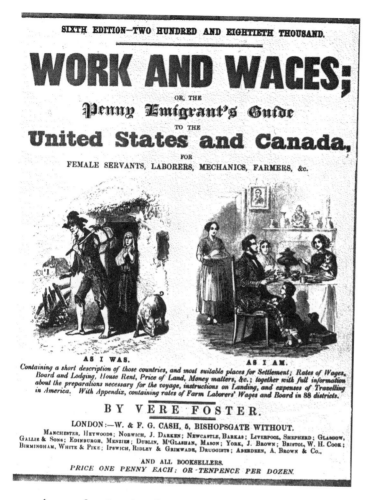

SIXTH EDITION—TWO HUNDRED AND EIGHTIETH THOUSAND.

WORK AND WAGES;

OR, THE

Penny Emigrant's Guide

TO THE

United States and Canada,

FOR

FEMALE SERVANTS, LABORERS, MECHANICS, FARMERS, &c.

AS I WAS.   *AS I AM.*

Containing a short description of those countries, and most suitable places for Settlement; Rates of Wages,
Board and Lodging, House Rent, Price of Land, Money matters, &c.; together with full information
about the preparations necessary for the voyage, instructions on Landing, and expenses of Travelling
in America. With Appendix, containing rates of Farm Laborers' Wages and Board in 88 districts.

BY VERE FOSTER.

LONDON:—W. & F. G. CASH, 5, BISHOPSGATE WITHOUT.

MANCHESTER, HEYWOODS; NORWICH, J. DARKEN; NEWCASTLE, BARKAS; LIVERPOOL, SHEPHERD; GLASGOW,
GALLIE & SONS; EDINBURGH, MENZIES; DUBLIN, M'GLASHAN, MASON; YORK, J. BROWN; BRISTOL, W. H. COOK;
BIRMINGHAM, WHITE & PIKE; IPSWICH, RIDLEY & GRIMWADE, DRUGGISTS; ABERDEEN, A. BROWN & Co.,

AND ALL BOOKSELLERS.
PRICE ONE PENNY EACH; OR-TENPENCE PER DOZEN.

The annual rate of emigration from Ireland rose in 1879 and doubled the *Family Emigration* following year to almost 100,000, remained high in 1881 and 1882 and jumped again in 1883. That year 300 emigrants assembled at Swinford work-house on 8 May and set out at six o'clock the following morning for Bally-haunis from where special trains took them to Queenstown (Cobh) and Galway. Over 200 went to Queenstown accompanied by M. J. Mellett and the remainder went to Galway with J. J. Carroll. The Allan Line steamer, *The Prussian*, bound for Halifax had already called at Blacksod Bay where it had picked up 400 emigrants from the barony of Erris, and in Galway 300 poor persons from Connemara boarded together with 100 from Swinford.

Those who had taken the train to Queenstown arrived there at 2 a.m. and *Swinford Emigrants* according to the *Cork Examiner* (Sat 12 May) 'had to lie in the streets until morning' with a large proportion of women and children in a 'pitiable' state.

However, a statement signed by some of the emigrants still ashore repudiated the charge, declaring that nobody was left on the streets on the night of arrival. The Queenstown passengers boarded the Anchor Line steamer, *Furnesia*, bound for New York.[62] A second group of 100 sailed on the *City of Rome* from Queenstown to New York on 26 May, and a group of sixty met in Ballaghaderreen, travelled to Belfast, and sailed from there to Quebec.[63] In 1884 the Allen Line sent their steamers in to Clew Bay. 'These arrangements were most successful and the expense and inconvenience of bringing the people to either Galway or Queenstown was thus avoided.' At the end of March that year 300 emigrants started from Swinford for Foxford where they took the train to Westport and boarded an Allan Line steamer bound for America. [64]

Condemnations

There was a certain ambivalence among the clergy about aided emigration. Matthew Finn of Swinford seemed unambiguously in favour of emigration in his letter to Vere Foster: 'Many parts of the west of Ireland are overcrowded. Either migration or emigration is certainly needed and as migration is very improbable, I am of opinion that many small and poor farmers would gladly emigrate if they had favourable prospects in other countries.'[65] Yet the same man signed a resolution of the Swinford deanery in March 1883 repudiating the emigrant ship as a remedy for continuing distress. 'We deem it cruel to push this remedy on our poor people who are a brave, noble, witty and generous race.'[66]

MacCormack's Pastoral

There was no ambivalence about MacCormack's condemnation of state aided emigration in his 1884 Lenten pastoral:

Emigration should be discouraged and discountenanced by all lawful means and the clergy of the west should keep a jealous and watchful eye upon the movements of those birds of ill-omen who are occasionally seen hovering about Union boardrooms ... Where the carrion is seen the vulture is soon on the wing. Their statements and promises should be largely discounted, if not discredited. They now come with larger gifts than before. They are now, forsooth, prepared to spare the ratepayers. Not a penny shall they demand for the deportation. But we have reason to doubt and fear those Grecian gifts ... Harrowing accounts of the misery of state-aided emigration have been written to friends at home and appeared in Canadian journals ... We should raise our voices in earnest protest against the deportation of our poor people to those inhospitable regions of the

62 *C.T.* 21 April, 12, 19 & 26 May 1883
63 *Telegraph or Connaught Ranger*, May 1883
64 *C.T.* 29 Mar 1884
65 NLI MS. 13552
66 *C.T.* 12 Mar 1883

British colonies ... Surely there is room enough for five million in this green isle of ours![67]

The *Connaught Telegraph* (26 April 1884) condemned Swinford Board of Guardians who 'lent themselves to the deadly policy of emigration ... as a result of the baneful workings of the Tuke Committee.' James Hack Tuke, a Quaker banker from York, produced a scheme for removing impoverished families from Mayo, Galway and Donegal. He raised £70,000 in Britain and provided assistance to almost 10,000 emigrant families between 1882 and 1884 who settled in the United States. The operations of the Tuke Committee were largely confined to the Clifden Union in 1882, but in 1884 it began to operate in the Swinford and Newport Unions. While success was reported from Belmullet and Newport Unions, emigration from Swinford Union was deemed unsatisfactory. Out of a population of 53,000 only 572 applied of which 312 persons (60 families) were accepted but not regarded as suitable for emigration, 'being for the most part labourers, widows with strong families, wives and children whose husbands and fathers were already in America, and evicted landholders'. The Tuke Committee preferred helping actual landholders to emigrate as it resulted in making more land available for those remaining.

Sydney Buxton, (probably one of those 'birds of ill-omen' referred to in MacCormack's pastoral), spent ten days in Swinford Union at the beginning of March 1884, from where he reported that MacCormack 'had denounced emigration and emigrationists in the strongest language. The Pastoral has been read by the priests from all the altars in the diocese "with emphasis".' Shopkeepers were strongly opposed to emigration and on a market day in Charlestown one of the principal traders posted a notice in the marketplace denouncing emigration.[68] Shopkeepers may well have been owed money by the emigrant families which they were unlikely ever to recover.

The opposition of the clergy is more difficult to explain. They undoubtedly favoured Vere Foster's scheme for the assisted emigration of girls because it not only improved the girls' own prospects but also improved the lot of their families at home by their remittances. The families assisted by the Tuke Committee to emigrate were a total loss to the country as their departure cut all ties with home. The *Freeman's Journal* never missed an opportunity to condemn state-aided emigration and the Tuke Fund while the *Connaught Telegraph* believed that 'parties engaged in those villainous proceedings should be held up to public reprobation.'

67 *C.T.* 1 Mar 1884
68 *Reports and papers relating to the proceedings of the committee of 'Mr Tuke's fund' for assisting emigration from Ireland* (private circulation, 1885) pp 181-184, 189

CHAPTER NINE

The Land War

It was against this background of famine and agricultural depression that the land agitation was launched in Mayo in 1879. Michael Davitt, who had been sentenced in 1870 to fifteen years penal servitude in Dartmoor for arms trafficking was released on ticket of leave in December 1877. Visiting his native county in February 1879 he discovered that a mass meeting was planned at Irishtown, near Claremorris, to put pressure on the landlord, Canon Geoffrey Burke, parish priest of Irishtown, to reduce his rents because of the depression. James Daly of Castlebar, proprietor of the *Connaught Telegraph* was the principal organiser, but Davitt framed the resolutions and provided the main speakers, Thomas Brennan an IRB man and John O'Connor Power, MP for Mayo. The meeting with over 7,000 attending on 20 April 1879, was a resounding success and the Canon, after this massive invasion of his sleepy little parish, immediately granted a reduction of 25% to his tenants.

News of this reduction spread throughout the county and demands poured in for meetings to be held in various districts. Davitt persuaded Parnell to address the first of these in Westport on 8 June. The ageing Archbishop MacHale of Tuam wrote a letter to the *Freeman's Journal* of 7 June warning against attendance at the Westport meeting but Parnell, a Protestant and thus more susceptible to Catholic episcopal censure, did not flinch. 'You must show the landlords that you intend to hold a firm grip on your homesteads and lands,' he informed the large gathering, 'You must not allow yourselves to be dispossessed as you were in '47.' Returning to Dublin by the night train, Parnell and Davitt were greeted at Castlebar, Balla and Claremorris stations by large enthusiastic crowds. The National Land League of Mayo was established in Daly's Hotel, Castlebar on 16 August with a Westport barrister, J. J. Louden, as president and James Daly as vice-president and an executive committee consisting of two members from each of the unions in the county.

Monster meetings continued to be held throughout the county, one at Balla on 15 August and another at Ballyhaunis on 31 August where there was a large representation from Kilkelly, Kiltimagh and Swinford. John O'Connor Power was the principal speaker in Ballyhaunis. Local clergy were forbidden to attend by the archbishop's nephew and secretary, Thomas MacHale, and the Augustinian friars refused to allow their Temperance Band to play, but the priests in Claremorris sent theirs. After the meeting O'Connor Power arrived in Ballaghaderreen on Monday night to begin a tour of his constituency.[1] The town was ablaze with bonfires and the administrator, Owen Stenson, introduced O'Connor Power who addressed the people from one of the windows of Queenan's Hotel. O'Connor Power spent two days in Ballaghaderreen as a guest of Stenson's whom he had first met when they were both travelling in the United States.

John O'Connor Power

O'Connor Power went on Thursday to Charlestown, where he arrived at three o'clock. 'On the front of their long car was a beautiful banner with on one side the motto "The Dawn of a New Era", with harp, wolf-dog, round tower and sunburst and on the other side, a representation of Erin, with the inscription "Welcome to one of Erin's faithful sons".' The Charlestown local band played them into town followed by a few thousand people and they drove to the parochial house where O'Connor Power was greeted by Thomas Loftus accompanied by neighbouring priests, John McDermott of Kilmovee, Peter O'Donoghue of Curry and curates, Thomas Doyle, J. Nelligan and Patrick Mannion. Loftus introduced the Mayo MP to the crowd and he was followed by James Daly who spoke about the current land agitation.

Charlestown

Then on to Swinford where they arrived at 8 p.m., greeted by torchlight processions and O'Connor Power addressed the gathering. The curates, Thomas Conlon and John Gunning paid their respects to the MP at Feeney's Hotel where he spent the night. On Friday he received a large deputation of traders in the boardroom of the workhouse and later called on the elderly Dean Durcan, before leaving for Ballina via Foxford.

Swinford

The land agitation was already producing some results locally. Charles Strickland informed the tenants on Lord Dillon's estate on 28 September that rents had been reduced by 30%. and a notice to this effect posted on the chapel gate at Ballyhaunis caused quite a stir. 'Bonfires were lit on every hilltop and village for miles around ... A large fire was set down opposite the house of Mr William Flynn ... who gave several half barrels of porter, in consequence of the good news, while the Ballyhaunis Temperance Band discoursed some beautiful music...'.[2] What was described as 'the greatest of the Mayo land meetings' was held on 5 October at Ballinrobe where O'Connor Power and Davitt were among the speakers.

Rent Reductions

1 *C.T.* 6 Sept 1879
2 *C.T.* 18 Oct 1879

Tubbercurry Meeting

Achonry diocese had its first Land League meeting a week later at Tubbercurry with an estimated crowd of 10,000.[3] The local priests did not take part, 'a matter much to be deplored', but however, Michael Conway, parish priest of Skreen in the neighbouring diocese of Killala, arrived at the head of 500 farmers, on foot and on horse, led by a splendid brass band. The Kilmactigue and Curry contingents, a few thousand strong, were led by Swinford Brass Band. Contingents came from Coolaney, Collooney and Mullinabreena and those from Gurteen and Ballymote were led by brass and fife and drum bands.

P. J. Sheridan from Tubbercurry chaired the meeting. James O'Connor, *The Irishman*, Dublin, proposed that a half year's remission of rent was absolutely necessary to save the people from ruin. Another speaker, O. J. Guinty from Leeds, was born on the banks of the Moy and had left Ireland twenty-eight years previously at the time of the Famine, 'a poor, helpless, shoeless boy'. He proposed that nobody should vote for any candidate who would not support peasant proprietorship, which was seconded by L. B. Colleran, introduced as 'a young man, a landlord in Mayo and Sligo, who had given a liberal reduction in rents.' James Daly proposed a pledge that 'not one of us will ever occupy a farm from which a tenant farmer was driven.'

National Land League

The Irish National Land League was founded in Dublin on 21 October with Parnell elected president, A. J. Kettle, Michael Davitt and Thomas Brennan, secretaries, and Joseph Biggar, W. H. O'Sullivan and P. Egan, treasurers, and in the weeks and months following meetings were held and local branches formed mostly in Connacht. The aims of the League were the reduction of rack rents and occupier-ownership of the soil and it was proposed that Parnell go to America to collect funds.

Aughamore Land Meeting

A meeting was held in Aughamore on Sunday 26 October.[4] Rain fell all day with unabated vigour and the ground was soaked, while thousands stood for hours under the downpour listening to speeches from Davitt, James Daly etc. John McDermott of Kilmovee moved the first resolution: 'Ireland is on the verge of bankruptcy, which means death by starvation for us and our little ones ... They should ask for relief from those who were fattened on their toil in past years.' More controversially, the priest added: 'Another class that should give reductions were the shopkeepers and the userers who were fat-

3   *C.T. & S.C.* 18 Oct 1879 Among those present: *Swinford:* Messrs Corley, A. Dolphin, P. J. Durkan, J. P. O'Connor, T. Callaghan, J. Timlin, C. McArdle, P. White. *Charlestown:* Messrs J. C. Brady, J. M. Henry, P. W. Mulligan, C. J. Henry, P. A. Mulligan. *Ballymote:* Messrs B. Coghlan, J. O'Brien, M. Judge, J. McDonagh. *Tubbercurry:* Messrs F. Cooke, Mullarkey, Jas. Connelly, P. J. Sheridan. *Gurteen:* Messrs Callely, J. McDermott, Mulrenan etc

4   *C.T.* 1 Nov 1879

tened on the poverty of the people.' A voice in the crowd shouted: 'The shopkeepers are the best friends of the tenant farmers' which was greeted with
cheers and Davitt declared that 'the shopkeepers of Ireland had stood between the people and the landlords'. An irate Kilkelly shopkeeper wrote to
the editor of the *Connaught Telegraph* (8 November) condemning McDermott and suggesting sarcastically 'if Canon John is satisfied with 13s 4d for
every pound previously demanded and faithfully exacted then I will respect
his motives and emulate his example.'

Gurteen Land Meeting on 2 November achieved national prominence.[5]   *Gurteen Meeting*
An estimated 18,000 attended with five bands, from Swinford, Boyle, Carrick, Ballymote and the local half parish fife and drum band. An immense
procession, over a mile long, was led by farmers of the better class on horseback, wearing sashes and rosettes and carrying banners emblazoned with
mottoes. A couple of hundred young men carrying mock pikes led the Tubbercurry contingent and Swinford, Charlestown and Ballaghaderreen were
represented by 'a splendid array of men'. Roger Brennan presided and was
joined on the platform by a half dozen other priests.[6] A letter of apology was
received from Michael Conway from Skreen who was prevented from attending by his bishop. 'The bishop and clergy of Achonry complained of my presence at Tubbercurry.'[7]

James McDermott of Bunninadden proposed that 'in consequence of the   *Peasant*
prevailing distress and the impending crisis of the coming winter, we, the   *Proprietorship*
tenant farmers of Sligo county, declare that a considerable reduction of rent is
necessary to save the people from starvation.' John Dillon declared that they
should not plead respectfully to the government for aid but 'should let them
know that they were dealing with men who could respect themselves'.
Michael Davitt took up the theme of peasant proprietorship proposed by
Denis O'Hara: 'The abolition of landlordism was the only remedy. The time
had come when the manhood of Ireland must spring to its feet and say it
would tolerate the system no longer ... Until the word 'landlordism' is written
out of the statute books, as in France and elsewhere, you will never be con-
tented or prosperous. Hold your farms. Let them serve you with notice to
quit, with ejectments. Let them if they like proceed in the courts. Defend
yourselves but don't allow them to evict you.'

5   *C.T.* & *S.C.* 8 Nov 1879
6   John McDermott, Kilmovee, James McDermott, Bunninadden & curates, Michael
    Keveney, Keash, Philip Mulligan, Collooney, Matthew Bourke, Bunninadden and Denis
    O'Hara, Ballaghaderreen
7   Such a complaint seems completely out of character for MacCormack. More than likely, it
    came from Michael Staunton of Tubbercurry who was opposed to that meeting

Contretemps   John McDermott of Kilmovee said that fixity of tenure should be insisted upon in the interval as peasant proprietorship would require a considerable time to be established, but James Daly accused McDermott of having changed his mind since the Aughamore meeting where he opposed peasant proprietorship and a shouting match ensued between the two, with Daly again accusing him of supporting King-Harmon. James Bryce Killeen, a Protestant barrister from Belfast, who drew attention to the presence of government note-takers, 'noting every word they said today for the purpose of putting them in dungeons', declared that 'he would like to see everyone there armed with a gun and knowing how to use it. The days of namby-pamby speaking were over.' Such violent language was bound to have serious repercussions for the speakers.

Kiltimagh Meeting   These monster rallies produced results in the form of rent reductions. Myles Jordan met his Gallen tenants in Swinford and offered them a reduction just two days before the important townspeople held a meeting to prepare for a Land League rally in the town.[8]

Some landlords in Kiltimagh had already promised to reduce rents before a spectacular Land League rally on Sunday 16 November of an estimated 20,000, addressed by James Daly and Westport barrister, J. J. Louden, and brass bands from Claremorris, Swinford and Ballyhaunis.[9] Triumphal arches spanned the streets with mottoes such as 'God save Ireland' and 'The priests and people forever', very much the theme chosen by the parish priest, Mathias Leonard, who presided. 'Their enemies would have them believe that the priests were separated from the people, that they had deserted the people.' A voice in the crowd shouted: 'The people won't desert the priests.' Leonard warmed to his theme. 'The priest loves the people. He lives for the people and would die for the people.'

Arrests   Three days later James Daly was arrested in Castlebar and James Bryce Killeen at Georges Place, Dublin.[10] The night before, Davitt received a message from the editor of the *Freeman* warning that he would be arrested the following morning and advising him to leave the country as his ticket of leave would be cancelled and he would be sent back to penal servitude. He ignored

---

8   *C.T.* 15 Nov 1879. John Flannery, Ballaghaderreen, gave a 25% and George Horkan, Liscottle, 20% reduction, Thomas Leetch, Kilkelly, gave 20% reduction to tenants in Gallen & Costello & McAlpines, 25% to tenants in Kiltimagh. *C.T.* 29 Nov & 27 Dec 1879. The land agent of McDonnell of Sragh, Carracastle attended at the hotel in Charlestown to receive rents and offered the tenants a reduction of 10% which they refused.

9   *C.T.* 22 Nov 1879, George Browne MP, Charles Bourke Jordan, Thornhill, Dr Roberts, and Mrs Stronge, an English lady

10 *C.T.* 22 Nov 1879

the advice and at five o'clock the following morning his lodgings at 83 Amiens Street were raided by Dublin Castle agents who arrested him on a warrant issued by Sub-Inspector McClelland of Tubbercurry. Davitt and Killeen were placed in a first-class carriage on the 9 a.m. train to Sligo, in the custody of a detective. The whole affair was managed so quietly that a railway official, recognising Davitt and referring to yesterday's *Freeman*, said he feared that Davitt would not be long at liberty. All three were taken before a resident magistrate and remanded in custody in Sligo jail for trial on the following Monday.

Parnell denounced the arrests and summoned an indignation meeting at the Rotunda. Anthony Dempsey of Balla with his family of six were to be evicted on or about 24 November and a huge demonstration had been planned by the League at the scene, with Davitt as the principal speaker. Parnell announced at the Rotunda that he would attend the Balla demonstration the following day. It turned out to be 'so extraordinary a demonstration of organised strength and determination that no attempt was made either to interfere with it or to proceed with the eviction.'[11]

Balla Meeting

Parnell had intended to proceed directly on Saturday from Balla to Sligo for the trial which was to begin on Monday. Less than two weeks earlier a committee had been set up in Swinford to organise a land rally in the town and invitations had been sent to T. D. Sullivan of the *Nation*, James O'Connor of *The Irishman* and, of course, James Daly among others.[12] Now Balla presented them with a chance of carrying off the biggest prize of all – Charles Stewart Parnell. The Swinford deputation waited on Parnell in Balla and persuaded him to attend the Swinford rally the following day.[13] It was a spectacular coup for the town. Parnell left Balla at 8 p.m. and was given an ovation in Kiltimagh which was illuminated in his honour. In Swinford the people turned out *en masse* to meet him about two miles from the town and, headed by the town's brass band (renamed shortly afterwards the 'Parnell Brass Band'), escorted him in.

Swinford Meeting

Bonfires blazed from the hillsides and the valleys and glens rang with 'Parnell! Parnell! Our chosen Chief.' On arriving opposite Mr Horkan's house, Parnell was taken from his carriage and carried on the shoulders of the people to Mr Mellet's house where he stayed. He addressed the vast assemblage from the window of Mellet's house and introduced Dillon who

11 Davitt, *Fall of Feudalism*, p 179
12 *C.T.* 15 Nov 1879
13 Messrs Dolphin, Mellet, Staunton, Corley and O'Connor, *C.T.* 29 Nov 1879

gave a brief address. Every word of both men was cheered to the echo. The town was brilliantly illuminated and all night long the heavens were rent with the plaudits of Parnell's name.[14]

Some 20,000 were present at the rally the following day, many coming from twenty to twenty-five miles away with contingents from Aughamore, Kilkelly, Balla, Kiltimagh, Tubbercurry, Castlebar, Kilmovee, Bohola, Foxford, Charlestown, Claremorris and Ballinrobe. 'Every faithful Soggarth Aroon rode at the head of each contingent.' Several arches spanned the streets with the inscription 'Welcome to Parnell' and the platform erected opposite Mr Gallagher's house in the centre of the square was gaily decorated with evergreens and bunting and the speaker's chair surmounted by a banner with 'God save Ireland. Remember '47'. Every man, young and old, wore on his arm and his breast a piece of crepe in memory of the Manchester Martyrs, whose anniversary occurred that day.

'Keep a Firm Grip...'   The curate, Thomas Conlon, took the chair in the unavoidable absence of the elderly Dean Durcan and he was joined on the platform by Parnell, Dillon, J. J. Louden, James O'Connor and various priests from Killasser, Charlestown, Kiltimagh, Tubbercurry and Ballaghaderreen. The first resolution proposed by P. J. Mellet and J. P. O'Connor strongly protested against 'the arbitrary arrest of Messrs Davitt, Daly and Killeen', pledging 'to sustain them by every legitimate means'. 'Do not be tempted into any acts of violence,' Parnell warned the crowd,

> Keep a firm grip on your lands; hold fast by your homesteads. Refuse to pay an unjust rent ... I do not advise you to pay no rent, but I advise you to pay only a fair one ... Remember Michael Davitt in his prison cell; recollect that he is suffering imprisonment because he has proved himself too powerful an advocate of your cause. And on this day, the anniversary of the Manchester Martyrs, when three of your countrymen were sacrificed in Manchester, I ask that you will remember the teachings of Michael Davitt, that the tenant farmers of Ireland should own the soil of Ireland.

Roger O'Hara of Killasser, seconded by John Dillon, called on landlords to give 'a liberal reduction of rents to their tenants who are unable to pay the present high rate in consequence of the failure of the crops and the low price of cattle and farm produce.' Other resolutions by Ambrose Dolphin and John Gunning requested public works, by A. J. Staunton and J. J. Louden in favour of peasant proprietorship and by Thos. A. Hickey, Dublin, and P. J. Mellet, calling for the restoration of the national parliament. In the evening the speakers and others were entertained to a sumptuous banquet in the hotel.

14 *C.T.* 29 Nov 1879

The trial, which began in Sligo on Monday 24 November, was described by Davitt as 'one of the most successful legal farces ever acted off a theatrical stage.' His own narrative remains the most entertaining account of it.[15]

The day's proceedings began by the Sligo Brass Band and a huge crowd escorting the prisoners from the county jail to the trial, the procession parading the whole town on its way to the court, like a newly arrived circus company The court was as crowded as a theatre with the attraction of a popular play, a large number of ladies being present. Then began the

Sligo Trial

Trial at Sligo Courthouse

15 Davitt, *The Fall of Feudalism in Ireland*, p 183

solemn farce of reading an indictment and the customary legal fray over points, precedents and previous judgments between the opposing counsel ... In this manner the first session of the magisterial investigation went on and ended, the sitting being adjourned until the following morning. Back we went to prison, the brass band leading, the police escorting, and the whole town following and cheering Parnell, Dillon and the prisoners. And when the "villains" of the piece were disposed of for the night in the jail, a public meeting was held in the town, addressed by Mr Parnell and others in speeches which rang with fierce denunciations of the prosecution, and the curtain was rung down upon the first act of the precious performance.

James Daly

James Daly, defended by J. J. Louden, was the first to be tried and in the end he was released on bail.[16] The news of his release spread rapidly through the country and, on his arrival in Charlestown, the parish priest introduced him to the vast crowd assembled around a large bonfire in the square while the band played national airs. In Swinford there was a great demonstration, with the band playing and bonfires blazing along the Sligo road. 'Not a hilltop from Muckelty to Ballaghaderreen and from Ballymote to Pontoon, that was not ablaze up to a late hour.'

Davitt

Typically, Davitt defended himself. He called the priests, Roger Brennan, John McDermott, and Denis O'Hara as well as John Dillon as witnesses to prove that he had not uttered at Gurteen a single word to excite violence but the court refused to hear them. He too was committed for trial but released on bail and left the court in the company of Parnell, Dillon and Louden. Later a band serenaded him while he dined at the home of Dr Michael Cox, seated between the head officer of the Sligo police and Parnell.

The 'Orange-Fenian'

But the farce became truly ludicrous with the trial of Killeen. He was defended by John Rea, a Belfast Protestant engaged by Joseph Biggar, who described himself as the 'Orange-Fenian Attorney-General of Ulster'. He was a six foot tall eccentric, with a massive head, a loud voice with a pronounced Ulster accent and, according to Davitt, 'a provocative manner which would drive a bench of Quakers into a militant mood of retaliation.' He insisted on addressing the presiding magistrate as 'Mr Promoted-Policeman', as he had formerly been one, and when the magistrate mispronounced a word, Rea was on his feet demanding to know 'whether it was permissible for a man in the pay of the Crown to murder the Queen's English?' When asked to produce witnesses, Rea called on Edward MacCabe, Roman Catholic Archbishop of Dublin and Edward Dwyer Gray, editor of the *Freeman*. When the presiding magistrate threatened to close the case, Rea called on John McDermott of

16 see account of trial, *C.T.* 29 Nov & 6 Dec 1879

Kilmovee. 'You are not unlike a Soggarth Aroon,' Rea told him, 'a little more ferocious though.' In the end Rea refused to offer bail and Killeen was physically carried by two constables to a carriage which took him back to jail.

Twenty-seven newspaper correspondents covered the trial and their reports not only appeared in the Irish and English press but also in the United States. Indignation meetings were held in Limerick, Cork, London, Leeds, Glasgow etc. and cable messages of support poured in from across the Atlantic. It was a spectacular propaganda triumph, according to Davitt. 'We could not have done the League work of propaganda and of covering the law with ridicule as effectively if we had spent £5,000 on the task.'

Propaganda Triumph

A Land League rally was held in Ballaghaderreen the following Sunday, 30 November, with Owen Stenson presiding and John Dillon, James Daly and James O'Connor among the speakers.[17] Sleet was falling and the air so cold 'that it would test the nervous temperament of a polar bear'. Nevertheless, an estimated 15,000-18,000 turned up, with five bands from Carrick-on-Shannon, Boyle, Swinford, Ballyhaunis and Ballaghaderreen. A dozen little boys mounted on donkeys carried green banners with the inscriptions 'The Young Blood' on one side and 'We Want Food' on the other. Each contingent was led by its parish priest, Charlestown by Thomas Loftus, Carracastle by Patrick Durkan and the Kilmovee contingent headed the procession led by John McDermott.

Ballaghaderreen

Denis O'Hara declared that 'the priests and people of Ballaghaderreen deeply sympathise with the tenant farmers in their great distress after three unfavourable seasons, the bad prices of cattle and farm produce and the fuel famine' and called on landlords for 'substantial reductions in rent'. Edward Connington from St Nathy's Seminary called on the people not to support any parliamentary candidate 'who will not join the native party in the House and vote for creating peasant proprietary'. That evening there was a dinner for the speakers, priests and other friends in Queenan's Hotel. At about 9 p.m. a constable arrived and asked the guests to disperse, and they naturally 'deprecated in strong terms this intrusion' and sent the constable packing, asking him to send in the Sub-Inspector.

Local branches of the Land League were established all over the diocese, fully supported by MacCormack. 'Let us make every legitimate effort to effect a change in the land laws of our unhappy country, to root the tenant in the soil.'[18] His opinion of the Land League was unequivocal. 'The cause is a good one; the grievance a real one; and the reform demanded a necessary

Land League Branches

17 *C.T. & S.C.* 6 Dec 1879
18 Lenten pastoral qtd in *S.C.* 14 Feb 1880

one.'[19] Carracastle set up a land league branch on 15 February 1880 with Patrick Durkan as president, and the curate, Patrick Mannion, as secretary, and people were urged to enrol as members to be prepared for impending evictions in Corragooly, Cranmore, Cloonmore, Castleduff and Ballintadder. At a land rally on 7 December Durkan was accompanied on the platform by at least eight other priests from the neighbouring parishes.[20] A land rally proposed for Killasser on 21 December was adjourned to early January. Over 200 tenant farmers of Toomore enrolled in the Foxford branch on 11 March.

League Fund

There was another urgent reason for establishing local branches. Just before Christmas 1879 Parnell, accompanied by Dillon, had set out for America originally to collect funds for the Land League, but with the growing famine at home the mission became focused on relief. Dillon's appearance at these fundraising functions had an enormous effect. His tall, thin frame, dark eyes, white face, and black beard, with hunger written on every line of his face, made an immediate impression on his audience who subscribed generously. £500 was raised at their first meeting in New York and dispatched to the League's headquarters in Dublin which distributed it among the branches most in need.[21] Charlestown received £25, Kiltimagh, two donations of £25 and 12 tons of Champion seed potatoes, and Ballaghaderreen, seed potaoes and £30. Kilkelly Land League, formed at the end of May, had twin aims, a pledge not to occupy farms from which tenants were evicted and 'to do all in their power to relieve the starving people from the terrible privations from which they are suffering.'[22]

Curry Meeting

The third monster rally held in County Sligo was at Curry on 18 January 1880 where the estimated attendance of 18,000 was made up of very large contingents from Swinford, Charlestown, Ballaghaderreen, Kilmactigue, Tubbercurry, Benada and Gurteen. Two government note-takers were protected by a posse of fifty policemen under the command of Sub-Inspector Egan from Sligo and 'the irrepressible McClelland of Tubbercurry'. Peter O'Donoghue who took the chair, accompanied on the platform by five parish priests and six curates from neighbouring parishes, told the crowd that ten or twelve families in the parish on the property of Messrs O'Rourke were threatened with eviction.[23] 'The tillers of the soil should be the owners of the soil they till and the national land movement, like a mighty earthquake, has shaken this island to its very centre.'

19 F. J. MacCormack to Mgr Kirby, 9 Dec 1880, Kirby Papers 507, ICR
20 *S.C.* 13 Dec 1879
21 *C.T.* 10 Jan 1879
22 *C.T.* 12 June 1880
23 *Parish Priests:* James McDermott, Bunninadden, Patrick Lowry, Achonry, Patrick Durkan,

L. B. Colleran spoke in favour of peasant proprietary and Malachy O'Sul-livan said Sligo should reject its two sitting MP's, King-Harmon and Denis O'Conor, at the coming election. Denis O'Hara told them that the new year had brought new life and new spirit to the movement. 'Three times Sligo had manfully spoken out. In Mayo every man had sworn never to cease agitating until the land in Ireland belongs to the people.' Loud cheering greeted his reference to MacCormack. 'If any patriotic bishop in Ireland deserved to be cheered their bishop did and everyone would wish him a long reign over the see of Achonry.'

Davitt was the principal speaker two weeks later, on 1 February, standing on a platform erected on the exact spot in Straide where he was born. It was an emotional home-coming.

Straide Meeting

> What wonder, standing here on the spot where I first drew breath, in sight of a levelled home with memories of privations and tortures crowding upon my mind, that I should swear to devote the remainder of my life to the destruction of what has blasted my early years, pursued me with its vengeance through manhood and leaves my family in exile today far from that Ireland which is itself wronged, robbed and humiliated through the agency of the same accursed system.

The usual contingents were present from all the surrounding towns, with some coming from as far as Ballinrobe and Louisburgh.[24] James O'Donnell, the parish priest, was in the chair and other speakers included Thomas Brennan, James Daly, J. J. Louden and P. J. Sheridan from Tubbercurry. Armed police from Castlebar, Ballyvary and Foxford protected the now customary government note-takers. Some eighteen months later, when Davitt was back in prison, this time in Portland Jail, and reminiscing on that day in Straide when he stood upon the ruins of his former home, the thought then uppermost in his mind was that he might yet live 'to have the satisfaction of trampling in turn upon the ruins of Irish landlordism.'[25]

About 5,000 attended a rally in Benada on 14 March as well as three bands, Swinford Brass Band, Ballymote Flute Band and Achonry Flute Band which had only been formed a short time previously. One banner depicted a prostrate landlord with Pat planting a foot on his neck and the cold end of a pike against his breast, with the motto 'Paying off old arrears'. Patrick Scully, who

Benada Meeting

Carracastle, Thomas Loftus, Charlestown, Patrick Scully, Kilmactigue; *curates:* Philip Mulligan, Collooney, Denis O'Hara, Ballaghaderreen, James Cullen, Kilmactigue, John Gunning, Gurteen, Patrick Mannion, Kilmactigue, Michael Keveney, Achonry. *C.T. & S.C.* 24 Jan 1880
24 *C.T.* 7 Feb 1880
25 *Jottings in Solitary*, TCD, Dav. P. 9639

took the chair, was accompanied on the platform, erected in a field opposite the convent grounds, by the parish priests of Curry, Charlestown and Carracastle as well as a number of curates. Speakers included Scully, Loftus of Charlestown and Durkan of Carracastle as well as P. J. Sheridan, Tubbercurry, Bernard Finn, Gurteen and Edward Gayer, editor of the *Sligo Champion*.[26]

General Election

When parliament was dissolved on 8 March, Parnell hurried back from America to prepare for the general election and news of his safe return was greeted in Ballymote and Tubbercurry with bonfires and all the windows illuminated.[27] Dillon was left to continue the fundraising tour with the intention of sending Davitt to join him later. The role of bishops and priests in the Irish elections was paramount. Priests of Swinford deanery, together with the bishop, sent a telegram to George Browne, one of the sitting members for Mayo, demanding that he be more frequent in attending parliament and generally more energetic, if he was to get their support. When he abjectly conformed they agreed to support him and O'Connor Power, and he was nominated in Castlebar by Bernard Durcan, while the parish priest of Castlebar proposed O'Connor Power.[28]

MacCormack attacks Parnell

In the event, however, Browne lost as J. J. Louden proposed Parnell at the last minute. MacCormack strongly criticised Parnell's intrusion into the contest in Mayo 'in opposition to the well-known wishes of the bishops, priests and, I believe, the vast majority of the electors of the county.'[29] He resented the arbitrary manner in which Parnell dictated to the Mayo electorate, describing him as having 'the ambition of a man who aspires to play the role of universal dictator,' and warned that the 'bubble of Mr Parnell's popularity might at any moment burst before the indignant spirit of Irish faith and fatherland'. He counted on the 'manly spirit of the priests and people of Mayo to teach Mr Parnell a lesson of prudence which he seems to miss so much at the present intoxicating stage of his political career.'

Two days later in Castlebar, Parnell tried to mend fences with MacCormack, whom he described as 'a most respected, loved and venerated prelate, a man whose name should be pronounced with love by every Irishman.' He deeply regretted that MacCormack and himself should appear to be on opposite sides.

> We are both really on the same side and when this little misunderstanding has been brushed aside as the thing of little moment that it is, you will see that no one will come forward with more joy and happiness than Dr Mac-

26 Also on the platform were Luke B. Colleran, Curry and Nicholas H. Devine, Tubbercurry. *S.C.* 20 Mar 1880
27 *S.C.* 27 Mar 1880
28 *C.T.* 27 Mar 1880
29 *F.J.* 8 April 1880 qtd in *S.C.* 17 April 1880

Cormack to congratulate the people of Mayo on placing myself and O'Connor Power at the head of the poll.

O'Connor Power came first with 1,645 votes, closely followed by Parnell with 1,560 while Browne only gained 628 votes. Parnell had intervened because there was a principle at stake since Browne had not accepted the party pledge. As Parnell was returned for three different seats he had to forego Mayo and was replaced by Isaac Nelson, a Presbyterian minister from Belfast, which left a bad taste in the mouths of many priests in Mayo, particularly the Archbishop of Tuam. 'I myself can never pardon Parnell, his putting in a toothless Presbyterian minister to represent Catholic Mayo'.[30]

The Sligo Convention on Wednesday 7 April was attended by all three bishops of the county, Killala, Achonry and Elphin, and a priest and two laymen from each parish. Thomas Sexton, who put himself forward at Parnell's suggestion, was chosen by seventy-one out of seventy-seven delegates.[31] Earlier that week Sexton had toured his constituency where he met particularly the local priests. He addressed a meeting outside the chapel in Coolaney on Sunday and the following day met Patrick Scully and the other priests in Tourlestrane. In Tubbercurry the platform party included Michael Staunton and his curate, Peter Lohan, as well as Patrick Lowry of Achonry, and his curate, Michael Keveney. In Gurteen he met the parish priest, Roger Brennan, and Denis O'Hara, Ballaghaderreen.[32]

A call was made at the Curry land rally in January that Sligo should reject its two sitting MPs, Captain E. R. King-Harmon and Denis O'Conor, at the coming election. King-Harmon had written to John McDermott of Kilmovee seeking his support and, still stinging from the rebukes he had received from James Daly on the Gurteen platform accusing him of having supported King-Harmon, McDermott took care to have his reply published in Daly's own newspaper. 'Your actions in the political field are well known and I am not such a traitor to my country as to pretend to see in them a motive for supporting you.'[33]

In his absence in America where he remained until July, John Dillon was returned for Tipperary, where his father, John Blake Dillon, had once been the representative. The general election was a personal triumph for Parnell, with the number of new members who looked to him for leadership considerably increased, insuring his election as chairman of the Home Rule Party.

Sligo Convention

Thomas Sexton
Weekly Irish Times
17 Mar 1883

30 Archbishop McEvilly to Mgr Kirby, 30 May 1883, Kirby Papers 123, ICR
31 *C.T. & S.C.* 10 April 1880
32 *S.C.* 10 April 1880
33 *C.T.* 10 April 1880. King-Harmon was ousted by Sexton

Bishops Divided   Members of the hierarchy had mixed views about the results of the election. Some were delighted that Ireland had returned sixty-three Catholics when not a single Catholic was returned for a constituency in England or Scotland. Patrick Moran, Bishop of Ossory, described Parnellites as 'extreme Home Rulers' and condemned them for opposing candidates, as in Mayo, chosen by the clergy and thus causing the bishops and clergy 'to bear a good deal of popular odium'.[34] Gillooly of Elphin had issued a circular exhorting the people 'to have nothing to say to these extreme politicians' and a number of people walked out in Roscommon when his vicar general read it from the altar. Moran decried the disunity among bishops: 'It would be well to call attention to the lack of union among our body in the matter of promoting Parnellism. It is useless for the bishops of one district to oppose it, if it is encouraged in other places.' He cited the diocese of Meath where the bishop ordered a collection to be taken up in all the churches to defray Parnell's election expenses in that county. 'How can we persuade the people that Parnellism is wrong after that?'

Land League
Meetings   Large Land League meetings continued to be held at various places in the diocese. A meeting at Mount Irwin in the parish of Kilfree on 6 June was called to protest against the eviction of Mrs Killoran, a tenant of Captain Thornhill and Francis McDonagh, a tenant of Alexander Sim, Collooney. Bands came from Boyle, Carrick, Achonry, Kilfree and Ballymote but there was no priest on the platform.[35] Kilmovee held a meeting in the chapel yard on 13 June and there was another in Bohola on 4 July where the display of banners was considerably reduced 'as a result of the poverty and wretched condition of the people'.[36] Between 4,000 and 5,000 people, as well as bands from Boyle, Ballymote, Kilfree and Killavil, were present at a land rally at the foot of Keash mountain on 25 July. [37] The two government note-takers were not allowed on the platform but were escorted into the middle of the crowd with a strong police bodyguard. Again there was no priest present on the platform but Mark Cooke of Keash sent a message wishing them well and asking that there be no violence. The chair was taken by a local tenant-farmer.

Ballaghaderreen
Meeting   Dillon was the principal guest speaker at a large meeting in Ballaghaderreen on 21 November and his sister, Christina, left a pen-picture of the reception he received in his ancestral home:

34 Moran to Mgr Kirby, 19 April 1880, Kirby Papers 200, ICR
35 Among the platform speakers were P. J. Sheridan, Tubbercurry, M. Loftus, Curry, J. Hyland and B. Finn, Gurteen, M. Judge, Ballaghaderreen, T. Mulligan, J. Coffee, J. O'Dowd, J. Leonard, J. McKeon. *S.C.* 12 June 1880
36 *C.T.* 10 July 1880
37 *S.C.* 31 July 1880

All the afternoon people were making preparations for a bonfire right in front of the house. They piled up a great quantity of turf and then a lot of barrels. It was finished quite early in the evening and they got impatient and set fire to it which was a mistake for it was still broad daylight. However, as soon as it was fairly lighted, they began building up a second and while they were working at this, a band marched up the street, placed themselves before the door and began to play. After a while the sun set, the moon rose and lights appeared in every window in the whole town. When the daylight was quite gone, they set fire to the second bonfire which made a splendid blaze and lighted up the whole street. At last, when a great crowd had collected, we opened the hall-door and Father O'Hara spoke from the steps introducing Johnnie. When Johnnie appeared at the door, there was a wild cheer and, of course, he had to make a speech ... Mrs Duff was awfully cross about the bonfires, she cant bear demonstrations of that

John and
Christina Dillon

kind and bands make her mad. She sat in her chair the whole evening and never once looked out and she persuaded herself that the fires made her room so hot that she did not sleep all night – which I don't believe.[38]

Six bands played at the main meeting with contingents marching in military formation, wearing sashes, rosettes and green caps. The platform was erected in the square 'in front of the handsome residence of Mrs Duff.' Edward Connington strongly condemned the government for prosecuting Parnell and the others as an attempt to deprive the people of freedom of speech. (The government had just instituted prosecutions against Parnell, Dillon, Biggar, T. D. Sullivan, Sexton, Brennan and Patrick Egan, for inciting the people not to pay rents.) Dillon and Denis O'Hara also spoke.

Other meetings were held in Kiltimagh the following Sunday, in Kilkelly in the middle of December and in Straide early in January 1881 with the platform erected once more on the ruins of Davitt's former home. The walls in Swinford and the surrounding towns at the end of March were plastered with posters, announcing a monster meeting in Swinford on 1 April.[39] Police and military were drafted in from all directions, only to discover that her Majesty's officials were the victims of an April Fool's joke.

Killasser Evictions   While these meetings were taking place, and indeed in spite of them, eviction notices continued to be served. Philip Langan and his family of seven, were evicted from their holding in Culduff, Killasser by their landlord, Daniel Keane in April 1879. 'The landlord has acted very cruelly in this case,' Thomas O'Brien, secretary of Killasser Land League informed headquarters. 'He has taken the land himself and left this poor family destitute of the means of living.' Patt Ford and his family of five were evicted in June in the same parish from a farm he held for forty years in Dromada Duke by Joseph McGloin of Foxford, agent of the landlord, Roger McCarrick of Cloonbarry, Co Sligo. Ford was sent to prison for seven days for repossession. McGloin also evicted the thirteen members of the family of Martin O'Brien from the same townland while Martin himself was in England [40] A large anti-eviction meeting was held on 13 June 1880 at Dunmanor to protest against the eviction of three families.[41] The Killasser fife and drum band led 3,000 men wearing green scarves and 'a train of cars from Castlebar, Foxford, Ballina, Swinford, Balla, Straide etc. occupied fully two miles of the road.' Roger O'Hara agreed to a request from the police that two government note-takers

38 TCD, Dil. P. 6457, Christina Dillon to Miss Knox, n.d. 1880
39 *C.T.* 2 April 1881
40 NLI MS. 17,709
41 *C.T.* 19 June 1880

be allowed on the platform. One of the speakers threatened to hold a meeting outside McGloin's house in Foxford.

Evictions took place elsewhere in the diocese, Aclare, Ballysadare, Curry, Gurteen, Keash, Kiltimagh, Meelick and Tubbercurry. [42] Fanny Howley, secretary of Curry Ladies' Land League, informed headquarters that three families, comprising twenty-five persons, were evicted on 25 May by R. St G. Robinson, agent of their landlord, Col. Richard Phibbs, Hydepark, London.[43] Just before Christmas, Charles Downing JP, armed with a Winchester rifle and accompanied by his steward and three others, served seventeen ejectment bills in Bonniconlon for non-payment of rent.

In Foxford and Kiltimagh the civil bill officer served 600 out of 700 bill processes within a month without the slightest molestation. All the tenants evicted in Kiltimagh belonging to the labouring class had paid their rents to middlemen who did not reimburse the landlord and, according to Thomas Carney, secretary of the local branch of the Land League, it appears to have been a device agreed between landlord and middlemen to evict the labouring tenants. Evictions also took place in towns. Patrick Staunton, the curate in Swinford, reported the eviction of Mrs Foy on 2 August by a pawnbroker called Meade. 'Some friends true to Land League principals put her back again'.[44] She became ill when she was harrassed by the pawnbroker and his son.

Martin Travers, secretary of Killaraght Land League, informed the Ladies' Land League that some landlords were putting pressure on prominent members of the local branch. His own landlord, Stephen Flanagan, son of Judge Flanagan, would not give Travers' father the grass of one cow on his farm. More importantly, the landlord party in Sligo attempted to muzzle the local press. Edward Gayer, editor of the *Sligo Champion*, complained to Thomas Sexton MP that he had been deprived of the contract for the county printing which he had held for a number of years because of his outspoken support for the Land League. 'The object is to crush an organ which has been in my hands a thorn in the side of a cruel landocracy.' [45]

Landlord Intimidation

So far the Land League agitation was one of 'passive resistance to the payment of rack-rents' but MacCormack for one was not convinced this could last indefinitely.

Passive resistance

42 see Appendix 35
43 NLI MS. 17,709
44 NLI MS. 17,709
45 Edward Gayer to Thomas Sexton, 9 July 1881, NLI MS. 17,709. Gayer attended Land League meetings all over counties Sligo and Leitrim, including those in Curry (18 Jan 1880), Benada (14 Mar 1880), Achonry (17 Oct 1880) and Ballymote (12 Dec 1880)

But we cannot expect that a popular movement upon a great question, vitally affecting millions of our poor people, would be carried on without some excess. Rarely, if ever, was such an agitation conducted without some abuse. And we can make allowances, when we remember the strong element of passion and prejudice invariably found in popular commotions.[46]

The bishop himself tried through his priests to direct the Land League movement in the diocese.

Since the very beginning of the land movement I have been endeavouring to keep the priests and people of this diocese as much as possible in harmony. I believed and still believe, in the prudence of sympathising with them, as far as we could do so without violation of principle, and of wisely directing them (the people) within certain safe lines, counselling order and justice, and abstention from outrage and violence, either in word or work.

Up to the end of 1880 his efforts had proved successful. 'I am happy to be able to state that in this diocese ... there has not been a single outrage on life nor on property, as far as I can learn, and most certainly no notable instance.' And all this despite the fact that there was no military detachment quartered in the diocese and very few extra police. This was to change dramatically in the early part of 1881.

Clogher
Riot
That year the police proceeded to Clogher on Saturday 2 April to protect a process-server, James Broder of Gurteen, serving writs on the estate of Arthur French.[47] Broder, armed with a bull-dog revolver, arrived outside the village accompanied by Constable Armstrong and three sub-constables, Walter Hayes, Michael James Donnelly and Patrick McNaughton, armed with rifles. They were confronted by thirty or forty persons, mostly women, boys and girls, with some men bringing up the rear. One young woman came forward. 'All we want are the processes', she said, 'and that you leave the roofs on our cabins for another year.'

What happened next is not entirely clear and depends very much on whose version is being related. At some point Constable Armstrong ordered his men to fire and two men were shot dead and a number of others wounded. The people then charged the police and seized Armstrong and Sub-Constable Walter Hayes. The whole fracas only lasted about ten minutes and left Armstrong dead with his skull crushed and Hayes seriously injured, knocked senseless on the road. When he recovered consciousness he made towards Mullaghroe but was intercepted by three young men and 'a man with a

46 F. J. MacCormack to Mgr Kirby, 9 Dec 1880, Kirby Papers 507, ICR
47 *C.T.* 9, 16 & 30 April 1881: J. C. McTiernan, 'A Fatal Affair at Clogher' in *Olde Sligoe*, pp 429-32; see also O'Rorke, *Sligo*, pp 381-2

whisker' who threatened to bash his brains out with a stone. Hayes pleaded with him, 'showing his scapular': 'if I had a priest you might dash my brains out.' A young woman, Mary Bermingham, intervened and saved his life (and later became his wife).

He had received five wounds to the head, one ear split and his hands bruised, while Armstrong had eight wounds to his scalp, both ears split and a contused wound on the arm. Dr Peyton told the inquest that he had been 'dreadfully beaten, that his skull was broken and in places the bones over-lapped each other.' Of those shot dead by the police, forty-five year old Joseph Corcoran, a tenant holding six acres from Thomas MacDermot, left a widow and six children. Brian Flannery, twenty-four years old and unmar-ried, supporting his father, mother and two sisters, was a tenant holding four acres from Arthur French.[48] According to the newspaper report Denis O'Hara 'was unceasing in his endeavours to alleviate the suffering of the people.'

There was a heavy military presence at the funerals of Corcoran and Flan-nery 'which were the largest ever seen in this part of the country'. The coffins were borne by young men to Kilcolman cemetery where Denis O'Hara and Edward Connington addressed the people 'and the entire multitude were moved to tears'. Ballaghaderreen Land League, with Denis O'Hara in the chair, passed a resolution the following Friday 'stigmatising the action of the police as most inhuman and unjustifiable firing on a unarmed crowd, most of whom were women and children.' The 'Buckshot Victim Fund' was opened for the relief of the families of Corcoran and Flannery, 'the first mar-tyrs of the land war' and subscriptions were received from MacCormack as well as Archbishop Croke of Cashel.

'Buckshot Victim Fund'

The inquest was held on Tuesday, 12 April, in the national school in Coolavin, with a large body of military and police present. John McDermott of Kilmovee and Denis O'Hara attended and John A. Curran, instructed by the solicitors of the Land League, acted for the next-of-kin. After an hour's deliberation the jury returned its verdict:

> That James Broder, Robert Armstrong, Michael Donnelly and Patrick Mc-Naughton feloniously, wilfully and of their malice aforethought did kill and murder the said Joseph Corcoran and Brian Flannery on 2 April and that Walter Hayes did feloniously kill and slay the aforesaid Corcoran and Flannery.

They were remanded in custody to Sligo jail to await their trial.

48 Those injured included Hugh Reilly, with buckshot wounds to the head, face and shoul-ders, Darby Duffy with similar wounds to the legs, Michael Casey with buckshot wounds to face and shoulder as well as a bayonet wound, Patrick Flaherty with buckshot wound, and Mrs Bridget Sharkey with a bullet wound in the head.

Kiltimagh Shooting

The Clogher riot was not an isolated incident. Three days later a similar incident involving shooting by the police took place at Knocknaskea in the parish of Kiltimagh.[49] John Kelly, the process-server in the Swinford division, with an escort of eleven RIC served writs on 5 April in Pollagh, Oxford and Cartoonbaun. At Knocknaskea a crowd of about 160 gathered and stones were thrown. Constable Roche ordered his men to fix bayonets and load. Kate Byrne, a young seventeen year old girl, was setting potatoes in a field nearby when she saw her grandmother, Bridget Madden, knocked down on the road by one of the police. She ran to help her and was fired on by Roche, receiving four gunshot wounds, one in the ankle, one in the knee and two above the knee. She did not regain consciousness until she was brought home.

Her father, William Byrne, a blacksmith, went to Kiltimagh, to get the dispensary doctor, Dr Bourke, but did not return. Apparently, he was recognised coming into Kiltimagh and taken into custody by Constable Roche. Kate's mother then sent her little son into town where he burst out crying that his sister was dying. Finally, Mrs Byrne went herself and was told that her husband had been arrested. Dr Bourke refused to go without a ticket, and when she got one he still refused to go because it was not the right one and when she got the right one, he still refused to go unless she provided a car. She then went to the local branch of the Land League and got the money for a car. Finally, when they reached the Byrne homestead after 10 p.m. Kate had been bleeding for seven hours. When the case came before Kiltimagh Petty Sessions on 18 May, Kate was carried into the court, fainted several times and was ordered home by the doctor. Later the adjourned case resumed but the judge refused to have Roche sent for trial and instead committed Kate and five other females for trial at the coming assizes.

Continuing Violence

Violent clashes between people and police continued throughout 1881. Fifteen members of the local branch of the Land League were summoned to Foxford Petty Sessions on 10 January for obstructing the police and the process-server in the discharge of their duty. They were indicted to the Castlebar General Assizes on 15 July. A force of 170 redcoats, a troop of cavalry and about fifty police were drafted into Foxford at the beginning of March during a trial for riotous assembly.[50] Some incidents ended tragically. When Henry McGloin of Aclare was on his way to Foxford Petty Sessions to proceed against some evicted tenants for resuming possession, he was confronted at Blackpatch by Andrew Jennings, an army pensioner, who pressed a

49 *C.T.* 21 May, 18 June & 2 July 1881
50 *C.T.* 5 Mar 1881

revolver into his ribs. The revolver misfired and McGloin shot and killed Jennings with his Winchester rifle.[51]

Over 170 police were concentrated on several estates in Kiltimagh in March.[52] Early in June the constabulary in Bonniconlon, backed up by a detachment from Ballina, ransacked the houses of members of the Coolcarney fife and drum band in an arms' search but no arms were discovered. Bernard Finn was arrested at Gurteen for a speech he made at a Land League meeting. In September, Casey, the Ballaghaderreen process-server, was escorted by 100 policemen from Charlestown to Kilmovee, thence to Carracastle and thence to Clogher. They were pursued by a huge crowd of women and children who threw stones and some women were arrested and two of them confined in Castlebar jail. Nevertheless, 'matters passed off without loss of life or limb on either side'.[53] When the police returned to Ballaghaderreen they were denied lodgings and smithies refused to work for them.

It was generally believed at the beginning of 1881 that the leaders of the Land League would be arrested in the near future. Davitt, in fact, was arrested on 3 February and detained in Portland Jail. The Ladies' Land League had been founded in New York by Fanny Parnell in October 1880 and, to ensure that the League continue to disburse its funds to evicted tenants, Davitt persuaded the executive at their meeting on 26 January 1881, against strong opposition from Parnell and Dillon, to sanction the formation of a provisional central committee of ladies, headed by Anna Parnell. The *Connaught Telegraph* (12 February) attacked the formation of the Ladies' Land League as 'ill-advised and unnecessary in the extreme'. 'God or nature never intended woman to take the advanced position in fighting for the emancipation of any nation or that the manhood of any nation could be so cowardly and demoralised as to entrench themselves behind the fair sex.' The ladies' central committee comprised seven members, two of whom were from Achonry, Anne Deane, Ballaghaderreen and Mrs P. J. Sheridan, Tubbercurry. [54]

Ladies' Land League

P. J. Sheridan, was one of the first to be arrested on 16 March 1881. A hotel-keeper in Tubbercurry, he was one of the leading organisers of the land agitation in the west and had been sent by the Land League to develop the organisation in the north of Ireland. On returning home to Tubbercurry to visit his wife who was ill, he was arrested on a warrant signed by the Lord

P. J. Sheridan

51 *C.T.* 6 May 1881
52 *C.T.* 12 Mar 1881
53 *C.T.* 1 Oct 1881: for other incidents mentioned see ibid 26 Feb, 12 Mar, 6 May, 11 June, & 27 Aug 1881
54 The others included Mrs Patrick Egan, Mrs J. E. Kenny, Miss Beatrice Walshe of Balla, Mrs John Martin of Newry and Mrs A. M. Sullivan of London.

P. J. Sheridan
Weekly Freeman
18 Dec 1880

Lieutenant. The police failed to get the requisite number of cars in Tubbercurry to convey Sheridan to the station in Ballymote and two cars had to be procured from Sligo. An immense crowd had gathered at the Ballymote station to cheer Sheridan on his way to Kilmainham. Sheridan's arrest was recorded in a local ballad.[55]

> *He spoke up for the tenants' cause and never changed his coat.*
> *His voice was heard round Sligo town and also Ballymote.*
> *But these wretches from the Castle watched this son of Granuail*
> *And from the bedside of his sickly wife they tore him off to gaol.*

A crowd of about 5,000, armed with spades, assembled in Tubbercurry on 5 May, led by banners and bands from Achonry, Tubbercurry, Kilmactigue, Killoran, Rooskey, Curry, Ballymote and Cloonacool, to cut Sheridan's turf.

> *But there are good hearts will think of him though far from sweet Sligo*
> *This is the truth you can't confute, for the public papers show*
> *How five thousand gallant Irishmen came headed by their bands*
> *And with their spades they made his turf and likewise sowed his lands...*
>
> *So cheer up, brave Mrs Sheridan, your good heart and be brave*
> *Your husband surely will come back, Kilmainham is no grave.*

Paris Fund

Patrick Egan, treasurer of the Land League, fearing the government might seize their funds, moved to Paris where he established the financial headquarters of the League. From there he furnished the Ladies' Land League with the bulk of their financial resources. Branches of the Ladies' League were formed throughout the country, including in Swinford on 25 February when over thirty women enrolled. They condemned the arrest of the 'brave Michael Davitt' and decided to hold a monster land meeting in Swinford at which Mrs Sheridan and Anne Deane would attend.[56] No less than three branches of the Ladies' Land League were formed in the parish of Ballymote, in Kilcrevin and Doo, in Emlaghfad and of course in Ballymote. [57]

Anna Parnell in Bohola

Anna Parnell arrived in Bohola to attend a Ladies' Land League meeting on Sunday 22 May, accompanied by bands from Swinford, Attymass and

55 Lines on the imprisonment of Mr P. Sheridan of Tubbercurry by N. McCarthy, Dil. P. 6819 316/91. See *S.C.* 1 Mar & 7 May 1881

56 President, Miss Kearns, vice-president, Miss Brennan, treasurer, Miss Strong, secretary, Miss Sarah Murphy *C.T.* 26 Feb 1881

57 *Kilcrevin & Doo:* Pres. Miss Maria O'Kane, Drumfin, V-Pres. Miss M. White, Kilmorgan. Treasurer, Miss M. Davey, do. Secretary, Miss Annie McGoldrick, Drumfin, assistant-Secretary, Miss M. Milmoe, Knockmenagh. Committee, Miss Braley, Kilmorgan, Miss Tighe, Knockmenagh, Miss Milmoe, Cloonlurg, Miss Bohan, Clooneen, Miss Kearns, Branchfield & Miss E. Tonry, Drumfin. *S.C.* 5 Feb 1881

Balla.[58] Anne Clarke read an address of welcome and the meeting, chaired by John O'Grady with Mathias Leonard of Kiltimagh also on the platform, thanked Archbishop Croke and A. M. Sullivan for their public defence of the Ladies' Land League. Archbishop MacCabe of Dublin had issued a pastoral on 13 March criticising the Ladies' Land League. 'They are asked to forget the modesty of their sex and the high dignity of their womanhood by leaders who seem utterly reckless of consequences.' Many bishops were embarrassed by the pastoral, particularly Croke, who declared that MacCabe's views were 'in opposition to the cherished convictions of a great and indeed, overwhelming majority of the Irish priests and people.' [59] In an open letter to A. M. Sullivan, who had rushed to the defence of the Ladies' Land League, Croke congratulated Sullivan for vindicating 'the character of the good Irish ladies who have become land leaguers' and challenging 'the monstrous imputations cast upon them by the Archbishop of Dublin.'

A vote of sympathy was passed at the Bohola meeting for those land leaguers who had been arrested, notably Michael Davitt and P. J. Sheridan of Tubbercurry. When Anna Parnell rose to speak, the men in the audience surged forward but she refused to speak unless the men let the women come to the front. 'Remember the condition of Mayo two years ago. You stood up for yourselves and you won the cause.' She described the shooting of Kate Byrne in Kiltimagh as 'the turning point in Irish history for this year.'

In fact, the turning point in Irish history that year was a completely different event. 'I see no prospect of tranquility', Bishop MacCormack had warned at the end of 1880, 'until the British government shall have passed a generous and thorough Land measure.'[60] At this point the people 'were awaiting with intense anxiety the turn of the tide, the settlement of the all-absorbing question in the approaching session of parliament.' On 7 April 1881 Gladstone introduced a major Irish land bill which, with its concept of dual ownership, offered substantial concessions to the tenants.

1881 Land Act

The Irish bishops, including MacCormack, at their meeting in Marlborough St presbytery at the end of April, unanimously approved the principles of the act but suggested numerous alterations. In particular, they requested that perpetuity of tenure should be granted to all tenants, that the protection of the bill should not be withheld from tenants owing arrears, that whenever a landlord demands an increase of rent which is refused by the tenant, the burden of proving that the present rent is not a fair one should be

58 *C.T.* 22 May 1881
59 *F.J.* 7, 12, 16, 18 Mar 1881
60 MacCormack to Mgr Kirby, 9 Dec 1880, Kirby Papers 507

cast upon the landlord, that in cases of eviction, some time should be given to the tenant to sell his tenancy and that steps should be taken to improve the conditions of agricultural labourers.[61] MacCormack himself, who was present that July in the gallery of the House of Commons when the land bill was before the committee of the whole house, was very impressed by Parnell who showed 'all the masterly skill and coolness of an able general'.[62]

SUPPLEMENT TO THE "WEEKLY FREEMAN"   APRIL 16TH 1881.

THE GENIUS OF THE BILL.

The above Picture accurately represents the "powerful influences" under which Mr Gladstone drafted his new Land Bill.

Dillon Arrested

Parnell, in fact, for tactical reasons treated the bill with reserve but Dillon, who rejected it out of hand, delivered an intransigent speech in County Tipperary urging the tenants not to pay excessive rents. He was arrested on 2 May for this speech and detained in Kilmainham prison where he was visited by Anne Deane shortly afterwards. She was impressed by the 'consideration and kindness of the governor,' but there was considerable public disquiet about the effect of imprisonment on his health. His family had a history of tuberculosis, a mother and sister had died from it years before and only the previous December his favourite sister, Christina, had fallen victim to it,

61 *C.T. & S.C.* 30 April 1881
62 *S.C.* 7 April 1883

while his brother, William, had to emigrate to Colorado to avoid the same fate. John was visited in prison by various people concerned about his health, including two English gentlemen, Mr Saunders and Dr Clarke. The visitors also proposed to visit Ballaghaderreen and Dillon wrote to Anne Deane requesting her to provide accommodation for them. 'Ballagh will become quite a famous city,' he told her.[63] Dillon's health continued to cause anxiety when he lost nine pounds, a serious loss for a man of six foot two whose normal weight was only ten and a half stone. He was released on 6 August on the grounds of ill health.

The Land Act became law on 22 August. It conceded the 'three Fs', fair rent, fixity of tenure and free sale. Fair rents were fixed for fifteen years by the quasi-judicial Irish Land Commission to which individual tenants and landlords could appeal for adjudication. A tenant paying his rent could not be evicted and he could sell his interest in the holding on the open market. The 1881 act recognised a form of dual ownership of the land between landlord and tenant and the great majority of the tenant farmers were happy with the new act and were prepared to desist from any further agitation. The stated aim of the Land League, however, was peasant proprietorship and it was in no way prepared to wind down its activities. Some of the poorer tenants, particularly in the west, were too deeply in arrears to clear their debts and thus could not benefit from the new act. Over 100,000 were in that condition and with these the leaders of the Land League were able to continue the agrarian agitation indefinitely.

The Three Fs

With the agitation continuing, the government decided to arrest Parnell on 13 October and detained him in Kilmainham jail. Many of the Land Leaguers, including Brennan and Kettle, were already detained there and were soon joined by Dillon, J. J. O'Kelly, Sexton and O'Brien. Chief Secretary Forster proclaimed the Land League as an illegal organisation on 20 October and over 800 local activists were detained without trial. One of these was Nicholas H. Devine of Tubbercurry, who was released early in March 1882 owing to ill-health. Thomas Lydon, a farmer and shopkeeper in Kilkelly, was imprisoned in Galway jail and while there was elected a Poor Law Guardian for the Aughamore division of the Swinford Union.

Kilmainham

From Kilmainham Parnell, Dillon, O'Brien, Kettle. Brennan, and Sexton signed a manifesto calling on farmers to pay no more rent but this was repudiated by the priests and bishops, the *Freeman's Journal*, the *Nation*, as well as many of the farmers who were content with the terms of the new land act.

No Rent Manifesto

63 Dil. P. 6885, John Dillon to Anne Deane, 6 July 1881

However, the situation had deteriorated so much that Gillooly of Elphin felt obliged to defer his *ad limina* visit to Rome in November.[64]

> Secret societies are spreading rapidly and great efforts are being made to prevent the people from following the guidance of the bishops. 'No Rent', 'No Land Courts', 'the liberation of Ireland from English tyranny' are now the watchword. The agitation has now become thoroughly revolutionary and the most brutal violence is being used to intimidate the people.

Gillooly set about establishing land committees in all parishes in his diocese to induce people to take advantage of the Land Act 'and to keep them out of illegal combinations'.

'Kilmainham Treaty'

While the leaders were in jail agrarian violence continued to escalate throughout the country. It was believed that only a freed Parnell could con-

Parnell and Dillon in Kilmainham *Vanity Fair* 1881

trol 'Captain Moonlight' and put an end to the violence that was stretching government resources to the limit. In April 1882 Parnell indicated that he was ready to make his peace with the government. An understanding was reached which became known as the 'Kilmainham Treaty' by which the government agreed to release the prisoners and introduce a substantial measure of relief for small tenants in arrears. Chief Secretary Forster resigned in protest. Parnell, Dillon and O'Kelly were released on 2 May and Davitt four days later from Portland jail. Parnell, Dillon and O'Kelly travelled over to Portland for Davitt's release on 6 May, planning to accompany him to London. There that evening they heard the news of the assassinations in Phoenix Park.

Phoenix Park Murders

The newly appointed Chief Secretary, Lord Frederick Cavendish, and the permanent Under Secretary, Thomas Henry Burke, were walking from the Castle to their residences in Phoenix Park when they were set upon and murdered by a group later identified as the Irish National Invincibles. Five of them were later hanged for the crime. James Carey, the informer, implicated several Land League organisers, including P. J. Sheridan of Tubbercurry, with

64 Gillooly to Mgr Kirby, 19 Nov 1881, Kirby Papers 425

the activities of the Invincibles.[65] Sheridan was said to be a member of the Invincible Directory and attended a meeting of the Dublin Directory disguised as 'Father Murphy' on his way to organise Invincible branches in the provinces. He agreed at the meeting for some weapons to be sent. Shortly after the assassinations Sheridan appears to have fled to America where he spent the rest of his life.[66]

There was an immediate outcry following the murders. MacCormack spoke for a large section of Irish opinion in a letter to the editor of the *Freeman's Journal* on 11 May condemning 'the treacherous and cowardly brutality of the foul and fiendish assassins': [67]

Reaction

> I am able to testify to the deep feelings of horror and indignation with which all (bishop, priests and people) are filled in view of that most disgraceful atrocity ... It is well that the Prime Minister should not look back from the work of conciliation ... To revert his policy or retard his projects of reform would crown the assassins' plot with success.

Gladstone did introduce a drastic coercion act which became law in July allowing in some cases trial without jury. But this was followed in the middle of August by the Arrears of Rent Act. Tenants with holdings of less than £30 valuation and owing substantial arrears which had accumulated over the bad years, were now liable for only one year's rent. The government agreed to pay half the balance and the landlord suffered the loss of the remainder. Some confusion existed in the early days of the act. 'The poor people are in a hopeless muddle about it,' according to Anne Deane who thought people should be sent to the large estates, like Dillon's, de Freyne's etc to instruct them. [68] Eventually, over 120,000 tenants availed themselves of the scheme. MacCormack penned an optimistic description of the state of the country in October 1883:[69]

Rent Arrears

> We are blessed this year with an abundant harvest and the condition of our poor country is promising well. The tenants will be able and willing to meet the just demands of landlords on the reduced scale of rents. The country is almost entirely free from agrarian outrage and peace is being rapidly restored in the war of classes.

Thus ended the first phase of the 'land war'.

---

65 Corfe, Tom, *Phoenix Park Murders*, p 137
66 See below, pp 284-5
67 qtd in *C.T.* 20 May 1882
68 Dil. P. Anne Deane to John Dillon, 19 Sept 1882
69 F. J. MacCormack to Mgr Kirby, 7 Oct 1883, Kirby Papers 181

CHAPTER TEN

Plan of Campaign

It became public knowledge early in 1883 that Parnell had debts totalling £18,000 obliging him to dispose of some properties in County Wicklow, and the idea of a testimonial was suggested and a committee formed to raise subscriptions from home and abroad. Among early subscribers were eight bishops, including Archbishop Croke, as well as three Achonry priests, Matthew Finn of Swinford, Peter O'Donoghue of Gurteen and Patrick Durkan of Carracastle.[1] MacCormack contributed £5 as an expression of his 'admiration for the brilliant service rendered by him to Ireland'.[2] He recalled watching from the gallery in the House of Commons in July 1881 when Parnell debated the Land Bill.

> It was a field day, great issues were at stake and Parnell was watching the fortunes of Ireland with all the masterly skill and coolness of an able general. There he stood inflexible among the cross fire of the enemy, a MacMahon[3] in intrepidity, a Sarsfield in dash and a Godfrey of Tyrconnell in unflagging perseverance to the end of the battle. I came away with the conviction that the Irish party was no small factor in the house, and that Ireland might count upon thorough exposure and ventilation of her grievances by that phalanx of energetic and eloquent men I saw mustered round the leader.[4]

George Errington, who had recently been appointed as chief secretary of the British embassy in Rome, immediately reported MacCormack's letter to Propaganda, suggesting that 'the comparisons of his with French and Irish military chiefs seem far-fetched, if not out of place, except in the supposition that the Parnellite movement may terminate in rebellion and foreign intervention.'[5]

The Vatican issued a circular, *De Parnellio*, to the Irish bishops deploring clerical support for the Parnell testimonial. 'The collection called the "Parnell Testimonial Fund" cannot be approved by this Sacred Congregation and

---

1 *F.J.* 9 April 1883
2 MacCormack to editor, *F.J.* 1 April 1883
3 General MacMahon was then President of France
4 qtd in *S.C.* 7 April 1883
5 SC Irlanda, vol 40, f 1111rv

consequently it cannot be tolerated that any ecclesiastic, much less a bishop, should take any part whatever in recommending or promoting it.'[6] The reaction in Ireland to the Roman circular was probably best described by McEvilly of Tuam:[7]

> It is right, however, to say in the interests of truth that this *furore* which unhappily has been excited, is *chiefly* owing to rumour, which has universally obtained, that it was brought about by English intrigue and English influence. There is nothing in this earth so calculated to madden the masses of the people – and these the most devoted Catholics, the most attached to the H. See – nothing so calculated to estrange them from any authority, temporal or spiritual, supreme or subordinate, as the idea that in any arrangements, England has anything to do. This I need not tell you (without attempting to justify or palliate it) arises from the undying recollection they have of the cruel wrongs inflicted on them, the terrible persecutions they suffered for over 300 years at the hands of England.

McEvilly, who did not share MacCormack's admiration for Parnell, was fully aware of the attachment the people felt for him. 'Right or wrong, the people are under the impression that it was owing to Parnell's action they have been rescued from the direst tyranny ever endured by a people from the landlord class.' This Roman intervention made little or no impact in Ireland and before the end of 1883 Parnell was presented with a cheque for £37,000.

MacCormack with McEvilly of Tuam and Gillooly of Elphin, arrived in Rome on 19 April 1885 after a twenty-one hour train journey from Cannes. Earlier that year he had written to Mgr Kirby in the Irish College a letter of introduction for Michael Davitt who also planned to visit Rome. 'He is by birth a child of the diocese of Achonry and one of her most distinguished children ... His name is deeply venerated by the great mass of the Irish race but nowhere more sincerely than here at home in his native diocese.'[8] 'I shall be pleased to meet him here,' he told Anne Deane, 'and show him in what esteem I hold him. It would delight you to hear a certain eminent prelate in London speaking of Michael Davitt during our trip.' [9] Early in May he met Davitt when he arrived from Naples but only spent part of a day in Rome before departing for Switzerland en route to Ireland.

MacCormack in Rome

> While he and I were together in one of the corridors of the Irish College, the Irish students rushed up, caught Davitt's hand and shook it with most

6   *C.T.* 19 May 1883
7   McEvilly to Kirby, 30 May 1883, Kirby Papers 123
8   F. J. MacCormack to Mgr Kirby, 2 Jan 1885, Kirby Papers (1885) 5
9   MacCormack to Anne Deane, 19 April 1885, Dil. P. 6892 (98)

Weekly Irish Times,
26 May 1883 (NLI)

hearty enthusiasm and then gave a cheer that could be heard up the Quirinal. I introduced Michael to the Archbishop of Tuam and to the dove of Elphin (Gillooly). He is looking well after his trip to the Holy Land. He got Masses offered at Jerusalem for his parents.[10]

In Rome Davitt also called on Croke of Cashel.

In all sixteen Irish bishops in Rome were entertained at a banquet in the Vatican on 8 May.

Today we dined at the Vatican, the guests of the Pope, and the Cardinal Secretary of State presiding in the name of His Holiness. The banquet was a splendid affair. There were five cardinals and forty all counted. I was received in private audience today by the Holy Father, and was alone with him for fully half an hour. We conversed in Latin and touched upon many subjects. I presented him £450 in the name of the diocese.[11]

Together with McEvilly and the Bishop of Galway, MacCormack returned home via Hamburg where they spent three weeks and on his return he was greeted enthusiastically in Ballaghaderreen by priests and lay people. A platform had been erected outside the cathedral and addresses were read from lay delegations from Swinford, Ballaghaderreen, Tubbercurry and Ballymote in the presence of almost every priest in the diocese. 'The nationalist sympathies of the prelate has endeared him to the people of his diocese.' [12]

10 MacCormack to Anne Deane, 8 May 1885, Dil. P. 6892 (99)
11 ibid
12 *C.T.* 4 July 1885

A general election was called in 1885. Parnell had established the Irish *1885 General Election*
National League (INL) in October 1882 which soon had branches all over the
country, providing Parnell with a countrywide organisation for his Home
Rule party. All candidates, before receiving the party's nomination, had to
sign a pledge that they would 'sit, act and vote' with the party. A convention
was called for each of the thirty-two counties attended by four representatives
of every local branch of the Irish National League and as many of the county's
priests as wished to attend. The Sligo convention at the end of October was
attended by a huge number of Elphin priests, with some from Killala as well
as no less than eighteen from Achonry, ten parish priests and eight curates.
Michael Staunton of Tubbercurry proposed Peter McDonald of Trinity College and he and Thomas Sexton were selected as candidates.

At the Mayo convention in Castlebar in the beginning of November,
Parnell himself took the chair and Denis O'Hara was appointed one of the
secretaries. Fourteen Achonry priests attended, eight parish priests and five
curates, including Thomas Loftus, the parish priest of Charlestown, who had
also attended the Sligo convention as his parish straddled the two counties.
There were also lay representatives from Charlestown, Ballaghaderreen, Bohola, Carracastle, Kiltimagh and Kilmovee.[13] Matthew Finn of Swinford
proposed Daniel Crilly of the *Nation* as candidate for North Mayo while
John Dillon, proposed by Denis O'Hara, was selected as candidate for East
Mayo. He had returned early in July from America where he had gone for
health reasons in early summer 1883 and had spent two years with his brother
William on a ranch about fifty miles from the city of Denver.

The election was a resounding triumph for Parnell, returning eighty-five *Parnell's Triumph*
Home Rulers in Ireland and one from Liverpool. The Liberals were exactly
eighty-six seats ahead of the Tories, leaving Parnell holding the balance of
power. Gladstone, the Liberal leader, a firm convert to a policy of home rule
for Ireland, introduced a Home Rule Bill early in April 1886 but failed to
bring his own party with him and the bill was defeated, leading to another
general election in July. Again Parnell and his party were returned with
eighty-six seats but this time, however, the Liberals were greatly reduced and
the Tories returned to power.

Poor seasons and falling prices in 1884 and the following years brought the *'Plan of Campaign'*
land question once more to the fore. A land purchase act (Ashbourne) had
been passed in 1885 which provided government loans to the tenant to purchase his holding at a rate which made the annual repayment less than the

---

13 *C.T.* 7 Nov 1885, see Appendix 36

previous rent. Parnell moved the Tenants' Relief Bill in September 1886 proposing an immediate review of the judicial rents and curtailing the power of landlords to evict if half the arrears and half the current rents had been paid. This measure was defeated by the government, sparking a new round of agrarian agitation. A 'plan of campaign' was drawn up in the autumn of 1886 and vigorously promoted at meetings throughout the country, mainly in the south and west, by John Dillon and William O'Brien, editor of the *United Irishman* and a dozen or so MPs.

Ballymote Meeting

William O'Brien was the principal speaker at a meeting in Gurteen on 10 October, with about 5,000 present and other speakers including the parish priests of Gurteen and Keash, as well as Denis O'Hara and the editors of the *Sligo Champion* and the *Roscommon Herald*.[14] Ballymote was occupied by a strong force of the Royal Irish Constabulary with orders to prevent a similar meeting taking place at the end of November.[15] A special excursion train had been laid on to bring in contingents and the police, unaware of the exact location of the meeting, lined up on the platform in Ballymote station. The train arrived but no one alighted. When the whistle was blown signalling the departure, the officer in charge ordered the police to board the train and follow the excursionists. The latter, as the train began to move off, leaped *en masse* from the train, while the puzzled police were whirled off towards Sligo. William O'Brien and J. J. O'Kelly addressed the meeting and by the time the police had finally returned to Ballymote and attempted to disperse the crowd, O'Brien advised them to go home quietly.

Dillon Tenants

A detailed description of the 'plan of campaign' appeared in *United Ireland* on 23 October. All tenants on an estate should agree on what was a fair rent and collectively tender that amount to the landlord or his agent. If the reduced rent was refused, it should be handed over to a trustee to constitute a fighting fund to suppport evicted tenants. One early test case was on the vast estate of Lord Dillon in East Mayo, extending from Ballaghaderreen in the east to Swinford and Ballyhaunis on the west and containing about 5,000 tenants paying annual rents of about £25,000. A meeting of the Ballaghaderreen branch of the Irish National League on 26 November, with Denis O'Hara in the chair and attended by John Dillon, William O'Brien and several hundred Dillon tenants, decided to adopt the 'plan of campaign' as published in the *United Ireland*. The tenants, who had sought a 25% reduction which was rejected by Hussey, Lord Dillon's agent, decided to hold weekly meetings, 'and show by their spirit that it is now or never' until Lord Dillon

14 *S.C.* 16 Oct 1886
15 *S.C.* 4 Dec 1886

settled with them.[16] Four offices were opened in Ballaghaderreen and rents were collected on every part of the Dillon property by three MPs, Crilly, Carew and William Redmond, who also collected rents in Kilkelly.

Tenants on other estates, such as two hundred on the Caddel and Costello estate in Gurteen, also adopted the 'plan'.[17] Denis O'Hara congratulated the Cloontia and Drimacoo tenants on the successful stand they made against their landlord, Jonathan Rashleigh of Cornwall. 'This was one of the best cases yet of the fear and dread the landlords have of the "plan".' [18] In Tourlestrane tenants of Roger McCarrick in Gortermone met his agent in Tubbercurry in December 1886 and asked for a reduction. 'Not one farthing', he replied and they left without paying. Fourteen tenants were served with ejectment notices on 28 December and decrees were obtained for possession, but in January 1887 the tenants adopted the 'plan of campaign' and lodged the rents less reductions in a war chest. They held out until the agent gave a 30% reduction for the 1886 and 1887 rents, with the landlord agreeing to pay all costs.[19]

As the Campaign continued tempers became frayed. A process-server was expected to post up ejectment notices on 1 January 1887 in the market square in Charlestown and police were drafted in to preserve the peace. When the first few constables arrived with Major T. K. Neild, the resident magistrate, Neild was mistaken for the process-server and brutally maltreated by an infuriated mob, whom the strenuous efforts of the parish priest were unable to restrain. Eight men were arrested and a few months later Neild, aged only forty-eight, died as a result of the beatings he received.[20] Several evictions were carried out in the barony of Gallen on the estates of Sir Roger Palmer, George A. Moore and Sir C. Gore and one eyewitness said he 'never beheld a more heartrending scene than to see young children cling to every available thing they could grasp at, to remain in the cabin that gave them birth.' Similar atrocities were carried out on estates between Swinford and Charlestown and over 100 police were drafted into Swinford for the Petty Sessions. [21]

Violence

In the village of Brackety on the summit of Slieve Horne on Lord Lucan's estate, Widow Kilgallon, Widow Mullany and Tom and Sarah Carolan were evicted. When word reached Kiltimagh, a large crowd set out for the place of eviction, led by the local fife and drum band and when they got there they

Evictions

16 *S.C.* 27 Nov & 4 Dec 1886
17 *S.C.* 1 Jan 1887
18 *S.C.* 29 Jan 1887
19 *S.C.* 18 Feb 1888
20 *C.T.* 8 Jan & 7 May 1887
21 *C.T.* 22 Jan 1887

heard that Widow Kilgallon was dying. 'A hundred stalwart hands burst the fastenings which the crowbar brigade had placed upon her door and she was returned to her bed.' A young woman darted from the crowd, seized the bailiff, placed a rope round his neck and attempted to hang him from a tree but he was rescued by the crowd. They and their band returned to Kiltimagh in triumph where all the houses were illuminated. [22]

MacCormack's
Support

The success of the 'plan' in any district depended very much on the support of the local bishop and his priests. MacCormack, in an interview with the *Daily News,* left little doubt about where he stood, though he claimed that the church tolerated the 'plan' rather than sanctioned it. 'There is a war of two classes going on. In a war many things must be tolerated that in a time of social peace could hardly be sanctioned. I could see no reason for restraining the priests in this diocese.' [23] The *Sligo Champion* had even less doubt about the bishop's support. 'It is an open secret that the movement had the entire sympathy of Dr MacCormack and his clergy.' [24]

Lord Dillon
Surrenders

Tenants of Lord Dillon, Lord de Freyne, Thomas Leetch and Roger Mc-Carrick held a meeting in Carracastle on 9 January 1887. En route to the meeting William O'Brien, accompanied by C. A. V. Conybeare, MP for Cornwall, and J. C. Shipman, an English barrister, stopped at the presbytery in Ballaghaderreen where they met Henry Doran, sub-agent of Lord Dillon. O'Brien nominated Conybeare and Denis O'Hara to enter into negotiations with Doran on behalf of the tenants and within ten minutes a written agreement was drawn up and signed undertaking to give a 20% reduction. 400 ejectments, prosecutions and writs for rents had been posted throughout the Dillon property during the previous ten days and the agreement undertook to reinstate all evicted tenants and pay the costs of all proceedings against tenants since the 'plan' had been adopted.

Carracastle Meeting

There was tremendous excitement when Denis O'Hara announced Lord Dillon's surrender at the Carracastle meeting. William O'Brien paid tribute to the tenacity of the Dillon tenants:

> What you have won you owe to the magnificent spirit of the Dillon tenants ... From the first day that John Dillon and myself opened this campaign here you have never faltered ... Today we are firing the last volley over the grave of landlordism in Ireland ... You owe something also to the fact that you have a true-hearted bishop in Dr MacCormack and that you have priests who like their bishop are not afraid to throw in their fortunes

22 *C.T.* 29 Jan 1887
23 qtd in *S.C.* 25 Dec 1886
24 *S.C.* 15 Jan 1887

with you as in the old days of struggle and persecution ... In a fight like this one man like Father O'Hara is worth a whole park of artillery and the whole Royal Irish Constabulary put together.[25]

The meeting was chaired by the parish priest who was joined on the platform by the parish priests and curates of Charlestown, Kilmovee and Curry, all part of the vast Dillon property. Later that evening the rents on the McCarrick and Leetch properties were collected and deposited with trustees.

A meeting was held in Keash on 27 March to urge tenants on the estate of Owen Phibbs of Corradoo to adopt the 'plan of campaign', in spite of the fact that the police had posted up placards proclaiming any assembly in the district. [26] Welcoming the MPs, Crilly and Sheedy to the meeting, the parish priest, Patrick Scully, declared that 'the men they had amongst them today brought Lord Dillon to his knees and I cannot see why they could not bring a petty little fellow in Keash to his knees.' The Phibbs estate consisted of 100 holdings averaging about twelve acres each and Crilly and Sheedy, as well as Martin Henry, the curate in Gurteen, and Jasper Tully, editor of the *Roscommon Herald*, all urged the tenants to adopt the 'plan'. Phibbs evicted two of his tenants, John Keane and John O'Connor, and their houses were occupied by 'emergency' men. The evictions were strongly condemned by the Gurteen and Killaraght branches of the INL and the victims were pledged all kinds of material support.

Keash Meeting

Patrick Scully
(*courtesy Jim Finan*)

A meeting was called on 17 May for the purpose of erecting National League huts for Keane and O'Connor and their families and contingents and bands arrived from Ballinafad, Ballymote, Gurteen, Kilfree and all the neighbouring districts with horses and carts and all the other necessary implements in abundance. Patrick Scully and his curate, Patrick McDermott, were there from an early hour and directed the workmen during the entire day, closely watched by a force of twenty-five policemen under the command of District Inspector Dale of Ballymote. Before the end of the day Keane's house was completed and O'Connor's greatly advanced, and Scully thanked all who had come. 'Let nothing satisfy you until landlordism is swept from the face of this land.' McDermott had received a letter from William O'Brien informing him that 'as long as there was sixpence in the chest of the League they will stick to the people of Keash and the tenantry of Phibbs.' [27]

National League Huts

25 *S.C.* 15 Jan 1887
26 *S.C.* 2 April 1887
27 *S.C.* 21 May 1887

The 'plan of campaign' continued in operation on the Phibbs estate for a number of months. Another demonstration on Sunday 14 August was attended by William O'Brien and John Ellis, MP for Nothingham, the parish priests of Ballymote and Bunninadden as well as two curates, Martin Henry, Gurteen and John Conlon, Achonry, and INL delegations from Ballaghaderreen, Ballymote, Culfadda, Cloonloo and Gurteen. Phibbs had sent a letter to Scully requesting to meet O'Brien to sort out the differences between himself and his tenants and after two hours' deliberations he capitulated.[28]

Coercion

To deal with the 'plan of campaign' the government decided to introduce in March a severe coercion bill to strengthen its hand in dealing summarily with boycotting, conspiracies against rent, intimidation, resistance to eviction, rioting, unlawful assembly and inciting others to commit any such crimes. The bill was bitterly opposed by the Irish members. It was denounced at a clerical conference in Tubbercurry on 11 April by MacCormack and twenty-one priests as 'oppressive, unjust and unwarranted in the present peaceable condition of the country' and they warned that the coercive legislation would drive the people from open combinations into secret societies.[29] It was wrong to deprive the people of the right to hold public meetings and to suppress all open legitimate combinations as these were the only ways that tenants could get reductions in the present exorbitant rents and thus save themselves and their families from eviction.

An estimated 10,000 were present with contigents from Swinford, Charlestown, Ballina, Foxford, Kilmovee, Kilkelly, Bohola etc at a demonstration in Straide organised on Sunday 22 May by the local INL branch to protest against the coercion bill.[30] Denis O'Hara and Michael Davitt told the crowd that the main aim of the coercion bill was to crush the movement that began in Mayo in 1879. The bill passed into law in July and in August the Irish National League was suppressed. A convention of the League in Sligo on 7 August was attended by delegates from twenty-five branches, more than half of which were from the diocese.[31] Davitt denounced the coercion act which 'did away with the three principles which are the very foundation of political liberty, legitimate combination, the rights of free speech and of public meeting.'

Persico Mission

John Healy, Coadjutor Bishop of Clonfert, had complained to the Vatican in December 1886 that boycotting was rife in Ireland and that priests were

28 *S.C.* 20 Aug 1887
29 *S.C.* 16 April 1887
30 *C.T.* 28 May 1887
31 Killoran, Bunninadden, Kilmactigue, Ballinacarrow, Ballymote, Keash, Tubbercurry, Achonry, Cloonloo, Gurteen, Collooney, Killaraght & Curry. *S.C.* 13 Aug 1887

deeply involved in the agitation. The Pope decided to send over his own representative, Monsignor Persico, to find out the true state of affairs and he arrived in Ireland in July 1887. He listened to both sides. He travelled by train to Sligo on Thursday 11 August and was greeted at the station by Laurence Gillooly and a number of priests, including Thomas Judge, a professor in Maynooth, and Dominick O'Grady, the curate in Carracastle. A number of people were invited to meet him while he was Gillooly's guest, among whom were a number of landlords, including Lord de Freyne, the O'Conor Don, Sir Henry Gore-Booth and Colonel Wood-Martin. De Freyne and Gore-Booth had estates in Achonry, the latter around Ballymote where he was generally well accepted. The *Sligo Champion* was hard put to justify their invitation: 'It is better to let exterminating rack-renters like Lord de Freyne and bigoted political outcasts like the O'Conor Don, make a case, if they have one, in an open and legitimate way, than to have their views presented at the Vatican, through the agency of lies and bribery.' Before leaving Sligo Gillooly and Persico visited Lissadell, the residence of Sir Henry Gore-Booth with whom they lunched.[32] Before the end of the year an English mission, headed by the Catholic Duke of Norfolk, was despatched to Rome, presumably to use papal influence to coerce the Irish clergy into withdrawing from the agitation. John Dillon reacted furiously:

> These very men who were now calling in this strange assistance to the back of the English government in Ireland were the men who only a short time ago used to say to Englishmen that Home Rule meant Rome Rule. What kind of rule meant Rome Rule now?' As Irish Catholics, although they revered the Pope as the head of their religion, they would 'no more take their political guidance from the Pope of Rome than from the Sultan of Turkey.[33]

Bishop Carr of Galway was appointed Archbishop of Melbourne early in 1887 and MacCormack received thirteen out a total of nineteen votes from the Galway clergy in the election of his successor. He was also recommended to Rome by all the western bishops as well as Carr himself who told Rome that he believed MacCormack possessed 'in an eminent manner all the qualifications requisite to rule with success the united diocese of Galway and Kilmacduagh.'[34] Carr and MacCormack had spent some time together as curates in Westport. MacCormack was transferred to Galway on 18 April 1887 and one of his last acts in Achonry was to appoint Denis O'Hara parish

MacCormack Transferred

32 *S.C.* 13 & 20 Aug 1887
33 *F.J.* 19 Dec 1887
34 SOCG 1026 (1887) ff 172rv,173r

priest of Kiltimagh following the death of Mathias Leonard, and he himself personally installed O'Hara on Sunday 20 February. [35]

Achonry Election   Achonry parish priests, presided over by Archbishop McEvilly, met in Swinford chapel on 13 June 1887 to elect a successor to MacCormack. Out of twenty votes, one was invalid, nine went to Denis O'Hara, eight to Michael Staunton of Tubbercurry, and one each to Thomas Gilmartin, professor of ecclesiastical history in Maynooth, and Matthew Finn of Swinford. The results were transmitted to Rome by the archbishop and also published in local newspapers.

Denis O'Hara   The name of Father O'Hara is best known to the people in connection with the Plan of Campaign of which he was fitly styled the "clerical Captain-General". Always a Nationalist of the most advanced type, he was from the cradle days of the Land League a prominent figure on its platform. As far back as the famous Gurteen meeting he stood by the side of Michael Davitt and was one of the most pronounced speakers on that historic occasion. Ever since it was to him western Leaguers looked for their cue. In public reports he was described as the soul of that movement west of the Shannon. He was the first to adopt the Plan of Campaign in Connaught. It will be in the recollection of our readers how he laboured day and night to fire the flagging zeal of priests and people on and around Lord Dillon's property. He organised a series of political gatherings around Ballaghaderreen and it was owing to the fire kindled on that occasion that the campaigning flame spread to the neighbouring counties. No one could doubt the purity of his motives through all this movement, and we congratulate those distinguished priests of Achonry who have shown their characteristic discrimination in placing at the head of the list for episcopal honours an untiring and unbending Campaigner.[36]

Denis O'Hara

That account may have done much to endear O'Hara to readers of the *Western People* but it was hardly likely to endear him to the Roman authorities. Which was why the British authorities, courtesy of John Ross of Bladensburg, had the *Western People* cutting promptly despatched to Rome. A second cutting from the same paper was also sent, giving an account of a speech by P. J. Smythe, the editor, at an Irish National League meeting in Newport, where he described how the police were 'struggling like bloodhounds on the leash, to spring upon the leaders of the Irish people'.

Last night I had the pleasure of accompanying the member for North Mayo on a moonlighting expedition. (Cheers and laughter). The authori-

35 *C.T.* 26 Feb 1887
36 *W.P.* 18 June 1887

ties need not be alarmed; there was no agent shot on the occasion, no bailiff's ears cut off; the object of our mission was a peaceable one. We were on a visit to the clerical captain-general of the Plan of Campaign, Father Denis O'Hara of Kiltimagh. (Loud cheers) Nevertheless, we were pursued for eight miles by a car-load of police, who scarcely left a booreen on the way that they did not search for us.[37]

The Connacht bishops met in Maynooth on 23 June to discuss the Achonry election and MacCormack, together with Tuam, Clonfert and Killala recommended the thirty-eight year-old O'Hara to Rome. Writing in Latin, they strongly defended his political activities:

Connacht Bishops

The sole object of his involvement in politics is to defend poor Catholic tenants who are unjustly and cruelly oppressed by Protestant landlords. Acting always with the advice and under the direction of his former bishop who counselled prudence, he stayed scrupulously within the limits of the law. Greatly admired by the people because of his zeal and care of the poor, he is oblivious of his own interest and his rejection at the present time would bring the church and the Holy See into disrepute. He always showed himself able in settling disputes in cases of justice as well as promoting Christian charity among the people.[38]

They were opposed to the nomination of an outsider, claiming it would create discord and unrest in the diocese which might take years to eradicate. In separate short submissions both Gillooly of Elphin and Healy, co-adjutor of Clonfert, rejected all three candidates as unsuitable: O'Hara, because of his political activities, Gilmartin, because of his youth – he was only thirty years old – and Gillooly considered Staunton's relationship with both priests and people unlikely to foster unity in the diocese.

From Portumna Healy sent a lengthier submission four days later to Cardinal Simeoni.[39] Strongly opposed to the Plan of Campaign and priests' involvement in it, his complaint to Rome led to the Persico Mission. He informed Simeoni that O'Hara was closely associated with Michael Davitt, the founder of the Land League, and was an active propagator of the Irish National League. He had become famous as the 'clerical captain-general' of the Plan of Campaign which had been condemned by the Irish supreme court as a 'criminal conspiracy'. He was a 'nationalist of the most advanced type', and his promotion to the episcopacy would be regarded generally by people as papal approval of the land war. Though Staunton was non-political

Healy's Letter

37 *W.P.* 11 June 1888
38 SOCG, vol 1028 (1888), ff 478rv, 479rv, 480r
39 SOCG, vol 1028 (1888), ff 482rv, 483r

and a learned theologian, 'he is said to be cranky (*asper*) and not above suspicion of being ambitious'. Gilmartin was the most suitable candidate, having been a professor in the diocesan seminary and later dean and now professor of ecclesiastical history in Maynooth and in spite of his youth had all the qualities necessary for a bishop.

McEvilly's Letter   McEvilly took up his pen again in defence of O'Hara, writing to Cardinal Simeoni on 1 July pointing out that while the majority of the Connacht bishops voted for O'Hara, no bishop voted for any of the other candidates.[40] McEvilly reiterated that O'Hara in his defence of the poor always remained within the limits of the law and always acted with the advice and guidance of his former bishop, 'who was universally acknowledged among his colleagues to be conspicuous for his prudence.' He then went on to describe in detail the background to O'Hara's political activities:

> Everybody knows that the poor Irish farmers of this region are unjustly oppressed. Commissioners appointed by the government to examine this serious question in a public enquiry, declared that taking everything into account, these poor tenants are compelled to pay annually twice the just rate for their lands and reduced the annual rents substantially in all cases and to a half in several cases.

> By the sweat of their brow these poor Catholic farmers made these sterile lands fertile and then were compelled to pay the full price for lands thus cultivated by their own labour. Thus, they are not only deprived of the reward of their labour, which cries out to heaven, but are even compelled to pay the full price for the improved condition of these lands produced by their own work. If they refuse, they and their families are driven into exile or into the hated workhouse, which a former prime minister, Mr Gladstone publicly described in the British parliament as a veritable sentence of death. As a result, our people depart in droves into exile every day and the population is reduced by a half or more.

It was to remedy this state of affairs and defend the rights of the poor that Denis O'Hara had fought so strenuously. McEvilly wondered whether it would be wise to reject such a worthy priest, especially since his former bishop, who knows him intimately, recommends him so strongly. If O'Hara had acted imprudently in exciting popular agitation against the law, McEvilly would never have recommended him. He cited one recent example of O'Hara's activities where he played the role of peacemaker between Lord Dillon and his tenants, and by using his influence to restrain the tenants, he

40 SOCG, vol 1028 (1888), ff 485rv, 486r

established a settlement between landlord and tenants acceptable to both sides and thus restored peace. Finally, McEvilly warned about a libellous letter sent to individual bishops. 'No one would be surprised if the same false allegations were also sent to the Holy See.'

It was a timely warning as the very next day, 2 July, such allegations were indeed sent to Rome contained in a lengthy document in English, unlike episcopal correspondence, which was normally written in Latin and, in fact, it is one of very few documents in English in this particular dossier.[41] The author, Patrick Staunton, then a curate in Ballymote and a younger brother of the candidate, professed to have been asked by several priests in the diocese to provide Rome with information on O'Hara. He claimed that O'Hara had a very poor academic record which he could vouch for personally as he had been a classmate of O'Hara in Maynooth. 'So low was the standard of success in his theological studies that they barely enabled his professors to pronounce him so far qualified to be admitted to Holy Orders.' McEvilly had already pre-empted this particular allegation, having informed Rome that he had taken care to examine with his own eyes the Maynooth College records where he had found that O'Hara had gained honours.

Staunton alleged that O'Hara, when he was curate in Kiltimagh, constantly quarrelled with the parish priest, Mathias Leonard, and the local doctor 'with both of whom he exchanged blows over a sick bed on at least two occasions.' 'During his time in that locality his relations with the parish priest and the medical doctor were the standing scandal of the parish.'

Next he turned his attention to O'Hara's lifestyle:

Staunton Letter

Patrick Staunton
(courtesy Dr Tom Staunton)

41 SOCG vol 1028 (1888), ff 487rv, 488rv, 489rv

He is a noted card player and gambler who at times when his bishop was absent gathered into his house all the noted card players, lay and clerical, for miles around. He plays all night long and for high sums – often he won or lost as high as twenty or thirty pounds sterling in a single night; and it is well known that frequently after spending the whole night at the cards, he rose up from the card table and walked straight to the altar to say Mass.

Nor did O'Hara's family escape criticism, alleging that his brother was a 'most disreputable drunkard' who was 'frequently dragged drunk through the public streets by the police.'

But his most trenchant criticism was reserved for O'Hara's political activities and 'his proclaimed hostility to the English Queen and the English government in Ireland.'

He is a politician of extreme views. He is a wild Land Leaguer and an out and out advocate of the 'Plan of Campaign'. Since the first days of the Land League he has been a familiar figure on its platforms. His wild words and extreme teachings always elicited the wildest cheers at these meetings. No paid orator of the Land League would venture to advise the strong measures, which he did to excited multitudes from public platforms. His thoughtless utterances have startled all prudent people. They were amazed to hear such words come from one whose duty was to preach peace and forbearance. His language went so far as to draw on himself the sharp attention of the government authorities who were responsible for the peace of the country and the lives of the people; and it is no secret that the government authorities warned the bishop that unless he restrained the wild speeches of Father O'Hara, they would be obliged to send Father O'Hara to prison.

At the Land League meeting in Curry in January 1880 O'Hara called upon women and children to resist government forces assisting process-servers 'until they would get bayoneted'. He urged men to replace then the bayoneted women 'and even in the teeth of the policemens' rifles resist and defend their rights to the last'. Such language was directly responsible for the Clogher riot on 2 April 1882 which 'sent a thrill of horror through the country' when two tenant farmers and one police sergeant were killed. 'It was told – not without a shudder – how on that occasion Reverend Denis O'Hara passed by the body of Hayes, the dying policeman, and refused to administer to him the last sacraments though requested to do so.'

Finally, Staunton accused O'Hara of having neither respect nor loyalty for the Holy See. When the Holy See issued a rescript criticising the clergy's involvement in the Parnell Testimonial Fund, O'Hara 'went about sneering at the motives that dictated the document and ridiculing in public the rescript'. He not only contributed himself to the fund but also organised a public subscription to it for which he earned the friendship and gratitude of the president of the Ladies' Land League.[42]

Such – please Your Eminence – is the character of the man whose name is now before you as a candidate for the episcopacy. A man destitute of the talents and learning so necessary for that high office, with nothing in his personal or family history to recommend him, but, on the contrary, much that good Catholics consider highly objectionable. A person who has sneered at and ridiculed the highest ecclesiastical authority and has publicly preached contempt and resistance to civil authority at the expense of the peace of the country and the lives of the people.

Staunton's letter probably did more harm to his brother's candidacy than to O'Hara. Rome was too long in the tooth to take such a document seriously. However, this was not the case with the next communication it received on the subject.

It was a letter, dated 9 July, from the Duke of Norfolk, England's senior Catholic aristocrat.[43] The letter in Italian, probably translated by the British embassy in Rome, contained very little that was new. Its importance derived from the status of the author rather than the contents. 'In ordinary circumstances it would never have occurred to me to interfere in any way in such an affair, but at the present time the nomination of the bishop of this diocese is a matter of the greatest importance.' Norfolk described O'Hara (whom he elevated to the dignity of Canon) as one of the most violent priests in the west of Ireland and claimed he was related to John Dillon, to whom he principally owed his election. He mentioned O'Hara's presence on the platform with Michael Davitt at the Gurteen meeting and his part in the Clogher riot where Sergeant Armstrong was killed. 'He never uttered a word of censure against those who had committed the crime.' O'Hara's nomination would be regarded as 'a public calamity not only by laity of good will but also by the good old priests of Achonry and the neighbouring dioceses.' On the other hand, Canon Staunton was a man of moderation and strength of character who had never taken part in the Plan of Campaign and 'had resolutely opposed P. J. Sheridan and his bloody comrades' in Tubbercurry.

Norfolk's Intervention

Meanwhile, MacCormack himself recommended O'Hara as a 'very self-sacrificing energetic priest, who has a great love of the poor, and a thorough ecclesiastical spirit,' a great church and school builder and a ready and willing

MacCormack's Letter

42 Anne Deane
43 SOCG, vol 1028 (1888), ff 496rv, 497v; another copy, f 494rv

preacher with an accurate knowledge of theology and canon law. 'In my experience I have not known a better priest.'[44] He then went on to deal specifically with the allegation that he was a politician of too advanced a type to be promoted to the episcopacy:

> In reply to the allegation I am able to testify that he consulted me, and got my sanction, before he took part in the several political and social movements that have engaged the priests and people for the last 6 or 7 years in this country. Father O'Hara always succeeded in keeping his flock from every kind of secret society, by guiding them through open legitimate combination. And the action he took was ever in the interests of the poor tenants, and has been uniformly successful.
>
> Hence, I am of opinion that Fr O'Hara would, if chosen, be a good bishop, would never compromise the episcopal character, or embarrass the Holy See, by any imprudent or injudicious opinions or actions.

Gilloolys Report   The next two documents to arrive in Rome were written in French, the first of which, dated 12 July, was penned by Gilloly of Elphin.[45] All the bishops of the province at their meeting on 23 June were agreed on the ineligibility of two of the candidates, Gilmartin because he was too young and Staunton because he was 'ambitious and dictatorial'. Staunton had voted for himself at the election and since then his brother, 'who is entirely under his influence, was engaged in destroying in a revolting manner the character of his rival, O'Hara.' He disagreed with his fellow provincial bishops about the merits and qualities of O'Hara and in fact, he believed that Achonry had no priest with the qualities necessary for the government of a diocese. Thus he opted for an outsider and this for two reasons. Firstly, the leaders of the Nationalist Party left nothing undone to promote the candidacy of O'Hara, using the Parnellite newspapers to influence the priests of the diocese and the bishops of the province. O'Hara was one of the clerical leaders of the Nationalist Party and thus closely linked to its political leaders. They used exactly the same tactics when Dublin was vacant and will doubtlessly do exactly the same every time a diocese becomes vacant. Their aim is understandable, to reward their clerical chiefs and make for themselves more zealous friends and defenders among the bishops and increase their influence in the church.

> This is precisely what makes me feel strongly the urgent necessity of resisting this dangerous form of dictation and intimidation by demonstrating that candidates who use or encourage it, will be judged unworthy of the episcopacy. If it is necessary, as I believe, in the difficult times in which we

44 MacCormack to Mgr Kirby, 7 July 1887, Kirby Papers 343, ICR
45 SOCG, vol 1028 (1888), ff 498rv, 499r

live, that a bishop has a sincere and active sympathy for the poor, it is no less indispensable that he be a man of recognised prudence and justice so that he can prevent excesses among his flock and maintain order among impulsive priests who love to lead people and seek popularity and who, if they were promoted to the episcopacy, would foster political agitation as our political leaders seek and desire. They would throw themselves into the political movement, cause unrest in society and degrade the church by subjecting it to the tyranny of the people.

O'Hara's promotion would be seen as a reward for his political views, which could not fail to provoke violent hostility on the part of the English government and people against the Irish clergy and even against the Holy See itself. This would have the effect of delaying indefinitely concessions from the government and parliament, particularly in the educational sphere. 'Would it really be prudent to provoke such hostility, especially in the present circumstances?'

The next communication also in French, dated 22 July 1887, was sent to Mgr Jacobini and signed by John Ross of Bladensburg.[46] Nothing is known of the author other than the details which emerged from his letter including his address, Victoria Barracks, Windsor which suggests that he was a military man. It appears that he was active in diplomatic channels, having visited Rome in the spring of 1886, where he was warmly received by Mgr Jacobini and had recently visited Dublin and had discussed Irish affairs with Mgr Persico on the previous Sunday when Ross gave Persico some documents 'on serious questions which ought to occupy his attention'. He described Persico's mission as 'to re-establish the peace which had been so shattered by the deplorable events which had taken place in this country'. He also knew Staunton whom he had met three or four years previously and whom he regarded as a moderate man who had his difficulties in Tubbercurry. 'In these difficulties he had always acted in a manner which safeguarded his principles while not too strongly opposing the opinions of the people.' Ross did not think that Staunton was a Nationalist, at least when he knew him three or four years ago. *John Ross of Bladensburg*

O'Hara was a completely different character, a violent and fanatical Nationalist. (Ross enclosed the *Western People* cuttings which described O'Hara as the 'clerical captain-general of the Plan of Campaign.') O'Hara in private life was a kind and good man 'and those who knew him loved him for his aimable qualities'. However, there was no doubt that he was the Nationalist

46 SOCG, vol 1028 (1888), ff 500rv, 501rv

Party candidate for the episcopacy. Ross also mentioned that O'Hara had been threatened with imprisonment but was not sure of the details. He thought it was in 1881 or 1882 and that Chief Secretary Forster had written to Dr MacCormack to restrain O'Hara but the letter may indeed have been written by Cardinal MacCabe. 'At least I believe it is a fact that a letter was sent to Dr MacCormack on the subject.'

Monsignor Persico

Mgr Persico wrote a few days later from Dublin where he was still engaged investigating the Plan Of Campaign.[47] Having obtained accurate information on the three candidates, he concluded that none of them was worthy of the episcopacy, O'Hara because he was an ardent Nationalist and playing an active role in the present agitation, the other two because they lacked the necessary qualities. He suggested that Rome should call for a new election but no decision was taken for the next few months and Persico wrote again on 1 November.[48] It was absolutely necessary to fill the vacancy as there were serious problems because the vicar-capitular, Matthew Finn of Swinford, was incapable of ruling the diocese. Neighbouring bishops had urged Persico to write to Rome and seek an immediate remedy.

New Election

Rome decided to hold a new election and wrote on 18 November to inform Archbishop McEvilly of their decision.[49] A new *terna* was to be elected, i.e. three new candidates, excluding the three previous candidates. McEvilly presided at this election which took place in Swinford on 12 December. Of the twenty votes cast (nineteen valid), Thomas Loftus of Charlestown got twelve votes, John Lyster, an Elphin priest and president of the diocesan seminary there, got four and there was one each cast for Matthew Finn of Swinford, John McDermott of Ballymote, and Owen Stenson of Bunninadden.[50]

Stauntons'
Intervention

Michael Staunton

Michael Staunton wrote on 23 December to Cardinal Simeoni expressing his opposition to the selection of Thomas Loftus and this was followed by a letter from his brother, Patrick, on 3 January 1888.[51] There was obvious collusion between the two brothers as not only did they make exactly the same criticisms of Loftus but they also outlined them in precisely the same order. The only difference was that Michael's letter was in Latin and consequently shorter, while his younger brother wrote in English and more expansively. Their first criticism of Loftus was that he was academically deficient. When he first presented himself at the age of twenty for admission to Maynooth he

47 SOCG, vol 1028, f 507r
48 SC Irlanda, vol 4
49 SOCG, vol 1028 (1888), ff 471r, 473v
50 SOCG, vol 1028 (1888), ff 464rv, 465rv: Acta, vol 258 (1888), f 56rv
51 SOCG, vol 1028 (1888), ff 474rv, 475rv & 509rv, 511rv

was rejected and only obtained entry the following year with great difficulty. In the twenty years since his ordination he never once preached a sermon nor gave a catechetical instruction. They also accused him of excessive drinking and card-playing with lay-people and prone to violent outbursts of anger. Recently he had severely beaten two men, one of them at a station-house, leaving them prostrate. (Loftus was a big man, standing six foot three!)

Furthermore, he was closely associated with Fenians, one of whose leaders was his brother, Michael Loftus, in whose house Fenians frequently held meetings. He was also active in the Land League and the Plan of Campaign and his victory at the clerical election was celebrated by bonfires wherever the Plan of Campaign was established. Loftus was also related to many of the parish priests in the diocese who canvassed vigorously for him:

> The clerical relations of Rev Thomas Loftus went around among the parish priests at the approach of the convention and, aided by the Land Leaguers through the diocese, gave them to understand that unless they voted for Rev T. Loftus the 'oblata' (offerings) on Christmas Day would be few, that the members of their flock would 'boycott' them, and that their revenues would suffer severely at the coming Christmas. To any person who knows the excited state of Ireland just now, it will be no wonder that these threats had their effect and that as a result of such terrorism Rev Thomas Loftus got 12 votes.

Patrick Staunton also added that after the election a memorial was addressed to the Holy See by the clerical relations of Loftus asking that no outsider be appointed.[52]

The bishops of the province were obliged to hold a meeting within ten days and submit their comments on the candidates with their recommendations to Rome. However, MacCormack of Galway, Gillooly of Elphin and McEvilly had already made arrangements to travel to Rome to celebrate the Pope's jubilee and asked and were given permission to hold their meeting in Rome, taking with them the recommendations of the other bishops in writing. The meeting took place on 30 December at the Minerva Hotel in Rome.[53]

Bishops in Rome

The comments of the bishops on forty-five year old Loftus bore out some of the criticisms levelled against him by the Staunton brothers but were expressed in much more moderate language. He had not been 'among the more learned students' in Maynooth and 'was very deficient in the duty of preaching'. Although he had never been seen drunk, he was fond of drinking and playing cards with lay-people often to a late hour at night. John McDermott

52 No such memorial was found in the Roman archives
53 SOCG, vol 1028 (1888), ff 466rv, 467rv, 468r; Acta, vol 258 (1888), ff 56v, 57rv, 58r

who was about fifty-five, had gained first place in his class in Maynooth and later taught theology for a number of years in All Hallows and in the Irish College, Paris. However, he was fond of money, much to the scandal of priests as well as lay people and did a lot of travelling.

John Lyster

John Lyster, who was about forty years old, (in fact, he was only thirty-eight) had also obtained first place in his class in Maynooth and had been granted an honorary doctorate by Leo XIII a few years ago. For fifteen years he performed with outstanding success the duties of professor and rector in the diocesan seminary of Elphin. The archbishop and the two other bishops present in Rome recommended him without reservation, as did Conway of Killala and Healy, coadjutor of Clonfert, in writing. Bishop Duggan of Clonfert, expressed no preference for any of the three candidates as, he said, he knew none of them. From Cork Mgr Persico wrote on 2 January 1888 expressing his preference also for Lyster. [54] Four days later Gillooly wrote a private letter to the secretary of Propaganda informing him that Lyster was the only one worthy to be nominated. By now there could be little doubt about the final outcome. At their general meeting on 23 January, the cardinals of Propaganda Fide, under their prefect, Cardinal Simeoni, recommended Lyster's appointment to the Pope and on 21 February 1888 John Lyster was appointed Bishop of Achonry.[55]

He was consecrated in Sligo cathedral on Low Sunday, 8 April by McEvilly, assisted by Gillooly and Healy in the presence of the Bishops of Derry, Ardagh and Galway and a large gathering of the clergy of both Elphin and Achonry. MacCormack preached the sermon and left little doubt where his sympathies lay with regard to the 'plan of campaign':

Here in this unhappy country, the poor, the oppressed are in a vast majority. How could the bishop remain passive when he saw the poor ground down by unjust laws, when he saw them hunted like vermin from the places assigned to them by God, when he saw the poor, who were made a little less than angels by God, made by their fellow-men a little less than beasts?

The *Freeman* commented:

Dr Lyster is an Irishman. He would be something less if in his sympathies he did not go out to the people in the infamies that are imposed on them today in the outraged name of the law ... If he sought a model ... we would commend ... the prelate who preceded him.[56]

54 SC Irlanda, vol 43, f 8r
55 Acta, vol 258 (1888), ff 53rv, 54r: SOCG, vol 1028, ff 461rv, 462r, 463r: *Hierarchia Catholica*, vol VIII, p 72
56 qtd in *C.T.* 14 April 1888

Five days later Lyster was received in the cathedral in Ballaghaderreen by the canons, clergy and a large gathering of people of the diocese.[57]

It was generally believed in Ireland that Rome would react favourably to the Irish situation and there was consternation when the contents of the papal rescript became known. It was issued by the Congregation of the Holy Office on 20 April while Mgr Persico was still in Ireland and without waiting for his full report. The 'plan of campaign' was denounced on three grounds, that it was unlawful to break contracts such as tenants had voluntarily entered into with their landlords, that the courts were available for those who sought rent reductions and that the funds for administering the 'plan' had been extorted from those contributing. The Roman condemnation may not have reflected Persico's thinking and Cardinal Manning told Dillon that Persico had no part in it. Certainly, the description Persico sent to Rome in November 1887 of Healy of Clonfert showed scant regard for that anti-Campaign bishop. 'This prelate is unpopular not only with the bishops but also with the people. In one instance while administering Confirmation in a parish, the people left the church *en masse* ... He would never be received as a bishop either in Clonfert or in any other diocese in Ireland.'[58]

Papal Rescript

The editorial of the *Sligo Champion* reflected the popular feeling: 'The papal rescript has filled the people of Ireland with dismay, anger and indignation. Rome has taken sides with Dublin Castle ...We have asked for bread; we have been given a stone.' Gurteen INL passed a resolution stating that 'His Holiness has again been made the victim of the British government and has been induced to denounce the Plan of Campaign and the boycotting of land-grabbers.'[59] John Dillon discussed with Archbishop Croke how they should react to the papal rescript, and a few days later an article, inspired by Croke, appeared in a newspaper arguing that the 'plan' would indeed deserve to be condemned if it fell within the categories mentioned in the rescript. As the whole document was based on a mistaken view of the landlord-tenant relationship, it could not possibly be regarded as applying to Irish conditions. Croke himself wrote later that year to Cardinal Simeoni warning him 'that as long as the Roman authorities believe or affect to believe that they understood better the real state of what is called the "Irish question" in all its aspects than the bishops and priests of Ireland, there will be very strong opposition to Roman opinions and intervention in our purely political affairs.'[60]

57 Udienze, vol 227, f 1027rv
58 SC Irlanda, vol 42, ff 886rv, 887r
59 *S.C.* 6 May 1888
60 SC Irlanda vol 43, ff 551rv, 552r

Dillon's Reaction   John Dillon launched a powerful attack on the papal rescript on 7 May:

> Are we to be freemen in Ireland or are we to conduct our public affairs at the bidding of any man who lives outside Ireland? ... I say without fear that if tomorrow, in asserting the freedom of Ireland, we were to exchange for servitude in Westminister servitude to the cardinal who signs that document or any body of cardinals in Rome, then I would bid goodbye for ever to the struggle for Irish freedom.[61]

At a later meeting in Dublin, referring to the possibility that priests might in future be prohibited from political activity, he insisted on the right of a priest to be a citizen as well as a spiritual leader:

> The attachment of the Irish people for their priesthood and for the See of Rome has survived the rack and the gibbet, but I doubt very much whether it would survive if we were to see the priest forbidden to sympathise with the poor and, as they were told to do by the Great Master, to denounce iniquity even when it was in high places. I say woe to the Catholic Church in Ireland if the priests are driven by the court of Rome from politics, and woe still more if we know it has been done at the bidding of a corrupt English ministry.[62]

Lyster's Response   However, Lyster's response was quite different. When he received the decree from Rome in May, he convoked a meeting of the clergy in each of the deaneries in the diocese, explained the decree to them and ordered all parish priests and curates to abstain from the condemned practices and to deter the people from participating in them. No ecclesiastic should preside or even be present at political meetings. When an encyclical letter on the subject was issued early in July, he had it translated and published and a copy sent to each individual priest with an accompanying letter from himself pointing out what their pastoral duty was. In this way 'all were warned, both clergy and faithful, that their conduct and behaviour should comply in every way with the teaching and warnings contained in the decree of the Holy Office and the Pope's encyclical letter.' He assured the Roman authorities at the end of November that since the day of his consecration early in April until now, no meetings were held in the diocese, no public speakers came there and no speeches were made in favour of the Plan of Campaign or boycotting. None of the clergy opposed the decision of the Holy See nor attended political meetings.

'All the people – the poorest and most wretched in all of Ireland – who heard the Holy See's warning in favour of the English government and cruel and inconsiderate landlords, even though they were disappointed

61 *F.J.* 8 May 1888
62 *U.I.* 26 May 1888

and saddened, and even, I might say, depressed, accepted it from their hearts.[63]

Lyster's account to Rome did not conform to the reality on the ground. While some more cautious priests may have used the Roman intervention as an excuse to withdraw, those as deeply committed as Denis O'Hara remained as active as ever. Others, like Martin Henry, the curate in Kilmovee, appeared to go into a state of denial. Warning local landlords and agents not to build a fool's paradise for themselves after recent events in Rome, he told the Kilkelly and Glan INL:

> Let them not imagine that our Holy Father the Pope had the smallest intention of preventing rack-rented tenants from looking after their just rights. No, my friends, Rome loves Ireland and she will never throw any obstacle in your way, while honestly and bravely defending you against the oppressor.[64]

Henry continued to direct the Plan of Campaign on the Gibbons' estate which had begun in 1887, and when a large number of ejectment notices were served in spring 1889, he met the agents of Mrs Gibbons and arranged a satisfactory settlement, six shillings in the pound for the last two years and the landlady to pay all costs.[65]

John O'Grady described to the Bohola INL 'the pitiful sight he himself witnessed' of the eviction on the estate of George A. Moore of Mrs Mc Nicholas and her family of nine, the eldest being nine years old and the youngest, seven weeks:

Bohola Eviction

> ... Their appearance outside from want and misery would take them back to the evil doings of landlords in '47 and '48. The only shelter the poor creatures had was the canopy of heaven. The sight, he felt sure, would bring tears from Balfour himself (if he had any to shed) and he was surprised that George A. Moore would disgrace the memory of his late-lamented father and he hoped he would put a stop to his agent and his base and brutal bailiff, Larry Sheridan, in trying to induce the land-grabber to take the homes of the poor, unfortunate evicted tenants.'[66]

The secretary, John P. O'Connor, suggested that Dillon should 'bring the conduct of Moore, the novelist and exterminator, under prominent notice' when parliament re-opened.[67]

63 SC Irlanda, vol 43, ff 553rv, 554r
64 *S.C.* 7 July 1888
65 *S.C.* 9 Mar 1889
66 *S.C.* 8 Dec 1888
67 27 Dec 1888, John P. O'Connor to John Dillon, Dil. P. 6219

Dillon, who continued to use strong language at meetings week after week urging tenants to join the 'plan', was arrested and sentenced to six months imprisonment in Dundalk on 20 June 1888. Kilkelly and Glan INL under Martin Henry condemned in the strongest manner the 'consigning of honest John Dillon to a lonely prison cell.' [68] The tag 'honest John Dillon', which remained with him throughout his long political career, may well have been coined here. Once in prison the old concern about his health reasserted itself and Lord Salisbury made the brutal remark that Dillon would be 'far more formidable dead than alive.'[69] By the middle of September, with less than half his sentence completed, there was a marked deterioration in the state of his health and the government decided to release him.

The 'campaign' funds were running dangerously low and Dillon had made up his mind while in prison that a major effort would have to be made to raise funds overseas. He had already informed William O'Brien that one of them had to go to Australia and that he was willing to go if O'Brien managed to stay out of prison. In spite of the fact that O'Brien was sentenced to four months in Clonmel jail, Dillon sailed on 6 March 1889 on a mission which was to keep him away from Ireland for the next thirteen months. During this period Anne Deane wrote frequently to him from Ballaghaderreen, keeping him informed of the news from Ireland and especially from her own neighbourhood. 'It will seem a very long time while you are away, but yet it is a great relief to me when I think you are out of Balfour's reach and away from this harsh horrible weather.'

Others were not so lucky. John Fitzgibbon, a shopkeeper and local activist in Ballaghaderreen, was given six months hard labour on 7 May. 'They are doing all they can to ruin him.' The Walshes from Kilmovee were prosecuted for threatening people who were working for a bailiff. 'There were three of them without a bit of land and all first rate campaigners.' She gave one of them the coat and vest Dillon had given her to give away 'and the poor little man seemed most gratified.' 'I give him all the credit for keeping Mrs Gibbons' tenants up to the fight.' Later the Walshe brothers were given two terms of imprisonment but by early August they were out again and 'as brave as ever'. By then John Fitzgibbon was also free. He had been imprisoned for two months in Castlebar jail but 'was none the worse for it' and his business had flourished while he was in. He continued to be shadowed by two policemen 'even going to Mass'.[70]

68 *S.C.* 7 July 1888
69 Lyons, *John Dillon*, p 97
70 Anne Deane to John Dillon, 21 & 27 Mar, 8 May, 19 June, 6 & 22 Aug 1890, Dil. P. 6885

Another name that figured frequently in Anne Deane's correspondance was Tom Towey of Barnaboy in the parish of Ballaghaderreen, one of the leading Plan of Campaign activists on the Dillon estate who paid a huge personal price. 'Tom Towey unfurled the Plan of Campaign on the Dillon estate three years ago and brought the noble rack-renter to his knees. Now Tom has been thrown on the roadside to perish.' [71] Nevertheless, he continued his agitation and the arrest of 'brave gallant Towey' was recorded in a local ballad describing how crowds followed the police to the station from where he was escorted to Galway jail.[72]

Tom Towey of Barnaboy

Towey appears to have been released by early August when Anne Deane described him as 'flourishing' and the INL continued to make grants to him as an evicted tenant. 'Tom Towey is the only prosperous man to be seen. The league is standing well to him.' [73]

Two other local men, Michael Morrisroe and Michael Rodgers, who were committed to Castlebar jail for two months, were celebrated in the same ballad which recounts how the Ballaghaderreen people saved Morrisroe's turf:

For grand Ballagh town, I pen it down and can't say half enough.
When they carried round about the town a hundred cribs of turf,
And the bands did play upon the way, till they got up, you know,
And built it up close to the house of Mr Morrisroe.

Towey of Barnaboy continued to be victimised and his plight was not helped when grants from central funds ceased in 1891. 'They are treating him harshly and trying to make an example of him and were it not for some children he has in America he would have starved since the grants ceased ... In the early days of the Land and National League he did good work and we would not like that he would suffer ...'[74] Towey was given a grant of £2 from central funds but his problems continued as he explained two years later to Dillon, then on a visit to Ballaghaderreen:

I am now in straitened circumstances, for owing to the tide affairs have taken in America, my children say they are out of employment and unable to aid me. Under heaven I have no one to whom I can appeal for assistance ... and you will pardon me for asking your kind attention to my plaint. I am a wounded soldier of the land war but I never surrendered or turned my back to the foe ... but should it lie in your power, I would with confid-

71 *W.P.* 25 May 1889
72 A New Song on Michael Morrisroe, Thomas Towey and Michael Rodgers, Dil. P. 6819 316/92
73 Anne Deane to John Dillon, 6 Aug & 9 Sept 1889, Dil. P. 6885
74 John Cawley to J. F. X. O'Brien, 17 & 19 Sept & 8 Oct 1891

ence and without other external pleadings, appeal to you in the hope that I have not been lowered on your list of friends.[75]

He was still soliciting and receiving grants the following year: 'I am sensibly aware of your many onerous duties and shy at the many troubles I have given you, yet I am emboldened to make this appeal in the hope you will not now at the eleventh hour cast me off but relieve me as was your wont.'[76]

William O'Brien

William O'Brien
(NLI P&D)

More Evictions

After his release from Clonmel jail, where he had been sentenced to four months and suffered harsh treatment for his refusal to wear prison dress, William O'Brien continued his agitation. He was prosecuted once more in the autumn of 1889 and detained this time in Galway jail. 'Poor Mr O'Brien is in prison again. I am glad he is received to Galway. He will not get bad treatment there and the prison is healthy.' Anne Deane's prediction proved accurate as she learned later from Bishop MacCormack.

'He was just after visiting Mr O'Brien and said to tell you you need not be uneasy. Every care is taken of him. The governor and his wife would do anything for him and he is well watched by friends. The Bishop told me not to speak about it but he thinks he was sent there with orders to let him have anything but his liberty. Please God he will come out all right.'

O'Brien, who even put on weight in prison, was released in time for Christmas which he spent with Archbishop Croke.[77]

Evictions continued to be carried out right across the diocese in the summer and autumn of 1889 while the menfolk were absent in England trying to earn the rent. Two women, both called Mellet, were evicted early in June from their holdings in Callow while both their husbands were away, one in England and the other in America. Bridget had seven in her family, the eldest fifteen and the youngest three, while Margaret had six in her family, the eldest also fifteen, and the youngest five. The jambs and sashes were taken out of their houses and the windows and doors built up with lime and mortar, to prevent them re-entering. Their landlord was a minor called Graham, whose agent, coincidentally, was also called Mellet, Michael J., from Swinford.

Eighty-seven-year-old Widow O'Neill was evicted from her home in Bohola which she and her ancestors had occupied for 150 years, on the instructions of her landlord, the novelist George A. Moore. She re-took possession of her

75 Thomas Towey to John Dillon, 4 Nov 1893, Dil. P. 6806
76 ibid, 27 April & 14 May 1894
77 Anne Deane to John Dillon, 28 Aug, 4 & 25 Sept & 25 Dec 1889

home for which she was fined ten shillings at the Swinford Petty Sessions and when she refused to pay was sent to Castlebar jail for seven days. In the same month, what the *Western People* described as 'a holocaust of eviction notices', was served on the Relieving Officer of the Swinford Union by Sir Roger Palmer and his nephew, Colonel Brabazon.[78]

There was renewed conflict on the Dillon estate in the autumn and winter of that year. 'The people are less inclined than ever to pay rents and Lord Dillon is going to evict.'[79] The evictions began on 8 September carried out by a posse of 100 policemen with bailiffs and emergency men and over 150 families lost their homesteads. 'In the majority of cases wives and children as well as aged parents were sent adrift upon the world while the breadwinners were away in England trying to earn the rent.'[80] Henry Doran, the bailiff, refused to stop the evictions. Deane painted a gloomy picture for Dillon:

Dillon Estate

> Yesterday and today the town is filled with police carrying out evictions over the Dillon estate ... the organisation is broken up and the priests can do nothing, but they are a worthless party here. I feel in a very bad state about the state of things all around but I despaired long ago of this place. Since Father Denis left everything has gone to the bad.

Later she told him: 'The Dillon tenants who are evicted have no one to help them. Father Keveney and Father Roger O'Hara are not much good for them.'[81]

In Australia Dillon followed the events at home with great interest:

> I was very much interested to hear about the evictions. Write anything fresh that occurs. I don't think that these people can expect much from the League because the estate broke away from the Plan and it would appear from your letter that Father Keveney has offered to pay costs.[82]

In Clooncarha in the parish of Kilmovee a girl, who was put out in a dying state, was attended by the curate, Martin Henry. P. J. Gordon, who was tried in Charlestown for advising several tenants who were evicted to resume possession of their homes, was sentenced to six months imprisonment.[83]

A convention of all INL branches on the Dillon estate was held on 17 October in Ballaghaderreen with each branch represented by a priest and three lay delegates. A resolution demanded a reduction of six shillings in the

Ballaghaderreen Convention

78 *W.P.* 8 & 15 June 1889; see also 3 Jan 1891
79 Anne Deane to John Dillon, 6 Aug 1889, Dil. P. 6885
80 *C.T.* 14 & 21 Sept 1889, *W.P.* 21 Sept 1889 Among those evicted were John Byrne and Mrs Donohoe, Ishlaun, John? Towey, Barnaboy, John Kilgariff and Luke Feeney, Kilkeeran, Pat Woods, Knockaconny, (Ballaghaderreen). Pat Morrisroe, Raherolus, Pat Craig, two families called Higgins and Pat Frain, Clooncarha (Kilmovee)
81 Anne Deane to John Dillon, 9 & 18 Sept 1889, Dil. P. 6885
82 John Dillon to Anne Deane, 17 Oct 1889, Dil. P. 6885
83 *C.T.* 28 Sept 1889

pound for all tenants and the re-instatement of those evicted or else there would be all out war. No deputation went to Hussey, Lord Dillon's agent in Loughglynn, but the resolution was sent by post. 'Lord Dillon's reply will be the signal for war or peace.' [84]

> The tenants on the Dillon estate are not paying but I have no confidence in them. All the priests are worthless as nationalists. Some creatures who owed three and four years (rent) were evicted and two were sent to jail today for retaking possession, a man and a woman. I believe the Dillons are not able to fight and if the people had any spirit they would have an easy victory.

She continued to be pessimistic. 'Lord Dillon's people are warning that they will fight this year but I don't depend on their leaders.' But she sounded somewhat more hopeful at the end of November:

> The Dillon tenants are on strike. They want the terms they got when the Plan was invoked. If they have any pluck at all they will succeed. The land-lords are in mortal terror of the Plan. They are wonderfully subdued all round.

A settlement was reached, brokered by Bishop Lyster, early in December and the tenants got reductions of six and four shillings in the pound. 'I can tell you I was heartily glad of the settlement. The League has enough on hands without the Dillon tenants.' Later she described it as a 'settlement in a kind of a way' as Lyster was not fit to manage land agents, the people were too weak and 'the priests are very worthless so nothing can be done.' [85]

Tenants' Defence Association

The Tenants' Defence Association, to raise more money for the relief of evicted tenants, was launched in October 1889. 'I see the new organisation is going to be started at last', Deane told Dillon, 'I hope it will do some good.' Denis O'Hara had formed a branch in Kiltimagh. 'It seems to me this Tenants' Defence Association is gaining great strength and that a large sum will be raised by it. William O'Brien seems to support it and (I) do not see that the government can touch it.'[86] Anne Deane was unaware that it was O'Brien's brainchild and that he had written to Dillon in the middle of June to inform him about it.

Mayo Convention

The Mayo county convention of the Tenants' Defence Association was held in Castlebar on Wednesday 15 January 1890 with Denis O'Hara and seven other priests from the diocese attending as well as lay delegations from

84 *W.P.* 26 Oct 1889 It was fighting talk but Anne Deane was not impressed
85 Anne Deane to John Dillon, 30 Oct, 12 & 27 Nov & 9 Dec 1889 & 12 Feb 1890, Dil. P. 6885
86 Anne Deane to John Dillon 9 Oct, 27 Nov & 26 Dec 1889, Dil. P. 6885

Attymass, Ballaghadereen, Bohola, Charlestown, Kilkelly, Killasser, Kilmovee, Kiltimagh, Midfield, Straide and Swinford and also a special delegation from the Swinford Board of Guardians. [87]

Letters of support from McEvilly of Tuam and Conway of Killala were read. Lyster, who had already sent his subscription to the Sligo convention, also wrote: 'Our people are not only within their rights in their present action but they are positively bound to defend their families and their homes against unwarranted and unjustifiable aggression.' Denis O'Hara proposed that the priests and delegates at this convention be hereby appointed secretaries and treasurers of the branches of the Tenants' Defence Associations in their respective parishes, where they were to summon meetings on 19 January to make arrangements for parochial collections a week later. 'I think you will also be surprised to see so much money raised for the Tenants' Defence Fund,' Anne Deane told Dillon, 'I hope it will go up to £50,000.' [88]

Dillon's Collection

Dillon himself was also enjoying success in his fundraising efforts in Australia. £1,000 was raised at a great meeting in Melbourne and a week later, £2,000 in Sydney. 'It will be all required to fight these wicked landlords who are trying to drive the people away.' [89] Dillon was surprised at the generosity of the Irish in Australia, particularly those in Sydney. 'Yesterday evening I spoke at a meeting in the suburbs of Sydney. There seems to be no bottom to the pockets of the Irish of Sydney. Think of our getting £250 last night after all that Sydney has given before now.' [90] When he finally turned for home by way of Honolulu and the United States his tour of Australia and New Zealand had collected over £33,000 by the time he reached Ireland on 20 April 1890. But in spite of the sum raised by Dillon and that collected by the new Tenants' Defence Association, money remained the perennial problem. The Plan of Campaign was costing in excess of £80,000 p.a. in supporting evicted families. To meet the on-going costs and to put an end once and for all to the constant nightmare of disappearing funds, Dillon and O'Brien planned a major tour of the United States in the autumn of 1890.

Blight Again

Meanwhile, another recurring problem raised its ugly head when the potato crop was once more struck by blight. 'The stalks are as withered today as they would naturally be on 1 October', according to the Swinford Board of

---

87 *C.T.* 18 Jan 1890 M. Keveney Adm Ballaghaderreen, M. Henry CC Kilmovee, J. O'Grady PP Bohola, Thomas Loftus PP Charlestown, P. Durkan PP Carracastle, J. Cullen CC Swinford, P. Hunt PP Straide. For lay delegations see Appendix 38. *Swinford Board of Guardians:* M.H. Jordan, A.J. Staunton, P. A. Mulligan, C. Davitt, J. Irwin

88 Anne Deane to John Dillon, 12 Feb 1890, Dil. P. 6885 In fact, it reached over £60,000

89 Anne Deane to John Dillon, 8 & 15 May 1889, Dil. P. 6885

90 John Dillon to Anne Deane, 17 Oct 1889, Dil. P. 6885

Blight Again   Guardians on 13 August, and at the end of that month they 'viewed with alarm the prospects of the coming winter and spring owing to the almost total failure of the potato crop.' From Kiltimagh the relieving officer, John Moran reported: 'I have not the slightest doubt in stating that the greater number of the small land-holders in my district will inevitably become desti- tute and that nothing less than a second Famine is imminent.'[91] Lyster and priests of the Swinford deanery called on the government to save the people from famine as the potato crop had failed entirely in all the parishes in the dean- ery. 'It is for those poor and hard-working people, so devoted to us and resplendent with noble virtues, that we are bound to appeal.' They urged the necessity of creating public works and particularly the construction of a line of railway between Claremorris and Collooney. [92]

Denis O'Hara was also troubled by the prospects. 'That there will be great distress everyone seeing the potatoes must admit. They are small and soft and rotten. I don't know any place in Ireland where the people are less able to meet a bad year than around Swinford.' He had some potatoes dug and in- spected by himself and a journalist from the *Pall Mall Gazette*. 'My honest opinion is that the potato crop is far worse this year than in '79.' He suggested holding a public meeting and wondered whether Dillon could attend it.

If you are going to America soon it would be well for many reasons that you would bring pressure to bear on the government to do something at

Market Street, Swinford

Market Street, Swinford.

91 Swinford Board of Guardians to John Dillon, 13, 19 & 26 Aug 1890, Dil. P. 6803
92 *C.T.* 30 Aug 1890

once. There are no persons of influence in this unfortunate Union and I fear there will be very little done for us if you do not help us.

If Dillon could come to a public meeting in Swinford it would draw public attention to the plight of that Union. 'The landlords could get a great squelching this winter. The people will not be able to pay rents.'[93] Lyster told Dillon that he had promised the Swinford deanery to write to or interview Balfour in connexion with the blight: 'It may not be much use; at the same time it is right, I think, to let these people see that we recognise their responsibility and we put it upon them.'[94]

The meeting took place in Swinford on Sunday 21 September with contingents from all the surrounding towns both inside and outside the diocese.[95] Dillon had left Dublin on Saturday and *en route* received addresses at Castlerea, Claremorris and Kiltimagh where he spent the night in the spacious new parochial house which Denis O'Hara had completed less than two years previously. Dillon and O'Hara were met by a dozen brass bands as they arrived from Kiltimagh. Westport Board of Guardians had appointed a delegation of eighteen Guardians from Westport, Louisburgh, Newport and Achill to discuss with Dillon what could be done 'in the present alarming state of the crops in the West.'[96]

Swinford Meeting

Dillon was scathing about the strong military presence in Swinford for the meeting, including two companies of the Royal Irish Fusiliers, two troops of cavalry from Dublin and 150 policemen, and soldiers were said to have been billeted 'in Mrs Cuniff's pig-stables on straw beds.'

> No greater crime or outrage has been committed, when a peaceful meeting of distressed people cannot assemble for the purpose of taking counsel with their representative, without being insulted and intimidated and outraged by this gigantic force of police and military ... £1,400,000 is spent each year on the police force ... If half of that was applied to useful purposes we would never have any distress in the country.[97]

Dillon urged the tenants to 'eat' the rent rather than starve:

> If I see that any man among the people of East Mayo has been base or

93 Denis O'Hara to John Dillon, 30 Aug & 1 Sept 1890, Dil. P. 6769
94 Dr Lyster to John Dillon, 5 Sept 1890, Dil. P. 6766
95 Balla, Ballaghaderreen, Ballina, Ballyhaunis, Bohola, Carracastle, Castlebar, Castlerea, Charlestown, Claremorris, Foxford, Killasser, Kilmactigue, Kiltimagh, Knock, Loughglynn and Tubbercurry. *C.T.* 27 Sept 1890
96 *Labour World,* 21 Sept 1890
97 Swinford INL later passed a resolution 'most strongly condemning Mr Balfour's action in sending soldiers to peaceable meetings at which were gathered a starving peasantry asking for work and not for alms.' *Labour World,* 11 Oct 1890

cowardly enough to pay an unjust and unfair tribute and then starve and see his children starve, he need look for no help from me. If we are willing to go into prison in the cause of the tenantry of Ireland I expect every man in this country to go into prison if need be rather than lie down like slaves and starve after paying some pampered landlord his rack-rent.

Denis O'Hara urged tenants to follow Dillon's advice:

The landlords of Mayo have taken away £400,000 within the past ten years ... They want the rent. They think it is the old story:

To labour hard, to labour late
To feed a titled knave, man,
And all the comfort that's for you
Is found beyond the grave, man.

... Our good bishop wrote more than once to the Chief Secretary asking him to send men around the district to see for themselves the distress ... It appears his answer is to send the military and the police ... If he (Dillon) is imprisoned, and it is almost certain that he will, there is a spirit abroad that nothing can imprison.

Martin Henry wondered why Ireland was a prey to recurrent famines:

How strange it is that Ireland is the only nation on the globe that suffers from this potato blight. The reason is, what God has given, man takes away. What you earn by the sweat of your brow is swallowed up by hungry rack-renters and exterminators ... We demand that the government come to the rescue. If they are not willing ... let them hand over the keys of the old house in College Green and we promise them that Irish brains and Irish courage will meet and effectively meet the difficulty.[98]

All speakers were convinced that the government should introduce public works immediately but Michael Davitt had doubts about the efficacy of public works to relieve famine.

The people hit hardest by the failure of the potato crop are not the people who pay the biggest rents. Neither are they the people to whom relief works will be of any benefit ... If relief works are opened it is not the starving peasant who finds enployment. It is the snug and comfortable farmer who combines road-making with farming during a long career of county jobbery to do the minimum of work for the maximum of pay.[99]

Such had been the widespread practice in previous periods of famine.

98 *C.T.* 27 Sept 1890
99 *L.W.* 27 Sept 1890

Dillon, accompanied by O'Hara, left for Ballaghaderreen on Sunday night and their car was so closely followed by a police 'shadowing' party, that they were run into by the police car, on pulling up at the hotel. When they arrived in Ballaghaderreen at 9.30 p.m. the town was illuminated with a huge crowd parading the streets led by the fife and drum band. The following day the country people flocked into town and assembled outside Monica Duff's clamouring for a speech and Dillon duly obliged. Extra police had been drafted in but despite the police tar-balls were thrown in dozens from backyards and archways and several persons were arrested and by 11 p.m. the spacious new barracks was crowded with inmates. [100]

Ballaghaderreen

There was a particular reason for the close police attention Dillon received. He had been arrested, together with William O'Brien, a few days before the Swinford meeting and both were now out on bail pending their trial and under continuous surveillance from 20 August to 8 October. On 9 October they were driven through Dublin city in broad daylight and spent the evening in a friend's house in Dalkey. At midnight they walked the few hundred yards to Dalkey Harbour, rowed quietly out to a small fishing vessel, slipped away under cover of darkness and made for France. Then on 15 October came the news that they had turned up at Cherbourg. After three days in France, they sailed for New York on 25 October and arrived there on 2 November. Their departure marked the end of the second phase of the land war. Shortly after they left, Ireland was rocked by a political bombshell which drove the agrarian agitation off the centre stage it had occupied since 1789.

*Dillon & O'Brien
Escape*

'The Plan of Campaign',
Vanity Fair, 1887

100 *C.T.* 27 Sept & 4 Oct 1890

CHAPTER ELEVEN

The Parnell Split

The Parnell Divorce

Captain O'Shea had filed a petition in December 1889 seeking a divorce from his wife and citing Parnell as co-respondent. Anne Deane wrote to Dillon, then on his fundraising tour of Australasia, to inform him about it:

> No doubt the O'Shea case has been cabled to all parts of the English-speaking world. What infamous people those are who are trying to ruin Mr Parnell! I trust he will confound them but it is enough to kill him and that is what the wretches want.

The liaison between Parnell and Kitty O'Shea was an open secret and had been suspected for years, at least by the leading members of the party and, presumably, Dillon. Later Deane on a visit to her old friend, Bishop Mac-Cormack, in Galway, wrote from there about O'Shea's writ against Parnell. 'It gave me a dreadful shock. I thought we were ruined but now the idea seems to be that he would come out of it and there is great sympathy for him. I am surprised how even Dr MacCormack speaks of it.'[1]

The Times Articles

It was widely believed by others as well as Anne Deane that the divorce case would collapse as *The Times* case had previously collapsed. *The Times* had run a series of articles from March to December 1887 under the heading 'Parnellism and crime' and the government by act of parliament established a special commission of three judges, which sat 128 times between October 1888 and November 1889, to investigate the charges made against Parnell and his closest political associates. *The Times* employed agents whom they sent, particularly to the United States, to track down witnesses among Land Leaguers and Fenians who might be persuaded for financial considerations to provide information to the commission against Parnell. However, the Home Rule Party put into place a fairly sophisticated counter-espionage system by which they successfully kept themselves *au courant* with the activities of these agents.

Patrick J. Sheridan

One of the agents, J. F. Kirby, approached Patrick J. Sheridan of Tubbercurry at his ranch in Spring Creek, Monte Vista, Colorado on 15 October 1888.[2] When the agent's message from Colarado was intercepted and decoded

1 Anne Deane to John Dillon, 7 & 22-26 Jan 1890, Dil. P. 6885
2 Sheridan appears to have emigrated from Tubbercurry in the early 1880s

at the Home Rule Party headquarters it caused some anxiety particularly to Parnell. Sheridan showed the agent a black bag containing letters from Parnell, Dillon, Davitt and others 'which would completely sustain *The Times* charges'. Sheridan wanted £20,000 – £10,000 down and the balance after he had given his evidence before the commission in London. Davitt, who had known Sheridan during the Land League days and was convinced that he was not that kind of man, crossed at once to Paris and cabled Thomas Brennan, former secretary of the Land League, then living in Omaha. Brennan went to see Sheridan in Colorado and Sheridan gave him a detailed account of his dealings with Kirby which Brennan subsequently published in the *New York Herald*.[3]

The Times wanted Sheridan to provide evidence that Parnell was party to the Phoenix Park murders and Sheridan was prepared to string their agent along with promises while he extracted damaging information from him on the dubious methods employed by *The Times*. Sheridan swore a statement before a public notary which was forwarded to Davitt on 3 June 1889:

> I deliberately entered into negotiations with Kirby as the *The Times* representative for the purpose of getting such information as I could from him as to the methods which *The Times* employs in getting up its case ... I have no information to give that would be useful to *The Times* or injurious to Mr Parnell or his friends.

In the end, the case against Parnell collapsed in November when it was discovered that Richard Piggot had forged the letter in which Parnell condoned the Phoenix Park murders. Parnell emerged from the whole affair with his reputation enhanced.

Thus when O'Shea filed his writ for divorce in the following month everybody believed that Parnell would once again emerge triumphant. Parnell himself had assured Michael Davitt that he would emerge from the ordeal without a stain on his honour. The trial went ahead in November 1890 but because he wanted to marry Kitty O'Shea Parnell made no move to defend himself and Mrs O'Shea prepared no defence either. The result was that O'Shea's biased and unflattering account went unchallenged in court and the court ruled in favour of O'Shea. Parnell's supporters, even those among the bishops, were slow to accept that they would have to disown him. *Divorce Trial*

The first to break ranks was Davitt in an editorial in his own newspaper, *The Labour World*, on 22 November: *Davitt's Editorial*

---

3   The account is reproduced in Davitt, *The Fall of Feudalism in Ireland*, pp 552-60

Mr Parnell is called upon to make a sacrifice ... to efface himself for a brief period from public life, until the time which the law requires to elapse before a divorced woman can marry, enables him to come back ... We urge him ... to withdraw for a few months from public life ... Every true friend of Home Rule ... in the three countries will expect Mr Parnell to perform this act of self-denial in the best interests of the Irish people and their cause.

The *Methodist Times* accurately predicted that the choice would be between Parnell or the Liberal alliance.

Of course Mr Parnell must go. If the Irish people are so degraded as to retain Parnell as their Parliamentary leader, they can do so, but in that case goodbye to Home Rule. So obscene a race, as in these circumstances they would prove themselves to be, would obviously be unfit for anything except a military despotism ... Unless the Liberal leaders in this country openly break with Parnell, the next election will be the most disastrous for the Liberal Party this century has known.

The *Cork Examiner* described the rising tide of opposition to Parnell: 'The cry becomes clearer, louder, more distinct that Mr Parnell must retire.'[4]

Committee Room 15

In spite of this, the parliamentary party re-elected Parnell as their chairman on 25 November and Gladstone responded by stating publicly that Parnell's continued leadership would make his own position untenable. As the *Methodist Times* had predicted, there was no possibility that Gladstone's

Parnell
Illustrated London News,
Nov 1880

nonconformist followers would tolerate a continued alliance with a leader who had been subjected to moral disgrace in the high court as Parnell had been. Parnell's continued leadership was debated in Committee Room 15 from 1 to 6 December when finally, the anti-Parnellites, forty-five in all, withdrew leaving Parnell with twenty-eight. When account is taken of absentees, like Dillon and O'Brien in America, the eventual breakdown was fifty-four anti-Parnellites to thirty-two Parnellites. Among the latter was Edward Leamy, the MP for South Sligo, while John Dillon, MP for East Mayo, though absent in America, leaned heavily to the anti-Parnellite side. Thus, the diocese of Achonry was split, at least in its parliamentary representatives.

4 qtd in *Labour World*, 30 Nov 1890

The bishops, though they could scarcely be seen as less censorious of Parnell's conduct than the English nonconformists, were persuaded by Archbishop William Walsh of Dublin to hold their fire until the parliamentary party reached its verdict. Finally, their standing committee, comprising the four archbishops and six bishops, including Lyster and MacCormack, issued a statement on 3 December: *Bishops' Statement*

> The Bishops of Ireland can no longer keep silent in the presence of the all engrossing matter which agitates not only Ireland and England alone but every spot where Irishmen have found a home ... Who is to be the leader of the Irish people – or rather who is not to be their leader? Without hesitation or doubt, and in the plainest possible terms we give it as our unanimous judgement that whoever else is fit to fill that highly responsible post, Mr Parnell decidedly is not ... The continuance of Mr Parnell as leader of even a section of the Irish Party ... we see nothing but inevitable defeat at the approaching General Election and as a result Home Rule indefinitely postponed, coercion perpetuated, the hands of the evictor strengthened, and the tenants already evicted left without the shadow of a hope of ever being restored to their homes.[5]

Croke of Cashel, up to now one of Parnell's staunchest supporters, was so thoroughly disillusioned that he virtually withdrew from public life and threw out a bust of Parnell which had stood proudly in the hallway of his palace in Thurles.

There was an immediate reaction throughout the country to the 'split'. The day after the anti-Parnellites withdrew from Committee Room 15 Kiltimagh INL under the chairman, Denis O'Hara, passed a resolution strongly critical of Parnell: *Kiltimagh Resolution*

> That we consider Mr Parnell's present attitude injurious to the Irish cause. His most recent conduct clearly shows that, provided he is allowed to remain as leader, he cares not how much dissension there may be in the party, or how many years Home Rule may be thrown back or what suffering may come on the noble campaigners throughout the country. That we believe that if Mr Parnell was unselfish enough to retire a week ago, our ranks would remain unbroken and our friends in England, with Gladstone at their head, would give us a measure of Home Rule at least as good as the one Mr Parnell accepted in '86. That as Dillon and O'Brien were the ones who did the work in Ireland for the past five years and saved the tenant farmers from the cruel, rack-renting landlords, we call upon our country-

5   *Labour World,* 6 Dec 1890

men to rally round the men who kept the flag flying when Mr Parnell could not be found.

They warned priests and people against contributing to the Tenants' Defence Association, of which Parnell was a treasurer, until they were sure how the money was to be expended.

Kilkelly and Glann

Martin Henry addressed Kilkelly and Glan INL the same day at Sonvolaun 'on the present unfortunate crisis in our National ranks':

> The Irish people were proverbally warm-hearted and in their generosity for past services they have been almost ready to sacrifice not only their individual interests but their hopes of national liberty on the altar of one man's passion and ambition. It is this feeling – a degenerated feeling of gratitude – which was responsible for the adhesion of a number of the Parnellite MPs to their leader. But when they have time to cool down and to look impartially upon the conflict into which they have been hurled, they will certainly admit that they would have acted more wisely if they had thought of their country first and of their leader after.' [6]

The feeling against Parnell was very strong and the meeting thought it would be better 'in the interest of our already prostrate country that Mr Parnell should resign at least for some time.' [7]

Swinford Split

Swinford Board of Guardians unanimously passed a resolution in favour of the anti-Parnellites 'lovers of faith and fatherland, protecting the Irish character.'[8] Parnellites held a meeting in Feeney's Hotel on 14 December 1890 which was reported in the *Freeman's Journal* and the local papers and caused 'much indignation' at a Swinford INL meeting a fortnight later under the chairmanship of the curate, Matthew Bourke. 'From reading it, an outsider would imagine that Swinford was heart and soul for Parnell.' The INL secretary, Francis Davitt, described those who had taken part in the meeting in Feeney's Hotel as being composed of 'landlords and cornerboys side by side ... and as incongruous an assemblage as ever met in Swinford to uphold a rotten cause' and condemned the meeting 'for taking on itself to express the opinions of the community which it did not represent'.

A tit-for-tat war of words ensued. The Parnellites sent a deputation to meet the curate and claimed that Bourke had disowned the condemnation. [9] At another INL meeting on 11 January a letter from Bourke was read declar-

6   *W.P.* 10 Jan 1891
7   *Labour World*, 13 Dec 1890
8   Proposed by C. P. Devitt and seconded by Thomas Carney. *C.T.* 3 Jan 1891
9   Deputation consisted of A. J. Staunton, M. J. Mellet, J. P. O'Connor, P. J. Campbell, Thomas Fitzgerald and Martin McNicholas. Other Parnellites included P. J. Horkan, Andrew Kelly and Michael Munroe

ing that he had nothing to do with 'the descriptive particulars as given by the secretary' but that as chairman he stood by the condemnation. P. J. Durkan PLG, who chaired the Parnellite meeting, was expelled from the INL[10] The 'split' was tearing local communities apart.

Bitter verbal abuse became the order of the day particularly in rival news- *Roscommon Herald*
papers. Shortly after the Committee Room 15 meeting Parnell crossed over to Dublin, broke into the premises of the *United Ireland* and dismissed the anti-Parnellite editor. The *Freeman's Journal* remained on Parnell's side and in March 1891 the anti-Parnellites founded their own daily, the *National Press.* Among the shareholders there were nine bishops, including McEvilly of Tuam and MacCormack of Galway as well as Denis O'Hara.[11] The *Roscommon Herald,* was violently anti-Parnell and Jasper Tully's editorial late in December 1890 was probably typical of the bitterness spawned by the 'split':

> The fight now is between Parnell and adultery and Faith and Fatherland, between the powers of hell and darkness and the powers of heaven and light. The priests with their crucifixes on their breasts will lead and head the men who step shoulder to shoulder with John Dillon and William O'Brien and Michael Davitt in a struggle as glorious as any Christian crusade to rid our land of the tyranny and blackguardism and scoundralism that ever threatened the existence of the nation and the common Christianity of the people. [12]

The *Connaught Telegraph* and the *Sligo Champion* were also anti-Parnell but much less strident than the *Roscommon Herald,* while the *Western People* supported Parnell but was much more moderate in its tone and even-handed in reporting speeches and resolutions from both sides. John Towey of Kilkelly described it as 'a most patriotic journal whose splendid advocacy of the sacred cause of Irish nationality and of its only leader deserves the undying gratitude of the Irish people the world over.' [13]

For Dillon and O'Brien there was not much point in remaining in Ameri- *John Dillon*
ca as their work of fundraising had been paralysed from the beginning of the crisis and was now disintegrating rapidly. It was decided that O'Brien should sail for France to try and reach a settlement with Parnell. He departed on 13 December while Dillon remained on in New York becoming more and more despondent with every news arriving from Ireland. 'I long with unspeakable longing to get out of politics and have done with the sordid misery of that

10 *C.T.* 10 & 17 Jan 1891: *W.P.* 3, 10, 17 Jan 1891
11 *W.P.* 16 Mar 1891
12 *Labour World,* 20 Dec 1890
13 *W.P.* 7 Mar 1891

John Dillon

life, and get to read and think and live at least for a few years before I die, but I fear it is too late now.' [14] Anne Deane felt the same:

I knew you were not fond of political life but I feared the dreadful shock you would have received would prey heavily on you and crush you completely ... I felt badly over this whole affair on public grounds and on your account but I was not at all unprepared for some contingency that might drive you out of politics. Mr Parnell has been behaving badly for the last five or six years and the Bishops are most unreliable in politics. [15]

Timothy Harrington, who had remained loyal to Parnell, had called to see her in Ballaghaderreen and the purpose of his visit may well have been to get her to influence her cousin in Parnell's favour. 'I see Mr Harrington too is desperately anxious to get you and Mr O'Brien to work in some way with Parnell but beware of them all. If you finally decide to retire I should be well pleased.'[16] Harrington had told her that the bishops had written to Parnell after Dillon had left for America in October 1890 'demanding of him as chairman to shut you and Mr O'Brien up about the Plan of Campaign.' 'After that piece of treachery I say no decent man ought to have anything to say to them again in political matters.' Harrington had great hopes that the 'split' would be patched up but Deane did not share his optimism: 'I believe Parnell would never enter any terms with you or O'Brien but that he feels he cannot go on without you and he is not to be trusted at all. He is in every respect a most untruthful and unscrupulous man.'[17] Dillon left for France on 10 January 1891 and arrived in Le Havre eight days later. The subsequent efforts of himself and O'Brien to heal the breach with Parnell, who had crossed over to France to meet them, proved a failure.

Ballymote Convention

A convention of all INL branches and GAA clubs in the South Sligo constituency was held in Ballymote on 4 January 'to pronounce an opinion on the present political crisis.' John McDermott was in the chair and eight other priests, three parish priests and five curates, as well as two MPs, David Sheehy and Daniel Crilly, were present.[18] There were delegations from twelve INL branches and five GAA clubs. The recently established GAA was particularly affected by the 'split'.[19]

14 'Diary', 20 Dec 1890, quoted in Lyons, pp 125-6.
15 Anne Deane to John Dillon, 3 Jan 1891, Dil. P. 6886
16 ibid
17 ibid
18 Owen Stenson PP Bunninadden, Patrick Scully PP Keash, Patrick Lowry PP Achonry, John McNicholas CC Ballymote, Patrick Conlan CC Keash, John Morrin CC Killavil, Patrick A. Filan CC Gurteen, Michael Doyle CC Ballaghaderreen
19 See Chapter Thirteen on 'split' and GAA: see also Appendix 37 for members of delegations

A dispute arose about whether the reporter of the *Freeman* should be allowed to attend. The curate in Keash, Patrick Conlan, opposed his presence but he was allowed in when McDermott threatened to leave the chair if he was expelled. The meeting, which was addressed by the two MPs, Patrick Conlan and Jasper Tully, editor of the *Roscommon Herald*, endorsed the action of the Irish Parliamentary Party in deposing Parnell whom the convention declared was no longer fit to lead the Irish people. The sitting MP, Edward Leamy, was condemned for supporting Parnell and called upon to retire.

A number of by-elections were bitterly fought between the opposing sides. *North Sligo By-Election* The first was savagely contested in Kilkenny late in December 1890 and both Parnell and Davitt were physically assaulted there. The anti-Parnellites won by just over 1,000 votes. The next took place early in April 1891 in the North Sligo constituency where Coolaney was an electoral division. At the Sligo convention on 19 March, attended by Lyster as well Gillooly of Elphin, Alderman Bernard Collery was chosen as the anti-Parnellite candidate. Michael Davitt addressed a large crowd in the Town Hall, Sligo in favour of Collery, whom he predicted would win by over 1,000 votes. The Parnellite candidate was V. B. Dillon, a cousin of John's and Parnell visited the constituency to campaign for him. On his way to Ballina he was greeted by a large crowd at the station in Foxford and later presented with an address by the people of Foxford at a meeting in Ballina on 23 March which claimed that there were 5,000 people in the Foxford district pledged to a man to Parnell with 'only three seceders in the place'.[20] Collery won but not by the margin predicted by Davitt. He polled 3,161 votes against 2,493 for Dillon.

Collery's victory was hailed with great celebrations in Swinford. There *Swinford Celebrations* were several bonfires, including two outside the presbytery, where a large meeting was held addressed by the two curates, Matthew Bourke and Daniel Gallagher who was particularly outspoken:

Sligo had inflicted a staggering blow to the Pretender ... The day would never come when those wicked men would succeed in dividing Faith from Fatherland. They heard talk of priestly dictation. The priests and bishops would not lead them on a wrong path as Parnell would lead them to suppose. There was not a black-hearted Orangeman in the constabulary but was on Parnell's side ... Their duty was to kill Parnell's rotten policy.[21]

Cornelius P. Davitt PLG spoke in a similar vein.

Passions ran high in the parish of Kilmovee where it appears the INL *Kilmovee* branch was highjacked by the Parnellites. All were in favour of Parnell at an

20 Anti-Parnellites were called 'seceders' by their opponents. *W.P.* 28 Mar 1891
21 *C.T.* 11 April 1891

INL meeting in Aghadiffin on Sunday 1 March, attended by a great portion of the people of the townlands of Aghadiffin and Cloonfaulus.[22] Roger O'Hara preached a 'scathing sermon' against them the following Sunday and the INL took up the parish priest's challenge at their next meeting in Uggool: 'We wish to remind the very reverend preacher in question that our fathers were Catholics, that we ourselves are Catholics, who like the priest himself, with God's help, would die for our religion if necessary, but we are not so ignorant as not to be able to draw the line between morals and politics and we hold that we have a perfect right to take any side we like in the present crisis.'[23]

They renewed their allegiance to Parnell, 'the illustrious chief of the Irish race' and pledged themselves to take 'no dictation in politics from any quarter'. A procession of 'schoolchildren and Healyites'[24] had been planned on St Patrick's Day to honour the national patron and the Parnellites decided to hold a counter-procession to honour the saint and Parnell. 'The meeting dispersed amid thundering cheers for Charles S. Parnell.'[25]

Irish National Federation

As the Irish National League (INL) was controlled by the Parnellites, a new body, the Irish National Federation (INF), was created by their opponents. A number of Achonry priests, including the two O'Haras, Denis and Roger, and Michael Keveney, Ballaghaderreen, attended the inaugural meeting in the Ancient Concert Rooms, Dublin.[26]

A branch of the Irish National Federation formed in Kilmovee on 2 March under the presidency of Roger O'Hara, condemned Parnell 'as a political trickster and his mad campaign as an outrage on common decency and the feelings of a thoroughly self-sacrificing people.'[27]

Other branches of the Irish National Federation were formed in Kilkelly and Glan, Keash, Ballaghaderreen and Gurteen. It was alleged that a meeting of the Gurteen Federation laid on free cars and promised free porter to con-

22 *W.P.* 7 Mar 1891
23 Thos. Regan, president in the chair. *Present:* P. Griffin, M. Cassidy, John Duffy, Jas. Mulligan, Nicholas O'Connor, M. Shiel, T. Duffy, Pat McCann, Dominick Griffin, James Duffy, Thos. Regan jr, John Duffy, T. McDonagh, Pat Duffy, M. Horan, Tom Horan, Thos. Freyne. *W.P.* 21 Mar 1891
24 Tim Healy was a particularly virulent critic of Parnell
25 John J. Craig to the Editor, Kilmovee, 16 Mar 1891, *W.P.* 21 Mar 1891
26 Others present: John McNicholas CC Ballymote, Martin Henry CC Kilkelly, Patrick Conlan CC Keash, Michael Grey, sec. Keash, Patrick Nerney sec. Culfadda, C. Burke sec. Kiltimagh, D. Murtagh, M. Sallant, do, M. Flanagan Ballaghaderreen. Apologies were received from Thomas Loftus PP and J. McDonnell CC, Charlestown. *W.P.* 21 Mar 1891
27 *Committee:* J. Coffey, John McDermott, Stephen Duffy, Thomas Finnegan, John Kilgariff, Jas. Doherty, Peter Shiel, Patrick Moran, Thomas O'Grady, Owen Connor, Neil Morley, M. Duffy. Also present: John Irwin PLG, M. Henry CC, Bernard Flannery, John Sheridan (ex-suspect). *W.P.* 7 Mar 1891

tingents coming from Ballaghaderreen. Jasper Tully, editor of the *Roscommon Herald*, vehemently denounced the Parnellites as did the curate, Patrick A. Filan. In a letter to the editor of *Western People* (2 May) an 'observer' remarked: 'His reverence should not descend to language about honest respectable men not sufficiently dignified for his sacred calling.' Parnellites were severely denounced from the altar in a parish church in the diocese early in April and a considerable number of parishioners left in protest. 'We forbear entering into more minute particulars of an incident which in every aspect must be considered unfortunate.'[28] Voices calling for restraint were rare. One from Edmondstown, Ballaghaderreen who signed himself 'an old peasant', urged all sides to close ranks and give up this internecine struggle: 'It grieves my heart to see "good men and true men" arrayed against each other. For the love of God, for the love of the country and for the dear old cause let us unite for in union there is strength.'[29]

Parnellites established the Parnell Leadership Committee to promote Parnell as leader and branches were founded in Swinford, Ballaghaderreen, Bonniconlon and elsewhere in the diocese, to fund and support the campaign. The Ballaghaderreen branch sent a cheque for £12 for the Parnell Leadership Fund to the *Western People* (4 April) with an accompanying letter signed by Edward Kelly, Michael Raftery, Edward Neary and James Howley:

Parnell Leadership Committee

> We desire to protest in the strongest manner ... against the foul and uncharitable language which from platform and elsewhere has been directed against Mr Parnell and his supporters. Through the medium of a series of scurrilous resolutions passed by a miserable clique it was made to appear that there was no independence in Ballaghaderreen.

Of thirty-three subscribers, almost half of them withheld their names, signing themselves simply 'Parnellites', suggesting that it may not have been wise to expose one's independence in Ballaghaderreen.[30] Swinford Parnell Leadership Committee sent a letter signed by Thomas Fitzgerald, president, P. J. Campbell, treasurer, and J. Mellet, secretary, together with a £10 cheque as a first installment. Again, as in the case of Ballaghaderreen, a substantial number of the subscribers preferred to remain anonymous.[31] Bonniconlon Parnell Leadership Committee was established in May under the auspices of the GAA club and was composed of members chosen from every townland in the parish.[32] A large and enthusiastic meeting was held in the main street of

28 *W.P.* 11 April 1891
29 *W.P.* 25 April 1891 Such appeals fell largely on deaf ears
30 *W.P.* 4 April 1891: see Appendix 39
31 *W.P.* 9 May 1891
32 See Appendix 39

Parnell in the West

the village on Sunday 24 May, even though the parish priest, Peter Harte, had spoken after Mass in opposition to it.[33]

Realising the powerful sentiments the Land League evoked in the west of Ireland, Parnell decided to celebrate the twelfth anniversary of its foundation by holding a monster meeting at Irishtown on Sunday 19 April. There were between 10,000 and 12,000 present, which the *Western People* (25 April) described as 'a seething mass of humanity'. Charlestown was the only part of the diocese represented at the meeting.[34] Julian Moore, a brother of the novelist and absentee landlord, George A., whose agent was then carrying out harsh and cruel evictions in Bohola, told the meeting that he heard a priest declare in a chapel that day that 'no good Catholic could attend a meeting called to support Parnell's leadership'. 'The greatest enemies the church ever had were her own unwise friends.' Moore hoped the day was not too distant when the priests would once more join with their 'old and trusted leader, Parnell'.

Parnell himself evoked the memory of former martyrs of the physical force tradition in the Irish struggle for independence. 'When Robert Emmet and Lord Edward Fitzgerald laid down their lives for their country they did not stop to think whether Ireland was a Catholic nation or not. The Nationalists of Ireland are the proud inheritors of those martyrs.' In the words of William O'Brien, he 'was falling back more and more on the hillside boys'. [35]

The following day Parnell travelled by train from Claremorris to Ballina for another monster meeting. A large crowd greeted him at the station in Foxford and later the Nationalist voters from that town and neighbourhood presented him with an address in Ballina.[36] A number of flags were displayed at the back of the platform, with the 'handsome banner from Foxford occupying the place of honour in the centre.' Addresses were also presented by the Swinford Parnell Leadership Committee, Bonniconlon GAA (and Band), and by the people of Attymass.[37]

In Ballina again Parnell continued to flirt with the physical force movement and seemed to be turning away from constitutionalism. Here he evoked the 1798 rebellion in Killala:

Men of Mayo and Sligo … you have reproduced the spirit breathed by your forefathers in 1798 when cheerfully in their thousands they gave up their lives shoulder to shoulder fighting with the gallant Frenchmen who

32 See Appendix 39
33 *W.P.* 16 & 30 May 1891
34 by E. Meehan.
35 William O'Brien to John Dillon, 15 Sept 1891, Dil. P.
36 See Appendix 39
37 See Appendix 39 for signatories

landed in Killala Bay, and just as the sacrifices you are asked to make today are small in comparison with those which your forefathers made, so you are determined to make them just as cheerfully as your ancestors rendered theirs, with the same energy, patriotism and courage to fight out this battle to the bitter end until we have won once more a united Ireland and a united Irish people.

Later that evening at a banquet in the Moy Hotel he repeated his now-famous dictum:

No man can fix the limits to the march of a nation; no man can say to a people who have within themselves the elements of greatness, "Thus far shalt thou go and no further." We have never pawned our birthright and never intend to.

Dillon in Jail Again

Meanwhile Dillon and O'Brien were back in prison and spared from the bitter in-fighting which was tearing the country apart. After their failed talks with Parnell in France on 12 February, Dillon and O'Brien had crossed to Folkstone where they were duly arrested and taken to Scotland Yard. Kilkelly and Glan INL condemned 'the cruel and hard-hearted action of Balfour in pouncing on the noble champions of the Irish race ere they could even rest a foot on Irish soil.'[38] From there Dillon and O'Brien were conveyed to Galway jail where they were detained for six months.

Prison for them at this point was a real haven. The authorities of the jail were friendly. They were comfortably lodged and their diet was carefully supervised by the prison doctor. Bishop MacCormack visited them several times and kept Anne Deane informed. 'I paid a long visit to the prisoners today and I am happy to be able to report that both are well. John is stronger than when I saw him in my previous visits. He has gained weight since and it tells in his appearance.'[39] Though they were not allowed to have newspapers, one way or another Dillon managed to keep abreast with what was happening outside. 'I am watching the Carlow election with great interest. If Parnell gets a good beating it will greatly increase our chance of making peace.' Dillon still hoped that a reconciliation was possible though the Carlow election had intensified the bitterness between the two sides. He was particularly depressed by the violent language used by the antagonists. 'There is not another example of the flood of villainy and filth to which a struggle of this kind is seen to give rise."[40]

38 *W.P.* 21 Feb 1891
39 Bishop MacCormack to Anne Deane, 23 July 1891, Dil. P. 6892
40 John Dillon to Anne Deane, 1 & ? July 1891, Dil. P. 6886

Released   The prisoners were released at 9.30 on Thursday morning 30 July. Shortly after nine MacCormack's carriage had been driven up to the front of the prison, followed a few minutes later by another carriage containing Mrs O'Brien and Miss Maud Gonne. All proceeded to the bishop's house where they breakfasted.[41] A few hours later Dillon addressed a Galway crowd:

> I say deliberately that my voice shall always be given in favour of welcoming any rational, patriotic and reasonable offer which comes from any quarter – I care not where – and which points towards a reunion of the national ranks in this country and the banishment of the demon of discord from the ranks of the people of Ireland. [42]

When news of the release of the prisoners reached Swinford, countless bonfires were erected on the surrounding heights and in every part of the town except the square which was occupied by the 'peelers'. District Inspector Allen attempted without success to stop the fires. Two large meetings were held the following Sunday, one in Kilmovee after first Mass and another in Kilkelly after the second Mass. Martin Henry expressed optimism that their release would heal the 'split': 'We are sure that their eloquent and statesman-like declarations made just outside the prison bars will quickly quell disunion, heal up old sores and make us once more a united people.'[43]

But in Mallow on 9 August Dillon and O'Brien took the decisive step of throwing in their lot with the anti-Parnellites and this, together with the defection of the *Freeman's Journal*, was a crushing blow to Parnell. Though his health was deteriorating rapidly he continued to cross over to Ireland weekend after weekend, addressing meetings all over the country. He addressed a meeting in Westport on Sunday 13 September at which Foxford was represented by J. Shiel and P. Boland while there was a sizeable contingent from Swinford. [44]

The following week William O'Brien was also in Westport addressing a meeting of anti-Parnellites and was presented with an address by the 'Nationalists of Swinford'.[45] Parnell was back in the west at the end of September, this time at Creggs, Co Galway where he urged his followers to fight on against all the odds and launched a series of rambling attacks upon his

Martin Henry

41 *W.P.* 1 Aug 1891
42 *F.J.* 31 July 1891
43 *W.P.* & *C.T.* 8 Aug 1891
44 J. E. Mellet, P. J. Campbell, M. McNicholas, J. J. Moloney, Thos. Moloney, P. J. Durkan PLG, J. Kearns, M. Munroe, T. Fitzgerald, R. J. O'Connor, J. J. Boland, J. Donegan, I. P. O'Donnell etc. *W.P.* 19 Sept 1891
45 Signed by Cornelius P. Davitt PLG, Patrick Doherty, Robert Furey, P. M. Henry, Patrick D. Harte, M. O'Callaghan, Michael Brennan, Charles Patten, Thomas Furey, Michael Gallagher

enemies. To Dillon all this was inexpressibly tragic. 'Parnell at Creggs yesterday, incoherent scurrility – sad, sad. He must be positively going mad.'[46]

Eight days later Parnell was dead. He had got wet at the meeting in Creggs
and was ill and feverish when he arrived home in Brighton a few days later
and was confined to bed. He died on the night of 6 October at the age of
forty-five. Following the announcement of his death, a number of his followers went to Brighton and arranged to have his remains brought to Dublin for
a public funeral. The funeral started from Brighton on Saturday 10 October
and arrived in Dublin the following day. Parnell's body lay in state in the City
Hall where he and Dillon had received the freedom of the city after their release from Kilmainham. From there the cortege set out for Glasnevin Cemetery with the coffin placed on the roof of a hearse. Behind the hearse came
Parnell's favourite brown horse, *Home Rule*, with Parnell's riding boots re-
versed, dangling from the draped saddle. Members of the GAA led the way
and contingents of them also followed. There were several carriages carrying
MPs and the Lord Mayor and Dublin corporation and finally 'a vast self-or-
ganised following of men and women'. Bands played the *Dead March* as it
moved slowly onwards through the streets. Brief halts were made at the place
where Robert Emmet was executed, at the old Parliament House and the O'-
Connell monument. An estimated 200,000 people attended the funeral.

Death of Parnell

Popular opinion largely exonerated Gladstone, Michael Davitt and above
all Parnell himself for the part they played in his downfall and premature
death. The church was to become the most widely accepted scapegoat for the
tragedy. *The Bishops and the Party / That tragic story made.*[47]

It was widely believed that the death of Parnell would bring the 'split' to an
end. On the day of the funeral the sole topic of conversation at a meeting of
the Glan and Kilkelly INF was the 'sad and lamented end of Mr Parnell' who
was described as 'undoubtedly a great man'. Martin Henry expressed the
hopes of many: 'Now may we at last expect that faction and disunion will
cease and that Irishmen will have the common sense and patriotism of once
more fighting shoulder to shoulder against the common foe and making our
native land a nation of freemen.' But the scars ran too deep to be healed
quickly. At Parnell's funeral the Dublin GAA Committee carried a floral
wreath with two shields, one with the words 'In memory of the Chief', and
the other 'An eye for an eye'. Another floral wreath from the Belfast Parnell
Leadership Committee had at the top the word 'Murder' worked mainly in
violets and at the bottom the word 'Revenge'. Peace-making was far from the

46 Diary of John Dillon, 28 Sept 1891, qtd Lyons, op. cit. p 143
47 W. B. Yeats, *Come gather round me Parnellites*, 1937

mind of the editor of the Parnellite newspaper, *United Ireland*, in the first issue after his death: 'Murdered he has been as certainly as if the gang of conspirators had surrounded him and hacked him to pieces.'

Ballaghaderreen
Meeting

Ballaghaderreen was the venue early in December for a meeting attended by Dillon and O'Brien. Michael Keveney thought that people locally would like to hear Tim Healy. 'He has never been in this direction and the belief that he would attend would help to swell the gathering.'[48] Dillon did not share Keveney's admiration for Healy who led the extreme Catholic wing of the party and as editor of the *National Press* launched attacks of unprecedented bitterness on Parnellites. Healy was not invited. Martin Henry again took up the theme of unification in Ballaghaderreen. 'Let us again unite under the old leaders and the old banner'. Keveney spoke in the same vein: 'We could understand in some degree the position of our opponents when Mr Parnell was alive but there is no shred of reason left now to justify them in the cause they are pursuing any longer.'[49]

Denis O'Hara

Denis O'Hara, 'a master of catch phrases', romanced in fine style about 'the boys of the old brigade' and claimed that Parnellites were the first to use abusive language, a view also shared by Dillon.

> Not a word of suspicion could be uttered against the members of the Parliamentary Party until the Split gave men who were not ashamed of anything, the chance of using shameful and shameless language ... They talk about their hillside men but years ago you had Dillon and O'Brien on the hillside and when Ireland wants the right sort of hillside men she will have Dillon and O'Brien and thousands of men like them ... During the anxious years of the past the only rest they ever got was within the walls of her Majesty's prison; the only winter quarters they ever had were the dungeons of Tullamore and Galway jails.

> Addresses were presented to Dillon and O'Brien at Ballaghaderreen presbytery by INF branches from Ballaghaderreen, Swinford, Kiltimagh, Kilmovee, Gurteen, Ballymote, Killaraght as well as both the INF and GAA in Glan and Kilkelly and Swinford Board of Guardians.[50] Returning that night from the meeting in Ballaghaderreen, the curate in Aughamore was assaulted in his carriage while crossing the bridge in Kilkelly between 7 and 8 p.m. and received two wounds on his head. The editorial in the *Connaught Telegraph* (12 December) strongly condemned the assault: 'The so-called "patriots" are determined ... to use the bloody weapons of assassination on the sacred persons of "clerical tyrants".'

48 Michael Keveney to John Dillon, 22 Nov 1891, Dil. P. 6770
49 *W.P.* 12 Dec 1891
50 *S.C.* 12 Dec 1891

Bitterness continued to manifest itself between Parnellites and their opponents. Swinford Board of Guardians passed a resolution early in March 1892 criticising a recent speech by Dillon in the House of Commons. The Board was evenly divided and Parnellites, taking advantage of the late arrival of their opponents, got the resolution through by eight votes to seven. Glan and Kilkelly INF, in spite of earlier aspirations of reconciliation, reacted savagely, describing the Swinford 'factionists' as 'toadies, lickspittles, grabbers, agents and a few shoneen landlords ... a begging and cringing clique.' A demonstration in Kiltimagh on St Patrick's Day at which Denis O'Hara presided also condemned the Swinford resolution and asserted that they had every confidence in 'honest John Dillon.'[51]

Swinford Board of Guardians

In March 1892 the *Western People* was advertised for sale and Denis O'Hara suggested to Dillon that the Party should buy it. 'In the hands of the present company it would surely give trouble at the General Election but having it on our side there would be a chance of winning North Mayo.' His advice was not taken but he planned to take some shares in the paper himself.[52] Subsequently, it appears that the *Connaught Telegraph* was acquired as it announced a change of management and editor in its issue of 25 June and later (2 July) that John Dillon had taken 50 shares in the company. At the general election convention in Castlebar Denis O'Hara recommended the *Connaught Telegraph* to the Nationalists of Mayo 'as the exponent of the policy and views of the Nationalist Party'. O'Hara appears to have been assigned the task of interviewing an editor who would be prepared to sign a guarantee to run the paper on the lines laid down by O'Hara, Dillon and two others nominated by them.[53]

Connaught Telegraph

Election fever was in the air and as the summer advanced and the general election approached nasty incidents occurred between rival parties. One such incident in Foxford threatened the survival of the Providence Woollen Mills which had been officially opened barely three months earlier. A Parnellite demonstration was held in the street and the parish priest, Michael O'Donnell, was booed and hooted as he passed by. Among the demonstrators were some of the employees of the Woollen Mills. The priests called to the convent and demanded that six of the workers be dismissed, the carpenter, John O'Donnell, Mary Henehan, a work teacher in the school, and four other girls, all belonging to well-known Parnellite families. John O'Donnell and Mary Henehan's father, Thomas, were members of Foxford Parnell Leadership

Foxford Dispute

51 *C.T.* 12, 19 & 26 Mar: *S.C.* 19 Mar 1892
52 Denis O'Hara to John Dillon, 15 Mar & 1 April 1892, Dil. P. 6769
53 Denis O'Hara to John Dillon, 2, 9, 11 & 21 Aug 1892, Dil. P. 6769

Committee.[54] The parish priest told the superioress, Agnes Morrogh Bernard, that he had informed Bishop Lyster and was acting on the latter's authority.

Agnes Stands Firm

Agnes suspended the six workers temporarily but refused to be intimidated, claiming that the mill was being made 'a party machine, a reward for good nationalists, "no others need apply"':

I felt bound to make a firm stand and I refused emphatically to agree to their demand. We Sisters of Charity have no politics ... I came here to help the poor, non-sectarian, non-political. So long as they require my help they shall have it and I will submit to no interference. We are not Sisters of Mercy under local authority. I am under that of my Superior General and recognise no other. If we are not allowed to do the work we came for, then we go ... I am ready to close down the mill, to leave on short notice and leave you the care of your own poor, the responsibility is with you.' [55]

The priests left dissatisfied.

Public Apology

A week later the curate returned to inform the superioress that her school was to be placed under interdict if the offending parties did not make a full apology. 'I repeated what I had said a week ago and added that I considered that my community was being badly treated. Our schools and grounds were private property and I would allow no action to be taken there that savoured of politics.' She did, however, concede that some of her employees had been rude to the parish priest and that a public apology would be made. She sent for the culprits and explained the position to them.

Agnes Morrogh
Bernard

I told them I would go with them next day and before the congregation after last Mass I would speak for them. It was a vital moment, the life or death of our work in Foxford depended on it. I insisted that the two priests should come to the church door, and there I made my first and last public speech, and read the apology I had written out for them:

'We have come to express our regret that any disrespect has been shown by us or anyone belonging to us to any of the priests as the ministers of God and our holy religion and humbly beg of you, Father O'Donnell, as our parish priest, and of you, Father Callaghan as curate, to allow the Reverend Mother to take us back into her employment which she promises to do as soon as we make this act of reparation for what has occurred.'

54 See Appendix 39
55 *The Memoirs of Mother Arsenius*, RSCG / H 26 / 449: Agnes Morrogh Bernard to Bishop Lyster, 24, 27 & 28 July 1892, RSCG / H 26 / 2 (2,3 & 4). See also Eugene Duffy, 'Mother Arsenius and the Eye of Providence' in *Survival or Salvation? A Second Mayo Book of Theology*, pp 89-90

Workers in Foxford
Mill, 1895
The Gentlewoman
14 Sept, 1895

All were forgiven except Mary Henehan, as the parish priest said that her case had been reserved to the bishop. There had been bad blood between her father, Tom, and the parish priest for some time and the Henehans were related to several of the townspeople. Denis O'Hara came and interviewed the Henehan family in the convent and succeeded in 'throwing oil on troubled waters' by getting them to agree to leave Mary's case in Agnes' hands. The parish priest had told Agnes that no one was to be received in the convent who was opposed to the parish priest, and particularly the Henehans. 'I told him plainly the convent doors would be open to every waif and stray – that we were a universal refuge for all.' The parish priest then threatened to leave the Sisters without Mass. Agnes wrote to Lyster whom she considered had 'so injudiciously acceded to the priests' demand'. The trouble began when the curate, Andrew Callaghan, came to the school on several occasions urging the Sister there to take 'decisive action' to get some of the parents of the children to change their political opinions. 'It is my firm opinion that the Foxford people can be led by kindness but never driven.'

Mary Henehan

A month later Lyster came to Foxford and after several hours Mary Henehan's case was resolved. In her *Memoirs*, Agnes later penned her own conclusion to the affair:

Dispute Resolved

'God arose and scattered His enemies' and our little barque once again weathered a violent storm, which had threatened to submerge our work, and leave the banks of the Moy as destitute as they had formerly been. And why? Because men allowed their political feelings to overflow, and because a couple of opponents booed, and their little girls thought they should do what their dadas did!

Michael O'Donnell, the priest at the centre of the row, died less than a year later in May 1893.

Conventions   At Sligo county convention in the Town Hall on 14 June Bernard Collery was chosen as the candidate for North Sligo and Thomas Curran, a native of Leitrim who had made his fortune in Sydney, Australia, for South Sligo. John O'Dowd of Bunninadden had been put forward as candidate for South Sligo at an earlier meeting in Ballymote, attended by many of the Achonry clergy, but at the county convention he withdrew in favour of Curran. Patrick Conlan, the curate in Keash, was the only clerical speaker at the convention. [56] At the Mayo convention in Castlebar on 27 June. 'vehement cheers greeted the appearance of John Dillon and the beloved parish priest of Kiltimagh.' [57] No less than sixty-one priests attended from the dioceses of Tuam, Killala and Achonry, ten of them from the latter.[58] There were lay delegations from every one of the parishes in the Mayo portion of Achonry.[59] Denis O'Hara proposed and Cornelius Davitt PLG Swinford seconded John Dillon as candidate for East Mayo.

Dillon took issue with Parnellite members of Swinford Board of Guardians who thanked Balfour for the relief received recently in that Union:

> The voters of East Mayo know that all the benefits that have been obtained for that district ... were won not by going down on your two knees by the roadside and begging and praying to have benefits conferred on you ... The people of Swinford invited me to a meeting there ... We came there to demand our rights and to insist that our people should not be allowed to starve. What is the result? A very short time after that came Mr Balfour cruising about the country on an outside car. In no constituency in Ireland was there so much spent by the Tory government as in the constituency of East Mayo. Nothing is to be won from English ministers or landlords by whinging and cringing and going down on your knees before them; but everything is to be won by combining together in defence of your rights and by standing like one man against the common enemy.

He told the convention that he would not be canvassing in East Mayo, leaving that to his friends, Denis O'Hara and Michael Keveney, while he intended to canvass in North Mayo where his presence was more needed

56 *S.C.* 18 June 1892
57 *C.T.* 2 July 1892
58 Roger O'Hara, Kilmovee, Thomas Loftus, Charlestown, John O'Grady, Bohola, Denis O'Hara, Kiltimagh, Patrick Hunt, Straide, Michael Keveney, Ballaghaderreen, Martin Henry CC Kilmovee, Bartholomew Quinn CC Kiltimagh, James O'Connor CC Ballaghaderreen, P. J. O'Grady CC Killasser
59 See Appendix 40

The *Connaught Telegraph* waxed eloquent on Denis O'Hara's talent of wooing an Irish audience:

> It is not a thing of art; it is a gift of nature and an outcome of the heart. He has caught some of the art and raciness of O'Connell as well as his earnestness and practical wisdom; and his cheery voice and open radiant face are fully in keeping with his other natural gifts.'

'Mayo was determined to fight the common enemy first, the landlords and Dublin Castle', he declared, 'and the people would take their own time to settle their own differences.' Of the 900 families he represented there were not three voters who would vote against Dillon.

Dillon in Kiltimagh

About a week later Dillon addressed a meeting in Kiltimagh. He had arrived from Ballina with Denis O'Hara with whom he stayed that night. A huge bonfire was erected in the old market place opposite the chapel and all the windows of the town were illuminated. 'I have always found consolation among the priests and people of patriotic Kiltimagh,' he told the crowd. He recalled the first occasion he visited the town with Parnell in 1879 when they were on their way from the Balla meeting to Swinford. 'The reception we got from your brave little town I will never forget.' [60]

Eight nomination papers were handed in from the diocese on behalf of Dillon. One was from Ballaghaderreen where the proposer was Bishop Lyster. The others came from Kiltimagh, Foxford, Kilmovee, Charlestown and Carracastle where the proposer in each case was the parish priest. Two nominations were handed in from Swinford. [61]

Election Results

At the time of the election Parnellites numbered thirty and they put forward candidates in forty-five seats, three of them in Mayo while no Parnellite contested North or South Sligo. When the election was over Parnellites were reduced to nine MPs against seventy-one anti-Parnellites. In many of the constituencies the Parnellite candidate suffered a massive defeat. In East Mayo John Fitzgibbon only gained 257 votes while in West Mayo O'Connor Power gained only a paltry 60 while his opponent got almost 8,500. Even the Tories who ran candidates in North and South Sligo did slightly better though Collery and Curran were returned with large majorities. Undoubtedly the role of the clergy was decisive. Lyster had told the clerical conference in Tubbercurry 'that everything must be done to support you and the party.' [62]

60 *C.T.* 9 July 1892
61 In one he was proposed by Matthew Bourke CC and seconded by Dr O'Grady and in the other he was proposed by James Cullen CC and seconded by Edward Dolphin with the assent of sixteen Nationalists. *CT.* 16 July 1892
62 Michael Keveney to John Dillon,(telegram) 28 July 1892, Dil. P. 6770

The general election of 1895 did not mark any great shift in the balance be-tween the parties. Parnellites went up from nine to eleven and anti-Parnellites went down from seventy-one to seventy. Sixty-one seats were uncontested in 1895 as against twenty-one in 1892.

Dillon's Marriage

Elizabeth Dillon
in 1900

John Dillon married Elizabeth Mathew in London on 21 November 1895. She was the daughter of Sir James Mathew, an English judge, who belonged to the same family as Father Mathew, the apostle of temperance. Dillon first met the Mathews in Killiney in 1886 where they and he were accustomed to spend their holidays. He later became a frequent visitor to the Mathew home in London during the sessions of parliament and while Elizabeth was infatu-ated by him from the beginning, John was so immersed in political life, and in and out of prison, he scarcely noticed his lovelorn admirer. It was almost nine years later when he finally proposed to her on 11 October 1895, setting their marriage for the following month. The first gift John gave Elizabeth was a pocket Testament that he used to take to Mass, marked in many places with his own hand. Nothing could have pleased her more. 'What made you know that I should love your little Testament more than any gift money could buy? It has you on every page and I stroke the pages softly and think that your hand has rested on them too.' [63]

Archbishop Croke was one of the first to send his best wishes: 'I congratu-late you heartily on the prospect before you. I hear the best things of your "intended". 'Tis time for you to step out. Anything that tends to your hap-pinness cannot fail to be a source of pleasure to me.' [64] The priests of the dio-cese formed a committee and presented the engaged couple with an inscribed silver tray. Lyster placed a notice of the presentation in the *Freeman*. 'The poor man was overflowing with tenderness towards you both', Anne Deane told Dillon.[65] Bishop MacCormack performed the marriage in Brompton Oratory in London, a quite wedding attended only by the Mathew family and Dillon's uncle, Charles Hart, and his cousin, Anne Deane, whose generosity in settling a large sum of money on Dillon made his marriage financially possible.

Roman Honeymoon

The newly-weds left at once for the continent where they spent a month, going by way of Paris, Avignon, Cannes to Florence and finally to Rome. There, on 12 December, they first called to St Isidore's, the Irish Franciscan college, where John's brother, Harry (Father Nicholas), was a member of the

63 Elizabeth Mathew to John Dillon, 24 Oct 1895 qtd Lyons, *Dillon*, p 257
64 Croke to John Dillon, 18 Oct 1895, Dil. P. 6766
65 Denis O'Hara to John Dillon, 19 Nov 1895, Dil. P.6769; Anne Deane to John Dillon, 24 Nov 1895, Dil. P. 6885

Order. Harry had only been recently ordained and the newly-weds arranged to attend his Mass and receive communion from him. Then they went to pay their respects to the rector of the Irish College. Here they learnt that Bishop O'Donnell of Raphoe, one of Dillon's most enthusiastic admirers among the bishops, was also in Rome, staying at the Minerva. The bishop later called on them and told them that both he and the rector were strongly of the opinion that the Dillons ought not to leave Rome without applying for a private interview with the Pope.[66]

The rector duly arranged for a private audience with Pope Leo XIII on the following Monday.

> Our audience with His Holiness was an immense success. Nothing could exceed the cordiality and affection with which he received us and the interview lasted almost a quarter of an hour altho' one of the cardinals was waiting outside for an audience. We were all copiously blessed and His Holiness was particularly gracious and affectionate to Bessie (Elizabeth).' [67]

They conversed with the Pope in French. 'He said "mais oui, mais oui" to everything', Elizabeth noted in her Diary, 'and fondled my hair with his tiny cold hand, and laid his other hand on John's black, smooth head.' In Irish affairs Rome had a tendancy to consult the English laity rather than the Irish party, as Dillon was only too well aware. In his interview with the Secretary of State, Cardinal Rampolla, who received them 'with effusion', he was particularly unimpressed by Rampolla's opening remark, 'Vous connaissez, sans doute, le duc de Norfolk?' When the Dillons pointed out that they were Irish Catholics, Rampolla tried to recover by referring to Archbishop Walsh as 'tres irlandais'. Dillon who thought that Archbishop's fault was that he was not nearly 'Irish' enough, replied coldly, 'Nous sommes tous hautement irlandais, Eminence' ('We are all proudly Irish'), and there the interview ended. [68]

Dillon must have wondered whether his furious reaction to the English mission to Rome headed by the Duke of Norfolk, at the end of 1887, had been reported to Rome when he had declared that Irish Catholics 'would no more take their political guidance from the Pope of Rome than from the Sultan of Turkey.'[69] Anne Deane was delighted with their visit to Rome and its 'crowning feature', the papal audience. 'All the priests in this quarter are greatly pleased and the poor people also. It will silence some people who might be inclined to comment on your want of respect for spiritual superiors.' [70]

66 John Dillon to Anne Deane, 13 Dec 1895, Dil. P. 6888
67 John Dillon to Anne Deane, 18 Dec 1895, Dil. P. 6888
68 Diary of Elizabeth Dillon, 13 & 29 Dec 1895 qtd in Lyons, *Dillon*, p 259
69 See above p 242
70 Anne Deane to John Dillon, ? Dec 1895, Dil. P. 6889

When they arrived back in Dublin, the house in 2 Nth Great George's Street had been completely redecorated and a cook and parlourmaid engaged by Anne Deane. The house belonged to Dillon's uncle, Charles Hart, who continued to live there until his death. Apart from an annual visit to Ballaghaderreen the Dillons lived and reared their family there. Visitors kept calling and there was a considerable amount of entertaining. One of their frequent guests was Denis O'Hara on his monthly visits to Dublin for meetings of the Congested Districts Board. So frequent were his visits that he was obliged to alert them whenever he was not coming. 'I am not going to Dublin this week', he informed John in 1900. 'Please tell Mrs Dillon not to put my name in the pot for Tuesday.'[71]

Mayo Visit Early in 1896 the newly-weds paid their first state visit to John's constituency in East Mayo. Anne Deane asked them to come on Wednesday, 29 January:

> The priests and people are preparing to give you a reception on that day and it would not do to come the day before and upset their arrangements ... All the priests of your division are coming. Of course it was not my duty to invite anyone but I told Father O'Connor[72] I would have dinner for anyone who came and I could see he was pleased at my taking them off his hands, as he is to have a great party in your honour on Sunday and you will have to remain. I only hope I won't have more than I shall be able to dine.[73]

'We shall go down prepared to stay over Sunday,' John told her. 'You must arrange that we go out some day to visit the Canon in Kilmovee. As I am resolved that Bessie (Elizabeth) shall not leave without putting in an appearance in Kilmovee.'[74] Canon Roger O'Hara had been the treasurer of the priests' committee which presented the Dillons with a silver tray.

On Wednesday they were met at the station in Ballaghaderreen by a brass band which paraded them to Anne Deane's house. There they were entertained to dinner which included among the guests no less than fifteen priests, which must have been an unnerving experience for the young bride. After Mass in the cathedral on Sunday, the crowd presented them with addresses of goodwill to which Dillon had to reply.

> So picturesque it was, to have the church porch behind us and the great crowd in front, and I loved to see John standing tall and commanding over the people with his head bare and his beautiful voice ringing through the air and penetrating everywhere. The addresses wished us all kinds of bless-

71 Denis O'Hara to John Dillon, 9 Dec 1900, Dil. P. 6769
72 Adm Ballaghaderreen
73 Anne Deane to John Dillon, n.d. 1896, Dil. P. 6888
74 John Dillon to Anne Deane, 25 Jan 1896, Dil. P. 6888

ings and that we might have heirs to perpetuate the noble race. No beating about the bush with the people of East Mayo.'[75]

Elizabeth did in fact provide an heir in August and several others, four boys and a girl, at frequent intervals during the next ten years. [76]

Dillon's Leadership

Justin McCarthy resigned the chairmanship of the parliamentary party early in 1896 and was succeeded by Dillon, who was proposed by McCarthy and seconded by Michael Davitt. Dillon was elected by thirty-eight votes to twenty-one. The latter were 'Healyites', followers of Tim Healy, a virulent opponent of Parnell who had many admirers, particularly among priests, one of whom may well have been Michael O'Donnell of Foxford. Agnes Morrogh Bernard described to Bishop Lyster how a group of boys, children of Foxford Parnellites, burned an effigy of Healy on the bridge over the Moy: 'when he got too hot for them, they dropt (*sic*) him into the Moy and our Sisters gave us an amusing description at recreation of the mortal remains of Tim floating down the Moy and getting stranded on the rocks.' [77].

Lyster may not have been amused by her account and it may well have contributed to the coolness that developed between them. Healy was strongly supported by the *Irish Catholic* which launched, in March 1896, a series of articles which were a sustained and venomous attack on Dillon. Dillon believed that Healy was constructing a clerical party and his first task as leader was to reduce the 'Healyites' to impotence. They were expelled from the committee of the party and from the Irish National Federation. Healy was later expelled from the party in 1900. By then Dillon had resigned as chairman in favour of John Redmond, leader of the Parnellites and the 'split' was formally brought to an end.

Anne Deane's Death

Anne Deane died on 3 July 1905 in her seventy-seventh year while she was convalescing in Dillon's Dublin home. Her remains were brought by train to Ballaghaderreen where they were met at the station by Lyster and several of the priests, including Denis O'Hara and Dillon's Franciscan brother, Father Nicholas. Her coffin was borne to the cathedral by about thirty-five young men, all members of the staff of Monica Duff and Co, and High Mass was celebrated the following morning by Denis O'Hara and attended by a large number of priests. Bishop MacCormack, who was administering confirmation in one of the remotest parishes of his diocese, was unable to attend and apologised for his absence 'which has been a distressing trial to me.'[78] Anne

75 Diary of Elizabeth Dillon, 3 Feb 1896, qtd in Lyons, *Dillon*, p 260
76 John Mathew, 1896, Anne Elizabeth, 1897, Theobald Wolfe Tone, 1898, Myles Patrick, 1900, James Mathew, 1902 and Brian, 1905.
77 RSCG / H 26 / 2 (3)
78 MacCormack to Mrs Dillon, 6 July 1905, Dil. P. 6889

Deane was buried in Straide, twenty-two miles away, where her husband lay and her remains were carried there in a splendid hearse, drawn by four horses, followed by about a hundred carriages and cars.

Davitt's Tribute   Among those who attended the funeral were Michael Davitt with his son, and Dr Douglas Hyde, the founder of the Gaelic League. Davitt was interviewed by the *Connaught Telegraph*:

> She was one of my dearest friends. I first made her acquaintance at the time of the Gurteen meeting in 1879 ... It was from Mrs Deane's house in Ballaghaderreen I started for that meeting and the chief speakers returned there after the demonstration ... Every prominent Nationalist of the last quarter of a century from Mr Parnell downwards was numbered among her friends and shared at some time or other the hospitality of her home. When the Ladies' Land League was formed in 1881 by Miss Anna Parnell, Mrs Deane was elected president ... She gave most generously of her means ... sound advice and clear judgement ... while the 'suspects' were under lock and key in Kilmainham.

Davitt described Anne Deane as 'a lady endowed with all the qualities which combine in showing God's best and noblest gift to man – an ideal woman.' [79]

Death of   Just four months later Michael Davitt himself was dead. He was only sixty
Michael Davitt   years old but the hectic life the one-armed Davitt was forced to lead to earn his bread and his deep involvement – in and out of prison – in the land war, took its toll.

Davitt had requested in his will, 1 February 1904, to be buried in Straide 'without any funeral demonstration'. The arrival of his remains at Foxford railway station was later described by an eyewitness.[80]

> The train, I remember was drawn by two engines, the St Patrick and the St Michael. The two engines and the long line of carriages were covered with black tapes. The leading carriage contained the remains of Michael Davitt. The next contained nothing but wreaths and floral tributes, and almost all the carriages were reserved. When the train stopped hundreds of passengers, including the whole Irish Party from Westminister, alighted. Many wore tall hats and black armbands. The hearse ... was drawn by four horses and there were ten brakes, six of which were reserved for the Irish Party, while others carried the wreaths ... Every horse-and-cart and trap for miles around was there, all filled to capacity with those who came to pay their last respects. Slowly the crowd moved to one side and the long walk to Straide Abbey, a distance of five miles, started. The stewards, with some young priests, kept

79 *C.T.* 8 July 1905
80 Michael Comer, 'The Funeral of Michael Davitt' in *Swinford Echo* 1967, p 60

the procession orderly. All along the road, people came from cabin and hamlet to see the funeral pass.

Davitt's death was a great personal loss to John Dillon. Ever since the Land League days when they first worked together they became close friends. They were soul brothers. 'To John it was the loss of one dearer than a brother', Elizabeth recorded. 'And what can I say of the desolation of his wife and children? That week when he lay dying was like a nightmare and remains in my recollection as a dream of misery.' [81] But an even greater tragedy lay in store for Dillon. A little over six months later, on 4 May 1907, Elizabeth herself died. A few hours before she died she received the Last Sacraments from John Conmee, a Jesuit from the nearby Belvedere College, on whom James Joyce was about to confer a dubious immortality. Two days before she had given birth to her seventh child, stillborn. Elizabeth and John had only been married for eleven years. On hearing the news Denis O'Hara immediately wired Dillon: 'Cannot find words to express my feelings of sorrow, regret and sympathy.' [82]

Death of Elizabeth Dillon

P. J. O'Grady with Keash Banner
(courtesy Jim Finan)

81 Diary of Elizabeth Dillon, 5 Nov 1906, qtd in Lyons, *Dillon*, p 267
82 Denis O'Hara to John Dillon, 5 May 1907, Dil. P. 6769

CHAPTER TWELVE

A Better Life

Distress The root cause of the poverty in the west, particularly in Mayo, was that too many people were trying to subsist on too little land. These districts were described as 'congested' because a high proportion of the people in them were restricted to patches of boggy or stony land from which it was impossible to do more than scratch the barest minimum necessary to keep body and soul together. When heavy rains in late summer damaged the potato crop, the staple diet of the people, the result was that 'distress', the official euphemism for famine or near famine, occurred and this was almost endemic in the west of Ireland. It was the distress of 1879 which sparked off the land war with the establishment of the Land League in that year and such distress was to occur again in 1890-91, 1894-95, 1897-98 and 1904-5.[1]

Blight struck the potato crop in the autumn of 1890. A large meeting in Kiltimagh with Denis O'Hara in the chair called on the government to 'come to our rescue seeing starvation and death staring us in the face.' The meeting wanted work, not charity: 'If we get work we are prepared to pay shopkeepers and landlords as far as we are able.' There were similar meetings in Ballaghaderreen and Monasteraden where the 'failure of the potato crop was absolute.'[2] 'Distress is actually in our midst', Bishop Lyster told the Bishop of Salford early in 1891, 'There are places limited in extent and not a few in number where at the present moment the people are dependent on the charity and pity of their immediate neighbours who are little better off than themselves.'[3]

1894-95 The potato crop failed again in the autumn of 1894 and early the following year Swinford Guardians, fearing 'a repetition of the famine scenes of '47', recommended that tenants be given employment on their own holdings, be paid with seed potatoes and be entitled to a reduction of rents for the following three years. 'It will take them that long to recover from the disastrous effects of this bad year ... unless some extraordinary relief works be opened

---

1 see Plan of Campaign p 262
2 *C.T.* 11 Oct & 8 Nov 1890
3 *W.P.* 14 Feb 1891

immediately in this Union, the Guardians will be utterly unable to cope with thousands of starving families.'[4]

By February they were receiving petitions for relief from numerous parts of the Union, one from forty families in Carnaculla fearing 'another repetition of '47 and perhaps a worse famine scene than '47 before May day next ...'[5] Other petitions were sent directly to the Under Secretary. [6] The relieving officers, inundated with pleas for help, asked the Guardians to appoint extra officers. 'Crowds of people are coming hourly to my door looking for relief in some shape', the relieving officer wrote from Charlestown, 'and I find it impossible to contend with this difficult task without assistance.' His colleague in Swinford asked for two assistants to cope with the increasing number of applicants for relief.[7]

Petitions

The harvest of 1897 was again a complete failure, as Denis O'Hara had predicted. 'Certainly the outlook for the coming year is gloomy enough. We have had constant rain for weeks. The people could not get down the crops and the potatoes that were put down in the lowlands have got soft and rotten and in a good many places the outlook is anything but encouraging.'[8]A relief fund was started in Manchester and over £6,000 was collected. 'It looks strange', O'Hara thought, 'that Manchester should be the only place where anything is being done to relieve the distress that prevails.' The Manchester Fund sent £450 to the Sisters of Charity in Foxford for relief works, as well as large consignments of clothing on several occasions which the Sisters distributed to the most needy. They also received a grant for their Bread Fund to feed children attending the convent schools. Funds came also from elsewhere and over thirty tons of seed potatoes were distributed among poor cottiers.[9] Maud Gonne visited Foxford in April and wrote an article in the *Freeman* describing conditions there and the work of the Sisters in relieving distress.[10]

1897-98

The Sisters of Charity in Ballaghaderreen and their superioress, Mrs Kelly, were doing equally good work among the poor:

Ballaghaderreen

> You could not believe all the Sisters have done and are still doing. They have a very large number of the poorest families on their lists, to each of whom they give a small allowance of meal, tea and other necessaries weekly

---

4 Resolutions of Swinford Board of Guardians, 1 & 29 Jan 1895, Dil. P. 6803
5 n.d. Feb & 4 & 5 Mar 1895, Dil. P. 6803
6 See Appendix 41
7 ibid
8 Denis O'Hara to John Dillon, 11 May 1897 & 15 Jan 1898, Dil. P. 6803
9 Charles Kennedy, £50 worth of oats, Belfast Ladies (procceeds of a Ball), £20, Anonymous, £25, Mr Ford, *Irish World*, New York, (per the Archbishop of New York), £200, Irish National Federation, Adelaide, £62. 'Annals of Foxford Convent', RSCG
10 *F. J.* 13 April 1898

Girl selling wool
in Foxford

and small as it is, it saves these creatures from starvation ... it is amazing all
they are able to do. They also give clothes to the school children in all the
schools, both to boys and girls (who are very poor) and in the town school
(the girls') their own, they supply lunch; plenty of bread and butter daily.
Mrs Kelly was in great spirits when I gave her Mrs Martin's £5 yesterday
and she told me that up to this she has never refused to relieve a needy
family and the money has come in, just like Mrs Martin's and Lady Mathew's, steadily in the most unexpected way and she is confident she will be
able to keep on until the crops come in. It is a great comfort to feel that all
this goes on. With all this the people are very poor and not able to resist
disease. So many die of illness who might be saved if they could get more
generous treatment. Mrs Kelly told me yesterday with great sadness that
there were two deaths from dire want which she did not hear of until it
was too late to save them. A great number of men have gone to England ...
and very little money is coming from America.[11]

1904-5   The potatoes failed again in the autumn of 1904 and by the following
spring distress was widespread. 'The month of February 1905 brought us face
to face with much destitution amongst the poor,' the annalist of Foxford convent recorded. 'The bad year in England and the destruction of the potato
crop now began to make itself felt.' The Sisters again received substantial help
'from a few tried friends' and purchased tons of seed potatoes for the most
destitute.[12]

11 Anne Deane to John Dillon, 9 May 1898, Dil. P. 6889
12 RSCG. A reporter from the *Freeman's Journal* visited the parishes of Swinford, Killasser,
    Charlestown, Kiltimagh and Foxford and wrote accounts of the famine there. *FJ.* 29 Dec 1904

Following periods of famine many tenants found themselves unable to pay their rents and evictions became commonplace. Collections were held in various parishes in 1893 for the Evicted Tenants' Fund. A collection was made throughout Charlestown parish during the last week in November culminating with a chapel gate collection on Sunday and the curate was confident that 'the people will take it up well'. John Dillon was delighted with the result in his ancestral home. 'Ballaghaderreen has done magnificently for the Evicted Tenants' Fund. It is really an amazing sum.'[13] Not all priests were as enthusiastic for the collection as Michael Keveney in Ballaghaderreen or the parish priest and curate in Charlestown. A Foxford man who sent ten shillings to Dillon for the fund complained that the parish priest had postponed the collection. 'I am very sorry to inform you that the priests here are very lukewarm Nationalists.'[14]

Some were deliberately singled out for eviction because they were political activists such as Dominick D. Regan on the Phibbs estate in Keash. He was one of the organisers of the Land League in Keash in 1880 and later a member of the local branch of the INL, and was now assistant secretary of Keash INF. He had organised sixty tenants in 1883 to take Phibbs to court to have a fair rent fixed. 'This man is victimised owing to the action he has taken both publicly and privately', according to Patrick Scully, the parish priest.[15] Regan, who was unmarried but supported two sisters, died after a short illness on 23 April 1895. Thomas Durkan of Bunninadden, 'one of the old guard in days gone by', who was evicted in March 1885, was still dispossessed over ten years later when he applied and was given a grant from the Evicted Tenants' Fund. There were five in his family ranging in ages from seven to eighteen and his farm was still unoccupied in May 1895, though 'grabbed' twice, first in 1886 and again in 1892, but the 'grabbers' were forced by public opinion to surrender possession.[16]

Evictions were carried out on the Dillon estate during the summer and autumn of 1892. Mrs Mary Gallagher of Drumnalasson, Ballaghaderreen was wakened at daybreak on 30 July by the sound of a number of men trying to level her house while her husband Ned and their son were away working in England. She appealed in vain to them to stop and, gathering a few sticks together, she made a shelter for herself and her family of eight, ranging in

13 J. J. McDonnell to John Dillon, 20 Nov 1893, Dil. P.6808; John Dillon to Anne Deane, 29 Nov 1893, Dil. P. 6887
14 Patrick Dunphy to John Dillon, 17 Dec 1892, Dil. P. 6819
15 M. Gray, secretary of Keash INF to David Sheedy, 15 Oct 1894; same to J. F. X. O'Brien, 13 June 1895, Dil. P. 6806
16 John O'Dowd to John Dillon, 24 April & 7 May 1895, Dil. P. 6807

ages from six to twenty-one. Seven families were evicted and three houses lev-elled on 17 September in Charlestown parish, including that of James Cooke of Lurga. Three families were evicted in Barnacuaige and four houses levelled at Carracastle, with Jackson and Stewart leading the 'crowbar brigade.'[17]

Dillon came to Charlestown to investigate the evictions and after address-ing the people opposite the chapel, drove to Lurga, accompanied by Tom Loftus and his curate, J. J. McDonnell. A large crowd had assembled there to build a wooden hut for James Cooke. The following day he visited the site of Mrs Gallagher's levelled house in Drumnalasson. She was then serving a prison sentence for digging up her potato crop and Dillon gave the eldest boy some money to buy dinner for the rest of the family and asked Anne Deane to find some clothes for them. Michael Keveney offered Hussey, Lord Dil-lon's agent, two years' rent if he restored the Gallaghers to their holding but to no avail.[18] Mrs Gallagher herself asked Dillon in July 1894 for a grant from the Evicted Tenants' Fund to help send a daughter to America. 'I hope not to be much longer in want of assistance when I get the most of my family in America.' By the beginning of 1896 her daughter was in America as well as her husband and son, but she was now very anxious to get her holding back and asked Dillon to help her.

Land-Grabbers

It had been 'grabbed' by a man named Fitzpatrick who was a blacksmith and carpenter who 'would throw up the holding if a little pressure was brought on him by way of a public meeting as he would immediately lose all his customers'.[19] Land-grabbers were particularly despised. Meetings were held every Sunday in Charlestown 'to protest against intending grabbers'. 'Sub-Inspector Allen has two police every Sunday and holiday outside Bush-field Chapel.'[20] Pat Murphy had been evicted in 1890 from his holding in Lowpark which was 'grabbed' by a man name Moffat who remained in pos-session in spite of all the protests. Murphy was convicted three times for tres-pass and on the last occasion got three months in prison. [21]

James Cooke of Lurga

The house of James Cooke of Lurga was one of the three levelled on 17 September 1892 and went up in a blaze when the roof was knocked down on the fire below. James himself, who was eighty years old, was away in England, leaving his elderly wife in the home. Denis O'Hara was particularly outraged:

17 Among those evicted: Pat Dunleavy (house levelled), Hubert Jordan, Barnacuaige, Tom Mulligan, Carn, (a prominent member of the local INF), Widow Halligan, Cashel, Mrs Doherty and James Cooke, Lurga. *C.T.* 17 & 24 Sept 1892
18 Michael Keveney to John Dillon, 13 January 1893, Dil. P. 6770
19 *C.T.* 29 Oct 1892, John Dillon to Anne Deane 27 Jan 1893, Mary Gallagher to John Dillon, 21 July 1894, Feb & 24 Nov 1896, Dil. P. 6806 & 6886

We have been told by John Dillon of a scene which is enough to make any civilised country ashamed, that the house where a human being dwelt had been set fire to over the head of that poor peasant. If they put us to it we will light a fire and light our torches in that flame and spread the flame through the length and breadth of the country ... If the landlords put us to it we will fight; we fought them before and beat them and it is not much trouble to do so now when we are at the winning post with plenty of life and plenty of energy remaining.' [22]

The Cooke saga continued for a number of years. The parish priest of Charlestown asked for a small grant from the Evicted Tenants' Fund for the Cookes who were almost starving, as Cooke had failed to get employment on the relief works in 1895.[23] Cooke was taken on the works but he had other problems according to his daughter, Mary. 'We are in sore need presently. My father was taken off the relief work a fortnight ago to spend a term of twenty-one days in Castlebar jail for no bigger crime than being inside the walls of the house that the rapacious tyrant Jackson threw and burned three years ago.' Cooke was only three days out of jail when he was fined twenty shillings or fourteen days in jail for trespassing on Lord Dillon's land. His daughter, who herself was fined ten shillings at the same court, complained that Lord Dillon's agent, Jackson, was taking both of them before every court for trespass.

She buried her elderly mother early in 1896:

So our fund of money has run ashore and to add to our misfortune, Jackson's spies goes about and threatens all kinds of vengeance on any persons who will give us entertainments. So we are without food or shelter or money to pay for either, dependent on the charity of some good-hearted people who takes us in, not knowing but it would cause their own rents to be refused if found out by Jackson.

Evicted a second time in June of that year, from the hut erected for them by the parish, they were without any shelter but the 'canopy of heaven'. 'So if your honour doesn't send us a grant or some relief, we must surely secumb (*sic*) under the weight of misfortune and poverty hanging over us.' Her father was arrested again and was once more an inmate of Castlebar jail and she had to spend most of the grant she received on clothes for him. He was back in jail in Castlebar in April 1897 for a further term of fourteen days. [24]

20 J. J. McDonnell to John Dillon, 20 Nov 1893, Dil. P. 6808
21 *C.T.* 29 Oct 1892
22 *C.T.* 19 Nov 1892
23 Michael Keveney to John Dillon, 6 April 1895, Dil. P. 6770
24 Mary Cooke to John Dillon, 16 Aug, 20 Nov, 1895, 29 Jan, 11 Mar, 22 June, 16 Nov, 16, 23 Dec 1896, 22 April 1897

Congested Districts
Board

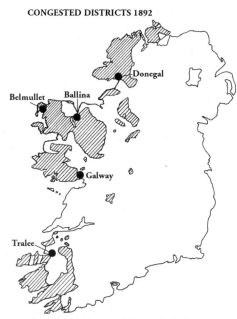

CONGESTED DISTRICTS 1892

The Land Act of 1891 broke new ground by establishing the Congested Districts Board (CDB) to relieve poverty in the south and west of Ireland. The Board introduced many schemes to improve the condition of the cottiers and attempted to encourage better methods of farming. An agricultural instructor was sent to Kiltimagh to advise nine landholders how to work a portion of their holdings. Good potato, oat and turnip seed were sold at cost price to farmers and certain agricultural implements, such as ploughs, harrows and rollers were lent or sold to cultivate holdings more thoroughly while considerable efforts were made to encourage drainage. However, difficulties were encountered, particularly in districts like Kiltimagh, where almost every able-bodied working man or lad was absent in England from June till October.

Swinford Example
Holdings

The Board co-operated with the Royal Dublin Society in maintaining ten example holdings in the neighbourhood of Swinford, where an agricultural instructor advised on rotation cropping so that the land could keep far more stock, and turnips and mangolds became common in the district. The experiment was discontinued at the end of 1895.

Tree-Planting

The Board also encouraged planting shelter belts of trees. At Denis O'Hara's request, some 350 holdings in his parish were planted in 1892 with small shelter plantations under the supervision of the Board's forester, and a similar scheme was operated in Bohola at the request of John O'Grady. Trees annually granted to the Sisters of Charity in Foxford were distributed among the cottiers. 12,500 forest trees, Scotch firs, larch, spruce, alder and sycamore were distributed in February 1902 in lots of 25, 50, 75 or 100. The Sisters had already distributed over 600 apple trees among seventy-two cottiers willing to cultivate small orchards.[25]

Home Improvements

For more than a hundred years there had been little or no improvement in the living conditions of poor cottiers. The twin evils of humans sharing their cabins with farm animals and the consequent manure heaps in front of the

25 RSCG

cabins continued to shock visitors to the West of Ireland, and concerted efforts were made during the last decade of the nineteenth century to encourage cottiers to discontinue these practices.[26] The Board offered inducements in 1894 to small occupiers in the Kiltimagh district to provide out-buildings for cattle, and by 1895 a number had been assisted in building cattle-houses, pig-styes, barns etc. Those who applied for grants had to give undertakings to discontinue the practise of keeping animals in their houses. Progress, however, was slow and by 1900 it was estimated that still five-sixths of the 4,300 tenants on the Dillon estate, extending through the parishes of Ballaghaderreen, Kilmovee, Carracastle and Charlestown, kept cattle in rooms occupied by themselves and their children. [27]

Once the animals had been evicted from the cabins it became necessary to erect shelters for them, particularly for the winter months. The convent in Foxford compiled annual lists of householders who built outhouses between 1898 and 1912, and these included names of householders from Meelick, Callow and Attymass as well from the parish of Foxford.[28]During that period 460 stables and 378 piggeries were built as well as new dwelling houses or old ones repaired. 277 householders added a new room to their homes and from 1903 many replaced earth floors with cement.

Outhouses

In the 1895 Winter Show of the Royal Dublin Society in Ballsbridge, thirty five entries in the vegetable section for the best six parsnips, best six carrots and best stone of potatoes, were confined to Foxford cottiers, and 300 prizes were awarded in February 1896 in the parish. The 159 entries in the garden section that year rose to 213 in 1898. 148 cottiers in thirty-five townlands competed for prizes for the best kept gardens in Foxford Agricultural Show that year.[29]

Agricultural Shows

The Board also established poultry farms to distribute among cottiers eggs for hatching. Some of the fifty-five Houdans purchased in France were dispatched to the convent in Foxford where the nuns enthusiastically instructed the country people in the rearing of poultry. Three incubators were in constant use, holding 50, 100 and 200 eggs, all from pure-bred stocks, and when the chicks were hatched they were given to cottiers to rear. They kept the pullets but gave back the cockrels to the Sisters, who also bought up at a shilling each all mongrel chickens, which were killed for table use to rid the countryside of them.

Poultry

27 CDB Ninth Report, p 18
26 see Chapter Four for efforts made by the Sisters of Charity in Foxford
28 RSCG/ H 26/ 111
29 Names and addresses given, RSCG/H 26/ 98 & 110

Eggs   Between December 1895 and April 1896, almost 38,000 eggs were bought from the cottiers with the new breeds of poultry. However, the market then was poor and prices low, so the Sisters opened a store for the eggs, had them packed and sent to Liverpool and other markets. Eighty Foxford cottiers sent eggs to the RDS Spring Show in 1896 and a hundred entered in the coloured, white and duck egg sections in the 1898 Spring Show. The egg market began to improve. A northerner named Hughes, an eggler who traded with Liverpool, went from village to village with a horse and cart buying eggs from cottiers, and by 1900 the trade had improved so much he acquired a motor lorry and later a second one. Villagers came down from their mountain homes to the nearest points where the lorries passed and sold Hughes their eggs and with the money bought 'tea, sugar, bacon, jams and a hundred other little luxuries'.[30] The Sisters of Mercy in Swinford were given a grant of about £190 in 1896 to assist them to provide fowl, poultry-houses, runs and other appliances for rearing and fattening poultry for educational purposes. [31]

Foxford Woollen Mills

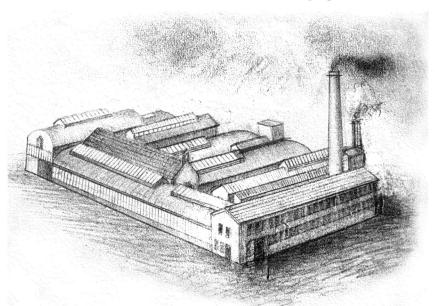

Foxford Woollen Mills   The Congested Districts Board liked to boast of the Foxford Woollen Mills as their most successful flagship, but much of the credit for its success lies elsewhere. It was the brainchild of Agnes Morrogh Bernard who moved from Ballaghaderreen to Foxford in 1891 and quickly realised the potential of the River Moy as a source of power for a woollen mills. One of the Sisters of

30 RSCG /H 26 / 449
31 CDB Fifth Report, p 12

Charity, Francis Columba Feeney, wrote to her cousin, Michael Davitt, for advice and he referred her to Peter White of the Irish Woollen Mills, Dublin, who in turn recommended John Charles Smith of Caledon Mills, Co Tyrone. Agnes wrote to Smith and he agreed to travel to Foxford at his own expense in June 1891 to discuss the project with her. Initially he scorned the idea but when she persisted he agreed to help her and the Catholic nun and the Protestant Orangeman were to prove a formidable combination.

The Mother-General of the Sisters of Charity, Mrs Margison, agreed to mortgage their head house in Milltown, Dublin to guarantee a loan of £5,000 which Agnes needed to get the project off the ground. She had already appealed to the CDB for a grant early in 1892 but was still awaiting their response. 'It appears the CD are now *ashamed* that *you*, a woman, have beaten them in generosity and done what they with their thousands to spend would not face for the poor congested creatures.'[32] However, the Board did give her in November 1892 a loan of £7,000 at 2½% interest repayable in eighteen years by fixed half-yearly instalments, and this was followed in April 1893 by a gift of £1,500. A capitation grant of £4,000 was provided for instruction in the technical school attached to the mills.

Already the mills were up and running when George Thomson of Huddersfield visited Foxford in 1893 at the request of the CDB. 'I found already in good working order a manufactory established on what I consider to be up-to-date principles of manufacture, engaged in the production of goods for which there is a large demand.'[33] The Board received an even more glowing report on the mills in 1894 from William J. D. Walker, a Co Down mill-owner, who assured them that they 'need have no anxiety about the investment'. Walker was particularly impressed by the 'enthusiasm of the devoted ladies in charge of each department' and their 'intimate personal contact' with the workers and the cheerfulness which pervaded the place. 'I shall conclude by saying that I have my Northern prejudices just as markedly accentuated as most men, and if the above report is favourable, it is not because I went there to praise what I saw, but because I have stated nothing but what I believe to be true.' [34]

When John Charles Smith died unexpectedly in January 1896, the Foxford Mills which he had helped so much to create was a viable venture. He had made no less than twenty-three visits to Foxford at his own expense and

John Charles Smith

32 Agnes Morrogh Bernard to Mrs Margison, 28 Oct 1892, RSCG/ H 26/ 1
33 Second Report of the Congested Districts Board, p 28
34 Full report reprinted in Denis Gildea, *Mother Mary Arsenius of Foxford*, pp 113-5 & *Work is Worship. Foxford 1892-1942*, pp 14-16

advised on the construction of the buildings, the selection of machinery, the purchase of raw material, the marketing of the finished product, methods of book-keeping etc. He had trained the Conroy sisters whom Agnes sent to his mills in Tyrone, and Agnes herself and another Sister also visited his mills to familiarise themselves with the process. Above all Smith had given them Frank Sherry whom he had trained as a manager and Sherry supervised the erection of the Foxford Mills and guided it to its ultimate success. On hearing of Smith's death the convent annalist wrote: 'Many thought his loss to the little factory would be well nigh irreparable and that soon the glowing hope of the new industry would fade away ... Divine Providence left him until all the initial difficulties were cleared away and fairly overcome'.[35]

The Connacht Exhibition

Successful advertising was the key to the growth of the Foxford Mills and to gain nationwide attention for this obscure Mayo village Agnes decided to hold an industrial exhibition there in September 1895. The Connacht Exhibition was a three-day event attended by a glittering array of distinguished guests including Lord and Lady Arran, the Lord Chancellor and Lady Ashbourne, the Lord Mayor of Dublin and Sir Horace Plunkett. The Lord Lieutenant would have attended had not his government been recently replaced. 'It was said that never before in Connacht had there been gathered together on so small a platform, men of so many divers opinions – Catholic, Protestant, Whig, Tory, Nationalist etc etc.' [36] Bishop Lyster declined an invitation to attend. 'Do you expect me to take off my hat and throw it in the air and shout for those people,' he told Agnes. She would, however, have expected him 'as a gentleman, to take off his hat to a lady', especially to Lady Arran who had done so much for the exhibition. Dean Staunton also refused to attend, which Agnes described as 'a second slap in the face for us' and she was obliged to rely on her old friend Denis O'Hara to be 'the man in the gap' and respond to speeches on their behalf.

The Countess of Arran from
The Lady of the House
15 Oct 1895

Prizes

The exhibition was divided into sections for the display of vegetables, flowers, poultry, dairy products, crafts, homespuns and textiles, with 2,025 entries in the various competitions. Exhibits came from as far as Dalkey, Kinsale, Cobh and Valentia. Prizes had been received from various organisations and enterprises. The London Irish Peasant Society donated twenty special prizes of five shillings each for the best gardens with the most productive returns, and 113 entries were judged by a three-man committee of inspection selected by Agnes, comprising the curate, Pat Conlon, Standish O'Grady

35 *Annals of Foxford Convent*, vol 1, p 46, RSCG
36 RSCG / H 26 / 449, pp 66-7

McDermott and Major Fair. Lord Clanmorris and Miss Charlotte La Touche donated prizes for replacing manure heaps with a garden for which forty competed. The Industrial Revival Movement, presided over by Lady Arran, secured prizes for hand-knitting, hand-spinning, hand-weaving, hosiery, embroidery, needlework, crochet, basketwork, carpentry and other crafts. There were prizes too for some rather quaint competitions such as the schoolboy who had the best patched and mended clothes and for the sister, mother or aunt who had done the patching. The regimental band of the Connaught Rangers played music at intervals over the three days.

Connaught Exhibition
in Foxford, 1895

The exhibition was an outstanding success and widely covered by newspapers and magazines. The *Freeman's Journal* described it as 'one of the most completely successful exhibitions of the kind ever held in Ireland' which it attributed to 'the phenomenal energy, determination and zeal of Mrs Morrogh Bernard', while the *Weekly Irish Times* wrote: 'Perhaps no more wonderful thing has ever occurred in the West of Ireland than the holding of the Industrial Exhibition in Foxford.' Lady Arran opened a 'Foxford Industrial Fund' with the aim of raising £1,000 to help relieve the crushing debt carried by the mills. In a belated attempt to recover from the dismay caused by his earlier fit of pique, Lyster contributed £100 to the fund. 'It was generally supposed,' Agnes later recorded, 'that a good many wires had been pulled and much pressure brought to bear on *Epus. Acha.* (the Bishop of Achonry) before so satisfactory a conclusion was reached.' [37]

Foxford Industrial Fund

37 RSCG / H 26 / 449, pp 65

The Foxford Mills continued to grow and came in for special praise from Charles Reid in his critique of the work of the first five years of CDB: 'It is a model in its working, fitted up with the latest machinery and turning out the best quality of stuffs in tweeds, serges, blankets etc. There is certainly no fault to be found with the management or the excellence of the fabrics.' Over forty women were then paid at an average rate of six shillings a week, but Reid

The Little Spinners
at the Connaught
Exhibition from
The Lady of the House,
15 Oct 1895

thought, however, that the commercial element could be improved by the employment of travellers to seek out markets. By 1900 two travellers were employed, one in England and one in Ireland, with the result that the demand exceeded the output of the factory. About 4,000 yards of tweeds, serges, flannels, blankets etc. were turned out weekly and over one hundred were employed all the year round at good wages. In addition about £3,000 was spent annually in the purchase of wool from local growers while £4,000 was paid for fine yarn imported. [38]

The Foxford Mills continued to go from strength to strength and by 1 November 1910, when it had paid the Board back the final of the thirty-six half-yearly instalments of the original loan received in 1892, it had earned both a national and international reputation for the quality of its product. That year the Board paid tribute to Agnes Morrogh Bernard and her manager: 'To her business capacity and enthusiasm at first, and subsequently to the able

38 Ninth CDB Report, p 41

assistance of Mr Frank Sherry, the manager of the factory, the unqualified success of this undertaking is due.' [39]

The Board had also made a loan of £3,000 in 1892 to the Sisters of Charity in Ballaghaderreen who had opened a knitting factory. The terms were the same as those given to the Foxford Sisters, who then employed forty-three hands while the Ballaghaderreen factory had ninety-two. They received a further £500 in April 1893 and members of the Board who visited the factory in that year, expressed themselves 'much pleased with the progress made and with the kind of goods that they saw in process of manufacture.' However, George Thomson, who visited the Foxford and Ballaghaderreen factories in 1893, expressed enthusiasm only for Foxford. The CDB Report of 1895 commenting on the remarkable progress made by the Foxford factory, added: 'We regret that we cannot yet feel assured of the success of the Ballaghaderreen Hosiery Factory.' It got into serious financial difficulties in 1905 and the Mother-General requested Agnes Morrogh Bernard to go there to resolve the problems, and she returned to Foxford before the end of the year when most of the problems had been resolved. [40]

Ballaghaderreen Hosiery Factory

CDB had made capitation grants in 1893 to both factories in Foxford (£1,500), and in Ballaghaderreen (£500), to maintain technical schools to provide instruction in the manufacture of woollen goods, hosiery, ready-made clothing and domestic service training. The full capitation grant was calculated on the standard attendance of 100 pupils in each technical school. William J. D. Walker's report to the Board in September 1894 was highly complimentary to the Foxford school: 'I was delighted with what I saw in the school and the apparent practical nature of the training. I noticed there was minute individual attention and great skill is displayed in drawing out the latent faculties of the children in such a way as to enable them afterwards to push their own way in the world.' [41] Walker also inspected the knitting, dairy and cooking departments in the school. Denis O'Hara's scheme in 1893 for providing technical instruction in Kiltimagh was approved by CDB and the building of the technical school there was completed in 1895.

Technical Schools

Home industry classes were established in parts of the congested districts. Lace classes began in 1902 in Kiltimagh, Gurteen and Benada where the Sisters of Charity also had a domestic training class. The following year Attymass had a lace as well as a domestic training class, most probably under the supervision of the Foxford Sisters, while Kilmactigue had a lace and

Home Industry Classes

39 CDB Nineteenth Report, p 35
40 Gildea, *Mother Mary Arsenius of Foxford*, pp 146-7
41 qtd in Gildea, op. cit., p 114

carpentry class. CDB reported in 1910: 'The demand for lace and crochet continues to be good and the earnings of the girls employed in the Board's classes are sufficient to make up in many of the poorest families the deficiency in receipts upon which depend whether the family is to make a painful struggle in poverty or to live in comparative comfort as regards the necessaries of life.' [42] Benada's lace class earned £2,252 10s. 5d. in 1911, the second highest earnings of some seventy-six classes in the country. There were other beneficial effects:

> The workers become neat, tidy and scrupulously clean: and their general appearance has improved wonderfully. This improvement has to a very large extent spread to the homes where much of their lace and crochet making is done, as the necessity for producing spotless and unstained lace and crochet was soon realised when it was found that prices depended upon a due regard for cleanliness.

For the most part the girls and women spent their earnings prudently, though the report added rather prudishly; 'It is true that a small portion of what these girls earn is spent on personal finery, but not to any extravagant or reprehensible extent.' [43]

Denis O'Hara

From the very beginning Denis O'Hara was an enthusiastic supporter of CDB and made suggestions which were very often adopted by the Board. It was not surprising that he became a member in 1895 and remained so until his death in 1922. He was described as 'an ideal inland-country representative, as he had a thorough day-to-day experience ... of a toiling population living

42 CDB Nineteenth Report, p 34
43 CDB Twentieth Report, pp 28-9

on small holdings inadequate for the support of their families' and whose men were obliged to migrate in thousands every year to England for harvesting work. [44] The Board consisted of about a dozen members usually headed by the Chief Secretary, and Denis, who was appointed by the then Chief Secretary, John Morley, served with his successors including Arthur and Gerald Balfour, George Wyndham, Augustine Birrell etc. and other well-known members such as Sir Horace Plunkett and Sir Anthony MacDonnell. The only other long-serving Catholic clergyman on the Board was Bishop Patrick O'Donnell of Raphoe. For the best part of twenty-seven years Denis attended the monthly meetings in Dublin, occasionally acting as a 'gentle, persuasive, practical and sensible' chairman. [45]

He persuaded the Board in 1897 to adopt the Parish Committee Scheme which aimed at inducing tenants to make improvements in their holdings, dwellings and surroundings with the help of small money grants. The scheme was administered by a parish committee, partly elected and partly *ex officio* such as clergymen of all denominations, Poor Law Guardians and landlords or their agents. Six members were elected by the rated resident landowners of the parish. Those who wished to make improvements applied to the committee, giving particulars of the proposed improvements and the amount of aid sought. The committee decided upon the application and made their recommendation to the Board who decided how much aid should be granted. If the improvements were sanctioned, the work was started and carried out under the supervision of a person appointed by the committee and when completed examined by one of the Board's inspectors.[46]

Parish Committee Scheme

CDB tried the scheme as an experiment in Swinford Poor Law Union during the period up to the end of December 1898 but later extended it to all 'those poor and populous parishes that lie between Foxford and Ballaghaderreen, covering an area of about 700 square miles, with a population of over 130,000. Almost the entire population of this great district consisted of very small tenants, each holding on average only five acres of very poor quality land, reclaimed from rock and bog.' Here grants amounting to £3,196 were made in 1897 and 1898:

Swinford Union

No one can pass through the districts in which these committees have been at work without noticing on all sides the new by-roads, extensive drains, and numerous small buildings with galvanised roofs which attest

44 W. L. Micks, *History of the Congested Districts Board,* p 179
45 ibid
46 CDB Sixth Report pp 26, 70-73

the success of the scheme and show that a real awakening of energy and industry has commenced amongst the small farmers and cottagers. [47]

Extension

Following its initial success in East Mayo, the Parish Committee Scheme was extended to the rest of the congested districts from Donegal to Kerry and by the end of March 1908 there were 848 committees in existence. From its inception in 1897 over £58,000 were given in grants, over 13,000 dwelling houses and almost 14,000 out-houses were erected or improved as well as roads and drains constructed or repaired. [48] By 1910 grants, varying from £20 in Achonry parish to £245 in Swinford, had been made under the scheme in some twenty parishes in the diocese, half in Sligo and half in Mayo. [49]

Land Purchase

The Land Act of 1891 provided a larger fund for state-aided land purchase but it lacked compulsory purchasing powers, as John Dillon had pointed out in Castlebar in July 1892: 'The Congested Districts Board should have power to buy up by compulsion large tracts of empty land in Mayo at a fair price and divide them into thirty or forty-acre farms for those in overcrowded districts.' [50] However, some 47,000 tenants, though much less than expected, utilised the Act to buy their farms. In practice, the process of buying was so complicated that tenants were easily discouraged, while landlords were alienated by the device of paying them not in cash but in land stocks.

Edmondstown Estate

One of the first estates to be purchased in June 1892, by Denis O'Hara and Michael Keveney, was the Costello estate at Edmondstown in Ballaghaderreen. The house was given to the bishop to be used as a diocesan college. [51] The demesne was purchased with the intention of dividing the estate into twenty-acre farms for local people and newspapers reported that the two priests had already created 400 peasant proprietors in the locality. [52] Over a year later Denis O'Hara had a 'long and most satisfactory interview' with John Morley, the Chief Secretary, who was 'greatly pleased' to hear his account of the Edmondstown tenants and Denis told him that Anne Deane had become security for the poorest of them. [53]

47 CDB Eighth Report, pp 27, 28, 29
48 CDB Seventeenth Report, Appendix XXXVI, p 148
49 *Co Sligo:* Kilmactigue, £125, Achonry, £20, Ballysadare & Kilvarnet, £70, Curry, £105, Kilfree & Killaraght, £120, Drumrat, £35, Emlefad & Kilmorgan, £30, Killoran, £25, Kilshalvey, Kilturra & Cloonoghill, £25, Cloonacool, £60. *Co Mayo:* Attymass, £55, Bohola, £80, Kilmovee, £180, Carracastle, £150, Kilconduff & Meelick, £245, Kilgarvan, £85, Killasser, £110, Killedan, £110, Toomore, £90, Templemore, £30. CDB Nineteenth Report, Appendix XI, pp 56-7
50 *C.T.* 2 July 1892
51 Now the bishop's residence
52 *C.T.* 18 June & *S.C.* 25 June 1892
53 Denis O'Hara to John Dillon, 3 Sept 1893, Dil. P. 6769

As holdings in congested districts were generally too small to make tenant purchase economic, CDB bought complete estates and rearranged, consolidated, and enlarged holdings, which were fenced and drained, before selling them to tenants. The Board purchased Lord Dillon's estate on 11 May 1899 for £290,000, which the Land Commission advanced to the Board in the form of Land Stock, and it took possession of the estate on 27 June 1899. It comprised over 90,000 acres with over 87,000 in Co Mayo, extending from Ballaghaderreen in the north-east to Ballyhaunis in the south and Charlestown in the north, and included the town of Ballaghaderreen and a portion of Charlestown within the boundaries of the estate.

Purchase of Dillon Estate

Anne Deane was delighted. 'There is great joy over the sale of the Dillon estate. It would be a sad disappointment if the towns are not included.' [54] The Dillon Estate was the first experiment in land purchase and settlement on a large scale made by the Board and their choice of that estate was no doubt largely due to the persuasive powers of Denis O'Hara, a long time advocate of the Dillon tenants. There were 4,300 tenants, of whom over half paid rents of £4 or less and a still larger majority were migratory labourers whose holdings were too small to support them. The gross annual rental of the estate was over £20,000.

The re-sale of the estate to the tenants proved much more difficult and time-consuming than anticipated. Some difficulties were bureaucratic. An inspector of the Land Commission normally inspected every one of the 4,300 holdings before the Commission could sanction the advancement of the purchase money. It was also necessary to rearrange and enlarge holdings or to stripe holdings. 'Frequently a single individual, by refusing to accept a new "striped" holding in lieu of a dozen patches of land among his neighbours' possessions, blocked the improvement of a whole townland, to his own no less than others' detriment.' Denis O'Hara suggested amendments to the Congested Districts Board Acts. ' We should get compulsory powers of striping where there are only a few cranks objecting and we should get the management of the turbary.' [55]

Re-Sale

Division of the turbary or bog on the estate presented exceptional difficulties as 2,500 of the 4,300 tenants had to get turf from a bog on the holdings of other tenants. This was eventually resolved by compensating the tenant from whose holding the turf is taken, by a reduction of rent or if he is a purchaser, by a lower price for the holding. The Board was also anxious to pre-

Turf

54 Anne Deane to John Dillon, May 1899, Dil. P. 6889
55 Denis O'Hara to John Dillon, 19 June, 8 & 9 July 1901, Dil. P. 6769

serve the game and fisheries on the original estate, a valuable amenity which might disappear once tenants were proprietors and game-keepers removed. Chief Secretary Wrench and Denis O'Hara met representatives of tenants to induce them to organise themselves to preserve the game.

As a result of these difficulties the level of sales to tenants was very low. By the end of March 1901 only 120 purchase agreements had been signed and a year later only 536. 2,500 purchase agreements had been signed by March 1903. Denis O'Hara was still not satisfied in 1904 with the clause on compulsory striping in the Chief Secretary's amending bill on the Congested Districts Board, i.e. no compulsory striping unless three-quarters of the tenants sign a request to this effect. 'According to this 3,200 of the Dillon tenants must sign before anything can be done.' He asked Dillon to seek to have it changed in Committee to 'three-quarters of the tenants affected by the striping.' [56]

A very large number of houses on the estate were built or improved by the Board, independently of all those built and improved under the Parish Committee Scheme which had been established for a number of years in all the parishes on the estate. The Board gave assistance in the form of roofing material, doors and windows to over 1,000 tenants who erected new buildings or improved old ones, and also undertook a massive drainage scheme on the Lung River, employing 500-700 labourers in the summer of 1905.

Wyndham Land Act George Wyndham, the Chief Secretary, introduced a new land bill in 1903 which encouraged landlords to sell entire estates and not just individual holdings, with sales taking place if three-quarters of the tenants on any given estate were in favour. The purchase money was advanced to the tenants by the state, to be repaid by annuities, and as an incentive to landlords to sell a bonus of 12% was offered on each sale. The bill was passed and became law by December 1903 and its immediate effect was to give an immense impetus to the transfer of land from landlord to tenant. An amending act, the Birrell Act, was passed in 1909 making land purchase compulsory. Denis O'Hara advised Dillon not to vote against it. 'If it can be passed in its entirety it will be a great bill and should settle the congested districts at least.'[57] Tenants eagerly seized the opportunity presented them by these two acts and between 1903 and 1920 nearly nine million acres changed hands and two million more were in the process of being sold.

56 Denis O'Hara to John Dillon, 18 July 1904, Dil. P. 6769
57 Denis O'Hara to John Dillon, 20 Nov & 8 Dec 1909, Dil. P. 6769

One of the architects of the Wyndham Act was Sir Anthony MacDonnell. [58] He was born in 1844 in Sragh in the parish of Carracastle, the son of Mark Garvey MacDonnell of Palmfield House, a local Catholic landlord. After attending Summerhill College and Queen's College Galway he joined the Indian civil service where he was rapidly promoted in the provincial government of Calcutta. He was reputed to have been largely responsible for the Bengal Tenancy Act which protected tenants from rack-renting and eviction. He was made a Knight Commander of the Star of India in 1893 and two years later appointed Lieutenant Governor of the United Provinces, ruling over a population of 40 million. He resigned in 1901 on health grounds and when the post of Under-Secretary became vacant in 1902 Wyndham asked the prime minister, A. J. Balfour, to offer it to MacDonnell.

Sir Antony MacDonnell

MacDonnell, a forceful personality, left Wyndham in no doubt about where his loyalties lay. 'I am an Irishman, a Roman Catholic, and a liberal in politics. I have strong Irish sympathies.' One of his brothers, Henry, was a priest in Mauritius and another brother, Dr M. A. MacDonnell, was a member of the Home Rule party and MP for Laois. He demanded to be given 'adequate opportunities of influencing the action and policy of the Irish government' and intended to concentrate on the settlement of the land question. Wyndham accepted these conditions and MacDonnell was appointed in October 1902 and became immediately involved in the preparations for, and the working of, the land act of 1903. He remained in his post until 1908, long enough to contribute to the solution of another Irish problem, the provision of University education for Catholics. That year an act was passed creating the National University of Ireland, comprising the three colleges of Dublin, Cork and Galway, while Maynooth became a constituent college. When he resigned in 1908 he took his seat in the House of Lords as Baron of Swinford.

MacDonnell, a somewhat autocratic administrator, favoured the abolition of the Congested Districts Board, dividing its functions between the department of agriculture and the Land Commission. During his term as Under-Secretary he managed to curb its independence, by subordinating it to the Chief Secretary's office, but after MacDonnell's departure the Board's sphere of action, particularly its powers in respect of land purchase, were considerably enlarged. In the following years the Board secured the sale of several estates in the diocese.

58 *Dictionary of Irish Biography*, Boylan, Henry, *Dictionary of National Biography*, p 198; F. S. L. Lyons, 'The Irish unionist party and the devolution crisis of 1904-5' in *Irish Historical Studies*, vol vi, no 21 (Mar 1948); Francis Shean, 'Lord McDonnell of Swinford' in *Swinford Echo* (1966), pp 95-6; Vincent Coleman, 'The MacDonnells of Palmfield House' in *Carracastle Then and Now*, pp 37-8

The estates of most landlords in Swinford were being mapped early in 1911 with a view to offering them to the Board but there was great dissatisfaction because General Brabazon did not have the town of Swinford mapped with the rural portion of his estate. 'If he persists in holding the town matters must be made hot for him.' [59] To exert influence on Brabazon, Edward Connington was persuaded to accept the presidency of the local UIL branch for that year. According to the parish priest of Foxford, 'Foxford and Swinford are the only towns that now remained unsold' in Dillon's constituency and 'the people of the town of Foxford wish to clear out Lord Clanmorris.' [60] By early 1913 George Brabazon's estate had been purchased by the Board as well as that of Hercules B. Brabazon in the same parish, and Swinford town as well as the demesne was included in the sale of George Brabazon's estate. Connington called a meeting of the townspeople to discuss the town's future.

The D'Arcy estate, close to Swinford town, was offered to the Board on condition that all rents due up to 1 May 1910 were lodged to D'Arcy's credit by 5 January 1911. They were lodged in Swinford bank in the names of Connington, James Spelman, his curate, and T. Morrin. Once D'Arcy had lodged all the documents necessary for sale to the Board the rents would be transferred to him. [61] Two years later the D'Arcy estate had still not been acquired by the Board and in the meantime a leading Swinford merchant had bought 200 acres of the estate for building purposes and a local medical doctor had also purchased some of the estate. Complaints were made to Dillon that 'such individuals are inflating prices and delaying sales.'[62] Meanwhile, the parish priest of Killasser informed Dillon in April 1911 that moves had been made towards the sale of all the estates except two in the parish.[63]

One of the very last landlords in the diocese to sell his estate to tenants was Colonel Henry B. Jordan of Thornhill, Kiltimagh. His tenants had withheld rent from him for two years until he had lodged maps with his solicitor preparatory to the sale. He lodged the maps in 1913 but when his tenants paid he refused to sell. [64] Denis O'Hara was scathing about the colonel's failure to do his duty during World War 1:

> There is no worse stamp of petty tyrant landlord now left than this Jordan.
> He always extracted every shilling he could from those unfortunate fellows
> ... He was training recruits in Cork for twelve months but he did not go

59 M. J. Leamy, Foxford, to John Dillon, 10 Jan 1911, Dil. P. 6822
60 Martin Henry to John Dillon, 7 Oct 1910, Dil. P. 6770
61 M. J. Leamy to John Dillon, 10 Jan 1911, Dil. P. 6822
62 P. O'Hara and P. Lenehan to John Dillon, 20 April 1913, Dil. P. 6822
63 J. J. McDonnell to John Dillon, 19 April 1911, Dil. P. 6822
64 J. P. O'Connor, Bohola, to John Dillon 23 June 1913, Dil. P. 6822

out himself and do any fighting. He now wants to fight his tenants. They are all wretchedly poor and I hope the League will help them. [65]

Jordan had thirty-two tenants, all migratory labourers, in Tooromin in the parish of Bohola[66] and in March 1916 he got twenty-six ejectment orders, telling O'Grady, the parish priest, that unless the tenants paid two years' rent and costs he would proceed with the ejectments. Denis O'Hara urged the tenants to stick together, that public opinion was on their side and that they would ultimately win the fight.[67] O'Grady called on the Under Secretary, Sir Matthew Nathan, to intervene and Nathan asked Denis to call on the

Plans by Henry Doran 1894

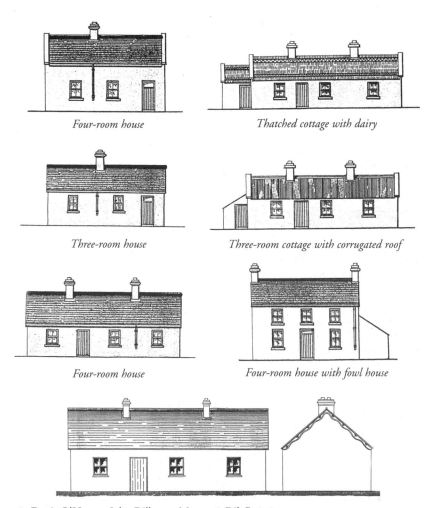

Four-room house

Thatched cottage with dairy

Three-room house

Three-room cottage with corrugated roof

Four-room house

Four-room house with fowl house

65 Denis O'Hara to John Dillon, 11 Mar 1916, Dil. P. 6769
66 See Appendix 42
67 W.P. 5 Aug 1916

Colonel. Jordan told him that he would not accept the Board's offer unless it satisfied him. Nathan summoned Jordan to Dublin but he remained stubborn and O'Grady called on the Chief Secretary, Henry Edward Duke, who promised to do his best, and even wrote to Prime Minister Asquith to complain about Jordan, but all to no avail.

Eviction Notices   O'Grady was daily expecting the eviction of twenty-nine families or 174 souls:

> God grant you may be instrumental in saving the poor tenants ... Every stone in their houses was picked up here and there and carried on their backs to build their little homes and out offices. They had no horses or donkeys or carts and no quarries convenient. Their story is heartrending. God help them! [68]

The eviction notices were finally served at the end of March 1917. 'For myself I am grieved that I failed, and much distressed that I have to witness sad scenes in this parish.' He gave a graphic description of a previous eviction he had witnessed here:

> It was in this wretched little estate I witnessed the first eviction and only eviction, the recollection of which will never leave my mind. I saw the aged venerable old man of eighty years, carried in a chair from his sick bed crying. Oh! The wail and lamentation of his daughter-in-law and five children. I shall never forget her husband stripted and bareheaded, crying and clasping his hands as if over a corpse, and going mad up and down the road, calling my attention to his house, every stone of which he carried on his back, wherever he got them, for there is no quarry in this bog. I assure you I can't suppress my strong emotions at the recollection of this harrowing scene I witnessed on the public road, and tremble at the thought of again witnessing more awful scenes. Ah if Mr Duke only witnessed the eviction I referred to, it would move him to tears. I can't believe he'll allow a large congested village to be desolated and the poor tenants to be driven from the houses they built themselves and from the little holdings they made and reclaimed by their persevering industry ... When Mr Duke was in the West I invited him to visit this wretched estate that he might see it and hear the poor tenants' tale... [69]

Final Solution   Three of the tenants, Michael Conlon, James King and Andrew Clarke were summoned to appear at Kiltimagh Petty Sessions on 19 November 1917 for non-payment of rent and failure to give up quiet possession of their holdings. Before the sitting Bohola Pipe Band played through the streets. O' Grady

68 John O'Grady to John Dillon, 14 Dec 1916, Dil. P. 6770
69 John O'Grady to John Dillon, 7 April 1917, Dil. P. 6770

gave evidence of his attempts to intermediate and failure 'to dent the colonel's obduracy'. The court was adjourned but eventually the colonel got decrees which he attempted to enforce at the end of August 1918 with the help of about a hundred RIC constables. Just as the bailiffs were about to carry out evictions, Dr Madden of Kiltimagh intervened declaring that a member in each family was ill and their removal might prove fatal. As a result the proceedings had to be abandoned for the day. Later the bitter dispute between the colonel and his tenants ended suddenly and unexpectedly when the colonel entered negotiations with the Bohola curate, Michael O'Hara, and Dr Madden acting for Dillon and reached a settlement. The final curtain was coming down on the long and protracted land war. By 1923 over three-fifths of all holdings in Ireland either had been or were in the course of being bought out and 72% of occupiers of land in the country had become or were in the process of becoming owners.

Swinford Town Crier, Stephen Bolingbroke, 1938. *(Photo Fr Browne SJ Collection)*

CHAPTER THIRTEEN

Going to Town

Market Towns

The social fabric of the diocese, as indeed much of rural Ireland, changed decisively in the course of the nineteenth century with the growth and expansion of a number of small market towns. Parishes were divided between their rural portions and their town portions with the latter playing an increasingly dominant role in social, economic, political and even ecclesiastical affairs of the parish. As the century advanced the rural portions were more and more perceived as hinterlands on which towns depended for their prosperity and the larger the hinterland the greater the prosperity. Some towns, like Swinford and Ballaghaderreen, also benefited from their proximity to completely rural parishes, like Killasser and Kilmovee.

Even the hugely popular agrarian movements which flourished in the later decades of the century were largely directed by townsmen. They played a dominant role in local Land League branches, Evicted Tenants' Defence associations and the numerous relief associations which sprang up to meet recurring famines. Membership of these groups was almost exclusively townspeople with an occasional benevolent landlord the sole rural representative. Labourers, cottiers and tenants who made up the great mass of the rural population did little else than fill the streets of the local town for huge land rallys to listen to speeches from priests, shopkeepers and other townsmen.

Social Life

The social life even of rural dwellers became more and more centred on towns, with Sundays, market-days and fair-days the highlights and 'going to town' a special event. The home-centred religion of the previous century, with its wakes, weddings, stations and patterns, gave way to a church-centred religion with parish missions and numerous new devotions. Churches were almost always built in towns and, in fact, were an important contributory factor to the growth of the town. New recreational activities were all town-based. The GAA mostly catered for townsmen, not only in its organisation but also in its sporting activities, with the odd talented country-boy recruited to play for the local town team. The Gaelic League was also patronised largely by town-dwellers. Amateur dramatics were exclusively a town phenomenon and later country boys and girls, when they could afford to, had to come to town to frequent dance-halls and cinemas.

A number of towns and villages, about ten in all, half of them towns and the other half villages, began to emerge and grow from about the middle of the nineteenth century. In 1837 they varied in population from 1,147 in Ballaghaderreen to 167 in Curry and 170 in Bellaghy.[1] Ballymote and Swinford had 875 and 813 inhabitants respectively, Tubbercurry, 650, Collooney, 553, Ballysadare, 546 and Coolaney, 326. Of an estimated population then of about 120,000 in the diocese, only about 5,500 or 4.5% lived in those towns or villages.

The main feature of a town was a weekly market. Some market towns had market houses, as Ballaghaderreen, described in 1837 as 'a commodious building' where a market was held every Friday, while Swinford had a 'good' market house which was used for markets on Tuesdays and the petty sessions

Population

Market Houses

on Wednesdays. The market house in Bellaghy was in the centre of the village and it was then planned to build one in Coolaney, while no such building was mentioned in either Collooney or Ballymote though both subsequently had one.

Four towns, Ballaghaderreen, Swinford, Collooney and Ballymote were described as 'post towns' while Ballysadare had a penny post as well as Tubbercurry with one to Ballymote. Apart from the Catholic chapel and the Protestant church, (a Wesleyan meeting house in Ballymote and a Baptist meeting house in Coolaney), other buildings in towns usually included a dispensary and a police station. There were three chief constabulary police stations in the diocese, one each in Ballaghaderreen, Swinford and Ballymote, which had the only bridewell in County Sligo, and ordinary police stations in Bellaghy, Collooney, Coolaney and Tubbercurry. A number of towns, including Ballymote, Collooney, Coolaney, Swinford and Tubbercurry had dispensaries.

Left: Market House, Collooney
Right: Market House, Ballymote

1   *Lewis' Topographical Dictionary;* neither Foxford nor Kiltimagh are listed in the dictionary which suggests that they were of insignificant size at the time

The status of a town was judged by the number of slated houses in it. In 1837 Ballaghaderreen, with its three principal streets, had about two-hundred houses 'all neatly built and slated.' as well as a courthouse and coastguard station. 'Many improvements have recently taken place in the town which is rising rapidly in importance.' Of the ninety houses in its one long street Collooney had only thirteen slated at that time, the rest being thatched. Such statistics may well have tempted Bishop McNicholas to move his residence in 1833 from there to Ballaghaderreen. Tubbercurry had also ninety houses, of which only fifteen were slated and a Protestant church built in 1830. Bellaghy, Coolaney, Curry and Ballysadare, consisted almost completely of thatched houses, seventy in Coolaney, forty-five in Ballysadare, thirty-four in Bellaghy and forty in Curry. The village of Benada consisted of about thirty 'cabins'. Over thirty years later Kiltimagh had only six slated houses. 'It was a conglomeration of straw-thatched dwellings, with a goodly percentage of hovels, poorly lighted and ventilated.' [2] There was no sanitary system and the town's water supply came from an open well. The small market square at one end of the town was described as 'a place of indescribable filth'.

Nearly all one hundred and fifty houses in Swinford were slated. 'We would not have a slated house in this town', the parish priest, John Coleman, stated in 1844, 'if the landlord had not taken it into his head to give them (the inhabitants) a lease of thirty-nine years and everyman built a house upon it and made it into a town without his (the landlord) laying anything out upon it.' Described as an 'improving' town, it consisted of one principal and two smaller streets. Swinford had also a station of the revenue police. The courthouse was described in 1846 as 'a good and convenient building lately erected and the Catholic chapel as 'an unostentatious but convenient structure'. The Protestant church of St Mary, a national school for boys and girls and barracks for the constabulary and revenue were the only other 'public establishments'. 'The place enjoys, at the present day, little importance from its trading transactions, and none from its architectural embellishments.'[3] The town had then one inn, seventeen public houses, four bakers, three drapers, two shopkeepers, two tailors, one butcher, shoemaker and blacksmith and a small number of professional people, including one doctor, two surgeons and one described as 'surgeon and apothecary'. The principal business establishment was John Mulligan & Co, merchants and importers of cotton, silk and woollen goods.

2   James O'Regan, *Articles Worldwide and Local*, pp 51-2
3   *Slaters National Commercial Directory of Irish, English and Scottish Towns*, 1846

Almost forty years later Swinford's main street received a favourable comment from a tourist:[4]

> What a splendid street the main street of Swinford is with some fine houses. About midway down the street there is a pretty cluster of aspens and spreading sycamores. The street is formed of that easy incline that hastens and sweeps its sewerage into the river at its base ... The houses are lofty and clean, its streets are well cleansed.'

The only industries mentioned in 1837 were located in the south Sligo end of the diocese. Ballysadare, with a population of 547, had two large two-wheeled corn-mills, Sim's 36-horse power and Culbertson's 70-horsepower, as well as some smaller ones and also a large bleaching mill as well as a green. Collooney too had a large bleaching establishment, a linen hall and an oatmeal mill.

Main Street, Swinford

MAIN STREET, SWINFORD.

Issued by Mellett, Swinford

Charlestown, the last town established in the diocese, was the brainchild of Lord Dillon's agent, Charles Strickland. The original town, Bellaghy, was just outside the boundary of the Dillon estate while most of the parishioners were Dillon tenants who were disadvantaged at markets in Bellaghy where their produce was last to be weighed and thus last to be sold late in the day. This was said to be the reason why Strickland announced in 1846 the creation of a new town. Three years later thirty-six houses had been built following a plan, with each house two storeys high and each street of houses provided with a back road. The national school in Bellaghy was transferred in January 1848 to

Charlestown

4   *C.T.* 23 Aug 1884

a new building in Lowpark and a few years later the site chosen for the church was also in the new town.

Many improvements were carried out in towns during the Famine as part of the programme of public works provided by the government to give relief to the starving. The back lanes and streets of Swinford were repaired in the winter of 1846-7 and sewer channels paved. The population of towns was not so greatly affected by the Famine as that of the surrounding countryside, and some towns particularly in County Sligo, such as Ballymote, showed an increase over that decade.

Lighting   Gas lighting was introduced early in the next century. Kiltimagh had an acetyline gas installation in 1909 when their ornamental street lamps were lit only on fair and market nights. At Christmas that year the first electric light bulb, which took the form of the star over the crib in the convent chapel, was switched on in Foxford. [5] Early in 1910 electric light was introduced into the Mills and the schools. It was powered by a dynamo and electric store battery which took four months to install at a cost of £1000.

Roads   Ireland, compared to many other countries, was well provided with roads from the end of the eighteenth century. Road construction was paid for by a county tax. The main coach roads had a metalling of broken stones with gravel borders and were 18-21 feet wide. Local roads from one market town to another were 15-18 feet wide, while other minor roads were still narrower at 12-15 feet wide. During the Famine the government launched a massive scheme of public works, consisting almost completely in road-making, which resulted in a huge improvement in the provision of roads either by repairing existing ones or constructing new ones.[6] Men were employed moving earth and transporting stones, while women and children were employed breaking stones, and work done by the destitute in workhouses very often consisted in breaking stones for road-making.

In the winter of 1846-7 the construction of about one hundred and fifty new roads or sections of roads was undertaken in the five baronies of the diocese, about fifty in each of the Mayo baronies of Costello and Gallen, about half that number in Corran and about fifteen in Leyny and the half barony of Coolavin. Some new sections of road were laid to avoid hills and many hills themselves were lowered and hollows filled in, such as along the entire line between Ballylahan and the crossroads at Barleyhill. So much roadwork had been done during the Famine that little more needed to be done for the rest of that century.

5   'Annals of Foxford', vol 2, RSCG
6   Swords, *In Their Own Words*, pp 429-37

In the pre-Famine period there was a regular mailcoach service between Dublin and Sligo, departing every evening at 8.15 p.m. from the Hibernian Hotel in Dawson Street, covering the 132 miles in fifteen hours, and after passing through Boyle, Collooney and Ballysadare, arrived in Sligo at 11 a.m. [7] It left Sligo at 2 p.m. and arrived in Dublin at seven the following morning. Some crossroad mails traversed the diocese, particularly one from Sligo to Castlebar, a distance of fifty-eight miles, which passed through Ballysadare, Collooney, Tubbercurry, Bellaghy and Swinford. It left Sligo at 9.50 a.m. and arrived in Castlebar at 5.25 p.m. Another mail plied between Ballina and Castlebar, passing through Swinford and Foxford.

Transport

Charles Bianconi ran his first coach service from Clonmel to Cahir in 1815 and by 1841 there were very few areas in the country that did not have access to a Bianconi car or other form of public transport. The 'Bianconi' was an

Bianconi Cars

Bianconi Car in Sligo

outside car, which was developed from the jaunting car, where passengers sat over the wheels facing out on both sides. In time it became the 'long car' which could accommodate twenty passengers. A small two-wheeled type was used on less frequented routes while the four-wheeled car was generally used on major routes such as Longford to Castlerea. The Bianconi car to Longford in 1846 left Swinford every day at 12.30 p.m. and passed through Ballaghaderreen. The 'Bianconi' remained the most used public transport until the last decades of the century when the railways began.

7   *Thom's Directory*

Shipping   Goods were transported mostly by water, and ports such as Sligo and Westport had a considerable volume of shipping both importing and exporting. In 1847 no less than twenty seven ships filled with emigrants sailed to Quebec from Sligo and five left from Killala for Canada. From January of that year to April 1850 twenty-three ships carried hundreds of emigrants from Sligo to New York. During the Famine much of the Indian meal, rice and other foods distributed in the west of Ireland were sent by the Quakers and other relief committees from Dublin to Longford by canal and there they were collected by carmen with their horses and carts sent by the various parish committees.

Railways   The Midland Great Western Railway to Sligo, opened on 3 December 1862, included a section which passed from Boyle to Ballymote, Collooney, Ballysadare and Sligo. The next station in the diocese, to open on 1 May 1868, was Foxford on the line from Manulla Junction to Ballina and Ballaghadereen, opened on 2 November 1874 on the nine-mile branch line from Kilfree Junction. Almost thirty years after the start of the Midland Great Western Railway line, the Claremorris to Collooney section of the Limerick-Sligo line was opened. Numerous meetings were held and resolutions passed, including one from Swinford Board of Guardians to the Lord Lieutenant in 1883, urging the necessity of constructing this line.[8] 'We have 400 sq. miles thickly populated and no line of railway.'

Large public meetings were held that year in Swinford, Charlestown and Tubbercurry, chaired by parish priests, pressing the government to give its support to the project. Denis O'Hara chaired a meeting in Kiltimagh in 1889 which urged the construction of this line as it would serve the Unions of Swinford and Tubbercurry, with a population of 80,000. 1890 was yet another bad year and Denis urged Dillon to bring pressure on the government to do something at once. 'If the line from Collooney to Claremorris were made it would give employment.'[9] Another large meeting in Kiltimagh at the beginning of October called on the government to come to their rescue with 'starvation and death staring us in the face' and begin the construction of the Claremorris-Collooney line.[10] Priests of the Swinford deanery had already passed a similar resolution.

Claremorris-to-Collooney   Eventually the appeals were heard and on the last day of 1890 the first sod was turned in Tubbercurry by Michael Staunton on the Claremorris-Col-

8   *C.T.* 21 July, 15 Sept. 1883, 27 June 1889
9   Denis O'Hara to John Dillon, 30 Aug 1890, Dil. P. 6769
10   *C.T.* 11 Oct 1890
11   Michael Comer, *Claremorris to Collooney Railway: The Burma Road: W.P.* 3 & 24 Jan; *I.T.* 3 Jan & *C.T.* 31 Jan 1891

looney line.[11] 2,000 men turned up in Swinford looking for work on the first day but only one hundred were taken on and the man in charge of the works had to get a police escort. 'There is great excitement and the men threaten to stop the work if they are not employed.' [12] Similar scenes were witnessed in Tubbercurry where the parish priest was called out at 7 a.m. to prevent a riot. Again 500 men were clamouring for employment in the streets of Swinford on Monday 19 January 1891 and 300 were put to work in the direction of Kiltimagh, but it was the old story once again. 'The men best off were the most pressing, the most persevering to obtain employment.' Before the end of January 900 men were employed along the line from Lislackagh outside Swinford in the direction of Charlestown. The workers did the fencing before laying the lines and were paid seven pence per yard for fencing, with a good worker earning twelve shillings a day.

Left: Carrowmore Station, 1961 *(courtesy H. C. Casserly) Right:* Leyny Station, 1975 *(courtesy R. M. Casserly)*

The Claremorris-Collooney line was officially opened on Tuesday, 1 October 1895 and large crowds gathered at each station to watch the first train arrive. The main stations along the forty-five-mile line were Kiltimagh, Swinford, Charlestown, Curry, Tubbercurry, Carrowmore and Leyny, with Claremorris and Collooney as termini. According to the advertised timetable, three passenger trains travelled daily in both directions leaving Claremorris at 9.35 a.m., 1.05 p.m. and 4 p.m. and from Collooney at 7.02 a.m., 10.21 a.m. and 4.35 p.m.

Bicycles were being produced in Britain from the 1880s but were expensive and did not become commonplace in Ireland until the beginning of the twentieth century. However, as early as 1888 the *Connaught Telegraph* published a letter from a correspondent in Ballyhaunis 'to draw the attention of the authorities to the nuisance of bicycling.' claiming that 'railway porters, corn-crushers and clog-makers' assembled in the town every evening at 8 p.m. for bicycle-riding.[13] 'Let their owners go to the country and indulge their fancies for bicycling without being a public nuisance. I hope the police

Bicycles

12 *I.T.* 3 Jan 1891
13 *C.T.* 28 Aug 1888

will no longer favour such dangerous games.' It is difficult to explain how those particular classes could have acquired bicycles when a standard model cost then £20, but they may well have been members of a club which were popular in the early years. A cycling club was formed in Kiltimagh in 1901 and bicycles were stored in a depot where they were cleaned, oiled and adjusted after use. 'Beginners are taught the art of using the wheel and when necessary members can have a bicycle on an easy payment system.' The same town had a Sinn Féin cycling club in 1906 and arranged outings to different towns including Straide to pay respect to Michael Davitt who had died that year.[14] Bicycles were to play an important role both in the 'War' of Independence and the Civil War.

Motor cars   Motor cars began to make their appearance early in the next century. Colonel Henry Jordan of Thornhill, Kiltimagh acquired one in 1905 at a cost

Swinford charabanc. Passengers include J. A. Mellett, J. Henry, D. S. Walsh, M. Hurst, M. Horkan, B. Cuniffe, E. Dolphin, M. Morrin, Jack Morrin *(courtesy Joe Mellett)*

14 *Kiltimagh*, pp 127, 135

of £750. Henry Doran of Kilmovee was also an early car-owner with Denis O'Hara one of his first passengers. 'I was saying to Doran a few days ago that we might run over on the motor some day next week to have a talk with you for an hour before you leave.' [15] The first car ever seen in Benada was in 1906 when the Viceroy, Lord Dudley, visited the orphanage accompanied by Bishop Patrick O'Donnell of Raphoe.[16] Dudley insisted on every child being given a ride in his car, making the orphans almost certainly among the earliest in the diocese to have had that experience.

The Gaelic Athletic Association was founded in 1884 and two years later a match under GAA rules was played in Ballaghaderreen.[17] The match, played in a field belonging to Anne Deane, lasted about two hours without either side scoring. Swinford GAA held weekly meetings in their own 'club room' in 1888 and decided in March to buy a new ball marked 'G.A. Association' and communicate with a Dublin firm with a view to acquiring jerseys 'and other requisites'. A letter was read from the Lord Mayor of Dublin, Thomas Sexton MP, thanking them for naming the club after him. Clubs adopted the names of prominent living politicians as well as long dead patriots.[18] Kilkelly club called itself after Michael Davitt while Charlestown was named Sarsfields. Ballaghaderreen was an exception calling themselves 'Faugh a Ballaghs' (Get out of the Way!) which was the slogan of the Connaught Rangers.

GAA

Swinford held a sports and pony races under the auspices of the GAA on St Patrick's Day. 'The Celtic Cross in national colours was conspicuously displayed.' A practice match – lasting two hours without any score – took place the following Sunday in preparation for entering the county competition. By mid April they had their jerseys and left from the club room 'rigged out in full colours.' Kiltimagh GAA club was formed at a meeting on 8 April, convened at the request of the county secretary, E. Lavin, who was elected chairman of the club, read the rules of the GAA, 'explained them ably and lucidly, gave an

15 Denis O'Hara to John Dillon, 18 Sept 1909, Dil. P. 6769

16 RSCG / H 13 / 91

17 *C.T.* 13 Nov 1886, see also *C.T.* 17, 24 & 31 Mar, 14 & 28 April, 5, 12 & 27 May, 2 June, 21 July, 3 Nov 1888, 27 Jan 1889; *S.C.* 15 Sept 1888, 5 Dec 1891; *W.P.* 7 Mar 1891; on clubs in different parishes see McGuinn, *Curry,* pp 70-82, Farry, *Killoran and Coolaney,* pp 112-13, *From Plain to Hill,* pp 154-59, *Keash and Culfadda – A Local History,* pp 161-75, *Kiltimagh,* p 98, Souvenir Programme, official opening of Fr O'Hara Memorial Park, Charlestown, 3 June 1951

18 Achonry Davitts and Red Hughs, Ballymote Round Towers, Bohola Tanners, Bunninadden Emmets, Charlestown Sarsfields, Coolaney Sarsfields, Currhownagh Wanderers, Culfadda O'Briens, Curry Liberators, Foxford Geraldines, Keash Emmets, Killasser Davis, Kiltimagh Volunteers, O'Donnell Aboos and Dillons, Kinaffe Brian Borus, Meelick Redmonds, Tubbercurry St Patrick's

account of the decadence of the old pastimes, with a history of the present wonderful reaction...' Charlestown also formed a club in 1888 with the help of the curate, John McNicholas, and a number of prominent townsmen.[19]

Tournaments

The County Mayo GAA held a convention in Ballina at the end of March and A. J. Staunton of Swinford was elected county treasurer. Arrangements were made for Castlebar Mitchels to play Kilkelly Davitts at Balla on 22 April, but the match never took place as Kilkelly could not field a team 'in consequence of many of their young men being then away in England.' Swinford Sextons played Ballaghaderreen Faugh a Ballaghs in Swinford on the same day. 'GAA is now in full swing in Mayo', according to the *Freeman*, 'and making rapid progress.' That summer two objections were lodged, one by Ballaghaderreen who were beaten by Castlebar by a point, and another by Ballina Stephens. Lodging objections following disputed results were to become a familiar feature of GAA tournaments.

Early Matches

Early matches were colourful affairs. When Swinford Juveniles played Ballina Stephens in June 1888, the Swinford convoy arrived in Ballina in 'a long string of brakes, cars and waggons laden with the stalwart Gaels of Swinford.' Headed by the juvenile fife and drum band, playing *God save Ireland,* they marched to the pitch 'all wearing straw hats of sombrero shape'. A few weeks later Swinford Sextons played Ballina Commercials. The Sextons left Swinford at 9.30 on the Sunday of the match, 'a procession of the captain and all his men in rich and rare colours and a tandem of two bays and an excellent whip leading, with a band brake and a dozen of side-cars, charmed with the music of Kearns' band.' Swinford won and the reporter singled out the captain, Staunton, and a half a dozen other players who 'made splendid kickings'. Swinford Sextons played Foxford Geraldines in September 1888 and despite the fact that Foxford had the services of three Australian rugby players, who were scholarship students in Oxford, Swinford won by 2 goals and 4 points to nil. About 3,000 attended a match in February 1889 in Kiltimagh between the local O'Donnell Aboos and Kilkelly Davitts, but the match was abandoned after fifteen minutes when a Kilkelly player dislocated his shoulder.

Rival Clubs

A second club was formed in Swinford, the Commercials, which suggests that it was composed mainly of shop-assistants, and the curate, James Cullen, was president in 1888. There may have been political differences between

19 Messrs Collins, George Harrington, Thomas Haran, John Marren, John E. Doherty, Thomas Peyton, Thomas Coen, John Gallagher, James Colleran, James Owens, Pat Breen, Matt O'Rorke, Thomas and John Cassidy, Thomas Tunney, Pat Phillips and James Parsons. Official Programme, 3 June 1951. I am indebted to John Gallagher SC, Dublin for drawing my attention to this programme which includes a history of the GAA in Charlestown.

members of the two clubs. 'Unlike the rival club in Swinford they (the Sextons) do not practise on the boycotted park of Colonel Brabazon nor have they for their referee a bailiff or detective.' Several larger towns, such as Ballina and Castlebar, had two or more clubs but even smaller rural areas were divided. Achonry had two clubs, Red Hughs and Davitts, and three differently-named teams in Kiltimagh, Volunteers, Dillons and O'Donnell Aboos, were mentioned in 1888 when the GAA was first established in the town. These local divisions were strongly criticised by the *Connaught Telegraph*: 'We will interfere in no local squabbles – in fact we are nearly disgusted with the whole proceedings of the GAA and all the unmanly shuffling and want of straightforwardedness to be seen in its workings in Mayo.' Nevertheless, there was a large attendance at the county convention held in the Moy Hotel, Ballina on Thursday 1 November 1888, with delegates from Kiltimagh, Charlestown, Ballaghaderreen, Kilkelly, Bohola, Killasser, Foxford as well as from both of the Swinford Clubs. A. J. Staunton was re-elected treasurer, while T. McNicholas from Kiltimagh and J. J. Glavey from Kilkelly were elected members of the county committee.

Like so many other groups in Ireland, the GAA became deeply divided as a *Parnell Split* result of Parnell's divorce in December 1890. It was particularly unfortunate for that organisation in Sligo and Mayo, as it had only been launched there with great enthusiasm a mere two years earlier. Countrywide the GAA tended to favour Parnell. In Achonry diocese different clubs were divided in their political loyalties. Delegates from five GAA clubs in South Sligo attended a convention in Ballymote in January 1891 which declared Parnell 'no longer fit to lead the Irish people'. There were no GAA representatives from the parishes of Achonry, Ballymote, Gurteen or Ballaghaderreen, though priests from these parishes were present.

The absence of a delegation did not necessarily prove that that club was Parnellite. There was no delegation from Ballaghaderreen though the curate, Michael Doyle, was there. Early in March he chaired a meeting of St Patrick's Temperance GAA club in Ballaghaderreen which passed a resolution strongly condemning Parnell: ' We consider after the scandalous revelations of the Divorce Court the continued leadership of Mr Parnell is impossible, as it would mean the destruction of the Home Rule cause and be injurious to the best interests of our country.' [20] The club placed its 'unabated confidence' in Archbishop Croke and Michael Davitt. There may well have been two clubs in Ballaghaderreen then and the Faugh a Ballaghs may have stayed loyal to Parnell.

20 *W.P.* 7 Mar 1891

Often the political leanings of a GAA club were determined by whether or not there was a strong clerical presence in the club. Such was the case in Keash and Culfadda club where the curate, Patrick Conlan, was president. On his departure to Ballymote later that summer he was described by the chairman of Culfadda O'Briens as 'the first man, clerical or lay in South Sligo, who took the initiative in stamping out the adulterer fox of the Divorce Court.' Conlan was elected vice-president of Sligo GAA at a convention in Ballymote later that year.[21] The County Mayo GAA governing body was pro-Parnell while individual clubs were probably divided. Bonniconlon GAA club was strongly Parnellite and later presented an address to Parnell when he visited Ballina.

The Split and the bitterness it entailed greatly retarded the growth of the GAA. It appears that no competitions were held in Mayo in 1893 as a result of which Charlestown decided to become affiliated with Sligo. When an East Mayo cycling club was formed in July 1894, one paper commented: 'Gaelic football was the popular sport for young men in this area, but it has been many a day since a ball was fielded here.' [22] However, it did recover and, with strong clerical approval and support, went on to become the dominant sporting activity in rural Ireland in the twentieth century.

Gaelic League

The Gaelic League was founded in 1893 by Eugene O'Growney, Eoin MacNeill and Douglas Hyde. MacNeill was an Antrim Catholic who worked in the civil service in southern Ireland and O'Growney was a priest and Professor of Irish in Maynooth. Douglas Hyde, the first president of the League, was born the son of a Church of Ireland rector in Sligo and grew up in Frenchpark, where he learned Irish and collected Irish stories and songs from the country people around. Ballaghaderreen was his nearest market town. Hyde's main aim was to liberate Irish culture from English influence. The purpose of the League was was to preserve and extend the daily use of the Irish language and the study and publication of Gaelic literature, as well as the creation of new works in Irish. Hyde believed that the League should be non-sectarian and non-political.

Kiltimagh

Gradually branches of the League were formed in towns all over the country. A branch was formed in Kiltimagh after a Sunday Mass in July 1898 with a local Protestant lady, Lottie MacManus of Killedan House, the driving force behind its formation. [23] She persuaded Denis O'Hara to preside at the inaugural meeting although he believed the revival of the language 'impracti-

21 *S.C.* 1 Aug, 5 Dec 1891
22 qtd in *Kiltimagh*, p 108
23 *C.T.* 18 July 1898 qtd in *Kiltimagh*, p 119; see also pp 120, 125, 126

cable and a sentiment.' 'From a utilitarian point of view it was useless; it would not help the possessor of it to any post or situation in the country, and was of no value to the boys and girls that were yearly migrating in thousands to America.' He simply hoped that it might do something to save the language from dying out in the parish.

About forty, many of them women, attended the first meeting, including surprisingly, Major H. B. Jordan who made 'a very generous subscription'. Michael O'Doherty, a local teacher and father of the future Archbishop of Manila, became one of its main Irish teachers and weekly meetings were held on Sunday evenings 'for a rehearsal of the week's studies'. Four new members were enrolled in August and students were divided into three groups depending on their knowledge of the language. Early in 1900 the new curate, William Byrne, just out of Maynooth 'where he distinguished himself as a writer and promoter of the Irish language', promised his active support. 'Irish was his first and fondest language' and he promised to use it in his daily routines where he could make himself understood. Byrne presided in May at a meeting where the guest of honour, Douglas Hyde, delivered a lecture in Irish. Hyde was delighted 'with the youthful portion of his audience' and complimented the boys' band for the pieces they selected. 'He exhorted the boys not to grow up as West Britons but as Irishmen in heart and soul by cultivating their national music and grand old language.'

Irish in Schools

From the very beginning the League ran a campaign for the introduction of the teaching of Irish into the schools. Before 1900 Irish in national schools was an extra subject which had to be taught outside normal school hours. Between 1900 and 1906 it became an optional ordinary subject for senior students who wished to learn it, provided the teacher was willing and able to teach it and other subjects were not adversely affected. The Sisters of Charity in Foxford began learning Irish in December 1900 to be ready to teach it the following May as an extra subject in the senior and infant schools, and in the autumn of 1902 the convent annalist recorded that 'Irish has been taught in all classes'.[24] Teachers in Kiltimagh parish were invited to a special meeting in June 1901 to discuss the question of teaching Irish in their schools. Michael O'Doherty, who chaired the meeting, was already giving classes in Irish in Kiltimagh national school where three of his students had been awarded prizes by the Gaelic League the previous January. All the teachers present at the meeting agreed to start lessons in Irish in the very near future.

24 RSCG 'Annals of Foxford', pp 63 & 75
25 RSCG 'Annals of Foxford', p 85

Douglas Hyde visited the convent school in Foxford in 1904 to present medals and prizes which the choir had won at Westport Feis. [25] 'He was more than surprised and delighted at the progress made here during the last ten years and made a long speech in Irish.' He also presented the Sister who taught music with a gold medal 'in recognition of her untiring work in the cause of the Irish music revival.' Hyde also attended Feis Achonry in Kiltimagh on 23 and 24 August 1905 where he acted as judge in the literary section. Lyster was patron and Denis O'Hara president, while his curate, Charles Gildea and Michael O'Doherty NT, acted as secretaries. There were over 1,000 entries in the various categories which was a big increase on the previous feis held in Charlestown. The feis was held in a different venue every year and was open to competitors from anywhere in the diocese. The Gaelic League in Kiltimagh and elsewhere continued to thrive with class numbers increasing. The services of a new Irish teacher, a native speaker, were procured in 1909 through the efforts of Pádraig Ó Máille, Gaelic League organiser, and 'some ardent Gaelic Leaguers in Kiltimagh, Swinford and Foxford'. Lottie MacManus was one of four delegates chosen to represent Connacht at an Irish language conference in Dublin in 1913.

From the second half of the nineteenth century the division between town and country became gradually more pronounced, even in the more remote and rural areas and this was especially the case in social and recreational activities. The Gaelic League was said to be essentially a townsmen's organisation. Small towns had a steadily growing population of shop assistants, bank clerks and members of other professions and their leisure needs caused something of a 'recreational revolution' in the last two decades of the century. The advent of amateur dramatic clubs was very much a town phenomenon.

One of the earliest clubs was formed in Swinford in December 1879.[26] Their first play, *The Colleen Bawn*, was staged on 2 January 1880 'on the second floor of the spacious new school of the Sisters of Mercy'. The programme also included a 'laughable farce', *Borrowed Plumes*, and music provided by the Swinford Brass Band. Later they travelled to Tubbercurry with their production. Three months later they produced another play, *Aurora Floyd*, and a farce, *Paddy Miles, the Limerick Boy* and a third play *Eileen Oge* after Christmas of that year, which they also staged in Tubbercurry and planned to bring

---

26 Patrick Mannion, hon. pres. Edward Dolphin, hon. vice-pres., C. P. McArdle, P. J. Durkan, treas., John Feeney, stage-manager, J. A. Henry, hon. sec., J. P. O'Connor, T. Corley, A. P. Dolphin, C. W. Armstrong, A. J. Staunton, Peter Horkan. *C.T.* 13 Dec 1879

to Castlebar.[27] During the decade 1880-90 Swinford club produced two plays a year, one at Easter and the other at Christmas, all staged in the convent schoolroom where 'the respectable inhabitants of the town were nearly all present'. All the actors were male and played female as well as male roles.[28]

The purpose of touring with these productions was to raise funds for local needs. The winter of 1879 was a period of widespread famine and Michael Staunton, a native of Swinford, had opened a relief fund in Tubbercurry which was greatly helped by the staging of *The Colleen Bawn* there by Swinford Dramatic Club. A new production by the Swinford club of the same play was staged in Kiltimagh in February 1888 together with a farce, *Barney the Baron*, in aid of the new church, and afterwards the cast were 'hospitably entertained' by Denis O'Hara. At Christmas 1889 they staged Dion Boucicault's *The Shaughraun* in Ballaghaderreen in aid of St John's new school there. [29]

Patriotic Themes

The themes of plays became more patriotic. *Robert Emmet* was staged in April 1889 by what was then described as Swinford Gaelic Dramatic Club. [30] Early in the following century Kiltimagh staged *The Rebel Chief* and the reporter wondered why it was so well received. 'Was it the popularity of some of the actors, its patriotic message or its dramatic value?' In September 1909 *Rory O'More*, a patriotic play set in the Ireland of 1798, was performed in the crowded Town Hall. By then the Kiltimagh Young Men's Society encompassed the dramatic club as well as the brass band whose repertoire included more and more national airs such as *A Nation Once Again*, as well as reels, jigs and hornpipes. The society put on 'a real Irish night' on 17 March 1910 with a play, *Irish Eviction*, followed by a concert with songs such as *The Croppy Boy*, *The West's Awake* and *Men of the West*. Later plays dealt with militant nationalistic themes such as the 1798 rebellion and it was an open secret that the monies raised were used to fund the local Volunteer company. By the end of 1916 the society had been infiltrated by the IRB and Denis O'Hara accused its president, Sean T. Ruane, 'of being the prime mover of a secret society, for which the dramatic club was a cover'.[31] Tubbercurry Dramatic Club produced *For Ireland's Sake* or *Under the Green Flag* for Christmas 1920.[32]

27 Casts included J. A. Henry, J. J. Timlin, A. P Dolphin. T. Corley, W. J. O'Connor, C. P. McArdle, P. Horkan, A. J. Staunton, J. A. Moloney, John Carroll, P. M. Horkan, J. P. Kyle and T. F. Cox. *C.T.* 27 Mar & 10 April 1880, 8 Jan 1881, *S.C.* 29 Jan 1881
28 Other plays included *More Blunders than One* and *Arrah-na-Pogue* or *The Wicklow Wedding* and a farce, *Boots at the Swan. C.T.* 12 Jan, 4 May & 21 Jan 1889
29 *C.T.* 18 Feb 1888 & 21 Dec 1889
30 *C.T.* 12 Jan & 4 May 1889
31 *Kiltimagh*, pp 137, 140-41, 158
32 *W.P.* 10 Jan 1920

Dramatic societies were formed all over the diocese in the first half of the twentieth century and many took part in the All-Ireland Drama Competition which was staged annually in Tubbercurry.

Convent Operas

Convents were enthusiastic promoters of amateur dramatics and school-children's productions formed part of the annual social calendar. When the Mercy Convent in Swinford celebrated its silver jubilee in 1881 it staged a theatrical *Marie Antoinnette*, performed by the school-children.[33] Later, when their boarding school became established, operas were produced annually and the arias and choruses of *Il Trovatore, La Traviata, The Bohemian Girl* and Gilbert and Sullivan's *Iolanthe, Mikado, Madam Butterfly* etc. became familiar in many homes. The St Louis convent annual production was widely acclaimed and *The Student Prince* in 1951 was attended by no less than four bishops, the Archbishop of Tuam and the bishops of Achonry, Elphin and Killala.

Bazaars

Bazaars were the most common form of fundraising while also providing entertainment. Almost every parish held a bazaar each year to raise funds for parochial purposes and so many were held that the bishop had to allot dates to each parish. Usually a bazaar lasted two days. Stalls were set up, presided over by the most important ladies in the parish. Over the previous months people were encouraged to donate gifts for sale at the bazaar and many business houses not only presented articles themselves but also canvassed contributions from their main Dublin or Belfast suppliers, many of whom were Protestant. The growing lists of contributors were published weekly in local newspapers, encouraging a certain level of competition.

Ladies at Kiltimagh
Bazaar, 1896

33 *C.T.* 17 Dec 1881

The Sisters of Charity held a bazaar on 22 and 23 October 1879 in aid of their new school in Ballaghaderreen.[34] 'The different stalls were presided over by Lady de Freyne assisted by the Hon. Miss Ffrench, Mrs Strickland, assisted by Miss Grehan, and Miss Ellison and Mrs Deane, assisted by Miss Duff and Miss Dillon.' The band of the Sligo Artillery played for the two days. Kiltimagh held its annual bazaar on 6 and 7 of January and in 1890 in aid of the new church.[35] There was a big number of stalls with valuable prizes on offer, a 'splendid display' of fireworks on the first day and a string band in attendance for the two days. In 1896 Kiltimagh bazaar was in aid of a technical school to provide training for would-be emigrants, particularly young girls going to America to work as domestic servants. Denis O'Hara hoped to raise £600 and issued a circular letter addressed to Irish emigrants overseas appealing for aid in connection with the bazaar. The well-known priest, Michael O'Flanagan, was guest of honour at a bazaar in Keash in April 1917 to clear off the debt on the parochial house and hall, and among a large number of prizes on offer were several 'fat sheep.' [36]

Annual summer outings by different societies were highlights on the social calendar.[37] Swinford Men's Sacred Heart Sodality annual picnic was a spectacular affair with over 100 members participating. [38] The convoy, consisting

Annual Outings

Swinford Men's Sacred Heart Sodality picnic to Pontoon, 25 June 1882 *(courtesy Mary Convey) Back Row:* T. Maloney, P. English, J. P. O'Connor, J. J. Henry, J. Kyle, M. J. Mulligan, T. Mulrooney, P. J. Durkin, F. Davitt, P. J. McNulty, A. J. Staunton, P. Horkan. *Middle Row:* Rev M. Burke CC, C. McGirl, M. Gavaghan, J. Henry, J. O'Reilly, P. Scully, P. McManus, C. Davitt, J. Durkin, M. Mellett, J. Staunton, J. Mellett, J. Horkan, J. Davitt, M. Heaney, J. Kerins, T. O'Connor, J. Flanagan, E. Dolphin, P. Jordan, J. Mulraney, A. McNulty, M. D. Gavaghan, M. Staunton CC *Front Row:* J. Brabazon, J. Munnelly, J. English, W. O'Connor, M. Doohan, T. Kerins, J. Mulligan, W. Furey, J Kerins

34 *S.C.* 1 Nov 1879

35 *Kiltimagh*, pp 102, 110

36 *S.C.* 28 April 1917; Denis Carroll, *They have fooled you again*, pp 62-64

37 *C.T.* 30 June 1883, 5 July 1884, 4 July 1885, 16 June 1888

38 1883 Committee: Peter Horkan, A. J. Staunton, E. Dolphin, James J. Henry, Dr O'Grady, P. J. McNulty, Charles McGirl, J. O'Brien, C. Davitt, M. McNicholas, John Feeny, F. Davitt, J. Davitt, P. J. O'Connor, J. Jordan, T. Fraine, J. Kyle, J. Henry, M. Mulligan, M. W. Doyle, P. Mitchel, J. Mulrooney, W. Staunton, P. Durkan, J. Flanagan, A. Browne, J. Brabazon, J. Mullany

of about twenty vehicles, led by the coach carrying the spiritual director and other clergy, and followed by a brake carrying the brass band under bandmaster, James Kearns, playing *God Save Ireland*. About fifteen side-cars followed with the banner of the confraternity displayed in the leading one. Bringing up the rear was a big black charger drawing a large dray cart laden 'with the choicest of sirloins, legs and hams mildly cured and full cases containing the best brands from Grisliers to Guinness'. Massbrook in Pontoon was the venue in 1883 with the picnic followed by a dance which lasted until 7 p.m., and before their departure the band struck up *Home Sweet Home*. They visited the Mountpleasant estate near Ballinafad in 1885 and toured the grand stables housing over a dozen racing thoroughbreds. Swinford Dramatic Society, accompanied by the curates, James Cullen and Walter Henry, went to Pontoon on a picnic in June 1888. The picnics were usually attended by the *Connaught Telegraph* reporter who wrote up the outing. Annual picnics continued to be popular events in the early decades of the next century and Pontoon continued to be the preferred destination. The Kiltimagh Young Men's Society held theirs there in August 1909.

Dances   At the turn of the century parochial halls were built and dancing became a popular pastime. Thomas Loftus had the old church in Ballymote converted into a hall named after him before he died in 1908. The White Hall in Keash was built in 1913. The curate in Foxford, Denis Gildea, went to America in 1923 where he spent almost two years collecting money to build what was

Town Hall, Swinford
(courtesy Joe Mellet)

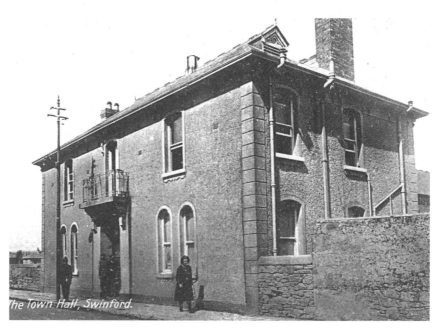

The Town Hall, Swinford.

later called the Admiral Browne Memorial Hall. Swinford was unusual in having a Town Hall, established by Dean Staunton and a number of towns-men who formed themselves into a limited liability company offering one thousand £1 shares to the public. Those owning thirty shares were eligible for election as directors. Built in 1909 with a two-storey front containing four large club rooms, a main concert hall with a large stage, beyond which was a supper room with accommodation for two hundred diners.

Early dances were mostly church-sponsored. A parish dance organised by Denis O'Hara in Kiltimagh in 1910 was described as 'one of the most brilliant social functions that took place in this part of the country for some time past.'[39] The dance, attended by about seven hundred, lasted from 6 p.m. until the early hours of the following morning. 'As many as 150 pairs could be seen dancing at the same time and the much esteemed pastor could be seen passing along the lines of dancing pairs, and now and again dropping a word or two from one to another, adding still more mirth to the occasion.' One of the highlights in the social calendar was the annual Benada charity concert and dance in aid of the orphanage run by the Sisters of Charity.[40] The concert began at 7.30 p.m. and lasted for three hours, and afterwards 'the ballroom filled with 200 dancing couples'. Supper began at 1 a.m. with the catering provided by the Sisters of Charity serving four hundred guests, seventy seated at each table. Dancing was resumed afterwards and continued until 8 o'clock in the morning. 'Several card tables were kept going all night.' The Directors' Dance in Swinford was an all-dress affair where many young ladies made their debuts while proud mothers thronged the gallery overlook-ing the dance-floor. Patrons came from all over Connacht.

Cinemas sprang up in towns throughout the diocese during the late thir-ties and early forties. The Savoy Cinema opened in Kiltimagh on 23 Septem-ber 1944 'to the delight of all who enjoy the wonders and excitement of mod-ern cinematography.'[41] The building had been completed for some time but due to the war the ESB refused to supply electricity and a local garage owner rigged up a car engine to supply power for the first films. The Lyric Cinema in Swinford had six evening shows every week, beginning at 8.45 p.m., as well as a children's matinee on Sundays at 4 p.m. The two-hour programme con-sisted of a short opening film and 'the big picture' with a change of films every two days. The main genres were westerns, detective stories, romances and an occasional horror film, all designed for family viewing. Some of the

Cinemas

39 *Kiltimagh*, p 141
40 *W.P.* 14 Jan 1922
41 *Kiltimagh*, p 219

greatest box-office successes, like *The Song of Bernadette, The Bells of St Mary's, Boys' Town, The Ten Commandments, Ben Hur, Quo Vadis* etc had religious or biblical themes. Hollywood produced its own 'soggorth aroon', portrayed by Bing Crosby in *The Bells of St Mary's*, which was enthusiastically received by priests and people on both sides of the Atlantic. For over thirty years 'going to the pictures' was one of the main sources of entertainment but with the advent of television in the early 1960s the days of the cinema were numbered. The Savoy Cinema passed into the hands of the parish council in Kiltimagh in 1977 to be used as a community centre.

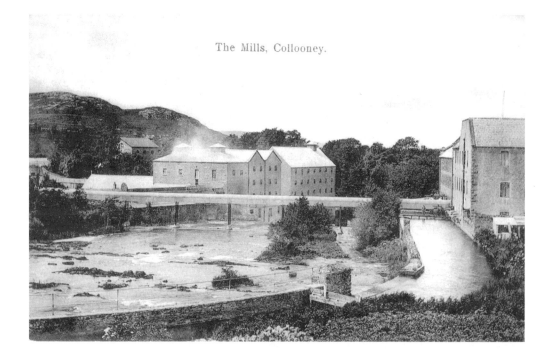

The Mills, Collooney.

CHAPTER FOURTEEN

A New Religious Landscape

Patrick McNicholas reported to Rome in 1822 that there were twenty-three parish chapels in the diocese, five of which were built since he became bishop in 1818.[1] They were very poorly furnished and many of the chalices were made of tin. Many of these old barn chapels, built at the end of the eighteenth and the beginning of the nineteenth century, continued in service during much of the latter. The era of his successor, Patrick Durcan (1852-1875), largely coincided with the period of church-building. 'About the time of the bishop's consecration, there were very few slated chapels in the diocese, whereas on the day of his death, there was not a single thatched house of worship within the length and breadth of Achonry, with the exception of that of Doo, which seemed left by a special disposition of Providence, to remind priests and people of all they owe to the prelate who went so lately to his reward.'[2] Thirteen churches and four chapels, as well as the cathedral, were built during that period.

Church-Building

Church of the
Assumption, Collooney

The Church of the Assumption in Collooney was erected in 1843, while Durcan was parish priest, on the site of the chapel erected in 1798 by Wat Henry.[3] The architect, Sir John Benson, was a native of the parish as was the builder and all the other workers, stonecutters, masons, plasterers, carpenters, plasterers etc engaged in the building. The spire of the church, built in the time of Durcan's successor, Terence O'Rorke, was completed in 1879 and extensive repairs and renovation were carried out in 1906.

Collooney

Four churches were built in the diocese in the decade 1850 to 1860, St Joseph's Church, Coolaney (1850), St Michael's Church, Cloonacool (1854), St James Church, Charlestown (1858) and Church of Immaculate Conception, Kilmovee (1859). The latter was dedicated on Sunday 9 October by Durcan while Archbishop John MacHale preached the sermon in Irish.[4] The

1   *SC* Irlanda, vol 23, ff 611r-614rv
2   T. O'Rorke, *Ballysadare and Kilvarnet*, pp 498-9
3   T. O'Rorke, op. cit. pp 108-10; *Catholic Directory* 1843; *S.C.* Jan 1843, 16, 23 Nov 1878 & 8 Jan 1879; *London Builder*, vol 19, p 722, 19 October 1861; *Irish Builder*, vol 48, p 688, 25 Aug 1906
4   *C.T.* 19 Oct 1859

architect, J. S. Butler, Dublin, designed the building in 'early decorated goth-ic style.' After the ceremony John Coghlan entertained the priests as well as 'a large number of the parishioners' to lunch at his residence. The Charlestown church, sometimes referred to as that of St Charles Borromeo, was designed by the London architects of Hadfield & Goldie.[5]

In the following decade six churches as well as the cathedral in Ballagha-derreen were built, Killavil (1861), Bohola (1863), Ballymote (1864), Gurteen (1866?),[6] Curry (1868?)[7] and Killasser (1868). Some of these churches were renovated rather than newly built. Durcan reported to Rome on 1 June 1862 that there were then thirty-four churches in the diocese, 'six of which had been renovated in the last few years'.[8]

Cathedral

The cathedral was consecrated and dedicated to the Blessed Virgin Mary and St Nathy on 3 November 1861.[9] The architect was George Goldie of the London firm of Hadfield and Goldie and the contractor was Charles Barker. Construction began in 1855 and was almost completed in 1860 when it was described as situated in a 'remote locality, out of line with railways and amidst a wide extent of bogs and comparatively sterile country.' The chapel which it replaced was described by Terence O'Rorke: 'A square barn like place – solid, substantial but ugly, hidden away in a gloomy part of the town sur-rounded by sombre trees; it had a cold flagged floor, three wretched galleries, a poor narrow altar and an unaccommodating sacristy. It was so ignoble in its accessories as to be unfit in any age like the present to serve for a place of wor-ship in the poorest parish of the diocese.'

The new cathedral was in the neo-Gothic style described as 'early English'. The high altar and tabenacle of Caen stone and Irish marble were still under construction late in 1860 in the workshops of Henry Lane, Dublin. The rere-dos was also to be made of Caen stone, 'encaiusted with enamelled tiles of rich colours'. 'Beyond the high altar no other fittings are as yet in progress – they will be undertaken by degrees.' These included the tower and spire which in fact were not completed until the early 1900s.

The bishop, who had considerable difficulty in completing the work, ap-plied to Rome in July 1863 for permission to leave Kilmovee vacant, following

---

5   *London Builder,* vol 16, 27 Mar 1858, p 214; *Dublin Builder,* vol 2, 1 Sept 1860, p 324; Douglas
     Scott Richardson, *Gothic Revival Architecture in Ireland* (typescript copy of doctoral dissert-
     ation), Yale University, II, 487 (1970)
6   foundation stone was laid by Durcan in June? 1866
7   McGuinn 1872
8   *SC* Irlanda vol 32, f 260rv
9   *The Dublin Builder & Architectural, Engineering, Mechanics and Sanitary Journal,* vol II
     (1 Sept 1860), p 327

the death of John Coghlan, and use the parish revenues, after 'suitably' paying a curate, for the refurbishment of the cathedral. Kilmovee was administered by James Barrett for the the following seven years. Durcan again applied to Rome in May 1865, this time for permission to retain the Jubilee offerings to be expended on the decoration of the cathedral 'on account of the difficult-ing of collecting the funds necessary for this work from the people because of their poverty.'[10] The total cost was estimated at about £5,000.

The Church of the Immaculate Conception in Ballymote was dedicated on Sunday, 4 September 1864.[11] Sir Robert Gore Booth, owner of the town and grandfather of Countess Markievicz, granted the site rent free. The foun-dation stone was laid on Wednesday 12 October 1859 after High Mass, at which Durcan presided and Terence O'Rorke preached. The architect, George Goldie of London, and the contractor, Charles Barker, were once more employed. Most of the estimated cost of the building, £2,743, came from natives of Ballymote in England. Scotland, the United States, Canada, and elsewhere and Denis Tighe wrote numerous letters to the *Sligo Champion* acknowledging contributions and report-ing on progress. Raffles were held locally for 'valuable prizes' ranging from a gold watch and chain to a pound note.

Ballymote

Original ticket 1862

Durcan, 'in full pontificals,' attended by Dr MacHale of the Irish College, Paris, performed the dedication in 1864 and the sermon was preached by John MacHale of Tuam. Special trains from the direction of Longford on one side and Sligo on the other and Bianconi cars from other districts insured a 'vast' congregation. There was an important attendance of the Catholic gen-try, including Charles and Mrs Strickland from Loughglynn House. Among the clergy attending was the Rev Mr Lohall of Collooney. The old chapel which was adjacent continued in use as a schoolhouse until 1914.

The Church of All Saints in Killasser was dedicated by Durcan on Sunday 8 November 1868 ' with all the solemn chant, benedictions and psalms pre-scribed by the Roman ritual.' The Sisters of Mercy from Swinford provided the music.[12] The architect was once again George Goldie. Terence O'Rorke, who preached the sermon, attributed the new church to 'zeal and energy' of John Finn, the parish priest, and also 'paid a very graceful and well-merited

Killasser

10 Udienze, vol 144, ff 1096v, 1097r, 1112r (1863); vol 151, ff 1619r, 1638r (1865)
11 Robert Flynn, *Church of the Immaculate Conception, Ballymote* (1983); *Dublin Builder*, vol 1, 1 Dec 1859, p 164, 3, 15 July 1861, p 577
12 *C.T.* 16 Nov 1868

compliment' to two landlords in the parish, John Nolan Farrell, Logboy and Roger McCarrick, Aclare, each of whom had contributed £100. The estimated cost of the new church was £1,200 contributed chiefly by the 'pence and shillings' of parishioners.

Attymass

Francis J. MacCormack, reported to Rome in January 1874 (on behalf of eighty-three year old Patrick Durcan) that there were then thirty-nine churches in the diocese, 'four of them built within the last two years.' [13] In August 1875 the bishop asked Rome for permission to leave Attymass vacant for three-to-five years, following the death of James Hurst so that the parish revenues, after paying a curate, could be used to build schools and a sacristy. [14] 'The faithful are so poor that they can scarcely pay the usual offerings for the support of their pastor.' Apparently the tactic proved remarkably successful. When John O'Grady, who administered the parish from 1876 to 1881, was transferred to Bohola in May 1881 it was reported that not only had he built a 'suitable' sacristy and six schools but also two teacher residences, as well as building a wall round the churchyard and erecting stations of the cross'. He also left 'a splendid parochial residence' to his successor.[15]

Carracastle

In the decade 1870 to 1880 six churches were built, Derrinacartha (1873), Cloonloo (1873), Killaraght (1875), Midfield (1876), Carracastle (1877), and Moylough (1878?)[16] St James Church, Carracastle was dedicated by MacCormack on Sunday 7 October 1877.[17] The building of this church 'was the work of many years begun and completed by the present zealous pastor of the parish', James Devine. The charity sermon was preached by 'the gifted pulpit orator' Pius Devine, a Passionist and the parish priest's nephew, and the collection made after the sermon realised a 'handsome sum'. The building of the church involved 'an outlay of money far in excess of what could have been contributed by the people of the parish who are comparatively poor.' The newspaper reporter waxed eloquent on the quality of Achonry churches: 'It is not in many dioceses, even in a country so remarkable for church building as Ireland, that the observant traveller is so agreeably struck both by the number and beauty of their churches as he is sure to be in the diocese of Achonry.'

Seven churches were built during the decade 1880 to 1890, Bushfield, Charlestown (1880), Foxford (1880), Doo, Ballymote (1880), Bunninadden (1881), Meelick, Swinford (1881), Mullinabreena (1884), Monasteraden (1884),

13 *SC* Irlanda, vol 37, ff 27r, 28r, 29rv
14 Udienze, vol 181 (1875), ff 879v, 888rv
15 *C.T.* 28 May 1881
16 McGuinn 1889
17 *The Mayo Examiner*, 27 Oct 1877. I am grateful to Vincent Coleman, Carracastle, for providing me with this newspaper cutting.

and Kiltimagh (1888). Cloonacool chapel was enlarged and substantially re-furbished and re-dedicated on 9 October 1881.[18] MacCormack reported to Rome in November 1882 that there were now forty churches in the diocese, 'nine of which were built or restored in the last decade'.[19]

The foundation stone of the new church in Foxford was laid by MacCor-mack in October 1877 and according to the *Connaught Telegraph* (4 September 1880) 'it was built with extraordinary rapidity thanks to the superhuman exertions' of the parish priest, Michael O'Donnell, and the contractor. Special trains were run on Sunday 25 September 1880 for the dedication performed by MacCormack, assisted by Hugh Conway of Killala. A Redemptorist from Dundalk, John Harbison, 'one of Ireland's greatest preachers', preached the charity sermon which lasted fifty-five minutes 'uninterruptedly'.[20] The church was still heavily in debt and it was hoped to liquidate some of it on that occasion.

Foxford

Harbison was one of four Redemptorists who gave a mission in the new church about a week later and he recorded that the building of the new church was the cause of some dissension in the parish, particularly between O'Donnell and McGloin, who was in charge of the building. 'There was a discrepancy between his figures and those of the parish priest.' Both were rec-onciled on the last day of the mission with the help of the bishop and Harbi-son. The church was still in debt over ten years later when Michael O'Don-nell organised a committee to run a bazaar 'to complete their beautiful new church'. The bazaar early in 1892, with the band of the Connaught Rangers providing the music, was 'a great success'.[21] The debt, however, continued to haunt his successors and in September 1909 Martin Henry left for America 'on a begging expedition in aid of his church'.[22]

A new chapel was dedicated by MacCormack who also preached the ser-mon in Doo (Kilcrevin), Ballymote on Sunday 5 December 1880.[23] It had been built in six months by the contractor, Patrick Harrington, at a cost of £600 and, according to the notice in the *Sligo Champion*, 'the good and gen-erous are earnestly requested to be present in person or by their subscription.' Due to famine that year it was impossible to raise money from the impover-ished parishioners, comprising 150 families, made up exclusively of 'herds, labourers and poor small families' and the only money collected locally

Doo Chapel

18 *S.C.* 15 Oct 1881
19 SC Irlanda, vol 39, ff 699r-705r
20 *C.T.* 2 Oct 1880
21 *W.P.* 11 April & 16 May 1891 & *C.T.* 9 Jan 1892
22 RSCG, 'Annals of Foxford'
23 *S.C.* 27 Nov 1880

amounted to £12 10s subscribed by thirteen families, while over £43 was collected 'from a few good and true friends from the town and neighbourhood of Sligo.' The site was provided by William Phibbs, Seafield and Christopher L'Estrange. In spite of the prevailing famine, the building of the new chapel had to be proceeded with as the congregation was then compelled to hear Mass in the open air. The old chapel, described as 'the very last thatched chapel in Ireland', had to be allowed to tumble down 'as the timbers were all rotten, the walls split and cracked, and several warnings were given of the risk to life'.

Meelick Chapel

Meelick chapel, which served about 500 families, was dedicated by MacCormack on Sunday 11 December 1881.[24] William Graham gave the plot at a nominal rent for 999 years and the contractor was Anthony J. Staunton, Swinford. 'The door, windows and chancel arch are painted Gothic; the altar, tabernacle and reredos handsomely wrought and finished.' Bernard Durcan, the parish priest of Swinford, who had died the previous March, left £100 in his will for the chapel. A special collection was taken up at the dedication and MacCormack gave £10, Anne Deane, £5, some thirty-four priests, £1 each, while lay-people contributed between £1 and 10s.[25] The church was re-roofed in 1928.[26]

Monasteraden

Denis O'Hara, then administrator in Ballaghaderreen, was the prime mover behind the building of the chapel in Monasteraden in 1884.[27] The high altar was presented by Thomas MacDermot of Coolavin. William Henry Byrne of Suffolk Street, Dublin, was the architect, the first of many commissions he obtained in the diocese, while James MacDonagh of Ballysadare was the builder and contractor.[28]

Monasteraden church,
West elevation
(courtesy W. H. Byrne)

24 *S.C.* 17 Dec 1881
25 For subscription list see *S.C.* 24 Dec. 1881
26 *Irish Builder*, vol 70, 1928, p E.506
27 O'Rorke, *Sligo*, p 383
28 W. H. Byrne & Son drawings, 1883-4; J. J. Tracey, unpublished Master of Architecture thesis, Queen's University, Belfast, pp 198-9

Mullinabreena

'The parish chapel of Mullinabreena stands as a monument to the utter disregard for the beauty of God's house', according to a letter to the editor of the *Sligo Champion* in 1882 (11 February). The writer gave a graphic description of the 'sorry structure': '... bog-scraws for ridge tiles, bog-scraws to fill up the many holes made by the late storms in its falling roof, with many patches of wall from which the plaster was blown and washed off, with the rotting sashes of its few and ill-shaped windows, with its loose jambs and creaking doors and with all its other abominations.' Stung by this criticism, Patrick Lowry replied that there was no point in wasting money repairing the old chapel which had been severely damaged in recent storms and four years earlier it had been decided to build a new chapel but the famine of recent years made it impossible to raise the funds. Galvanised into action, work began on a new chapel in 1883 'and was pushed so vigorously by Father Lowry, who was its architect, builder, and clerk of works, all in one, that it was opened for worship on the 9th November 1884.'[29] It was dedicated by MacCormack with Matthew Finn of Swinford preaching the sermon. The stain glass windows were made in Bruges and the high altar was of white marble and Caen stone. The total cost amounted to £1,500, of which the people of the parish contributed £500. Lowry appealed through the columns of the *Sligo Champion* to the outside public to attend the dedication hoping 'that the towns and districts around will pour in an overflowing congregation who will assist by their generous contributions, to relieve the house of God of the debt that still hangs over it'.

Kiltimagh

The church in Kiltimagh was dedicated by Lyster on Sunday 16 December 1888.[30] It was built on the site of the old chapel which was demolished in February 1887 and Denis O'Hara once more called on the architect, William Henry Byrne. MacCormack, now Bishop of Galway, preached the sermon and 'on this occasion, even surpassed his previous efforts of proverbial eloquence, and held his thousands of listeners spellbound with delighted admiration.' He expressed surprise at seeing 'such a splendid edifice erected' as it was not two years since he appointed O'Hara to Kiltimagh. The collection on that occasion amounted to over £500. The church cost £3,320 15s 8d of which the people of the parish had contributed £1,160 by the following December. [31] O'Hara held a bazaar on 6 and 7 January 1890 where he hoped to clear the debt 'with the generous help he has got from friends at home and

29 *From Plain to Hill,* pp 19-20; O'Rorke, *Sligo,* p 125
30 *S.C.* 22 Dec 1888 & *C.T.* 8 & 22 Dec 1888; *Kiltimagh,* p 93 with drawing of church; W. H. Byrne & Sons drawings, Pile 12; *Irish Builder,* vol 58, 1916, p 153
31 Denis O'Hara to Editor of *Connaught Telegraph,* 14 Dec 1889

abroad.' From 1914-16 the side aisles were extended, a new altar, font and communion rails installed and an entrance porch built containing mortuary chapel and baptistry.

Kiltimagh church 1888
(courtesy Betty Solon)

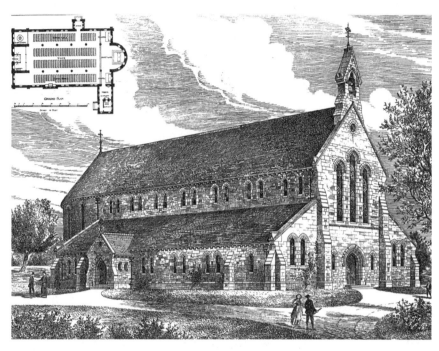

Swinford   Matthew Finn laid the foundation stone for the new church in Swinford in 1889 built on the site of the old chapel. The architect was once again William Henry Byrne, and the builder was John Mulligan, Swinford.[32] The new church was dedicated on 15 March by MacCormack while Lyster preached the sermon on this occasion and the choir was provided by the local Mercy Sisters. The high altar of pure Carara marble was a memorial to the late Mrs Patrick Corley who had left £100 for that purpose. The cost of the building was estimated at £4,000 of which the debt remaining was £1,600 and the collection taken up at the dedication came to £500, with the two bishops giving £25 each. [33] Dean Finn was absent from the dedication due to an illness from which he never recovered. He died on 7 June without ever cel-

32 W. H. Byrne & Son drawings; *The Builder*, vol 60, 21 Mar 1891, p 236; Edmund Sharp's publicity booklet (1920s) p 18

33 *W.P.* 21 Mar 1891. *Collectors:* Dr O'Grady, J. P. Mannion, solr, M. J. Corley, Timothy Corley, A. J. Staunton, P. J. Durkan, J. P. O'Connor, P. Fitzpatrick, M. J. Mellet, Edward Dolphin, Bernard Cuniffe and Thomas O'Connor. Subscription runs to over three newspaper columns in *W.P.* 28 Mar 1891

ebrating Mass in his new church, where he was buried opposite St Joseph's altar. [34] St Joseph's Church, Rooskey (Carracastle) was dedicated on 18 January 1891. [35]

The Church of Our Lady of the Holy Rosary in Kilmactigue was dedicated by Lyster on Sunday 2 October 1898.[36] The church was designed by W. H. Byrne, in a 'mixed gothic-romanesque style' and although some portions of

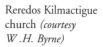

Kilmactigue

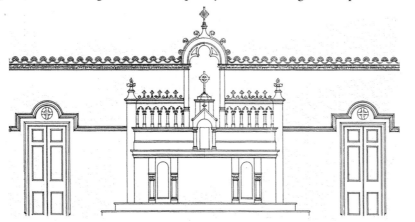

Reredos Kilmactigue church *(courtesy W .H. Byrne)*

the old church were retained it was 'to all intents and purposes an absolutely and entirely new edifice.' A beautiful marble high altar was presented by Bishop McGoldrick of Duluth, USA, a native of the parish, to commemorate his parents. Three stained glass windows behind the altar were presented by three other native priests of the parish, Tom Loftus of Ballymote, John O'Grady of Bohola and a priest in America. There was then an outstanding debt of £800 and 'the result of his lordship's appeal was that £400 was collected within a very brief period.' Bishop Healy of Clonfert was the preacher, Batty Quinn, administrator of the parish and the curate, William E. Flynn.

Lyster reported to Rome in October 1895 that there were then forty-nine chapels in the diocese.[37] The number in each parish ranged from five in Swinford and four in Ballaghaderreen and Kilmactigue to one in Attymass, Bonniconlon, Bohola, Straide, Coolaney and Kiltimagh. There were then four convents in the diocese, each of which had its own chapel. The population of the diocese was then just under 90,000 and there were forty-eight

34 *W.P.* 13 June 1891
35 *W.P.* 7 Feb 1891; see subscription list in *W.P.* 14 Feb 1891
36 *C.T.* 8 Oct 1898
37 N.S. vol 69 (1895) ff 140rv, 141rv, 142r. Swinford, 5, Ballaghaderreen, 4, Kilmovee, 3, Kilfree, 3, Collooney, 3, Kilmactigue, 4, Tubbercurry, 3, Keash, 2, Ballymote, 2, Bunninadden, 2, Charlestown, 2, Curry, 2, Achonry, 2, Carracastle, 2, Killasser, 2, Foxford, 2, Attymass, 1, Bonniconlon, 1, Bohola, 1, Straide, 1, Coolaney, 1 and Kiltimagh, 1

priests. In the seventy-three years since McNicholas reported to Rome in 1822, the number of churches in the diocese had more than doubled. The great church-building era in the diocese was the thirty years 1861-91 beginning with the cathedral in Ballaghaderreen and ending with the church in Swinford. Only ten new churches were built in the twentieth century. [38] During this period some churches, such as Bonniconlon (1908), Achonry (1913), Bunninadden and Callow (1931), were either remodelled or renovated by the architect, Rudolph Maximilian Butler. [39]

Pew Rents   It was customary up to about 1880 to charge parishioners for their seats in the chapels and pew rents, as these charges were called, were used to keep the chapels in repair. There was very limited seating accommodation in the older smaller chapels for large parish populations where only the better-off parishioners could reserve seats for their use. Matthew Finn took a case to court at the Ballymote Quarter Sessions in January 1880 to recover the pew rents for the chapel at Doo. [40] His curate, John O'Neill, was in charge of the chapel in Doo from 1877 until his death in 1879 and during that time he collected pew rents amounting to £7 8s 9d. His mother, who had administration of his will, despite several requests from Finn, refused to return the money and hence the court case which found in favour of the plaintiff. The money was probably urgently required as the new chapel in Doo was then under construction and when it opened in December 1880 only one-third of the floor, made of 'coal-tar in a bed of good mortar', had new seats.

Gurteen Sacrilege   The assignment of pews could and did cause bitterness and serious division within a parish. A group of men 'forcibly and violently' removed and smashed into pieces seats from the church in Gurteen on Sunday 24 January 1882.[41] That day the seats had been rented for the coming year by the newly

Gurteen church
(courtesy W. H. Byrne)

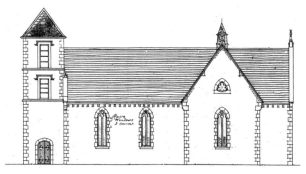

38 Achonry (1901), Ballinacarrow (1903), Straide (1916), Tubbercurry (1933), Brusna (1950), Toomore (1952), Culfadda (1959), Kilkelly (1962), Urlaur (1969), Attymachugh (1980)
39 *Irish Builder*, vol 55, 7 & 21 June 1913, pp 388 and 415 (Achonry & Bunninadden)
40 *S.C.* 24 Jan 1880
41 *S.C.* 4, 11 Feb & 4 Mar 1882; *C.T.* 25 Feb 1882

appointed parish priest, Peter O'Donoghue, who was probably unaware that this matter had caused great dissatisfaction among parishioners for the previous two years. Now, apparently, their anger boiled over. In his Lenten pastoral that year MacCormack asserted that the culprits had so behaved 'all because they failed to constitute themselves a committee of management over the seats' and he placed the church under interdict. 'No longer is the Holy Sacrifice offered up within its precincts or the sacraments administered.' The sacrilege was made a reserved sin and those who perpetrated it could not be absolved without reference to the bishop himself. Twenty-six men were later accused and tried for the offence at Mullaghroe Petty Sessions.[42]

Another striking new feature in the religious landscape of the diocese was the foundation of convents from the second half of the nineteenth century onwards. The Convent of Mercy in Swinford was the first convent established in the diocese when two Mercy Sisters, Monica Martyn and Emily Coppinger, arrived from Tuam on 5 June 1855.[43] It was the brainchild of Bernard Durcan who had appealed the year before for aid to build a convent, and three weeks after the arrival of the two Sisters it was blessed and opened on 1 July by his brother the bishop. The site, leased by Captain H. Brabazon, was colourfully described over twenty-five years later in an obituary tribute to Bernard:[44] 'The spot on which it was built was the receptacle of all the dead dogs and cats of the town. It was here the crowd assembled on fair and market evenings, to see card-sharpers and thimble-riggers at their games, to see actors dance and tinkers and cudgel-men decide the issues of the day with the blackthorn.'

Swinford Mercy Convent

Monica Martyn was only twenty years old and had just been professed in Tuam by Archbishop John MacHale, taking Aloysius as her religious name. She belonged to a branch of the well-known Galway landlord family and had entered the convent two years previously at the age of eighteen. Emily Coppinger, who was born in Liverpool and said to be a direct descendant of the Duke of Norfolk, had entered at the same time, though she was then twenty-seven. After spending a short time in Swinford she returned to Tuam where she remained until her death in 1904.

First Sisters

---

42 Hugh O'Donnell and Thomas Leonard, Gurteen, Andrew Walshe, Ballymote, James O'-Gara, Bartly Casey, Thomas Cawley, Batty Sherlock, John Marran, Dominick Farrell, Pat Muldoon, Pat Flynn, James Scanlan, Pat Henry, Mark Henry, Michael Reed, Dominick Lee, Pat Lee, Owen Carr, John Henry, John Jordan, John Lydon, Thomas Callaghan, Owen Rogers, James Bruen, Pat Cox and Thomas Kelly. *S.C.* 4 Mar 1882
43 Phyl Clancy, *A Journey of Mercy*
44 *C.T.* 14 May 1881

The first postulant, Catherine Graham, arrived in November 1855, a few months after the foundation of the convent, and in the following ten years fourteen others joined, five of them in 1858. Most, if not all, of those entrants, were from County Galway and were probably known to Monica Martyn. The second postulant who entered in March 1856 was Mary Dooley from Shrule, Co Galway, the first of five sisters to enter the convent and also in 1861 the first member of the community to die. Her sister, Teresa, who entered in 1859 died in 1862 and the three other sisters who followed later went on a mission to Australia.

Monica Martyn
Martyn continued as superioress for the first eighteen years. Bernard Durcan presided over the first election, held in May 1864, and over subsequent elections in 1867 and 1870 when she was again re-elected. In February of that year the bishop wrote to Rome seeking a dispensation for her because according to the Mercy statutes the superioress could only be elected twice. [45] MacCormack presided over the 1873 election when there were about twelve members in the community, and when nobody received a majority, he appointed Magdalen Hession as the new superioress. Martyn, who was then only thirty-eight, did not, apparently, take kindly to being reduced to the ranks. Like many founders of convents in that period with a similar family background, she had formidable leadership qualities which she was not prepared to hide under a bushel. She refused to accept the new superioress and drew two or three other Sisters into rebellion with her. MacCormack referred the case to Rome in 1874 seeking advice on how he might 'prudently' act to resolve the matter. [46]

Australia
Resolution of the problem came in a rather surprising development the following year. The Bishop of Sandhurst in Australia came to Ireland hoping to get some Irish nuns to come and work in his diocese. He looked for volunteers from the original Mercy convent in Baggot Street but they had none to offer and suggested that he approach the convent in Swinford. They may well have been informed of the problem there. His visit to Swinford resulted in Monica and two others, including one of the Dooley sisters, Kate, leaving for Australia. Two other Dooley sisters later went to Australia. After establishing a flourishing convent and school in the diocese of Sandhurst, Monica, accompanied by her life-long friend, Kate Dooley, accepted an invitation in 1892 to make another foundation, this time in Tasmania. There the foundress of the Mercy Convent, Swinford died in 1899 at the age of sixty-four.

45 Udienze, vol 164, f 117r
46 SC Irlanda, vol 37, f 28r

Sisters Divided

Her departure for Australia did not altogether resolve the problems in Swinford where the Sisters remained divided during a period of instability which followed. Elections frequently failed to produce a majority in favour of any one candidate, obliging the bishop to appoint the superioress. When Nannie Dooley, left for Australia in March 1887 mid way through her term as superioress, the subsequent election failed to produce a majority. MacCormack appointed Margaret O'Hagan on 5 May 1887 but eighteen months later she 'mysteriously' disappeared. Lyster, who had replaced MacCormack, wrote to Rome in March 1889 about O'Hagan, then living in the diocese of Shrewsbury in England and seeking release from her vows. [47]

Two months later he wrote to Cardinal Simeoni about another Swinford nun, Helen Perrin(s). [48] She was about forty years old, had spent twenty years in the convent and was now seeking a dispensation from her vows. She gave as her reasons that she never had a vocation, that she could no longer accept the burden, wished to return to secular life and even marry. Recommending that Rome give the necessary dispensation, Lyster argued that she was a bad example to the other nuns.

Visitation

Worried about the lax state of Swinford convent, Lyster carried out a visitation in August 1890 and issued a number of directions: 'In accordance with the customs of the Sisters of Mercy, the gates of the convent should be closed each evening at 4 p.m. Visitors should not be admitted after that hour, nor should any of the Sisters leave the convent except those from the Workhouse returning to their duties in that institution.' [49] He also directed that 'no public theatricals, parties or dances' be permitted in the convent schools. In fact, Swinford Dramatic Society staged plays there in January and April 1889 and at the January presentation 'the respectable inhabitants of the town were nearly all present' when the music was provided by the Mechanics Band from Ballina. [50] In fact the dramatic society had been staging their plays there regularly for ten years since their inception and, in spite of Lyster's directive, again staged their play in the convent schoolrooms in January 1892.[51]

Evangelista McCarthy

Lyster decided to look outside the diocese for a new superior. Eventually, through the influence of Agnes Morrogh Bernard of the Sisters of Charity, he procured the services of Margaret (Evangelista) McCarthy who had just com-

47 ICR, Kirby Papers (1889), 80
48 Udienze, vol 232 (1889), ff 1016v, 1026rv. Probably the same person as Victoria Perrin who entered in December 1869
49 The Board of Guardians had appointed in 1883 two of the Sisters as nurses in the Workhouse hospital. *C.T.* 5 May 1883
50 *C.T.* 12 Jan & 4 May 1889
51 *C.T.* 13 Dec 1879, 8 Jan 1881

pleted in 1891 a six year term as superioress of St John's Convent, Tralee and he appointed her superioress in Swinford on 2 September 1891. She returned to Tralee in 1896 where she had again been elected superioress, but after another six-year term there, she returned again to Swinford in 1902 and from then until her death in 1926 was elected superioress at every subsequent election.

The numbers in the community increased from 1902 with two or three new postulants received every year, many of them from Cork and Kerry. Two new branches were opened in the diocese, Ballymote in 1902 and Collooney in 1909 and Morrisroe reported to Rome in 1917 that Sisters in the three houses totalled fifty. A new national school was built in Swinford in 1905 and

1926 St Ann's Laundry van with Eddie McHugh and Packie Brennan (courtesy Phyl Clancy RSM)

a girls' secondary school began the following year with a new building by 1912. Brabazon Park House with some land was acquired in 1916 and the Sisters opened a Rural Domestic Economy School. Shortly before her death, in 1925 St Ann's steam electric laundry was built on the convent grounds, providing much-needed local employment particularly, for women and girls. At her funeral the people of Swinford carried her body through the streets of the town. After her death the convent continued to thrive and the numbers continued to grow with some postulants received each year.

Sisters of Charity Benada

One of the last official acts of Mary Aikenhead, foundress of the Sisters of Charity, was to sign in Easter 1858 a document accepting the property of Benada Abbey consisting of a manor, about 900 acres of land and the rents which went with it. [52] It was the ancestral home of the Jones family since the

---

52 'Annals of Benada'. RSCG / H 13 / 91; Sarah Atkinson, *Mary Aikenhead: Her Life, her Work and her Friends*, pp 413-25; Katherine Butler, *The Story of Benada;* T. O'Rorke, *Sligo*, pp 145-148

early seventeenth century when their Welsh ancestor acquired the confiscated Augustinian abbey in Benada. Later descendants converted to Catholicism and when the last owner, Daniel Jones, died in 1845, leaving his widow, Maria and six children, three boys and three girls, five of them were destined to enter religious orders. Daniel and James became Jesuits, Mary and Georgina, Sisters of Charity, and Elizabeth, a Mercy Sister in the diocese of Elphin. The remaining son, Freddy, died of consumption in 1853 at the age of thirty.

Jones' Donation

With their mother's consent the family decided to donate the property to the Sisters of Charity and Camillus Sallenave, accompanied by another religious and two domestic Sisters, arrived in Benada on 28 August 1862. Patrick Durcan, assisted by Laurence Gillooly of Elphin, dedicated the convent chapel on 8 October and shortly afterwards they began their regular visitation of the sick poor in the neighbourhood. Maria Jones continued to live there until her death in 1865.

They opened a school for boys and girls in June 1863, a year after their arrival, and also prepared children in the parish church twice weekly for the reception of the sacraments. After acquiring a jennet and trap they extended their sick visits to the workhouse in Tubbercurry in 1866 at the invitation of the parish priest, to the churches in Curry and Moylough in 1868 and in 1872 to Cloonacool.

Our Lady of Benada

Daniel Jones visited Rome at the end of 1865 bringing with him a letter of introduction from Durcan to Cardinal Barnabo.[53]

Father Jones has rendered valuable service to religion in my diocese: he has founded in it a convent of the Sisters of Charity at his own expense and he has assigned a considerable portion of the family estate as an endowment to this convent ... There is in the convent a beautiful statue of the Blessed Virgin Mary representing her Immaculate Conception and the favour that Father Jones wishes to obtain from the Holy Father is an indulgence for those who shall recite certain prayers before the statue.

Mary Aikenhead had signed a document with the family in 1858, stipulating that a statue of the Madonna be placed over the high altar in the Sisters' oratory and honoured under the title 'Our Lady of Benada'. Each Sister in the convent was to recite daily in front of the statue the *Memorare*. Daniel Jones visited Benada for the last time in 1869 and died in June of that year at the age of fifty-three.

Daniel Jones SJ
(courtesy Thomas Flynn)

53 SC Irlanda, vol 35, ff 393rv, 394v; Lettere, vol 356 (1865), ff 561v, 562r; Udienze, vol 150, f 1237r

Convent Closed   Benada convent became a direct casualty of the famine conditions prevailing in the winter of 1879. The Sisters' only means of support were the rents paid by the Jones' tenants which had been donated to them with the property by the family. The Land League, founded that year, encouraged tenants to withold their rents and made no exception for the Benada convent. Many landlords reacted by evicting non-paying tenants but according to the convent annalist, 'eviction could not ever find a place in the thoughts of a Sister of Charity'. They had no alternative but to pack up and leave and return to Dublin. The convent closed in February 1880 and the house in Benada remained unoccupied for almost two years.

Even before leaving Benada, the Sisters had tried to create employment for local girls by introducing in March 1863 the hand weaving of linen and later, in 1867, purchased a fly-loom for this purpose. If they were to return to Benada they had to find an income to leave them independent of the rents and so they decided to establish a grant-endowed industrial school. The Sisters returned on 15 August 1881.

> Great joy was testified by the people of the neighbourhood at the return of the Sisters – two triumphal arches were erected, one of which bore the appropriate if somewhat amusing legend 'Virgins welcome home', the village band played for hours together and the day was wound up by a torchlight procession really very effective.

Industrial School   That day the foundation stone of the industrial school was laid by MacCormack, who himself contributed £700 towards the project. It was opened in July 1882.

> At first there was some difficulty in getting the places filled, owing to the ignorance and general backwardness of the people about, who never having seen an establishment of the kind imagined that their darlings would be subjected to harsh treatment and prison discipline. These fears were very soon dispelled by the sight of the children in their comfortable clothing (above all the boots!), the contrast they presented with the deplorably neglected and dirty state in which most of them were admitted, being indeed very striking. If there were now vacancies for hundreds they would easily be filled. Many a poor mother comes to beg a corner for her little ladies and goes away with a sad heart on hearing they have no chance.[54]

The following year the inspector, Sir John Lentaigne, 'expressed much pleasure at the evident happiness and good order of the children' and later inspectors re-echoed his sentiments. Mr Fagan in December 1900 'expressed his

---

54 'Annals of Benada', RSCG / H 13 / 91

satisfaction at the healthy happy appearance of the children and the cleanliness of the institutions' and the school was very highly placed in his public reports. On his last visit in September 1904 'he publicly congratulated the children on the advantages they were receiving' and at his request nine of the children were sent in 1905 to Sligo to be examined by Lady Aberdeen 'and returned with flying colours'. The convent annalist was unequivocal: 'Nowhere are there better and more healthy children than in Benada. Years pass without a single death, this, where all are orphans or destitute from delicate parents, is a very marked care of the Sacred Heart to whom all thanks for the health, happiness and prosperity of Benada is due.' [55]

With the help of a grant from the Congested Districts Board, the Sisters started a lace-making school for local girls, who flocked to become apprentices, attracted by the prospect of earning money. By the autumn of 1901 there were about 300 girls employed in the school and Benada was carrying off the top prizes for lace-making at the Dublin Horse Show. Demand for lace declined during World War 1 and knitting was introduced. Later still, Benada specialised in producing vestments and altar linen.

Lace-making

Patrick Durcan had invited the Sisters of Charity to open a convent in Ballaghaderreen and his coadjutor, MacCormack, laid the foundation stone of the Convent of the Sacred Heart on the Feast of Corpus Christi 1874. [56] The convent cost £6,500 to build and MacCormack contributed £500 from his

Ballaghadereen

Convent of the Sacred Heart, Ballaghaderreen

<hr>

55 'Annals of Benada', RSCG / H 13 / 91.
56 Denis Gildea, *Mother Mary Arsenius of Foxford*, pp 61-79; Maire McDonnell-Garvey, *Mid-Connacht*, pp 92-101; see Appendix 13

own private funds, while two priests, Owen Stenson and Thomas Loftus, collected another £500 in America. The Mother-General, Mrs Margison, gave an endowment of £3,000 which came from the Galway estates of Colonel Gore Ousley Higgins, whose sister, a member of the community, had a life interest in the rents from the property, which the Order gave for the maintenance of the Ballaghaderreen convent. The Sisters of Charity accompanied by the Mother-General and MacCormack, who had boarded the train in Newtownforbes, arrived at Ballaghaderreen station on 24 April 1874 where they were greeted by a large crowd.

Agnes Morrogh Bernard The superior of the new convent, Agnes Morrogh Bernard, was the daughter of a Co Cork Catholic landlord and an English woman, Francis Mary Blount and in fact Agnes herself was born in Cheltenham. She was educated in Laurel Hill convent in Limerick before she went to finish her education in Paris where she spent two years living in a convent in the Latin Quarter run by English nuns. From there she returned home and for a few years led the life of a young lady of the manor. She entered the novitiate of the Sisters of Charity in Harold's Cross, Dublin in 1863 and was professed three years later. For the next eleven years she was assigned to various posts in Dublin before leaving for Ballaghaderreen.

In Ballaghaderreen the Sisters immediately began their pastoral work of visiting the sick poor in their homes and preparing young people, and sometimes adults, for the reception of the sacraments. In fact, during their first year five hundred adults were confirmed. They were also much in demand to catechise the young in the outlying parishes, and in summertime parish priests sent their own broughams to bring them to their churches. The convent school was built in 1879 and later a laundry, a dairy and a kitchen, where local girls were taught house-keeping skills which were to prove invaluable when they later emigrated to America to be employed as domestic servants.

Industrial School The Sisters received a grant in 1886 to set up an industrial school where they taught seventy-five girls, taken mostly from workhouses in different parts of Mayo. A handloom was acquired in 1889 and the girls both in the national and the industrial schools were taught the art of weaving as well as knitting, needlework, dressmaking and buttonmaking. With a loan from the Congested Districts Board they set up a knitting factory employing ninety-two hands.

Foxford Denis O'Hara was toying with the idea of establishing a convent in Kiltimagh and two Sisters of Charity came down from Dublin in 1890 to discuss the matter with him. The plans fell through and Anne Deane called on the Mother-General in Dublin, urging her to set up a convent in Foxford where she had lived before her husband's death. [57] She agreed, promising to lend £1,000 on which Deane agreed to pay the interest for five years. The bishop wrote to the Protestant police sergeant in Foxford asking him if there was any house available in the district 'suitable for a lady with small means and a family of ten or twelve' and as a result the parsonage was secured for £400 from Mrs Jackson, widow of the late Protestant Dean. The convent was opened and blessed by Lyster on 26 April 1891 with Agnes Morrogh Bernard superioress and four other Sisters, Wall, Smollen, Meyler and Doran. They took over the girls' national school from the former teacher who had just retired. Within a year of arriving in Foxford the woollen mills were in operation. [58]

Agnes Morrogh Bernard

Denis O'Hara arrived unannounced in the St Louis Convent in Monaghan on 19 October 1896.[59] 'Mother Xaviour found him standing in the parlour, a tall figure instinct with an almost fierce determination, who, in reply to her greeting, declared without a word of preamble: "I'm not moving out of this until you promise me Sisters for Kiltimagh!" When he left Monaghan that evening he had received the desired promise and made all necessary arrangements.'

St Louis Sisters

In fact, three years earlier Denis O'Hara had already made plans to establish a convent in Kiltimagh when he described to John Dillon his scheme for benefitting 'the congested district of Kiltimagh'. [60]

O'Hara's Plan

'I am applying for a grant for building a dairy ... that is where the people would bring the butter fresh from the churn without salt and there would be a machine here for blending all up together. I would have nuns specially trained who would take charge of the dairy and who would go out into the houses in the country and show the people how to keep the milk and make the butter. I would also have attached to the convent a kitchen and a laundry where girls would be taught to wash and cook. This would be of the greatest benefit to girls remaining at home and to those going to America. I would also have a poultry farm where people could get the best breeds of fowl for table and for laying purposes. All could be done for £500.'

57 RSCG, 'Annals of Foxford'; Gildea, *Mother Mary Arsenius of Foxford*, pp 87ff
58 See pp 317-323 for history of Foxford Woollen Mills and other work of Sisters of Charity in Foxford
59 Sr M. Pauline, *God Wills It*, ch 28; Frank McCarrick, 'Father Denis O'Hara, a short biography', ch 8 (unpublished thesis); *Kiltimagh*, p 112
60 Denis O'Hara to John Dillon, 3 Sept 1893, Dil. P. 6769

Denis confidently expected to get his scheme sanctioned by the Congested Districts' Board at their next meeting on 13 October 1893, and all this long before he had found any nuns to set up a convent in Kiltimagh. Why he chose the St Louis Sisters to undertake this work remains a mystery, as their later work in Kiltimagh and elsewhere suggests that their speciality was more the education of 'young ladies'.

Begging Letter   Work began on building a convent with architect William H. Byrne who had already designed the new parish church and contractor Mr Dwyer. Denis issued a circular letter appealing for funds for the convent with its infant and technical schools, particularly from Irish emigrants in America. [61]

> Most of the children of the parish have to emigrate and I want to have them trained before they go away ... Our girls leave home and land in New York without knowing a single thing about cooking, washing or house-work of any kind. They have to begin on the lowest wages and put up with the hardest work. I know you have in your hearts a love for the dear old land and for our poor Irish girls who must cross the ocean to earn a livli-hood ... To what more deserving charity can a few dollars be given than for properly training your own kith and kin?

He promised those who made a contribution to have their names read out from the altar, to offer Mass once a month for their intentions and to enter their names in a book to be kept in the convent 'so that the nuns may ever re-member them in their prayers.'[62]

St Louis Convent, Kiltimagh

61 NLI Amy Mander Papers, Ms. 24,526; W.P. 14 Nov 1896
62 A number of these books are now kept in the parochial house in Kiltimagh. I am grateful to Paddy Kilcoyne for this information.

Four St Louis Sisters, Philomena Lynch, Augustine Roch, Liguori Cloran, Joseph Hickey and two postulants, Kathleen O'Callaghan and Frances Mc-Grath, accompanied by Denis who boarded their train at Collooney, arrived in Kiltimagh on 14 September 1897. They were met at the station by a large crowd, including Lyster, all the priests of the deanery and the school children dressed in white and drawn up in processional order by the ladies of the town. The nuns were brought to the church in the bishop's carriage where after Benediction, he delivered a welcoming address. They lived in St Aidan's school until the convent was completed. *Sisters Arrive*

The Congested Districts Board gave O'Hara a grant of £1,000 for a technical school which was completed in 1895.[63] A lace school was established by the nuns and one of its exhibits, a collarette, won first prize at the Horse Show in 1899 and was purchased by the Lord Lieutenant's wife. The school continued to carry off prizes at subsequent shows and by 1901 girls employed at lace-making were earning from ten to twelve shillings a week and were also trained in housekeeping to prepare them for a career in America.

A boarding school 'for young ladies' was established, offering a wide curriculum, including five languages, English, French, Latin, German and Italian, music (piano, harp, violin and guitar), singing, drawing, painting, dancing, domestic economy, including cookery, plain and fancy needlework and dressmaking.[64] Already by 1900 there were fifty boarders in the school and so many applicants that extensions were planned for dormitories, class halls, recreation rooms and a large hall. When Denis brought the whole school on a visit to Foxford Woollen Mills in June 1913, the group comprised 22 nuns and 118 boarders. This boarding school which attracted girls from all over Ireland, most of them the daughters of well-to-do shopkeepers and professional classes, was the longest lasting legacy of the St Louis Sisters in Kiltimagh. *Boarding School*

Five Marist Sisters, Angela Cox, Agatha Keane, Anastasia Murray, Martha O'Dowd and Melanie Quinlan, arrived in Tubbercurry on Saturday 28 September 1901 and were met at the station by Lyster and a number priests and brought to their newly furnished convent where the bishop celebrated Mass.[65] Four of the five sisters had made their novitiates and were professed in France, while Melanie Quinlan had been professed in London. The Order's first house in Ireland was founded in Carrick-on-Shannon in 1873. Lyster had invited the Marists to Tubbercurry to take charge of the girls' national school and the infant school for boys, and the curate, Michael Doyle, in his sermon the *Tubbercurry Marists*

63 2nd Report of Congested Districts Board, p 28
64 See Chapter Sixteen and Appendix 11
65 *Marist Centenary Magazine;* see Appendix 10

following day took the opportunity 'to mark his appreciation of the spirit which actuated the teachers who voluntarily and cheerfully consented to the arrangements.' The Sisters began their classes in the national school on 1 October.

Lyster laid the foundation stone of the new convent on 9 October 1904 and the Mass on that occasion was celebrated by the Bishop of Ardagh, while the Bishop of Elphin preached the sermon. The building designed in a French style was completed two years later. The Sisters received considerable financial help from Edward Joseph Ormsby Cooke and his sister, Marie Louise, who took up residency in the convent after their property was destroyed by the Black and Tans in June 1920. [66]

Marist Convent, Tubbercurry *(courtesy W. H. Byrne)*

The church in Achonry was thoroughly institutionalised by 1917 when Morrisroe proudly reported to Rome that there were then eight convents with a total of 155 nuns, fifty-seven Sisters of Charity in three convents, fifty Mercy nuns, also in three convents, thirty-eight St Louis nuns in Kiltimagh and sixteen Marist nuns in Tubbercurry. The diocese then had fifty-six secular priests, and eighteen clerical students, for a population of about 80,000. [67]

Brothers

There were also two communities of Brothers, each with four members, the Marists in Swinford and the De La Salle in Ballaghaderreen. The De La Salle Brothers were the first to arrive in the diocese, having been invited by Lyster in 1890 to take charge of the boys' national school in Ballaghaderreen which they renamed St John's Monastery School. They remained until 1985 and during that time sixty-six Brothers taught in the school and twelve natives of the diocese entered the Order.[68] The Marist Brothers came to Swinford where they took charge of the boys' national school in 1901 and remained

66 See Chapter Eighteen, pp 465-9
67 ASV Congregazione Consistoriale, Relationes Diocesium 5 (1917)
68 See Appendix 15. I am indebted to Pius McCarthy for information on the De La Salle Brothers.

until 1918 when nineteen Brothers had worked there. The Franciscan Brothers began teaching in the boys' national school in Foxford in 1924 and remained for eight years, leaving in 1932.

Religious Sisters and Brothers not only made a major contribution to education in the diocese, they also contributed hugely to the devotional life of the people. The Sisters, in particular, were avid collectors of the numerous religious novelties sweeping the country from the late nineteenth century on as a result of parish missions, and enthusiastically promoted them among their pupils and their families. They played a major role in what has become known as 'the devotional revolution'.

Tubbercurry Church, front elevation *(courtesy W. H. Byrne & Sons)*

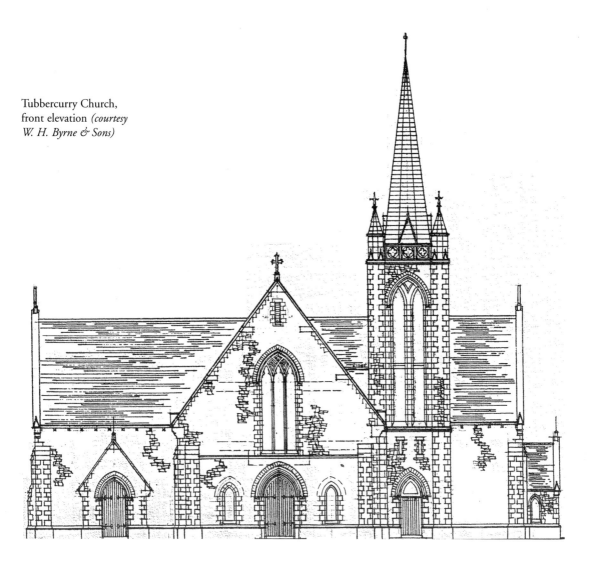

CHAPTER FIFTEEN

Devotional Revolution

Parish Missions

A huge transformation took place in the devotional life of people in the diocese somewhere between 1870 and the end of the century, a transformation which was to remain unaltered until the Second Vatican Council. This 'devotional revolution' was largely the result of parish missions.[1] Patrick Durcan reported to Rome in 1862 that missions lasting three weeks were given by Jesuits in certain parishes.[2] In fact, by then two parish missions had been given in the diocese by Jesuits, one in the newly-opened cathedral in Ballaghadereen from 12 May to 2 June 1861 and another three years earlier from 16-30 May 1858 in Swinford where the bishop's brother, Bernard, was parish priest. Bernard had represented the aging and ailing McNicholas at the Synod of Thurles, which had strongly recommended parish missions. Other Jesuit missions were held in Swinford in 1866 (30 September-14 October), 1873 (1-23 May) and 1877 (March) and in Kiltimagh in March 1877.

Tourlestrane

The only other Jesuit mission in the diocese was held at Tourlestrane in 1867 (19 May-2 June). Of the four Jesuits, Healy, Fortescue, Corcoran and McEnroe, one was given lodgings in the administrator's house and the other three were accommodated by Michael Mullarkey of Drumartin. The Sisters of Charity provided the liturgical music and also cooked for priests from neighbouring parishes who assisted in hearing confessions. During the mission two processions took place, one in honour of the Blesssed Virgin Mary and the other in honour of the Blessed Sacrament.

'Little Mission'

A 'little mission' lasting only a few days was given by a single Jesuit, Fr Corcoran, in Benada in May 1673. Morning Mass celebrated by the missioner was followed by an exhortation and then three or four other Masses by visiting priests. After breakfast confessions were heard for several hours by six or seven neighbouring priests as well as Bishop MacCormack. The Litany of the Saints was recited while the priests were at dinner. The Rosary was recited at 6 p.m. followed by a sermon, Benediction and the singing of the Litany of the Blessed Virgin Mary. 1,000 people received communion during the

1 The phrase was coined by Emmet Larkin in 'The Devotional Revolution in Ireland, 1850-75', *American Historical Review*, vol 77, no 3, (June 1972)
2 SC Irlanda, vol 32, f 260rv

mission. On the last day there was a procession in honour of the Blessed Virgin in the convent grounds, followed by a sermon and Benediction given from an altar erected under the trees.[3]

Sermons

The outstanding feature of missions were the sermons, then rare oc-curences in parish liturgies. The Sisters of Charity complained that the first two years they spent in Foxford and attended the parish church they never heard a sermon from either the parish priest or curate. [4] People loved listen-ing to public speeches, and orators of the day tended to be loquacious by modern standards. Sermons frequently lasted an hour or more and with any-thing less people often felt cheated. Different preachers became noted for dif-ferent topics. Subjects included the existence of God, the purpose of life, the Blessed Eucharist, Mary, the Mother of God etc., while sin was a major topic with special emphasis on local vices such as drunkenness, dishonesty, gam-bling and faction-fighting.

Sex

Among local vices, sexual immorality was rarely listed in missioners' chronicles. Priests in Stranorlar informed the Jesuits in 1870 that the parish had not 'an instance of an illegitimate child in the last thirty years.'[5] Morris-roe reported to Rome in 1922 that there had only been two instances of con-cubinage (unmarried people living together) in the whole of the diocese in the previous thirty years.[6] Dancing, however, was listed as one of the local vices in Swinford in 1894 and Ballaghaderreen in 1898. Redemptorists spe-cialised in sermons on sexual morality, which they referred to as their 'partic-ular' instructions, and the sexes were rigidly segregated for these sermons. The second Sunday of the mission in Curry in 1894 was reserved for married men, and the following Monday for married women, while another morning each was alloted to single women and single men.

Hell

The high point of the mission was often the sermon on the 'Last Things', death, Last Judgement, eternal reward and punishment, particularly with Redemptorists noted for their 'fire and brimstone' sermons on hell. Graphic descriptions of the torments of hell were a rhetorical device used by mission-ers to terrify the listener with fear and induce his conversion. One Redemp-torist missioner recalled that the Irish loved 'strong sermons that filled them with the holy fear of God.' 'The more terrifying the sermon, the more the people loved it.' [7] While the thrust of the preacher was often to provoke in

3   RSCG / H 13 / 91, 'Annals of Benada'; Kevin A. Laheen, *Jesuits in Killaloe*, Appendix
4   RSCG / H 26 / 449, p 38
5   *Collectanea Hibernia*, no 41, p 154
6   ASV, Congregazio Consistoriale, Relationes Diocesum, 1922
7   John Sharp, *Reapers of the Harvest*, p 162

his audience the fear of God's wrath, leading to their confession and repentance, it was somewhat balanced by reference to God's mercy.

Confessions   A great part of the mission was taken up with confessions. Three Redemptorists, Condon, McCormack and O'Farrell, 'continued from 6 a.m. until late at night in the confessional' in Kiltimagh in 1881.[8] Upwards of 13,000 confessions were heard in the parish of Elphin in 1863. Confessions began there in 1876 at 7 a.m. until Mass at 8 a.m., resumed from 10 a.m. to 12 noon, 1.30 p.m. to 3.30 p.m. and finally 8 p.m. to 9.30 p.m., a total of six and a half hours each day. Large numbers of priests from surrounding parishes assisted the missioners, seventeen during the first week, twenty during the second and over thirty the last week. This practice was repeated elsewhere, at the Oblate mission in Tubbercurry in 1886 where 'a large number of the clergy of the neighbouring parishes attended', and during the last week of the Franciscan mission in Coolaney in the winter of 1889 when Lyster and several priests from neighbouring parishes heard confessions.[9]

'The very first day we sat to hear confessions', a Jesuit recorded at a mission in County Cork in 1874, 'the boxes were thronged and we had to leave many behind us that day and the succeeding days unheard'. He had a similar experience in Derry in 1873 where at the end 'the rush was so great that twice the number of priests who came to our aid would have been required.'[10] People sometimes took extraordinary steps to insure that their confessions were heard. Men began queuing up at the confessionals at one o'clock in the morning in Tipperary and some in Kilmallock, Co Limerick in 1883 got into the chapel through a window in the middle of the night to get a place in the confessionals the next day.[11]

In some parishes, such as Castlerea in 1873, confessional tickets were issued to penitents each day and were collected each evening from the different confessors and the number noted down. The tickets insured that parishioners were given priority over outsiders – described by one missioner as 'fine fat fish from other waters' – who often availed themselves of services provided by a mission in a neighbouring parish. Parish priests later favoured opening up their missions to surrounding parishes, much to the displeasure of missioners like the Redemptorists in Castlerea in 1887 where the church was 'filled with but comers and goers for the day, who, when they had heard a few sermons, three generally, and their confession over, went home to let their friends come for the day.' Philip Mulligan favoured admitting all-comers to confes-

8   *C.T.* 17 Sept 1881
9   *S.C.* 2 Oct 1886 & 21 Dec 1889
10 *Collectanea Hibernica*, vol 42, pp 132, 147
11 Sharp, pp 152-3

sions in Curry in 1894, leaving the disappointed Redemptorists to conclude it was 'only a huge station ... a hullabaloo mission'.[12]

Irish

In the last decades of the nineteenth century many people, particularly in rural districts like Newmarket, Co Cork in 1874, were Irish-speaking. 'Nearly all the people here speak Irish and they have a decided preference for the native tongue, for although they understand English well and speak it also, they would be better pleased to confess their sins in Irish.'[13] The situation was probably similar in most parishes in Achonry. One of the Passionists, Pius Devine, a native of the diocese, preached in Irish in Ballaghaderreen in May 1869, and the three Redemptorists in Tourlestrane in 1881 thought that if they had twice as many missioners and one or two able to speak Irish, 'the missioners would not have laboured so much in vain.'[14]

Requiem Day

One day in each mission, usually Saturday of the first week,was set aside for special remembrance of the dead, the dying and the sick, when there was always an unusual high attendance. An open coffin was placed close to the altar rails and the congregation was invited to put into it the names of those to be prayed for. The catafalque, altar and candles were all draped in black for the solemn requiem high Mass offered for the deceased of the parish. In a sermon on purgatory, people were reminded of their duty to remember in their prayers their deceased relatives and the faithful departed in general. After the sermon the prayers of the church were said over the empty coffin which was incensed and sprinkled with holy water. Confessions were heard during the entire day.

Offerings

Offerings or entrance charges were taken up at the various exercises of the mission and amounts varied from one parish to another.[15] Described as 'extremely modest' in one parish in 1870, while 'a halfpenny or nothing at all' was recommended at evening devotions in another, and no collections at any of the other exercises with none at all on 'requiem day'. An impressed Jesuit missioner wrote in his diary. 'Would that others would go and do likewise.' The Jesuits also admired the system in Kildare in the summer of 1871 where two 'rusty' boxes were placed at the chapel gates and the tariff of a penny for the floor and sixpence for reserved seats was left completely optional. 'All who choose can pass the collectors without paying a fraction and enter the house of God without a word being said to them.'

12 'Apostolici Labores', Dundalk, 1, pp 172-3 & 324 qtd in Sharp, pp 219-20
13 *Collectanea Hibernica*, vol 42, p 147
14 'Chronica Domestica et Apostolici Labores', Dundalk, vol 1 (1876-98), pp 98-9 qtd in John Sharp, *Reapers of the Harvest – The Redemptorists in Great Britain and Ireland*, p 211 who mistakes Kiltimagh for Kilmactigue.
15 *Collectanea Hibernica*, no 41, pp 161, 189, 193, 211, 214

A penny was charged at each of the exercises on weekdays in Donegal in the winter 1871-2 and threepence and sixpence on Sundays. In a parish in the north of Ireland in 1872, 'numbers of the parishioners held back from the sermons unable (as they said) to meet the tariff' which was lowered in the middle of the week with 'a visible improvement at once'. One parish priest's manner of collecting was described as 'unique', standing by the collection-box, chatting or reading. 'The people pass by without let or hindrance, and give or give not just as they please. Some lay down coppers, others silver, others nothing at all.' The parish priest appeared oblivious to what was being given, though the missioner was convinced that in reality he was 'wide awake'. The Sisters of Charity paid a contribution of 12s 6d at the 1892 Oblate mission in Foxford 'as an entrance fee' for some of their workers who 'were miserably poor.' 'The mission opened on Sunday and on Tuesday evening the poor things eager to attend were refused admittance. Another 2s 6d was sent up at once and a good many odd pennies had to be found before the end.'[16] The money collected during the mission was used to pay the expenses of the mission and the honorarium, usually £10, given to each missioner.

Agnus Deis

An Agnus Dei (Lamb of God), a small article made of red flannel, was a pious object or sacramental distributed by missioners to those attending and for which there was a tremendous demand. 'Their anxiety to procure the Agnus Dei is beyond anything, and having procured it they kiss and hug it as a real treasure. Those who have relatives in America or out of Ireland think their fortune made if they can only get an Agnus Dei to send them.'[17] The anxiety to procure them in Meath in 1869 was 'intense and universal' and the following year people in Kilkenny were said to be 'ravenous' for them,

Agnus Deis *(courtesy Mary Ann Bolger)*

16 RSCG / H 26 / 449
17 *Collectanea Hibernica*, no 41, p 173. See also pp 163, 165, 195, 209

while the Jesuits in Dingle in 1872 were 'devoured' for Agnus Deis. 'The anxiety to possess themselves of Agnus Deis was nowhere greater than in Roscommon.' Young people about to emigrate came to get them before embarking.

From almost the very beginning, missions attracted vendors of medals, scapulars, rosaries, pious books and other holy objects, who set up their stalls on roads leading to the chapel and even in the chapel yard. McNicholas had asked Rome as early as 1821 for faculties to bless scapulars of the Blessed Virgin Mary, the earliest request of such a kind from the diocese, and later he sought faculties to bless and attach indulgences to rosaries, crosses, crucifixes

Vendors

Mission stall

and medals. But there was a huge increase, particularly from the last decades of the nineteenth century, in the use of these 'pious objects' as important devotional aids, and Durcan, MacCormack and Lyster all wrote to Rome requesting faculties to bless these objects and power to communicate the same faculties to their priests. [18] Vendors were generally welcomed by priests of the parish and missioners who laid aside a portion of each day to enrolling in the various scapulars and blessing medals and other pious objects.

Profits were sometimes quite modest. In Meath diocese in 1870 'the vendors of beads etc made a very poor market, scarcely enough to pay their expenses to and from.' Very occasionally, as in Monasterevin, Co Kildare, they were banned by priests in the parish. 'The vendors of pious books and other

18 Udienze, vol 59, ff 604rv, vol 101, ff 887r, 910r, 911v, vol 120, ff 2721r, 2758r, vol 179, f 1470r, vol 187, f 1339r, vol 212, ff 1036rv, 1061r, vol 245, ff 2388r, 2411rv

pious articles are not allowed to erect their stalls in the chapel yard. No welcome here for them from the priests who have shopkeepers of their own in this line whom they patronise.' Over the years these vendors furnished almost every house in the country with its religious art – holy pictures and statues – of little or no artistic merit but of great religious significance.

Confraternities   Towards the end of the mission, people were enrolled in confraternities to keep them involved by providing weekly devotional meetings and an opportunity for monthly communion. People were thus moulded into what was described as 'lay religious'. Each Order had their own favourite confraternities. Jesuits promoted the 'archconfraternity in honour of the agonising heart of Jesus for the dying' while Redemptorists had two, the archconfraternity of the Holy Family and the archconfraternity of Our Lady of Perpetual Succour. The Holy Family was the only confraternity allowed by Philip Mulligan in Curry in 1894 and the Redemptorists urged it strongly, with the result that all in the parish joined.[19] Other popular confraternities were the Immaculate Heart of Mary and the Sacred Heart confraternity. All Dublin parish priests unanimously acknowledged, according to John Harbison in 1874, that confraternities 'are by far the best and the most practical work for the Irish working class that has yet been tried in Ireland.'

The earliest recorded confraternitiy in Achonry was of the Blessed Virgin Mary of Mount Carmel. Bernard Durcan asked Rome in 1851 for faculties to bless habits for that confraternity in Swinford and power to enrol both sexes in it, and six years later renewed his request. His brother the bishop sought similar faculties around the same time. [20]

The Children of Mary was very popular among girls and women and mostly promoted through convents. It was established in the convent in Benada in 1865 and in their sister convent in Foxford soon after its foundation with over 200 members shortly afterwards. Swinford had regular Children of Mary retreats in the 1880s but by 1894 it was in a 'delapidated condition' and revived during the Redemptorist mission, with the membership increasing by about 200.

Children were also recruited into confraternities or associations such as the Holy Childhood and Children of the Angels. The Sisters of Charity in Ballaghaderreen established the Apostleship of Prayer and Holy League of the Heart of Jesus in 1887 to help 'in moulding them to piety' because they were not 'ripe enough yet for the sodality of the Children of Mary'. By the early decades of the twentieth century, there were four annual retreats in Foxford,

19 'Chronica Domestica' Dundalk, p 325
20 Udienze, vol 114, ff 1012rv, vol 120, ff 2721r, 2758r, vol 126, ff 1291v, 1319r

one for male mill workers and the others for the sodalities of the Children of Mary, Christian Mothers and the Children of the Angels.

MacCormack called on priests and people in his Lenten pastoral in 1884 'to stamp out that appalling vice of drunkenness which is a stain on our national character.' [21] As drinking was often cited as one of the abuses prevailing in most parishes, it is not surprising that missioners encouraged the formation of temperance societies. A branch of St John's Temperance Society was formed in Ballymote at the beginning of September 1876 during a Redemptorist mission and later a fife and drum temperance band was established. Swinford had a temperance society in 1886 when over a hundred members took part in their annual picnic to Pontoon, [22] while Carracastle had its own temperance hall and Ballaghaderreen a GAA temperance club.

Temperance

Carracastle
Temperance Branch
*(courtesy Vincent
Coleman)*

Three Redemptorists were employed by Lyster for about six weeks from 12 September to 31 October 1909 to launch a temperance crusade throughout the diocese, and they preached in every parish in the diocese except Charlestown, Bonniconlon, Attymass and Curry, which were having missions about the same time. [23] Agnes Morrogh Bernard made her own particular contribution to the crusade, making arrangements with some shopkeepers in

Temperance Crusade

21 *C.T.* 1 Mar 1884
22 *C.T.* 26 June 1886
23 ADA, Bishop Lyster Book

Foxford in 1910 to sell tea made by the Sisters in urns and supplied to the shops at the May fair. Eighty-five gallons of tea were consumed at the fair, as well as numerous ham sandwiches also made by the Sisters. Afterwards most shops sold tea and sandwiches on fair days. Coffee, according to the convent annalist, was looked down upon by country people as much inferior to tea.[24]

Carracastle Temperance Band with Philip Mulligan *(courtesy Vincent Coleman)*

Close of Mission

The mission ended with a sermon on perseverance, followed by the solemn renewal of baptismal vows, with all the people holding lighted tapers. After the papal blessing there was a short procession of the Blessed Sacrament, then the acts of reparation and consecration to the Sacred Heart, and finally Benediction of the Blessed Sacrament. There was usually great sadness on the last day of the mission and people were loath to see the missioners depart. Large crowds often accompanied them to the local railway station. Jesuit missioners in Omagh in 1869 'were accompanied to the train by a sobbing and weeping multitude of poor people', and were given an even more spectacular send-off from Castlecomer, Co Kilkenny later that year.

'Having driven about three miles of the road we came up to a band of 500 honest colliers who had left their work to thank us and bid us farewell. Each had a green branch and the party was preceded by a grand banner on which was inscribed in large gold letters 'Farewell to the Jesuit Fathers'. Their shouts were really deafening and it required all our eloquence and

24 RSCG, 'Annals of Foxford'

ingenuity to dissuade them from following us to Carlow. All along the road for a mile or so from that spot, we met poor creatures kneeling at the side of the road to get a last glimpse of us and wish us "God Speed"... nowhere except in Ireland could such a spectacle be met with.'

Mission Crosses

On the first occasion of a mission in a parish, as in Swinford after the 1858 Jesuit mission, a cross was erected near the church entrance to commemorate the event. Crosses were usually made of stone but sometimes also of wood. Bishop Durcan solemnly blessed the 'handsome massive oak cross' erected in Tourlestrane in September 1867 to commemorate the Jesuit mission given earlier that year. [25] The funds for the cross were raised by the Jesuit, Daniel Jones, formerly of Benada Abbey and two charity sermons were preached on the occasion, one in English by a Jesuit, the other in Irish by John Brennan, parish priest of Tubbercurry. The Passionist mission in Charlestown in 1874 was commemorated by the erection of a large wooden cross in front of the church in the presence of 10,000 people. At the end of a mission in Bunninadden in 1891 given by the Oblate Fathers, 'a large and beautiful memorial crucifix was erected within the church, with the usual indulgences, and was solemnly blessed by the bishop, who was attended by the missioners and the rest of the clergy.' [26] Before such crosses were blessed, a sermon was preached on the sufferings of Christ during his passion, like one in Ballina by the Jesuit, John Dwyer, noted for his sermons on Christ's passion. 'The sermon produced the deepest emotion. During the whole of it sobs were heard from different parts of the church and many of the congregation were plunged in grief and tears.' [27]

James Higgins PP
Charlestown with
Mission Cross, 1874

Reconciliation

After the blessing of the cross a ceremony described as the 'reconciliation of enemies' took place, with no one allowed to kiss the cross unless he was first reconciled with his enemy. One poor man, during this ceremony in 1870, asked his offender to shake hands with him but the latter refused and the former went ahead and kissed the cross. The other man then ran after him, shook his hand and he in turn kissed the cross. [28] At the end of the

25 RSCG / H 13 / 91, 'Annals of Benada'
26 Oblate Missionary Record, (1891), p 32
27 *Tyrawley Herald*, 7 June 1855
28 *Collectanea Hibernica*, no 41 (1999), pp 156-57

mission people were exhorted to visit the mission cross daily for forty days to pray in thanksgiving for blessings received during the mission and, by offering three Our Fathers, three Hail Marys and one Glory be to the Father, they could gain an indulgence of five years. 'The devotion of the poor faithful Irish to these crosses is inconceivable. Every day in the year they are seen kneeling and praying most fervently before them in spite of rain and storm and mud. No fury of the elements is capable of interfering with their devotion to the sign of Redemption and the memorial of the graces bestowed on the parish during the mission.' [29]

Success or Failure   Some Orders, particularly the Redemptorists, kept diaries with detailed accounts of the missions they gave and their verdicts on the success or failure of each mission. They pronounced their mission in Tourlestrane in 1882 'a most decided failure' while the one in Ballaghaderreen in 1889 was 'a most brilliant success.' The jury remained out on the 1880 mission in Foxford which the chronicler placed in the 'don't know' category. [30] In reaching their verdicts, certain tangible results were taken into account such as the number who attended, the numbers of the 'lapsed' who returned to the fold, of couples 'living in sin' who had their unions regularised and the number of conversions to Catholicism during the mission. As the population in most Achonry parishes was overwhelmingly Catholic converts were rare, though there was one at the 1889 mission in Ballaghaderreen. One couple living in concubinage in Foxford in 1880 were joined in legitimate marriage. Of the 'immense' population in Swinford in 1894 'all made their mission but two or three hardened cases, one a solicitor of the town and the others moneylenders'.

Passionists   As two members of the Passionist Order, Pius and Arthur Devine, were natives of Achonry and nephews of the parish priest of Carracastle, James Devine, it was hardly surprising that the Order was invited to give missions in the diocese. [31] Pius Devine preached in Irish at a three-week mission, 2-23 May 1869, in the cathedral in Ballaghaderreen assisted by Sebastian Keens, Gregory Callaghan and Dominic Neill. His brother, Arthur, was one of a foursome, with Alphonsus O'Neill, Sylvester McManus and Malachy Graham, who gave a three-week mission, 3-24 May, in Charlestown in 1874. There were 9,000 communicants and on the final day 10,000 received the papal blessing in the open air. Between 1860 and 1868 the same Order gave eight retreats in the Mercy convent in Swinford.

29 qtd Laheen, p 133
30 'Chronica Domestica' Dundalk, pp 68 & 98
31 Information supplied by Andrew O'Loughlin, Archivist, Mount Argus

Four Redemptorists gave a mission in Ballymote in September 1876 [32] and in Kiltimagh at the end of the month. A three-week mission was conducted in Foxford in October 1880 by four Redemptorists.[33] The success of the mission was hampered by the poverty of the people and the distance many of them had to go to the church. 2,648 persons received communion. One of the Redemptorists, John Harbison, considered Foxford 'the most God-forsaken place he had ever been in, the country people so ignorant that they scarcely knew right from wrong.' The missioners called on the Sisters in Ballaghaderreen and urged them to pray that a convent would be established in Foxford. Three Redemptorists, Condon, McCormack and O'Farrell gave a mission in Kiltimagh in 1881, beginning after 11 o'clock Mass on Sunday 11 September. [34] They preached after Mass every morning and at 2 p.m. gave instruction to the children. Parishioners over-crowded the church in the evenings.'

Three Redemptorists, Palliola, Frohn and Power, gave a three-week mission in Tourlestrane in September 1882.[35] The local abuses were described as 'missing Mass and supreme ignorance'. There was a 'scanty' attendance of between three and four hundred in the evenings while the morning attendance was somewhat larger but there seemed to be a different crowd every day because everyone received communion each day (8,000 in all), whereas the norm was once for each person during the whole mission. The Redemptorists themselves heard 1,800 confessions.

Redemptorists

'Gigantic Station'

'The bishop called in a dozen of his neighbouring priests, and crowds principally of women poured in from all parts to attend this gigantic Station. In the midst of such bustle and confusion the Fathers cannot vouch that all the parishioners succeeded in making their confessions, as the secular staff of confessors admitted all-comers. There are strong reasons to fear that numbers, specially men, did not come up at all.'

The Redemptorists themselves thought that the mission was 'undoubtedly a most decided failure.'

'The parish extends over an area of 30 miles in circumference, and though the principal chapel is in the centre, as the people are all poor, starved, naked etc, they found it too far for them to go. September was the most ill-chosen month of the year, because of the gathering of the harvest and secondly because of the dampness of the evenings ... If six Fathers had

32 *S.C.* 21 Feb 1880
33 'Chronica Domestica', Dundalk, vol 1, pp 67-8; RSCG / H 26 / 449
34 *C.T.* 17 Sept 1881
35 'Chronica Domestica', Dundalk, vol 1, pp 97-9

been sent, one or two able to speak Irish, and if the mission had been given in the three chapels of the parish that were four miles apart, then the missioners would not have laboured so much in vain.' [36]

Curry   The mission in Curry was given by three Redemptorists, Hall, McNamara and Peters, for two weeks, from 6-20 May. The population of the parish was 3,000, of whom a few were non-Catholics, and the Redemptorists thought the people 'simple, innocent, God-fearing, primitive' and in a 'rather backward' spiritual state:

Their idea of a mission was that of a big station – 2 or 3 sermons to be heard and their usual confession ... The PP did not interfere in the little details of the mission, but he did in what was really important for the success of the mission. The neighbouring PPs too – with him – wanted all their people to be heard whether they had been to sermons or not and

esp(ecially) their petty little "well to do's". The weather was awful throughout – cold and very rainy. Yet the bad weather, throwing back the work in the fields, was rather a help to the success of the mission as it made work impossible for the people. No one of the parish lived more than 5 English miles away, but many made less distance than this an excuse. The season would have been suitable had not the time of year been

Curry church

unusually bad. 7-30 (a.m.) for morning Mass and 7 (p.m.) for evening sermon suited. The usual ceremonies in honour of the Bl(essed) Sacr(amen)t & B(lessed) V(irgin) Mary took place. The children had their mission – Mass at 9 o'cl(ock) with instr(uction) – general communion. The married men had their special instr(uction) on 2nd Sunday – married women Monday morning – young women another morning & young men on another. Confessions by missionaries 68, (by others 12,000!! As calculated by themselves). Twenty priests heard nearly every day.

The attendance at first poor, grew with time, so that overflow services had to be held in the open-air. The church was crowded with penitents during the day. The vast majority of these crowds, made up of parishioners and outsiders, was heard by the clergy at (the) rate of a hunt and not minding

36 'Chronica Domestica et Apostolici Labores', Dundalk, vol 1 (1876-98), pp 98-9 qtd in John Sharpe, *Reapers of the Harvest – The Redemptorists in Great Britain and Ireland,* p 211

whether their penitents attended (the) mission. The mission in a word was a hullabaloo mission where the people of the parish did not get fair play and for many it was only a huge station and the PP would not hear of the mission being any longer than a fortnight. Had we been 3 weeks there and been able to confine ourselves to the parish and allowed to follow our rules, our traditions & the injunctions of our H(oly) Father, the mission might have been the most successful ever given in Ireland. But "propter bonum commune" (for the common good) – that of our future missions in Achonry & in the West – it was judged better by Rector not to fight but to yield and do what we could. The PP expressed himself delighted and was all through most cordial. The priests who assisted thought the mission a wonder and spoke of the good done as something quite new to them as confessors ... Though many of the parishioners are away in summer and at home in the winter, yet, it may be said, that when Curry has been stirred up (by) a real mission or two a regular confraternity may succeed there as it has elsewhere under like difficulties.

Three Redemptorists, Geoghegan, McNamara and Bannon, gave a three week mission in Swinford later that year from 16 September-7 October. Before the mission the spiritual state of the people was thought to be 'rather backward in the matter of instruction'. Dancing was the local vice resulting from the practice of holding a raffle for a duck or a hen to help some poor person and the raffle was always followed by a dance. Many men in the neighbourhood had not yet returned from England. The poverty of the people and the distances many of them had to travel were obstacles to the success of the mission and matters were not helped by the decision of the parish priest. 'The Pastor did not put on a high charge but there was no free place for the poor and there was no making the suggestion to him without coming to a rumpus.' A ten day mission was given to the children and sixty of them made their First Communion. During the mission 7,400 received communion, while the three Redemptorists heard 1,664 confessions. *Swinford*

The Redemptorists gave two missions in Ballaghaderreen, one in 1889 and the other nine years later. Three Redemptorists, Geoghegan, Graham and O'Brien gave a three-week (3-24 Feb.) mission in 1889.[37] The missioners were informed that the local abuses were 'night dances & 'porter-sprees' and neglect of Mass when over in England'. For the last fortnight of the mission there were no fewer than eighteen priests hearing confessions. The three Redemptorists themselves heard 2,600 confessions while the others heard at least *Ballaghaderreen*

37 Dundalk, 'Labores Apost. Externi Anni 1889'

6,000. 8,200 received communion and 1,100 at the children's general communion. 'The mission was a most brilliant success. The earnestness of the good people to attend the sermons and to get to confession was extraordinary.'

Nine years later the Redemptorists returned to Ballaghaderreen for a three-week mission in February 1898, but in the meantime missions given by Franciscans and Dominicans accordng to the Redemptorist chronicler, were 'without much success'. The local vices still remained the same. 'There was a little drinking at fairs and too much dancing.' The attendance in the beginning was poor due to the bad weather and an outbreak of 'flu which prevented country people making the journey daily. 'Towards the end people got more enthusiastic and overcame all difficulties nobly so that this mission rivalled the great mission 9 years previous.' The three Redemptorists, O'Laverty, Routledge and Murray, heard 2,700 confessions between them, while 3,300 were heard by other priests. Over 6,000 received communion.

Oblate Missions

There was 'an unusually large attendance' at the mission in Tubbercurry conducted by the Oblate Fathers in autumn 1886 and 'a large number of the clergy of the neighbouring parishes attended' and assisted in hearing confessions. [38] Three Oblate Fathers, Nicholl, O'Dwyer and Furlong gave a three week mission in Bunninadden in May 1891. Lyster was present from the first Monday until the close of the mission and together with many priests from neighbouring parishes heard confessions everyday. 8,000 people went to confessions, about half of them from outside the parish. The Sodality of the Sacred Heart was established in the parish with 500 members enrolled by the bishop. These three were joined by a fourth Oblate, Brady, for a two week mission in Foxford in October 1892. [39] It concluded with the renewal of baptismal vows when all the congregation held lighted candles. The Oblates gave a retreat in Ballaghaderreen in 1894.

Franciscans

A number of missions were given in different parishes in the diocese by three Franciscans in the winter of 1889-90. They spent Christmas with Anne Deane in Ballaghaderreen because of her connexion with the Order – John Dillon's brother, Henry, was then studying to become a Franciscan. [40] One of the missions took place in Coolaney and it was reported that a great number of people had to cross a dangerous river in storms of rain and hail to get to the mission 'and yet they brought the maimed, the blind and the sick on their

38 *S.C.* 2 Oct 1886: Information on missions in Kiltimagh, Foxford and Ballaghaderreen supplied by Michael Hughes OMI, Inchicore. On Bunninadden mission see Oblate Missionary Record (1891) p 32
39 Oblate Missionary Record (1892) p 393; *C.T.* 12 Nov 1892
40 *S.C.* 21 Dec 1889; Anne Deane to John Dillon, 25 & 26 Dec. 1889, 7 Jan 1890, Dil. P. 6285

backs across this river.' During the last week of the mission, Lyster and several priests from neighbouring parishes heard confessions. 1,200 were enrolled in the scapular of the Immaculate Conception and 1,000 in the Cord of St Francis, a Franciscan Third Order. A similar mission was held in the parish of Achonry where 1,600 were enrolled in the scapular of the Immaculate Conception and 1,300 in the Cord of St Francis.

The Dominican mission in Tourlestrane in 1895 was 'splendidly attended'.[41] During the fortnight 7,000 received communion and confirmation was administered. In February 1903 a three-week mission was given in Foxford by Vincentian Fathers. 'It was splendidly attended, people coming from miles around.' Less than a year later, in January 1904, a parish retreat lasting a week was given by two Vincentians and again the attendance was 'phenomenal'. Lyster attended on the last day. [42] He informed Rome in October 1905 that during the year missions had been held 'in almost half the diocese'.[43] Missions continued as a regular and highly popular feature of parish life in the first half of the twentieth century.

Up to fairly late in the nineteenth century the Sunday Mass was almost the only public religious act in a parish. Redemptorists in Tourlestrane found in 1882 that 'the only sign of religion is a Mass on Sunday' and missing Mass was one of the principal vices there. Lack of proper clothing prevented many adults of poorer classes from attending Mass and little had changed since the beginning of the century when McNicholas made his first report to Rome in 1822. [44] 'The poorer people rarely frequent the chapel in wintertime because of lack of clothes; however, they are accustomed to recite prayers at the time the sacrifice of the Mass is offered in the chapels.' Redemptorists explained that the bad turnout at Tourlestrane mission resulted because 'the people are all poor, starved, naked etc.' But there were other lesser reasons for missing Mass as they found 'non-attendance at Mass for slight excuse fairly commomplace' in Curry in 1894.[45] Congregations were segregated, with men on the gospel side (the left side facing the altar) and women on the other side, 'the epistle side'. Men were bare-headed in church while women wore hats or otherwise covered their heads. Seating was limited – only about a dozen benches in Tourlestrane in 1867 – and available only to those who could

Sunday Mass

41 'Annals of Benada', RSCG / H 13 / 91
42 RSCG 'Annals of Foxford Convent', vol 1 (1891-1905) pp 76-7, 83-4
43 N.S. vol 323 (1905), ff 819rv, 820rv, 821rv. For missions in the diocese 1904-10 see ADA, Dr Lyster, Book E & Appendix 43
44 SC Irlanda, vol 23, ff 611R-614rv
45 'Chronica Domestica', Dundalk, vol 1, pp 98 & 322

afford to pay pew rents, so a considerable portion of the congregation stood either inside or outside the church. The priest said Mass in Latin with his back to the people, attended by a boy server who made the responses having learned them parrot-like in the national school. Some of the congregation followed the Mass by using a missal with an English translation printed side by side with the Latin, but most used the occasion to say the Rosary or other private prayers. Mass was followed by certain devotions, as in Charlestown in 1892. 'After Mass Fr McDonnell addressed the congregation and gave Benediction. When Benediction was over an old gentleman began to recite the Rosary and the people joined in, while children assembled in Sunday school in another part of the church.' [46]

Sunday Sermons   Sermons were fairly rare, partially because most priests had to 'binate' i.e., said two Masses on Sundays, each in chapels a considerable distance apart, and all the while fasting from the previous midnight. Agnes Morrogh Bernard and her companions who attended parish Masses in Foxford for two years after their arrival there in 1891, never heard a sermon in all that time. 'The curate had a delicate throat and the old PP never preached.' [47] A complaint was made to Rome in 1888 about Thomas Loftus of Charlestown, admittedly by a hostile witness, that it was more than twenty years since he was ordained and had not yet preached his first sermon. [48]

Politics   When sermons were preached they bore no connection to the gospel of the day and sometimes not even to other religious matters, but frequently referred to political and topical issues. Denunciations from the altar were commonplace. The Fenian, John Duffy, was denounced by name from the altar by a parish priest in Co Sligo, and Fenianism itself was condemned by many priests including Roger Brennan in Gurteen and Matthew Finn in Ballaghaderreen.[49] After the Parnell 'split' Roger O'Hara preached a 'scathing sermon' in Kilmovee against the Parnellites in the parish [50] and John O'Grady launched a tirade from the pulpit against Sinn Féin supporters in Bohola in 1917, calling them 'a lot of corner boys'.

In an age when priests played a leading role in politics, always present on political platforms with leading politicians, it was not suprising that they should use their pulpits to air their views nor was it unacceptable to people or politicians like John Dillon. 'Woe to the Catholic Church in Ireland if the

46 *Irish American*, 3 Sept 1892 qtd in *C.T.* 17 Sept 1892
47 RSCG / H 26 / 449
48 Patrick Staunton, C.C. Ballymote. SOCG, vol 1028 (1888), ff 474rv, 47RSCG / H 26 / 449
49 *The Irishman*, 5 Dec 1868; *Irish People*, 8 April 1865
50 *W.P.* 21 Mar 1891

priests are driven by the court of Rome from politics'.[51] Priests also used their altars to defend the poor against cruel evictions by landlords and in this they had the whole-hearted support of bishops like MacCormack, who said at his successor's consecration, 'How could a bishop remain passive when he saw the poor ground down by unjust laws, when he saw them hunted like vermin from the places assigned to them by God ...' [52]

Parish missions introduced a considerable number of new devotions all over rural Ireland which were often enthusiastically promoted by convents in their locality. The new parish churches were adapted and furnished to cater for these new devotions which, by the end of the nineteenth century, considerably changed religious practice. The older home-centred religion had given way to a church-centred religion. This also coincided with the growth in size and importance of the towns, the continuous rural depopulation and the increasing number of clergy and religious.

New Devotions

The Sisters of Charity, when they first came to Benada, found that 'young persons and children of both sexes were considered exempt from attending Sunday Mass.' 'No boy or girl under 14 or 15 was seen in church. Parents thought that their sons should go to church when closing their teens and their daughters when of marriageable age, or when they considered it prudent to dress them out and let them be seen in public with a view to their settlement in life.' Poverty and the consequent near nakedness of many, particularly the young, made their attendance at Mass well-nigh impossible. When visiting the sick the Sisters found it 'only too true that these poor little children were unable to leave their wretched hovels for want of proper covering and were huddled together near the miserable fire like so many animals.' [53]

Children's Mass

To encourage children and young people to attend Mass special children's Masses were introduced, usually at the instigation of nuns. Children's Mass began in the cathedral in 1882 under the direction of the Sisters of Charity. 'There is an attendance of between 400 and 500 children at the Mass said specially for them on Sundays in the cathedral and followed by catechism taught by the students from the seminary and male and female teachers from the national schools, two Sisters superintending, one the boys and the other the girls, to whom they lend small penny prayer books every Sunday to train them to follow the Mass and to prevent their talking and gaping around.' [54] From then on children's Masses were extended to other parish churches

51 *U.I.* 26 May 1888
52 *C.T.* 14 April 1888
53 'Annals of Benada', RSCG / H 13 / 91
54 RSCG 'Annals of Ballaghaderreen'

especially in towns, though surprisingly there was no such Mass in Foxford until 1 November 1914. [55] Upwards of 300 children, boys on one side and girls on the other, sang during the Mass which was followed by catechism taught by six Sisters and twelve or fourteen teachers from different country schools.

Stations of the Cross

The earliest ornamentation introduced into churches appears to have been Stations of the Cross. Bishop Durcan asked Rome in December 1854 for faculties to erect with the usual indulgences Stations of the Cross, and powers to communicate the same to priests of the diocese. When the new church in Kilmovee was opened in October 1859, the walls were lined with a 'series of framed engravings, representing the stations of the cross' and three years later the parish priest, John Coghlan, asked Rome for faculties to attach indulgences to them. [56] The devotion does not seem to have caught on very quickly as in 1875 and again in 1885 MacCormack was still asking for the same faculties.[57]. Between 1876 and 1885 Stations of the Cross were erected in Swinford and ten other churches in the diocese. [58] Morrisroe told Rome in 1817 that it was customary to perform the Stations of the Cross publicly on Fridays during Lent. [59]

Blessed Sacrament

Up to the last decade of the nineteenth century, the Blessed Sacrament was not reserved in many parish churches in the diocese but kept in the homes of parish priests and curates as had been the custom now for centuries. This was to facilitate priests to make sick calls, particularly at night. The older chapels served solely for Sunday Masses and little else, with all other sacraments administered in the homes of recipients. Towards the end of the century a gradual change took place and the Blessed Sacrament was retained in more and more churches. MacCormack reported to Rome in 1872 that it was kept in 'several' churches and his successor reported that it was kept in thirteen churches in 1895. [60]. In May that year it was kept in Tourlestrane church from the last day of the mission. [61]

Benediction

Benediction was the devotion most associated with the Blessed Sacrament. The consecrated host was exposed to the view of the congregation by placing it in a glass case in a monstrance or highly ornate stand. After singing two

55 RSCG 'Annals of Foxford'
56 *C.T.* 19 Oct 1859
57 Udienze, vol 120 ff 2721r, 2758r; vol 141, f 2198r; vol 180, ff 148r, 195r; vol 212, ff 1036rv, 1061r
58 Cloonacool (1876), Swinford (1876), Killavil (1877), Meelick (1878), Benada (1878), Lough Talt (1878), Attymass (1879), Killasser (1880), Carracastle (1884), Coolaney (1884), Monasteraden (1885). ADA, Lyster Book
59 ASV, Congregazio Consistoriale, Relationes Diocesium 5 (1917)
60 18 Jan. 1874, SC Irlanda, vol 37, ff 27r, 28r, 29rv; 9 Oct 1895, N.S. vol 69, ff 140rv, 141rv, 142r
61 'Annals of Benada', RSCG / H 13 / 91

Latin hymns, *O Salutaris* and *Tantum Ergo*, the monstrance was incensed and the priest solemnly blessed the people using the monstrance, giving the ceremony its name. This was followed by the recitation by the priest of the 'Divine Praises' each of which was repeated by the congregation and the ceremony concluded with a final hymn. Jesuits noted at their mission in Co Cork in 1873 that 'Benediction of the Blessed Sacrament was a novelty to the people when we came into the parish.' In fact the early missioners brought with them instruments, such as the monstrance, necessary for the ceremony. Benada Sisters not only provided music for Benediction at the Jesuit mission in Tourlestrane in 1867 but all else required, 'the parish not possessing anything necessary for that rite'. Gradually from the last two decades of that century Benediction became a familiar and frequent feature of parish devotions, most often coupled with the Rosary in what was called 'evening devotions' during the months of May and October. Benediction also took place after Last Mass on special Sundays and feastdays.

Other devotions associated with the Blessed Sacrament included Adoration, Holy Hours and *Quarant' Ore*. Adoration took place on special occasions when the Blessed Sacrament was 'exposed' in the monstrance placed at the centre of the altar which was greatly illuminated by rows of lighted candles and decorated with a profusion of flowers. The devotion most frequently associated with Adoration was called a 'Holy Hour', i.e., an hour spent in alternating vocal and silent prayer, concluding with Benediction. *Adoration*

Quarant' Ore or the Forty Hours devotion consisted of Adoration extending over a period of two days and one night, and was first celebrated in the diocese in Foxford convent on the occasion of the centenary of the the Sisters of Charity in August 1915. [62] It began with High Mass presided over by Morrisroe, assisted by the Bishop of Killala, Dean Connington of Swinford and ten other priests, and on the final day there was a *Missa cantata* (sung Mass). Gradually the devotion spread to parish churches throughout the diocese, including Foxford parish church in September 1918 when a constant stream of 'men wearing white scarves kept up adoration in the sanctuary while the Children of Mary did the same outside the rails.'

Some of the new devotions, particularly Benediction, required music and towards the end of the century choirs were established in parish churches. Kiltimagh had a choir and an organist soon after the new church opened and at Mass on Christmas Day they performed an impressive repertorium including Mozart's *Kyrie*, Schmidt's *Gloria* as well as *Adeste Fidelis* and *Ecce Panis*. *Choirs*

62 RSCG 'Annals of Foxford', vol 3, p 49

Charlestown had a choir at the same time. [63] The convent choir replaced the parish choir in Foxford in 1903 and on Christmas Day they sang the Mass with a full orchestra, brass instruments, cellos etc which, not surprisingly, 'charmed' the congregation. [64]

Christmas Crib

The Christmas crib was another novelty whose earliest recorded appearance in the diocese was in Benada convent in 1870 where it created a lot of excitement. It had a similar effect in Ballaghaderreen in 1885 when the Sisters set up a crib in the infant school. 'The room was crowded every evening when men and women from town and country, poor and well-to-do, all joining in the devotions with the greatest recollection. Many a sin was avoided during those evenings by the young men who, very likely, would have otherwise spent the time in the public house.' The Rosary was said at intervals during the day while the main devotions took place in the evening with Rosary, hymns and Benediction. [65] Kiltimagh ladies set up a crib in 1892 in front of the Blessed Virgin altar. [66]

Corpus Christi

One of the highlights of parish missions from the very beginning were processions, usually two, one in honour of the Blessed Virgin and the other in honour of the Blessed Sacrament, which caused great excitement among

Sacred Heart procession, Kiltimagh 1896

country people for whom it was a complete novelty. They were very simple affairs, usually comprising a short walk around the church with the priest carrying the Blessed Sacrament or a statue of Our Lady. Later they became a feature of parish life with the May procession in honour of Our Lady and the larger Corpus Christi procession on that feastday in June. The Corpus Christi procession had its origins in medieval Italy where inhabitants believed that by carrying the Blessed Sacrament through the streets of their towns and villages, they would be preserved from the plagues which frequently ravaged them.

63 *C.T.* 31 Dec 1892
64 RSCG, 'Annals of Foxford'
65 RSCG, 'Annals of Benada', 'Annals of Ballaghaderreen'
66 *C.T.* 31 Dec 1892

Corpus Christi
procession, Foxford 1913

That procession began in Achonry diocese in the very last years of the *Foxford*
nineteenth century with the earliest one recorded in Kiltimagh in June 1892.
The women's Sacred Heart Sodality walked in the procession. 'The banners
of the different guilds were carried and the school-children were dressed in
white with wreaths of flowers on their heads and bouquets in their hands.' [67]
The Foxford procession was obviously the creation of the Sisters of Charity,
who had at their disposal the wherewithal to mount an impressive display.
Three hundred took part in the procession on 15 June 1901, largely confined
to the convent grounds where little children threw flowers on the road before
the monstrance with the Blessed Sacrament carried by a priest under a
canopy. The choir sang *Lauda Sion* with every alternate verse being played by
the brass band. These remained the main features of the procession which
grew in grandeur and numbers as the years passed.

The bishop and dean were present the following year when Martin Henry
carried the Blessed Sacrament through the town. [68]

'The people turned out *en masse* and decorated the streets and their houses
most tastefully. Even the Protestants closed their shop and donned their
best attire to honour our common Master ... A very handsome altar was
erected at the entrance to the mill yard ... draped in red and cream and
shoals of flowers and evergreens ... another altar was arranged at the Grotto

67 *C.T.* 25 June 1892
68 RSCG 'Annals of Foxford'

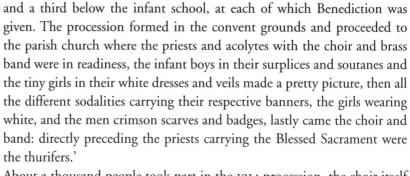

Canopy bearers at Swinford Corpus Christi procession c. 1943. *Front:* Bernie O'Connor, Paddy Frain, *Middle:* Dominick Casey CC, Patrick Higgins PP, —, *Back:* Jack Dorris, —, W. Mellet, Michael James Horkan

Communion

First Communion

and a third below the infant school, at each of which Benediction was given. The procession formed in the convent grounds and proceeded to the parish church where the priests and acolytes with the choir and brass band were in readiness, the infant boys in their surplices and soutanes and the tiny girls in their white dresses and veils made a pretty picture, then all the different sodalities carrying their respective banners, the girls wearing white, and the men crimson scarves and badges, lastly came the choir and band: directly preceding the priests carrying the Blessed Sacrament were the thurifers.'

About a thousand people took part in the 1914 procession, the choir itself made up of 200 boys and girls and a guard of honour for the Blessed Sacrament of 'six or eight young men wearing white scarves trimmed with gold fringe.' There were also a corps of two hundred of the recently formed Volunteers wearing green sashes. 'Handsome arches bearing suitable mottoes crossed the streets.' Elsewhere, such as Swinford, in later years, the guard of honour of about a dozen men, chosen from the upper echelons of town society or those with such aspirations, wore dress suits and took it in turns to carry the four-postered canopy. Corpus Christi became an annual occasion when shopkeepers painted their premises, emptied their shop windows of display goods and replaced them with altars and religious pictures, and townspeople toured the town the evening before to see who had the best display.

Up to the end of the nineteenth century, people continued to frequent the sacraments of confession and communion only twice a year, Christmas and Easter. Little had changed since the previous century and most of the rural population continued to receive the sacraments at the twice yearly stations in their localities. As national schools became widely established all over parishes, stations in the diocese were held in schools rather than houses, a change greatly welcomed by the people who found the expenses of holding a station in their home very burdensome. Stations continued to be held well into the next century even though the need for them had largely ceased to exist, but priests were reluctant to abandon their traditional 'station dues'. In more modern times their survival became assured with the revival of home Masses.

Young persons and children of both sexes were considered exempt from attending Sunday Mass.[69] In 1864 the Sisters prepared forty-one persons in Tourlestrane, ranging in age from fourteen to twenty-five, for their first confession and eighty for first communion. In 1881 a large number of boys, 'almost

69 RSCG / H 13 / 91, 'Annals of Benada'

young men', made their first communion in Tourlestrane, and two years later forty girls ranging in age from fourteen upwards made theirs. The Sisters had the same experience in Ballaghaderreen between 1876 and 1882 where 'children often grew up to 18 or 20 years of age without making their first confession'[70]

The Benada Sisters began to prepare younger children from seven years upwards, first in Tourlestrane church and later in neighbouring churches. They prepared twenty-seven girls for first communion in Tubbercurry in 1866, believing that there should have been three times that number 'but there seems to be a great apathy for religious instruction among the people'. The boys and girls they taught in Cloonacool received their first communion at the end of November 1867. *Preparation*

> Girls are almost all dressed in white – all at least wear white muslin veils – and both boys and girls are conspicuously adorned with first communion medals, suspended from scarlet strings. The boys are ranged in rank on the gospel side and the girls on the epistle side. Afterwards the children process to the national school for a substantial breakfast of bread, butter and tea and some small treat in the way of sweetmeats.

The priest joined them for breakfast and afterwards they went back to the chapel for the renewal of their baptismal vows and benediction.

The Sisters extended their work to Curry and Moylough in 1868 and in July 1873 John O'Grady, the curate in Charlestown, invited them to prepare children there, sending his own horse and car for them. 165 children made their first communion there that August. The Ballaghaderreen Sisters also set up large classes of boys and girls to prepare them for the sacraments, and they too were invited by neighbouring parish priests to help them. Some priests sent their cars a couple of times a week during the summer to bring them to their churches, where children from different schools were assembled and put through a course lasting five or six weeks. They also visited country schools in Ballaghaderreen on two days a week 'which secures that every child in the locality is visited within the month'.

400 made their first communion in the cathedral in Ballaghaderreen on the first Sunday in Lent in 1882 and 120 boys and girls made their first communion in Monasteraden in summer 1893, while a large number made theirs in Derrinacarta chapel and in the cathedral, 'the Sisters always being present on the occasion and taking care to have a good breakfast for the communicants.' First communions sometimes took place during parish missions. Forty

70 RSCG, 'Annals of Ballaghaderreen'

made their first communion at the Redemptorist mission in Tourlestrane in 1882, 360 in Ballaghaderreen during the 1889 mission and 60 at the 1894 mission in Swinford.

Sacred Heart
Sodality

Towards the end of the nineteenth century, attempts were made to encourage more frequent communions. Benada Sisters found in the early 1860s that only two or three people received communion on the first Sunday of the month in the parish chapel. Ireland was consecrated to the Sacred Heart on Passion Sunday 1873 and devotion to the Sacred Heart became widespread with parish missions playing a central role. Branches of the Sacred Heart Sodality were established in many parishes and members undertook to receive communion on a specified Sunday each month. There were usually two branches in each parish, men's and women's, each with its own banner and sash and particular Sunday for reception of communion when members occupied the front seats in church.

Sacred Heart League,
Kiltimagh 1896

Tourlestrane and
Kiltimagh

Benada Sisters organised a sodality in Tourlestrane in 1873 and had the Blessed Sacrament exposed after Mass on certain Sundays, followed by a Holy Hour. Members contributed sixpence a year for Masses celebrated for their intentions on the First Fridays. Sisters and children in Benada were enrolled in the League of the Sacred Heart in May 1888 and before the end of the year there were 600 members with 60 *Messengers* distributed each month. Poor people called to the convent looking for the Sacred Heart badge. The women's branch in Kiltimagh had a retreat in January 1892 during which 700 women received communion. [71]

71 *C.T.* 16 Jan & 25 June 1892

Swinford had a thriving branch of the men's Sacred Heart Sodality in 1881, *Swinford*
with one of the curates acting as spiritual director, and for most of the following decade its annual outing was one of the highlights of town's social calendar.[72] There was also a women's branch of the sodality. Shortly afterwards
they appear to have fallen into decay, as Redemptorists found the sodalities
there in 1894 'in a delapidated condition'. They preached on the subject and
succeeded in enrolling 700 women as well as 400 men in a branch which
they 'established and organised' for them. Earlier that year they suffered a set-
back in Curry where there was no sodality 'nor would the PP have any.' [73]

In his Lenten pastoral in 1892, Lyster exhorted his parish priests to estab- *First Fridays*
lish the First Fridays novena to encourage devotion to the Sacred Heart.[74]
The devotion began in Foxford in April of the following year though Michael
O'Donnell was very reluctant to introduce it despite pressure from Agnes
Morrogh Bernard. [75] 'He was a holy old man in his own old-fashioned way,
not going at all with the revival of devotion in recent times. "Don't they go to
confession twice a year at the stations", he used to say of the people, "some of
them once, and some of them not at all, when they go harvesting to England. If
they stay there for three years they come back without much religion".' After
two years and 'much persuasion' the Sisters succeeded in getting him to start the
First Fridays which was attended by about thirty people. On the second occasion
in May 'the old priest was there in his church, but lying dead in his coffin'.[76]

Confirmation was very much the Cinderella of the sacraments. When *Confirmation*
McNicholas made his first visitation of the diocese he found that it was twenty
years since confirmation had been administered in some parishes. 'As often as
I administered confirmation, the faithful in vast numbers flocked enthusiastically to the different chapels, bringing me the greatest happiness.' [77] However, confirmation remained exceptional and there were probably many people in the first half of the nineteenth century who were never confirmed at
all. People in Ballaghaderreen had a strange view of it. 'Many were under the
impression that the longer they put off receiving the sacrament of confirmation, the greater would be the spiritual advantage derived from it and that it
would wash their souls like a second baptism. When undeceived on this
point, 700 adults were confirmed last October (1882), many of them being
married men and women.' [78]

72 *C.T.* 7 May 1881, 24 June 1883, 5 July 1884, 4 July 1885
73 'Domestica Chronica', Dundalk, pp 325, 341
74 *S.C.* 5 Mar 1892
75 RSCG, 'Annals of Foxford' & H 26 / 449
76 'the old priest' was in fact only fifty-six years old, a mere five years older than Agnes herself
77 SC Irlanda, vol 23, ff 611r-614rv
78 RSCG, 'Annals of Ballaghaderreen'

Special efforts were made during parish missions to encourage people to come forward for confirmation, and often on the last day the sacrament was administered to large numbers of adults as well as young people. 300 were confirmed in Tourlestrane at the 1867 mission, 976, many of them adults, at the Passionist mission in Charlestown in 1874, 520 at the mission in Bally-mote and 342 in Kiltimagh in 1876. 828 were confirmed at the Redemptorist mission in Foxford in 1880 and 770 at the mission in Ballaghaderreen in 1881. Of the 270 confirmed in Tourlestrane at the Redemptorist mission in 1882, 190 of them were children. A staggering 1,496 were confirmed by Lyster at the 1889 mission in Ballaghaderreen, of whom about one half were adults, and he confirmed 407 on the last Sunday of the mission in Swinford in 1894. [79]

Abductions   Abductions of females were widely practised in pre-Famine Ireland, with or without the complicity of the girl involved. A girl thus compromised was regarded as having lost her marriage prospects and had little alternative but to marry her abductor. These abductions were usually highly organised and sometimes used considerable force. Forty to fifty armed men came to Widow Rooney's house in the neighbourhood of Ballymote just after Christmas in 1833. They smashed all the windows and a considerable part of the furniture, knocked the widow down with the butt end of a musket, stabbed her brother in the thigh, before forcibly carrying off the daughter of the house. They were pursued by the police from Templehouse who succeeded in rescuing the girl and arrested five, including the intended husband.

At midnight on 22 November 1836, a party of about forty men broke into William Kelly's house in Lisnaskea, about a mile from Aclare and forcibly took away his sister 'contrary to her wishes'. Again she was rescued by the po-lice who arrested nine men whom Daniel Jones committed to Sligo jail to await trial. Some abductions were more spontaneous affairs. Elizabeth Com-mins of Ballylahon was making her way home in October 1836 from a shoe-maker who had just measured her for a pair of shoes. She decided to take a shortcut when she encountered James Maloney Jr who forceably dragged her across two fields to his father's house, where he detained her against her will. A boy who was with her ran and told her uncle who came with a few friends. Maloney, armed with a pitchfork, refused to surrender the girl but was even-tually overpowered. 'The girl's person had not been violated' and when the police arrived the abductor had absconded. [80]

79 Confirmations at other missions: 1889, Coolaney, 80 adults; Mullinabreena, 102 adults; 1890, Foxford, 300 children; 1891, Bunninadden, 350 mostly children; 1892, Foxford, 300 children; 1898, Ballaghaderreen, 120 adults

80 Constable J. Whittaker to Inspector General, 29 Dec 1833 & 25 Nov 1836, OP Sligo 1834 & 1836: Constable David J. Barry to Inspector General, 14 Oct 1836, OP Mayo 1836

Arranged marriages were the norm in the diocese for much of the nine-teenth century, a custom which John Blake Dillon took a very poor view of, as he told Adelaide, then on a visit to Ballaghaderreen in 1849. [81]

> I shudder at the thought of what men and women are brought to in that country. I have never known a single case in which a man loved the girl he was married to. This holy union has become amongst that degraded peo-ple a mere traffic and it is invariably negotiated in the same spirit as men purchase an ox or a horse, and would you believe it, Ady, that I have heard Dean Durcan ... maintaining that these cold prudential marriages are more in accordance with religion than those which are prompted by love.

Offerings made to priests on the occasion of marriages, while graded ac-cording to the circumstances of the couple, were generally substantial sums and gave rise to a certain amount of resentment. Fees were also charged for marriage dispensations, which MacCormack told Rome in 1875 was an 'im-memorial custom' in Ireland. Dispensations were required by couples of mixed religion or those within forbidden degrees of relationship and bishops had to seek faculties from Rome to grant these dispensations. McNicholas asked for faculties in 1821 to grant dispensations to couples related to each other, pointing out that such marriages were permitted by civil law and, if re-fused, the Catholic couple would have recourse to a Protestant minister. Rome usually granted the faculties for a fixed period of time, normally six years, and for a specified number of cases. A clandestine marriage had taken place earlier in the presence of a suspended priest and as such a marriage was valid in civil law 'it would be very dangerous for the parish priest to declare it invalid or to grant permission to either of the couple to enter into a new marriage'. [82]

Fees for dispensations were substantial and were paid to the bishop, who sometimes justified them on the grounds that they discouraged people from entering such unions. A niece of Denis Tighe got a dispensation in 1870 to marry her cousin from Bishop Gillooly of Elphin who demanded £100. [83] The girl's father complained to Rome, demanding restitution of the money and Mgr Kirby of the Irish College was asked to write to the bishop 'inviting' him to return the fee.

A widow in Kilkelly wanted to marry the first cousin of her deceased hus-band but Roger O'Hara and the bishop refused her request for a dispens-ation and her brother wrote directly to Pope Leo XIII in 1891, seeking a dispens-ation as the couple were now 'living in sin'.[84] John MacDermott asked Rome

81 John Blake Dillon to Adelaide, 16 July 1849, qtd in Ó Cathaoir, *John Blake Dillon*, p 119
82 SC Irlanda, vol 23, ff 354rv, 355rv
83 SC Irlanda, vol 36, ff 686rv, 687rv
84SC Irlanda, vol 45, f 383r

for a dispensation in 1888 for a Ballymote couple related within the forbidden degrees of kinship as otherwise it would cause a major scandal since the marriage had already taken place and the woman was pregnant.[85] MacCormack sought a dispensation in 1886 for a mixed marriage where the girl's parish priest had assured him that the couple would be married in a Protestant church by the Protestant minister if the dispensation was refused.[86]

Nuptial Mass   Marriages continued to be celebrated in homes well into the nineteenth century and even when celebrated in churches there was no nuptial Mass until the last decades of the century. A newspaper account of a marriage in Collooney in August 1882 mentioned that the ceremony included 'the special marriage Mass'.[87] The bride was Miss O'Rorke, probably a niece of the parish priest, Terence, who lived next door to his brother John who owned a public house. The clerical connection probably explains why the marriage was attended by 'a considerable number of priests from neighbouring parishes' and also the celebration of the nuptial Mass 'but too rarely witnessed, unfortunately in this country'. It was something of a 'society' wedding to judge from the celebrations in Collooney.

> The time between the dejeuner and the departure of the happy pair was used by the inhabitants of the village in erecting flags on neighbouring hills and triumphal arches, festooned with branches, flowers and streamers. The carriage that bore them to the station was met by many hearty manifestations on the road and when they took their seats in the train they were accompanied by the blessings of the poor and the ringing cheers of the crowd that thronged the station.

Death   Many of the customs surrounding death remained the same as in the previous century. People attached enormous importance to the 'last sacraments' and sick calls dominated the life of priests. The importance of their presence at death-beds was greatly enhanced when they acquired the power to bestow a plenary indulgence with their final blessing to dying penitents, giving them the hope of a complete remission of punishment in the next life. [88] Wakes were held in homes with the remains of the deceased laid out, though wake-games were gradually phased out under continuous pressure from priests.

Keening women appear to have survived well into the century. Adelaide, the widow of John Blake Dillon, lost her young daughter, Zoe, who died of consumption in Ballaghaderreen in April 1869. [89]

85 Udienze, vol 226 (1888), ff 325v, 350rv
86 Udienze, vol 216 (1886), ff 36v, 57rv & 183r, 199r
87 *S.C.* 5 Aug 1882
88 Udienze, vol 120, ff 2721r, 2758r, vol 150, f 1198r & vol 170, f 1478r
89 25 April 1869, Adelaide Dillon to Miss Knox, Dil. P. 6457

My comfort is sitting and praying in the room where dear Zoe – all we have left of her is – and listening to the alternate prayers and cosherings of two old women who go on incessantly and sometimes edify and again absolutely make me smile. "Ah! Cushla Ma'chree och ochone sure she's in heaven – sure it's happy for you – she's with God and the Blessed Virgin and her own father, alanna – ocoo muscha musha we'll be all together in heaven soon with the blessing of God and the help of the Blessed Virgin." It's all true and as my poor old women are really saints in their own humbled resigned quiet way – their predictions and prayers comforted me.

A High Mass was celebrated in the cathedral for Zoe Dillon.

The remains were always taken to the church on the evening before burial took place. In one very unusual case in Swinford in 1881, people stayed all night with the remains in the church. [90] The deceased was a young man who was a member of the Sacred Heart Sodality and his remains were carried to the chapel by other members of the sodality who remained there from 11 p.m. to 7 a.m. next morning, 'reciting alternately the Rosary and the stations of the cross'. Solemn requiem high Mass was celebrated at 11 a.m. and was followed by the funeral, with members of the Sacred Heart sodality 'wearing their handsome red green bordered scarves', carrying the coffin.

High Mass required four or a minimum of three priests, celebrant, deacon, sub-deacon and master of ceremonies, and could only be the norm in parishes with at least two curates. There is some evidence to suggest that there was a two-tiered system in operation, where the better-off classes had requiem high Masses while others had to be content with low Masses. In any event it was usual to offer a stipend to each of the three or four priests involved in a high Mass which would put them beyond the reach of the poor.

High Mass

The status of the deceased was often judged by the number of priests at the funeral. Fifteen priests of the diocese attended the funeral of Daniel Mullarkey of Drumartin in Tourlestrane in 1889. [91] Besides being an extensive farmer employing a large number of labourers, he was also the rate collector and relieving officer. 'The cortege extended nearly a mile with over eighty vehicles and an immense crowd on foot' and the morning of the funeral eight low requiem Masses were said by visiting priests in the home of the deceased. Priests from neighbouring parishes celebrated Mass in the Staunton house in Swinford on the morning of the funeral of Patrick Staunton in 1884. [92] Surprisingly, the two priests, Michael and Patrick, did

90 *C.T.* May 1881 (funeral of Ambrose P. Dolphin)
91 *C.T.* 9 Mar 1889
92 *C.T.* 22 Mar 1884

not officiate at the high Mass for their father but sat in the choir with the rest of the clergy.

Masses were said by visiting priests in Swinford convent chapel 'from an early hour' on the day of a nun's funeral and at 11 a.m. the office for the dead was recited followed by solemn requiem high Mass. [93] The funeral was led by a cross bearer with acolytes and thurifer, followed by priests chanting the *Miserere*, then the coffin carried by members of the Sacred Heart Sodality, and finally the nuns drawn up in twos. When Patrick Cuniffe, the curate in Ballaghaderreen, died of the 'flu in 1891 at the age of thirty, his remains were taken to Swinford convent chapel where the office of the dead and high Mass took place. [94] 'His remains were robed in white vestments and in his wasted hands was the delicately wrought chalice presented to him a few months ago by the members of Ballaghaderreen Sacred Heart Sodality.' 'During the influenza epidemic he was almost always on horseback going about from house to house anointing and consoling. The fact that he caught the disease himself did not prevent him continuing his labours and he took to his bed only when he was no longer able to walk and then it was too late.'

Mass Offerings
On the occasion of a death, friends gave Mass offerings 'for the repose of the soul' of the deceased. Agnes Morrogh Bernard suggested to John Dillon that he should have what were called 'Gregorian' Masses offered for Mrs Deane, i.e. thirty Masses on thirty successive days, without missing a day. 'It is well authenticated that St Gregory was promised, that those for whom those Masses were offered, called the Gregorian Masses, would obtain the release from purgatory of the soul for whom the Masses were offered.'[95] Gregorian Masses were usually said by religious orders where there were several priests in the community. During the fourteen years Agnes spent in Ballaghaderreen convent Mrs Deane had hundreds of Masses offered for Dillon which she had asked Agnes to send to various religious orders.

Anniversaries
It was customary to have an annual Mass, presided over by the bishop, for the deceased priests of the diocese. It was also a long-standing custom to celebrate Mass one month after the death of individual priests, the Month's Mind, as well as anniversary Masses. This custom was later adopted by the better off families in parishes. Such Masses could be high or low, though in the larger parishes like Swinford and Ballaghaderreen, high Mass became the norm in the twentieth century.

93 *C.T.* 2 Feb 1884
94 *W.P.* 24 January 1891
95 27 Aug 1905, Agnes Morrogh Bernard to John Dillon, Dil. P. 6889

CHAPTER SIXTEEN

Educating the Elite

The exact origins of the college in Ballaghaderreen are difficult to uncover. Terence O'Rorke claimed that Patrick Durcan made his early classical studies in Swinford and later in the 'diocesan school' in Ballaghaderreen which he left in 1812 for Maynooth.[1] This was more than twenty years before Mc Nicholas had decided to make Ballaghaderreen his capital. Shortly after becoming bishop of the diocese in 1818, Patrick McNicholas set up a clerical seminary to meet a very urgent situation he encountered. 'I found fifteen junior priests ordained for four or more years, who had never followed a course of studies, wandering here and there to the great scandal of the laity and damage to clerical dignity.'[2] He brought them together in a 'fairly commodious building in a secret place.'[3] A modest tax was imposed on parish priests to support the upkeep of this establishment. This seminary probably did not survive once its immediate purpose was achieved. However, six years after McNicholas had transferred to Ballaghaderreen there was said to have been a 'good seminary' there under his patronage, described in 1854 as the 'diocesan college' though Patrick Durcan made no mention of this institution in his report to Rome in 1862.[4]

Diocesan Seminary

The Intermediate Education Act of 1878 resulted in the appointment of a seven-member unpaid board to distribute the annual interest on one million pounds to the managers of intermediate schools. The monies were distributed according to the performances of individual students at the annual examinations set by the board and most went to the managers of the schools though a smaller portion of it went to the individual successful students in the form of prizes and exhibitions. The first countrywide intermediate examinations were held in 1879. The whole purpose of this 'payment by results' approach of the Intermediate Education Act was to assist Catholic secondary schools while pretending not to do so. Unlike the primary system of education, the intermediate system was denominational from its very inception.

Intermediate Schools

---

1 O'Rorke, *Sligo*, vol 2, p 112
2 SC Irlanda, vol 23, ff 611r-614rv
3 It is believed to have been the former home of Archbishop Philip Phillips in Cloonmore.
4 *Catholic Registry* 1939

Lodgings   Edward Connington was transferred from his curacy in Killasser to Ballaghaderreen to take charge of the college there, the first priest to do so. Francis J. MacCormack described the college in Ballaghaderreen in 1882 not as a diocesan seminary but a 'diocesan school with a pious and learned priest in charge where thirty youths attend daily who are taught Latin, Greek, English and mathematics, and almost all are candidates for the priesthood.' [5] The 'pious and learned priest' was the newly ordained Thomas Gilmartin who succeeded Connington in 1881. MacCormack was anxious to establish a proper diocesan college. 'The necessity of a new seminary' was the subject chosen by Gilmartin for the prize English essay in June 1882.[6] Gilmartin remained in charge of the college until September 1884 when he was appointed dean in Maynooth College. Michael Coleman succeeded him in the Ballaghaderreen college which Lyster later referred to as a 'seminary near the cathedral reserved for ecclesiastical students only who in the past lodged in private houses.'

Edmondstown College
students, May 1895

Edmondstown   This college moved in September 1893 to the former Costello residence in Edmondstown which had been purchased by Denis O'Hara and Michael Keveney in 1892 with the rest of the estate.[7] The estate was divided up among the tenants while the mansion and demesne land was given to the bishop for

5   SC Irlanda, vol 39, ff 699r-705r. Except where it is otherwise referenced, the information on the diocesan college is taken from Martin Jennings, 'St Nathy's College: Historical Background' in *St Nathy's College Journal* 1996, pp 9-18
6   *C.T.* 1 July 1882
7   *C.T.* 18 June & *S.C.* 25 June 1892

use as a diocesan college. James Daly, who was in charge of the college in Edmondstown, described 'the situation of the college as most healthy; its recreation grounds are spacious and well laid out, its class hall, refectory, dormitories, bathrooms and all internal arrangements are most perfect in their kind; a very moderate pension will be charged and nothing will be left undone to secure the happiness, comfort, moral and intellectual training of its students.' The future bishop, Patrick Morrisroe, was one of the teachers in Edmondstown.

Lyster described the move to Edmondstown in his report to Rome in 1895: 'So great was the poverty of the flock there was no way that a seminary could be built. In these straitened circumstances I left the episcopal buildings and handed it over for use as a seminary so that there exists now a suitable seminary where twenty-eight youths are housed and study the humanities, ancient and modern languages, mathematics and the elements of philosophy.' [8] Lyster resided at the Abbey at Kilcolman on the Sligo road but Rome seemed under the impression that he had given up his own residence to be used as a seminary. Ever conscious of preserving what it liked to refer to as 'episcopal dignity', Rome insisted that Lyster reverse his decision but he, however, quickly pointed out that he had never given over his residence to be used as a diocesan seminary.

In his Lenten Pastoral in 1896 Lyster appealed to all parishes for funds to equip a larger college, and he acquired in 1898 the old military barracks built at the beginning of the nineteenth century which was to become the permanent home of St Nathy's College. He reported his acquisition to Rome in 1900 and informed Propaganda that there were now four priests and fifty students in the seminary. [9] A major rebuilding programme was undertaken by Lyster's successor, Patrick Morrisroe from 1914 to 1916. The college was now capable of housing eighty students and had seventy-five when Morrisroe made his first report to Rome in 1917. [10] There were five priests on the staff, the president and four teachers who lived in the college as well as three lay teachers who lived outside. To cater for the increasing demand for student accommodation a new wing was added in 1941 with 150 students, rising to 190 four years later and eventually to about 200 boarders with about sixty day boys. After the introduction of free post-primary education in 1967, the number of boarders declined while the number of day boys increased. [11]

The Barracks

8   N.S. vol 69, ff 140rv, 141rv, 142r
9   N.S. vol 189, ff 818rv, 819rv, 820r, 821v
10 ASV Congregazione Concistoriale. Relationes Dioecesium 5
11 See Appendix 20 for list of teachers

St Nathy's College
1912-13, front elevation
(courtesy W. H. Byrne)

Convent Schools

From the very beginning, post-primary education in the diocese was the exclusive domain of religious. The earliest schools were established by the St Louis Sisters in Kiltimagh, the Sisters of Mercy in Swinford and the Marist Sisters in Tubbercurry. Later the Sisters of Charity opened secondary schools in Foxford, Benada and Ballaghaderreen. The Mercy Sisters gradually expanded their system to include Ballymote, Ballysadare/Collooney, Gurteen and Ballaghaderreen, while the Marist Sisters in Tubbercurry opened a second school in Charlestown.

'For Young Ladies'

Shortly after they took up occupancy in their new convent in Kiltimagh in July 1898, the St Louis Sisters planned the establishment of a boarding school 'for young ladies'.[12] According to their own prospectus 'careful attention will be paid to the health, manners and deportment of the young ladies, and no efforts will be spared to give them habits of order and neatness, that they may return to their houses both accomplished and useful in all that regards the duties of a woman's sphere.' The course included English, French, German, Italian and Latin, music (piano, harp, violin and guitar), singing, drawing, painting, dancing, domestic economy, plain and fancy needlework, dressmaking etc. All this was to form part of the Intermediate System of Education.

St Louis Successes

Very quickly they began to make their mark, gaining three distinctions in 1902 including one pupil winning the gold medal for English composition. Three years later another pupil in senior grade English achieved the highest score in all Ireland, the 'blue ribbon' of the Intermediate System. In fact that year Kiltmagh was placed fourth in Ireland among Catholic girls' schools, surpassed only by the Dominican Convent in Eccles Street, Dublin, the St Louis in Monaghan and the Ursulines in Cork. It was rated seventh in 1907, carrying off two exhibitions, three book prizes and a special prize. Some pupils won university scholarships in the following years and went on to take

12 Much of the information on the St Louis boarding school is taken from Peter Sobolewski and Betty Solon (eds.) *Kiltimagh Our Life & Times*, see Appendix 27 for list of teachers

degrees in University College, Galway which was described in 1913 as 'purely a man's' college up to comparatively recently. One pupil gained a second class exhibition in experimental science in 1915, the only convent girl in Ireland to do so. Each year the *Freeman's Journal* published the Intermediate lists of prizes and exhibitions and with the Kiltimagh school figuring so prominently it attracted boarders

First group of Swinford Sisters for Jefferson City, Aug 1960
Front L to R:
Srs Carmel, Bernardine, Peter and Teresa.
Back L to R:
Sr Magdalene, Mother Clare, Sr St John

from all over the country. The two daughters of the executed labour leader, James Connolly, arrived as boarders in September 1916 and their mother spent a night in the convent when she visited them the following year.

Under the new native Irish government, special emphasis was placed on the teaching of Irish and the Kiltimagh school quickly gained distinction in this field, winning the Dáil Cup in 1925 awarded to a school in each province for proficiency in Irish. They were second in Ireland in 1934 and the following two years gained first place, carrying off the All Ireland Irish Shield.

The Convent of Mercy in Swinford set up an Intermediate School for girls in 1906. [13] A boarding school was established in 1912 and attracted boarders from all over the country. At first they were accommodated in Brabazon Park House but in the twenties and thirties new boarding facilities were built in the convent grounds.

Mercy Schools

Mercy Sisters from Swinford made a foundation in Ballymote in 1902 and ran an infant and primary school there for many years. Rose Gonley started a private secondary school on the Keash Road in 1939. The convent entered consultations with Gonley, and after receiving sanction from the department of education in 1942, decided to open a secondary school. The staff consisted of two nuns, one of whom was the principal, and Rose Gonley. Fifteen girls enrolled in September of that year, eighteen the following year and by 1944 there were fifty-two pupils who paid £3 per term.

About the same time a secondary school was started in Collooney where the Mercy Sisters had been established since 1909. It was transferred on 8 September 1943 to Ballysadare where the Sisters had been left a property. A new three-room school was opened in 1953 to accommodate the forty

13 Phyl Clancy, *A Journey of Mercy*. Information on the secondary schools in the diocese run by the Mercy Sisters is taken from this source; see also Appendix 26 for list of teachers

students then attending. In 1954 Mercy Sisters made a foundation in Gurteen in a house donated to them by Nicholas O'Rafferty, a parish priest in Seattle and a native of Culfadda, and immediately opened a secondary school for girls. A new school was built and opened in January 1956.

Sisters of Charity   A fee-paying school, St Joseph's Intermediate, was opened by the Sisters of Charity in Ballaghaderreen in 1933. It was amalgamated in July 1944 to the primary school as a 'Secondary Top' which was non-fee paying as the constitution of the Sisters of Charity obliged them to give priority to the poor. Over 100 girls were enrolled in the 'Secondary Top' by 1946 and a new school building was opened in 1947? (49). With the introduction of free post-primary education, the school reverted again to a secondary school in 1964. The Sisters of Charity were replaced by the Sisters of Mercy in 1971.

Banada Abbey Secondary School was opened as a co-educational school in 1958.[14] Pupil numbers greatly increased with the introduction of free transport in 1976 which had an important impact on schools situated in rural areas. When the Sisters left Benada in 1987 the school was transferred to the care of the diocese and a board of management was appointed. In the last decade of the school's existence the number of pupils increased to 450 and in all 2,651 pupils received their secondary education here. It closed in June 2002 after amalgamation proposals were agreed with the Marist Convent, Tubbercurry, and it now forms part of St Attracta's Community School in Tubbercurry.

The Sisters also had a secondary top attached to their girls' primary school in Foxford which catered for sixty girls prior to the erection of St Joseph's Secondary School which was officially opened in October 1961. Built by the Sisters without grants at a cost of £45,000 it catered for 270 pupils and was co-educational from the beginning. The Sisters of Charity severed their connection with the school in 1992 and at present the school has 350 pupils and twenty-five members of staff.[15]

Tubbercurry   The Marist Sisters were invited by Lyster to take charge of the girls' national school and the infant boys' school in Tubbercurry which were then housed in the old Carrowntubber building. The new convent national school was opened in 1911 and from the very beginning took in boarders, many of whom remained on to take matriculation or the King's Scholarship which were open examinations. Besides their classes in the national school the Sisters gave lessons to fee-paying students in art, music, French, shorthand and typing.

14 Information from Michael Collins. For list of teachers see Appendix 24 and for list of pupils see David McVeigh, *For the Record: Banada Abbey Secondary School 1958-2002*
15 See Appendix 25 for list of teachers

They were keen to open a secondary school under the Intermediate Act to facilitate their boarders but were opposed by Morrisroe who, it was said, did not wish them to provide competition for the St Louis boarding school in Kiltimagh. Morrisroe finally relented in 1914 and the Sisters developed a secondary system. Their numbers increased and a new wing was completed in 1927 with another wing added two years later. [16]

Apart from St Nathy's College only one other place, Swinford, attempted to provide post-primary education for boys, first with a secondary top staffed by the Marist Brothers 1901-1918 and later by the St Joseph's/St Patrick's College.[17] As early as 1895 Latin and Greek were taught in the boys' national school in Swinford by the curate, Francis Benson, though the National Board

Swinford Marists

St Patrick's College, Swinford, football team *Back L to R:* Seamus Campbell, Brian Rowley, Edward Lydon. *Middle:* Brendan McNulty, Pádraic Brady, Patrick Ruane, Seamus Curry, – McHugh, Jimmy McDonagh, Jimmy Conlon. *Front:* Julian Conlon, Donal Keane, Joe Campbell, Conal O'Neill, Jude Walshe, Tommy Walsh, Miko Greally, Joe O'Connell *(courtesy Joe Mellet)*

of Education refused to pay Result Fees for it. When the Marist brothers took over in 1901 the school quickly became a secondary top with students remaining on in to their mid-teens, some taking the King's Scholarship to qualify for places in teacher training colleges and others matriculating for the university. This school reverted to its traditional primary school status when the Marists left in 1918.

A co-educational secondary school, St Anthony's, was set up by Maura Cahill in 1936 in Charlestown in a prefabricated building close to the present town hall and among the students were a number of boys from Swinford who cycled to Charlestown each day.[18] It was not well-received by the church au-

Charlestown Co-Ed

16 See Appendix 22 for list of teachers
17 See Appendix 15 for list of Marists
18 Mícheál Campbell, John Curry, John Donegan, Tom Egan, Colm Lambe, George Mullis, Desmond & Laurence O'Neill, Pat Staunton & Luke Tunney. I am indebted to Mícheál Campbell for this information

thorities, not only because they frowned on co-education for that age-group but also because they resented intrusion by the laity into what was then regarded as a clerical domain. The Marist Sisters in Tubbercurry were invited in 1942 to take over the running of this school, which was now exclusively for girls and in 1953 the convent and school building moved to its present location in Lowpark.

Guinane's School

Jim Guinane, a native of Limerick, was a teacher in the co-ed school in Charlestown in 1941 when he married his wife, Kay, also from Limerick. After the Marist takeover, some parents begged him to open a school for their sons, whom they could not afford to send as boarders to St Nathy's College. He secured a disused bakery in Swinford belonging to Katie Daly and decided to open a secondary school for boys there. When he called on Ambrose Blaine in Charlestown to inform him, the parish priest told him he would have to get permission from the bishop. When he called on the bishop this permission was refused. Later a letter from Morrisroe was delivered to him by hand: '... If and when the bishop is satisfied that there is need for a secondary school in the Swinford area he will take steps to provide it in the manner approved by the church authorities.' Guinane decided to go ahead and, when he inserted an advertisement in a local paper announcing that St Joseph's Secondary School would open in Swinford in September 1942, 'all hell broke loose' according to his widow. Patrick Higgins denounced him from the pulpit in Swinford and warned the congregation 'of dire consequences if they supported this man or his school.' [19]

Morrisroe's Threat

Worse was to follow. In August 1942 he received another letter from Morrisroe:

Dear Mr Guinane,

You are still, it seems, persisting in opening the Swinford Secondary School, contrary to the bishop's express prohibition.

Once more I formally notify you that it is the right of the bishop to establish schools in his Diocese for Catholics and that if you disregard this right, I shall be obliged to place the school under the ban of Interdict. This means that those associated with the school or teachers will be disbarred from the reception of the sacraments and that pupils or their parents may also incur punishments of the church for their disobedience to their ecclesiastical superiors.

August 19th 1942 + P. Morrisroe

(Bishop of Achonry)

19 *Sunday World*, 9 June 1974, p 16; *Western Journal* 2 and 9 Feb 1979

Despite the threats, Guinane opened his school and twenty-five boys turned up on the opening day, but clerical denunciations continued and on one occasion one of the curates used his car to block boys on their way to school and ordered them to go home.

Guinane and his little school were in fact more wanted than the clergy realised or at least were prepared to admit. A number of women in Swinford made no secret of their strong support of Guinane and a deputation went to Ballaghaderreen to make their views known to the bishop.[20] It was said that he offered their sons free places in St Nathy's if they withdrew their support from Guinane's school but some of them not only declined this tempting offer but in fact later sent their sons to boarding schools outside the diocese rather than to St Nathy's.

Women's Protest

Because of the church's opposition to his school, the Department of Education refused to sanction it and Guinane, realising it was a lost cause, sold his desks and other equipment and moved with his family to Sligo where he found employment in the Grammar School. To placate the continuing disquite in Swinford over his treatment of Guinane's school, Morrisroe instructed the chaplain there, Jack O'Neill, to open a secondary school for boys. A room was acquired in the Town Hall and the first class of ten boys was received in September 1945, with Jack O'Neill teaching all subjects. At the beginning of the second year, it became clear that Morrisroe's intention was to allow the school to fizzle out, as no provision was made for the appointment of a second teacher for the new class. If that was his intention, it was thwarted by O'Neill employing a homebased university student, Kevin Henry, whom he paid out of his own pocket to supervise one class while O'Neill taught the other.

Coláiste Pádraig

With the death of Morrisroe in 1946, the Swinford school began to thrive with the appointment of additional staff.[21] Classes continued to be held in the Town Hall until Easter 1950 when a new college was completed and opened. When Jim Guinane, now teaching in Summerhill College, opened his newspaper that day and saw a photgraph of the official opening, he was very upset. 'That should have been my school', he told his wife. Francis Stenson, who had been appointed by Morrisroe's successor as parish priest of Swinford in 1946 undertook a tour of the United States in 1951-52 to raise funds to to pay off the debt on the new college.

"All I ask of you is, that wherever you may be, you will remember me at Holy Communion and at the foot of the Altar."

Sacred Heart of Jesus
Have Mercy on the Soul of
Very Rev.
Francis Canon Stenson
D.D., P.P., V.F.
Swinford, Co. Mayo
who died on 13th. August 1968.

20 Mrs Twomey, Mrs Josephine McManus, Mrs Barbara O'Connell, Mrs Maggie Campbell and Mrs Aggie Curry.
21 See Appendix 21 for list of teachers

Vocational Schools   The Vocational Education Act was passed in 1930 and Vocational Education Committees (VECs) were established in each county with the purpose of providing vocational and technical education for boys and girls. Each VEC had fourteen members, five to eight of whom were members of the local rating authority while the others were selected from employers, trade unions etc. A chief executive office was charged with making and implementing proposals. Vocational schools were under secular control and non-denominational. Boys were taught woodwork and mechanical drawing and metal work as well as rural science, while girls learned domestic science which included cookery and needlework, as well as shorthand and typing, commerce and business. English and Irish were taught to both sexes. They followed a two year course leading to a Group Certificate which was introduced in 1943. Most vocational schools began presenting students for the Intermediate Certificate in 1967 and for the Leaving Certificate two years later.

Vocational education classes began in St Brigid's Hall in Ballaghaderreen in October 1935 when thirty-five students enrolled, and later a vocational school was built by the Roscommon Vocational Education Committee which opened in October 1939. Swinford Vocational School was built and opened in 1954. A deputation from Kiltimagh went to Castlebar in November 1957 to put their case to the County Mayo Vocational Committee for a vocational school in the town and one eventually opened in September 1964. The vocational school began in Charlestown the following year and closed at the end of the 1983-84 school year.

Co-Education   Boys were admitted to the Mercy convent school in Ballymote in 1955, making it the first co-educational school in Connacht. The Sisters built a new school, Coláiste Mhuire, with five classrooms, a domestic science kitchen and cloak rooms, which was blessed and officially opened in September 1957. The Mercy school in Gurteen admitted boys in 1958 and ten years later was amalgamated with the vocational school. Ballysadare Mercy school became co-educational in 1966. With the introduction of free secondary education the Marist school in Charlestown was given permission to enrol boys. For a number of years the Marist Sisters in Tubbercurry were coming under increasing pressure to admit boys but were refused permission by Bishop Fergus. With the Education Act of 1967 attitudes began to change towards co-education and boys were finally admitted in the Marist schools in Charlestown and Tubbercurry (1973). With the resulting increase in numbers the boarding school in Tubbercurry was gradually phased out and finally closed in 1983.

As boarding schools were phased out more and more schools became amalgamated. The vocational school in Swinford was amalgamated with Meán Scoil Mhuire agus Phádraig in September 1992, Coláiste Raifteirí in Kiltimagh and the St Louis convent school the following year and in 1996 the three schools in Ballaghaderreen, St Nathy's College, St Joseph's convent school and the vocational school were amalgamated.

Amalgamation

Ballaghaderreen College staff, 1909; front row, Ambrose Blaine (left) and 'Doc' Henry

CHAPTER SEVENTEEN

The War Years

The Volunteers The General Election in December 1910 left eighty-four Irish nationalists holding the balance of power between the Liberals with 271 seats and the Tories with 273 seats. The Parliament Act of 1911 reduced the veto of the House of Lords to a power to delay for two years. All this paved the way for a third attempt to pass a Home Rule bill, which was introduced by Asquith in April 1912. This in turn led to the determined opposition of Ulster unionists, led by Edward Carson, which was demonstrated in the signing of the Solemn League and Covenant in Belfast on 28 September of that year, and followed on 31 January 1913 by the formation of the Ulster Volunteer Force, 100,000 men who were to be trained and eventually armed. Copy-cat reaction in the south led to the formation of the Irish Volunteers. The idea was originated by UCD professor, Eoin MacNeill, who wrote an article entitled 'The North Began' which appeared on 1 November 1913 in the Gaelic League newspaper, *An Claidheamh Soluis*. At a mass meeting in Dublin on 25 November, the Irish Volunteers were formed and between three and four thousand recruits enrolled on the spot, and this rose to about 75,000 within six months.

Gun-running Arms, purchased in Germany, were landed in Ulster, at Bangor, Larne and Donaghadee, on the night of 24-5 April 1914 and were distributed over the province within twenty-four hours. The Irish Volunteers followed suit, landing at Howth in broad daylight on 26 July and under the very noses of the police and troops, a cargo of arms and ammunition, purchased in Germany by Darrell Figgis and transported to Ireland by the amateur yachtsman, Erskine Childers. Sir Roger Casement, who had become a member of the governing body of the Volunteers, was largely instrumental in raising the money for buying the arms. But unlike the Ulster gun-running, the Howth episode ended in tragedy. When the troops marched back to Dublin they clashed with the crowd that followed them and at Batchelor's Walk fired on them, killing three people and wounding thirty-eight.

Redmond Take-Over Meanwhile, John Redmond, the leader of the Parliamentary party, manoeuvered to bring the Volunteers under his control. Dillon, acting for Redmond, met MacNeill, who left him with the impression that he was 'extremely muddlehead'.[1] MacNeill raised an objection to Michael Davitt, son of the Land Leaguer, one of Redmond's nominees to the governing body of the Volunteers. Finally twenty-five members nominated by the parliamentary party were added to the provisional committee which acted as the governing body of the Volunteers. This move was resisted without effect by the republican element on the committee, the IRB who had twelve members on the committee and were now outvoted by the Redmondite nominees. They were now known as the Irish National Volunteers but the seeds were sown for a future split.

The Volunteers spread rapidly throughout the country so that by July there were about 160,000 members. A meeting was held in Kiltimagh early in June 1914, under the chairmanship of Dr T. J. Madden, where a resolution was adopted calling upon every man in the district capable of bearing arms to join the Volunteers. Subsequently about 150 names were submitted for enrolment and on Friday 25 July, provisional officers of the Volunteer corps were appointed.[2] The following Monday a special meeting was convened in Kiltimagh to protest about the brutal murders at Batchelor's Walk. 'Our brothers in Dublin have only to command their brother Volunteers in Connaught and "the men of the West" will be with them.' After the meeting some 200 men formed up in the Market Square and marched in silence through the principal streets of the town preceded by a detachment of boy scouts bearing torches. Kiltimagh shopkeepers agreed in August to close their premises at 8.30 pm on four evenings each week so that they and their employees could take part in drilling exercises. The local correspondent suggested that it set a headline which should be followed by other towns. A large consignment of rifles arrived in Kiltimagh early in October and was displayed in Murtagh's shop-window, and Captain Murphy obtained a substantial quantity of ammunition in November.

Similar Volunteer corps were formed elsewhere in the diocese. In Foxford 200 Volunteers wearing green sashes took part in the 1914 Corpus Christi procession, marching behind the Blessed Sacrament.[3] South Sligo was slow

Kiltimagh

Corporal Patrick Carroll, Attavally, Kiltimagh *(courtesy Betty Solon)*

1 Dillon to Redmond, 28 May 1914: qtd Lyons, *Dillon*, p 351
2 This account of Kiltimagh Volunteers is from Peter Sobolewski and Betty Solon, (eds) *Kiltimagh, Our Life & Times*, pp 150-51; *provisional officers:* Captain Michael Murphy, Lieutenants J. Corcoran and T. Brennan; *section commanders:* T. Ruane, J. McDonagh, B. McTigue, and J. T. Somers
3 RSCG, Annals of Foxford Convent vol 2 (1905-15)

to take up the Volunteers. No corps was formed there before May 1914 but a corps was formed in Ballymote at the end of July. However, the situation changed dramatically after the Volunteers were taken over by the Irish Parliamentary Party so that by September there were forty-four corps in the county with almost 5,000 Volunteers.[4] There was a full attendance at the weekly meeting of the Swinford Volunteers, under the command of P. O' Connell, on Sunday 31 January with M. J. Hurst presiding and the secretary, M. J. McNulty, informed the meeting that the first consignment of rifles for target practice was expected the following week. An 'imposing display' of Volunteers marched from the Hibernian Hall to Cloonlara for target practice on Sunday 14 February. [5]

World War   The First World War began on 4 August and, in a highly charged atmosphere in the House of Commons, Redmond pledged Ireland's support for the war, urging the government to remove its troops, leaving it to the Volunteers to defend the country. Dillon did not receive Redmond's declaration with much enthusiasm but it caused an immense sensation in the House, with some Tories thanking him afterwards 'literally with tears in their eyes'.[6] Dillon and Redmond met Lord Kitchener, Secretary of State for War, about the best means of using the Volunteers but he was only interested in recruiting them for the regular army and Dillon was indignant at the suggestion. A big meeting was planned in Ballaghaderreen in mid-September. 'I don't think it would be prudent,' Denis O'Hara warned Dillon, 'to give any advice to the Volunteers about going to the front. If any of them wish to go, let them go by all means, same as the others who may go.' [7]

Home Rule   The Home Rule Bill was finally placed on the Statute-book and received the royal assent on 18 September but it was accompanied by a Suspensory Act, preventing its operation until after the war. The news reached Kiltimagh the following day:

> On September the 19th, a day that had been dark and rainy in the morning, I was waiting outside a shop in the little town when I saw Father Denis O'Hara coming towards me with a telegram in his hand. His step was swift, his fine face was triumphant. There was always a look of dignity and power about him and both showed now in the pose of his head, his erect figure, in the line of his mouth, in his commanding good-souled eyes. 'The Home Rule Bill was signed at twelve o'clock today by the King,'

4   Michael Farry, *The Aftermath of Revolution, Sligo 1921-23*, p 4
5   *W.P.* 6, 13, 20 Feb 1915
6   Lyons, p 357
7   Denis O'Hara to John Dillon, 13 Sept 1914, Dil. P. 6769

he said. And then after a pause. 'At last! After all these years.' He gave me the telegram to read. It was from Mr Dillon.[8]

Priests of the diocese, at their conference in Tubbercurry on 30 September, passed a motion, proposed by John Gunning of Tubbercurry and seconded by Philip Mulligan of Curry, congratulating John Redmond and the Irish Party for achieving Home Rule.

Volunteer Split

Partially as a reaction to the passing of the Home Rule Bill, and inspired by Carson's appeal to the Ulster Volunteers to enlist for service overseas, Redmond made a speech in County Wicklow on 20 September urging the Volunteers not merely to defend the shores of Ireland but to go 'wherever the firing-line extends, in defence of right, of freedom and of religion in this war'. [9] The immediate outcome of this speech was a split in the Volunteer movement, as a result of which a minority of about 12,000 followed Patrick Pearse and Eoin MacNeill and others into a separate organisation, retaining, however, the name 'Irish Volunteers', while the great majority, roughly 160,000, remained with Redmond, but were known thenceforward as the 'National Voluneers'. The majority of Volunteers in County Sligo sided with Redmond.

Dillon did not share Redmond's enthusiasm for the war but he did agree that the price Ireland had to pay for Home Rule was loyalty to England in its present struggle as he declared in Ballaghaderreen:

> I am England's friend in this war and as long as she stands by that Bill (Home Rule) and keeps faith with Ireland, any influence I can exercise in this country will be used to its uttermost to induce people to stand by England and keep faith with her and to prove to England that the bond of Ireland is something more than a scrap of paper.[10]

Patrick Reilly, Cartron, Kiltimagh, Ambulance Corps U.S. army *(courtesy Betty Solon)*

Conscription Scare

Before the end of the month some alarm was caused in Bohola by a newspaper report, according to John O 'Grady:

> The *Irish Independent* has led people here to believe that the conscription laws shall be enforced immediately and that after a week no young man will be able to go to America ... I hear fifty young men left Kiltimagh station a few days ago for America. The *Independent* has excited the people, indeed ... set them mad. I have written to this paper to say ... they were

8   L. MacManus, *White Light and Flame*, pp 98-9
9   Lyons, p 359
10 *F.J.* 6 Oct 1914

acting cruelly ... I'll refer to this on Sunday next and consider it a duty to allay the excited feelings of the poor people.[11]

Conscription was not in fact introduced into Ireland.

'Gallant Little Belgium'

Germany invaded Belgium in August 1914 and the fate of 'gallant little Catholic Belgium' produced an emotive response all over Ireland, with special church collections held throughout the country. Swinford convent school put on an entertainment in January 1915 in aid of the Belgian relief fund and collections were held in all parishes in the diocese, yielding sums ranging from £8 in Bonninconlon to £85 in Ballaghaderreen. In all over £735 was collected and Morrisroe sent a cheque for that sum to Cardinal Mercier, the Belgian primate.[12]

Recruitment

A recruiting campaign was organised and many young men in the diocese enlisted for active service. One of the first was Timothy Corley who enlisted in his hometown, Swinford, in the autumn of 1914, while others enlisted in Sligo, Boyle and Ballina and one, John Flemming of Tourlestrane, went all the way to Galway to enlist. The Irish Guards, with their regimental brass band, held recruiting meetings at the end of April 1915 in Collooney, Bunninadden, Tubbercurry, Coolaney and Ballymote where the meeting was chaired by the parish priest, Batty Quinn.[13] The Connaught Rangers held meetings in the same towns in mid-June and in Ballaghaderreen early in September.[14] The same regiment with their regimental band held a large recruitment meeting in Swinford on Tuesday 25 January 1916, and one speaker referred to how splendidly Ballina had responded to the call to arms. 'There was not a street in the town but had a DCM (Distinguished Conduct Medal). These men were all heroes and the mothers who sent them to defend the Empire were heroines of the truest type.' The Rangers were accompanied by Lt Michael O'Leary from Cork, an Irish war-hero who had been awarded the Victoria Cross for outstanding bravery on the field of battle. O'Leary made a strong appeal for recruits, especially to farmers' sons and shop assistants, who had no excuse for holding back.

In the first six months of the war over 50,000 flocked to the colours countrywide and another 25,000 over the following six months. By then there were 450 in the army from the Swinford police district.[15] One large contingent of volunteers left Swinford early in July 1915. A dance was held in their honour on the night before their departure and the following day there was

11 John O'Grady to John Dillon, 20 & 22 Oct 1914, Dil. P. 6770
12 *W.P.* 30 Jan & 20 Feb 1915
13 *S.C.* 8 May 1915
14 *S.C.* 19 June & 18 Sept 1915
15 T. R. McNulty to editor, *W.P.* 18 Sept 1915

'an immense gathering at the station with vociferous cheering'.[16] Commenting on the great numbers of his parishioners who had joined the army, Denis O'Hara said early in April 1916: 'Mr Dillon's constituency had proved itself one of the best recruiting grounds in Ireland.'[17] 1,175 had enlisted from Mayo and 1,116 from Sligo by November 1916.

There were occasional protests. At one of the Connaught Ranger meetings in Ballaghaderreen, on Sunday 14 November 1915, O'Leary and the regiment were hooted at by some local Volunteers as they were leaving the town after the meeting. As a result, permission for the Volunteers to drill was withdrawn by the local magistrate, but the Volunteers later repudiated the charge.[18] Young men were circularised by the Lord Lieutenant urging them to join the army. A meeting in Tubbercurry on 5 November, called by Patrick Dyer, drew a large attendance of the local shop assistants thirty-two of whom signed a document declaring that they would only join up when Ireland had a free and independent government. Dyer was arrested on 15 November and imprisoned for one month in Mountjoy. On his release he was given an enthusiastic reception in Tubbercurry and presented with an Address by the local corps of the Irish Volunteers. [19]

Protests

Those who volunteered for active service came from a wide spectrum of social backgrounds. While many of those who enlisted were the sons of small farmers or labourers, others belonged to the better-off classes in the towns. M. J. McNulty was the assistant clerk of Swinford Board of Guardians when he received his commission as a lieutenant in the Connaught Rangers in November 1915, and James B. O'Connor was the youngest member of the Swinford District Council when he joined the Cadet corps about the same time. Capt J. P. Roache was pension officer in Charlestown as was J. S. Clarke in Swinford, while Mr Marks was cashier in the Provincial Bank there. Two sons of a national teacher in Cortoon, Charlestown, volunteered, Thomas J. Marren, himself a teacher in Inchicore, Dublin, and his brother, Jack, a third-year medical student. Bombardier Edward Harte was the son of M. J. Harte, a teacher in Knocks national school in Killasser. At least one teacher volunteered himself, Joseph O'Dowd, who was principal of Doocastle NS when he joined the Connaught Rangers in 1915. [20]

Background

16 Among the volunteers were J. P. O'Callaghan, Joe O'Connor, and Frank Whiston, a Gaelic footballer. *W.P.* 10 July 1915
17 *W.P.* 8 April 1916
18 *S.C.* 20 & 27 Nov & *W.P.* 27 Nov 1915. The repudiation was signed by P. J. Ryan, J. J. Coleman, B. J. O'Gara, J. Morley, J. Gannon, T. McCormack, T. F. O'Hara, John Coleman, J. O'Kelly, P. Freyne, T. Cuniffe, Joe Flannery (Hon. Sec.) *W.P.* 11 Dec 1915
19 *S.C.* 20 Nov, *F.J.* 1 Dec 1915 & *W.P.* 1 Jan 1916
20 *W.P.* 21 July, 25 Sept, 27 Nov, 4 Dec 1915, 10 Mar & 26 Aug 1917; *S.C.* 17 June 1916

Brothers   Like the Marrens from Charlestown, some families provided more than one son for the front. Widow Canavan of Kiltimagh had three sons in the Dublin Fusiliers while Mrs Browne of Main St had also three sons in the army. When Tom Kneafsey of Swinford joined the Irish Guards in October 1915, his brother had already enlisted in the same regiment. [21] In Tubbercurry four brothers of the Mannion family, Philip, Michael, John and Tom, enlisted as did another four brothers, the sons of J. W. Scott of the Fisheries in Ballysadare. 'I would not believe the number of young men from Turlough parish who had joined the army,' John Conroy told Dillon. 'In fact there are few families in the parish who have …not some member in the army.' Conroy listed eighty-three recruits among whom were four sets of two brothers and three sets of three brothers. The description of Turlough was probably similar to that of the neighbouring Achonry parishes. In Knockmore parish adjoining Foxford, there were thirty-three recruits from the village of Shraheens alone. Five men, William Bourke, James Morley, Michael Ansboro, Ignatius Morley and Martin Morley, joined the army from the small village of Carroward in Bohola and six young men in the village of Tooromin were said 'to have answered the call at the outbreak of hostilities.' [22]

Regiments   While many of those who volunteered for active service joined the Connaught Rangers, others, like the Kneafseys of Swinford, joined the Irish Guards and a host of other regiments both Irish and English. Of six Kiltimagh men who enlisted in 1915, three joined the Connaught Rangers, one the Dublin Fusiliers and the other two the South Lancashires and the West Riding Regiment, York.[23] Other Irish regiments listed included the Leinster Regiment, the Royal Irish Rifles, the Royal Irish Liverpool Rifles, the Irish Brigade, etc., while English regiments included the Royal Garrison Artillery, Durban Light Infantry etc. Many of those who enlisted in England were probably emigrant or migratory workers and often joined English regiments, like Thomas Kearns and James Kennealy of Kilkelly who enlisted in Liverpool and Lancashire in the East Lancashire and South Lancashire Regiments respectively. But even here they often joined Irish regiments, like Martin Groarke of Swinford who enlisted in Manchester in the Royal Dublin Fusiliers and Michael Flynn and Thomas Welsh of Foxford who enlisted in Edinburgh in the Irish Guards and the Connaught Rangers respectively.

21 *W.P.* 18 Sept & 16 Oct 1915; *Kiltimagh*, p 159
22 John Conroy to John Dillon, 14 Mar, 20 Oct 1916 & 5 Nov 1917, Dil. P. 6771; *Kiltimagh*, p 161
23 *Kiltimagh*, p 155

Three Achonry priests volunteered as chaplains. Felix Burke, a curate in *Chaplains*
Ballaghaderreen, served four years as chaplain in the 16th Irish Division and
was named in Field Marshall Sir Douglas Haig's despatches for distinguished
service and devotion to duty on the field. While home on leave in October
1916 he gave a lecture in Keash entitled 'The Big Push.' [24] Michael Louis
Henry had taught in St Nathy's College but was a curate in Kiltimagh when

Chaplain Felix Burke
(courtesy James McGuinn)

John Francis Campbell, Swinford, US
Chaplain *(courtesy Mairéad Regan)*

he volunteered as chaplain in April 1916. He was presented with an address
illuminated by the St Louis nuns and a beautiful chalice by Dr Madden who
said he'gave a splendid example to the young men of the locality.' [25] Henry, a
former student at the Irish College, Salamanca, where he had a distinguished
career, obtaining a double doctorate, was affectionately known as the 'Doc'.
It was later said that he was court-martialled for his pro-German sympathies
but, be that as it may, when he returned to Ireland he became an active IRA
supporter in the Anglo-Irish War.[26] M. J. Mullins, son of Patrick Mullins,
Ballinacarrow, who was ordained in Maynooth in December 1916, joined the
army as a chaplain after Christmas but the following October was in a conva-
lescent home in England after what was described as 'a long and dangerous
illness' in a French hospital.[27] Another native of the diocese, John Francis

24 *W.P.* 28 Oct 1916 and 3 Mar 1917: see also John Doherty, *Achonry Priests in the Twentieth
    Century* (unpublished typescript)
25 *W.P.* 8 April 1916
26 Maurteen Brennan, in O'Malley Notebooks, P17b / 133, AD UCD
27 *S.C.* 27 Oct 1917

Decorated

Campbell of Swinford, was the first priest in the diocese of Philadelphia to volunteer, in 1917, for the US army.

A number of Achonry volunteers were decorated for gallantry at the front. One of the first to be awarded the Distinguished Conduct Medal (DCM) in September 1915 was twenty-seven year old Private John Henry from Culmore, Swinford. In the same month, J. S. Clarke, the former pensions officer in Swinford was also awarded the DCM and promoted to sergeant. In June 1916 the former pensions officer in Charlestown was awarded the Military Cross as was Edward Harte of Knocks, Killasser [28]

Died in Action

Joe Leydon of Collooney, serving with the Irish Guards in France, was killed in action on 24 August 1914 and became the first Co Sligo casualty of the war. Two days later thirty-two-year-old Corporal Michael Ansboro from Kiltimagh (though a native of Bohola) also lost his life in France. For the next four years the dreaded news of death at the front was received in homes in every parish of the diocese. By August 1915 local newspapers were reporting casualties at the front, H. M. MacDermot, the son of The MacDermot of Coolavin, killed a few months after he had volunteered, as well as four from Killasser and two from Swinford.[29] When Lance-Sergeant Patrick O'Connor from Collooney was killed in action in October 1915, his mother received letters of sympathy from the King and Lord Kitchener. [30]Sergeant John Francis McGuinn's parents in Tubbercurry received a telegram signed by Kitchener when he died from wounds while serving with the Irish Guards: 'The King commands me to assure you of the true sympathy of His Majesty and the Queen.' His personal belongings, including 'scapular, rosary beads, copies of the *Messenger* and the crucifix that he held clenched in his right hand as he died' were sent home to his mother, and later Chaplain Ambrose McGrath found his prayer book. 'I knew him very well serving my Mass in barracks and church and was an exemplary Catholic.' [31]

Casualties in 1916 included Lance-Corporal Martin Higgins, killed in action in the Dardanelles, and Lance-Corporal D. Mulholland, the nineteen-year-old son of the foreman in Morrisroe's bakery in Charlestown. A former RIC constable, Martin McKenzie, from Carrowcrom, Bonniconlon, was killed in action in the autumn of 1917 and his Rosary beads was enclosed with news of his death. Capt. J. P. Roache, the former Charlestown pension-officer,

28 W.P. 11 Sept 1915; 10 Mar and 17 July 1917
29 S.C. 28 Aug 1915. *Killasser:* Sgt Duffy, Leinster Regiment; Private Loftus, Lancashires, Privates Corr and Sweeney. *Swinford:* Sgt Michael O'Hara and Private James Gallagher, Connaught Rangers. W.P. 4 & 11 Sept 1915
30 S.C. 13 Nov 1915
31 James McGuinn, *Sligo Men in the Great War,* pp 84, 85, 87

and Private John Henry of Culmore, both of whom had been decorated, were killed in action in France. On entering the trenches on 27 November Henry had a presentiment of his death and gave his watch to Corporal Kneafsey of Swinford who later gave it to his mother. Two others died from diseases contracted at the front, Driver John Alexander Allen from Tubbercurry of typhoid fever in Salonika in 1916, and Sergeant James Mullen from Bonniconlon of meningitis in 1917. [32]

Wounded

Thomas Malley of Kiltimagh was wounded when the Connaught Rangers were engaged on 14 September 1915. From his hospital bed he wrote to his wife – they had only been married a short time before he left for the front: 'I will be for the front again in about a week. I do not mind when it is for my King and country – may God save it! Ask all your friends to pray for me, and write to Mother and tell her I am well. May God bless you all.' Lt Dermot A. M. MacManus of Killedan House, Kiltimagh, was wounded at Gallipoli. Among the wounded in 1917 were J. B. O'Connor, J. F. McNicholas and Private M. Clarke from Swinford, Privates J. McGettrick and E. Shannon, Ballymote, Privates J. Merrigan and J. Regan, Ballaghaderreen. John Golden of Kiltimagh was seriously wounded in the leg, which he lost subsequently. He did not expect to survive as he was losing an enormous amount of blood but believed that the weight of his dead comrades on top of him, prevented him bleeding to death. [33]

Prisoners of War

Others became prisoners-of-war in Germany. Private Joe King, a Connaught Ranger from Bunninadden, was a prisoner-of-war at Limburg on 8 March 1915.[34] Private Halligan of Swinford town was a prisoner-of-war there in July and by mid-September there were at least four other prisoners-of-war from the diocese in the same camp.[35] A concert was held in Swinford early in July in aid of the Connaught Rangers' prisoners-of-war in Germany.

U.S. soldiers in Flanders, 1917. Extreme right, Tom Fleming, Broaha, Curry *(courtesy James McGuinn)*

32 *W.P.* 22 Jan & 19 Feb 1916, 5 Aug 1916, 7 July, 13 Oct & 15 Dec 1917
33 *Kiltimagh*, pp 153 & 163; *W.P.* 31 July 1915, 26 April & 15 Sept 1917
34 *S.C.* 24 April 1915
35 Sgt Duffy, Kilmovee, Private J. Horan, Glentavraun, Kilkelly, Private Timmons, Charlestown, Private James McCann, Uggool, Kilmovee. *W.P.* 7 Aug & 20 Nov 1915

Migratory
Labourers

There were reports of bad treatment of Irish migratory labourers in English towns in the spring of 1916. They had difficulty getting food and lodgings and sometimes their lives were in danger. Given the number of young men from Turlough parish who had enlisted in the army, John Conroy believed it was very unfair to treat Irish workers badly. 'Most of the old men will go to England this year and leave the young fellows at home.'[36] But there was soon to be a more serious pretext for English anger against the Irish.

1916 Rebellion

On Easter Monday, 24 April, about 1,400 Irish Volunteers, under the command of Patrick Pearse, together with 200 of the Citizen Army, under James Connolly, seized the General Post Office in Dublin and occupied a number of other places including the Four Courts, Boland's Mills, Jacob's Biscuit Factory and St Stephen's Green. It was a bank holiday and many of the English garrison were at the races at Fairyhouse. When news of the Dublin rebellion finally reached the rest of the country, there was shock and disbelief. People in Kiltimagh found it difficult to believe when Denis O'Hara declared on Tuesday evening that 'John MacNeill had seized the General Post Office yesterday and ran up the republican flag.' [37] In fact, MacNeill had taken no part in the insurrection, having issued countermanding orders when he first learned of the proposed rising. In Foxford 'no news had come through for ten days, except wild unreliable rumours.'

Ruins of G.P.O., Dublin, as seen from top of Nelson's Pillar

NLI (Valentine
Collection R27,448)

36 John Conroy to John Dillon, 14 Mar 1916, Dil. P. 6771
37 *Kiltimagh*, p 156

Frank Sherry, manager of the Foxford Woollen Mills, also 'found it difficult to believe, but unfortunately it was too true.' He was one of the few people from the west of Ireland who was an eye-witness of the events of that
week. [38] Sherry, who had come to Dublin with one of the mill hands, arrived
out at Ballsbridge on Easter Monday to prepare the Foxford stall for the
opening of the Spring Show on Tuesday. There, they heard of 'the Sinn Féin
rising in the city', as a result of which they became trapped in Dublin for ten
days until Wednesday 3 May with plenty of time to observe the events,
though their movements were restricted by the military. Sherry kept a record
of the happenings which began on Wednesday 26 April, as a letter addressed
to Agnes Morrogh Bernard, but as there was no possibility of posting it, continued it as a day-to-day diary. [39]

Wednesday, 26 April: When he heard that Liberty Hall had been blown up
that morning by the military, he commented 'one "Wasp's Nest" cleared out'
leaving little doubt where Sherry's sympathies laid. That day he went out to
Ballsbridge to make sure that the Foxford exhibits were safe and secure. Close
by two houses were occupied by insurgents:

> Some thousands of soldiers just arrived as far as Ballsbridge now. They
> were met at the Bridge by a fusillade of shots from one of the houses which
> they (the Sinn Féiners) are in possession of. At the moment I do not know
> how many casualties, but there must be a great number. The soldiers are
> lying across the road. They are just after coming from England and march-
> ing from Kingstown. They are clearing all the civilians out of the vicinity
> and out of the houses just now – so they must be preparing for a real at-
> tack. We are about 300 yards from the house from which the Sinn Féiners
> are firing, but we are under cover here on the gallery. Terrible firing going
> on now, no civilians allowed to cross Ballsbridge ...

They had to return to their hotel by way of Donnybrook and up Leeson
Street to St Stephens Green:

> Stephen's Green is not clear yet. There were shots fired while we were com-
> ing along. Just now machine guns are firing madly down about Sackville
> Street (O'Connell Street). There are about six tram cars, a dozen motor
> cars, bread carts and other carts, some ordinary cars, and one dead horse
> blockading Stephen's Green. The windows in the Shelbourne and several
> other houses are riddled with bullets. Noblet's at the head of Grafton
> Street is wrecked and all looted. Tyler's and several other houses in

38 T. F Keane, Killasser House, who had also come to Dublin for the Spring Show, wrote a
    lengthy article, entitled 'Dublin during Insurrection' in the *Western People*, 13 May 1916, p 5
39 Frank Sherry to Agnes Morrogh Bernard, 26 April 1916, RSCG / H 26 / 75

Sackville Street are wrecked and looted. Lawrence's and two or three other houses are burned down. Slept well during the night and heard very few shots ...

Heavy Artillery

Thursday, 27 April: Early in the morning they went back to Ballsbridge where they found about 500 soldiers sleeping around the gallery and so could not get near their stall. The soldiers left in about an hour and before the next crowd came in, Sherry and his companion got everything packed up and stored away safely in a corner of the gallery.

About 3 o'clock today a naval gun with gunners arrived at Ballsbridge. After resting and feeding the horses etc. they passed on to Haddington Road when they started to fire. The firing of this gun and rifles was something terrible to hear for about three-quarters of an hour. We were looking at them in the distance from Landsdowne Road. Of course we would not be allowed any nearer them. We came up Landsdowne Road and Baggot Street, along Stephen's Green and down Grafton Street without incident or interruption, until we came within twenty yards of the hotel, when a soldier ordered us to go in by a side door. Not a soul is allowed to pass down this street, there are soldiers at each corner.

Looting

It is very sad to go down Grafton Street and see the looting. At least a dozen houses are completely cleared out by the women, boys and girls actually carrying everything away wholesale. I understand the same thing is going on in several places through the city. It is now 7 o'clock and no one allowed outside doors – firing going on all over the city.

John Dillon who was penned into his house in North Great George's Street, a few hundred yards from the GPO, made a similar observation on Tuesday:

All yesterday afternoon and again this morning, a steady stream of women, girls and young children have passed up this street, laden with loot – clothes, boots, boxes of sweets, etc. etc. It is horrible to see some well-dressed respectable girls laden with loot. Just now a woman passed with a baby's perambulator piled with boots.[40]

Sherry's comment later proved accurate:

It is supposed to be a bigger thing and will be more difficult to put down than most people imagine. When the big guns were going I could compare it to nothing but continuous very heavy thunder. The Sinn Féiners have possession of the GPO, Jacob's Factory, Royal College of Surgeons in Stephen's Green, as well as several houses all over the city, and seem all out to die, so that it will take some time to clear them.

40 qtd Lyons p 370

From the hotel the sky is red from a fire down towards Sackville Street, but *Fires Raging*
we cannot tell where it is. All lights are ordered out in the hotel by the military. Terrible rifle shooting all around the place here. Have gone to bed,
but it is difficult to sleep with such firing all around the house.

Friday, 28 April: 'Slept a little off and on. The firing kept up all night and
is still going on now at 6 o'clock.' They were not allowed to leave the hotel all
day and had no way of finding out what was going on. They heard that fires
were raging in Sackville Street and Henry Street. 'The sky is simply blazing
over towards Sackville Street, just now 10 o'clock.'

Saturday, 29: April: Sherry tried to get to Kingsbridge station to see if *Surrender*
trains were running but he was stopped by the military who told him there
were none. He got to Harcourt Street station but there were no trains running there either. He tried to get out to Ballsbridge but, having been warned
that he might not get back, he stayed put.

At 4 o'clock this evening the military got word that the Sinn Féiners had
surrendered, and all the soldiers were ordered to fire no more, but to keep
their position and keep loaded. I believe the Leaders have surrendered, but
very likely some of them will never surrender. The shooting is going on
still all over the city, but not as much as usual at time of going to bed. No
one allowed on the streets after 7.30 and all lights out.

Sunday, 30 April: They have just surrendered in the Royal College and
Jacob's and are taken prisoner to the Castle. The soldiers are withdrawing
from around this quarter, so we have been able to get as far as O'Connell
Bridge. All O'Connell Street (*sic*) is burned from Hopkin's to the Pillar, including Hopkin's and Clery's. In fact, all that block, right back to the next
street, the GPO, Metropole Hotel, Elvery's and several others on the opposite side (are burned). The trouble is still going on at Westland Row and
around that quarter, as well as snipers all over the city, but the general
opinion is that they will have it well in hand tomorrow. No one is allowed
out of the city without a pass, and then go at their own risk. No trains
running anywhere yet, but we are hoping to get away by Tuesday and hope
we will not be disappointed.

Monday, 1 May: Sherry tried in vain to get a pass to go home, but people *In Ruins*
were allowed to move through certain areas of the city without a pass.

All Abbey Street, all Henry Street, with the exception of Arnott's, which
we were not able to get up to, all both sides of O'Connell St as far as the
Pillar, and six or seven houses farther up on Clery's side, are all a heap of
ruins. I fear Arnott's is also burned, but am not sure. Then, there are

dozens of houses all over the city in the same state, and I believe hundreds broken up and looted. The sight would really make one sad.

Tuesday, 2 May: Sherry and his companion went to the Castle in the morning and succeeded in getting passes without difficulty which not only permitted them to return home by train the next day but also enabled them to go through all the metropolitan area that day:

We went all through the city to see the destruction, which is really a sad sight to behold. Some 200 houses with all their contents burned to the ground, as well as hundreds of houses battered with shot and shell, and without a whole pane of glass left in them. The streets of the city are literally strewn over with glass where they are not covered with bricks and mortar and debris of every description.

We made our way to Ballsbridge, by the direct Kingstown route. This road is lined with soldiers on both sides all the way to Ballsbridge, and we had to show our passes every 100 yards or so. Many houses on this route are also levelled to the ground, some by fire and others by shell. Blood over the road in various places. We found our goods all right on the gallery at Ballsbridge. Some hundreds of soldiers are sleeping around the gallery and in various places through the Show Grounds. All the Ballsbridge grounds are full of military, munitions, guns of various descriptions, horses, mules, field kitchens – in fact, everything on a war footing.

Back to Foxford

Wednesday, 3 May: Sherry and his friend arrived at Broadstone Station an hour before the first train to leave the city in ten days was due to depart. Even so there were at least a hundred people waiting before them. Only those with passes were allowed to board the train, which departed at 9.30. There was a welcoming party to meet them when they arrived at Foxford, all eager to hear their story 'as no news had come through for ten days, except wild, unreliable rumours. During that evening and next day we gave a history of our experiences, and the loss of life and property which had taken place – something which we hope never to see again.'

Charlestown Reaction

When the news reached Charlestown on Sunday 30 April of the unconditional surrender of the insurgents, 'much jubilation took place to mark the satisfaction of the people.' The streets were 'brilliantly illuminated with electric lamps' and the local band paraded the town with the Boy Scouts carrying the Belgian flag. 'The people of the district condemned it (the rebellion) in vigorous terms.' The Charlestown reaction was probably typical of most areas. The *Western People* described the events of Easter Week as 'a mad enterprise'. The *Sligo Champion* was equally condemnatory: 'Those outside the movement can see no justification for the action of the insurgents. It is regrettable from every point of view.' [41] Some of the Charlestown anger directed at the insurgents might have been caused by a shortage of bread in the town as no yeast could get through from Dublin. [42]

In the six days of fighting 450 people were killed and 2,614 wounded. 318 of those killed, and 2,217 of the wounded were insurgents or civilians of whom the official figures made no distinction. Martial law was introduced and a general round-up of 'suspects' all over the country was ordered. These included everyone who had incurred official suspicion in the previous two years. It was 'a crass psychological blunder' on the part of the British authorities as it conferred the mantle of revolutionary on a large number of people throughout the country who neither had knowledge of or involvement in the events of Easter Week. The full consequences of herding innocent people into camps alongside dedicated revolutionaries would be seen in the years that lay ahead. 'It would appear', the *Sligo Champion* stated in its editorial, 'that martial law as at present applied in the peaceful districts of Ireland, is calculated to foment rather than lessen rebellious sentiment.'[43] Over 3,000 were swept into the net although about half of these were released after interrogation, and the remainder sent to Britain for internment.

Aftermath

John Shouldice from Ballaghaderreen, who seems to have taken part in the rebellion in Dublin, was sentenced to death which was later commuted to five years imprisonment.[44] Seán Corcoran, a shop assistant in Murtagh's, Kiltimagh, was arrested and charged at a special court in Kiltimagh 'for attempting to cause sedition and disaffection among the civilian population' on 26 April. He was detained in Castlebar jail but later interned with fifty-three others in Wandsworth Prison. Corcoran's arrest resulted from a jocose remark made in the Hibernian Bank during the Rising, and on being searched a copy of the IRB oath was found in his possession. Corcoran was later transferred to Frongoch in Wales from where he was released in August.[45] Among some 200 prisoners transferred from Dublin to Knutsford Detention Barracks in England were two men from the diocese, M. Savage, a barman from Ballysadare, and M. Murphy NT, Rinbane, Curry.[46] A detachment of Sherwood Forresters swooped on Ballaghaderreen on 11 May and arrested over twenty young men, some of whom were later released. Those detained were

Interned

41 *S.C.* 20 May 1916
42 *W.P.* 6 May 1916
43 *S.C.* 20 May 1916
44 *W.P.* 13 May 1916
45 *W.P.* 6 May 1916. See *Kiltimagh*, pp 156, 158
46 *W.P.* 13 May 1916

later deported to England and held in Frongoch internment camp.[47] 'The prisoners appeared in the very best of spirits and were given a very enthusiastic send-off at the station by a large crowd.'[48] Most of them were released at the end of July or the beginning of August.[49] By then many of the internees had been released and the remainder were released at Christmas.

Executions

The authorities further squandered their chance of exploiting the unpopularity of the Rising by the manner and severity of the punishment of its leaders. Fourteen of them were executed in Dublin and these executions were spun out over ten days, from 3 to 12 May, which allowed time for the public attitude to change from outright condemnation to feelings of compassion for the victims and anger against the authorities. The *Sligo Champion*, a staunch supporter of Redmond, summed up the widespread revulsion at the executions. 'A sickening thud went through the heart of Ireland at each fresh announcement.' [50]

Dillon's Opposition

John Dillon vehemently opposed the executions, realising that the effect on public opinion might be disastrous in the extreme. He crossed to London and delivered a speech to a hostile House of Commons on 11 May in an effort to stop the executions: [51]

> You are letting loose a river of blood and make no mistake about it, between two races who, after three hundred years of hatred or strife, we had nearly succeeded in bringing together ... We have risked our lives a hundred times to bring about this result. We are held up to odium as traitors by the men who made this rebellion, and our lives have been in danger a hundred times during the last thirty years because we have endeavoured to reconcile the two things and you are washing out our whole life work in a sea of blood.

English MPs were outraged when he appealed to the Prime Minister to stop the executions:

> But it is not murderers who are being executed; it is insurgents who have fought a clean fight, a brave fight, however misguided, and it would have been a good thing for you if your soldiers were able to put up as good a fight as did these men in Dublin – three thousand men against twenty-thousand with machine-guns and artillery.

47 P. J. Ryan DC, John J. Coleman, James Cuniffe, John F. Morley, Thomas O'Hara (Flannery's), T. Cooney (Flannery's), Bertie Shouldice (Flannery's), Bartley O'Gara, Joseph Kelly, Joseph Flannery, and Thomas McCormack (newsagent & baker)
48 *S.C.* 20 May 1916; *W.P.* 20 and 27 May 1916
49 *W.P.* 29 July 1916
50 *S.C.* 20 May 1916
51 Lyons, pp 381-2

In the short term, Dillon's speech seemed to have had little effect. Further executions took place the next day, including that of James Connolly who was so ill that he could not stand, and was shot seated in a chair. In September his two daughters, Inagh and Maura, were sent as boarders to the St Louis Convent in Kiltimagh and his widow later spent a night in the convent and was visited by Denis O'Hara. [52]

There was a growing sympathy for the executed leaders and a requiem high Mass for the repose of their souls was offered in Ballymote on Monday 12 July in the presence of a large congregation[53] but during the rest of 1916 there was no remarkable change in public opinion in favour of Sinn Féin. 'The feeling in my district and in the country generally is sound in favour of the Irish Party with the exception of a few cranks here and there.'[54] Denis O'Hara believed towards the end of that year that 'the country seems to be getting back to commonsense'.[55]

At a meeting in the Town Hall in Swinford in January 1917, chaired by Dean Connington and with sixteen other priests on the stage, Dillon spoke of the executions and the part he played in trying to prevent them:

Speech in Swinford

> We stopped the executions and saved the lives of twenty and probably thirty-five men who would have been shot only for our action ... I went to the Castle and saw Sir John Maxwell to stop the executions ... The next thing we did was to stop the courtmartials. But for the Party action there would be at least three hundred men in penal servitude instead of eighty-six ... We obtained the release of over 2,000 untried prisoners.[56]

Connington's intervention probably revealed the changing public opinion in the period since the events of Easter Week: 'Other people have just as much a right to their opinion as we have and the chances are equal that their opinion is just as correct, as good and as sound as ours, and we have no right, because a man differs from us, to call him a knave and a fool.'

His view, however, was not shared by his bishop. Morrisroe's Lenten Pastoral in February 1917 condemned the 1916 Rising as a 'domestic tragedy' which 'if the authors had been fully alive to its consequences they would, if inspired with the sentiments of God-fearing men, have stayed their hands.' He was grateful that at least the people of his diocese were 'free from complicity in this hapless enterprise.' He also commented on the changing public opinion:[57]

Morrisroe's Pastoral

52 *Kiltimagh*, pp 158, 160
53 *S.C.* 15 July 1916
54 John Conroy to John Dillon, 29 Aug 1916, Dil. P. 6771
55 Denis O'Hara to John Dillon, 7 Nov 1916, Dil. P. 6769
56 *W.P.* 27 Jan 1917
57 *W.P.* 24 Feb 1917

The excessive severity employed to end the turmoil had left behind irrita-
tion and resentment and those, who at first abhorred the rash venture,
were afterwards turned into active sympathisers with the victims, but compassion for a culprit did not mean approval of his crime ... It was a sense of
righteousness and not the shedding of blood that should decide the fate of
nations struggling to be free.

By the time of the anniversary of the 1916 Rising public opinion, particularly
among the younger generation, had noticeably changed, as Lottie MacManus
noted in her diary:

Throughout the country, from the spires of Catholic churches, from town
halls, the tricolour flag waved. Sometimes the police got down a flag;
sometimes they failed. I saw it waving over Swinford's Catholic church. Their
rifles had not moved it. I saw it over the church in Cuiltemach (Kiltimagh)
... Everywhere in Ireland young men were running up the flag.[58]

Sinn Féin Clubs

Sinn Féin clubs began to sprout up all over the diocese. Swinford had a
Sinn Féin club at the beginning of July 1917 when a large attendance was reported at the club meeting in Swinford Town Hall, and fifty-three new members were enrolled in the club a week later.[59] The curate, Michael Connolly,
was elected president in January 1918, with Pat O'Hara and Michael Campbell, vice-presidents.[60] In the last months of 1917 and the early months of
1918, there were reports of clubs in Foxford, Kiltimagh, Aclare, Carracastle,
Cloonacool, Kilkelly, Hagfield, Bushfield, Curry, Ballaghaderreen, Attymass,
Bonniconlon and Bohola. Almost a hundred members of the Carracastle
Sinn Féin club marched on the last day of 1917 to their new and spacious club
rooms, where their president's address was followed by a dance. Mayo County
Convention of Sinn Féin was held at Balla on Wednesday 19 September and
was attended by delegates from twenty clubs including Kiltimagh, Swinford
and Ballaghadereen.[61]

South Sligo

South Sligo Sinn Féin executive was formed by delegates from eight areas
in April 1917 and by July there were fifteen clubs. It was reported in September that 'the Sinn Féin movement has spread all over the county', with forty-
three clubs at the end of December. Meetings, lectures and *aeríochtaí* were
held all over the county. The last six months of 1917 saw a tenfold increase in
Sinn Féin membership both in Sligo and Mayo. Interest in the movement
was then said to be beginning to wane. [62]

58 *White Light and Flame*, p 124
59 *W.P.* 14 & 21 July 1917
60 Treasurer, P. Durkan, secretaries, A. Mulrooney and P. J. Henry. *W.P.* 2 Feb 1918
61 *W.P.* 4 Aug, 7 Sept, 22 Sept,13 Oct,17 & 24 Nov, 19 Dec 1917, 19 Jan and 2 Feb 1918
62 Farry, *Aftermath*, pp 5-6

Public meetings were held in Keash, Gurteen, Achonry, Killoran and Cloonacool in June 1917 and Sinn Féin clubs were formed, in some cases with the 'active co-operation of the clergy'. P. J. O'Grady was elected president of the Countess Markievicz Club formed in Keash on Sunday 10 June. Delegates from nine clubs, as well as representatives from Tourlestrane and Cloonloo, attended the South Sligo Sinn Féin Alliance in the Town Hall in Tubbercurry on Sunday 24 June with Pádraic Ó Domhnalláin, professor of Irish in Summerhill College, in the chair. [63] Seventeen were listed as members of the Achonry Sinn Féin club in July and a hundred were enrolled in the Moylough club in August. Clubs were formed in Ballysadare and Collooney on Sunday 26 August and reported in Doocastle and Bunninadden in October. By then the club in Mullinabreena had over 200 members. One of the last clubs to be formed in South Sligo was in Ballinacarrow on Sunday 4 November. [64]

P. J. O'Grady
(courtesy Jim Finan)

Sinn Féin held large demonstrations in several towns in the diocese in the autumn of 1917.[65] About 5,000 people carrying banners, led by bands and preceded by 200 men on horseback wearing Sinn Féin sashes, marched through Ballymote in military formation on Sunday 23 September to protest against the treatment of Irish political prisoners. The meeting was chaired by Alec McCabe and speakers included D. A. Mulcahy. P. Ó Domhnalláin, J. J. Clancy, J. Cogan, Sean O'Ruane, Thomas McGowan and Sean McMorrow. Eoin MacNeill was the principal speaker at a demonstration in Swinford on the following Sunday, attended by representatives of numerous clubs many of whom arrived on bicycles carrying Sinn Féin flags.[66] Four bands provided music, Kiltimagh Brass and Bohola Pipers as well as fife and drum bands from Cloonoghill and Attymachugh. MacNeill told the crowd that while it was no secret that he did his best to prevent the Easter Week Rising, he was not ashamed to pay tribute to those who died. The meeting ended with the singing of the *Soldiers' Song*.

Eoin MacNeill in Swinford

About 4,000 attended a demonstration in Tubbercurry on Sunday 7 October. Sean Milroy was the principal speaker on Sunday 4 November in Kiltimagh where about 3,000 attended the demonstration. Milroy, who was presented with an address by T. Ruane on behalf of the Kiltimagh James

63 Tubbercurry, Mullinabreena, Emlanaughton, Ballymote, Achonry, Keash, Culfadda, Gurteen and Moylough
64 *S.C.* Sept, 20 Oct & 3 Nov 1917, 2 Feb 1918. The complete membership of Mullinabreena Sinn Féin club listed by townland is published in *S.C.* 2 Feb 1918
65 *W.P.* 29 Sept, 6 & 13 Oct, 10 Nov 1917; *S.C.* 13 Oct 1917, 2 Feb 1918
66 Kiltimagh, Bohola, Cloonoghill, Attymachugh, Cashel, Tubbercurry, Ballaghaderreen, Castlebar and Foxford

Connolly Sinn Féin club, referred to an article in the *Daily Mail* which expressed concern about the state of religion in Ireland because young priests identified with Sinn Féin. Pádraig Ó Domhnalláin and M. Murphy of Curry, who was recently released from Frongoch internment camp, were the principal speakers at a demonstration in Curry at the end of January. [67]

Carracastle Clashes

Several clashes between Sinn Féiners and Nationalists were reported in 1917 from Carracastle where Philip J. Mulligan, the parish priest, was an enthusiastic Sinn Féiner. [68] The United Irish League had arranged to hold a meeting outside the chapel after last Mass on Sunday 29 April, but they found Sinn Féiners in possession of the church steps. Mulligan introduced Pádraig Ó Domhnalláin, who spoke in Irish but was vigorously boohed and the Sinn Féiners were forced to withdraw. Another clash between Sinn Féiners and Nationalists occurred on Sunday 29 July outside Tonroe schoolhouse, when the tricolour carried by the Sinn Féiners was snatched and trampled underfoot. 'Fusillades of stones were exchanged' and several widows in the school were broken. Another incident occurred on Friday 17 August when a large *meitheal* of Sinn Féiners with twenty-five horses and carts, delivering turf to the parish priest and bearing Sinn Féin flags, received a hostile reception in Barroe from a number of the villagers. Trouble was averted when the police arrived and removed the flags. A letter to the *Western People* (1 Sept), signed 'Nationalist', declared that nobody from the village had interfered with the carts but that it was the police who had rushed the carts as they passed the barracks and snatched the flags.

P. J. Mulligan, Carracastle *(courtesy Vincent Coleman)*

Bohola

A Sinn Féin meeting was planned in Bohola for Sunday 16 December 1917, and the previous Sunday John O'Grady launched a tirade from the pulpit against them, calling them 'a lot of corner boys'. He had already refused the school for a Sinn Féin concert. However, as was becoming the pattern all over

67 *S.C.* 2 Feb 1918
68 *W.P.* 5 May, 4 Aug and 1 Sept 1917

the diocese, his curate, Michael O'Hara, was an enthusiastic Sinn Féiner and as Dillon's local agent was only too aware, 'a curate in a parish has a good deal of influence with the young men especially when he gets up plays etc. as Father O'Hara did.' The president of the Sinn Féin club was a local carpenter and drummer in the Pipe Band. 'He was wavering and I'm sorry to say he went over and he was always a good nationalist, but I expect the influence of the curate prevailed.' Another curate, Michael Connolly in Swinford, was 'a very advanced Sinn Féiner' and made many converts in the half-parish of Midfield, for which he was responsible. [69]

Michael O'Hara

Early in 1918 a number of Sinn Féiners from Ballina, with a small contingent from Bonniconlon, met the congregation after Sunday Mass in Attymass. [70] John Moylett, president of Ballina Sinn Féin club climbed a wall to address the crowd and when he had finished the parish priest, Walter Henry, also mounted the wall and spoke to the people:

Attymass

> Talk of establishing a republic was the merest moonshine ... If an attempt was made by force to establish a republic, it would simply mean the drenching of the country in blood and slaughter a million times worse than Easter Week.. It was what Cardinal Logue called "a mad and foolish dream" ... The true hope of the country lay in constitutional methods. It was by these means and through the Irish Party, that they won the land, broke down the power of the landlords and accomplished other great reforms.

While the priest was speaking the Sinn Féiners tried to interrupt him by going through 'military evolutions' on the edge of the crowd and singing the *Soldier's Song.*

Sinn Féiners tried to address the crowd as they emerged from Mass in Kilmovee on 21 March 1918, but they were not given a hearing, the crowd hooting and jeering at them, and had to move about 500 yards away before they could hold their meeting. Michael Vincent Hardy from Foxford addressed the meeting: 'I went out in Easter Week and stood behind a rifle and I am prepared to do the same tomorrow if necessary.' A similar incident occurred in Kilkelly the following day. Later in June Hardy was charged in Castlebar with 'unlawful assembly and creating disaffection among his Majesty's subjects.' [71]

Kilmovee

Arthur Griffith was the principal speaker at a Sinn Féin meeting in Foxford on Easter Sunday, 31 March 1918, with about a thousand present, mostly young people, from Ballina, Bonniconlon, Swinford, Bohola etc.[72]

Griffith in Foxford

69 John Conroy to John Dillon, 9 Dec 1917 & 14 Feb & 20 July 1918, Dil. P. 6771
70 *W.P.* 23 Feb 1918
71 *W.P.* 29 June 1918
72 *W.P.* 6 April 1918

'Throughout the world little nations were coming in to their own and other nations almost forgotten had sprung back again into existence.' He warned England that she would never enforce conscription on Ireland 'The great bulk of the congregation at last Mass', according to the parish priest, 'returned home immediately and did not wait for the meeting,' and he thought there was no support from business people or farmers. Francis Ferran, the local doctor, a 'most rabid Sinn Féiner' was the prime mover behind the meeting. 'I am sure it is in view of the election that he is making the move.' [73] In fact, Ferran and three others were later charged in Ballina 'with taking part in an unlawful assembly'. When the judge offered to release them on bail, they refused and were removed to Sligo Jail. [74]

Ballaghaderreen Incident

In the early hours of Monday morning, 7 May 1917, Constables Francis Leahy and Joseph Sheridan were on patrol in Ballaghaderreen when they found Joseph Kelly with three companions 'behaving in a disorderly fashion' outside a pub.[75] The constables ordered them to go home and when Kelly refused they arrested him and took a revolver from his pocket. But he had a second revolver and shot Leahy in the thigh. The four were later courtmartialed and Kelly was sentenced to two years hard labour. After five months he went on hunger strike and was released, returning to a big welcome in Ballaghaderreen.[76] The two constables later claimed compensation in the Four Courts.

De Valera in Ballaghaderreen

Countess Markievicz, accompanied by among others Éamonn de Valera and Darrell Figgis, was given the freedom of Sligo on 22 July 1917. Later they went to Ballaghaderreen where they addressed a large Sinn Féin meeting with contingents and bands coming from a wide area. 'They stood for an absolutely free and independent Ireland.' De Valera told the crowd. 'They were not dreamers and meant to get what they wanted.' [77]

Dillon Elected Leader

John Redmond died on 6 March 1918 and less than a week later Dillon was elected chairman of the Irish Parliamentary Party. To Denis O'Hara Dillon was 'the leader who never lowered the flag. May he live to see it float over a free and independent Ireland.' Several priests from the diocese sent letters of congratulations, including Morrisroe. 'I hope your uncompromising and enlightened patriotism will rally all genuine Irishmen in sound policy for national rights.' [78]

73 Martin Henry to John Dillon, 25 Mar 1918, Dil. P. 6770
74 Others were William Sears, editor, *Enniscorthy Echo*, William O'Leary Curtiss, journalist, Dublin, Pádraig Ó Domhnalláin, *W.P.* 6 July 1918
75 Thomas Flannery, Henry McAlister and John Irwin. *S.C.* 12 May and 1 Dec 1917; *W.P.* 4 May 1918
76 *S.C.* 1 Dec 1917
77 *S.C.* 28 July 1917

Conscription had been introduced in England in January 1916 and there was a threat to impose it on Ireland at the end of that year. 'I am afraid the "Conscription" question is not yet fully laid to rest,' Denis O'Hara told Dillon, 'but if it is brought up, I hope you will be able to kill it ... The Party will recover its prestige in the House and in the country by taking a strong line and making an earnest fight.'[79] But the threat remained. By spring of 1918 war weariness was setting in and morale falling when the Germans launched an offensive on the western front. 150,000 extra troops were needed and Ireland was the only place where there were sufficient young men still available. A Conscription Bill was introduced in the House of Commons on 9 April and was passed within a week, despite the protests of the Irish Party. Dillon, the new leader, attacked it fiercely warning the government that they would not get the slightest reinforcement in this way. 'All Ireland as one man will rise against you.' He then led his colleagues out of the House as a protest.

Public meetings were held all over the diocese in the middle of April, with five on Easter Sunday alone in Foxford, Killasser, Kilmactigue, Largan and Tubbercurry. Martin Henry presided in Foxford where over 2,000 Volunteers paraded. One of the groups came on bicycles from Kiltimagh where about a hundred men and boys had assembled in Market Square 'after a bugle had sounded' and marched to Mass in military formation. Four of them were later charged in Castlebar with illegal drilling.[80] In Killasser, where the parish priest also presided, the notable feature of the meeting was how 'Nationalists and Sinn Féiners closed ranks in face of the common danger.' Thomas Quinn, Adm. Tourlestrane, waxed eloquent in Tubbercurry in the presence of 'several thousand' on the relationship between the priest and people:

> Through all the web of Irish history ... one golden thread has ever shone with undiminished lustre – the uncompromising, the unwavering, the unpurchaseable adherence of the Irish people to the Irish priest and the fidelity of the Irish priest to the Irish people ... All of nationality that Ireland has ... has now ... gathered itself together and identified itself with Ireland's irrepressible Catholicity ...

Both D. J. O'Grady, and his curate, Roger O'Donnell, addressed a meeting in Bunninadden. [81]

The parish priests of Attymass and Foxford as well as the parish priest and

78 James Henry, Adm. Ballaghaderreen, Martin Henry PP and James Spelman CC Foxford and Michael Keveney PP Charlestown. *W.P.* 16 & 23 Mar 1918
79 Denis O'Hara to John Dillon, 7 Nov 1916, Dil. P. 6769
80 John Walshe (bicycle mechanic), Patrick Jordan, Daniel Sheehy (solicitor's clerk), and William McHugh. *W.P.* 20 April 1918
81 *S.C.* 20 April 1918

curate of Bonniconlon were among the many priests on the platform at a huge anti-conscription meeting in Ballina on Easter Monday.[82] Easter Tuesday, 16 April, was Ballaghaderreen's turn and there were no less than fifteen priests on the platform with the administrator, James Gallagher, who presided.[83] Morrisroe, who was absent in Tuam, sent a telegram: 'Wholehearted sympathy with united action against mad proposal of government.' Over 2,000 men and 200 women, led by a number of bands, marched in military formation through the principal streets.

Mansion House Conference

An anti-conscription conference in the Mansion House, Dublin, on 18 April was attended by representatives of virtually the whole spectrum of Irish nationalism, including Dillon and Devlin as well as de Valera and Griffith, and a pledge was drafted binding those who took it to resist conscription 'by the most effective means at their disposal'. The standing committeee of the Irish bishops publicly proclaimed that the Irish people had the right to resist conscription. Prayers were offered at all Masses on Sunday, 21 April, asking God to save the country from the implementation of conscription and the anti-conscription pledge was taken by thousands of people outside the chapel doors. 'Defying the right of the government to enforce compulsory service in this country, we pledge ourselves solemnly to one another to resist conscription by the most effective means at our disposal.'

Pledges

Meetings were held in Swinford, Collooney, Ballysadare, Charlestown and many other parishes. Denis O'Hara believed that 'there never was more determination or more loyalty amongst the people.'[84] Michael Keveney, who presided at the meeting in Charlestown on Sunday 21 April, told the crowd that a collection would be taken up on the following Sunday in aid of the National Defence Fund, and that a Defence Committee would be elected by the people to give instructions how the people were to act if an attempt was made to enforce conscription. All day streams of people signed pledges and by Monday over 3,000 of both sexes had signed. [85] A considerable amount of money was collected in each parish. £700 was raised in Swinford, while the half-parish of Meelick collected £210. Tourlestrane, Kilmactigue and Largan combined raised £220.

---

82 Walter Henry PP Attymass, Martin Henry PP Foxford, Andrew Callaghan PP and Anthony Kirrane CC Bonniconlon. *W.P.* 20 April 1918

83 O'Beirne, James McKeon, Patrick J. Casey, John O'Dowd, Ambrose Blaine, O'Dea, Patrick O'Donnell, Eugene Foran, Roger McCarrick, Kelly, Philip J. Mulligan, Mullaney, Dominick McGowan, James O'Connor, Denis Gildea and Canon Geraghty. *W.P.* 20 April 1918

84 Denis O'Hara to John Dillon, 26 April 1918, Dil. P. 6769

85 *W.P.* 27 April 1918

John Dillon addressing
Anti-Conscription
meeting,
Ballaghaderreen 1918

A monster anti-conscription meeting was held in Ballaghaderreen on Sunday 5 May when Dillon and de Valera shared the same platform and Michael O'Flanagan, the curate in Crossna, was also among the speakers.[86] The administrator, James Gallagher, presided and the attendance was estimated at over 15,000. A letter was read from Morrisroe who called for unity: 'Whatever success has been achieved is due to the magnificent unity and solidarity that has prevailed ... May God grant that all contentious subjects be left in abeyance until the crisis is past.' Dillon took up the same theme: 'Drop all the quarrelling and stand together as one man in a frank and friendly spirit.' He advised the people to set up a committee attached to each chapel. 'The time may come when you may have to look for directions to the priests.' De Valera also emphasised the necessity for unity: 'There is no difference between Mr Dillon and his party and Sinn Féin as regards the necessity of fighting conscription.' This was to be the last time these two men were to share a common platform.

Ballaghaderreen Meeting

Demonstrations by women against conscription were held in Collooney and Curry on Sunday 9 June, and a large demonstration in Tubbercurry organised by Cumann na mBan on the following Sunday. A procession took place after Mass with women carrying flowers and singing hymns, which was followed by the Rosary and Benediction and hundreds of women signed the pledge.[87]

Womens' Action

86 *W.P.* 11 May 1918
87 *S.C.* 15 & 22 June 1918

Arrests

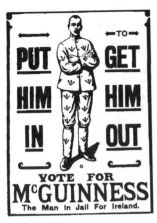

Election poster, 1917
(NLI)

Great War Ends

Because of the strength of the anti-conscription movement the government appointed Field-Marshall Lord French as Lord Lieutenant and shortly after he arrived in May he issued a proclamation and arrested anyone suspected of 'intriguing' with the Germans. Virtually the whole of the Sinn Féin leadership (with the exception of Michael Collins) were arrested on the night of 17 May. Seán Corcoran and Thomas Ruane from Kiltimagh were interned in Lincoln Jail, where de Valera was also a prisoner. John Shouldice of Ballaghaderreen was also arrested and, later on in June, Alec Mc Cabe was re-arrested and deported after completing a sentence he served in Sligo Jail in connection with land raids.[88] One of the first results of these arrests was to ensure the election from his prison cell of Arthur Griffith in the East Cavan by-election. 'Put him in to get him out' was the slogan which was later to become familiar in the general election at the end of that year. Early in July the government banned the Volunteers, the Gaelic League and any other organisation thought to have sympathies with Sinn Féin.

The Great War finally came to an end on 11 November 1918. The young men who had been cheered as they volunteered for the front a few years before, returned home to a changed Ireland where they were seldom welcomed as heroes. Many of them never returned. By the time the Great War ended on the 'eleventh hour of the eleventh month' in all about 430 young men from the diocese had died. [89] They were destined to be forgotten by all except their immediate families and their 'supreme sacrifice' never publicly acknowledged, as it has been ever since elsewhere in Europe for other nationalities who died. Swinford parish had the highest total of casualties with over fifty, followed by Ballaghadereen with almost forty and Ballymote with a few less. The vast majority of these deaths occurred on the western front in the killing fields of France and Flanders. There were in excess of sixty casualties in the diocese as a result of the Battle of the Somme which began on 1 July and ended on 18 November 1916. Swinford alone suffered twelve casualties, four on the very first day, two of whom were brothers, John and William Philbin. Four others, one each from Doocastle, Charlestown, Carracastle and Ballymote, were also killed on that day.[90] Ballaghaderreen lost eleven at the Somme and Ballymote eight.

88 *S.C.* 22 June 1918
89 See Appendix 44
90 Privates Thomas Gallagher and William Durkan, Swinford, Thomas Curley, Doocastle, Anthony McHale, Charlestown, Michael Finn, Carracastle and John Duffy, Ballymote

But there were some casualties further afield. The first battalion of the *Mesopotamia*
Connaught Rangers, made up almost exclusively of men from the West of
Ireland, received orders at the end of 1915 to leave the Western front for modern Iraq, called then Mesopotamia, which formed part of the Ottoman Turkish Empire. They embarked at Marseilles on 11 December and disembarked
almost a month later at Basra in the swamps of southern Iraq. From there
they set out on a six-day trip on paddle steamers up the Tigris River to the
front lines at Kut. For the next three months numerous and costly attempts
were made to break through the Turkish lines. About a dozen men from the
diocese died or were killed in action on this front, many of them in April
1916. At the end of that month a cholera epidemic broke out among the
ranks and within a few days most of the battalion was stricken. Private
Michael Downey of Charlestown was one of those who died. Just at this time
the sick and demoralised troops received their first news of the Easter Rising.

Elsewhere about seventeen died at Gallipoli and a further two in the adjoining Dardanelle Straits. Seven died at Salonika, a Greek port on the
Aegean Sea, all but one of them on the same day, 7 December 1915.[91] They
were all members of the fifth battalion of the Connaught Rangers. Two privates, Charles Kilpatrick, Ballymote, and Martin Walsh, Charlestown, died
in the Persian Gulf. Three others died in Egypt, Privates Michael Clarke,
Aclare, Michael John Judge, Ballymote and Acting-Sergeant Hubert Ginty,
Swinford. Judge was killed only two weeks before the war ended and Ginty
on 9 November 1918, a mere two days before the armistice.

The end of the war paved the way for calling a general election and polling *General Election*
date was set for 14 December. The prospect of nationalist fighting nationalist
in this election caused apprehension and dismay among some, particularly
churchmen and especially in the north, where unionists might be the victors
as a result. Cardinal Logue persuaded nationalists to divide such seats among
themselves. The Bishop of Raphoe, one of Dillon's oldest and warmest supporters, tried to persuade him to stand down all his candidates but Dillon
replied that the Irish people would regard such behaviour as cowardice in a
political leader.

Sinn Féin had nominated de Valera as their candidate in East Mayo to op- *Search for Unity*
pose Dillon, thus making this constituency the eye of the storm where the
two leaders met head-to-head. Denis O'Hara discussed the nationalist *versus*
nationalist prospect with Dean Connington and made a suggestion to Dillon:

91 Corporal Patrick Higgins and Privates Thomas Gara, Ballaghaderreen, Edward Mullen,
   Ballysadare, Thomas Kennedy, Curry, Thomas Leonard and John McHugh, Swinford and
   Charles Lundy, Tubbercurry

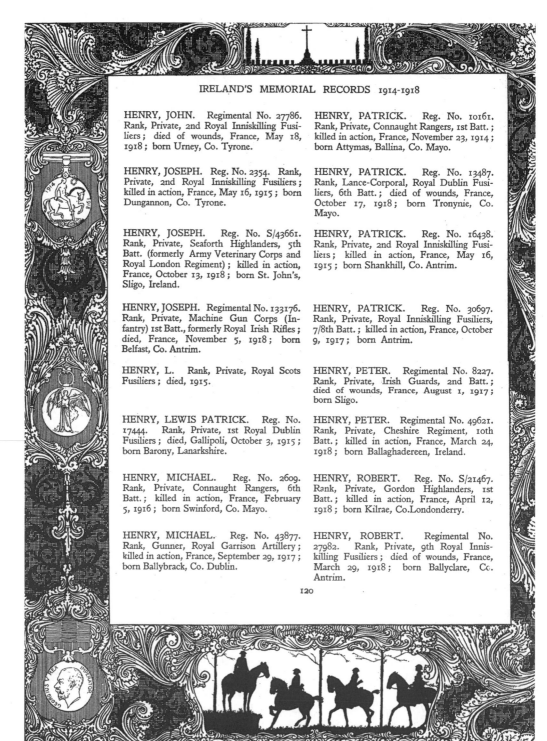

IRELAND'S MEMORIAL RECORDS 1914-1918

HENRY, JOHN.   Regimental No. 27786. Rank, Private, 2nd Royal Inniskilling Fusiliers; died of wounds, France, May 18, 1918; born Urney, Co. Tyrone.

HENRY, JOSEPH. Reg. No. 2354. Rank, Private, 2nd Royal Inniskilling Fusiliers; killed in action, France, May 16, 1915; born Dungannon, Co. Tyrone.

HENRY, JOSEPH.   Reg. No. S/43661. Rank, Private, Seaforth Highlanders, 5th Batt. (formerly Army Veterinary Corps and Royal London Regiment); killed in action, France, October 13, 1918; born St. John's, Sligo, Ireland.

HENRY, JOSEPH. Regimental No. 133176. Rank, Private, Machine Gun Corps (Infantry) 1st Batt., formerly Royal Irish Rifles; died, France, November 5, 1918; born Belfast, Co. Antrim.

HENRY, L.   Rank, Private, Royal Scots Fusiliers; died, 1915.

HENRY, LEWIS PATRICK.   Reg. No. 17444. Rank, Private, 1st Royal Dublin Fusiliers; died, Gallipoli, October 3, 1915; born Barony, Lanarkshire.

HENRY, MICHAEL.   Reg. No. 2609. Rank, Private, Connaught Rangers, 6th Batt.; killed in action, France, February 5, 1916; born Swinford, Co. Mayo.

HENRY, MICHAEL.   Reg. No. 43877. Rank, Gunner, Royal Garrison Artillery; killed in action, France, September 29, 1917; born Ballybrack, Co. Dublin.

HENRY, PATRICK.   Reg. No. 10161. Rank, Private, Connaught Rangers, 1st Batt.; killed in action, France, November 23, 1914; born Attymas, Ballina, Co. Mayo.

HENRY, PATRICK.   Reg. No. 13487. Rank, Lance-Corporal, Royal Dublin Fusiliers, 6th Batt.; died of wounds, France, October 17, 1918; born Tronynie, Co. Mayo.

HENRY, PATRICK.   Reg. No. 16438. Rank, Private, 2nd Royal Inniskilling Fusiliers; killed in action, France, May 16, 1915; born Shankhill, Co. Antrim.

HENRY, PATRICK.   Reg. No. 30697. Rank, Private, Royal Inniskilling Fusiliers, 7/8th Batt.; killed in action, France, October 9, 1917; born Antrim.

HENRY, PETER.   Regimental No. 8227. Rank, Private, Irish Guards, 2nd Batt.; died of wounds, France, August 1, 1917; born Sligo.

HENRY, PETER.   Regimental No. 49621. Rank, Private, Cheshire Regiment, 10th Batt.; killed in action, France, March 24, 1918; born Ballaghadereen, Ireland.

HENRY, ROBERT.   Reg. No. S/21467. Rank, Private, Gordon Highlanders, 1st Batt.; killed in action, France, April 12, 1918; born Kilrae, Co.Londonderry.

HENRY, ROBERT.   Regimental No. 27982. Rank, Private, 9th Royal Inniskilling Fusiliers; died of wounds, France, March 29, 1918; born Ballyclare, Co. Antrim.

120

What the Dean and myself proposed was that the priests of this diocese, and not merely of East Mayo, should be asked their opinions regarding the advisability of having a meeting to pass a resolution calling upon the leading nationalist politicians to come together to formulate a common policy. I had hoped that we would agree in suggesting that two or three bishops, six priests and twenty laymen, ten from each party, would be asked to form a committee for this purpose.[92]

At the time of writing only half of the priests had answered though replies from East Mayo had been received from all except three.[93]

Every one who wrote approved of the suggestion saying it may do good, it can do no harm. It would make no matter who were the representative laymen selected – whether they were Sinn Féiners or supporters of the Party – there would be no party politics allowed to be discussed. The only question to be considered would be the resolution calling on the leading nationalists to come together. If all, or practically all, approve I think we should give them an opportunity of coming together though there will be little time now for doing this.

Denis warned Dillon that he would have a very small following in the next parliament and that very few of the Party would survive in the south and west:

There is scarcely a safe seat in the west. The young fellows and the young girls will in almost every place go in for Sinn Féin and will all work everything, whilst the others will do little or nothing except perhaps to vote ... You should at your first meeting in Dublin or elsewhere say that you had letters from all parts of the country saying that all sections in the country wished to have and longed for unity and that as far as you are concerned, there was nothing you so much desired, and that if a few of the bishops would only take it into their hands to help in selecting those who should be likely to bring about this unity, you would have some hope of success. Make it clear, in any case, that if there is to be a fight amongst nationalists, the fault is not yours.

Martin Henry of Foxford expressed disappointment that no united action was arranged. 'Could not the Irish Party remain from the House of Commons for a limited time, say during the present government.'[94] He may have thought that to adopt the abstentionist policy of Sinn Féin would improve the electoral prospects of the Party. The usual Party convention was to be

92 Denis O'Hara to John Dillon, 16 Nov 1918, Dil. P. 6769
93 Philip Mulligan and his curate in Carracastle and James Jordan CC Killasser.
94 Martin Henry to John Dillon, 20 Nov 1918, Dil. P. 6770

held in Swinford but Dillon's old friend, Dean Connington, refused to preside telling Denis O'Hara that he had made up his mind not to take any part in the election, as his people were so divided amongst themselves. [95] Morrisroe, according to Denis, had no intention of preventing priests joining in a joint address with parish priests to the electors, as was wrongly reported. [96]

Election Campaign Dillon began his campaign in East Mayo at the end of November and soon got a foretaste of how bitter the contest was going to be. He was greeted as usual at the station in Ballaghaderreen by several hundreds of his supporters and a few bands who paraded him to his residence. However, green republican flags were waved from some houses along the route and there were cries of 'Up de Valera'. The next day, Sunday 24 November, he opened his campaign in Kilmovee with Roger O'Hara in the chair and joined on the platform by five other priests including his brother, Denis. [97] Dillon spoke of the part he had played on behalf of the prisoners after the Easter Rising: 'When the Sinn Féiners got into jail they came to me and I got them out. Sixteen men from Ballaghaderreen were locked up and ill-treated in an English jail. They wrote to me ... I never rested until I got them out of jail.' He played a major part in preventing the execution of de Valera who 'would have been lying in unconsecrated ground were it not for me. He was one of twenty-five men condemned to death and they were determined to shoot him when I crossed over to London in 1916, and were it not for Redmond and myself, he and twenty-five others would have been shot.'

Dillon went on to contrast the achievements of the Irish Party over thirty-five years with the virginal record of Sinn Féin. 'The Sinn Féin policy had been built and founded upon misrepresentation and lies, and it brought nothing to the people from its outset but misfortune and misery and suffering.' Denis O'Hara told the meeting that Eoin MacNeill, Arthur Griffith and Éamon de Valera were opposed to the Easter Week rebellion 'but it was only fair to Mr de Valera to say that when he found his friends in trouble he thought it would be too bad that he would not be amongst them.' Michael Keveney of Charlestown also spoke.

At the same time, about a hundred yards from where Dillon was speaking, Sinn Féin held a meeting of de Valera's supporters. The main speaker was Pádraig Ó Domhnalláin who spoke first in Irish. 'Ireland would never be at peace until she was restored to her original status as a free and independent

95 Denis O'Hara to John Dillon, 17 Nov 1918, Dil. P. 6769
96 Denis O'Hara to John Dillon (telegram), 21 Nov 1918
97 Michael Keveney PP Charlestown, James Gallagher Adm Ballaghaderreen, Patrick Boland CC Carracastle and William Flynn CC Kilmovee. *W.P.* 30 Nov 1918; see also *Kiltimagh*, p 165

nation.' He assured his audience that de Valera and Sinn Féin had the support of the vast majority of the Irish people including 'many bishops, priests and thinking people'. It must have been a deep personal disappointment to Dillon when Michael Davitt's son, Cahir, addressed a Sinn Féin meeting in Ballaghaderreen and spoke strongly in favour of de Valera. [98]

Six parish priests joined Dillon on the stage in Swinford Town Hall on Tuesday 26 November.[99] Some Sinn Féiners entered the hall to try to prevent the speeches and Thomas Campbell, a solicitor, jumped up on the stage and 'vigorously heckled' Dillon. Dillon agreed to allow Campbell speak after he himself had finished but when Campbell did speak, he went on for over thirty minutes. Denis O'Hara was also heckled but gave as good as he got. 'He had spoken in Swinford when soldiers were lined up on the streets and when some of those interrupting were in their cradles. He had been identified for the last forty years with every movement for the good of the country.' He recounted what Michael Davitt had told him after coming back from a meeting in Swinford. 'I declare to you, Father Denis O'Hara, some of them are not worth fighting for. Of all the places I went, I never saw such blackguardism – I was pelted with stones – as in the town of Swinford.' O'Hara 'was sorry to say a few of that kind were still here.' The local curate, Michael Connolly, himself an enthusiastic Sinn Féiner, unsuccessfully tried to persuade the hecklers to desist, telling them: 'We have no free country if we have no free speech.'

Swinford Meeting

The parish priest, Peter Cawley, spoke in Straide at a meeting of Dillon's supporters on 1 December of the dissension among nationalists caused by Sinn Féin. 'Sinn Féiners said they have given a new soul to Ireland. They have given the soul of dissension. They had disturbed the peace of districts. They had entered into the family circle and divided father and son.' Denis O'Hara addressed a large meeting of his parishioners in Kiltimagh on the same day: 'Mr de Valera told them the only hope for Ireland was in the armed young men of the country. Was there any sane man in Ireland today who thought Ireland could win absolute independence from England by force of arms?' He underlined the enormous contribution Dillon had made over the years: 'He was four times in jail, had collected thousands of pounds in America to relieve distress in the country and sustain the national movement. He had fought with Davitt and Parnell and had assisted in procuring for Ireland the great reforms which had been won during the past thirty-five years.' [100]

Straide and Kiltimagh

98 *S.C.* 7 Dec 1918
99 *W.P.* 30 Nov 1918
100 *W.P.* 7 Dec 1918

Nominations

The nominations for East Mayo took place in Swinford on Wednesday 4 December and twenty-two nomination papers were handed in on behalf of Dillon and seventy-five for de Valera. [101] Dillon was proposed by Denis O'Hara and seconded by Dr Madden, Kiltimagh, while other nomination papers were signed by the parish priests of Kilmovee, Killasser, Straide and Foxford as well as the administrator in Ballaghaderreen and the curate in Carracastle.[102] De Valera was proposed by the Swinford curate, Michael Connolly, and Pat O'Hara, Swinford and was represented also by Connolly as well as Thomas Campbell and T. B. Doyle, Ballaghaderreen. The curate in Foxford, Denis Gildea, delivered a speech in Swinford on that day in favour of de Valera's candidacy which was later printed as a leaflet and circulated in the constituency.[103] In South-Sligo the sitting MP, John O'Dowd, who was proposed by James Daly, parish priest of Mullinabreena, and Thomas Quinn of Tourlestrane, was nominated for the Irish Party while about sixty papers were handed in for the Sinn Féin candidate, Alec McCabe, one of whose proposers was the parish priest of Keash, P. J. O'Grady.[104]

Charlestown

Two meetings were held in Charlestown, one on Sunday 8 December and the other on the following Wednesday.[105] Michael Keveney addressed the first and was subjected to several interruptions from Sinn Féiners. He invited questions from them and said in reply that 'his honest belief was that all this talk about an Irish Republic was simple moonshine ... He could not understand under the sun what was to be gained by abstention. If the Sinn Féiners win a majority in this election they will get you, not a Republic, but martial law and possibly another rebellion.'

Priests' Warning

Nine of the eleven parish priests from the East Mayo side of the diocese signed a resolution warning the people about the disastrous results of the Sinn Féin policy of abstention from the British parliament.[106] Firstly, Ireland would be replanted with soldiers, secondly, Carson and his followers would be left to represent Ireland at the Peace Conference in Versailles and finally, it would result in the imposition of 'Godless education' on the country.

Intimidation

Dillon was already becoming aware of what he called 'organised intimidation' by supporters of Sinn Féin. 'Young bands of roughs are going round the roads at night shouting that they will burn down any house that votes Dillon,

101 *W.P.* 7 Dec 1918
102 Roger O'Hara, John J. McDonnell, Peter Cawley, Martin Henry, James Gallagher and Patrick Boland
103 *W.P.* 12 Dec 1918
104 *S.C.* 7 Dec 1918
105 *W.P.* 14 Dec 19186
106 Of the remaining two, Dean Connington remained aloof and neutral, as he had promised, while Mulligan of Carracastle was a committed Sinn Féiner

and threatening to destroy cattle ...'[107] One of Dillon's correspondents, refer- ring to what he called 'the Swinford blackguardism' thought it might be counter-productive. 'I believe it has done more good than harm.' In some in- stances the Irish Party supporters gave as good as they got. The same corre- spondent described to Dillon what happened when Sinn Féiners from Fox- ford, Ballyvary and surrounding areas attempted to hold a meeting in Straide: 'They received cruel usage and none of them returned the road they came. I'm told that pipes, money and coats are to be found from Straide to Ballylahan Bridge. One coat was made into stripes and tarred with "vote for John Dillon" and hung up. All the walls about Straide and Ballylahon are tarred with "Vote for John Dillon".'[108]

While almost all the complaints about Sinn Féin intimidation came from Irish Party activists, there can be little doubt there was some justification for them. Keveney warned Dillon not to come to the meeting in Charlestown as it would almost certainly be broken up. 'Thousands would come from Curry, Carracastle and Swinford to affect this.' In spite of this warning and with characteristic disregard for his own safety, Dillon came. Keveney had cau- tioned Dillon not to infer from these threats that his prospects at the poll were not good. 'Young fellows who would take part in this opposition have sent their mothers to assure me that notwithstanding they will vote for you.' Keveney had asked the Under Secretary to send a strong military force to Charlestown and urged Dillon to get military forces sent all over the division on polling day, Saturday 14 December. 'There will be intimidation of a most formidable kind employed throughout the division on Saturday.'[109] The same story came from Kiltimagh where Denis O'Hara reported that the people 'are frightened out of their minds and the young fellows are going round every night ... threatening them, if they don't vote Sinn Féin.' The parish priest of Killasser thought it absolutely necessary that there should be mili- tary patrols along the roads on polling day and particularly at all the cross- roads. Denis O'Hara thought that five or six motor cyclists or even three or four at every crossroads would be enough.[110]

The Sinn Féin campaign was superbly organised. Apart from the numer- ous Sinn Féin clubs that existed in every parish, umbrella bodies were estab- lished to co-ordinate the campaign. The East-Mayo Sinn Féin Executive had been formed in Swinford Town Hall on 10 November 1917, and the South-

Sinn Féin Campaign

107 John Dillon to T. P. O'Connor, 6 Dec 1918, qtd Lyons, p 451
108 John Conroy to John Dillon, 28 & 29 Nov 1918, Dil. P. 6771
109 Michael Keveney to John Dillon, 3 & 7 Dec 1918, Dil. P. 6770
110 Denis O'Hara to John Dillon, 9 & 10 Dec 1918, Dil. P. 6769

Sligo Sinn Féin Alliance in the other constituency in the diocese.[111] At the very end of that year, John Shouldice presided at a meeting of the East-Mayo Convention where twenty Sinn Féin clubs were represented. The Central Council of Sinn Féin had prepared a plebiscite of the adult suffrage and issued books, each containing 180 names. Pat O'Hara told the Executive that a thorough organisation was essential in East-Mayo because they would have to confront John Dillon, 'none of your two-pence-halfpenny MPs'.[112] John Shouldice was appointed in January 1918 director of elections in the constituency, which was divided into four sections with a separate organiser for each section.[113] The organisers were to arrange that every parish had canvassers to ask every person of eighteen years and over, male and female, Catholic and Protestant, Sinn Féiner, Nationalist and Unionist, to sign.

Polling Day   There were 21,635 voters on the electoral register, of whom 8,237 were women who were voting for the very first time in this election. A number of violent incidents were reported on polling day, Saturday 14 December.[114] Nationalist voters and election agents in East-Mayo were sometimes attacked, and large boulders and bottles placed on the roads leading to Charlestown to impede motor cars carrying Dillon supporters to the polling station, while the tyres of some cars were slashed. In Swinford and Foxford the drivers of such cars were attacked and stoned. Eight Sinn Féiners were reported to be carrying 'serviceable sticks' as they patrolled the streets of Ballaghaderreen, although the administrator, James Gallagher, congratulated the people for keeping the polling trouble-free. Roger O'Hara, now over eighty years old, drove into Ballaghaderreen at the head of a large body of voters from Kilmovee where Dillon was thought to have secured a substantial majority.

Elsewhere the story was very different. On the very day of polling Denis broke the bad news to Dillon:[115]

> I hope they have not done quite as badly elsewhere as we have done here. I am sorry to say we could not have done worse. I did think we might get something like half but we are far from this. They were simply terrorised into voting Sinn Féin. One man told me he was met by two men on his

---

111 *W.P.* 17 Nov 1917
112 *W.P.* 5 Jan 1918
113 Frank Shouldice, Ballaghaderreen for Ballaghaderreen, Kilmovee, Carracastle and Rooskey: P. Henry, Swinford, for Swinford, Killasser, Charlestown, Meelick & Midfield. Kiltimagh Sinn Féin club was to appoint an organiser for Kiltimagh, Bohola, Ballyvary, Straide South, Kilkelly and Glan, and the Foxford club to appoint an organiser for Foxford and Straide North. *W.P.* 2 Feb & 2 Mar 1918. See Appendix 45 for names of officers and delegates at East-Mayo Executive in Swinford on 24 Feb 1918
114 *W.P.* 21 and 28 Dec 1918
115 Denis O'Hara to John Dillon, 14 Dec 1918, Dil. P. 6769

way to vote, each of whom told him his life would be a short one if he did not vote for de Valera. The cry of 'vote for the man in prison' and 'vote for de Valera and no taxation' had the desired effect ... it is sickening and disheartening to see what condition the country is in after forty years of uphill fight.

One Sinn Féin activist remembered a different picture of polling day in Kiltimagh, when women voted for the first time. 'Everywhere there was order and good humour. The few known supporters of Dillon received friendly greetings from their opponents.'[116]

Two days later O'Hara, confirming the news that Dillon had done badly in Kiltimagh, commented on the remarkable number of people who had voted as illiterates: 'All the old people had voted as illiterates and everyone of them almost voted Sinn Féin. They were terrorised no doubt by the young people, but one would expect some little gratitude and some little pluck.' By voting as illiterates they had to declare their preference aloud and thus it would become public knowlege and prevent possible future harassment. O'Hara claimed that over 500 voted as illiterates in the Kiltimagh polling station and well over 2,000 in the whole electoral division. 'There is no better proof of the intimidation practised at the election.'[117] 2,407 polled in Kiltimagh and O'Hara thought that Dillon did not get more than 500. 'You got scarcely one at all from Bohola parish and they had more than a third of the whole.'[118] Of the 1,103 voters on the register there only 615 voted. 'I think we may take it that most of the voters who did not come to the poll stopped away on account of threats of some kind, and that they were supporters of yours.'[119] An 'abnormal number of illiterate voters' were reported in Charlestown where de Valera gained a substantial majority. [120]

Illiterates

The counting took place in the Marist Brothers' school in Swinford on Saturday 27 December and among the counting agents for de Valera were the Elphin priest, Michael O'Flanagan, and Dr Ferran of Foxford.[121] De Valera received 8,975 votes and Dillon 4,514, giving Sinn Féin an almost two-to-one majority.

Results

116 L. McManus, *White Light and Flame*, qtd in *Kiltimagh*, p 166
117 Denis O'Hara, 26 Dec 1918, Dil. P. 6769
118 Denis O'Hara to John Dillon, 19 Dec 1918, Dil. P. 6769
119 Denis O'Hara to John Dillon, n.d. 1918, Dil. P. 6769
120 *W.P.* 21 & 28 Dec 1916
121 Others were P. Beirne, Ballaghaderreen and P. Henry, Swinford. Dillon's counting agents were J. J. Morrin, solicitor, Swinford and P. O'Donnell, Charlestown. The election agents were T. Campbell for de Valera and P. J. Mulligan for Dillon. *W.P.* 4 Jan 1919

Alec McCabe

In South Sligo, the other constituency in the diocese, Alec McCabe won a decisive victory, when Sinn Féin garnered eighty-two per cent of the votes. He was a native of Keash where he had been principal of Drumnagranchy national school until he was dismissed because of his political activities. A member of the Supreme Council of the IRB in 1914, he was arrested in November 1915 at Sligo station where he was found to be in possession of explosives. At his subsequent trial he was found not guilty by a jury and returned home to a hero's welcome. He was prominent in organising Sinn Féin clubs all over the constituency and also spearheaded a conacre campaign. Early in 1918 about 500 Sinn Féiners, led by three bands, marched from Bunninadden for about twenty miles where McCabe commandeered, in the name of the Irish Republic, portions of grazing farms to let at £2 or £3 an Irish acre. For these and other activities, he and others were arrested, tried and detained in Sligo Jail and on completion of his sentence McCabe was re-arrested and deported.

Alec McCabe

While he was interned in England a large party of young men from the Ballymote district lifted and pitted his potato crop at the end of October, the third time there was such a gathering. In the week leading up to polling-day, Michael O'Flanagan from Elphin addressed a Sinn Féin meeting in Gurteen and Pádraig Ó Domhnalláin a similar one in Mullinabreena in support of McCabe.[122]

John O'Dowd

The defeated candidate was the incumbent John O'Dowd, a merchant in Bunninadden whose son was a priest in the diocese. He was assaulted on the eve of polling-day and wounded, requiring four stitches in his head. Four men were subsequently charged at a special court in Sligo 'with divers other evilly-disposed persons to the number of five or six' who were armed with stones and other offensive weapons on the occasion.[123] O'Dowd later claimed that a 'murderous attack' was made upon him which almost cost him his life because he refused to withdraw from the contest and leave Sinn Féin unopposed. 'I was subjected to a symptomatic boycott by the Sinn Féiners for years afterwards. My house and premises were raided and robbed five or six times and cash and goods taken on each occasion.' Some years later and in straitened circumstances, the former Irish Party MP was reduced to the indignity of writing to Dillon, his former colleague, seeking a handout. Dillon sent him £20.[124]

Immaculate Heart of Mary, pray
for us. 100 days.

Sweet Heart of Jesus, be
Thou my love, 300 days,
each time.

Sacred Heart of Jesus, I
place all my trust in
Thee. 300 days.

In Loving Memory of
VERY REV.
John Canon O'Dowd, P.P.,
FOXFORD,
WHO DIED
On the 7th January, 1949

122 *S.C.* 16 Feb, 22 June, 2 Nov & 14 Dec 1918
123 Andrew Grehan and John Quigley, Rathnarrow, Patrick Richardson and Martin Foley, Ballinacarrow. *S.C.* 21 Dec & *W.P.* 21 & 28 Dec 1918
124 John O'Dowd to John Dillon, 24 July 1924, Dil. P. 6759

Countrywide, the Irish Party was almost entirely wiped out, reduced to only six seats, five of these in Ulster, four of which were contests between Unionists and Nationalists. The fifth was in West Belfast where Joe Devlin defeated de Valera by more than 3,000 votes. Of 105 seats Sinn Féin won seventy-three. Such a decisive victory for Sinn Féin and such a massive repudiation of the Irish Party cannot be explained in terms of the superior organisation of the Sinn Féin campaign, of which there can be no doubt, or by the use of intimidation which there certainly was. It was now almost forty years since the heady days of the Land League when John Dillon and Denis O'Hara first emerged into the limelight. The younger generation, both of priests and lay people, who played such a crucial role in the Sinn Féin victory, had not forgotten what Dillon and O'Hara achieved then and later. They were too young to have ever known about it.

Decisive Victory

De Valera addressing
Anti-Conscription
meeting,
Ballaghaderreen 1918

CHAPTER EIGHTEEN

The 'War' of Independence, 1919-21

The Dáil
In January 1919 the newly elected Sinn Féin members, following Arthur Griffith's doctrine of abstention, refused to take their seats in Westminster and instead assembled in Dublin, but because thirty-four of them were still in prison there were only twenty-seven present at this first meeting of the Dáil. The Dáil re-assembled on the the first of April and by then some of the prisoners, including de Valera, had escaped, while the remaining prisoners were released by the government in March. As a result there were fifty-two members present. De Valera was elected prime minister or 'president', with eight other ministers including Griffith, Michael Collins, Cathal Brugha, Countess Markievicz, Count Plunkett, W. T. Cosgrave and Eoin MacNeill. A number of meetings were held until the government suppressed the Dáil in September 1919. Cosgrave, who was Minister of Local Government, set about persuading county and borough councils to transfer their allegiance to Dáil Éireann, which soon became a reality when Sinn Féin secured a dominant majority on these councils as a result of the local elections of 1919.

Sinn Féin Courts
The Dáil also created the so-called Sinn Féin courts to arbitrate in difficult cases, especially dealing with land disputes, and by the summer of 1921, several hundreds of them were functioning throughout the country. Such courts were reported to be operating in Charlestown and Foxford in the summer of 1920 where 'most of the litigants have decided to submit their grievances to Sinn Féin courts'. The same report stated that 'similar tribunals are functioning with the greatest success' in many other districts in East Mayo. In Swinford the Volunteers picketed the Quarter Sessions and 'induced many litigants to submit their cases to Sinn Féin courts' while such courts were said to be the 'norm' in Ballaghaderreen. [1]

Volunteer Policing
By then local branches of the Volunteers had assumed the role of policing communities. 'Ireland sober, Ireland free' was their maxim and they raided several houses in Aclare and arrested notable poteen-makers and the following Sunday displayed some twenty stills outside the chapel gates. A typewritten notice was posted up in Ballaghaderreen in May 1920 stating that anybody

---

1 *W.P.* 5 June, 3 & 17 July 1920

guilty of robbery of any kind, of raiding private houses for arms, of nocturnal visits to houses for the purpose of intimidation and of sending threatening letters, would be dealt with by the IRA.[2] About the same time there were reports that the IRA were apprehending petty thieves in Ballymote. [3] Later in the year three men were arrested in Tubbercurry by the Volunteers and charged with attempting to set fire to the Protestant church. The first one arrested was taken blind-folded in a car and arraigned before a republican courtmartial where he confessed and implicated the others. The accused were fined and the money given to Rev Mr Beckett to be used for whatever charitable purpose he wished. [4]

As a result of such developments, the RIC became demoralised and at the beginning of 1920 the government began to recruit a new body to support them which became notorious as the 'Black and Tans', a name derived from a famous hunt in the south of Ireland. Originally they were intended to fill the vacancies which amounted to about 1,500 but as the situation deteriorated their numbers increased and about 7,000 had been taken into service by the end of August 1922. They were police, not soldiers, but not surprisingly they attracted many ex-soldiers who had been disbanded at the end of the World War. *'Black and Tans'*

A second body – consisting for the most part of ex-officers – were recruited in the summer of 1920 as an auxiliary division of the RIC and by the following summer they amounted to about 1,500. They were popularly known as the 'Auxiliaries' and almost as equally detested by the people as the Black and Tans. This hatred was by no means universal, as one IRA activist described the Auxiliaries in Tubbercurry as 'a decent lot' and another declared that 'the Tans walked out with the best looking girls from the village of Kiltimagh.' [5] In all, the combined government forces amounted to about 40,000. *Auxiliaries*

Against these were ranged about 15,000 Volunteers who after 1916 were heavily infiltrated by the IRB. Michael Collins estimated that the active element among the Volunteers, known as the IRA – the Irish Republican Army – never amounted to more than 3,000. The clashes between IRA and the government forces were sporadic and fragmented, and in the diocese of Achonry scarcely deserves the name of 'war' at all. There, most of the summer and autumn was spent holding *aeraíochtaí* in various parishes, and most police activity in Sligo, in fact, consisted in futile attempts to enforce bans on *Aeraíochtaí*

2   *W.P.* 22 May 1920
3   Farry, *The Aftermath of Revolution, Sligo 1921-23*, p 10
4   *W.P.* 2 Oct 1920
5   AD UCD O'Malley Notebooks / P 17b / 109 & 133 (Maurteen Brennan and Tom Carney)

aeraíochtaí and meetings 'likely to cause disaffection'.[6] An *aeraíocht* in Benada on Sunday 28 June was addressed by Prof Ó Domhnalláin and Alec McCabe TD. [7]

Mrs Pearse

Mrs Pearse, the mother of Patrick and Willie, was the guest of honour on Sunday 7 September at Foxford *aeraíocht* which was in aid of St Enda's, Rathfarnham, the school founded by Patrick.[8] Martin Henry, who introduced Mrs Pearse, said he knew her and her sons for a long time and had dined in her house. A newspaper report claimed that Patrick Pearse had often visited Foxford and that Willie had built and designed the high altar in the parish church. [9] Mrs Pearse gave a lecture in Swinford Town Hall the following Saturday and attended the Ballaghaderreen *aeraíocht* the next day. [10]Large numbers of older people from the mountain side who spoke Irish attended Aclare *aeraíocht* on 12 September and the curate in Bonniconlon, Anthony Kirrane, addressed them in Irish. 'The two fights for freedom and the language must go side by side and should be found to strengthen and reinforce each other at every step.' The local Volunteer Corps kept order. [11]

Gurteen Incident

The first violent incident in the diocese was recorded in Gurteen on Sunday 16 November 1919. Pádraic O'Hegerty, a Sinn Féiner from Mayo, accompanied by Dr D. J. Doyle, left Gurteen by car to address a meeting in Cloonloo and later another meeting at Killaraght chapel. On returning the RIC attempted to stop the car but the owner, Dominick O'Grady, drove the car at high speed and broke through the police barrier. The retreating car was riddled with bullets and Dr Doyle was wounded in the leg, while O'Hegarty and the other occupant, Jim Hunt of Moygara, escaped injury. O'Grady deposited his passengers in Gurteen and went on to Edmondstown, where he had been commissioned to bring Bishop Morrisroe to Ballymote. On returning to Gurteen, O'Grady was warned that six policemen were 'approaching on bicycles at high speed' and jumping back into his car made another high speed escape. The next day Jim Hunt was arrested and conveyed under escort to Sligo. [12]

Post Office Raids

Most local IRA activity consisted in raids on post offices and mail trains. Half a dozen armed men held up the mail train between Ballaghaderreen and

6 Michael Farry, *The Aftermath of Revolution, Sligo 1921-23*, p 11
7 *W.P.* 12 July 1919. Another *aeraíocht* was held in Callow about the same time
8 Speeches also from T. B. Doyle, Ballaghaderreen, Michael O'Hara CC Bohola, Denis Gildea CC Foxford and Dr Ferran, Foxford. *W.P.* 13 Sept 1919
9 *W.P.* 6 Sept 1919
10 *W.P.* 20 Sept 1919
11 *W.P.* 25 Sept 1920. Kirrane later entered the Redemptorist order
12 *W.P.* 22 Nov 1919: AD UCD, O'Malley Notebooks, P17b/133

Kilfree Junction at Island Road Station on 8 May 1920, rifled the mail bags and seized all letters addressed to the Ballagaderreen police. Cloontia, Bunninadden and Kilmovee post offices were raided on 14 May and £20 and £32 pension money taken by armed men. Twenty masked men took £40 from Carracastle PO while the post offices in Lisacul and Bohola had £60 and £25 taken. Later that summer a train was held up at Carramore Station and a large box addressed to the military in Tubbercurry seized, while the mail train from Ballymote to Aclare was also raided and RIC correspondence taken.[13]

Attempts were made by the IRA to force shopkeepers to refuse to serve the military and RIC but these were largely futile for the simple reason that the latter had more firepower than the IRA. In the summer of 1920 traders in Ballaghaderreen were warned by the IRA. against serving the military and on one occasion on being refused in a pub, the military drew their own pints. Duff's and Flannery's were visited and warned that, if they did not serve goods to the military and RIC their premises would be occupied by the military within twenty-four hours.[14] Notices were put up in Tubbercurry in September warning people not to supply goods to the police.[15] Pressure was also put on railwaymen to refuse to work trains carrying munitions or armed police or military. As a result of such refusals some of them were dismissed causing them considerable hardship and collections for them were taken up in Curry and Cloonacool.[16]

Military Boycotted

Remote RIC barracks were particularly vulnerable to attacks by the IRA and the authorities decided to withdraw their personnel and concentrate them on better-protected barracks in the main towns. Often abandoned barracks like Bohola were then burned down by the IRA. Described as a 'military manoeuvre involving several Volunteer companies' which even included setting up roadblocks 'on the night of the eve of Ascension Thursday, May 1920', Bohola turned out to be something of a botched affair. [17] Despite having been advised to use paraffin oil, petrol was sprayed over a wooden floor in a room in the barracks where a fire was burning. An explosion followed and three of the Volunteers were badly burnt.[18] Michael Collins (whose sister was married in Bohola) was said to have been annoyed when he heard of the incident. Aclare, Curry and Cloonacool barracks were closed early in August and

RIC Barracks Attacked

13 *W.P.* 15 May, 31 July & 14 Aug 1920
14 *W.P.* 17 July 1920
15 Farry, *Aftermath*, p 10
16 *W.P.* 31 July 1920
17 Statement of Senator Sean T. Ruane for the Bureau of Military History, in *Kiltimagh*, p 173
18 Seán Corcoran, Tom Carney and – Mooney. Corcoran and Mooney were treated by Dr Ferran of Foxford and Carney was treated by Dr M. Staunton, Swinford.

Frank Carty

the policemen were brought in to Tubbercurry, which now had a complement of almost thirty. Aclare barracks was burned down the night the twelve policemen left. [19] In November the Inspector-General was awarded £1,000 compensation at Castlebar Quarter Sessions for the destruction of Kiltimagh RIC barracks. [20]

Some members of the RIC were supportive of the local IRA. Michael McHugh of Foxford who had been six years in the force by August 1920, was described in an IRA report as 'perfectly dissatisfied with his present status and would resign but for the greater good will remain on.'[21] The same report mentioned two constables in Swinford, Mullaney and Laing, who were 'anxious to help'.

Frank Carty Rescued

A reported one hundred IRA from Tubbercurry, Collooney and Ballymote as well as Sligo town spectacularly rescued Frank Carty from Sligo jail on Saturday 26 June.[22] The locks on the front gate were broken with crowbars, the warder held up and forced to hand over the keys and Carty sprung from his cell. Carty was born in Clooncunny, Mullinabreena, joined the Volunteers in 1914 and became prominent in the Tubbercurry area. He took part in a raid for arms on Perceval's at Templehouse for which he was later arrested.

Swinford Hold-Up

At the end of June, two members of Swinford RIC, Constables Scully and Gleeson, went to Kilkelly barracks to relieve Constable Laing. On returning that night, Gleeson and Laing were attacked at Derryronane by armed and masked men, thrown off their bicycles, relieved of their revolvers, ammunition and handcuffs, and locked up in a nearby barn from which they were released an hour later by some locals. [23]Possibly as a result of this incident a military detachment arrived in Swinford in the middle of July which, it was alleged, made 'an unprovoked attack on the inhabitants of the town, letting volley after volley of rifle fire on the houses, terrifying women and children.' [24]

---

19 AD UCD O'Malley Notebooks / P 17b / 137 (Jack Brennan); *W.P.* 14 Aug 1920
20 *Kiltimagh*, p 173
21 AD UCD P7 /A / 40
22 *W.P.* 3 July 1920; AD UCD, O'Malley Notebooks/ P17b/133 & 137 (Tom Scanlon and Jack Brennan)
23 *W.P.* 10 July 1920
24 Letter to the editor of the *Irish Independent*, signed by J. J. Horkan and A. Flatley, secretaries of the Swinford Traders' Association, reproduced in *W.P.* 24 July 1920

A similar incident occurred in July at Curry. [25] Three policemen were return-*Curry Hold-Up* ing by train from Sligo where they had given evidence against Tom Dunleavy who had been arrested in Kilmovee. The train was surrounded by half a dozen armed and masked men at Curry station and the policemen were taken off, stripped of their caps, belts, tunics and batons, and detained for some hours in a disused house. Later they were obliged to walk back to Tub-bercurry in shirts and trousers.

At Carricknagat, Ballysadare near the Teeling monument, on 2 August *Carricknagat* 1920 about thirty IRA from the Tubbercurry, Collooney and Ballymote bat-*Ambush* talions under Frank Carty, ambushed an RIC party cycling from Bunninad-den to a court in Tubbercurry. Two policemen were captured and locked up in an outhouse. Among those who took part in the ambush were Maurteen Brennan, Mick O'Hara from Aclare, Tom Scanlon, Harry Benson and Paddy Gilmartin. [26]

'Doc' Henry also seems to have taken part in this ambush. A former *'Doc' Henry* British army chaplain, Michael Louis Henry was generally known as 'Doc', as he had acquired two doctorates (some say three) in Salamanca where he was educated and ordained. After the war he became curate in Curry and one prominent IRA activist, Maurteen Brennan, later claimed that he consulted him whenever he was planning any attack. He and other members of the IRA also availed of the 'Doc's' spiritual services. When going to confession to him, Brennan took off his hat. 'Put on your hat,' 'Doc' told him, 'you are a sol-dier.' For the same reason he would not permit Brennan to kneel down to re-ceive absolution. Some of the leading IRA activists on the run, such as Mick O'Hara and Frank Carty, took refuge in his house which was raided several times by the RIC.

It was also raided by the Auxiliaries after they came to Tubbercurry in the spring of 1921. The officer second in command of the Auxiliaries, nicknamed 'Tiny', was 6 foot 6 inches tall and, coincidentally, had served with 'Doc' in the same regiment in the British army during the Great War. Both of them had been in a tight corner on one occasion and had become close friends. They renewed their acquaintanceship when 'Tiny' led a party of Auxiliaries in a raid on 'Doc's' house. 'I believe you are friendly to the IRA,' 'Tiny' re-marked. 'I believe you are correctly informed,' answered 'Doc'. Their friend-ship rekindled and 'Doc' was made an honorary member of the officers' mess in Tubbercurry where a place was always reserved for him which put him 'in

25 *W.P.* 31 July 1920
26 AD UCD O'Malley Notebooks / P 17b / 137 (Jack Brennan); P 17b / 133 (Maurteen Brennan)

a damn awkward spot'. Brennan described the Auxiliaries in Tubbercurry as 'a decent crowd' and after 'Doc's' visits he was always driven home in an open car by Colonel Johnston, who kept two bombs and two revolvers on the car seat. Jim Hunt of Gurteen described 'Doc' as chaplain to the IRA and 'the only clergyman in Ireland who qualified for a pension'. When he died as parish priest of Straide in 1947, he was given an IRA funeral. [27]

Foxford Threat

Agnes Morrogh Bernard wrote to Sir Horace Plunkett early in September telling him that she feared the Woollen Mills would be attacked by the military. Plunkett approached 'the young Englishmen in the Castle who seem to be at the moment running the machine.' They undertook to call the immediate attention of the authorities locally responsible to the necessity of preventing 'the outrage you had been warned might occur'. 'I told those I met the romantic story of your wonderful enterprise and they said that it seemed inconceivable that anybody under any circumstances whatsoever would do it harm.' Plunkett was aware that a large number of co-operative creameries had been wrecked by the military and 'that new breed of peace-preservers commonly known as the 'black and tans'. [28]

Ratra Ambush

In the autumn of 1920 the struggle entered a new and more violent phase in which the first fatal casualties were recorded. IRA ambushes were set up to waylay small RIC patrols, usually on bicycles, and other such soft targets, and were usually followed by reprisals carried out on the nearest town. On Wednesday morning 1 September a party of four constables and a sergeant on bicycles were ambushed by the Gurteen IRA battalion under Jim Hunt at Ratra crossroads, on their way from Ballaghaderreen to Frenchpark for the Petty Sessions.[29]. Two of the constables, Edward Murphy, a native of Knock, and McCarthy, a native of Clare, as well as one of the Volunteers, Capt Thomas McDonagh of Cloonloo, were killed. Murphy, twenty-four years old, the eldest of eight children of a small farmer, had only joined the RIC two years previously and helped to support his family. His parents, William and Kate, later claimed compensation for the loss of their son and were awarded £800.[30]

Reprisals

That night a great part of Ballaghaderreen was wrecked as a reprisal. [31] Morrisroe condemned the shootings the following Sunday and extended his

27 AD UCD O'Malley Notebooks / P 17b / 133 (Maurteen Brennan and Jim Hunt)
28 Horace Plunkett to Agnes Morrogh Bernard, 9 Sept 1920, RSCG / H 26 / 170
29 Constables Martin Cooke, Edward Murphy, Hopely and McCarthy and Sergeant Burke
30 *W.P.* 4, 11 & 6 Nov 1920
31 Flannery's was extensively damaged as well as the premises of Patrick Beirne, James Cuniffe's, J. J. Coleman's, J. O'Reilly's, Mrs Regan's, Hanley's, Miss O'Rourke's, J. Swift's, Roger's, Durkin's and the Sinn Féin Club. *W.P.* 4 & 11 Sept 1920

sympathy to the relatives of the deceased. He also condemned the reprisals. The bishop later described the devastation. 'A few weeks ago Ballaghaderreen was a model of neatness, cleanness and commercial enterprise. Now it is in a sad plight indeed. At its top stands the ruins of a burnt courthouse, in the middle are the charred remains of a once flourishing business establishment, and here and there as you go along delapidated shop fronts stare you vacantly in the face.' [32]

Another ambush took pace at Chaffpool near Ballymote on Thursday, the last day of the same month.[33] That morning a lorry with six policemen, as well as District Inspector Brady and Head-Constable O'Hara, had left Tubbercurry for Sligo. Returning that evening via Bunninadden in a Crossley tender, they were ambushed at Leitrim Hill near Chaffpool Post Office, by the Tubbercurry IRA battalion who riddled the tender with a hail of bullets. Head Constable O'Hara was injured in the leg and Constable Brown received a slight flesh wound. But D. I. Brady was hit three times in the back and rushed to Tubbercurry where the curate, Felix Burke, gave him the Last Rites before he died. He was only twenty-one, had already served with distinction as an officer in the Irish Guards in the World War, after which he joined the RIC in Monaghan. He had just transferred to Sligo at his own request and, in fact, was already dead when the *Western People* announced his appointment to Tubbercurry on 2 October. He was the son of Capt Louis Brady, former harbour master in Dublin and nephew of the former MP, P. J. Brady.

Towards midnight on the same day, four heavy lorries loaded with military entered Tubbercurry, firing off their rifles and proceeded to ransack the town, concentrating on the houses of anybody with known IRA associations. [34] Howley's premises was the first to be visited but the attempt to set the place alight proved unsuccessful. E. J. Cooke's was next and 'all that was left of it the following morning was a smoking debris'. P. J. Gallagher's and John Coleman's were 'completely wrecked'. Others had their windows smashed. [35] The military then proceeded to the creameries in Ballyara and Achonry and the latter was burned down.

Fear continued to reign in Tubbercurry and when reports reached the

Chaffpool Ambush

District Inspector
Brady (NLI)

*Tubbercurry
Ransacked*

32 Morrisroe to Canon Gunning, 6 Oct 1920, *W.P.* 16 Oct 1920

33 *W.P.* 9 Oct 1920 & 29 Jan 1921; AD UCD O'Malley Notebooks / P 17b / 137 (Jack Brennan)

34 *W.P.* & *S.C.* & *Irish Independent* 9 Oct 1920; John C. McTernan, 'Night of Terror in Tubbercurry' in *Olde Sligoe*, pp 533-7; *Marist Convent Tubbercurry, Centenary Magazine*, pp 165-7

35 Gallagher Bros., Cryan Bros., Luke Armstrong's, Mrs Marren's, T. Madden's, M. Cunnane's, P. Heneghan's, J. Mullarkey's, J. Hunt's, J. Dunleavy's, T. E. Guthrie's and Philip Durkin's. *W.P.* 9 Oct 1920

Capt Brady's funeral
to Glasnevin cemetry.
Irish Independent,
Oct 5 1920 (NLI)

town on the following day, Friday, that police reinforcements coming from Sligo had been fired on at Tubbertelly, 'women and children were flying in terror of what another night might bring forth, while several found shelter and comfort in the local convent.' Among those who took refuge in the Marist convent was E. J. Cooke and his sister, Marie Louise. Both of them continued to live there for the rest of their lives and bequeathed a considerable sum to the convent.

Two days after the town was ransacked an *Irish Independent* reporter, who found that 'ruined shops were still smoking', described the terrified atmosphere in the town:

> We found little knots of people standing at several corners, others in close proximity to the ruined buildings – all discussing from various standpoints what had happened. The fright of the whole thing has not yet passed. It appears to be a living horror night and day. With these people it will no longer be an effort of the imagination to arrive at the meaning of reprisals. They have tasted the bitterness of which they had only read and heard before. It is the reality of such a scene that impresses one.[36]

Letter to America   Bridget Gilmartin of Main Street wrote on 5 October to her daughter, Nora, in the United States:

> Tubbercurry is destroyed. Thanks a thousand times to saints Peter and Teresa our cabin is spared and ourselves are uninjured so far ... We were sitting all the time in our own kitchen expecting every minute to be our last, until at last one of the soldiers stood at our door and fired two shots into Mullarkey's hardware shop just opposite our house (where Cryan

36 Reprinted in *S.C.* 9 Oct 1920; McTernan, *Olde Sligoe*, p 536

lived when you left here). At that time we three were almost senseless with fright and we crawled as best we could out to the stable where we remained until all was over ... Oh Nora, the soldiers that night were like so many demons let loose from hell. As they broke the fine plate glass fan lights and windows they were calling out the Sinn Féiners and saying "Where are they, the bloody swine?" ... It's a blessing after all we have gone through that there is nobody killed or wounded ... and we are almost certain it was the rosary that night that saved us when the houses on both sides were looted and destroyed ...[37]

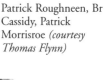

Patrick Roughneen, Br Cassidy, Patrick Morrisroe *(courtesy Thomas Flynn)*

Louis Brady, the father of James, wrote a letter from himself and his wife to Canon Gunning which he read out at Mass on Sunday 10 October:

I want to tell you that neither of us entertain the least feeling of ill-will towards anyone in connection with the tragedy. God's holy will be done: it was His way of bringing Jim to Heaven. We forgive from our hearts whoever was responsible for this deed wherever they came from. My wife and I were deeply grieved to learn of the reprisals that have taken place in your parish. No useful purpose is served by such conduct and if anything, would now make my poor boy unhappy to know he was the innocent cause of injury to anyone. Asking for your prayers and those of your congregation for my boy and his heart-broken mother and father.[38]

Gunning also read out a letter from Morrisroe conveying his sympathy to the people 'for the frightful horrors to which they have been subjected' and condemning the action of those who took part in the ambush:

Morrisroe's Letter

'...These fine fellows, so stainless and pure in most ways, will under the delusion that they are doing a service to their country, imbue their hands in the blood of a brother and speed the bullet that leaves wife without husband, child without father, and that will perhaps – most awful reflec-

37 *Olde Sligoe*, pp 536-7
38 *W.P.* 16 Oct 1920

tion of all – send a soul for which Christ died into the presence of its Maker without a moment's time for preparation ... I appeal therefore, to my people not to be led astray into wrong courses certain to provoke reprisals that the government appears to connive at, and that will surely follow perhaps in a more terrible form on the slightest excuse.[39]

Count Plunkett

The bishop's letter was published in the *Irish Times* (13 Oct 1920) where it came to the notice of, among others, Count Plunkett, father of the executed 1916 insurgent. [40] Plunkett took strong exception to the letter – 'a sorry document' – and queried the logic of Morrisroe's argument:

> On what grounds do you declare the attacks made by Ireland on her enemy to be crimes? The Irish people resisted conscription and the Irish bishops declared they were in their right, thereby affirming the will of Ireland to be Ireland's law – a very safe proposition. The same national will, by a great majority, elected a national parliament pledged to the Irish Republic and appointed a ministry, including a Minister of Defence, in control of our national army. The allegiance of all Irishmen is due to the national government which functions in spite of England's force ... England's occupation of Ireland is a crime: the Irishman who helps her rule by word or deed is a criminal: the policeman or other English agent who informs on Irish Nationalists or arrests them or otherwise interferes with their liberty and the execution of their duty to Ireland, must take the consequences of his treachery or warfare. I wonder when will some of you Irish bishops come to understand that your denunciation of acts of war carried out by your own people against the English murderer and robber, who hold our country down by force, is an offence against humanity, against justice, against the rights given us by God? Our people face England's worst every day: they will not yield while life lasts: their heroism is moving a hard world. Can you do no better than denounce them?

In another draft of his reply, Plunkett declared that if a bishop in Poland, Belgium, Bohemia or Hungary had expressed Morrisroe's opinions 'he would run the risk of being either expelled by the people or recalled by the Pope.'

The shooting of D. I. Brady came before the Quarter Sessions in Tubbercurry in January 1921 where a claim for compensation for the loss of their son was made on behalf of his family. Counsel for the family stated that Brady was 'a Catholic and had as strong and as keen a love for his country as the men who had done him to death.' His family were awarded £2,000.[41] Later damages

39 *W.P.* 16 Oct 1920
40 Count Plunkett to Bishop Morrisroe (2 drafts), 13 Oct 1920, Plunkett Papers, NLI Ms. 11408
41 *W.P.* 29 Jan 1921

were awarded to some of those whose properties were damaged or destroyed during the reprisals. E. J. Cooke was awarded £40,000 and Mrs Kate Armstrong and the Misses Howley also received sizeable compensation. [42]

Eight lorries loaded with military returned to Tubbercurry on Monday 25 October. Having surrounded the town they made an exhaustive search of almost every house in the town including that of Canon Gunning and his curate, Felix Burke.[43]

Wednesday 3 November was the fair day in Ballymote. Sergeant Patrick Fallon was returning from Millstreet, where he lived with his two daughters, his wife having died three years previously. Unarmed, he was confronted within a hundred yards of the RIC barracks by two men and shot through the heart. The assassins melted into the fair day crowd. Fallon was given the Last Rites by the chaplain in Ballymote, Charles Carney, assisted by Canon Quinn. 'After the shots were fired there was a wild stampede from the town. Country people left hurriedly and in a short time the streets were deserted and all the houses were quickly shuttered.' Fearing reprisals few people remained in Ballymote on Wednesday night. [44]

Ballymote Shooting

Teeling St, Ballymote c. 1900 (courtesy Bob Flynn)

At about 8 p.m. six lorries of armed military arrived in the town. The creamery was set alight and two other houses were burned down, D. Hannon's and the bakery of John A. Dockery. The local police actually helped to extinguish the flames. [45] The town had the appearance of 'a deserted village' the follow-

'A Deserted Village'

42 *W.P.* 5 Mar 1921
43 *W.P.* 30 Oct 1920
44 *W.P.* 6 & 13 Nov 1920
45 D. I. Russell, D. I. McBride, Head Constable Cahill, Constables Needham, Madden, Moran and Kelly. *W.P.* 13 Nov 1920

ing day which although market day all the houses were closely shuttered and business completely suspended. Towards evening there was another exodus from the town. Many sought refuge in the convent while others left for the country.

Sergeant Fallon's funeral took place on Friday. The coffin was borne on the shoulders of his comrades and Canon Quinn, assisted by Thomas Gallagher and Charles Carney, read the prayers at the graveside. Fallon, a native of Galway, with almost thirty years service in the RIC, came to Ballymote five years previously from Mullaghroe where he received a presentation on departing. He left three daughters, the youngest thirteen years old and the eldest seventeen, a teacher in England. That day large notices were displayed in the town which read: 'Another Sinn Féin victory. Three orphans doubly bereaved.'

Military Raids

During the end of 1920 and the early months of 1921 raids were made by the military in several places in the diocese and several arrests were made all over East Mayo. A detachment of the Highland Regiment descended on Charlestown on the fair day 10 December and captured Andrew Flatley, a prominent Sinn Féiner from Swinford who had been on the run for some months. The crown forces swooped on Gurteen, searched a number of houses and made some arrests. Thomas E. McCarrick, a shop assistant in Howley's, Tubbercurry was arrested in his bed and a loaded revolver was found in a coat thrown over the bed, and a document detailing the arms and ammunition of the sixth battalion of the Sligo IRA brigade. McCarrick was court-martialled in Derry early in March and refused to recognise the court. John Durkin, a motor driver from Tubbercurry arrested at the same time as McCarrick, was released without charge after six weeks in Sligo jail. Many members of Tubbercurry Rural District Council were also arrested. A party of a dozen armed policemen, mounted on bicycles, visited Aclare on Monday 14 February and proceeded to search all the houses and premises in the town. [46]

46 *W.P.* 11 Dec 1920, 8, 22 & 29 Jan & 26 Feb 1921. Among those arrested: *Charlestown:* A. Flatley, F. O'Doherty. *Swinford:* J. Rowley NT, J. Comer DC. *Killasser:* T. Keane DC, Kilduff, P. Keane, do, - Naughton. *Kilkelly:* J. J. Beirne, M. J. Cafferky, C. Lydon, Dunleavy, Sunvolaun, T. Cafferky. *Kiltimagh:* Messrs T. Lavin, Connolly, McTigue and Carroll. *Gurteen:* Joe Tansey, Thomas Jordan, Robert Broder, Patrick Mulligan, John Flynn & James Keegan. *Tubbercurry RDC:* Joseph Gavaghan, Aclare, James O'Grady, Kilmactigue, James P. Cahill, Cully, Patrick Phillips, Curry, Patrick Coleman, Coolaney, Joseph Hunt, do, John O' Donnell, do, Thomas Cawley, Dechomade, Bunninadden, Joseph Doohan, Quarryfield, M. J. Hunt, Coolaney, Hugh Kerins, Achonry, John Feely, Bunninadden and James Gannon, Carnagoppal. *Aclare:* John Ginty (student in All Hallows), John Leonard Tourlestrane, M. J. O'Hara DC Aclare, Joseph Gavaghan, Claddagh, James O'Grady, Stonepark.

On Sunday 20 February curfew came into force in Tubbercurry between 9 *Curfew*
p.m. and 6 a.m. and all pubs were to close at 6 p.m. A party of Auxiliaries
took up quarters in the town to help the RIC enforce the curfew. Three men
armed with revolvers shot into the army camp early in April and the following day the military imposed a new curfew beginning at 8.30 p.m. which was
still in force at the end of April, causing hardship to those working on the
land, tilling and turf-cutting as the evenings grew longer. Fairs and markets
were also prohibited which affected equally both town and country people. [47]

A curfew was imposed on Foxford in May after some roads leading to the *Foxford*
town had been trenched. People were confined to their homes after 6 p.m.
and the use of bicycles without permits from the armed forces was strictly
forbidden. The May fair was prohibited, causing considerable hardship to
farmers as they could not dispose of their cattle nor get grazing for their surplus stock. Agnes Morrogh Bernard wrote early in June to District Inspector
McGarry in Swinford, pleading that the June fair should be allowed. She
pointed out that the curfew regulations were causing great hardship to her
mill workers:

> Heretofore, the workers could cycle to their homes for their meals, and
> after working in the mill could do nearly a half-day's work on their bog,
> saving turf, and in their little plots gardening and farming, and the factory
> girls used to enjoy a good long walk in the dusk of the twilight after a hard
> day's work ... In the interests of common humanity – not to speak of jus-
> tice or charity – both these regulations, involving so much hardship,
> should be removed. [48]

There was little McGarry could do about it and he admitted to Agnes that
he had not been consulted about the curfew 'which put him in an awkward
position as he had been on friendly terms with the locals.' [49] By this time the
IRA had launched an attack on Foxford barracks which was followed by the
usual reprisals. [50]

Agnes wrote to the commander-in-chief of the British forces in Ireland,
General Sir Neville Macready, asking him to allow the June fair and to relieve
them of the curfew or have it extended to 11 p.m. She enclosed a letter, signed
by the two priests, Martin Henry and Denis Gildea. 'We earnestly hope that
the peaceful people of the parish will be relieved of the curfew regulations at
least to the extent of two further hours and the ban on our local fair usually

47 *W.P.* 26 Feb, 5 Mar, 9 & 30 April 1921
48 qtd Gildea, *Arsenius*, pp 178-9
49 RSCG / H 26 / 178
50 See below, p 479

held on 25 June.' Macready told her that 'it may be possible to ease matters in your part of the country' and promised her that he would speak to General Jeudwine on the matter. 'If such takes place, I hope that the inhabitants will prevent further outbreaks, which would of course necessitate a reimposition of those restrictions which are irksome to you all.' Macready's letter was in fact delivered by hand to Agnes by General Jeudwine, who was motoring to Swinford, accompanied by Col. Tweedy. [51]

Police Attacked

About midnight on the eve of St Patrick's Day a police patrol in Ballymote was fired on by three or four armed men and Constable O'Brien, born in England of Irish parents, was wounded and died the next morning. A civilian named Molloy of Lissinanny, after being struck in the head by a revolver butt, was arrested in connection with the shooting. [52]

According to the official report, the RIC barracks in Collooney was attacked at 3.30 a.m. and the doors of the barracks were blown in by explosives. A fierce fight ensued for nearly two hours when the raiders were beaten off. There were no police casualties and it was not known if any of the attackers were wounded. [53]

Swinford Atrocities

The military carried out a number of atrocities in Swinford in the middle of March.[54] Three officers and two sergeants, all very drunk, visited the

Chapel St, Swinford
(courtesy Joe Mellet)

Chapel Street, Swinford.

51 Agnes Morrogh Bernard to General Sir Neville Macready, 20 and 27 June 1921, General Macready to Agnes Morrogh Bernard, 7 July 1921 (copy), Agnes Morrogh Bernard to General Macready, 3 Aug 1921 (copy). RSCG / H 26 / 174
52 *W.P.* 26 Mar 1921, AD UCD P7/A/40
53 AD UCD P7/A/52
54 *W.P.* 11 Feb 1921

home of James Curry, a railway porter, on 16 March and put him up against a wall with a revolver to his head. Every time he failed to say 'Sir' he was beaten and kicked, causing bleeding. They found a Child of Mary cloak belonging to his sister and told him to wipe off the blood with it but he refused, 'not wishing to desecrate it'. They put the cloak around him and took him out to be shot but Curry burst away from them and managed to escape. He was treated by Dr McCarthy for bruises and 'a gaping wound on his left side.'

On the same night at 11.30 p.m. the military broke into the bedroom of Martin Dunleavy, a law clerk in Swinford, beat him with whips on the head and shoulders, and after wrecking his house took away some papers. He and his brother, Peter, were brought to the army huts, beaten again with revolver butts and horse whips, and then marched through the town to the convent railings where they met other prisoners. At the chapel gate they were again beaten. Lieutenant Harte, who was in charge of the soldiers, asked Dunleavy for the names of the local IRA men and Sinn Féiners, and when he refused Harte caught him by the throat and threatened to shoot him. Harte asked him 'was he intellectual?' 'Fairly', replied Dunleavy. 'Are you an RC?' 'Yes' he replied. 'If you are you cannot be an intellectual,' declared Harte.

Four days later, Pat Reilly was taken to the army huts, beaten with whips and thrown into barb wire and then marched through the town 'with a tong of a whip in a noose round his neck' and thrown into a river. On the same day the military burst in the door in the Kilbride Cottages of the house of James Clarke, knocked down his father and pulled James from his bed. He was kicked and beaten and later thrown into a river. Reilly and Clarke were treated by Dr Michael Staunton and were later, together with the two Dunleavys, awarded compensation at the Swinford Quarter Sessions. [55]

The home of P. J. Henry, assistant clerk of the Swinford District Council was raided by the military at the end of May. He was taken to the army camp where he was kept until 11 p.m., then with two others marched through the streets to a river where he was beaten with whips and clubs. His clothes were torn off him and thrown after him into the river. He managed to recover his overcoat and and continued down the river until he came near the town. Curfew was then on and he had difficulty in avoiding the night watches as he made his way home. Shortly afterwards he left home and did not return until the Truce was declared on 11 July. [56] Anyone of the foregoing incidents may

55 Pat Reilly, £90, James Clarke, £125, James Curry, £75, Martin Dunleavy, £90, Peter Dunleavy, £90. *W.P.* 11 Feb 1922
56 Henry was later awarded £110 compensation at the Swinford Quarter Sessions where the judge stated that Henry 'did not exaggerate in any way.' *W.P.* 11 Feb 1922

have been the occasion when the military rounded up the inhabitants of the town, lined them up and forced them to sing *God Save the King* before forcing them to cross a stream under machine-gun fire.[57]

Kiltimagh Terrorised

British soldiers, principally from the Scottish Fusiliers, descended on Kiltimagh on 22 March with fixed bayonets and rounded up shop-owners, including John and William McDonagh, assistants and others, up to thirty in all.[58] Two soldiers broke into the house of Edward Jordan in James' Street, a disabled ex-serviceman, and ordered him to get up off the sofa. He told them that he had been wounded twice at the Battle of the Somme but they pulled him out and marched him through the streets. Patrick Moloney, an ex-navy man, who had been all through the war, was treated similarly. The soldiers went to the railway station and apprehended John Forde, a railway porter. They asked him who were the men on the platform who took the 11.40 a.m. train to Claremorris and when he refused to tell them they beat him for half an hour. Another railway porter, Thomas Haran, and Michael Mulvanny, boots at the Railway Hotel, got the same treatment and all three were marched into town to join the others. Two national school teachers, Francis P. Quinn and James Carroll, were also seized as were nineteen-year-old Thomas Costello, Patrick Walsh, Joseph Hegarty and Thomas Begley, a motor mechanic.

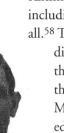

Private Edward Jordan, James' Street, Kiltimagh (*courtesy Betty Solon*)

They were all lined up against the railings of the Hibernian Bank and marched to the market square. 'Calling them "bloody swine" they were ordered to kneel down, kicked, cursed and rolled in the mud in which they were forced to rub their faces for ten minutes.' Quinn later said that the language used was 'the most obscene he had ever heard.' The young chaplain, Edward O'Hara, who happened to be buying something in a shop, was ordered out and when he refused, a soldier stuck the point of a bayonet in his back and drove him out. Somebody managed to get word to Denis O'Hara in the presbytery where he was having dinner with an elderly Canon from a neighbouring parish. The old priest begged him to stay where he was, lest he might be killed but Denis answered, 'I must go to my flock.' When he approached the commanding officer he was completely ignored.

The men were marched about a mile to a river on the Swinford road and made to lie in the water for ten minutes. Moloney, the ex-navy man, said to the officer in charge, 'This is a nice way to treat a man who has been all through the war.' The officer replied that he had been in the war himself but

57 AD UCD, O'Malley Notebooks / P 17b / 109 (T. Carney)
58 The following account is taken from L. MacManus, *White Light and Flame*, reproduced in *Kiltimagh*, p 177 & *W.P.* 11 Feb 1922

did not like Moloney drilling with rebels. However, he let him go. The teacher, Quinn, later contracted double pneumonia which resulted in bronchitis. The men were then ordered to run and shots were fired after them. Some of the victims were later awarded from £50 to £500 compensation at the Quarter Sessions in Swinford in February 1922. [59]

Next day Denis went to Claremorris where he made a formal complaint to Col. Tweedy, the officer-in-command, who refused to believe that his men could behave in such a way but reluctantly agreed to make enquiries. A few nights later – it was actually Good Friday – a lorry with soldiers came into town about midnight. Denis was awoken by the sound of the lorry stopping opposite his house. Hearing the tramp of feet in his driveway, he got up, looked out and saw uniformed soldiers approaching his door. He slipped out by the back door and hid in the hay in the stable while bullets were fired through his hall-door before the soldiers went back to the lorry.

Denis O'Hara Attacked

Some time later two officers of the Scottish Fusiliers arrived at the presbytery in Kiltimagh, ostensibly to hold an enquiry into the incident. A local Protestant lady, Lottie MacManus, happened to call to the presbytery while they were there and Denis invited her to join them in the study. There he regaled her and the officers with stories, some of them humorous, of Land League days. Suddenly, he stopped. 'Standing very erect, he raised his fine head, and in a tone of great dignity said, "They used to be gentlemen, the officers in the British army! ... It was uniformed men who fired into my house".'

Morrisroe presided at the usual clerical conference in Swinford on 29 March and priests and bishop took this opportunity to issue a strong condemnation of the attack made on Denis O'Hara. 'There is no need to tell the Irish people who Denis O'Hara is ... People of all shades of opinion in East Mayo respect and revere Father O'Hara; and while he is now, as always, a most outspoken Parliamentarian, the leaders of Sinn Féin have always borne willing testimony to his sincerity and are amongst his greatest admirers and closest personal friends.' An attempt was made to blame the incident on members of the IRA but 'the bishop and priests repudiate that allegation as a calumny, and declare that they are convinced beyond any shadow of reasonable doubt, that the perpetrators of the crime were servants of the Crown.' [60]

Condemnation

---

59 Edward Jordan, £300, Patrick Moloney, £65, John Forde, £70, Francis P. Quinn, £380, James Carroll, £100, John McDonagh, £50, William McDonagh, £50, Thomas Costello, £500, Thomas Haran, £50, Michael Mulvanny, £200, Thomas Begley, £50, Patrick Walsh, £280. Joseph Hegarty's claim was adjourned as he was unable to attend. *W.P.* 11 Feb 1922
60 *Kiltimagh*, p 178

Ballaghaderreen
Funeral

Sergeant Coughlan from Ballaghaderreen was shot dead in an ambush near Westport and his remains were brought to Ballaghaderreen on Good Friday, 25 March, where they lay in the cathedral mortuary chapel. The following day was the fair day and the streets were crowded, and as the police lorries in the funeral cortege moved slowly through the crowds some policemen levelled their revolvers at men in the crowd, compelling them to remove their hats as a mark of respect. [61]

Round-ups

Several roads around Tubbercurry were trenched by the IRA at the end of March and the military rounded up young men in Cully and compelled them to fill in the trenches. IRA notices were found posted up on the Market House in Charlestown and the military rounded up all the male adults and warned them that they would be held severally responsible for any outrages committed in the district. [62]

Kilmovee Shooting

On Holy Thursday night a member of the IRA, James Mulrennan from Lisacull, was shot as he was cycling through Kilmovee. He was taken to Philip Duffy's pub where he was given the Last Rites by the curate, James O'Connell, and then removed by the crown forces to an unknown destination. His brother was then in custody in Boyle Barracks. [63]

Sean Corcoran Shot

A party of policemen and soldiers were carrying out a routine search at Crossard near Ballyhaunis on 1 April when they were approached by two men pushing bicycles. [64] One of the policemen accompanied by one of the Argyle and Sutherland Highlanders, mounted their bicycles, approached the men and called on them to halt. One of the men, Seán Corcoran, drew a pistol from his pocket and fired at the policeman but his revolver jammed. The policeman returned fire and wounded Corcoran fatally. Corcoran, a manager in Dominick Murtagh's in Kiltimagh, was Commandant of the East Mayo IRA Brigade. His companion, Michael Mullins, the son of a local teacher, was arrested.

Corcoran's remains were removed the following Sunday from Ballyhaunis to Kiltimagh church where they lay surmounted by a tricolour for three days. A guard of honour of the local Volunteers kept vigil day and night while Rosaries were recited at intervals. All business in the town was suspended and schools closed. After solemn requiem high Mass on Tuesday, in the presence of fifteen priests, the coffin was carried by Volunteers to the republican plot in Kilkenure cemetery. A large force of soldiers and police posted outside the church presented arms as the coffin passed and Denis O'Hara thanked the

61 *W.P.* 2 April 1921
62 *W.P.* 2 April 1921
63 *W.P.* 2 April 1921
64 *Kiltimagh*, p 176; AD UCD O'Malley Notebooks/ P 17b/ 113 (Johnny Greely)

commanding officer of the crown forces for their salute. At the graveside the Last Post was sounded and two volleys were fired over the grave.[65]

An RIC party from Ballina was ambushed in Bonniconlon on Sunday 3 April by the Ballina battalion of the North Mayo IRA brigade. [66] About fourteen policemen, all travelling in a Crossley tender, stopped a short distance outside the village and all except four, who remained behind to protect the Crossley tender, went on foot to a dance in the local school. A few minutes later, those who remained behind were fired on and Constable Hankins, an Englishman, was seriously wounded. The police took cover and returned fire and the ambushers dispersed. All males at the dance were searched by the police who threatened to shoot them if they did not disclose the whereabouts of four missing men. The IRA claimed that they would have attacked the main police party at the dance but that it would have endangered the other people there. Next day the military, armed with machine-guns, arrived in Bonniconlon. Patrick Lawrence was questioned in the street about the ambush, and he and John Cawley were beaten with rifles and thrown into a river several times. Cawley, who was kept in the river for half an hour with shots fired over his head, later contracted pneumonia.[67] Nothing was burned or destroyed in Bonniconlon.

Bonniconlon Ambush

Three armed and masked men, wearing trench coats and gaiters, carried out a robbery of the Hibernian Bank in Charlestown on 7 April taking £5,000.[68] They had kidnapped the manager, Mr Flood, from the Imperial Hotel, and the cashier, Mr Mulligan from the Commercial Hotel, to gain access to the bank. It appears that the money from the bank raid never showed up in the coffers of the IRA who made several arrests in the Charlestown and Swinford districts in connection with the robbery.

Charlestown Bank Robbery

A few days later police from Swinford travelling by car at high speed had a narrow escape when they got stuck in zig-zag trenches cut across the road between Cloonmore and Curry. The car was a complete wreck. Two of the constables made their way back to Swinford to get help and two others remained with the car. They went to the nearest house where they took two men as hostages who were released when the military arrived. As they were hoisting

Narrow Escape

65 *W.P.* 9 & 16 April 1921, *Kiltimagh*, p 176. For a somewhat different account of the funeral, see L. MacManus, *White Light and Flame*, reproduced in *Kiltimagh*, p 179

66 O/C N. Mayo Brigade to A/G, 10 April 1921, AD UCD P7/A/38 (Mulcahy Papers) and P7/A/52; *W.P.* 4 Feb 1922

67 Both were later awarded compensation at the Ballina Quarter Sessions, Lawrence, £200, and Cawley, £450. *W.P.* 4 Feb 1922

68 *W.P.* 16 April & 18 June 1921; AD UCD P7/A/53: O'Malley Notebooks / P 17b / 109 (T. Carney) Carney said the raid took place 'the night that Corcoran was killed' i.e. 1 April

the car on to a lorry, they were fired on from the direction of Cloonmore wood and replied with machine-gun fire. [69]

Two RIC constables, Kelly and Hetherington, who were engaged on despatch work, were taken off the Dublin train at Ballysadare on Tuesday 19 April, shot dead and their despatches taken. Kelly was a native of Sligo and Hetherington from County Tyrone. Three officers and two soldiers on the train were also held up and disarmed and two were killed, one because he had

Ballysadare Station, 1938
(courtesy H. C. Casserly)

directed the Auxiliaries in carrying out reprisals and the other because he was in the wrong place at the wrong time. [70]

When Constable Stevenson was shot in Ballyhaunis, many residents fled to the neighbouring towns or to the countryside fearing reprisals. A deputation of the leading merchants waited on the military and on behalf of the people of the town disassociated themselves from the shooting of the constable and assured them that no Ballyhaunis men had taken part. The town was almost completely deserted, with business suspended, fairs and markets prohibited and a curfew imposed from 7 p.m. daily. [71]

A police patrol from Ballaghaderreen came upon a group digging trenches across the road at Tonroe (Carracastle?) on Friday night 13 May, who when called on to surrender opened fire. The police returned fire and the diggers withdrew leaving behind them spades, shovels, pickaxes, crowbars, two bicycles and several coats. When reinforcements arrived, the police gave chase and three arrests were made. Others were seen to be carrying two who had been wounded. The police suffered no casualties. [72]

69 AD UCD P7/A/53
70 *W.P.* 23 April 1921; O/C Sligo Brigade to A/G, 1 May 1921. AD UCD P7/A/38 (Mulcahy Papers): P7/A/53
71 AD UCD P7/A/53
72 AD UCD P7/A/53

Four days later, on Tuesday 17 May, a daring raid was made by the IRA on Ballaghaderreen police barracks. Three men under the command of Jim Hunt commandeered the midday mail train from Sligo to Dublin and forced the driver to stop the train on a bridge over the Frenchpark road about eighty yards from the barracks.[73] From there the IRA opened fire on the barracks. The police replied and after a lively exchange the train backed down the line. Later that day a big search was launched and after a stiff fight Hunt and another man were captured. They were found in possession of mail taken in a raid in Kilfree on the same day. [74]

Daring Raid

In their search for IRA suspects, the Sunday Mass congregation became a favourite target for the military during the first six months of 1921, up to the Truce. Mass was interrupted in Kiltimagh in the middle of January when Denis O'Hara informed the congregation, which contained members of both Sinn Féin and the IRA, that British soldiers were surrounding the church. O'Dowd, a local RIC constable, was posted at the door to point out the known activists as they emerged. Denis led the way and as he passed O' Dowd, he whispered, 'If ever you had a blind eye, have it now.' O'Dowd duly failed to spot any activist. Girls had given their hats and coats to suspects and with the crowd pressing closely round them they escaped detection.[75] Crown forces rounded up the greater part of the congregation after Mass in Gurteen on Sunday 8 May and after being searched and questioned they were all released except four.[76] All males in the congregation at Monasteraden chapel on the feast of Corpus Christi, 26 June, were taken out, questioned and searched but later released. Early in July crown forces rounded up over 200 males while Mass was being celebrated in Bunninadden church and marched them to Tubbercurry where they were compelled to move obstructions on the roads. [77]

Chapels Searched

Agnes Morrogh Bernard wrote from Foxford early in February to the divisional commissioner of police in Galway regarding the proposed transfer of the local RIC sergeant, Brady. 'Our district is and has been very quiet and the people consider that a great deal of credit is due to Sergeant Brady here, who has the reputation of being very tactful and diplomatic.' She asked that Brady be left on in his present position and the commissioner acceded to her request. [78]

Foxford Atrocities

---

73 Jim Hunt, a native of Gurteen and well-known handballer, joined the RIC in 1910 but resigned in 1914 and joined the Gurteen IRA Company in 1917
74 *W.P.* 21 & 28 May 1921; AD UCD O'Malley Notebooks/P 17b/ 133AD; P7/A/53
75 *Kiltimagh*, p 176
76 McDonagh, Flynn and two named Hunt
77 *W.P.* 14 May, 4 June & 16 July 1921
78 Agnes Morrogh Bernard to R.T.Q. Cruise, 9 and 12 Feb 1921, (copy) RSCG / H 26 / 171

The peace in Foxford was shattered a few months later when the RIC barracks was attacked on the night of 24 May. [79] Dublin Castle reported the following day: 'At 3 a.m. yesterday, Foxford (Mayo) barracks were attacked by a number of men armed with rifles and bombs. The attack was beaten off at 4 a.m. There were no police casualties.' All roads leading to the town were reported to have been trenched, bridges blown up and trees felled. Two days later, Friday 27 May, the military seized a number of local people. Three of them, Dr Dunleavy, Martin Gaughan and William Moran, were taken to Claremorris, two others, Patrick Gaughan and Patrick McKenna, were taken to Swinford and four others, James Connolly, Thomas Stephens, John Higgins (a clerk in the Woollen Mills) and Patrick Smith, were detained in Foxford.

East Main St, Foxford

The two prisoners in Swinford, Pakie Gaughan and Patrick McKenna, were taken outside the town at about 10 p.m, forced to strip and painted green, white and yellow. Even their scapulars were taken from them. Thrown into a river which flows near Swinford and their clothes after them, they were compelled to keep their heads under the water and when they raised them to breathe they were beaten with rifles and stones. Shots were fired over their heads. Eventually the military departed for Foxford and the victims, more dead than alive, set out for Foxford. After walking two miles they reached Gallagher's house in Cloongullane where they were given hot drinks and dry clothes.

At midnight the military, under Capt Grant, arrived in Foxford and took the prisoners out of the barracks and marched them to the bridge over the Moy. Ordered to strip, 'the scapulars were contemptuously torn from their

79 *W.P.* 28 May and 4 June 1921; Gildea, *Arsenius*, pp 173-9

necks'. "Do you think these rags will save you?" they were asked.' They also were painted green, white and yellow all over their bodies. After being ill-treated for about half an hour they were compelled to mount the parapet of the bridge and forced to jump into the river – a fall of about 18 feet. 'People heard the screams of the unfortunate victims but were afraid to come out of their houses.' [80] They crawled under one of the arches of the bridge where they clung for about two hours until they were sure that the military had de-parted. Then they crept out and made their way naked to the house of a Protestant, Miss Neill. All four were put in one bed while Miss Neill ap-proached her neighbours in search of clothes and they were still there at 4 or 5 a.m. when Mrs Connell arrived with clothes.

After Foxford the military continued on towards Ballina to the village of Shraheens, about four miles from Foxford.[81] There they dragged out of bed Mr Loftus, assistant teacher in Shraheens NS, stripped him naked, covered him with eggs, milk and flour and forced him to go up a chimney. He was then taken to Lacky Kelly's house where he and Kelly's son were beaten.

Some of the Sisters of Charity who were making sick calls on Saturday saw the Foxford victims and 'returned very much upset by the sad sights they wit-nessed' which galvanised Agnes into action. She instructed Denis Gildea to draw up a report which was entitled 'Diabolical Atrocities by Swinford Mili-tary Officers' detailing what happened on that Friday night, which she sent to Sir Horace Plunkett. 'A word from the new Lord Lieutenant might relieve the whole situation and compel military officers to act as common Chris-tians.' She also sent a copy to Monsignor Descuffi suggesting that he translate it for Italian papers. 'This report will give you a faint idea of what poor un-protected and inoffensive people have to endure from the military and Black and Tan parties.' Another copy was sent to a priest nephew, Eustace Morrogh Bernard, asking him to get it published in the *Westminister Gazette, Manches-ter Guardian* and *Daily News* and to approach Cardinal Bourne to contact the Lord Lieutenant. [82]

Agnes Takes Action

Col. Dell, who was on a fishing holiday in Pontoon, called to see the Mills and Agnes used the opportunity to give him a copy of the report which he promised to forward to Capt Grant's superior officer, Col. Tweedy in Clare-morris. She followed this up with a letter to Dell thanking him for his help while at the same time making a number of important observations: firstly,

80 Agnes Morrogh to Sir Horace Plunkett, 31 May 1921, RSCG / H 26 / 174 (1)
81 'Further Military Atrocities' RSCG / H 26 / 174 (7)
82 Agnes Morrogh Bernard to Sir Horace Plunkett, 31 May & 3 June 1921 (copies); same to Mgr Descuffi, 31 May 1921 (copy); RSCG / H 26 / 174 (1 &10)

there was no doubt that such terrorism was sanctioned by the Cabinet, secondly, officers will be loyal to their brother officers and thus no shortage of witnesses to prove that Capt Grant was not in Foxford on that night, and thirdly, that an investigation might incite the officers in Swinford to take the lives of the victms. She cited what happened to Denis O'Hara when he reported a similar case of terrorism to Col. Tweedy. Dr Conor Maguire, who had seen the victims on Saturday 28 May, could testify to their condition and there were at least eight other witnesses who heard and saw what happened who could testify to the accuracy of her report. 'Shopkeepers would be afraid to testify as their premises would be burned. We are living in sad times.'[83]

Straide Attrocity   Atrocities, however, continued to be perpetrated and on the very day that Agnes had written to Sir Horace Plunkett another was taking place in Straide.[84] It was the fair day there but people were unaware that the fair had been prohibited by the military. Just before midday fifteen fully armed soldiers under Lieutenant Harte arrived from Swinford on bicycles. The women were ordered home and about thirty men were lined up. Three of them, Willie Sheerin from Straide and two brothers, John and James (?) Smyth from Grallach, were taken from the line-up, stripped naked, beaten with canes, and each slung by two soldiers into a stream near the old church. It was only a few inches deep and full of stones. Lieutenant Harte watched from the bridge with a smile on his face and when the parish priest, Hugh O'Donnell, arrived on the scene he was ordered off threateningly. The three young men denied that they were Volunteers or Sinn Féiners. 'They then blasphemously asked them "did they know Jesus?"' The report added that 'this particular form of attrocity was most popular with the Swinford military.'

Inquiry   District-Inspector J. E. McGarry from Swinford called on Agnes on 2 June with a telegram from Sir Horace Plunkett: 'I am in communication with persons in authority upon whom I can rely to get the truth of all that has happened in Foxford.' A second telegram arrived the same day, informing her that an inquiry had been ordered but that it would take some time as a full inquiry was going to be made. It finally took place in Foxford on Wednesday 8 June with a presiding judge from Galway 'who seemed anxious to get the truth'. There was great excitement with motors and military lorries going to the barracks, putting witnesses, who had seen what happened to the victims on the bridge, on the alert. 'All the people are so cowed down by terrorism', Agnes told Horace Plunkett, 'that they are afraid to say the simple truth such

83 Agnes Morrogh Bernard to Col. Dell, 1 June 1921, RSCG / H 26 / 174 (4)
84 RSCG / H 26 / 174 (9)

as it stands.' [85] The day before, two sergeants called on the parish priest, Martin Henry, to give him notice of the inquiry which was to start at 10 a.m. the following morning but they did not encourage him to attend saying that it might only lead to trouble for him and for others. The victims themselves were only notified shortly before curfew began and two of them were absent. A motor car was sent for Smyth to take him to Swinford where the president was to dine and a car was also sent to take Connolly (who was a native of Hollymount) to Claremorris where he and Dr Conor Maguire would be examined by the president on his way back to Galway. Miss Neill and Mrs Connell gave evidence.

The cases of Patrick (?) and John Smyth, Grallach, Willie Sheerin, Straide and Kelly, Shraheens were also heard in Foxford Barracks on 13 June.[86] Patrick Smyth had been told by the police that 'it would be better not to give evidence against the military who would be on his track'. Smyth told them that he would give evidence of everything that happened and 'not take one word from it'. His brother John's left hand had swollen considerably since he had been thrown into the river three times. Kelly of Shraheens also gave evidence and his sister was a witness for him.

Members of the court visited Gallagher's house in Cloongullane on Friday 17 June where Pakie Gaughan and Patrick McKenna were assisted after their maltreatment in Swinford.[87] For some unknown reason the court note-taker took Gallagher's evidence phonetically, perhaps to ridicule it. Gallagher, who was a man of some means as the owner of a two-story house, told the court that Gaughan and McKenna had visited him on the night in question.

Q. "Were they alright when they entered?"
A. "Throth they wornt."
Q. "How were they?"
A. "They wor the mosht awful sights ye ever saw."
Q. "How?"
A. "Any clothes they had on them were dhreepin wet and dirty."
Q. "Did you see any paint on them?"
A. "Paint is it? Wait till I go up sthairs and show ye the shirts they had on them, tho' me woman washed them three times: but shure the paint is on them yet."
Q. "Oh! Don't mind showing us the shirts, we'll take your word for it; were their clothes wet?"

85 Agnes Morrogh Bernard to Sir Horace Plunkett, 9 June 1921, RSCG / H 26 / 174 (11-12)
86 RSCG / H 26 / 174 (16)
87 RSCG / H 26 / 174 (17)

A.   "Well, wet is no word for it – wet, dirty and mucky."

Q.   "Did you give them any refreshments?"

A.   "Well, we did our besht for them and gav them something to warm them and we gev them any dhry clothes we could spare."

Q.   "Did they return you the clothes?"

A.   "Throth then they did, thim are daicent bhoys. They sint thim back again."

Q.   "Well, thanks very much now. It corresponds to what we heard in Foxford. Sign this."

A.   "Well maybe ye'd give me a permit for me bicycle now?"

Q.   "Oh that's not our business – Goodday."

Sequel   Towards the end of June Agnes wrote to the commander-in-chief of British forces in Ireland, General Sir Nevil Macready, thanking him for the two sworn inquiries held in Foxford barracks.[88] She enclosed a statement from James Connolly, one of the victims who was absent from the Foxford inquiry and also a statement from Martin Henry and Denis Gildea asserting their belief in the innocence of the ill-treated young men. The priests were present at the inquiry and 'were appalled at the injuries inflicted on the six young men'. Agnes followed up with another letter to Macready expressing disappointment that there was not a full inquiry into the innocence of the ill-treated boys. 'We are convinced and have proof of their innocence.'[89] When General Jeudwine, accompanied by Col. Tweedy, visited the convent on 14 July to deliver a letter from General Macready, they told Agnes that 'they did

Nun and boy in
Foxford Mills, 1896

88   Agnes Morrogh Bernard to General Macready, 20 June 1921, RSCG / H 26 / 174 (20) (copy)

89   Agnes Morrogh Bernard to General Macready, 27 June 1921 (copy), RSCG / H 26 / 174 (21)

not like the work they had been at in this country.' Agnes commented: 'It would never subdue our people.' Jeudwine and Tweedy were on their way to Swinford, presumably to deliver a rebuke from Macready to Capt Grant.[90]

Some months later Agnes wrote to Sir Horace Plunkett thanking him for having taken 'such a deep and kindly interest in securing full light being thrown on the case of the Foxford men' and informing him of the verdict of a case for compensation taken by the victims at the Swinford Quarter Sessions.[100] Judge Doyle, who presided, said it was 'the worst case that had been brought before him of the escapades of the military'. He awarded the six £350 each with costs and would have given them their full claim but that 'the pockets of the ratepayers required due consideration.'

The military stopped Dominick Grogan of Tavraun on the road to Kilkelly on 5 June and threatened to shoot him.[101] Shots were fired over his head 'which cut branches off the trees' and one of them put the point of his rifle under his nose saying: 'Smell that; that's powder; that's the stuff to give you.' They beat him with rifles and kicked him 'shouting like wild beasts' until he was unconscious, and when he regained consciousness threw him into a thorn bush. Anthony Harrison received similar treatment on the same occasion, as Annie Jane Reid witnessed and later gave evidence at Swinford Quarter Sessions where both Grogan and Harrison were awarded £100 compensation.

Kilkelly Atrocities

Thomas Tarpey, a tailor in Kilkelly, was cutting a suit of clothes when four Tans walked in and one of them knocked him down saying, 'You will burn no more barracks when I am done with you.' He was forced to say that he would have nothing to do with Sinn Féin. Five times they marched him up and down the streets of Kilkelly, knocked him down while handcuffed and dragged him through the mud. He told the judge at Swinford Quarter Sessions that he could not live at home afterwards until the Truce was signed. Dr Lyons told the court that Tarpey 'was bordering on insanity' as a result of the ill-treatment. He was awarded £225 compensation.

That evening, some girls were sitting on a fence in Groarke's garden in Rabaun, Castlesheenaghan when they were approached by 'five or six disorderly soldiers'. The girls fled into the house but as they did Kate O'Malley was shot in the wrist. Later at Swinford Quarter Sessions she said she had

90 Agnes Morrogh Bernard to General Macready, 20 June & 3 Aug 1921 (copies), RSCG/ H 26 / 174 (20 & 26)

100 Agnes Morrogh Bernard to Sir Horace Plunkett, 4 Nov 1921 (27) (copy) RSCG / H 26/ 174 (27)

101 Descriptions of the following incidents are compiled from the evidence given by the victims at Swinford Quarter Sessions in spring 1922 as reported in the *Western People* 11 Feb 1922. As they were seeking compensation allowance should be made for some exaggeration.

been planning to go to America 'but now her prospects were blighted' as her hand was useless. Dr McCarthy of Swinford had her sent to hospital for ten weeks and later she was moved to Sir Patrick Dunn's Hospital in Dublin. She was awarded £1,000 compensation.

Charlestown

John Haran of Mullinamadogue, Charlestown was awarded £100 compensation by the same court. About a dozen soldiers came to his house, pulled him out of bed, brought him to a bridge and after beating him severely, threw him over the bridge into two feet of water. This was repeated three times until he became senseless. John Carroll of Bushfield, who was awarded £90, had been seized at a fair in Kiltimagh and questioned about the shooting of officers in Dublin. Although he knew nothing about it except what he had read in the newspapers he was, nevertheless, given the usual treatment.

The Truce

A number of other incidents occurred in the diocese in June and early July before the Truce was signed.[102] Two lorries carrying huts for the Auxiliaries in Tubbercurry were held up on 13 June near the town by armed men who set the lorries on fire. Some RIC constables from Ballymote on their way to Collooney were fired on and when they returned fire the attackers escaped through a wood where reinforcements from Tubbercurry failed to find them. Constable Moffat was fired on by two armed men while attending a sports meeting on Friday 8 July in Ballaghaderreen. He rolled over on his face and opened fire on his attackers. 'A wild stampede followed and soon the field was clear of both players and spectators.' [103]

On the same day one of the last incidents in the 'war' occurred in Carralavin, a small village midway between Ballina and Bonniconlon, where the dead body of Sergeant Foody was found by a postman. He had a number of bullet wounds and a label round his neck, 'Revenge for Dwyer and The Ragg.' Foody had been stationed at the RIC barracks in The Ragg, Co Tipperary, where two brothers called Dwyer were shot.[104] Foody, a native, had recently bought a farm near Bonniconlon. He was the last casualty in the diocese of the 'war' of Independence as the Truce came into operation three days later on 11 July. By then there had been a total of thirteen fatalities in the diocese and one other outside the diocese, an RIC constable from Ballaghaderreen. In all nine RIC were killed as well as two of the military and three Volunteers.

102 AD UCD P7/A/53
103 *W.P.* 9 July 1921
104 AD UCD P 7 / A / 53

CHAPTER NINETEEN

The Civil War

Following the signing of the Truce on 11 July 1921, the few IRA who were still on the run emerged from their hideouts and were generally welcomed as heroes who had defeated the might of the British Empire. They quickly took advantage of their new found celebrity and during the six months of the Truce period they became the leading force in local politics.[1] They were honoured guests at public functions and basked in the adulation that was accorded to them as 'gunmen'. A football match at Benada *aeraíocht* between the IRA and the local team was attended by 'several IRA officers in uniform, all of them looking well in their dark green.' [2] 'The gunmen came out of the struggle victorious' which makes one wonder what might have happened if they had lost the match.

Truce

Countess Markievicz was the guest of honour at the Tubbercurry *aeraíocht* in September.[3] She told the crowd that she could see that 'the west was awake' by the number of trenched roads she had to cross, the broken bridge at Curry, the burnt barracks and the scene of the Chaffpool ambush, which she had visited. She exhorted the men to be sober: 'Young men of the IRA must keep their lives pure, clean and sober. No man who drinks can be sure of himself or safe with a gun in his hand' which was the reason, she believed, that de Valera was a teetotaller. Breaches of the Truce were recorded in Tubbercurry late in August and early in September when shots were fired at the barracks and the police replied with a heavy bombardment, causing considerable damage to Howley's premises.[4] In a separate incident a police patrol was fired on and two policemen, Constables Kenny and Walsh, wounded.

Countess Markievicz

The day after the Truce was signed Michael Marren, the officer in command of the IRA battalion in Ballymote, was drowned while swimming at Strandhill and his body was washed ashore five days later, on Sunday 17 July. The funeral of the 'dead hero' was an impressive affair testifying to the ikon status now enjoyed by the IRA. The funeral cortege was led by Ballymote

IRA Funeral

1 Farry, *Aftermath*, pp 17-35
2 *S.C.* 27 Oct 1921
3 *W.P.* 1 Oct 1921
4 *W.P.* 11 Sept 1921

Brass and Reed Band playing the *Dead March* on the ten mile journey to Ballymote, where some 2,000 Volunteers with draped Sinn Féin armlets, marching four-deep, formed a guard of honour together with Cumann na mBan wearing Sinn Féin rosettes. All schools and business houses in Ballymote, Tubbercurry and Ballaghaderreen were shut as was the creamery in Gurteen. Twelve priests attended the solemn requiem Mass. Canon O'Connor of Gurteen spoke at the graveside: 'A nobler soul, a braver soldier, or a more fearless champion of the Irish cause never breathed the breath of life.' [5]

Gurteen Altercation   Later, O'Connor became embroiled in a bitter row with the Gurteen IRA battalion. They had set up a training camp in Kilfree in September and on Sundays marched to Mass in Gurteen in military formation and took up

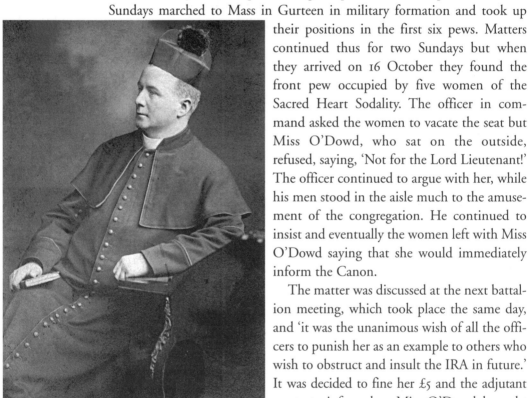

their positions in the first six pews. Matters continued thus for two Sundays but when they arrived on 16 October they found the front pew occupied by five women of the Sacred Heart Sodality. The officer in command asked the women to vacate the seat but Miss O'Dowd, who sat on the outside, refused, saying, 'Not for the Lord Lieutenant!' The officer continued to argue with her, while his men stood in the aisle much to the amusement of the congregation. He continued to insist and eventually the women left with Miss O'Dowd saying that she would immediately inform the Canon.

The matter was discussed at the next battalion meeting, which took place the same day, and 'it was the unanimous wish of all the officers to punish her as an example to others who wish to obstruct and insult the IRA in future.' It was decided to fine her £5 and the adjutant wrote to inform her. Miss O'Dowd brought

James O'Connor
(courtesy John Doherty)

the letter to the Canon. He immediately sent the letter to the Department of Defence explaining to them that Miss O'Dowd was head of the Ladies' Guild of the Sacred Heart Society and that it was normal for them to occupy the front seat, 'from which they were peremptorily ordered out' on their communion Sunday. 'I think you will agree that anything like this should not have occurred in the church.' The Department of Defence passed his letter

5   *W.P.* 30 July 1921

on to the Chief of Staff to have the matter investigated and he in turn passed it on the Adjutant-General.

He wrote to William Pilkington, the commanding officer of the Sligo brigade, demanding that the officer responsible be immediately suspended as he 'was not fit to be a compa-ny officer much less a battal-ion officer.' An explanation for his conduct was to be sent on and an official apology to be made to Miss O'Dowd and Canon O'Connor.[6] Pilkington asked that a stay be put on the suspension as he regarded both the O/C and Adjutant in Gurteen as 'particularly good officers' and because Canon O'Connor was 'particularly aggressive in his opposition and the hostility he displays to the I.R.A.' He thought it would be very bad and unfair to see these officers punished 'because of the representations of a man who is the enemy of the cause', but he promised to make enquiries and send on a report as soon as possible.[7]

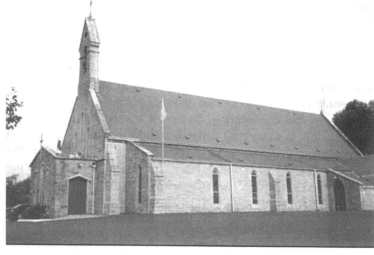

St Patrick's Church, Gurteen

The report was duly compiled.[8] 'O'Connor is a man who, since the repub-lican movement started in Gurteen in 1916, was an open and bitter enemy of the cause and on several occasions criticised and ridiculed publicly from the pulpit the men who went forwarding the cause in the area and never let slip an opportunity when he could insult the commanding officer or the men carrying out the local civil administration.' Miss O'Dowd was the sister of the president of the local Ancient Order of Hibernians, 'a long and bitter enemy of ours and the bosom friend of the Canon's' and O'Dowd was used 'as a willing tool by the Canon to make the Volunteers a cause of ridicule before the congregation'.

Early in November O'Connor wrote to Cathal Brugha, Minister of Defence, regarding fresh troubles in his parish. [9] The IRA commandant was going round the parish saying that 'he would make it hot' for O'Connor

6 Adjutant-General to O/C Sligo, 20 Oct 1921; Mulcahy Papers / P7 /A / 33
7 O/C Sligo Brigade to Adjutant-General, 21 Oct 1921
8 Batt. H.Q. Gurteen to Brigade H.Q. Sligo, 27 Oct 1921
9 Canon O'Connor to Cathal Brugha, 2 Nov 1921

because of his complaint about the incident in the church. 'Well, you know, and every sensible man knows, that no layman, no matter what his station may be, can be allowed to usurp the position of the Parish Priest in the discharge of his ecclesiastical duties, but incredibly this young man thinks otherwise.' A Christmas prize draw was to be held to raise money to pay off the church debt but the IRA stated that it could not go ahead 'without their express permission.' A dance in St Patrick's Hall on 1 November was picketted by the IRA who turned people back on roads leading to the dance and shots were fired. 'Now surely this cannot be the orders of Dáil Éireann? I consider it most ruffianly conduct ... I feel that an apology is due to me and my people from the body we have always helped and served.'

The Adjutant General passed on O'Connor's new complaints to the commanding officer of the Sligo Brigade who in turn communicated them to the Gurteen battalion for their comments. They detailed instances of O'Connor's hostility to the Republican movement. [10] He had described Commandant Tansey and other officers in 1916 as 'brainless men ... the blind leading the blind and that he would keep the young politicians in their places.' When Tansey wished to give Capt Murphy of Kilfree Company a military funeral in November 1918, O'Connor refused to allow the coffin to be carried by his comrades, saying that 'he had too much respect for the deceased to allow his remains be carried by them.' O'Connor described the shooting in Thurles of RIC District Inspector Hunt, a native of Gurteen, as ' a diabolical murder and unchristian and unIrish to shoot a man in the back.' However, when his own parishioners, Jim Hunt, Dr Doyle and Dominick O'Grady, were fired on by the police outside his own chapel, O'Connor remained silent.[11] Some time ago a letter from O'Connor was read in Killaraght chapel describing Sinn Féiners as 'blackguards'. Eventually, the whole affair seems to have petered out and the Chief of Staff was informed early in December that there was nothing in the files to show that disciplinary action had been taken against the Gurteen officer or that an apology had been given to O'Connor.[12]

Collooney Dispute   Another dispute took place between republicans and the clergy in Collooney in November.[13] The curate, Michael Durcan, was accused of having 'imperial sympathies' and a 'feeling of prejudice against the national language of Ireland' when he said in a sermon that some people in the parish were 'putting the language movement before the cause of their spiritual

10 O/C 4th Batt. to Brigadier, Sligo, 21 Nov 1921
11 See above p 428
12 M/S to C/S, 9 Dec 1921
13 Farry, *Aftermath*, p 35

salvation.' The parish priest had already angered the Gaelic League by refusing to let them use the national schools for Irish language classes and the Irish language teacher complained about him in a letter to a newspaper. As a result most of the teachers withdrew from his Irish classes and the IRA imposed a boycott on two schools.

A number of IRA training camps were set up in the diocese 'where rank and file in addition to officers and NCOs were put through a course of camp training.' The numbers ranged from twenty-four officers at the Coolaney camp to 120 at a large camp in Cloonamahon Sanatorium. Other camps were established at Tubbercurry workhouse, Kilfree and Culfadda. In East Mayo a large training camp was established in Oldcastle near Swinford where about 100 men at a time attended a three week course. Brian MacNeill, son of Eoin MacNeill, attended this camp. [14] Two officers were sent down from GHQ in Dublin in November to inspect the camps with a view to setting up a new divisional structure in County Sligo. The result was the establishment of the 3rd Western Division, consisting of five brigades, two of which, South Sligo (4th Brigade) and East Mayo (5th Brigade), comprised almost the totality of Achonry diocese. The only exceptions were Foxford, Attymass and Bonniconlon which belonged to the 4th Western Division. William Pilkington became O/C of the 3rd Division and Brian MacNeill, Quartermaster General with Frank Carty O/C of South Sligo brigade and Tom Carney, O/C of East Mayo brigade.

IRA Training

The Treaty was signed in the early hours of Tuesday 6 December 1921 and approved by the Irish cabinet by four votes to three on the following Thursday. South Sligo Comhairle Ceanntair met in Ballymote under the chairmanship of Dr J. A. Flannery on Sunday 1 January 1922, voted forty-five to three in favour of the Treaty and requested their TDs, Alec McCabe, Frank Carty, Tom O'Donnell, Seamus Devins and Dr Ferran, to vote for the Treaty. Tubbercurry Sinn Féin club voted nineteen for and seven against, while clubs in Killavil, Cloonloo and Gurteen requested their TD, Alec McCabe, to vote for ratification of the Treaty.[15] The Dáil ratified the Treaty by sixty-four votes to fifty-seven on 7 January and two days later the Pope expressed his 'relief and joy' at the news. In the Dáil McCabe and O'Donnell voted in favour of the Treaty while Ferran, Devins and Carty against. The Irish Free State Provisional Government was established on 14 January.

The Treaty

In County Sligo most of the IRA took the anti-Treaty side, Jim Hunt of Gurteen being one of the few prominent IRA who was pro-Treaty. The 3rd

14 O'Malley Notebooks, P 17b / 113 (Johnny Greely)
15 *W.P.* 7 & 14 Jan 1922; *R.H.* 7 Jan 1922

Mickeen Howley,
Johnny Walsh,
Jim McHale
(*courtesy Betty Solon*)

Western Division broke away from the army GHQ and when anti-Treaty IRA officers attended the Army Convention on 24 March, despite a ban from the Provisional Government, the 3rd Western Division sent eighteen delegates and William Pilkington was elected a member of the executive. One prominent anti-Treaty member of the IRA later claimed that the majority of East Mayo IRA were opposed to the Treaty. 'The majority of the people accepted the Treaty and the priests were 90% against us.' Another one claimed that over 50% and under 75% of the members of Sinn Féin clubs were in favour of the Treaty. [16]

16 Tom Carney & Johnny Greely, AD UCD O'Malley Notebooks, P 17b / 113

Some prisoners had been released early in December.[17] 356 political prisoners were released from Irish jails on 12 January 1922. Among these was Jim Hunt of Gurteen. When he arrived home he was greeted by large crowd including TDs, Alec McCabe and Tom O'Donnell, five bands and Volunteer companies in uniform.[18] A banquet was held in Gurteen later in February to welcome home the internees, of whom almost thirty came from the Gurteen battalion area, one of whom, Bernard Brennan from Lincoln Jail, and the guests included General Seán McKeon and 'Doc' Henry, the curate in Curry. [19]

Prisoners Released

The Auxiliaries began to withdraw on 13 January. Three days later Charlestown RIC barracks (which was housed in the Town Hall since the original barracks was burned down) was seized by by about 100 IRA men who were doing a three-week training course at the camp in Oldcastle near Swinford. Almost sixty rifles were seized and the following day three IRA men went to the railway station in Kiltimagh where they attempted to seize more arms. They had filled an uncoupled waggon with arms when they were surrounded by British troops but managed to escape.[20] Swinford barracks was vacated early in February and occupied by the IRA. Three days later a large armed party of IRA under Commandant Mulrenan, marched into Ballaghaderreen where the RIC barracks was handed over by District-Inspector Godfrey and the Sinn Féin flag raised over the building.[21] Later that month Ballymote barracks was also formally handed over to the IRA.

Auxiliaries Withdraw

With the occupation of former RIC barracks the IRA also assumed their policing role. When Commandant M. J. O'Hara searched every licensed premises in Tubbercurry for poteen, the *Western People* (25 March) wished the Commandant and his men 'success in their efforts to stamp out this evil' and the Volunteers in Swinford damaged some premises when enforcing a 'closing order'.[22]

The IRA also contributed to the general growth of lawlessness after the departure of the RIC. A group of local IRA men robbed the bank in Charlestown of over £5,000 on 1 February and some of them had taken part in a similar robbery in April of the previous year.[23] Tom Carney of the East-

Bank Robbed Again

17 John Ginty & J. O'Hara, Aclare from Ballykinlar Camp, Charles Lydon & Michael Cafferky from same and Patrick Dunleavy & Martin Casey of Kilkelly from Rath Camp. *W.P.* 17 Dec 1921
18 Gurteen, Cloonloo, Monasteraden, Edmondstown and Killaraght
19 *W.P.* 21 Jan & 18 Feb 1922
20 Eugene Kelly, M. & Dan Sheehy. P /17b /113 (Johnny Greeley): *W.P.* 21 Jan 1922
21 *W.P.* 11 & 18 Feb 1922
22 P. O'Hara's, John P. O'Connor's, Edward Henry's, T. P. O'Connor's & Mr Smyth's. *W.P.* 15 April 1922
23 *W.P.* 25 Feb & 4 Mar 1922; AD UCD O'Malley Notebooks / P /17b /109 (Tom Carney)

Mayo brigade launched a search and brought the culprits before a republican court in Swinford on 1 March where they were charged and sent to Sligo jail to await their trial.[24] While there they made statements which led to the recovery of most of the money, of which £800 was found in a bag of meal in one house. 'We got most of the money in bags of meal', Tom Carney recounted later, 'and there, like as in a pirate story, in the corner of a field twelve steps up and twelve steps down ... was buried a couple of hundred pounds from the second raid.'[25] The bank gave the IRA £500 for their 'good police duty'.

The prisoners also made statements about the first bank raid which implicated the local battalion O/C and the ex-adjutant of the brigade. The battalion O/C had £80 in a cannister and pleaded that if he was allowed keep the money he would leave for the USA. The IRA did not wish to expose him and he went to Dublin where he joined the CID. One of the prisoners made a statement alleging that one of those who received the stolen money was a brother-in-law of the bishop whom Carney described as 'imperial Bishop Pat Morrisroe, the worst bishop in Ireland'.

The IRA also tended to impose their will on democratically elected bodies. A large body of Volunteers with the curate, Fr Walsh, presented themselves at a meeting of Swinford District Council where Walsh advocated that road maintenance should be carried out by employing young men of the district. The Volunteer captain insisted they would undertake the repair of the roads whether they had the approval of the Council or not, to which the chairman replied that if they acted like that the Council might as well retire. The Volunteers intimated that they would not allow contractors undertake the work and the contractors stated that 'they did not want to stand in the way of the young men who had done so much for the country.'[26]

Election Campaign   Though the date of polling had not yet been finalised, preparations for the general election campaign began early in March in south Sligo. Pro-treaty supporters held a conference, chaired by Alec McCabe TD, in Collooney on 13 March and a director of elections for the Sligo-East Mayo constituency was appointed. At the same time the anti-Treaty side, with their three outgoing TDs, Frank Carty, Seamus Devins and Francis Ferran, held a meeting in Tubbercurry where a pro-Treaty election committee was also set up. South

24 Michael (Wallace) Frain, Bulcaun, Edward McCormack, do, James McDonagh, Kilgarriff, Michael Mulherin, do, Thomas Haran, Killeen, James Reilly, Cloonoghill and John Haran, Charlestown. Two others were arrested but escaped from Swinford, John Drudy, Bulcaun and Michael Kiggins, Kilgarriff. *W.P.* 4 Mar 1922
25 P 17b / 109
26 *W.P.* 18 Feb 1922

Sligo pro-Treaty meetings were held on the last two Sundays in March and Tom O'Donnell was the principal speaker. The anti-Treaty campaign was opened with a meeting in Swinford on St Patrick's Day.

A pro-Treaty meeting was arranged for Castlebar on Sunday 2 April at which Michael Collins was to be the principal speaker and a determined effort was made by the anti-Treatyites to prevent the meeting taking place. Posters were torn down, all the main roads were blocked, railway lines ripped up and excursion trains held up. The Sligo train could not get past Kiltimagh and the driver was obliged to back the train to Swinford. Notwithstanding, large crowds made their way to Castlebar and at 3 p.m. when the meeting began there were about 3,000 present in the Mall.

Collins in Castlebar

Collins received 'a mighty ovation' when he mounted the platform.[27] Thomas Campbell, the Swinford solicitor, stood on a lorry about thirty yards from the platform, surrounded by a number of young men in uniform and he and others continuously heckled Collins in an attempt to prevent him speaking. An IRA officer mounted the platform and proclaimed the meeting. After delivering part of his speech, Collins retired to the hotel with his sister, Mrs Joe Sheridan of Bohola, and during his absence the anti-Treatyites sang continuously the *Soldier's Song* to prevent other speakers being heard.

When Collins returned, Campbell continued to heckle him, declaring that he had questions to put to Collins. Collins repeatedly asked him to give him the questions which were written down but Campbell refused and angry exchanges between the two men followed. 'Didn't you stone Davitt in Swinford?,' Collins asked, 'Who supplied the Black and Tans in Swinford?' Campbell called Collins 'a loyal subject of King George'. 'Your conduct is worthy of your record' Collins retorted angrily, 'but you took good care to be in jail when there was danger. You are here for making noise and that is all you can do.' Another speaker, Tom O'Donnell TD, asked: 'Where was your rifle, Campbell, for the last two years?'

There was now great excitement and feeling was running high. An attempt was made by a number of young men, some in uniform, to rush the platform. Alec McCabe TD whipped out his revolver and those rushing the platform also drew their weapons and for a moment it looked as if there would be a shoot-out. Some men jumped from the platform and fled:

> '...at least six shots rang out in quick succession, causing the wildest com-
> motion. Women screamed, some fainted and others became hysterical.
> There was much panic and a dash for cover by those on the outskirts of
> the meeting, but the great bulk of the people held their position ...'

27 *W.P.* 8 April 1922.

Collins succeeded in calming the crowd and commenting on the 'scandalous conduct' at the meeting, he declared that this was not the freedom for which they had risked their lives: 'Let the people decide and if the verdict is in favour of the opposition, they won't find me behind. I will stand with the people as I always did, no matter what their position was.'

Griffith in Sligo   Another pro-Treaty meeting was planned for Sligo on Easter Sunday, 16 April and Arthur Griffith was to be the principal speaker. [28] All public meetings and political demonstrations were proclaimed on 7 April by William Pilkington, O/C of the breakaway 3rd Division, and the Mayor of Sligo telegraphed Griffith to inform him about the proclamation. Griffith wired back that Dáil Éireann had not authorised any interference with the right of public meeting or free speech. 'I, as President of Dáil Éireann, will go to Sligo on Sunday next.' On Thursday night prior to the meeting Alec McCabe led a column of Provisional Government troops into Sligo and occupied the jail. Anti-Treaty troops were drafted in from all over the 3rd Division and a hundred came by train from South Sligo and occupied strategically placed public buildings. Fearing a bloody encounter, the Bishop of Elphin tried unsuccessfully on Saturday to arrange a truce between the opposing factions.

Griffith was due to arrive on the Saturday evening train but he left the train at Carrick-on-Shannon where he was met by General Seán McKeon with Provisional Government troops who escorted him to Sligo that night. On Sunday morning a convoy of about forty government troops from Dublin stopped outside an hotel occupied by the IRA and an exchange of fire took place lasting about ten minutes. Three of the IRA were wounded, one of whom was Michael Mullin of Bunninadden. About fifty well-armed men supported by an armoured car were dispersed along the converging streets and occupied all the principal hotels, the post office, four of the banks and several houses at street corners, including the offices of the *Sligo Independent*.

The meeting went ahead in the afternoon with about 2,000 present and besides Griffith, the speakers included Darrell Figgis, Thomas O'Donnell and Alec McCabe. 'The people had a perfect right to reject the Treaty', Griffith told the crowd. He would advise them not to do so but if they did he would follow them. He was not going to surrender the freedom of speech 'to any junta that set itself up in Ireland'. Seán McKeon said he was there as a soldier 'not to speak for or against the Treaty but to uphold freedom of speech. The army must be the servant and not the dictator of the people.' All passed off without incident and the meeting was followed by a banquet with the Dublin party departing by train the following day.

28 Farry, *Aftermath*, pp 59-61; P7/B/199

Anti-Treaty soldiers
in Sligo at
A. Griffith meeting

On 14 April Rory O'Connor and the anti-Treatyites occupied the Four *Bishops' Statement*
Courts. The Irish bishops viewed with alarm the claims being made by certain elements within the army and issued a statement on 26 April:

> The cause of our present scandals and turmoils is the unconstitutional pol-
> icy of certain leaders, who think themselves entitled to force their views
> upon the nation, not by reason but by firearms ... Among the principles
> they defend is the claim that the Army or any part of it can, without any
> authority from the nation as a whole, declare itself independent of all civil
> authority in the country ... Young men connected with this military revolt,
> when ... they make war are parricides, not patriots; when they shoot their
> brothers, they are murderers, and when they injure property, are robbers
> and brigands.[29]

Following the army split, individual members of the IRA were obliged to *Tubbercurry IRA*
declare their allegiance. In Tubbercurry battalion disciplinary action was
taken against those who were pro-Treaty and a 2nd Lieutenant was reduced
to the ranks and eight soldiers courtmartialled and given fourteen days' hard
labour in Boyle barracks. Two others who had been imprisoned in Tubbercurry escaped and later attended a GAA dance at Carrowrile school. The IRA
from Tubbercurry arrived at the dance and 'a hand-to-hand encounter followed'. Shots were fired and injuries were sustained by some, one 'so seriously
injured that the Last Sacraments had to be administered'. Four arrests were
made including the two escapees. [30]

29 *W.P.* 29 April 1922
30 Among those wounded were George, James and Patrick Armstrong and John Gormley.
   P7/B/197, 6 April 1922: Farry, *Aftermath*, p 55

Jim Hunt Arrested   Some incidents could be best described as curtain-raisers to the Civil War which was about to follow. On 2 May a group of five, led by Brigadier Jim Hunt, went to Cloonoghill, Charlestown to organise an official IRA company there. Anti-Treaty IRA, under Adjutant Nealon, opened fire on them. They did not return the fire but agreed to go voluntarily to Tubbercurry where they were detained overnight. Before being released their arms and car were confiscated.[31] Nealon's patrol included Capt Haran, Lts M. Carroll, J. Cahill and three ASUs of twenty men.[32] A number of violent incidents were reported during May and June. At the end of May a farmer's wife in Sonnagh, Charlestown was shot dead after a political argument and a man was arrested. [33]

Collins-de Valera Pact   Collins and de Valera signed a pact on 20 May by which it was expected that all the outgoing TDs would be returned unopposed which in fact removed the Treaty as an issue in the election. The pro-Treaty supporters in South Sligo-East Mayo felt justifiably aggrieved as it left them with two TDs while their opponents had three, despite the fact that the majority of voters were pro-Treaty. Electioneering virtually ceased when the pact was announced although de Valera toured the constituency addressing meetings in many places, including Tubbercurry, Ballymote and Kiltimagh. There was general apathy on polling day and when the votes were counted in South Sligo-East Mayo it was found that the anti-Treatyites got 56% and the pro-Treatyites 30% though the pro-Treaty side had the satisfaction of seeing Alec McCabe top the poll. This was the only constituency in the country where the anti-Treatyites had a majority, but the contest was uneven as the pro-Treaty side had only two candidates as against their opponents' three.

Four Courts   After the election the new government felt it had a mandate to attack the occupants of the Four Courts, which they did on 27 June. About a month earlier Rory O'Connor and Liam Mellowes had attended a Sunday Mass in Monasteraden. [34]. Three days later the Four Courts surrendered and 150 were taken prisoner. The attack on the Four Courts marked the beginning of the Civil War. Frank Carty formed an active service unit (ASU) of twenty-four men in the 4th brigade of the 3rd Western Division and arrested prominent local pro-Treaty leaders, transferring them to Castlebar for detention. [35]

---

31 Hunt's party consisted of Captains Finn, Sweeney, Brennan and O'Connor as well as from Tubbercurry, P. Scanlon, M. Moriarty and T. Brennan.

32 *W.P.* 13 May 1922; Farry, *Aftermath*, p 63

33 The dead woman was Mrs James Kelly and Michael McIntyre of Sonnagh was arrested. *W.P.* 3 & 10 June 1922

34 They accompanied Mollie Flannery Woods, a former contributor to the *Freeman*, and a native of Monasteraden. *W.P.* 10 June 1922

35 'Diary of Activities of 4th Brigade, 3rd Western Division from beginning of hostilities to 30 Nov 1922', P 69 / 33 (17); hereafter 'Diary of Activities'

Twenty-eight-year-old Thomas Ruane, vice-Brigadier of the East-Mayo *Kiltimagh*
IRA brigade, was one of the first casualties of the Civil War in the diocese. A *Shooting*
bitter feud had existed in the brigade for some time and a split occurred during the 'war' of Independence. 'Both sides went on the run,' Tom Carney
recounted later, 'with a greater hatred of each other than they had of the
Tans.' [36] Ruane was the leader of the the unofficial side. An incident occurred
in Kiltimagh on 30 April in which Ruane, by now on the pro-Treaty side, was
involved. That Sunday two men were reading a Free State poster on one of
the gate pillars outside the church in Kiltimagh when they were confronted
by an anti-Treatyite. An argument arose and revolvers were drawn and Ruane
who tried to separate the parties, was shot in the index finger. His house was
raided the following night and attempts were made to arrest him but failed
because he was armed. 'The men retired but intimated that they would call
again.' [37]

They kept their promise. At 10 p.m. on 29 June a party of republicans
entered the premises of his father, Simon Ruane.[38] It was the fair day in
Kiltimagh and Thomas and his brother, James, had spent the day working in
the shop. The intruders produced revolvers and attempted to arrest the
brothers and when James tried to seize one of the revolvers he was shot in the
back. Thomas was dragged outside where he was shot and wounded. One of
the raiders, twenty-year old Moran from Bohola, was also shot and died
within minutes.[39] Both Ruane brothers were moved to Castlebar but doctors
failed to locate the bullet in Thomas and when blood poisoning set in, he
died on Wednesday 5 July.

Foxford had become completely cut off when the bridge over the Moy and *Foxford Mills Closed*
those at Ballylahon and Cloongullane were blown up. Agnes Morrogh
Bernard had no alternative but to shut down the Woollen Mills on Saturday
1 July and she gave a notice to Martin Henry and his curate, Dominick
Casey, to be read at all Masses: 'Owing to the stoppage of trains and posts we
are forced to shut down this mill until communications are opened again and
normal business conditions resumed. We have already large stocks on hands
and we cannot afford to increase same.' [40] She shared her disappointment

36 O'Malley Notebooks / P17b / 109 (Tom Carney) and 113 (Johnny Greely)
37 *W.P.* 6 May 1922; *Kiltimagh,* p 182
38 E. B. J. Seery to Dept of Defence, 27 July 1922, P7 / B / 73 (Seery was a Custom and Excise
   officer in Kiltimagh and was requested by S. T. Ruane to report the death of his brother,
   Thomas.)
39 He was buried in Bohola graveyard on 1 July. His cap and belt was placed on the coffin
   which was borne by a detachment of the IRA. L. MacManus, *White Light and Flame,* p 221
40 P7 / B / 73, 1 July 1922

Notice, signed by Agnes Morrogh Bernard, closing Foxford Mills

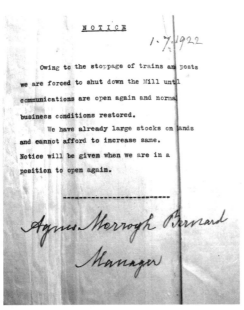

NOTICE

1.7.1922

Owing to the stoppage of trains and posts we are forced to shut down the Mill until communications are open again and normal business conditions restored.

We have already large stocks on hands and cannot afford to increase same.

Notice will be given when we are in a position to open again.

Agnes Morrogh Bernard
Manager

with Mother-General: 'After struggling so hard for the last thirty years, and keeping it open in spite of the War and the Black and Tans, it is our own Irishmen who are bringing poverty into this locality. In another fortnight many poor men with large families depending on their weekly wages in the mill will be starving.'[41] The mills then employed 300 hands who were breadwinners for 1,000 people. 'There are nightly arrests of Volunteers loyal to GHQ and civilian supporters of the government, accompanied by fusillades of gunfire to frighten women and children.' Understandably, the people of Foxford became 'very hostile' to the republicans and were 'looking anxiously forward to their deliverance by national troops'.[42]

Collooney Captured

Carty's republicans, with assistance from other areas, captured the government post at Collooney on 1 July after a two-hour fight with no casualties on either side. Thirty-three prisoners were captured and transferred to Castlebar and some guns and ammunition seized. At Carricknagat, a half mile from Collooney, the following day they captured, without a shot being fired, a party of fourteen government troops travelling from Athlone to Sligo. Again the prisoners were sent to Castlebar and on this occasion 13 rifles, 1,300 rounds of ammunition and a lorry were seized. Two days later, on 4 July, Carty's men attempted without success to take the government post at Gurteen and in the engagement one of his men was mortally wounded.[43]

Railways Disrupted

Republicans continued to use the guerrilla tactics that they had originally employed in the war against the British forces. Their principal targets were the lines of communication especially roads and railways, and bridges were blown up and roads trenched. The Midlands Great Western Railway reported on 1 July that Foxford bridge had been blown up and that the line had been cut at Ballysadare where it was feared that an attempt might be made to blow up the viaduct there. 'These breakages practically put the Sligo line out of action.'[44] Carty's engineer did in fact blow up the bridge at Ballysadare on 1

41 Agnes Morrogh Bernard to Mother General, 5 July 1922, RSCG / H 26 / 87
42 Report of Dr Dunleavy, Foxford to Chief of Staff, 11 July 1922, AD UCD P7 / B / 109;
   P7 / B / 73
43 'Diary of Activities 1, 2, & 4 July', P 69 / 33 (17)
44 P 7 / B / 23 1 July 1922

July and his brigade diary for the week 4-11 July recorded that they destroyed 'enemy lines of communication' throughout their area. 'In all there were eleven large bridges demolished, several culverts opened and trenches cut, and trees felled on all the main roads likely to be of use to the enemy.'

The breakdown in railway communications very quickly caused hardship, particularly in towns. The parish priest of Ballymote asked the station-master in Sligo on 8 July to run a train to Ballymote with foodstuffs. The republican commander in Sligo also ordered him to run the train, promising to remove a mine that was laid on the line and he threatened to blow up the signal cabin in Ballymote if he did not comply. The station master asked the company what he was to do and he was told that 'orders of Irregulars' officers were not to be obeyed by you' and that the company would only run trains on that line 'on instructions from the military authorities acting under the Provisional government.' Disruption on rural railways was also causing hardship in Dublin and arrangements were made with some station masters to collect milk to be conveyed to the city. [45]

It was reported from Enniskillen on 20 July that no trains ran between Sligo and Collooney since 1 July 'by verbal order of the officer commanding the Irregulars in that district.' 'Passengers on their trains are being searched and goods are being looted in a very thorough fashion by the Irregulars ... Both life and property have not been safe lately in the district.' At Enniskillen station the railway company held a large quantity of foodstuffs intended for areas in the West which urgently needed them.[46] Ballaghaderreen station was closed for most of the month of July.

Mines were laid on Ballysadare bridge on 3 July but were taken up again and trains ran between Kiltimagh and Sligo. There were two breaks on the line between Claremorris and Kiltimagh. A train was sent from Tuam on 8 July to the point of obstruction beyond Claremorris and the agent in Kiltimagh sent a train from his end to the obstruction, thus enabling passengers to be conveyed to Collooney. At Collooney uniformed republicans took possession of the train and ordered it to be taken to Sligo. A goods train which had arrived the day before at Kiltimagh returned in the Sligo direction but was taken over by republicans in Tubbercurry. Afterwards they used the train to carry foodstuffs from Sligo to Tubbercurry, Swinford, Kiltimagh and intermediate stations. [47]

Ballymote Cut Off

Collooney to Claremorris Line

45 MGW Rly, 6, 9 & 10 July 1922, P 7 / B / 23 & 98
46 S.L. & N.C. Rly, 22 July 1922, P 7 / B / 23
47 Dermot Fawsitt's railway report, 28 July 1922, P 7 / B / 109

A rail was removed from the line between Charlestown and Curry on 11 July, replaced but removed again on 24 July. Two rails were removed between Curry and Tubbercurry on 15 July and the same day a permanent way between Carramore and Leyny was damaged by explosives, which happened again on 24 July. A pair of rails was taken out and another pair pulled out of position on the line between Curry and Tubbercury. A signal cabin and connections at Charlestown were damaged and three nights later the signal cabin was completely burned down.[48] It was reported that a masonry underbridge on the Claremorris to Collooney line had been blown up on 23 July, that there was an unexploded mine on another bridge and that two overline bridges between Claremorris and Kiltimagh were also blown up. Thirty-two old sleepers were placed across the rails between Charlestown and Curry stations on 25 July and the railway ganger was informed that there was a mine laid under the sleepers.

Mails Disrupted

The railway company asked the military authorities to have the mine removed. On 3 August it was reported that bridges on the Claremorris to Collooney line had been repaired but on the following day armed men would not allow the rails to be repaired at Curry station. Some days later when the lines between Charlestown and Curry were being repaired, armed men forced the workers to remove a rail and throw it down a slope. The line between Claremorris and Kiltimagh was again broken on 13 August but repaired three days later.[49] Early in August the C-in-C of the government forces informed the postmaster-general that it was 'quite impossible' to insure military protection for mail cars or trains carrying mails from Claremorris on the Sligo line. He suggested that the postmaster in Claremorris should get in touch with the local troop commander and try to arrange with him to have the mails conveyed to Swinford, Kiltimagh etc when troops were going to these places.[50] Later that month rails on the line between Ballina and Foxford were torn up, telegraph poles and wires cut and men sent to carry out repairs were fired on. The company had to suspend the service between Manulla Junction and Killala as the military authorities were unable to afford the necessary protection to workers.[51]

Battle of Collooney

National troops leaving Markrea Castle on 13 July were ambushed at Rockwood by Carty's republicans who killed three, wounded ten and captured thirteen – the whole party except one who escaped.[52] Two of those

48 GS & W Rly, 3 Aug 1922, P 7 / B / 23
49 GS & W Rly, 25, 26 & 27 July, 3, 4, 8, 12, 17 Aug 1922, P 7 / B / 23
50 C-in-C to Postmaster-General, 3 Aug 1922, P 7 / B / 25
51 MGW Rly, 21 Aug 1922, P 7 / B / 23
52 'Diary of Activities 13 July', P 69 / 33 (18)

killed were commandants while Commandant Reynolds and Capts Connolly and McPartland were taken prisoner. The republicans also captured the 'Ballinalee' armoured car which provoked an immediate reaction from the government forces. That day General Seán McKeon took between 300 and 400 troops by train from Athlone to Collooney and completely surrounded the town. The attack began at about 6.30 p.m. the following day, Friday 14 July:

An ultimatum was sent to the O/C of the Irregulars and a note to Rev M. Doyle PP to get the citizens to surrender ... The people having left, an attack was launched and after four hours fight, the Irregulars surrendered one post and evacuated the remainder, taking to the hills under Commandant Frank Beirne, who with twenty-three others were captured at 8 a.m. this morning ... In all 70 prisoners were captured, with a huge supply of arms, ammunition and bombs ... The town is only slightly damaged. The Church of Ireland suffered most, owing to a party of ten Irregulars having taken up positions in it. Prisoners were liberated, including Capt Connolly who was wounded in the ambush reported above.[53]

Protestant Church, Collooney

The republicans claimed that about forty of their men, including two commandants, were taken prisoner.[54] 'Twelve men, including Vice-Brigadier Brehony, OC of the garrison, Comdt Coleman and our Lewis-Gunner (with gun) broke through the enemy investing lines and effected their escape.' Their claim that casualties on the goverment side included eleven killed and sixteen wounded appears to be something of an exaggeration.

It was reported that Mrs Terence McSwiney and Mrs Kathleen Barry attended the republicans wounded in Collooney, one of whom,twenty-two year old Patrick Mullen of Carralabin, Bonniconlon, died later in the Mater Hospital, Dublin.[55] His coffin, draped with the tricolour, was placed before the altar in Bonniconlon church where it remained during all Masses on Sunday. At the last Mass the curate, Edward O'Hara, paid a tribute to him and he was given a military funeral to Kilgarvin cemetery where the Rosary was recited in Irish.

Government troops under the command of McCabe, Lawlor and Farrelly, attacked the republican post in Ballymote on 16 July. The attack lasted over an hour when the republicans set fire to the post and surrendered. [56]

53 Report of Seán McKeon, 15 July 1922, P7 / B / 109 & 114
54 'Diary of Activities, 14 July'
55 *W.P.* 22 July & 9 Sept 1922
56 'Diary of Activities', 16 July'

Clonalis Castle
Captured

A column of national troops with armoured car and 18-pounder arrived in Castlerea on the morning of Friday 21 July while a train carried a large number of troops to within two miles of the town. They began an attack on Clonalis Castle at 6 a.m and shortly after noon the republicans occupying the house surrendered and an estimated 300 were taken prisoner.[57] 'The people shouted with joy and cheered "Up McKeon". They were especially pleased with some captures and actually threw their hats (in the air) and danced in the streets.' [58]

With the arrival of the national troops life was returning to normal. 'Farming operations have been resumed ... There is more freedom in travelling, especially for women and children who have been held up in the war zone for several weeks ... Motor cars are scarce and the old outside car has become a popular feature once more.' [59]

Ballyhaunis
Relieved

From there Lawlor pushed on towards Ballyhaunis, one column going by train and the other by road. They arrived there about 10.30 on Sunday morning and again were given a rousing reception:

Barrack Street, Swinford
(courtesy Joe Mellet)

'...thousands rushed out from all sides. I was pulled from the car, seized and carried shoulder high through the town. I did not get away for three-quarters of an hour and they carried me to an hotel where I had to make a speech ... There was no stop to them. They cheered and shouted "Up

57 22 July 1922, P7 / B / 73; another report put the number of prisoners at 60, 25 July 1922, P7 / B / 73
58 Dispatch of General Lawlor, 21 July 1922, P 7 / B / 109
59 *Sunday Independent*, 23 July 1922

McKeon" and "Up Collins" everywhere. Having got the troops fixed up in time to go to Mass the Canon, who had got the news from Prof Whelan, preached "false prophets to have arisen amongst you" and delivered a sermon saying how Maguire was a false prophet and that Seán McKeon's men were the elect. The people applauded in church.'

Lawlor then advanced on Claremorris, eleven miles away. 'All along the road people were collected cheering our troops very much.' [60]

In the middle of July it was planned to send a military expedition by sea from Dublin to Westport with the objective of controlling the area between Ballina, Castlebar and Sligo which included Foxford, Ballaghaderreen and Ballymote. [61] It was hoped to clear the railway line from Claremorris via Tubbercurry to Sligo and to capture republican forces operating in that area. The expedition was to consist of 600 men with 150 bicycles, 600 rifles, six machine guns, 130,000 rounds of ammunition, an armoured car, one eighteen-pounder, one three-ton lorry and one week's rations for 600 men. The plan was to leave 200 men to defend Westport, and to send three cyclist parties, each numbering fifty, to descend on Castlebar following three separate routes while the main body of 100 followed the main road.

Westport Expedition

The expedition, under Capt O'Malley, left the North Wall at 8 p.m. on Saturday 22 July and arrived in Westport Bay at 2 a.m. on Monday 24 July. [62] The pilots from Westport initially declared that the boat was too long to land at the pier but eventually agreed to attempt the landing, which was successfully accommplished at 6.40 p.m. The landing created 'wild panic' among the republican ranks. 'There was a stampede simultaneously from Westport and Castlebar where many of the Irregulars rushed off clad only in shirt and trousers.' In Westport, where they found the barracks on fire after republicans had evacuated it, the national troops were given 'a great reception' by the townspeople. Early on Tuesday morning they set out for Castlebar and when they arrived there at noon they found it already occupied by General Seán McKeon.

Working from Castlebar and Westport the national troops pursued the republicans and made several arrests in Foxford and elsewhere, and a strong detachment took control in Foxford. 'The joy in Foxford knows no bounds as the Irregulars' regime had threatened to ruin the Woollen industry. The village is bedecked with bunting in honour of the advent of the National troops.' It was hoped to re-open the mills shortly.[63]

60 General Lawlor to General Seán McKeon, 25 July 1922, P 7 / B / 109
61 Memorandum on Westport expedition, 17 July 1922, P7 / B / 73
62 Report of Capt O'Malley, 25 July 1922, P7 / B / 73
63 Report, 31 July 1922, P7 / B / 73

Ballaghaderreen Occupied

Republicans occupied Ballaghaderreen at the beginning of July and remained in occupation of the town for three weeks with their headquarters in John Dillon's house.

Formerly, the inhabitants of Ballaghaderreen were strong supporters of de Valera's policy, but the ordeal they have gone through owing to the Irregulars' occupation has completely altered their views. For three weeks all business was suspended and there was no communication with the outside world. At one time there were 200 Irregulars in the place and shops and private houses were ransacked by them ... There was much hardship among the poorer classes.

The same report stated that they laid mines opposite Dillon's house, at Flannery's corner, the courthouse and at other important centres. Four bridges near the town were destroyed and another one close to the bishop's palace. Morrisroe denounced these activities and declared that 'the wilful destruction of bridges etc would be treated as a reserved sin in the diocese.' [64]

It was reported on 22 July that they were preparing for a long siege and that they went to Frenchpark and took all the provisions they could get. 'The people around Ballaghaderreen are in a plight for provisions as all the merchants in Ballaghaderreen have ceased to do any business.' [65] As the national troops approached, the republicans left Ballaghaderreen at 6 p.m. on Wednesday 26 July 'in stolen cars and lorries' and the national army entered the town the following day.

Tubbercurry Captured

Tubbercurry was occupied without resistance by the national troops on 28 July and again republicans left as the troops approached. Some prisoners with arms and ammunition were taken, including Vice-Brigadier Harry Brehony.[66] From now on national forces occupied the towns in County Sligo while republicans took to the hills and adopted guerilla tactics. In the week 4-12 August republicans set up three ambushes, two on the Ballymote to Sligo road and one on the Ballymote to Tubbercurry road, but the ambushes were foiled, they claimed, by civilians revealing their positions to government forces. During that week republicans also sniped at government posts in Tubbercurry, Collooney and Ballymote.

Battle of Swinford

National troops in Swinford were attacked by a large party of republicans led by Tom Carney on Wednesday 2 August. [67] It was the fair day. About

64 28 July 1922, P7 / B / 73; *R.H.* 22 July 1922
65 22 July 1922, P7 / B / 73
66 G.H.Q. statement, 29 July 1922, P7 / B / 73; 'Diary of Activities, 28 July', P 69 / 33 (18)
67 *W.P.* 5 August 1922; P 7 / B / 73, 4 Aug 1922; O'Malley Notebooks / P /17b / 109 (Tom Carney) and 113 (Johnny Greely)

forty-five national soldiers occupied the old RIC barracks with seventeen republican prisoners, both civilians and active members. Republicans seized fifteen of the richer pro-Treaty shopkeepers of Swinford and sent an ultimatum to the barracks, stating that if the prisoners were shot republicans would shoot every member of the garrison. The garrison replied that they would release the prisoners if republicans withdrew from the town. A second ultimatum was sent demanding the release of the prisoners within ten minutes and this time the prisoners were released. Then the battle began and lasted a few hours until the roof of the barracks caught fire and the occupants surrendered. Some republicans were shot dead in the encounter and a large number of the garrison were wounded. About forty rifles were seized.

Reinforcements were sent from Ballina to re-occupy Swinford on the same day but they were ambushed midway between Ballina and Swinford. Commandant Scally and Volunteer J. Traynor (Fermanagh) were killed and Capt Connolly and Volunteer Mike O'Donnell were wounded. [68] When the troops opened fire with a machine gun, the republicans hoisted the white flag and surrendered and five were taken prisoner. [69] Later that evening national troops re-occupied Swinford.

Free State prisoners in Swinford

68 Scally was from Ballymahon where his funeral later took place, *Irish Times*, 7 Aug 1922
69 Commandant James O'Boyle, Foxford, P. Molloy, Foxford, M. Walsh, Straide, John Dooher, Larganmore, Foxford. *W.P.* 5 Aug 1922

National troops from Ballina were ambushed in Killasser on Tuesday 8 August. The battle lasted three and a half hours and eighteen republicans were taken prisoner.[70] Two casualties among the government troops were reported and the dead body of a republican was later found in a turnip field.

Ballinamore Round Up

Government forces attempted to round up republicans but it was a protracted and difficult task as they could easily melt into their surroundings where they had a number of safe houses and committed supporters. Troops under General Lawlor left Ballina at 2 a.m. on 14 August with the 'Big Fella' armoured car and spent hours scouring the area between Kiltimagh and Swinford searching for republicans.[71] Several houses were raided in Kiltimagh. General Lawlor and Comdt Coyle, who travelled ahead of the main convoy in a motor car, were ambushed by a large party of republicans at Ballinamore. However, the 'Big Fella' and the main body of troops arrived quickly on the scene and the republicans surrendered. Thirty-seven republicans were taken prisoner and brought to Ballina.[72] 'It is considered that the capture of these leaders will break the backbone of the resistance in East Mayo.' The troops also seized thirty-seven rifles, fourteen revolvers, thirty-two bombs, a large quantity of ammunition and important documents, including charts and maps. They returned to Ballina via Swinford 'where the national forces were received with great enthusiasm by the people who rushed from their homes with hot tea for the troops.'

Scarce Supplies

Republicans continued to disrupt road and rail transport. The Ballymote to Gurteen road was made impassable as the republicans had blown up a railway bridge in August and for a week the town was completely cut off and supplies of food ran very low. The mail car from Ballymote to Aclare was held up so often that it was said that the horse drawing the car stopped automatically every time he encountered a group of two or more men. Supplies were also in scarce supply in Tubbercurry and as there were no trains merchants had to send carts to other towns to try and replenish their stocks. With no newspapers people were unaware of what was happening elsewhere.[73]

70 Comdt P. Finn, Adj. D. Caulfield, Capt John Robinson, Capt P. J. Keenan, Capt Thomas McGarry, Lieut W. Foley, Lieut James Charleton, QM. P. Laraghan, QM. Martin Gallagher, QM. M. Dooney, Stephen Sheerins, J. J. McDermott, Joe McGowan, James Brennan, James Brady, Charles McDonagh, John Peyton, and Pat Hunter. *W.P.* 12 Aug 1922
71 P/7/B/73, 15 Aug 1922; *W.P.* 19 Aug 1922
72 Among those captured were Comdt Dan (Dynamite) Sheehy, Comdt Peadar Deignan, Section Comdt Dunleavy, brigade QM Henry McNicholas, Comdt James Henry and Volunteers, T. Jordan, Thomas Browne, M. Hunt, M. Duddy, P. Convey, M. Groarke, E. Walsh, T. McNeela, Denis Killackey, - Beehan, P. Moran, P. Duddy, M. Brennan, J. Duddy, J. McNicholas, J. Carroll, P. Carroll and J. Deacy. *W.P.* 19 Aug 1922
73 *W.P.* 12 and 19 Aug 1922

Michael Collins was shot dead on 22 August and Foxford sent a delegation to attend his funeral.[74] A solemn requiem Mass was offered in the parish church on Monday 28 August attended by nine priests, a large congregation and a military guard of honour comprising over 200 Volunteers. Bohola race committee cancelled the annual race meeting and passed a resolution of sympathy to their chairman, Joe Sheridan, whose wife was a sister of Collins, expressing 'the great loss the Irish nation had sustained by the death of such a leader.' The directors of Swinford Town Hall also passed a resolution of sympathy to Mrs Sheridan and all business houses in Swinford and Tubbercurry were closed. A few weeks earlier, when Arthur Griffith had died Foxford also sent representatives to his funeral and had a solemn requiem Mass celebrated in the parish church.[75]

Death of Collins

During the remaining months of 1922 republicans carried out a number of ambushes. On 25 August Frank Carty lured a party of forty-four national troops from Tubbercurry into an ambush in which the whole force was captured, one soldier killed, three wounded and arms and ammunition, including forty rifles and a Lewis gun seized. One report claimed that the national column was decoyed into the ambush by a priest for Carty, but the republican report stated that the troops were lured out by a bogus dispatch sent to Tubbercurry revealing the whereabouts of two officers of their ASU. [76]

Ambushes

Dr Francis Ferran and Frank Carty

National troops travelling in a Crossley tender from Ballyhaunis were ambushed about a mile from Kilkelly on Wednesday 6 September and a number of them wounded. They returned fire and the engagement lasted three hours. When the wounded were being removed to Ballyhaunis a large body of republicans were seen in the hills but they launched no attack. Three republicans were taken prisoner.[77]

74 Dr Dunleavy, J. Mulhern, J. McDonnell, J. Higgins, Mrs Jones, Miss L.M. Gaughan. *W.P.* 2 Sept 1922
75 Patrick Jones and Frank Dorr. *W.P.* 2 Sept 1922
76 'Diary of Activities, 25 Aug, P/69/33 (19); Conroy, Athlone to D/I (telephone), 26 Aug 1922, P/7/B/73. 25
77 Brig. Adj. James Vesey, Capt Peter Donnelly and Capt. Luke Traynor (Taylor?). Among the wounded national troops were the driver, Cloonan, Sgt McGuinness and Corporal Gorman P7/B/73, 7 Sept 1922, *W.P.* 9 Sept 1922

John Durcan, Curry

Carty's ASU with the 'Ballinalee' armoured car entered Tubbercurry the following day and tried unsuccessfully to capture the garrison. They launched an attack on Ballymote barracks on 13 September which began at 4 a.m. and lasted about an hour. Two government soldiers on duty in the streets were overpowered and disarmed but the republicans were forced to retreat and one of them, Adjutant John Durcan of Curry, was shot dead. The republicans retired to billets in the vicinity of Lough Talt. [78]

Foxford Casualties

Ten days later two Foxford men, Capt Tom Healy (Pontoon) and Volunteer Sean Higgins, were killed by republicans in an ambush in Erris. When their remains were returned to Foxford they were met by a large crowd at the station and brought to the church where a guard of honour remained all night. Solemn requiem Mass the following day was followed by a military funeral by soldiers of the 2nd Battalion, led by the Foxford Brass Band, to the 'patriots' plot' in St Michael's cemetery. The funeral oration was given by Dr Dunleavy followed by a firing party and the playing of the Last Post. Michael Collin's sister, Mrs Sheridan of Bohola, was amongst those present at the funeral. [79]

Swinford Attacked

Swinford was attacked on Sunday night 1 October by republicans who had surrounded the town.[80] The garrison, who occupied strong positions at the station, the workhouse and the convent grounds, replied with machine guns and rifles. The exchange continued from 11 p.m. to 6 a.m. when the attackers retreated towards Kilkelly, pursued by national troops who claimed to have brought down two fugitives.

A flying column of national troops returning from Charlestown on Saturday 14 October was ambushed at Carracastle and in the engagement, Jim Mulrenan of Lisacull, who had been the republican commanding officer in Ballaghaderreen during their occupation of the town, was shot dead. Two months later his brother, Patrick, a prisoner in Costume Barracks, Athlone, died from wounds received there. [81]

Arrests

At the end of August a party of national troops under Colonel-Commandant McCabe captured twelve republicans in the Ballaghaderreen

78 'Diary of Activities, 13 Sept', P/69/33 (19); *W.P.* 16 Sept 1922
79 Higgins was one of the six victims of the Black and Tan atrocity in Foxford in the previous May. *W.P.* 23 Sept 1922
80 P/7/B/74, 3 Oct 1922
81 P/7/B/74, 17 Oct 1922; *W.P.* 21 Oct & 16 Dec 1922

area, as well as a quantity of arms, ammunition, Mills bombs and two motor cars.[82] Seán McKeon with troops from Athlone joined forces with Lawlor in Tubbercurry on the night of 14 September and, with about 700 men, equipped with two field-pieces and two armoured cars, swept the Ox Mountains from there to Coolaney searching for Carty and his republicans. Carty, who had received prior intelligence of the operation, demobilised his men with instructions to 'lie low' to avoid capture and as a result only one republican was captured. They remained demobilised from 15 September to 4 November, much to the annoyance of General Liam Lynch. 'The enemy must not be permitted,' he informed William Pilkington, O/C of 3rd Western Division, 'to roam freely through his area.'[83] A number of republicans were arrested in Ballaghaderreen in the second half of September and those held in Ballymote were transferred to Athlone. [84]

At the end of October hundreds of national troops with the 'Big Fella' armoured car arrived in Ballyhaunis and from there 200 troops, under Comdt Francis Symons went in the direction of Aghamore and Kilkelly. In Aghamore they captured a party of republicans including Comdt Michael Mullins. They occupied Kilkelly on Saturday night 28 October and the following day arrested some republicans including Comdt Johnny Greely 'the most noted leader of the republicans in East Mayo'.[85]

Kilkelly occupied

Eight republicans were captured in a round-up near Tubbercurry on 1 November and, believing that enemy spies were informing on them, Carty decided to take drastic action. Four armed men arrived at 2 a.m. on Saturday (Sunday) 5 November in Powelsboro at the house of Matt Hunt, a fifty-year-old farmer, father of ten, two of whom were three-month old twins. [86] They took him from his bed and ordered him outside. 'He called for a drink of holy water before he went out.' One of the armed men was left behind to guard the family until about 5 a.m. when shots were heard. On the same night armed men came to Michael O'Connor's house also in Powelsboro and took

Tubbercurry Shootings

82 P/7/B/73, 26 Aug 1922
83 William Pilkington to Chief of Staff, 10 Dec. 1922 and Chief of Staff to O/C 3rd Western Division, 19 Dec 1922; 'Diary of Activities, 15 Sept-4 Nov', P/69/33 (20)
84 *Ballaghaderreen:* J. J. Coleman, J. Feely, Joe Morley, Joe Towey, Bob Flannery, George Mahon, – O'Dowd (son of ex-Sgt O'Dowd), – Coffey, – Flynn, P. Doyle (Duff's), – Kirrane or Kirwan (Flannery's), – Moran (electric light station, brother of Moran, Crossna, executed in Mountjoy), Dominick McCoy, Edmondstown, – Geever, Cloontia, McGeever, Charlestown, etc. *W.P.* 23 Sept 1922. *Transferred from Ballymote:* Section Comdt Pat McAndrew, Bonniconlon, Pte James Judge, do, Pte Pat Crean, do, Pte Michael Flynn, Tubbercurry, Pte Dan Gallagher, Ballymote. *W.P.* 30 Sept 1922
85 P/7/B/74, 30 Oct 1922
86 P/7/B/74, 8 Nov 1922; Report of Western Command to C-in-C, 8 Nov 1922, P/7/B/110; *W.P.* 18 Nov 1922

out his son, twenty-seven year old James Joseph as well as his brother, Patrick. On his way out James asked for a priest to attend them before they were shot. One of the brothers, Patrick, was sent back to the house where one of the armed men kept guard until shots were heard at 5 a.m. Both bodies were found a few hours later by people on their way to Sunday Mass. The report of the Western Command which described Hunt and O'Connor as 'local volunteers of the national army', stated that they 'appear to have been terribly mutilated before being shot as there heads were completely battered in.' A label was found near their bodies with the words 'Convicted Spy. IRA.' The republican diary recorded the killings with clinical detachment: 'With the approval of the Divisional Command we executed two enemy spies at Moylough, Tubbercurry.' [87]

Cloonacool Man Shot

A detachment of twelve national soldiers from Ballymote barracks, under the command of Alec McCabe, accompanied by Capt Conway and Capt Boles from Tubbercurry, arrived in Cloonacool the following night to search for the killers. They searched a number of 'disloyal' houses and in one found a shotgun and some ammunition. Then they approached the house of creamery manager, Frank Scanlon, which was close to the house of the prominent republican, Jack Brennan.[88] Frank's wife, Eleanor, who heard them approaching, warned her husband and he fled out the back as she was opening the front door. He was called on to halt and when he did not two shots were fired. When his wife rushed out she was stopped by the military and she begged them to send for a priest but they said it was not necessary as he was not dead. Later they told her that they had sent a car for a priest but no priest came. An hour later she found the dead body of her husband about thirty yards from the back door. McCabe claimed that Scanlon 'was constantly associating with republicans in Cloonacool and a close personal friend of Jack Brennan's' whom he was probably going to warn when he was shot. On the following Wednesday all businesses in Tubbercurry were closed for the funerals of Hunt and O'Connor and their coffins were draped with tricolours as they were brought to Rhue cemetery. Scanlon was also given a funeral of 'imposing dimensions.'

Reign of Terror

McCabe reported that at this time a young man in Curry, a strong government supporter, was taken and kept out all night which left him 'speechless from severe shock'. 'A column of about fifty men under Carty is making a circuit of the Tubbercurry area leaving a trail of blood behind them.' Notices were posted on Moylough chapel on Sunday 12 November that

87 'Diary of Activities', 4 Nov, P/69/33 (20)
88 Report of Col Comdt McCabe, 7 Nov 1922, P/7/B/114

people giving information to government forces would be shot, and similar notices signed IRA were posted extensively around Tubbercurry warning people against speaking to national soldiers on penalty of being taken from their homes and shot. [89] These warnings, coupled with the two killings by Carty, had an immediate effect and the republican diarist recorded his satisfaction with the result of the executions: 'This action had the effect of completely breaking up the enemy spy system in this area, especially in the district between Tubbercurry and Ballymote.'[90] Eight inhabitants of Tubbercurry took refuge in Markrea Castle which was occupied by government troops and Alec McCabe reported that 'there were crowds coming in from the terrorised area to Ballymote and Tubbercurry barracks. Don't know what to do with them.' [91]

National troops were ambushed on Tuesday 7 November between Swinford and Foxford by a party of about eighty republicans, said to be commanded by Frank Carty. [92] The troops returned fire and it was reported that seven republicans were killed and several others wounded while three of the national troops who were wounded were later discharged from hospital. Early in December a party of five national soldiers travelling by car from Tubbercurry to Ballymote was ambushed by a section of Carty's ASU at Powelsboro, about a mile from Bunninadden. The engagement lasted only five minutes and two of the soldiers were killed and one wounded.[93]

Callow Ambush

A twelve man section of a republican ASU held up the mail train from Dublin to Sligo about a mile from Ballymote on the Dublin side on 14 December.[94] All the letters were censored and 'some important enemy intelligence reports' captured. Five national soldiers travelling from Boyle to Markrea Castle were taken prisoner and three rifles, 400 rounds of ammunition and other equipment seized. The engine was then uncoupled from the train and sent full speed in the direction of Sligo without driver or fireman but points furthest distant from Sligo station were split and the engine travelling at 50 m.p.h. was derailed and hurtled down an embankment.

Train Held-Up

A CID man, 'Pepper' McDonnell from Carracastle, who was stationed in Swinford, drove to Charlestown on the evening of Friday 22 December.[95] His

Charlestown Shooting

89 *W.P.* 18 Nov 1922, P/7/B/74
90 'Diary of Activities, 4 Nov', P/69/33 (21-2)
91 Report of McCabe, 7 Nov 1922, Mulcahy Papers, P/7/B/114
92 P/7/B/74. 8 and 9 Nov 1922
93 Capt Brennan and Volunteer Clarke were killed and Capt Dolan was wounded. The other passengers included the driver, Gannon, and Volunteer Kenny. *W.P.* 9 Dec 1922
94 Report of Adj Seán Ginty, 14 December 1922: P/17a/119: P/7/B/74, 15 Dec 1922
95 P/7/B/74 3 Jan 1923; *W.P.* 6 Jan 1923

car was immediately surrounded by armed men who shot McDonnell in the arm but he succeeded in drawing his revolver and in the exchange a young man called Kilroy from Curry was shot dead. In the republican report of the incident, Kilroy managed to fire twice and wounded McDonnell in the side and hand but as none of the other republicans were armed McDonnell made good his escape.[96] Kilroy was buried in a cemetery about a half a mile from Tubbercurry which was strongly garrisoned by national troops who made no effort to interfere with the funeral the following Sunday and he was given full military honours by a large party of armed republicans marching in military formation.

Courtmartialled

Also in Curry at the same time, a sixty-year-old farmer, called Durcan, from Bunnacranagh, whose son was in the national army, was shot and wounded in his bed.[97] The shooting was disowned by republicans and the perpetrator, Brennan, was forced to stand outside Curry chapel on Sunday 12 January with a placard round his neck signed by Carty, stating that he had been courtmartialled by republicans. Brennan was later expelled from the brigade area.

Carty's Colunm

Dr O'Donnell, the medical officer of Sligo Garrison, informed the office of the Commander-in-Chief in Dublin on 21 December that Carty was operating in a block between Sligo, Ballina, Charlestown and Tubbercurry and that it would take three to four hundred men to capture him and his column. 'Carty's column operating in that area has terrorised the people to such an extent that they will give no information whatever.' [98]

An unnamed officer reviewed the situation in north-west Sligo where Carty and the republicans controlled all Co Sligo between Ballina and Ballysadare: [99]

> They move about as they please and commandeer everything they require. They are nearly always in Enniscrone and Bonniconlon and make periodical raids on the shops in Easkey and Dromore West ... They always have sentry groups at the townlands of Cloonta and Carna near Bonniconlon who can review from the hills all roads from Ballina so all Irregulars get timely warning and clear out ... The Irregular headquarters in this area are at Gleneask House about two miles due north of Lough Talt. Carty is generally there. In addition, the principal resting place is in the row of houses running from north to south on the slopes of the Ox Mountains in Clookeelaun Bog.

96 Report of Seán Ginty, 14 Dec 1922, P 17a / 119
97 P/7/B/74, 3 Jan 1923; P/17a/119, 14 Jan 1923; *W.P.* 13 Jan 1923
98 P/7/B/75, 21 Dec 1922
99 P/7/B/75, 29 Dec 1922

The civilian population in this area consisted of three classes. Larger farmers and nearly all shopkeepers who were suffering severely would support strong action to get rid of the republicans. On the other hand, the moderate size farming class had everything to gain from the absence of ordered control as they paid no rates or rents and had a supply of goods and provisions looted from the shops for which in return they housed republicans. The poorer class of farmers depended for their livelihood on the sale of turf which was well-nigh impossible with roads blocked and cut up. 'They suffer great hardship and are secretly hostile.'

Sligo anti-Treaty column

Enormous quantities of treacle arrived in Sligo and Ballina from Liverpool and Glasgow and during Christmas week the officer saw six horse carts in line loaded with treacle leaving Ballina alone. The treacle, nominally for cattle, was in fact used for making poteen. 'This Christmas the countryside from Sligo to Connemara was not alone drunk but demented from this stuff.' Republicans licensed certain houses where it was sold at sixpence a glass and was 'as plentiful as water'. With or without poteen social activities during the Christmas period were severely curtailed. Morrisroe asked that no dances or similar gatherings be held in the diocese due to the disturbed conditions prevailing and the festive season in Ballymote was described as 'very tame and dull'.[100]

Poteen

1923 began with republicans continuing their guerrilla activity.[101] They sniped at the government post in Tubbercurry on 1 and 4 January and on 25

Guerrilla Activity

100 Farry, *Aftermath*, p 138
101 'Diary of Activities, 1, 4, 25 & 30 January', P/17a / 119

January a sniper shot dead one of the garrison. At the end of that month Carty's ASU held up the mail train from Sligo to Dublin between Collooney and Ballymote, censored the mails and seized government intelligence reports. The train was derailed and the engine blown up by a land mine.

Glore Ambush   Republicans were more active in East Mayo, setting up an ambush at Glore bridge on the Swinford to Kiltimagh road on Wednesday 17 January. [102] About sixty soldiers from the Swinford garrison had gone to Kiltimagh to attend the funeral of one of their number, twenty-five-year-old Capt James Higgins,

and forty-five republicans under Brigadier Tom Carney planned to ambush them as they returned to Swinford after the funeral. Meanwhile a Ford car approaching from the direction of Swinford was stopped by the republicans who directed it up a by-road 'where other civilian cars were detained'. The driver, Michael Byrne from Swinford, 'made a dash for Kiltimagh' and shots were fired. One of the passengers in the back seat, Christopher Farrell of Dublin, a representative of Power's Whiskey, was hit and mortally wounded. Byrne stopped and was forced to take a by-road where he was told he could get a priest and a doctor a few miles away. It eventually brought him to Knock where he sought the services of the parish priest.

The approach of the cars and lorries carrying the troops from Kiltimagh was signalled by 'a lady waving a handkerchief from a hill top' and they were met with a fusillade of bullets. They took cover behind a ditch and returned fire. The attack began at 4 p.m. and continued until 8 p.m. when reinforcements with artillery arrived from Claremorris and forced the ambushers to retreat. The troops suffered a number of casualties including Commandant McCann, O/C Swinford garrison, Capt Benson of Kiltimagh, Volunteer Clarke and Volunteer Thomas Browne from Kiltimagh who died later from

Capt James Higgins,
National Army
(courtesy Betty Solon)

his wounds. All of them were removed to the hospital in Claremorris.

There were also some 'young ladies' from Swinford travelling with the troops in a car, driven by Vice-Brigadier Byrne, with Commandant McCann. It was reported that an explosive was thrown into the car and one of the girls,

102 Report of East Mayo Brigade, 27 Jan 1923, P/17a/119; O'Malley Notebooks (T. Carney), P/17b/109; *W.P.* 27 Jan 1923; *Kiltimagh*, pp 184-5

Mary Frances Smyth, only daughter of a Swinford hardware merchant, was 'shockingly mutilated' and lost an eye. She was also taken to Claremorris hospital where she was visited by General Seán McKeon who said that 'there was no chivalry in the murder of the little innocents and there would be no chivalry shown as far as he was concerned.' Regarding Miss Smyth, republicans claimed that 'the enemy press reports were entirely inaccurate.'

Tom Carney was wounded in the lung and lost a good deal of blood while he was being taken in an ass and cart to a farmer's house. He was attended by pro-Treaty Dr Tighe from Kilkelly who told him that he had only a 20-1 chance of surviving. The curate in Kilkelly, Matthew Leonard, also attended him and Carney found him 'very nice'. Later Carney was taken to a house about a mile from Ballaghaderreen, where a son and daughter were doctors and another daughter a nurse and was kept there for two weeks and then brought to Archdeacon O'Hara's house in Kilmovee. Roger O'Hara (whom Carney described as 'a terrible reptile') was then in his mid-eighties and the housekeeper, a Limerick girl called Maggie Collins, was 'really the acting PP and every one was afraid of her'. She put Carney to bed in the parochial house where he was unable to move for three weeks and when he was able to get up in March Maggie gave him one of the Archdeacon's trousers as he had nothing to wear.[103]

Roger O'Hara

Round-Ups

By now the war had degenerated into a number of minor actions by republican columns such as disruption of rail and telegraph communications, burning of houses of government supporters and other low-risk activities. The entry in the diary of activities for the East Mayo brigade on 16 March read: 'Portion of the roads strewn with tacks of glass to retard enemy cycling patrol.'[104] Republican activity was severely curtailed by the frequent large-scale sweeps of their areas by government forces, like that carried out along the Ox Mountains from 6-13 April.[105] Government troops estimated at about 1,100 blocked all access and egress to the mountains between Ballysadare and Ballina on the north side and on the south side from Coolaney to Lough Talt and right into Bonniconlon. Signallers were placed at various vantage points along the mountains and on 10 April they carried out a house-to-house search. Carty's republicans, who were concentrated in the mountains, were well aware of the troops' movements and largely eluded capture. Prior to this

103 O'Malley Notebooks (T. Carney), P/17b/109
104 P/69/30 (170)
105 Report of Enemy Round-Up on the Ox Mountains, Adj. 3rd Western Division to O/C Western Command, 16 April 1923, P/69/30 (88-91)

sweep government troops had taken control of Aclare and captured five members of a republican ASU in the mountainous district around Aclare. In East Mayo they occupied Charlestown and Kilkelly.

Last Fatality   One of the last fatalities in the diocese was thirty-one year old Peter Mc Nicholas of Bridge Street, Swinford.[106] He left Charlestown on Wednesday 25 April with five others in a Ford car driven by by Sgt John Douglas Garnett on their way to their headquarters in Claremorris and about two miles beyond Kiltimagh, near Murneen schoolhouse, the car was fired on and Mc Nicholas hit in the head. The driver accelerated from 15 to 30 m.p.h. and when he reached Claremorris McNicholas was attended by a doctor and a priest but died in the early hours of the following morning in Claremorris hospital. Just a month later, on 24 May, Frank Aiken, the republican Chief of Staff, issued a call to his men to dump their arms, which effectively brought the Civil War to an end. Republicans continued on the run for some time afterwards but were gradually rounded up. William Pilkington was arrested while cycling unarmed outside Ballymote a month after the Dump Arms Order, and M. J. O'Hara of Kilmactigue, commandant of the Tubbercurry battalion, was captured in a dug-out in Skreen, while Commandant Dominick Benson of Ballysadare suffered the same fate. [107]

Deaths   It is estimated that about fifty-four people in County Sligo lost their lives during the civil war, twenty members of the government army, twenty-three republicans and eleven civilians. [108] Most of these deaths (38) occurred in the first three months of the war with only eight deaths from January to May 1923. There were only thirteen named fatalities in the Mayo part of the diocese but at least as many more deaths were reported where victims were not identified. Of the thirteen identified, eight belonged to the government forces, four were republicans, and one civilian.

Religion   There was a strong religious sense amongst the participants on both sides in the Civil War and even a certain amount of puritanism, particularly among the leaders. Confession was high among the priorities of men who lived frequently in the shadow of death. 'Before the attack (Boyle) all our lads went to confession,' Commandant Johnny Greely of the republican East Mayo brigade later recounted. [109] Going to confession was often a sign that an ambush was imminent. 'Pilkington was seen in Sligo at confession about two weeks ago,' it was reported towards the end of 1922.[110] William Pilking-

106 *W.P.* 5 May 1923
107 P/69/107
108 Farry, *Aftermath*, p 93
109 O'Malley Notebooks, P/17b/113
110 Interview with Dr O'Donnell, 21 Dec 1922, P/7/B/75

ton, the republican commanding officer of the 3rd Western Division, was described by Ernie O'Malley as 'very religious, a fighting saint.' [111] The republican 4th Western Division covered North Mayo which included Foxford, Bonniconlon and Attymass. In July 1922 an ASU from this division collaborated with the 3rd Western Division in attacks on Collooney, Gurteen, Markrea Castle and Boyle. 'From 2-10 September we have continually changed billets, got confessions on two occasions, communion once and attended Mass twice.' They had already got confessions in a private house at the end of August from the curate of Mulranny.[112]

When Michael Mullin of Bunninadden was shot and wounded in Sligo on the occasion of Arthur Griffith addressing a meeting there, General Lawlor recited an act of contrition in his ear before he was attended by a Dominican priest. Usually care was strictly taken to insure that wounded opponents were given access to spiritual assistance. At Rockwood ambush on 13 July 1922, where three were killed and eleven wounded, the republicans released one driver 'to procure spiritual and medical aid.' Again on 30 November when republicans ambushed five government soldiers on the Tubbercurry-Ballymote road and wounded four of them, they sent the driver, the only one to escape injury, to Bunninadden 'for spiritual and medical aid'. This was duly recorded in the republican diary of activities compiled by the adjutant of the 4th Brigade, Seán Ginty of Aclare, a former seminarian in All Hallows. [113]

Spiritual Assistance

This concern for the spiritual welfare of combatants was not always evident. The huge terror caused in the Tubbercurry area by Carty's shooting of the two alleged spies in Powelsboro was probably due at least partially to the victims having been denied the ministrations of a priest prior to their execution. When government forces under Alec McCabe shot the creamery manager in Cloonacool, his wife asked them to send for a priest, and she stated at the inquest that they told her 'they had sent a motor for the priest but no priest came.' [114] In the propaganda war, each side accused the other of denying their victims spiritual assistance. Such an accusation was made against republicans at the Glore ambush where the commercial traveller was shot. The driver was not allowed to proceed to Kiltimagh for the obvious reason that he could warn the soldiers of the ambush awaiting them but was, however, allowed to follow a side road to Kilkelly and eventually got a priest in Knock.

On one occasion a priest was impersonated. [115] On Saturday 26 August

111 Ernie O'Malley, *The Singing Flame*, p 50
112 'Diary of Activities, 4th Western Division, 1 July-19 Sept 1922', P/17a/121
113 'Diary of Activities, 4th Brigade, 3rd Western Division, 1 July-30 Nov 1922', P/69/33 (17)
114 *W.P.* 18 Nov 1922
115 *W.P.* 2 Sept 1922

Patrick Nealis of Kilnamanagh, Ballysadare was taken from his home by three republicans and driven to a house in Skreen. He was told to prepare for the priest as he was going to be shot. A man dressed as a priest entered the house on Sunday morning and beckoned to Nealis to follow him into a room where he would hear his confession. Later Nealis said that the man 'smelt strongly of drink and staggered about'. However, he went through the formality of making his confession. The man posing as a priest had particular difficulty when giving absolution 'stuttering and stopping and muttering'. Nealis was then taken back to the Collooney crossroads where he was shot five times and wounded in the chest, hip and shoulder but later recovered. Morrisroe referred to this incident in his pastoral the following Lent and roundly condemned the impersonation of a priest.

Perhaps the most fitting epitaph on the Civil War came from the pen of a Kiltimagh writer: [116]

Darkness and fear over the land. All is weird, unnatural. Men's eyes filled with scales: men's hearts hardening. Hatred and malice and lies abroad. Children learning to be spies. Suspicion everywhere. This is the awful Civil War.

Priests
There were some early attempts at reconciliation. The parish priest and four curates in Castlebar signed a letter to the newspaper calling for the release of republican prisoners: [117]

Taking into consideration that Christmas is approaching, the holy season of peace and goodwill, and that the Republican Party have abandoned their attitude of armed hostility, we are of the opinion that the release of the political prisoners would help to restore peace and unity once more to our beloved country.

Such attempts by priests were rare and doomed to failure.

Most Achonry priests, with probably three exceptions, Philip J. Mulligan, Denis Gildea and 'Doc' Henry, followed the lead of their bishop, Morrisroe, 'one of the most determined opponents of republicanism.' [118] A leading republican in East Mayo described the 'imperial' Morrisroe as 'the worst bishop in Ireland'[119] Morrisroe advised the people not to vote for Sinn Féin in the general election in 1923 as it would mean the country would face a repetition of the horrors of 1922, and again in 1925 he sent a similar message to a Cumann na nGaedheal meeting in Ballaghaderreen suggesting it would be a

116 Lily MacManus, *White Light and Flame*, p 223
117 P/69/34 (137), Dec 1923
118 Patrick Murray, *Oracles of God*, pp 166-167
119 O'Malley Notebooks (T. Carney), P/17b/109

'suicidal act' to vote against the government. In 1927 he nominated his local Cumann na nGaedheal candidate.

In these election campaigns some Achonry priests were outspoken in their condemnation of the republicans. Thomas H. Quinn of Ballymote, one of the leading Cumann na nGaedheal campaigners in County Sligo, described republicans in 1925 as 'renegades and traitors, knaves and tricksters, who are false to every trust, law and honour' and advised the people to reject republicanism with 'its anarchy, red ruin and destruction'. Walter Henry of Killasser clashed with the famous republican priest, Michael O'Flanagan, at a meeting in Callow when he told O'Flanagan to remove his clerical collar and advised people not to listen to him. Michael Connolly of Curry compared Frank Carty at a Cumann na nGaedheal meeting there to Judas Iscariot who 'did great work and then went wrong'.[120] The bitter legacy of the Civil War was to retard normal political evolution in the country for much of the century and probably enhanced the dominant role exercised by the church over Irish society.

120 *Irish Independent*, 21 Feb and 2 Mar 1925; *R.H.* 14 Mar 1925; see Murray, *Oracles*, pp 117-19

Aftermath

The church in Achonry continued to expand in the numbers of its clerical and religious personnel, while at the same time its population declined dramatically as a result of emigration. In 1881 the population of the diocese stood at 104,490 with just over forty priests. The population declined every decade by 10-12,000, falling to 82,705 by 1901. Seventy years later it had more than halved again to 40,000 while there were seventy-one priests working in the diocese as well as thirteen Passionists resident there, with two diocesan priests working elsewhere in Ireland and four abroad. The ratio of priest to people went from 1 to 3,777 just before the Famine to 1 to 666 in 2000. The decline in the number of Protestants was also dramatic, falling from 2,734 in 1881 to a mere 400 in 1980.

Vocations

Vocations to the priesthood and the religious life in the diocese flourished for much of the twentieth century. It was not unusual for almost half a Leaving Cert class in St Nathy's College to opt for the priesthood, while in convent secondary schools a sizeable number of girls, including many of the brightest and best, chose the religious life. From the early decades of the century there were so many vocations to the diocesan priesthood that most of the priests had to serve lengthy periods abroad before a position could be found for them in the diocese.[1] In fact up to the 1960s no priest was appointed to a parish in the diocese immediately after ordination. Those few who did return to the diocese immediately had special academic qualifications and were appointed to teaching posts in St Nathy's. In 1930 alone there were thirty Achonry priests serving temporarily abroad. One of them, Thomas McGettrick from Killavil, was on loan to Nigeria where he opted to stay and later became Bishop of Ogoja. In fact, not surprisingly, about a third of over a hundred Achonry priests who served abroad chose to stay in their adopted countries. Some seventy others returned, many of them after fairly long stints abroad. James Edward O'Hara spent fourteen years in Los Angeles before returning to become dean in St Nathy's. James Hyland spent ten years in Melbourne before he was recalled. Martin McManus from Killasser spent eleven

James Hyland

---

1   see John Doherty, *Achonry Priests in the Twentieth Century* (unpublished typescript 1999)

years in Nigeria before he was recalled to the diocese in 1949. He later returned to Nigeria where he spent a further nine years before he returned to fill several posts in the diocese before becoming parish priest in Bonniconlon where he died.

Female religious communities continued to thrive. The Mercy Sisters received almost ninety postulants in the fifty years from 1927-1977, with one most years, often two and sometimes three. A peak was reached in the late fifties and early sixties with four postulants received in Swinford for each of the years 1959 and 1960 and six in 1961.[2] New branches were established within the diocese, Ballysadare (1942) and Gurteen (1954) and abroad in Jefferson City (1960). The other religious communities probably experienced a similar influx during that period. The Marist Sisters established a community in Charlestown in 1942 when Sisters came from Tubbercurry to take charge of a girls' secondary school. The convent was built in Lowpark in 1953 and up to the present twenty-five Marists have served there, while over 180 have ministered in Tubbercurry.[3]

Mercy novices and postulants, Swinford 1960
Front row L-R:
Angela O'Grady,
Enda O'Donnell,
Anselm McNicholas,
Colman Noonan,
Ambrose Shiels,
Declan Chambers,
Ligouri Kelly
Back row L-R:
Vincent Haran,
Andrew Lally,
Vianney Mullen,
Philip Sherlock,
James Lowther,
Joachim Gallagher
(courtesy Phil Clancy)

Sisters of St John of God of the St Therese province in Australia established in 1936 a juniorate in Ballinamore House, the former residence of the Ormsby family, a short distance from Kiltimagh. The juniorate continued from 1936-42 and again from 1959-65 and almost 160 girls from all over Ireland

Sisters of St John of God, Ballinamore House

2   See Appendix 12; information provided by Phyl Clancy RSM
3   See Appendix 10; information provided by Alvarez Kelly SM

began their religious training there for missionary work in Australia.[4] The Order's novitiate moved there in 1942 because of the Second World War and Morrisroe officiated at the reception of eight novices in February 1844. The noviate remained until 1947 when it was transferred to Subiaco in Western Australia. The Sisters set up a nursing home in Ballinamore in 1943 and this continued until 1959. Ballinamore House and grounds were given by the Order to the Western Care Association as an outright gift in 1974 for the care of children with disabilities. Four of the Sisters agreed to help in caring for the handicapped and continued to work there until 1986 while living in Main Street, Kiltimagh.

Ballymote   The Sisters opened in 1953 a maternity nursing home in Castle Lodge in Ballymote which also catered for convalescents and those suffering from minor illnesses. It became a nursing home for the elderly in 1971 which continues to exist, with Sisters working there though the administration was transferred in 2001 to the North Western Health Board. In all, thirty-four Sisters of St John of God ministered in Ballymote since 1953.

The Passionists   The Passionists opened St Joseph's Retreat House in 1943 in the former seat of the Meredith family in Cloonamahon near Collooney, becoming the

Cloonamahon House

only religious order of priests in the diocese.[5] The number in the community ranged from about six to fourteen and, while their main function was to preach missions in various parts of the country, they also catered for local re-

4   See Appendix 14; information provided by Mary Eugenia Brennan SJG
5   See Appendix 16

treats. Apart from the superior, bursar, cook and farm manager, six of the community of twelve in 1971 were described as missioners / retreat directors.

Unquestionably, Achonry's most outstanding contribution in the twenti-eth century was in the mission fields.[6] Over one thousand priests, nuns and brothers, all natives of the diocese, whose names are recorded in this volume, served as missionaries in all four continents. Probably many other names are omitted as they have no longer relatives in their native parishes to record their memory. Many nuns, particularly, entered the religious life overseas and only by scouring the records of these convents – a task way beyond the scope of this work – could their connection with Achonry ever be known. Some parishes had extraordinary records. It was said of Tourlestrane – and not without some justification – that there was scarcely a house in the parish that had not produced one or more religious vocations, many of whom became missionaries. With sixty-three missionary priests it had easily the highest number of any parish in the diocese. In all, the diocese produced 467 priests for the missions and just over one hundred more nuns (568). Swinford had the greatest number with 169, almost three-quarters of whom were nuns, fol-lowed by Ballaghaderreen with almost a hundred. Surprisingly, Curry was a close third, with two-thirds of them nuns. Kiltimagh and Kilmovee also had impressive numbers.

They went all over the world: almost 350 to the United States and Cana-da, about 300 to Great Britain, almost 120 to Africa and 80 to Australia and New Zealand. Of those who went to Africa, many worked in Nigeria and South Africa while others ministered in Kenya, Uganda, Ghana, Zimbabwe, Zambia, Sierra Leone, Liberia, Ethiopia, Egypt, and Tanzania. Smaller num-bers went to Asia, particularly to China, Hong Kong, Korea, Japan, India. Pakistan and the Philippines, and to Peru, Mexico, British Guyana, Brazil, Ecuador and Paraguay in South America. Others went to Mauritius, Malaysia, Fiji and Papua, New Guinea. Some fifty natives of the diocese worked in con-tinental Europe, in Belgium, France, Spain, Portugal, Italy, and Germany.

Some missionaries ministered in several countries, sometimes even in dif-ferent continents. Michael E. Coleman from Killasser, who spent four years as president of St Nathy's College, later joined the Jesuits and worked in South Africa, China and Australia where he died in 1920. Andrew Kelly from Swinford was chaplain to the British Army in Burma and later spent ten years in Peru before ending his life as parish priest of Charlestown. Mary Flannelly from Attymass, who was professed in 1952 at the age of twenty-one, served in

Missions

6   see Appendix 17

Australia, the United States, India, England, Malta and Scotland. Francie Cawley, who taught for years in St Nathy's, worked in Peru for six years and a further eighteen in Jamaica. Teresa Dempsey from Killasser, who was professed in 1971, worked in Uganda and Kenya in Africa as well as India and the United States.

Only one lay missionary, Mary Costello of Creaggagh in Kiltimagh who went to Iceland, is recorded here. There were probably others. Over 60,000

Catherine McManus OP, 1882-1933

people emigrated from the diocese in the ninety years between 1881 and 1971. They made a huge contribution to the Catholic Church all over the English speaking world, particularly in Great Britain, the United States and Australia. Unlike the priests, most of the nuns whose names are recorded as serving in the United States, Canada, Australia, New Zealand, Great Britain and elsewhere in the English-speaking world, like the McManus sisters from Derryronane in Swinford, entered the religious life after they had emigrated to these countries.

By the time the Second Vatican Council met in 1962 to revive an ailing and declining church, particularly in countries in Europe such as France, Italy, Germany etc, the Achonry church was alive and well and at the very peak of its institutional achievements. Church practice among all age groups and classes was virtually 100%. Masses became more numerous as the number of priests increased. Swinford then had a minimum of five daily Masses, two in the parish church and one each in the convent, hospital and domestic economy school. On most mornings there was also one or more requiem high Masses for funerals or anniversaries, requiring the participation of at least three priests. Any priest surplus to those requirements availed of the convent chapel to say his private Mass and even that managed to muster a congregation of sorts. The 'devotional revolution' resulted in a religious practice dominated by private prayer, and even Mass became an occasion for many to say Rosaries and novenas and other special prayers directed at solving personal problems or achieving individual ambitions.

The church's control over recreational activities was very pervasive and generally undisputed. Dances were not permitted during Lent and Advent and were never held on Saturdays, insuring that there would be no unfair competition with Confessions and preparation for Sunday Mass. Cinemas also remained closed on Saturdays for the same reason. Priests were patrons or presidents of almost every club and society based in their parishes. The parish priest was officially listed in 1959 as patron of eight different commit-tees in Swinford, including race committee, Town Hall club, badminton club, tennis club, boxing club, GAA, agricultural show committee and young farmers' club. The only exceptions were the golf club, where he ceded his po-sition to the bishop, settling for the lesser role of president, the ICA, for obvi-ous reasons and the East Mayo Anglers which comprised members from sev-eral parishes.[7] While the position of patron or president was purely titular, it was sufficient to insure that the club or society would be scrupulously metic-ulous in complying with clerical wishes and, besides, other priests in the parish acted as chairmen and played much more active roles in these clubs.

But there was a downside to this spectacularly successful church, some-thing not always as evident to contemporaries as to later generations. It was a priest-dominated church, with clericalism and authoritarianism rampant and the laity reduced to the 'pray, pay and obey' category. Clerical attitudes tended to mirror those prevalent elsewhere in society. Teachers, doctors, gardaí etc were all more or less authoritarian but, more importantly, so were parents in their homes. While there were unquestionably some excesses or abuses, the paternalism practised by priests and others was largely benevolent and ac-cepted as such.

Bishop Morrisroe receiving sodalists in Ballaghaderreen Convent *(Photo Fr Browne SJ Collection)*

7   *Swinford Echo*, No. 1 (1959)

Appendices

Patrick McNicholas	Mar 1818 - Feb 1852
Patrick Durcan	Oct 1852 - May 1875
Francis J. MacCormack	Nov 1871 - May 1875 Coadjutor
	May 1875 - 1887 Bishop
John Lyster	Feb 1888 - Jan 1911
Patrick Morrisroe	June 1911 - May 1946
James Fergus	Feb 1947 - Mar 1976 retired. Died Mar 1989.
Thomas Flynn	Jan 1977 -

APPENDIX 2: PROTESTANT BISHOPS OF TUAM, KILLALA AND ACHONRY

James Verschoyle	6 May 1810 - 13 April 1834 (Killala & Achonry)
Thomas Plunket	1839 - 1866 (Tuam, Killala & Achonry)
Charles Brodrick Bernard	1867 - 1890
James O'Sullivan	1890 - 1913
Benjamin John Plunket	1913 - 1919
Arthur Edwin Ross	1920 - 1923
John Orr	1923 - 1927
John Mason Hardin	1927 - 1931
William Hardy Holmes	1932 - 1938
John Winthrop Crozier	1938 - 1957
Arthur Hamilton Butler	1958 - 1969
John Coote Duggan	1970 - 1985
John Robert Winder Neill	1986 - 1997
Richard Crosbie A. Henderson	1997 -

APPENDIX 3: CATHOLIC DEANS/VGS

James Henry	1826 - 1831
Patrick Durcan	1831 - 1852
Bernard Durcan	1852 - 1881
Matthew Finn	1881 - 1891
Michael Staunton	1892 - 1910
Edward Connington	1910 - 1935
James O'Connor	1935 - 1944
James Gallagher	1947 - 1950
Ambrose Blaine	1951 - 1971
James Colleran	1971 - 1978
John Francis O'Hara	1978 - 1982
Patrick Higgins	1982 - 1991
Michael McGuinn	1991 - 1997
Robert Flynn	1997 -

APPENDIX 4: PROTESTANT DEANS

Arthur Henry Kenny	1812 - 1821
William Greene	1821 - 1824
Theophilus Blakely	1824 - 1839
Edward Newenham Hoare	1839 - 1850
Hervey de Montmorency	1850 - 1872
William Jackson	1872 - 1875
Arthur Moore	1875 - 1882
Hamilton Townsend	1883 - 1895
George Abraham Heather	1895 - 1907
Thomas Gordon Walker	1907 - 1916
Thomas Allen	1916 - 1927

Since 1927 the bishop of the diocese has also been Dean of Achonry

APPENDIX 5: PRIESTS OF ACHONRY, PARISH BY PARISH

Attymass

Parish Priests

Michael O'Brien	c.1776 -1794?
?	
Peter Brennan	1832 - 1835
Denis O'Kane	1835 - 1844? [1]
Michael Flynn	1845 - 1847
James Hurst	1848 - 1875
John O'Grady Adm.	1876 - 1881
Edward Meehan	1881 - 1894
Edward Connington	1894 - 1897
Martin Henry	1897 - 1901
Walter Henry	1901 - 1920
Roger O'Donnell	1920 - 1934
James Jordan	1934 - 1945
Peter O'Callaghan	1945 - 1953
Gerard Hannan	1953 - 1960
James Henry	1960 - 1970
John A.McGarry	1970 - 1973
Patrick Higgins	1973 - 1978
Thomas Gavigan	1978 - 1986
Michael Giblin	1986 - 1991
Thomas Colleary	1991 - 2002
Thomas Mulligan	2002 -

Roger O'Donnell

Curate

Francis Clarke	1893

Administrators

Ballaghaderreen

Michael Farrell PP	1803 - 1817
?	
Patrick Durcan	1820 - 1823

---

1   1840, ED 1/61, no.32, ED 2/32, f.163

Ballaghaderreen

Patrick J. Roughneen

?	
Bernard Durcan	pre 1832 - 1836 [2]
Denis Tighe	1836 - 1849
John Howley	1850 - 1855
Matthew Finn	1854 - 1861
Vacant	1861 - 1864
Matthew Finn	1864 - 1869
Roger O'Hara	1870 - 1872
Thomas Conlon	1873 - 1876
Owen Stenson	1877 - 1881
Denis O'Hara	1881 - 1887
Michael Keveney	1887 - 1895
James O'Connor	1895 - 1905
James Gallagher	1905 - 1922
James Spelman	1922 - 1926
Patrick J. Roughneen	1926 - 1943
Frank Stenson	1943 - 1947
James Hunt	1947 - 1951
Thomas A. McVann	1951 - 1966
Michael Carty	1966 - 1970
James Lafferty	1970 - 1977
Michael Cryan	1977 - 1980
Christy McLoughlin	1980 - 1985
John Doherty	1985 - 1987
Patrick Peyton	1987 - 1992
Padraig Costello	1992 -1995
Michael Reilly	1995 -

Curates

Denis Tighe	pre 1832 - [3]
Thady Mullaney	pre 1832 - 1836 [4]
James Gallagher	1836 - 1837
Luke Duffy	1836
Patrick Keegan	1836
Patrick Hyland	1839
Patrick Spelman	1840 - 1843
Patrick McNicholas	1844 - 1848
John Howley	1847 - 1849
Patrick Roddy	1850
Matthew Finn	1852 - 1856
Patrick Coffey	1856
Matthew Leonard	1857 - 1861
Patrick Davey	1859 - 1863
Peter O'Donoghue	1862 - 1864
Roger O'Hara	1865 - 1869
Thomas Conlon	1870 - 1876
Owen Stenson	1873 - 1876

2   ED 2/32, f.19
3   ED 2/32, ff.13 & 19
4   ED 2/32, ff/13, 19 & 48

Denis O'Hara	1877 - 1881	*Ballaghaderreen*
Thomas Bowler	1881 - 1883	
Michael Keveney	1882 - 1887	
Bartholmew Quinn	1887 - 1888	
Patrick Cuniffe	1888 - 1891	
Michael Doyle	1889 - 1895	
Andrew Callaghan	1888 - 1889	
James O'Connor	1893 - 1895	
Daniel Gallagher	1896 - 1897	
Michael O'Flanagan	1896 - 1897	
Thomas O'Hara	1897 - 1898	
Michael Harte	1898 - 1905	
John Hurst	1899 - 1890	
James Gallagher	1901 - 1905	
Thomas M. Gallagher	1904 - 1905	
Patrick Higgins	1905 - 1906	
Michael Durcan	1906 - 1912	
Thomas Gallagher	1903 - 1905	
Denis Gildea	1911 - 1918	
John O'Dowd	1913 - 1919	
James Spelman	1919 - 1922	
Thomas Morrin	1922 - 1924	
Francis O'Connor	1926 - 1941	
Patrick J.Roughneen	1924 - 1926	
Paul O'Grady	1928 - 1938	
James McVann	1939 - 1942	
Bernard O'Hara	1939 - 1940	
James Hunt	1941 - 1947	
Thomas McVann	1942 - 1951	
Joseph Henry	1948 - 1955	
Michael Carty	1951 - 1966	
Patrick Feely	1955 - 1966	
James Lafferty	1966 - 1970	
John Doherty	1966 - 1976 & 1981 - 1985	
John G.Walsh	1971 - 1981	
Christopher McLoughlin	1976 - 1980	
Peter Gallagher	1980 - 1985	
Thomas Mulligan	1985 - 1990	
Francis Henry	1985 - 1988	
John Geelan	1989 - 1990	
Joseph Gavigan	1990 - 1991	
John Glynn	1990 - 1997	
Padraig Costello	1991 - 1992	
Michael Reilly	1992 - 1995	
Patrick Henry	1992 - 1999	
John Durkan	1995 - 1997	
Patrick Holleran	1997 - 1998	
James Brett	1998 - 2003	
Michael Maloney	1999 - 2000	
Vincent Sherlock	2000	

Ballymote   *Parish Priests*

Patrick Grady   1811 - 1817
Francis Boland   1817 - 1823
Patrick Durcan   1823 - 1832 [5]
Brian O'Kane   1832 - 1848
Denis Tighe   1849 - 1877 [6]
Matthew Finn   1878 - 1881
John MacDermott   1881 - 1894
Thomas Loftus   1895 - 1908
Edward Connington   1909 - 1910
Batty Quinn   1911 - 1920
Tom Quinn   1921 - 1943
P. J. Roughneen   1943 - 1970
Peter Harte   1970 - 1973
John F. O'Hara   1973 - 1982
Robert Flynn   1982 - 2002
Gregory Hannon   2002 -

Curates

Bartholmew Keirns?   1818
Matthew Healy   1830 - 1833
Denis Tighe   1832 - 1834 [7]
Bernard Egan   pre 1836 -1839
John Coghlan   1839 - 1844
James Higgins   1844 - 1846
John Finn   1846 - 1848
Patrick McNicholas   1848 - 1849
Patrick O'Connor   1849 - 1850?
John Browne   1852 - 1853
James Devine   1853 - 1854
James Barret   1855 - 1863
Michael Ivers   1864 - 1866
James McDermott   1865 - 1876
Patrick? Staunton   1875 - 1876
Patrick McDonald   1876 - 1878
Michael? Staunton   1876 - 1877
Philip Mulligan   1879 - 1880
John O'Neill   1879
Edward Meehan   1880 - 1881
James Cullen   1881 - 1885
Patrick Staunton   1886 - 1889
Michael Doyle   1889
John McNicholas   1889 - 1891
P. J.O'Grady   1889 - 1894
Patrick Conlan   1892
John Morrin   1894 - 1896
Patrick Filan   1894

5   17 Mar 1832, Durcan still there. ED 1/79, no.3
6   4 April 1849 D. Tighe PP. ED 1/79, no.112
7   ED 1/79, no.16; ED 2/41, ff.13 & 47

Patrick O'Grady	1895	*Ballymote*
Dominick O'Grady	1895 - 1898	
Daniel Gallagher	1898 - 1904	
Patrick Hewson	1900 - 1901	
Patrick Moran	1900 - 1901	
John Breen	1901 - 1902	
Patrick Boland	1902 - 1903	
Roger O'Donnell	1903 - 1904	
Henry Dillon	1905 - 1906	
Thomas M. Gallagher	1906 - 1931	
Patrick Mulligan	1908 - 1909	
Edward Henry	1911 - 1912	
Charles Carney	1919 - 1921	
Anthony Durcan	1922 - 1934	
Bernard O'Hara	1931 - 1939	
James McVann	1934 - 1939	
Philip J. Durkin	1939 - 1943	
Walter Casey	1939 - 1943	
Joseph Henry	1943 - 1947	
Peter Coleman	1943 - 1947	
Denis O'Hara	1947 - 1949	
Luke Molloy	1947 - 1951	
John F. O'Hara	1949 - 1968	
Thomas Gannon	1951 - 1954	
Michael F. McGuinn	1951 - 1955 & 1964 - 1978	
Patrick A. Higgins	1955 - 1960	
Andrew Kelly	1960 - 1964	
Sean Tiernan	1968 - 1978	
Dudley Filan	1978 - 1982	
Dermot Burns	1978 - 1986	
Patrick Lynch	1986 - 1988	
Dan O'Mahony	1988 - 1994	
James McDonagh	1994 - 1995	
Joseph Caulfield	1995 - 1999	
Gabriel Murphy	1999 -	

Parish Priests

John C. Duffy	1978 - 1991	
Gregory Hannon	1991 - 2002	
Thomas Colleary	2002 -	

Dudley Filan

Ballysadare

Parish Priests

Peter Cooke	pre1836 - 1844	*Bohola*
Thomas McNicholas	1844 - 1860	
Thomas Judge	1860 - 1881	
James Cullen Adm	1881	
John O'Grady	1881 - 1926	
Patrick Higgins	1926 - 1935	
Thomas P. Gallagher	1935 - 1955	

Philip Durkin

Bohola

Philip Durkin	1955 - 1966
Thomas A. McVann	1966 - 1968
Patrick O'Leary	1968 - 1972
Martin McManus	1972 - 1978
Patrick Finan	1978 - 1986
Farrell Cawley	1987 - 1994
Padraig Costello	1994 -

Curates

Patrick Lyons	1836
James Higgins	pre 1838 - 1844 [8]
Patrick Groarke	1844 - 1847
Patrick O'Connor	1848 - 1849
Vacant	1850 - 1857
Thomas Judge	1857 - 1858
?	
Michael D. Staunton	1869 - 1870
Vacant	1870 - 1872
John Gallagher	1873 - 1874
Patrick Staunton	1874 - 1875
Vacant	1875 - 1885
Francis Benson	1885 - 1887
Francis Hannon	1887 - 1888
Vacant	1888 - 1902
Edward Henry	1902 - 1906
Henry Dillon	1906 - 1907
Patrick Higgins	1907 - 1913
James McKeon	1913 - 1915
Michael O'Hara	1916 - 1923
Louis Henry	1924 - 1926
Felix Burke	1926 - 1927
Peter Callaghan	1931 - 1945
John F. O'Hara	1945 - 1947
Peter Coleman	1948 - 1953
Thomas Gavigan	1953 - 1957
Gerry Henry	1956 - 1960
Louis Dunleavy	1961 - 1962
Denis O'Hara	1962 - 1964
Liam Cawley	1964 - 1965
James Finan	1965 - 1966
Patrick Kilcoyne	1967 - 1978
Luke Carney	1978 - 1989

Parish Priests

Patrick McNicholas	c.1780 - c.1819
Thady Mullaney	pre 1836 -1844 [9]

---

8   15 Oct 1838 and 7 Nov 1839, ED 2/32 ff.68 & 114: However, the *Catholic Registry* 1839 lists Higgins as curate
in Kiltimagh.

9   30 July 1844 Mullaney was replaced by Egan. ED 2/32, f.137

Bernard Egan	1844 - 1859
William Jones	1860 - 1864
Sodan Martin	1865 - 1870
Harte Peter	1871 - 1896
Connington Edward	1897 - 1904
Callaghan Andrew	1905 - 1919
John McKeon	1919 - 1927
Hugh O'Donnell	1929 - 1934
Michael Durcan	1934 - 1941
Peter O'Harte	1941 - 1943
Matthew Leonard	1943 - 1951
James Shryane	1951 - 1958
Peter Harte	1958 - 1970
James Henry	1970 - 1978
Martin McManus	1978 - 1987
John Doherty	1987 - 1992
Thomas Towey	1992 -

Curates

Daniel Gallagher	1892 - 1893
John McKeon	1893 - 1895
Vacant	1895 - 1902
Henry Dillon	1902 - 1904
Patrick Higgins	1904 - 1905
William Harte	1905 - 1911
Patrick Boland	1912 - 1916
Anthony Kirrane	1916 - 1923
Eddie Morahan	1919 - 1921
Eddie O'Hara	1922 - 1939
James McGrath	1922 - 1929
Thomas Loftus	1939 - 1943
James B. Walsh	1943 - 1948
Paddy O'Leary	1948 - 1951
Padraig O'Grady	1951 - 1958
Vincent Burke	1958 - 1964
Andrew Johnston	1964 - 1966
Martin McManus	1966 - 1968
Farrell Cawley	1968 - 1971
Thomas Frain	1971 - 1973
Thomas Towey	1973 - 1974
Dermot Burns	1974 - 1977
Michael Gallagher	1977 - 1981
Denis McManus CSSP	1981 - 1982
Eamon Hanniffy	1982 - 1983
Padraig Costello	1983 - 1987

Parish Priests   *Bunninadden*

| Mark Rush | c.1780 - 1817 |
| John Doddy | 1817 - 1822 |

Bunninadden	Bernard O'Kane	1822 - 1832 [10]
	Thomas Healy?	pre1835 [11]
	John Corley	1832 - 1839
	James Henry	1840 - 1852
	John Browne	1852 - 1858
	James Henry	1858 - 1876
	James McDermott	1877 - 1881
	Owen Stenson	1881 - 1901
	P. McDermott	1893
	Dominick O'Grady	1901 - 1918
	Thomas Quinn	1918 - 1920
	Peter Cawley	1920 - 1924
	William Flynn	1924 - 1939
	Felix Burke	1939 - 1943
	Patrick Wims	1943 - 1951
	Luke Molloy	1951 - 1970
	Peter Coleman	1970 - 1980
	Gerard Henry	1980 - 1992
	Patrick Peyton	1992 -

Curates

Patrick Spelman	c.1832[12]
Thomas Healy	c.1835[13]
John Finn	1837 - 1846
John Browne	1847 - 1852
Luke Hannon	1854 - 1855
William Jones	1856 - 1859
Mark Cooke	1860 - 1865
Michael Dolan	1862
Patrick Davey	1866 - 1868
Patrick Lowry	1868 - 1869
Patrick Scully	1869 - 1874
John O'Grady	1875
John Gunning	1876
James Murphy	1877 - 1878
Matthew Burke	1879 - 1882
Edward Connington	1882 - 1886
Patrick Cuniffe	1886 - 1890
John Morrin	1890 - 1894
Patrick McDermott	1894 - 1895
Patrick Morrisroe	1895 - 1896
Arthur Devine	1897
Philip Mulligan	1898 - 1899
Dominick O'Grady	1899 - 1901

10 25 June 1832. ED 2/41, ff.4 & 73
11 ED 2/32, f.57. John Corley is also mentioned as an applicant. O'Rorke states that Corley succeeded O'Kane, in which case Thomas Healy may have been his curate. *Sligo*, p. 199
12 ED 1/79, no.5
13 ED 2/32, f.57: see above

Michael Durcan	1901 - 1902	*Bunninadden*
James McKeon	1903 - 1905	
Roger O'Donnell	1905 - 1920	
Patrick Wims	1921 - 1923	
Michael O'Hara	1924 - 1928	
Charles Carney	1928 - 1944	
James B.Walsh	1937 - 1938	
Edward Gallagher	1940 - 1943	
Denis O'Hara	1945 - 1947	
Paul O'Grady	1947 - 1949	
John F. O'Hara	1948 - 1949	
Thomas Foy	1949 - 1950	
Martin McManus	1950 - 1952	
James E.O'Hara	1952 - 1973	
Patrick Peyton	1972 - 1976	
Thomas Johnston	1976 - 1978	
Francis McMenamon	1978 - 1979	
Francis Henry	1979 - 1980	
Eugene Duffy	1981 - 1982	
Dudley Filan	1982 - 1985	
James Johnson	1986 - 1987	
Padraig Costello	1987 - 1991	
William O'Connell	1992 - 1993	

Parish Priests

Thomas McNicholas	1830 - 1844	*Carracastle*
Denis O'Kane	1844 - 1852	
James Henry	1853 - 1858	
James Devine	1858 - 1878	
Patrick Durcan	1878 - 1908	
Philip J. Mulligan Adm.	1902 - 1910	
PP	1910 - 1927	
John McKeon	1927 - 1930	
Edward Henry	1930 - 1939	
John O'Dowd	1939 - 1943	
Thomas Morrin	1943 - 1944	
Michael O'Hara	1944 - 1948	
Eugene Foran	1948 - 1955	
Anthony Durcan	1955 - 1964	
Denis O'Hara	1964 - 1968	
John F.O'Hara	1968 - 1973	
Walter Casey	1973 - 1978	
Sean Tiernan	1978 - 1978	
Robert Flynn	1978 - 1982	
James Gavigan	1982 - 1986	
John G.Walsh	1987 - 1999	
Joseph Caulfield	1999 -	

Anthony Durcan

Carracastle	*Curates*	
	William McHugh	1835
	?	
	John Gallagher	1847 - 1848
	Mark Healy	1850
	James O'Donnell	1852 - 1853
	Patrick Groarke	1854
	Patrick Coffey	1857
	Dominick O'Grady	1858 - 1859
	Patrick Davey	1860 - 1861
	William Boland	1862 - 1863
	Vacant	1864 - 1865
	James Keveney	1866 - 1867
	John O'Neill	1868 - 1870
	Patrick Hunt	1871 - 1872
	Thomas Horan	1872 - 1873
	Matthew Burke	1874 - 1876
	James Cullen	1876 - 1878
	Patrick Mannion	1878 - 1881
	Francis Benson	1882 - 1882
	Peter Lohan	1882 - 1884
	Patrick McDermott	1884 - 1886
	Peter Lohan	1886 - 1887
	Dominick O'Grady	1887 - 1888
	Francis Benson	1888 - 1894
	Peter Cawley	1894 - 1895
	Michael Fanning	1895 - 1896
	Edmund Corbett CM	1896 - 1897
	Patrick Shinnick	1897 - 1899
	Timothy O'Dwyer	1900 - 1906
	Michael O'Harte	1906 - 1908
	Michael Connolly	1908 - 1916
	Patrick Boland	1917 - 1920
	Peter O'Callaghan	1920 - 1931
	Dominick Casey	1931 - 1934
	Thomas Loftus	1934 - 1939
	James B.Walsh	1939 - 1943
	James Henry	1943 - 1949
	Michael McLoughlin	1947 - 1948
	James Flannery	1949 - 1954
	James Lafferty	1954 - 1966
	John A.McGarry	1966 - 1970
	Patrick Kilcoyne	1970 - 1971
	Thomas Colleary	1971 - 1972
	Vincent Burke	1972 - 1974
	Martin Jennings	1974 - 1975
	Padraig Costello	1975 - 1978
	Walter Casey	1978 - 1983
	Francis Henry	1983 - 1985
	Anthony Flannery	1985 - 1986
	Vincent Sherlock	1987 - 1990

Parish Priests

Dominick Phillips	c.1803 - 1822
Patrick McDonnell	1825
Michael Filan	1825 - 1828
William McHugh	1828 - 1848
James Higgins	1848 - 1878
Thomas Loftus	1878 - 1895
Michael Keveney	1896 - 1920
John McDonnell	1920 - 1922
Charles Gildea	1924 - 1937
Ambrose Blaine	1937 - 1948
Eddie O'Hara	1948 - 1950
Francis O'Connor	1950 - 1973
Edward Gallagher	1973 - 1978
Andrew Kelly	1978 - 1990
Liam Cawley	1990 - 2003
Thomas Johnston	2003

Curates

Patrick Groarke	1842 - 1843
Michael Muldowney	1845 - 1848
John Gallagher	1850 - 1854
Vacant	1855 - 1859
Patrick Davey	1859 - 1860
Paul Henry	1862 - 1866
Peter Harte	1867 - 1868
Michael O'Donnell	1868 - 1869
John O'Grady	1870 - 1874
Patrick Hunt	1875 - 1876
Edward Meehan	1877 - 1878
Patrick Scully	1879 - 1880
Michael Cawley	1881 - 1882
John Morrin	1882 - 1884
John McNicholas	1885 - 1889
John McDonnell	1889 - 1897
James McKeon	1898 - 1899
Matthew Devine	1900 - 1904
Patrick O'Donnell	1905 - 1906
Patrick Bradley	1906 - 1908
Henry Dillon	1908 - 1912
Thomas P. Gallagher	1913 - 1927
Denis Gildea	1927 - 1932
John Kirwin	1932 - 1950
Edward Doherty	1932 - 1933
James B. Walsh	1934 - 1936
?	
James Lafferty	1950 - 1951
Thomas Gavigan	1950 - 1951
Patrick Higgins	1951 - 1955
Gerard Henry	1951 - 1956

Edward Gallagher

James B. Walsh

Charlestown

Thomas Vesey	1955 - 1961
Thomas Gavigan	1956 - 1971
James P. Walsh	1961 - 1963
John Doherty	1962 - 1963
Michael Cryan	1963 - 1970
Dudley Filan	1968 - 1973
John McNicholas	1970 - 1975
John Doyle	1974 - 1975
Thomas Towey	1975 - 1977
Bernard Mulkerins	1976 - 1977
Farrell Cawley	1977 - 1985
Patrick Holleran	1984 - 1987
Thomas Colleary	1985 - 1990
Sean Lodge	1988 - 1989
Andrew Kelly	1990 - 1992
John Durkan	1991 - 1993
Michael Giblin	1992 - 2000
James Brett	1994 - 1997
Adrian McHugh	1997 - 1999
Michael Maloney	2000 -

Collooney

Parish Priests

Walter Henry	1794 - 1805
James Henry	1805 - 1833
Patrick Durcan	1833 - 1852?
Terence O'Rourke	1854 - 1907
Edward Connington Adm	1904 - 1907
PP	1907 - 1909?
Michael Doyle	1911 - 1924?
Peter J., Cawley	1926 - 1942
Patrick J. Casey	1942 - 1953
Thomas Morrin	1953 - 1970
James Hunt	1970 - 1978
Patrick Higgins	1978 - 1991
Thomas Johnston Adm	1991 - 1992
Joseph Spelman	1993 -

Curates and Chaplains

John McNulty	c.1812 - 1815 [12]
John Doddy	c.1812 - 1815 [13]
Denis Tighe	1834 [14]
Michael O'Flynn	pre1836 - 1844
Patrick McDonnell	1841
Dominick O'Connor	1842 - 1848
Mark Healy	1845 - 1848
James Devine	1849 - 1853

12 O'Rorke, *Ballysadare*, p. 488
13 ibid
14 18 Feb 1834, ED 1/79 no.28

Patrick Groarke	1849	*Collooney*
William Jones	1854	
Luke Hannan	1855 - 1857	
Patrick Lohan	1858 - 1868	
Peter Lohan	1869 - 1876	
John Gunning	1877 - 1878	
Philip Mulligan	1879 - 1887	
Arthur Devine	1888 - 1890	
Francis Benson	1888	
Dominick O'Grady	1889 - 1893	
James Finn	1891 - 1895	
Mark Dempsey	1895 - 1899	
Patrick J.O'Grady	1896 - 1999	
John McKeon	1900 - 1903	
Peter Cawley	1900 - 1901	
Henry Dillon	1902 - 1904	
Patrick O'Donnell	1904	
Patrick Casey	1905 - 1912	
Patrick Mulligan	1911	
Michael Durcan	1913 - 1922	
Paul O'Grady	1923 - 1927	
Matthew Leonard	1928 - 1930	
Francis Stenson	1931 - 1943	
James Shryane	1931 - 1940	
Thomas Foy	1941 - 1943	
Gerard Hannon	1943 - 1947	
Neil O'Donnell	1944 - 1948 & 1961-1967	
James P. Walsh	1947 - 1961	
Gerard Henry	1948 - 1951	
James Lafferty	1951 - 1954	
Michael Cryan	1954 - 1957	
Christopher McLoughlin	1957 - 1963	
John Doherty	1961 - 1962 & 1963 -1966	
John C. Duffy	1966 - 1978	
Padraig O'Grady	1967 - 1973	
Patrick Towey	1973 - 1978	
Michael Giblin	1978 - 1986	
Thomas Johnston	1987 - 1991	
Vincent Sherlock	1992 - 1995	
John Maloney	1996 -	

Parish Priests		*Coolaney*
Robert Dillon	1790 - 1808	
Daniel O'Connor	1808 - 1825	
Matthew Healy	1825 - 1836	
Paul Henry	1836 - 1848 [15]	
Patrick Hurst	1848 - 1861 [16]	

15 1 June 1846 Hurst replaced Henry as school manager because of 'delicate health'. ED 2/41, f.112
16 2 Feb 1848. ED 1/79 nos.80,105 & 106

Frank O'Connor

John Kirwin

Coolaney	Luke Hannan	1861 - 1869?
	Patrick Lowry	1869? - 1878
	Patrick McDonald	1878 - 1904
	Daniel Gallagher	1904 - 1910
	Matthew Devine	1910 - 1922
	Michael Durcan	1923 - 1934
	Peter O'Harte	1934 - 1941
	Frank O'Connor	1941 - 1950
	John Kirwin	1950 - 1954
	James B.Walsh	1954 - 1963
	Walter Casey	1963 - 1968
	John O'Neill	1968 - 1975
	John McNicholas	1975 - 1986
	Dudley Filan	1986 - 1991
	Patrick Kilcoyne	1991 - 1999
	Patrick Holleran	1999 -

Curates

	Daniel Hurst	1840 - 1841
	Patrick Hyland	1842
	Michael McCawley	1843
	John Gallagher	1844 - 1846
	Patrick Hurst	1846 - 1849
	?	
	Philip Mulligan jnr	1894 - 1895
	Andrew Callaghan	1895 - 1896
	Michael Harte	1896 - 1897
	Thomas Quinn	1897 - 1901
	John Humphries	1902 - 1903
	Patrick Boland	1904 - 1905
	?	
	Daniel Devine	1916 - 1919

Curry	*Parish Priests*	
	Anthony McNamara	1786 - c.1792
	James Filan	?-1830
	John O'Flynn	1830 - 1856
	John Howley Adm	1855
	John Howley	1856 - 1867
	Peter O'Donoghue	1867 - 1881
	Thomas Conlon	1881 - 1889
	Philip Mulligan	1889 - 1930
	John McKeon	1930 - 1931
	Thomas Gallagher	1931 - 1944
	Thomas Morrin	1944 - 1953
	John Kirwin	1953 - 1968
	Thomas Loftus	1968 - 1977
	James Lafferty	1977 - 1991
	Michael Joyce	1991 - 1998
	Martin Jennings	1998 -

Curates

Luke Duffy	1837 - 1839
Dominick O'Connor	1840 - 1841
Roger Brennan	1842 - 1848
John Brennan	1848 - 1852
Michael Cawley	1852 - 1856 [17]
James Barrett	1857 - 1858
Patrick Killoran	1859 - 1865
James McDermott	1865 - 1866
Michael Ivers	1866 - 1867
Patrick Davey	1867 - 1871
Philip Mulligan	1871 - 1872
Owen Davey	1872 - 1875
Denis O'Hara	1875 - 1876
Peter Lohan	1876 - 1878
Edward Meehan	1879 - 1880
J. Nelligan	1879 - 1880
John Gunning	1880 - [18]
Patrick Mannion	1880 - 1881
Patrick Hunt	1882 - 1887
Edward Connington	1887 - 1895
Philip Mulligan jnr.	1895 - 1896
Matthew Devine	1895 - 1898
Patrick O'Donnell	1899 - 1903
John Humphries	1904 - 1906
Patrick J. O'Grady	1906 - 1911
William Harte	1908 - 1913
Edward Henry	1911 - 1912
James Jordan	1912 - 1918
Patrick Mulligan	1913 - 1918
Thomas Morrin	1916 - 1919
Peter Callaghan	1917 - 1920
Louis Henry	1920 - 1923
Edward Morahan	1920 - 1923
Michael Connolly	1923 - 1931
Dominick Casey	1924 - 1930
James Hyland	1931 - 1934
Anthony Durcan	1934 - 1944
Edward Gallagher	1944 - 1947
Thomas Loftus	1947 - 1952
Martin McManus	1952 - 1957
Patrick Finan	1957 - 1966
Peter Coleman	1966 - 1970
Andrew Kelly	1970 - 1978
Thomas Flanagan	1978 - 1980
Peter Coleman	1980 - 1990
James Lafferty	1991 - 1999

17 ED 2/41, f.167
18 DCA CH 1/39/416

Foxford   *Parish Priests*

James Henry	pre-1833 - 1840[19]
John Corley	1841 - 1852?
P. J. O'Connor	1852 - 1861
James Halligan	1862 - 1864
Patrick Davey	1865 - 1866
Mark Cooke Adm.	1866 - 1869
Michael O'Donnell	1869 - 1893
John Gunning	1893 - 1901
Martin Henry	1901 - 1924
Patrick J. Casey	1925 - 1943
John O'Dowd	1943 - 1949
Thomas Curneen	1949 -1955
Eugene Foran	1955 -1958
James Shryane	1958 -1960
Gerard Hannan	1960 -1978
Michael Keegan	1978 -1983
Michael F. McGuinn	1983 -1995
Peter Gallagher Adm	1995 -1997
Andrew Johnston	1997 -

Curates

Bernard Egan	1834 [20]
Michael O'Donnell	1839
Patrick Hyland	1843 - 1850
Patrick O'Connor	1851 - 1853
Vacant	1853 - 1872 [21]
John Gunning	1872 - 1874
John McNicholas	1880 - 1884
Vacant	1875 - 1879
Walter Henry	1888 - 1889
Andrew Callaghan	1889 - 1893
Patrick Conlon	1893 - 1896
James Finn	1896 - 1897 [22]
Peter Cawley	1898 - 1899
Mark Dempsey	1899 - 1900 [23]
William Harte	1900 - 1904
Matthew Devine	1904 - 1909
Peter O'Harte	1910 - 1913
James Jordan	1911 - 1912
James Spelman	1915 - 1918
Denis Gildea	1918 - 1927
James Shryane	1924 - 1925
Felix Burke	1928 - 1929

19 ED 2/32, f.146
20 ED 2/32, f.2
21 No curate listed in *Catholic Registry* in 1854
22 became a Protestant
23 went to America

		Foxford
James McGrath	1930 - 1943	
Paul O'Grady	1944 - 1947	
John A. McGarry	1947 - 1949	
Patrick Feeley	1948 - 1955	
Walter Casey	1949 - 1950	
Michael McLoughlin	1955 - 1966	
Padraig McGovern	1957 - 1959	
Patrick Towey	1960 - 1973	
Michael Gallagher	1969 - 1970	
Cornelius Gordon	1970 - 1973	
Myles Roban	1973 - 1974	
Dudley Filan	1973 - 1978	
Patrick Higgins	1973 - 1973	
Eamon Cullen	1974 - 1975	
John Doherty	1976 - 1981	
Gerard Hannan	1978 - 1986	
Joseph Caulfield	1981 - 1982	
Dan O'Mahony	1982 - 1987	
Joseph Caulfield	1988 - 1995	
Joseph Gavigan	1992 - [Secondary School]	
Michael F.McGuinn	1995 - 1996	
Christopher Ginnelly	1998 -	

Gurteen

Parish Priests

Frank Cunnane	c.1803
Roger McDermot	c.1816
Peter Brennan	1834 - 1854
Roger Brennan	1854 - 1880
John McDermott	1881 - 1882
Peter O'Donoghue	1881 - 1896
Patrick Lowry	1896 - 1905
James O'Connor	1905 - 1944
Thomas Gallagher	1944 - 1955
James Colleran	1955 - 1968
Thomas A. McVann	1968 - 1978
Patrick Towey	1978 - 1992
John Doherty	1992 -

Curates

P. Duffy	1836
Roger Brennan	1840 - 1841
Bernard Egan	1842 - 1843
John Coghlan	1844 - 1846
John McDonnell	1847 - 1850
Patrick Roddy	1852 - 1858
John McDermott	1859 - 1860
Dominick O'Grady	1860 - 1861
Matthew Leonard	1862 - 1864
Patrick Killoran	1864 - 1868

Gurteen	Patrick Lowry	1868 - 1869
	James Keveney	1871 - 1876
	Patrick Hunt	1877 - 1880
	J. Horan	1880 - 1881
	Michael Keveney	188? - 1882
	John Browne	1882 - 1885
	Patrick Conlan	1882 - 1885
	Martin Henry	1885 - 1886
	Patrick Conlan	1886 - 1888
	Patrick A. Filan	1887 - 1890
	Bartholmew Quinn	1889 - 1890
	Walter Henry	1894 - 1897
	Arthur Devine	1894 - 1895
	Michael Durcan	1898 - 1899
	Philip Mulligan	1900 - 1901
	Dominick McGowan	1900 - 1905
	Hugh O'Donnell	1903 - 1904
	Michael Harte	1905 - 1906
	John McKeon	1905 - 1908
	Edward Henry	1908 - 1911
	John McKeon	1912 - 1919
	Edward Henry	1921 - 1925
	John Casey	1926 - 1939
	James Shryane	1929 - 1930
	Philip Durkin	1931 - 1934
	Michael O'Hara	1934 - 1943
	James McVann	1939 - 1941
	James Shryane	1941 - 1951
	Eddie O'Hara	1943 - 1948
	James B. Walsh	1948 - 1952
	James Henry	1952 - 1960
	Paddy O'Leary	1960 - 1968
	James Walsh	1963 - 1964
	John Wims	1964 - 1968
	Michael McLoughlin	1968 - 1977
	Martin McManus	1968 - 1972
	John Doherty	1972 - 1973 [24]
	Charles Doherty	1973 - 1989
	Michael Giblin	1977 - 1978
	Thomas A. McVann	1978 - 1981
	James Flannery	1982 - 1991
	Don Shelly	1989 - 1990
	Tommie Mulligan	1991 - 1997
	John Durkan	1997 - 2001
	Stephen O'Mahony	2001 - 2002

Killaraght   Up to about 1851 Killaraght was a separate Parish.
Constantine Cosgrove was Parish Priest from 1836 or earlier to 1851.

24 Columban Priest

Parish Priests   *Keash*

Richard Fitzmaurice	1796 - 1831
James O'Hara	1831 - 1851
Constantine Cosgrove	1851 - 1872
Mark Cooke	1872 - 1880
Patrick Scully	1881 - 1901
Dominick O'Grady	1901 - 1912
P. J. O'Grady	1912 - 1920
William Flynn	1920 - 1924
Edward Henry	1924 - 1928
James Hyland Adm.	1928 - 1931
Michael Connolly	1927 - 1944
Anthony Durcan	1944 - 1955
Peter Harte	1955 - 1958
Edward Gallagher	1958 - 1973
John A. McGarry	1973 - 1985
Christopher McLoughlin	1985 - 1990
James Finan	1990 -

Curates

Bernard Egan	1840 - 1841
Patrick McDonnell	1841 - 1842
John McDonnell	1843 - 1846
David O'Hara	1847 - 1855
Vacant	1856 - 1857
Luke Hannon	1858 - 1861
Dominick O'Grady	1861 - 1869
Vacant	1870 - 1873
Matthew Burke	1873 - 1874
Edward Meehan	1875 - 1876
Thomas Doyle	1877 - 1878
Michael Keveney	1878 - 1880
James Murphy	1880 - 1881
Peter Lohan	1882 - 1885
Patrick McDermott	1885 - 1888
Patrick Conlan	1888 - 1890
Felix Gallagher	1891 - 1893 [25]
Andrew Callaghan	1891 - 1894?
Daniel Gallagher	1893 - 1898
Peter Cawley	1896 -1897
William Harte	1899 -1900
John Humphries	1900 -1901
Patrick Boland	1901 -1902
Roger O'Donnell	1903 -1904
James McKeon	1905 -1913
Edward Henry	1913 -1915
Felix Burke	1915 -1916
James O'Connell	1917 -1919
Thomas Morrin	1920 - 1921

25 S.C. 26 Aug 1893

Keash	Felix Burke	1921 - 1926
	Louis Henry	1927 - 1938
	Edward O'Hara	1939 - 1943
	Thomas Gannon	1943 - 1950
	Paul Cryan	1948 - 1954
	James Flannery	1954 - 1981
	Patrick Lynch	1981 - 1985
	Farrell Cawley	1985 - 1986
	Thomas Flanagan	1986 - 1988
	Roger McDonagh	1989 - 1993
	John Geelan	1993 - 1999
	James Gavigan	1999 -

Killasser

Parish Priests

Roger McCarrick

	Michael O'Brien	? -1815
	?	1815 - 1830
	John McNulty	1830 - 1848
	John Finn	1848 - 1872
	Francis J. McCormack	1873- ?
	Roger O'Hara	? -1881
	Thomas Judge	1881 - 1900
	John McDonnell	1900 - 1920
	Walter Henry	1920 - 1945
	Roger McCarrick	1945 - 1952
	Edward Morahan	1952 - 1963
	James B. Walsh	1963 - 1971
	Patrick Feeley	1971 - 1980
	Sean Leonard	1980 - 1988
	Patrick Lynch	1988 - 1994
	Dan O'Mahony Adm	1994 - 1997
	PP	1997 -

Curates

Thomas Horan

	John Coghlan	pre1836 -1839
	Patrick Hunt	1840 - 1841?
	James Hurst	1843 - 1849?
	Patrick Groarke	1851 - 1853
	Vacant	1853 - 1857
	James McGirr	1857 - 1858
	Michael Dolan	1859 - 1861
	Vacant	1861 - 1862
	Michael O'Donnell	1863 - 1867
	Peter Harte	1868 - 1869
	John O'Neill	1870 - 1872
	Thomas Horan	1873 - 1874
	Vacant	1874 - 1877
	Edward Connington	1877 - 1878
	Thomas Bowler	1879 - 1881
	Patrick Hunt	1881 - 1882

Francis Benson	1883 - 1885
Thomas Doyle	1886 - 1887
John Horan	1887 - 1888
Andrew Callaghan	1888 - 1890
Patrick O'Grady	1890 - 1894
James McKeon	1895 - 1897
Roger O'Donnell	1897 - 1902
James Spelman	1899 - 1900?
Arthur Devine	1902 - 1917
Patrick Wims	1917 - 1918
James Jordan	1918 - 1934
James Hyland	1934 -1943
Patrick Towey	1942 -1943
Hugh McHugh	1944 -1947
Michael Carty	1943 -1945
Michael Carty	1948 -1951
Andrew Kelly	1951 -1960
Padraig McGovern	1960 -1966
Michael McLoughlin	1966 -1968
Thomas Gavigan	1968 -1971
Michael Gallagher	1971 -1972
Padraig Brennan	1972 -1978
Dan O'Mahony	1978 -1982
Paul Keane	1982 -1983
Pat O'Connor	1983 -1983
Leo Henry	1983 -1986
Dermot Meehan	1986 -1994

Killasser

Patrick Feeley

Parish Priests

James Feighny	-1818
Robert Hepburne	-1842 [26]
Thady Mullaney	1844 - 1846
John Coghlan	1846 - 1863
James Barrett Adm.	1863 - 1870
Matthew Finn	1871 - 1877
John MacDermott	1877 - 1881
Roger O'Hara	1881 - 1924
Martin Henry	1925 -1939
William Flynn	1939 -1943
Felix Burke	1944 -1951
James Hunt	1951 -1970
Michael Carty	1970 -1985
Thomas Lynch	1985 -1987
Gregory Hannan	1988 -1991
Michael Gallagher	1991 -1995
Padraig Costello Adm	1995 -1995
Farrell Cawley	1995 -

Kilmovee

26 Hepburne was a curate in Swinford in 1822

Kilmovee   *Curates*

Luke Leydon OP	c. 1816 - 1833
Bernard Egan	pre-1836 [27]
Patrick Sharkey OP	1839 - 1841
P. J. O'Connor	1842 - 1847
Patrick Groarke	1847 - 1848
M. Healy	1849
William Jones	1850 - 1853
James O'Donnell	1854 - 1855
John Gallagher	1856 - 1861
Michael Ivers	1862 - 1863
William Boland	1864 - 1865
Henry Anderson	1865 - 1866
John Gallagher	1867 - 1871
Patrick Hunt	1872 - 1874
Patrick Scully	1875 - 1878
Thomas Doyle	1879 - 1882
Arthur Devine	1882 - 1887
Patrick Hunt	1887 - 1888
Martin Henry	1888 - 1895
James Finn	1895 - 1896
Michael O'Flanagan	1897 - 1898
John McDonnell	1898 - 1900
William Flynn	1900 - 1919
Patrick Bradley	1912 - 1914
Matthew Leonard	1916 - 1927
James O'Connell	1921 - 1943
Michael O'Hara	1927 - 1933
Philip Durkin	1934 - 1938
Louis Henry	1938 - 1943
Charles Carney	1943 - 1945
Patrick Feeley	1945 - 1947
Gerard Hannan	1947 - 1953
James Henry	1949 - 1951
Thomas Loftus	1952 - 1954
Paul Cryan	1954 - 1966
James Gavigan	1955 - 1956
Patrick O'Leary	1957 - 1960
Patrick Higgins	1960 - 1973
Patrick Feely	1966 - 1970
Thomas Gavigan	1971 - 1978
Thomas Lynch	1973 - 1985
Paddy Kilcoyne	1978 - 1985
Dermot Burns	1986 - 1993
Gabriel Murphy	1993 - 1997
Thomas Mulligan	1997 - 2002
John Glynn	2002 -

27 No curate listed in Catholic Registry in 1837

Parish Priests   *Kiltimagh*

Patrick Grady	c. 1818 -1826
James McNicholas	1826 - 1836?
Bernard Durcan	1836 - 1846 [28]
Daniel Mullarkey	1846 - 1862
Matthew Finn	1862 - 1864
Matthew Leonard Adm.	1865 - 1869
Matthew Leonard	1869 - 1887
Denis O'Hara	1887 - 1922
James Gallagher	1922 - 1950
Matthew Leonard	1950 - 1960
Dominick Casey	1960 - 1968
John Walsh	1968 - 1975
John O'Neill	1975 - 1980
Michael Cryan	1980 - 1995
James Gavigan	1995 - 1999
Patrick Kilcoyne	1999 -

Curates including Chaplains in Kiltimagh & Ballinamore

Francis Burke	c.1817
Michael Muldowney	pre-1836 -1837
James Higgins	1838 - 1839 [29]
John Gallagher	1840 - 1844
John Brennan	1844 - 1848 [30]
?	1848 - 1850
Patrick McNicholas	1850 - 1853
James Halligan	1854 - 1857
Peter O'Donoghue	1858 - 1861
Vacant	1861 - 1873
Denis O'Hara	1873 - 1877
Matthew Burke	1877 - 1879
J. Nelligan	1879 - 1880
Arthur Devine	1880 - 1882
Martin Henry	1882 - 1884
John Morrin	1885 - 1887
Michael Coleman	1888 - 1890
Bartholmew Quinn	1890 - 1893
Thomas E. Judge	1893 - 1895
Martin Henry	1895 - 1897
Walter Henry	1897 - 1899
William Byrne	1900 - 1901
Philip J.Mulligan	1901 - 1902
Patrick Higgins	1903 - 1904
Charles Gildea	1905 - 1919
Matthew Leonard	1914 - 1915
Louis Henry	1915 - 1916
Peter Callaghan	1916 - 1918

28   29 July 1846 transferred to Swinford. ED 2/32, f.112
29   transferred to Bohola c.Oct 1839. ED 2/32, ff.112 & 114
30   transferred 19 Jan 1848. ED 2/32, f.11

Kiltimagh		
Edward O'Hara	1919 - 1921	
Peter O'Harte	1921 - 1933	
Patrick J. Roughneen	1922 - 1924	
Bernard O'Hara	1925 - 1930	
Thomas Loftus	1931 - 1933	
John O'Dowd	1934 - 1939	
Denis O'Hara	1934 - 1943	
James Henry	1937 - 1943	
Paul O'Grady	1939 - 1944	
James McGrath	1944 - 1950	
Patrick O'Grady	1944 - 1945	
John A. McGarry	1944 - 1947	
Michael Carty	1945 - 1948	
Andrew Kelly	1948 - 1949	
Patrick Finan	1948 - 1949	
Martin McManus	1949 - 1950	
Patrick Higgins	1949 - 1951	
John C. Duffy	1950 - 1951	
James E. O'Hara	1951 - 1952	
Edward Gallagher	1951 - 1958	
James B. Walsh	1952 - 1954	
Michael Cryan	1953 - 1954	
Peter Coleman	1954 - 1966	
Robert Flynn	1954 - 1954	
A. Sands	1955 - 1955	
Patrick O'Grady	1958 - 1967	
Denis O'Hara	1958 - 1960	
John G. Walsh	1961 - 1971	
Patrick Finan	1966 - 1978	
Farrell Cawley	1967 - 1968	
A. Doody	1968 - 1969	
Luke Lynch	1969 - 1969	
Gerard Henry	1969 - 1979	
Gerry Neylon	1978 - 1978	
Thomas Towey	1978 - 1979	
Thomas Flanagan	1979 - 1986	
Patrick Holleran	1979 - 1983	
Padraig Brennan	1984 - 1991	
Michael Quinn	1991 - 1993	
Michael Quinn	1993 - [Secondary School]	
Adrian McHugh	1993 - 1998	
John Glynn	1997 - 2002	
John Durcan	2002 -	

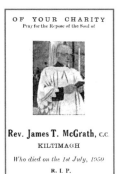

OF YOUR CHARITY
Pray for the Repose of the Soul of

Rev. James T. McGrath, C.C.
KILTIMAGH
Who died on the 1st July, 1950
R. I. P.

Mullinabreena	*Parish Priests*	
	Owen Duffy	c.1786 -1814
	Dominick O'Hara	1814 -1834 [31]

31 O'Hara died in 1834 having retired from bad health 'some years previously'. O'Rorke, *Sligo*, p. 123. However, he was still listed as PP in the *Catholic Registry* in 1837 and 1839

James Gallagher	-1850 [32]	*Mullinabreena*
Patrick Spelman	1850 - 1864	
Patrick Roddy	1864 - 1866	
John McDermott	1866 - 1869	
Luke Hannon	1869 - 1878	
Patrick Lowry	1878 - 1895	
James Cullen	1895 - 1900	
Barrtholmew Quinn	1901 - 1911	
James Daly	1911 - 1921	
Matthew Devine	1922 - 1949	
Paul O'Grady	1949 - 1949	
Dominick Casey	1949 - 1960	
John Walsh	1960 - 1969	
Walter Casey	1969 - 1973	
Padraig O'Grady	1973 - 1992	
Thomas Johnston	1992 - 2003	
James McDonagh	2003 -	

Curates

James Gallagher	1832 - 1843 [33]
John Brown	1844 - 1846
Patrick Roddy	1847 - 1849
Patrick Groarke	1849 - 1850
Vacant	1851 - 1858
Martin Sodan	1859 - 1862
Roger O'Hara	1863 - 1864
Peter Harte	1865 - 1866
Edward Meehan	1872 - 1876
Thomas Horan	1875
John O'Neill	1877 - 1878
Patrick Staunton	1879 - 1880
James Keveney	1881
Michael Cawley	1882 - 1885
Patrick Conlon	1886 - 1888
Thomas Doyle	1889
Daniel Gallagher	1890 - 1892
Dominick O'Grady	1892 - 1894
John McKeon	1895 - 1899
Patrick O'Grady	1900 - 1905
Thomas P. Gallagher	1905 - 1912
Edward Henry	1912 - 1919
Felix Burke	1914
Patrick Boland	1920 - 1931
Denis Gildea	1932 - 1936
Gerard Hannon	1937 - 1943
Thomas Gannon	1937 - 1943
Patrick Feely	1944 - 1946

32 25 Mar 1850 Spelman replaced the deceased Gallagher as school manager. ED 2/41, ff.20 & 67. O'Rorke dates the changeover as 1849
33 ED 1/79, nos.10 & 18

Mullinabreena	Patrick Finan	1947
	Michael McLouglin	1948 - 1954
	Michael F. McGuinn	1955 - 1964
	Vincent Burke	1964 - 1971
	Thomas Johnston	1972 - 1973
	Michael Gallagher	1973 - 1977
	Dermot Burns	1977 - 1978
	Thomas Colleary	1978 - 1985
	Michael Reilly	1985 - 1990

Straide	*Parish Priests*	
	John McHugh	pre-1836 - 1855
	James O'Donnell	1856 - 1888
	Patrick Hunt	1888 - 1915
	Patrick Higgins Adm.	1915 - 1916
	Peter Cawley	1917 - 1920
	Hugh O'Donnell	1920 - 1929
	Felix Burke	1929 - 1939
	Patrick Wims	1939 - 1943
	Michael Louis Henry	1943 - 1947
	James Hyland	1948 - 1949
	Philip Durkin	1949 - 1955
	Thomas Loftus	1955 - 1968
	John Wims	1968 - 1978
	Francis McGuinn	1978 - 1983
	Padraig McGovern	1983 - 1994
	Dermot Burns	1994 -

	Curates	
	John McLoughlin	1841 [34]
	Francis Benson	1886 -1887
	Francis Hannon	1887 -1888
	John McKeon	1909 -1911
	Patrick Higgins	1914
	Charles Carney	1938
	James Flannery	1948

Swinford	*Parish Priests*	
	Patrick O'Connor	c.1780 -1803?
	John Brown	-1805[35]
	James Henry	- 1805
	?	1805 - 1817
	John Coleman	1817 - 1846
	Bernard Durcan	1846 - 1882
	Matthew Finn	1882 - 1891

---

34 ED 2/32 f.145

35   O'Rorke states that James Henry was assistant to Fr Brown PP Swinford, an uncle of John Brown PP
     Bunninadden 1853-1858. Henry succeeded Brown and remained until 1805 when he transferred to Collooney.

Michael Staunton	1891 - 1910	*Swinford*
Edward Connington	1910 - 1935	
Patrick Higgins	1935 - 1947	
Francis Stenson	1947 - 1968	
James Colleran	1968 - 1978	
Paul Cryan	1978 - 1988	
Sean Leonard	1988 - 1998	
Michael Joyce	1998 -	

Curates

James Henry	c.1803 [35]
Robert Hepburne	c.1822 [36]
Constantine Cosgrove	- 1836
James Higgins	1836 - 1838
Michael Muldowney	1838 - 1843?
Patrick Spelman	1845 - 1850
James Devine	1845 - 1848
James Hurst	1849 - 1851
Michael Ivers	1851 - 1857
Michael Cawley	1855 - 1856
Patrick Lohan	1857 - 1859
James Halligan	1858 - 1861
J.Burke	1860 - 1861
Martin Sodan	1862 - 1863
Mark Cooke	1862 - 1863
Patrick Lowry	1863 - 1866
William Coleman	1863 - 1871
Michael D.Staunton	1867 - 1876
Owen Davey	1872 - 1873
Philip Mulligan	1873 - 1879
Thomas Conlon	1879 - 1881
John Gunning	1879 - 1880
Patrick R. Staunton	1881 - 1885
Matthew Burke	1881 - 1893
Michael Coleman	1882 - 1884
Francis Hannon	1885 - 1887
James Cullen	1886 - 1895
Walter Henry	1890 - 1893
John Morrin	1891 - 1892
Daniel Gallagher	1893 - 1895
Francis Benson	1895 - 1896
Andrew Callaghan	1896 - 1905
Michael Harte	1897 - 1898
Henry Dillon	1898 - 1900
Michael O'Doherty	1899 - 1900
John Hurst	1901 - 1903
Peter Cawley	1902 - 1911
James Spelman	1907 - 1913

35 see above
36 SC Irlanda vol. 23, ff. 661rv, 662v

Swinford	James Jordan	1907 - 1910
	Patrick Boland	1908 - 1911
	Denis Gildea	1909 - 1910
	P. J. O'Grady	1911 - 1912
	P. J. Casey	1913 - 1925
	Patrick Mulligan	1913 - 1914
	Peter F. O'Harte	1916 - 1917
	Anthony Durcan	1914 - 1921
	Michael Connolly	1917 - 1921
	John Kirwin	1920 - 1922
	Paul O'Grady	1922 - 1923
	Patrick Higgins	1922 - 1926
	Charles Carney	1924 - 1926
	Thomas Morrin	1925 - 1943
	James Hyland	1927 - 1928
	Thomas P. Gallagher	1927 - 1936
	Gerard Hannan	1929 - 1936
	Denis Gildea	1937 - 1941
	James Hunt	1937 - 1940
	Dominick Casey	1941 - 1950
	James Hyland	1944 - 1948
	John O'Neill	1941 - 1952?
	John Wims	1948 - 1964
	Edward O'Hara	1948 - 1948
	John Wims	1948 - 1964
	Denis O'Hara	1949 - 1957
	John A. McGarry	1956 - 1966
	Michael Keegan	1964 - 1978
	Paul Cryan	1966 - 1978
	James Gavigan	1978 - 1982
	Padraig Costello	1978 - 1983
	Gregory Hannon	1982 - 1988
	Michael Reilly	1983 - 1985
	Patrick Kilcoyne	1986 - 1991
	Stephen O'Mahony	1987 - 1990
	Patrick Holleran	1990 - 1996
	Peter Gallagher	1997 -
	James McDonagh	2000 - 2003
	James Brett	2003 -

Tourlestrane	Administrators	
	Daniel Mullarkey	pre-1833 - 1847 [37]
	James Higgins	1847 - 1848
	Roger Brennan	1848 - 1854
	James Devine	1854 - 1858
	John Brennan	1859 - 1860
	Patrick Roddy	1860 - 1864

37 ED 2/41, ff. 10 & 68

Peter O'Donoghue	1864 - 1867
*Thomas Loftus	1868 - 1878
*Patrick Durcan	1868 - 1878
Patrick Scully	1878 - 1880
John Gunning	1881 - 1893
Bartholmew Quinn	1893 - 1901
Thomas H. Quinn	1901 - 1919
Charles Gildea	1919 - 1922
Patrick J.Wims	1922 - 1935
Matthew Leonard	1935 - 1943
Michael O'Hara	1943 - 1944
Peter Harte	1944 - 1955
Joseph Henry	1955 - 1956
Joseph Higgins	1956 - 1970
Michael Cryan	1970 - 1977
Michael McLoughlin	1977 - 1978

It would appear that they were Joint Adms

Tourlestrane

Joseph Henry

Parish Priests

Michael McLoughlin	1978 - 1988
Liam Cawley	1987 - 1990
Christy McLoughlin	1990

Curates and Chaplains

Patrick Hurst	1833 [38]
James Hurst	1836 - 1842
Patrick Hurst	1842 - 1846
Thomas Judge	1846 - 1857
Michael Ivers	1858 - 1861
John Gallagher	1861 - 1866
Thomas Loftus	1866 - 1868
Patrick Lowry	1867 -1868
Patrick McDonnell	1868 -1874
James Cullen	1872 -1873
Patrick J.McDonald	1874 -1876
James Furlong	1876 -1878
J. Greene	1878 -1879
James Cullen	1879 -1881
J. Murphy	1879 -1881
John Horan	1881 -1887
John Browne	188? -1882
J. Dawson	1882 - 1884
Patrick Filan	1885 - 1886
Thomas Doyle	1887 - 1888
John McDonnell	1887 - 1889
Patrick McDermott	1888 - 1892
William Flynn	1893 -1900
Patrick Morrisroe	-1893
Mark Dempsey	1893 - 1894

38 ED 2/41, ff. 23 & 88; ED 1/79, no. 23

Michael O'Donoghue	1894 - 1895
P. Sherlock	1895 - 1896
Patrick Shinnick	1896 - 1897
Edward Doherty	1898 - 1899
James Spelman	1900 - 1906
James McKeon	1900 - 1902
John Breen	1903 - 1904
William Harte	1904 - 1905
Michael Durcan	1906 - 1907
Patrick Higgins	1906 - 1907
Patrick O'Donnell	1907 - 1909
Felix Burke	1907 - 1913
John O'Dowd	1909 - 1912
William Harte	1913 - 1925
Michael O'Hara	1913 - 1915
Edward Morahan	1916 - 1917
Edward O'Hara	1918 - 1919
Patrick Wims	1919 - 1921
Francis Stenson	1922 - 1923
John Casey	1924 - 1925
Philip Durkin	1925 - 1931
James Shryane	1926 - 1928
Luke Molloy	1929 - 1947
Matthew Leonard	1931 - 1938
Luke Molloy	1939 - 1947
Joseph Henry	1940 - 1943
Patrick O'Leary	1947 - 1948
Thomas Vesey	1948 - 1949
Edward Gallagher	1948 - 1951
Patrick Finan	1949 - 1957
Thomas Gavigan	1951 - 1953
Vincent Burke	1954 - 1957
Michael Cryan	1957 - 1963
James Colleran	1958 - 1959
Dudley Filan	1960 - 1963
Christopher McLoughlin	1963 - 1976
Louis Dunleavy	1963 - 1964
Liam Cawley	1965 - 1987
Dan O'Mahony	1976 - 1978
John Horgan	1978 - 1979
Anthony Flannery	1980 - 1982
Seamus Colleary	1984 -to present
Michael Gallagher	1986 - 1991
John Geelan	1991 - 1993
Roger McDonagh	1993 - 2001

Tubbercurry   *Parish Priests*

Patrick Henry	1806 - 1815
John McNulty	1815 - 1830 [39]
James McHugh	1830 - 1859

John Brennan	1859 - 1869
John McDermott	1869 - 1877
Michael D. Staunton	1877 - 1891
Patrick R. Staunton	1891 - 1912
John Gunning	1912 - 1926
James Spelman	1927 - 1940
Denis Gildea	1940 - 1948
Ambrose Blaine	1948 - 1971
Joseph Higgins	1971 - 1986
James Gavigan	1987 - 1995
Patrick Lynch	1995 -

Curates and Chaplains

James Gallagher	1836
Dominick O'Hara	1836
Patrick Spelman	1836 - 1839
Patrick Hyland	1839 - 1841
John Browne	1841 - 1843
Michael Cawley	1844 - 1851
John Brennan	1852 - 1858
Michael Cawley	1858 - 1859
Patrick Roddy Adm.	1859 - 1860
John Burke	1861 - 1862
Martin Sodan	1863 - 1865
Patrick Durcan	1865 - 1867
James Keveney	1867 - 1869
Edward Meehan	1870 - 1872
John O'Neill	1873 - 1876
Patrick Staunton	1876 - 1878
Peter Lohan	1876 - 1882
Thomas Doyle	1882 - 1886
Edward Connington	1886 - 1887
Philip Mulligan	1887 - 1889
Patrick Staunton	1890 - 1891
John McNicholas	1891 - 1894
Dominick O'Grady	1894 - 1895
Michael Doyle	1896 - 1911
Peter Cawley	1911 - 1916
Peter O'Harte	1917 - 1921
Felix Burke	1921 - 1922
Anthony Kirrane	1922 - 1925
John O'Dowd	1925 - 1933
Dominick Casey	1934 - 1940
Peter Harte	1934 - 1941
Edward Morahan	1941 - 1951
Walter Casey	1944 - 1948
Niall O'Donnell	1948 - 1961
John A. McGarry	1949 - 1955

Tubbercurry

Denis Gildea

Ambrose Blaine

39   McNulty transferred to his native Killasser. O'Rorke, *Sligo*, p. 133.

Tubbercurry	John C. Duffy	1952 - 1966
	Thomas Flynn	1956 - 1964
	Gerard Henry	1961 - 1969
	Cornelius Gordon	1964 - 1970
	Padraig McGovern	1969 - 1983
	James Gavigan	1971 - 1977
	Padraig Peyton	1982 - 1985
	James Finan	1983 - 1989
	Frank Gallagher	1987 -to present
	Ambrose McLoughlin	1990 - 1994
	Gerard Davey	1995 - 1999
	John Geelan	1999 -

Priests outside the Diocese at present
Gerard Davey, Rossport, Co Mayo in Killala Diocese
Eugene Duffy, Western Theology Institute, Galway
John Maloney, Catechetics course, Dublin
Dermot Meehan, St Patrick's College, Maynooth
Ronan Murtagh, Western Theology Institute, Galway
Paul Surlis, Crofton, Maryland, USA
Liam Swords, Hollybank Ave, Ranelagh, Dublin

Retired Priests
Padraig O'Gady, Ballymote, Co Sligo
Paul Surlis, Crofton, Maryland, USA
Patrick Towey, Gurteen, Co Sligo

Non Diocesan Priests who served in the Diocese and are now retired
Ambrose McLoughlin, Lough Talt, Aclare, Co Sligo
Frank Gallagher, Tubbercurry, Co Sligo
Roger McDonagh, Gurteen, Co Sligo

APPENDIX 6: PROTESTANT RECTORS, VICARS AND CURATES

Rectors
See Protestant Deans, Appendix 4, who were incumbents up to 1870

Achonry	George Abraham Heather	1871 - 1907
	Frederick William O'Connell	1907 - 1910
	Audley Alfred Ost	1910 - 1923
	Thomas Allen	1923 - 1927
	John Charles Forrester	1927 - 1929 (Rector of Achonry & Killoran)
	Herbert James MacReady	1930 - 1944
		1948, united with Tubbercurry
		1960, united with Kilmactigue

Curates		
	William Tyndall	c.1826
	John Nicholson Constable	1870
	William Reid Keillor	1906 - 1907

Vicars

Joseph Seymour	1811 - 1850
Anthony Thomas	1855 -
James Little	1867 - 1889

Castlemore ceased to be a parish and was united to Emlaghfad

Vicars

John Garrett	1806 - 1855
Arthur Moore	1855 - 1882
Thomas Gordon Walker	1882 - 1910
William Lindsell Shade	1916 - 1918
Charles John Algernon Harris	1918 - 1929
Isaac Hill McCombe	1930

1960 Emlaghfad, Killoran & Killaraght united.
1974 above united to Ballysadare

Curates

Henry Garrett	1836
Peter R. Foley	1870
Hawtrey Browne	1871
William John Haire	1877
Thomas Gordon Walker	1880

Vicars

Joseph Verschoyle Jr	1817 - 1820
Thomas Kingsbury	1820 - 1821
William Handcock	1821 - 1829
Charles Molloy	1829 - 1832
George Trulock	1832 - 1834
Lewis Potter	1834 - 1838
William Newton Guinness	1838 - 1857
William Chambers Townsend	1858 - 1872
Joseph Barker	1872 - 1876
Edward Francis Hewson	1879
William Newton Guinness	1884 - 1892 (2nd time)
Samuel Johnston	1892
George Fitzherbert McCormick	1904
William Lee Mather Gaff	1935
Ralph Montgomery	1956 - 1969

Curates

Claudius Huston	1818
George McClelland	1832
John Maguire	1838
Nicholas Whitestone	1844
Robert Hamilton	1856
John Fish	1860
Alfred Burton	1870 - 1873
John Charles Spencer	1904

Ballysadare	Chaplains	
	11 Nov 1849, chapel-of-ease built by E. J. Cooper	
	Lewis Potter	
	Robert Hamilton	1854
	William Brennan	1886 - 1895
	William Frederick Fitzgerald	1895 - 1899
	George Fitzherbert McCormack	1899
	Arthur Charles Rogers	1905

Coolaney (Killoran)	Vicars	
	Joseph Verschoyle Sr	1818 - 1862
	Hamilton Townsend	1862 - 1895
	Robert John Noyes	1896 - 1904
	Thomas Allen	1904 - 1927
		1927, united to Achonry, 1960 united to Emlaghfad, 1961 Glebe house and lands at Rathbarron sold, 1974 held by the incumbent in Skreen, 1975 united to Achonry and Tubbercurry.
	Herbert James McCready Bryan	1960
	Vivian Edwy Kille	1966
	Curates	
	John Stack	1807
	Arthur Huston	1842
	George Garrett	1852
	J. Willis	1873
	Robert Alexander Geddes	1876
	Joseph Russell Little	1878
	C. Townsend	1882
	Richard Huggard	1886
	William Evans Colvin	1889
	Thomas McVeagh	1891
	William John Haire	1895

Gurteen (Killaraght)	Vicars	
	James Elwood	1836
	Thomas Lindsay	1876 - 1877
	Daniel George Hayes Croly	1877
	William John Haire	1878 - 1917
	Arthur Manning	1917 - 1923
		1923 united to Emlaghfad. 1 Jan 1961 services discontinued.
	Curates	
	Francis Burke	1862
	Archibald Matthews Haire	1911
	Victor Frederick Lindsay	1912

Kiltimagh (Killedan)	Vicars	
	John Cromie	1805 - 1809 (as in Straide)
	John Meara	1809 - 1816 (as in Straide)
	John O'Rourke	1817 - 1849 (as in Straide)
	Mark Anthony Foster	1849 - 1873 (Rector of Killedan & Bohola)
		1873 united to Kilconduff

Vicars   *Straide (Templemore)*
John Cromie   1805 - 1809
John Meara   1809 - 1816
J. Gorges   1815 - 1817
John O'Rourke   1817 - 1849
William Jackson   1849 - 1866
William Oliver Jackson   1866 - 1871
John Gough Eames   1872 - 1881
John Walter Costello   1881 - 1896
Theophilus Patrick Landey   1896 - 1915
Charles Edward McQuaide   1915 - 1945
Thomas Quigley   1946
                               1946 united to Kilmoremoy & Castleconnor

Curates
Thomas Bell   1806
A. Thomas   1816 (also curate in Kilconduff)
Anthony Ormsby   - 1830
George Giles   1830 - 1835
Thomas de Veres Coneys   1835 - 1841
George Huston Mostyn   1841 - 1857
James H. Watson   1857 - 1866
Adam Gordon Farquhar   1866

Vicars   *Swinford (Kilconduff)*
Thomas Radcliffe   1805 - 1807
Joseph Burrows   1807 - 1821
E. Davis   1821 - 1827
Hon. George Gore   1827 - 1844
Benjamin Wilson Eames   1844 - 1871
John Nicholson Constable   1872 - 1888
David Patton Kinghan   1888 - 1908
Francis Travers Cockle   1909 - 1926
                               1926 united to Straide

Vicars   *Tourlestrane*
James Neligan   1802 - 1835   *(Kilmactigue)*
William Tyndall   1835 - 1847
Arthur Knox Huston   1847 - 1871
Peter Foley   1871 - 1872
John Walter Costello   1872 - 1881
Edward Symons   1884 - 1925
                               1925 united to Tubbercurry

Permanent Curates (in parish of Achonry)   *Tubbercurry*
George Huston Mostyn   1832 - 1841
Dominick Browne   1842
John Hamilton   1842 - 1865
James Jackson   1866 - 1870
Michael Shea   1870 - 1871
                               1870 - 1873 (Rector)

Tubbercurry	Thomas Leader Hanson	1873 - 1879
	Robert Alexander Geddes	1879 - 1882
	Alexander Thomas	1882 - 1888
	George Patton Mitchell	1889 - 1891
	Simon Carter Armstrong	1891 - 1892
	John Geddes	1892 - 1902
	Henry Acheson	1902 - 1909
	Thomas Alexander Beckett	1910 - 1925
	Edwin Symons	1925 - 1932
	Ivan Ridley Kirkpatrick	1933 - 1937
	Desmond Charles O'Connell	1938 - 1942
	Cyril Godfrey Wilson	1942 - 1945
	Paul Quigley	1945 - 1949
	James Mansel Egerton Maguire	1949 - 1955
	Walter Cyril Spence	1955 - 1966
	William Desmond Henderson	1966 - 1976
	Joseph Alfred Ambrose Condell	1976 -

Note. 1960 Achonry united to Tubbercurry, 1974 Kilmactigue included in group as well as Killoran in 1975

Attymass & Bonniconlon (Kilgarvan) belonged to the parish of Ballina (Kilmoremoy)	*Vicars:*	
	Joseph Verschoyle	1817 - ?,
	Joseph Verschoyle Jr	1857 - 1867
	Weldon Ashe	1867 - 1874
	Henry Acton Fleming	1874 - 1879
	William Skipton	1879 - 1903
	Frederick Dobbin	1903 - 1908
	John Francis Maurice Nash	1908 - 1925
	Theophilus Patrick Landey	1925 1927
	Robert Duggan	1927 - 1929
	Charles John Algernon Harris	1930 - 1942
	William James Ewart	1942
	John Ernest Leeman	1965
	John Luttrell Haworth	1976
	Frederick Charles Jameson	1979

Note. 1952 Straide grouped with Kilmoremoy

	Curates:	
	Claudius Huston	- 1829
	Francis Kinkead	1837
	John Lees	1847
	John Ribton Gore	1850
	Arthur Moore	1852
	Andrew Tait	1857
	James White	1862
	Richard Clarke	1864
	Pitt Johnston	1865
	Henry James Meyler Sibthorpe	1870
	James Fitzgerald	1870
	Robert Young Lynn	1871
	James Carmichael	1873

David Anderson	1877
Thomas Samuel Chapman	1878
Harloe A. Theodore Phibbs	1880
H. L. B. Benson	1882
John Lee Ralph	1883
Thomas Skipton	1885
Henry Chester Browne	1891
James Leonard Poe	1894
John Charles Spencer	1900
John Francis Maurice Nash	1903
Percival Doherty Irwin	1907
William Perry Roche	1910
Edwyn F. Heaton Thomas	1913
Cecil D. Clarke	1915

Irish College, Paris

APPENDIX 7: ACHONRY STUDENTS IN THE IRISH COLLEGE, PARIS

Durcan, Bernard, changed from Maynooth, ord. 1825*

Higgins, James, b.1797, Cullagh, ent. 28 Nov 1831, left 23 April 1833, d.Charlestown, 1878

Spelman, Patrick, Ardmile, ent. 24 Oct 1833

Healy, Matthew, Ballymote, ent. 20 Jan 1834, left for Ireland 5 April 1835

Ruane, Patrick, 29 Jan 1839, left 1 May 1841

Grealy?, Dominic, ent. 4 Oct 1853, sub-diaconate 19 Dec 1857

Dolan, Michael, ent. 4 Oct. 1853, sub-diaconate 19 Dec 1857

O'Donnell, Michael, ent. 24 Dec 1858, called out 15 May 1863, ord. in Maynooth

Henry, Paul, ent. 24 Dec 1858, called out Aug 1862, ord. at home

Hart, Peter, ent. 26 Oct 1860, called out 30 May 1865, ord. in Maynooth

Scully, Patrick, ent. 18 Jan 1863, delicate, left 7 Feb 1868, ord. at home

Burke, Matthew, ent. 19 Sept 1865, ord. at home July 1872

Gunning, John. ent. 6 April 1868, ord. Pentecost 1873

Mannion, Patrick, ent. 24 Oct 1872, ord. at home 1878

Coleman, Michael, ent. 22 Sept 1876, ord. at home, summer 1882

Duffy, John, ent. 17 Oct 1879, delicate, left 4 April 1881

Daly, James, ent. 12 Jan 1882

Cooke, Edward, ent.21 Sept 1882, left *ad vota saecularia* June 1884

McNicholas, Thomas, ent. 8 Oct 1882, left *ad vota saecularia* June 1885

Flynn, William, ent. 24 Sept 1885, ord. in Ireland 1890

Devine, Matthew, ent. Sept 1887, ord. Dec 1893

Healy, Thomas, ent. Sept 1890, died in college, April 1891

McKeon, Peter, ent. 25 Sept 1891, died of meningitis in college 11 April 1893

Boland, Patrick, ent. 20 Sept 1895, ord. 6 June 1891

Gaughan, John, ent. 17 Sept 1897, left *ad vota saecularia* Sept 1900

Gallagher, William Joseph, ent. 13 Sept 1901, withdrawn June 1904

O'Hara, Edward, ent. Sept 1907, left the college at the request of superior 28 July 1911, ord. later**

O'Connor, Francis, ent. 18 Sept 1908, ord. in college in June 1914

Dunne, Patrick, ent. 19 Sept 1913, transferred to Maynooth 1914

Battle, John Charles, ent. 30 Sept 1920, ord. priest for Glasgow 30 May 1926

McVann, Thomas, ent. Oct 1922, ord. 3 June 1928

Gallagher, Edward, ent. 27 Sept 1923, ord. in college 1926

O'Leary, Patrick, ent. 1926, ord. May 1932

O'Donnell, Thomas Francis, ent. 1930, asked not to return Sept 1934

Hurst, John, Carrowmacarrick, Coolaney, ent. 29 Sept 1933, ord. 1939

Feeley, Patrick, Tourlestrane, ent. 29 Sept 1935, ord. 1939

McNicholas, John, Church St, Swinford, ent. 29 Sept 1935, ord. Maynooth 6 June 1941

McLoughlin, Michael, Streamstown, Ballysadare, ent. 1935, ord. Maynooth 22 June 1941

Finan, Patrick Joseph, Killaraght, Ross, Lisserlough, Roscommon, ent. 1935, ord. Maynooth 22 June 1941

Cryan, Paul, Teeling St, Ballymote, ent. 23 Sept 1937, ord. Maynooth 22 June 1941

McLoughlin, Patrick Ambrose, Glenree, Bonniconlon, ent. 6 Oct 1938

Lang, Michael Anthony, Main St, Swinford, ent. 6 Oct 1938, died at home on vacation

Gavaghan, Anthony Thomas, Aclare, ent. 6 Oct 1938, ord. 1944, d. Attymass, 28 July 1986

Hughes, Michael Henry, Main St Foxford, ent. 6 Oct 1938

McGuinn, Michael Francis, Curry, ent. 6 Oct 1938

*   Had to leave Maynooth before beginning theology because of bad health. He was ordained a priest on the recommendation of the president and went to the Irish College, Paris to complete his studies. *C.T.* 14 May 1881

** Edward O'Hara left the college on 28 Dec 1911 at the request of the superior. The entry in the student register states that O'Hara was ordained later, became a military chaplain and was killed during the Great War. In fact Edward O'Hara was ordained on 1 June 1913, served all his life in Achonry and died in November 1950 as parish priest of Charlestown.

APPENDIX 8: ACHONRY STUDENTS IN THE IRISH COLLEGE, ROME

McNicholas, Patrick, ent. 21 Nov 1836, left 29 April 1841

Sweeney, Luke, b. 27 Sept 1887, ent. 28 Sept 1905, d. 20 May 1906 from typhoid and TB and buried in college tomb in Campo Verano, Rome

Lynch, Stanislas, Kiltimagh, b. 29 April 1886, ent. 28 Sept 1905, ord. 24 April 1910, D.Ph, left 22 May 1911, went to Philippines with Bishop O'Doherty, but left later and married in Southwark

Hyland, James, Kiltimagh, b. 1886, ent. 27 Sept 1907, ord. 1913, d. Straide 1949

Roughneen, Patrick J., Kiltimagh, b. 1892, ent. 3 Nov 1909, ord. 1916, d. Ballymote 1970

Dunne, Patrick, Carrowreagh Knox, Tubbercurry, b. 1893, ord. 1919, d. San Diego 1960*

Hannon, Gerard, Keash, b. 1900, ent. 10 Jan 1919, ord. 1924, d. Foxford 1987

O'Hara, Denis, Cloonacool, b. 1900, ent. 31 Oct 1919, ord. July 1924, left June 1925, d. Carracastle 1968

Horkan, Martin Thomas, Ballydrum, Swinford, ent. 23 Oct 1926, left 17 June 1932, ord. Brentwood, England, 15 Aug 1932

*Doherty, Edward, Mullinabreena, b. c. 1903, ord. 1928, d. Mullinabreena 1998

McGarry, John, Collooney, b. 1910, ent. 24 Oct 1928, ord. 1934, d. 1994

Madden, Louis, Kiltimagh, ent. 5 Nov 1939, b. 1918, ord. 1944, R.A.F. chaplain, d. 2001

McLoughlin, Christopher, Bridge St, Ballina, b. 1931, ent. 11 Oct 1951, ord. 1957

Kennedy, John, Main St, Foxford, ent. 10 Oct 1962, left *ad vota saecularia* 29 June 1965

Peyton, Patrick, Attymass, b. 13 April 1948, ent. 11 Oct 1967, ord. 24 June 1972

Geelan, John, Cloonloo, Gurteeen, b. 7 Sept 1954, ent. 9 Sept 1985, ord. 11 Dec 1988, left June 1989

Durkan, John James, Swinford, b. 2 April 1962, ent. 10 Sept 1987

Murtagh, Ronan, Tubbercurry, b. 4 Mar 1971, ent. 1 Oct 1999?

*   Not recorded in student register

APPENDIX 9: ACHONRY STUDENTS IN THE IRISH COLLEGE, SALAMANCA

Irish College,
Salamanca

O'Dwyer, William, Bohola, left and later became Mayor of New York and
   US ambassador to Mexico
Henry, Michael Louis, Killavil, b. 1874, ord. 1906, d. Straide 1947
Jordan, James, Crennane, Ballaghaderreen, ord. 1906, d. Attymass 1945
Blaine, Ambrose, Parke, Co Mayo, b. 1883, ord. 1906, d. Tubbercurry 1971
Reid, Patrick, b. Advarna, Ballaghaderreen 1887, ord. 1911, d. Ballyhaise, Kilmore diocese 1912
Wims, Patrick, Rathdooney, Ballymote, b. c.1888, ord. 1912, d. Bunninadden 1951
Shyrane, James, Ballaghaderreen, b. 1891, ord. 1914, d. Foxford 1960
O'Hara, Bernard, Aclare, b. 1894, ord. 1918, d. 1940
O'Hara, John Francis, Aclare, b. 1906, ent. 1925, ord. 1931, vice-rector 1935-45,
   d. Ballymote, 1989
Howley, Thomas, Charlestown, ord. 1931, Southwark diocese, d. 1993
Carty, Michael, Coolaney, b. 1910, ord. 1934, d. 1991
Vesey, Thomas P., Barroe, Carracastle, b. 1915, ord. 1950, d. 1962

APPENDIX 10: MARIST SISTERS

Charlestown*

Brennan, Breege: Brennan, Conrad: Brennan, Ildefonse: +Brett, Perpetua: Carr, Osana:
Carter, Darerca: +Cosgrove, Francis: +Costelloe, Philippine: Coyne, Rose: +Cullen, Teresa:
+Dodd, Brendan: +Duffy, Canisius: +Duignan, Stephen: +Durkin, Angela: +Farrelly, Emily:
+Finneran, Aidan: Flynn, Amadeus: +Flynn, Nicholas: +Gannon, Veronica: +Gavigan,
Cecilia: +Gilfillan, Thomasina: +Gilmartin, Elsie: Gilmartin, Joan: Gorman, Mary: +Griffin,
Fergus: +Hunt, Mercedes: Keaney, Asicus: +Kelly, Alvarez: Kelly, Modesta: +Kearns, Fanchea:
+Kiernan, Albert: Kiernan, Mary Patrick: +Lohan, Cassian: +McCarrick, Adrienne: +Moran,
Donal: +Murtagh, Calasanctius: +O'Connor, Ignatius: O'Connor, Maura: O'Flynn, Emer:
O'Halloran, Mary: +O'Reilly, Leo: +O'Rourke, Peter: Prenderville, Alacoque: +Quinn,
Gregory: +Regan, Nessa: Regan, Scholastica: +Reynolds, Ursula: +Richardson, Mary: Rooney,
Gemma: Ryan, Caitriona: +Ryan, Moira: +Towey, Marie de Lourdes: +Varden, Marie
Annunciata: +Walsh, Cletus: +Wims, Margaret Mary: Wrynne, Anthony.
*   Names supplied by John Doherty
+   Served also in Tubbercurry

Tubbercurry, 1901- *

Benson, Longinius: Blundell, Richard: Boland, Catherine: Brett, Felicitas: Brett, Perpetua:
Burke, Dunstan: Burke, Rita: Byrne, George: Byrne, Gertrude: Callaghan, Matthew: Cawley,
Georgina: Cogan, Margaret Mary: Cogan, Rosarii: Columb, Lawrence: Cosgrove, Francis:
Costello, Philippine: Cox, Angela: Crowe, Columba: Cullen, Teresa: Cummins, Margaret
Mary: Dodd, Brendan: Doyle, Florine: Duffy, Canisius: Duffy, Gonzaga: Duignan, Stephen:
Durkin, Angela: Earley, Ciaran: Euphemia, Sr: Farrelly, Emily: Finneran, Aidan: Finneran,
Eileen: Fleming, Eugenie: Flood, Adelaide: Flynn, Nicholas: Gannon, Gileesa: Gannon,
Veronica: Gavigan, Cecilia: Gavigan, Mary de Lellis: Gildea, Leo: Gilfillan, Thomasina:
Gilmartin, Elsie: Gilmore, Catherine: Griffin, Fergus: Griffin, Regis: Hanley, Ludgard: Henry,
Benen: Higgins, Fintan: Hourican, Austin: Hourican, Brigid: Hunt, Mary: Hunt, Mercedes:
Hyland, Felicity: Jennings, Mary Malachy: Johnson, Mary: Jordan, Catherine: Keane, Agatha:
Keaney, Eleanor: Keaney, Raphael: Kearns, Fanchea: Keaveny, Eudoxie: Keenan, Theresa:
Kelly, Alvarez: Kelly, Elizabeth: Kenny, Inez: Kiernan, Albert: Kirrane, Sylvester: Lavin,
Martin: Lavin, Raymond: Lawrence, Terence: Layden, Imelda: Layden, Maureen: Leyden,
Asicus: Lohan, Cassian: McCarrick, Adrienne: McCartin, Sr: McCormack, Anne:
McCormack, Marcelline: McDermott, Christina: McGrath, Simon: McGuinness, Brigid

Tubbercurry, 1901-   Mary: McKeon,, Adrian: McKeon, Ambrose: McKeon, Camillus: McKevitt, Pacome: McManus, Marcelline: McManus, Miriam: McNabola, Mary Josephine: McVeigh, Regina: Mangan, Hubert: Mangan, Melanie: Mary Martha, Sr (?): Maye, Maria: Moran, Donal: Mulligan, Margaret: Murray, Anastasia: Murray, Dominic: Murtagh, Calasanctius: Murtagh, Mary Imelda: Naughton, Honoria: Niland, Myra: Noone, Cornelius: O'Boyle, Claire: O'Connor, Aideen: O'Connor, Edmund: O'Connor, Ignatius: O'Donnell, Colman: O'Dowd, Martin: O'Gorman, Denis: O'Gorman, Mary Presentation: O'Gorman, Stephanie: O'Halloran, Philomena: O'Hara, Wilfrid: O'Malley, Edward: O'Reilly, Leo: O'Reilly, Marie: O'Riordan, Beatrice: O'Riordan, Philomena: O'Rourke, Eunan: O'Rourke, Peter: O'Sullivan, Dermot: Polycarp, Sr: Poole, Edmund: Quinlan, Melanie: Quinn, Gregory: Reddington, Muredach: Regan, Celestine: Regan, Nessan: Reid, Jarlath: Reynolds, Brigid: Reynolds, Ursula: Richardson, Mary: Ryan, Moira: Rynn, Anthony: Rynn, Dominic: Scott, Wenceslaus: Sharkey, Patricia: Stuart, Lawrence: Sweeney, Brigid Mary: Tracey, Geraldine: Towey, Marie de Lourdes: Varden, Marie Annunciata: Verdon, Pancras: Walsh, Angela: Walsh, Cletus: Walsh, Eucharia: Walsh, Venantius: Wims, Bertrand: Wims, Margaret Mary:
   * Names supplied by Alvarez Kelly RM

APPENDIX II: ST LOUIS SISTERS, KILTIMAGH *

Kiltimagh   Agnew, Una: Armitage, Margaret: Armstrong, John: Barneville, Evangelist: Boland, Donatus: Bolger, Veronica: Brennan, Stephen: Bresnahan, Victoire: Brett, Margaret Mary: Brett, Teresa: Brophy, Donal: Broughton, Nora: Burns, Emmanuel: Byrne, Baptist: Campion, Hyacinth: Canty, Rupert: Carey, Margaret: Catherine Mary, Sr: Clancy, Louis Marie: Clancy, Nessa: Cloran, Liguori: Coleman, Fabian: Colleran, James: Connolly, Liam: Connolly, Terence: Conroy, Andrew: Corish, Rosalie: Corr, Colman: Cox, René: Cummins, Marie Clare: Cunnane, Lucina: Curran, Stanislaus: Curran, Xavier: Delaney, Mary: Dillon, Bernice: Dobbin, Vivian: Dolan, Lonan: Doyle, Carthage: Duffy, Audrey: Duggan, Jarlath: Durkan, Gabrielle: Eaton, Bernardino: Emmanuel, Sr: Evans, Genevieve: Evans, Ita: Finan, Mary: Finan, Mary (superior): Fitzgerald, Mary Margaret: Flannery, Joy: Foley, Betty: Foley, Clare: Foley, Kathleen: Fox, Ancilla: Fullam, Fiona: Gibbons, Agnellus: Gibbons, Caitriona: Gildea, Elizabeth: Gill, Benen: Gilmartin, Angela: Gilmartin, Euphemia: Gleeson, M. de Sales: Hickey, Gertrude: Hickey, Roch Joseph: Higgins, Aida: Higgins, Aidan: Higgins, Aloysius: Holton, Eymard: Hughes, Venard: Hyland, Magdalene: Jordan, Sheila: Joyce, Cleophas: Joyce, Dominic: Judge, Immaculata: Keane, Francis: Kearney, Darerca: Kelly, Anne: Kelly, Columba: Kelly, Declan: Kelly, Patrick: Kelly, Theresia: Keneghan, Teresa: Kenny, Caitriona: Kett, Senan: Lee, Priscilla: Lillis, Ethna: Loftus, Gertrude: Lynch, Mary Philomena: McCluskey, Dorothy: McDermott, Brigid: McDermott, Gerard: McDevitt, Marie: McDonald, Rosario: McEnnis, Claudine: McGrath, Loretto: McGrath, Louis: McGreal, Davnet: McGreal, Marion: McGuinness, Eileen: McGuinness, Philomena: McHugh, Alberta: McHugh, Antonio: McKenna, Benedict: McKenna, Comgall: McKiernan, Mary: McKiernan, Proinnsias: McMahon, Dorothy: McNally, Kathleen: McNally, Mairead: McNama(ra)?, Dympna: McNicholas, Mochua: Maguire, Maureen: Mallon, Ernan: Maloney, Patricia: Mansfield, Ailbe: Marie, Josephine, Sr: Marie Louise, Sr: Martin, Annuntiata: Minogue, Oliver: Mitchell, Brendan: Mitchell, Casimir: Mitchell, Mercy: Moen, Dympna: Molloy, Fidelis: Monaghan, Gervase: Morrin, Isobel: Morrin, Nathy: Morris, Eileen: Morris, Ivor: Muldoon, Christina: Mulligan, Eugene: Murphy, Padraig: Nealon, Christopher: Noone, Aloysius: Noone, Evangelista: O'Boyle, Carol: O'Boyle, Teresina: O'Brien, Justin: O'Callaghan, Madeline: O'Callaghan, Realeno: O'Connell, Eucaria: O'Connor, Áine: O'Connor, Mary: O'Daly, Chrysostom: O'Doherty, Bernadette: O'Doherty, Imelda: O'Donnell, Aengus: O'Driscoll, Carmelita: O'Flynn, Marius: O'Gorman, Philippine: O'Hanlon, Fionnuala: O'Hara, Denis: O'Higgins, Philomena: O'Keeffe, Concepta: O'Keeffe, Treasa: O'Malley, Connla:

O'Reilly, Ercnat: O'Reilly. Lorcan: O'Sullivan, Maeve: Owens, Xavier: Owens, Inez: Power, Clement: Quinn, Theophane: Raferty, Cyril: Regan, Helen: Roche, Mary Augustine: Ryan, Aideen: Sexton, Attracta: Sharkey, Bernadette: Sleon, Kathleen: Smyth, Stella: Staunton, Anne: Stephens, Columcille: Stuart, Laurentia: Tierney, Eilís: Toal, Melíosa: Toolan, Anne: Walsh, Ignatius: Warde, Joseph: Woods, Paulinus: Woulf, Ethna.

Kiltimagh

* Names supplied by Paddy Kilcoyne

APPENDIX 12: SISTERS OF MERCY *

Aherne, Nannie (Vincent), Holy Cross, Co Tipperary, ent. 1886, d. 1916
Andrews, Margaret (Brigid), Gravois Mills, Missouri, USA, ent. 1965
Blewit, Mary (Muredach), Callasdashin, Co Mayo, ent. 1909, d. 1965
Bourke, Teresa (Aquinas), Kinagrelly, Collooney, Co Sligo, ent. 1943
Breheny, Kathleen (Assumpta), Keash, Ballymote, Co Sligo, ent. 1946
Brennan, Brigid (Fidelma), Portroe, Nenagh, Co Tipperary, ent. 1909, d. 1974
Brennan, Catherine (Josephine), ent. 1874, d. 1916
Brosnan, Ellie (Brigid), Odorney, Co Kerry, ent. 1893, d. 1914
Casey, Mary (Edan), Hagfield, Ballaghaderreen, ent. 1889, d. 1944
Casey, Mary (Evangelist), Monasteraden, Ballaghaderreen, ent. 1899, d. 1938
Casey, Mary Teresa (Teresita), Coolbock, Riverstown, Co Sligo, ent. 1928,
Cashman, Madge (Columba), Ballyheigue, Co Kerry, ent. 1903, d. 1932
Cassidy, Maureen (Veronica), Ballymote, Co Sligo, ent. 1949
Cawley, Rosaleen (Patrick), Kilnamonagh, Collooney, Co Sligo, ent. 1940
Chambers, Bernadette, Ballymote, Co Sligo, ent. 1961
Chambers, Ellen (Declan), Ballymote, Co Sligo, ent. 1960
Clancy, Philomena (Consilio), Main St, Clifden, Co Galway, ent. 1949
Coen, Margaret (Emmanuel), Culfadda, Ballymote, Co Sligo, ent. 1951
Coleman, Annie (Peter), Corbally, Co Cork, ent. 1891, d. 1922
Coleman, Cecilia (Nathy), Rathbarron, Co Sligo, ent. 1895, d. 1954
Comyn, Margaret (Liguori), ent. 1858, d. 1865
Conway, Nancy (Teresa), Conway's Cross, Riverstown, Co Sligo, ent. 1907, d. 1909
Coyle, Mary Assumpta, Belmullet, Co Mayo, ent. 1973
Cryan, Patricia (Rosarii), Ballymote, Co Sligo, ent. 1944
Cuffe, Anne (de Porres), Glencullen, bangor Erris, Co Mayo, ent. 1961
Cuniffe, Annie (Oliver), Swinford, Co Mayo, ent. 1919, d. 1950
Daly, Agnes (Margaret Mary), Ballymote, Co Sligo, ent. 1891, d. 1943
Deignan, Margaret (Imelda), Birr, Co. Offaly, ent. 1928, d. 1986
Doherty, Brigid (Carmel), Charlestown, Co Mayo, ent. 1945
Donagh, Marian Concepta (Concepta), Drogheda, Co Louth, ent. 1920, d. 1985
Dooley, Alice (Columba), Shrule, Co Galway, ent. 1878
Dooley, Kate Mary (de Sales), Shrule, Co Galway, ent. 1862, d. 1932
Dooley, Mary (Gabriel), Shrule, Co Galway, ent. 1856, d. 1861
Dooley, Mary Teresa (Stanislaus), Shrule, Co Galway, ent. 1859, d. 1862?
Dooley, Nannie (Stanislaus), Shrule, Co Galway, ent. 1871
Dore, Margaret (Laurentia), Glyn, Co Limerick, ent. 1908, d. 1968
Dorr, Catherine (Bernadette), Foxford, Co Mayo, ent. 1927, d. 1980
Duffy, Kathleen, Collooney, Co Sligo, ent. 1973
Dunleavy, Brigid (Bernardine), Kilkelly, Co Mayo, ent. 1941
Durkan, Anne (Bernard), ent. 1858, d. 1868
Durkan, Kathleen (Immaculata), Rathnamagh, Crossmolina, Co Mayo, ent. 1942

Swinford

Kathleen Breheny,

Swinford   Durkan, Lilly (Agatha), Rathnamagh, Crossmolina, Co Mayo, ent. 1941

Flannery, Freda (Ursula), Kilkelly, Co Mayo, ent. 1936

Flatley, Margaret (Columbanus), Leckee, Foxford, Co Mayo, ent. 1920, d. 1973

Foody, Mary (Giovanni), Knockanillaun, Ballina, Co Mayo, ent. 1965

Gallagher, Margaret Mary (Sacred Heart), Masshill, Tubbercurry, Co Sligo, ent. 1965

Gallagher, Mary Amelia (Gertrude), Killasser, Co Mayo, ent.?

Gallagher, Mary (Dolores), Laghey, Co Donegal, ent. 1945

Gallagher, Mary (Joachim), Kinagrelly, Collooney, Co Sligo, ent. 1955

Gardiner, Pauline, Killavil, Co Sligo, ent. 1951

Gavin, Agnes (Damien), Swinford, Co Mayo, ent. 1970

Graham, Mary (Alphonsus), Cork, ent. 1893, d. 1949

Graham, Catherine (Joseph), ent. 1855, d. 1911

Griffin, Kate (Celestine), Castletownbere, Co Kerry, ent. 1913, d. 1928

Gould, Mary (de Sales), Dingle, Co Kerry, ent. 1898, d. 1972

Hayes, Mary (Attracta), Gurtroe, Co Limerick, ent. 1894, d. 1940

Henry, Mary (Xavier), ent. 1876, d. 1913

Hession, Kate (Magdalen), Galway, ent. 1859, d. 1915

Hickey, Margaret (Annunciata), Mullingar, Co Westmeath, ent. 1946

Hogge, Mary (Loreto), Derroon, Ballymote, Co Sligo, ent. 1963

Horan, Evelyn (Martinian), Gurteen, Co Sligo, ent. 1965

Horan, Margaret (Vincent), Gurteen, Co Sligo, ent. 1959

Houlihan, Anne (Columba), Knock, Ennis, Co Clare, ent. 1943

Judge, Mary Catherine, Dromore West, Co Sligo, ent. 1977

Kearney, Mary (Michael), Ballincleminsey, Causeway, Co Kerry, ent. 1904, d. 1955

Keating, Delia (Francis), Kilnamona, Co Clare, ent. 1917, d. 1967

Kelly, Kate (Gabriel), Carradine, Kiltimagh, Co Mayo, ent. 1932

Kelly, Mary (Finian), Lettermullen, Co Galway, ent. 1942

Kelly, Sarah (Bernard), Carradine, Kiltimagh, Co Mayo, ent. 1934, d. 1993

Kelly, Veronica (Liguori), Midfield, Swinford, Co Mayo, ent. 1959

Kennedy, Kate (Catherine), Glenfesk, Co Kerry, ent. 1916, d. 1974

Kerrins, Helen (Paul), Dromard, Co Sligo, ent. 1964

Kilcawley, Maura (Attracta), Ballinacarriga, Ballymote, Co Sligo, ent. 1942

Kilcoyne, Catherine Philomena (Collette), Killavil, Co Sligo, ent. 1961

Killoran, Margaret (Joseph), Bunninadden, Co Sligo, ent. 1963

Kirwan, Cecilia (Gertrude), Galway, ent. 1862, d. 1917

Kyle, Maggie (Anthony), Swinford, Co Mayo, ent. 1902, d. 1967

Lafferty, Teresa (Rose), Kilmovee, Co Mayo, ent. 1938

Lally, Maureen (Andrew), Islandeady, Castlebar, Co Mayo, ent. 1958

Leavy, Mary (Kevin), Ballysadare, Co Sligo, ent. 1968

Lowther, Nora Imelda (James), Cooneel, Ballina, Co Mayo, ent. 1958

Lydon, Margaret (Regina), Ballyfarnon, Co Roscommon, ent. 1954

McCann, Margaret (de Lourdes), Derryronane, Swinford, Co Mayo, ent. 1947

McCann, Maureen (Scholastica), Bunninadden, Co Sligo, ent. 1968

McCarrick, Bernadette (Nathy), Mullinabreena, Co Sligo, ent. 1970

McCarrick, Brigid (Celsus), Loughill, Tubbercurry, Co Sligo, ent. 1913, d. 1949

McCarthy, Alice (Paul), Swinford, Co Mayo, ent. 1901, d. 1957

McCarthy, Josie (Finbar), Charleville, Co Cork, ent. 1902, d. 1932

McDonnell, Evelyn (Alphonsus), Kilmovee, Ballaghaderreen, Co Mayo, ent. 1967

McDonnell, Mary (Leo), Kilmovee, Ballaghaderreen, Co Mayo, ent. 1961

McEniry, Ellen (Lelia), Bruff, Co Limerick, ent. 1906, d. 1946

McEniry, Minnie (Augustine), Bruff, Co Limerick, ent. 1900, d. 1971
McGinnity, Margaret (Aidan), Drumguilla, Castleblaney, Co Monaghan, ent. 1965
McMorland, Margaret (Paschal), Callagraphy, Ballintrillick, Co Sligo, ent. 1951
McNamee, Mary (Margaret Mary), Bridge St, Loughrea, Co Galway, ent. 1953
McNicholas, Brigid (Elizabeth), Swinford, Co Mayo, ent. 1970
McNicholas, Frances (Anselm), Swinford, Co Mayo, ent. 1960
MacNiffe, Kate (Francis), ent. 1875
Madden, Mary (Joseph), Limerick, ent. 1920, d. 1962
Martin, Monica (Aloysius), Galway, ent. 1855, d. 1899
Meagher, Alice (Augustine), ent. 1857, d. 1861
Molloy, Mary (Mary), Attymass, Co Mayo, ent. 1910, d. 1959
Molloy, Sheila (Laboure), Lisananny, Ballymote, Co Sligo, ent. 1963
Moran, Margaret (Jarlath), Onnagh, Ballyhaunis, Co Mayo, ent. 1910, d. 1965
Moylan, Elizabeth (Patricia), ent. 1883, d. 1910
Mullen, Maureen (Vianney), Ballymote, Co Sligo, ent. 1959
Murphy, Bridie (Ita), Ehane, Co Kerry, ent. 1903, d. 1935
Murphy, Irene, Cork, ent. 1977
Murray, Margaret (Mercedes), Coolea, Macroom, Co Cork, ent. 1947
Nealis, Mary (Lassara), Kilnamonagh, Collooney, Co Sligo, ent. 1908, d. 1946
Noonan, Monica (Coleman), Buttevant, Co Cork, ent. 1913, d. 1924
Nugent, Brigid (Teresa), Kilkeady, Tubber, Co Clare, ent. 1939
Nugent, Helena (Clare), Kilkeady, Tubber, Co Clare, ent. 1927, d. 1989
O'Brien, Catherine (Teresa), ent. 1858, d. 1884
O'Callaghan, Maria (Scholastica), Cork, ent. 1890, d. 1937
O'Connell, Lizzie (Aloysius), Headford, Killarney, Co Kerry, ent. 1916, d. 1939
O'Connell, Mary (Veronica), ent. 1858, d. 1904
O'Connor, Eliza (de Chantal), ent.1861, d. 1900
O'Connor, Kathleen (Benignus), Cahirciveen, Co Kerry, ent. 1902, d. 1970
O'Connor, Marian (St Ann), Ballinacarrow, Co Sligo, ent. 1955
O'Dea, Mary Francis (Philomena), Kinvara, Co Galway, ent. 1927
O'Donnell, Anne (Malachy), Ballygoran, Co Laois, ent. 1909, d. 1966
O'Donnell, Kathleen (Peter), Carrowrile, Lavagh, Co Sligo, ent. 1939
O'Donnell, Mary (Enda), Carrowneaden, Collooney, Co Sligo, ent. 1960
O'Dowd, Katie (Rose), Bunninadden, Co Sligo, ent. 103, d. 1924
O'Grady, Mary (Ethnea), Mahanna, Boyle, Co Roscommon, ent. 1909, d. 1970
O'Grady, Bernadette (Angela), Killasser, Swinford, Co Mayo, ent. 1959
O'Grady, Mary Eithne (St John), Killasser, Swinford, Co Mayo, ent. 1957
O'Grady, Nora (Perpetual Succour), Cloonacool, Co Sligo, ent. 1920, d. 1973
O'Grady, Teresa (Agnes), Killasser, Co Mayo, ent. 1936
O'Halloran, Anne (Albeus), Fedamore, Co Limerick, ent. 1907, d. 1965
O'Halloran, Barbara (Cecelia), Lower Abbeygate St, Galway, ent. 1924, d. 1985
O'Halloran, Eileen (Stanislaus), Fedamore, Co Limerick, ent. 1916, d. 1978
O'Hara, Teresa, Sligo (Liguori), ent. 1865
Oliver, Noreen (Monica), Tullinacurra, Swinford, Co Mayo, ent. 1968
O'Malley, Teresa (Patrick), Sligo, ent. 1910, d. 1938
O'Reilly, Sabina (Angela), Galway, ent. 1883, d. 1946
O'Riordan, Kate (Brendan), Tralee, Co Kerry, ent. 1892, d. 1895
O'Shaughnessy, Kathleen (Dominic), Oughterard, Co Galway, ent. 1937
O'Shea, Augusta (Martha), Kilrecle, Loughrea, Co Galway, ent. 1923
O'Sullivan (Gerard), Elizabeth, Newcastle West, Co Limerick, ent. 1919, d. 1980

Swinford

Kathleen O'Donnell

Teresa O'Grady

Bernadette O'Grady

Swinford   Perrin, Lizzie (Aloysius), 1858, d. 1868?
Perrin, Victoria (Gonzaga), ent. 1869, d. 1919
Power, Kate (Bonaventure), Crusheen, Co Clare, ent. 1912, d. 1970
Power, Mary (Catherine), ent. 1856, d. 1910
Regan, Angela, Kilmovee, Co Mayo, ent. 1934
Reidy, Margaret Mary (Celestine), Shanagolden, Co Limerick, ent. 1940
Reilly, Nora (Camillus), Gurteenamore, Claremorris, Co Mayo, ent. 1916, d. 1959
Reynolds, Bridie (Athanasius), Cloonkeary, Ballymote, Co Sligo, ent. 1961
Riordan, Kate (Kevin), Killarney, Co Kerry, ent. 1911, d. 1961
Scanlon, Brigid (Christina), Upper Carrigans, Ballymote, Co Sligo, ent. 1950, d. 1986
Scanlon, Eileen (Baptist), Bunninadden, Co Sligo, ent. 1966
Scollard, Katie (Raphael), Ballybrannaigh, Tralee, ent. 1904, d. 1955
Scully, Kate (Berchmans), Ballymote, Co Sligo, ent. 1916, d. 1976
Sheehan, Kate (Joseph), ent. 1873, d. 1877
Sheridan, Monica (Benedict), Port Clarence, Bithingham, Stockton, England, ent. 1933, d. 1987
Sherlock, Brigid (Philip), Brislough, Boyle, Co Roscommon, ent. 1958
Shiels, Attracta (Michael), Corhober, Ballymote, Co Sligo, ent. 1961
Shiels, Catherine (Pius), Corhober, Ballymote, Co Sligo, ent. 1953
Shiels, Josephine (Ambrose), Corhober, Ballymote, Co Sligo, ent. 1960
Stack, Ellen (Dympna), Kilflyn, Co Kerry, ent. 1907, d. 1970
Sullivan, Ellen (Brigid), Kenmare, Co Kerry, ent. 1914, d. 1963
Sullivan, Kate (Elizabeth), Kenmare, Co Kerry, ent. 1908, d. 1967
Sunney, Anne (Brendan), Annabeg, Collooney, Co Sligo, ent. 1907, d. 1972
Tobin, Mary (Magdalen), Rathkeale, Co Limerick, ent. 1917, d. 1954
Torsney, Margaret Mary (Magdalen), Gadden, Collooney, Co Sligo, ent. 1957
Walsh, Barbara (Dorothy), Cloongulaune, Swinford, Co Mayo, ent. 1931, d. 1975
Watson, Mary (Virgilius), Lismoyle, Athlone, Co Westmeath, ent. 1913, d. 1964
Whelan, Nora (Baptist), Stradbally, Co Waterford, ent. 1901, d. 1958
Wims, Catherine, Collooney, Co Sligo, ent. 1974
Winters, Margaret Mary, Cork, ent. 1973

Superiors 1885 - 2002

Monica Martyn	1855 - 1876
Kate Hession	1873 - 1876
Cecilia Kirwin	1876 - 1882
Mary Teresa Dooley	1882 - 1887
Agnes Hagen	1887 - 1888
Mary Henry	1888 - 1891
Margaret McCarthy	1891 - 1896
Mary Casey	1896 - 1899
Sabina O'Reilly	1899 - 1902
Margaret McCarthy	1902 - 1926
Mary Casey	1926 - 1932
Sabina O'Reilly	1932 - 1938
Mary Casey	1938 - 1944
Monica Noonan	1944 - 1950
Nora Whelan	1950 - 1953
Helena Nugent	1959 - 1965
Monica Sheridan	1965 - 1968

Helena Nugent	1968 - 1974	*Swinford*
Teresa O'Grady	1974 - 1980	
Attracta Shiels	1980 - 1986	
Veronica Cassidy	1986 - 1992	
Attracta Shiels	1992 -	

Convent of the Sacred Heart 1971 - 1994   *Ballaghaderreen*
Brosnan, Francis, Cassidy, Maureen (Veronica), Chambers, Ellen (Declan), Coen, Margaret (Emmanuel), Coyle, Mary, Cryan, Patricia (Rosarii), Cuffe, Anne (de Porres), Dunleavy, Brigid (Bernardine), Durcan, Lily (Agatha), Foody, Mary (Giovanni), Gallagher, Mary, Gallagher, Mary (Dolores), Haran, Evelyn (Martinian), Houlihan, Anne (Columba), Kilcoyne, Phyllis, Lafferty, Teresa (Rose), Lydon, Margaret (Regina), McCann, Maureen (Scholastica), McCarrick, Bernadette, McNicholas, Frances (Anselm), O'Donnell, Mary (Enda), O'Grady, Mary Eithne (St John), O'Shaughnessy, Kathleen (Dominic), Reynolds, Bridie (Athanasius), Scanlon, Eileen (Baptist), Shiels, Attracta (Michael), Shiels, Kathleen (Pius), Torsney, Margaret Mary (Magdalen)

St Nathy's College 1950 –
Gallagher, Mary E., Hogge, Mary (Loreto), Kelly, Veronica (Liguori), Kilcawley, Maura (Attracta), Lally, Maureen (Andrew), McNamee, Mary (Margaret Mary), Molloy, Sheila (Laboure), Mullen, Maureen (Vianney), O'Sullivan, Brigid, Power, Kate (Bonaventure)

Convent of Our Lady of the Rosary 1902 –   *Ballymote.*
Ahearne, Nannie (Vincent), Brehony, Kathleen (Assumpta), Casey, Mary Teresa (Teresita), Cassidy, (Calasanctius), Cassidy, Maureen (Veronica), Cawley, Rosaleen (Patrick), Chambers, Ellen (Declan), Clancy, Philomena (Consilio), Coyle, Mary, Daly, Agnes (Margaret Mary), Dore, Margaret (Laurentia), Dorr, Catherine (Bernadette), Dunleavy, Brigid (Bernardine), Durkan, Kathleen (Immaculata), Durkan, Lily (Agatha), Flannery, Freda (Ursula), Gallagher, Mary, Gallagher, Mary Amelia (Gertrude), Gould, Mary (de Sales), Hogge, Mary (Loretto), Horan, Margaret (Vincent), Houlihan, Anne (Columba), Kearney, Mary (Michael), Keating, Delia (Francis), Kelly, Kate (Gabriel), Kelly, Mary (Finian), Kennedy, Kate (Catherine), Kerrins, Helen (Paul), Kilcawley, Maria (Attracta), Kilcoyne, Catherine Philomena (Collette), Kilcoyne, Phyllis, Killoran, Margaret (Joseph), Lafferty, Teresa (Rose), Leavy, Mary (Kevin), Lydon, Margaret (Regina), McCann, Josephine, McCann, Margaret, (de Lourdes), McCarrick, Bernadette (Nathy), McGarty, Rita, McNicholas, Frances (Anselm), Molloy, Mary (Mary), Moran, Margaret (Jarlath), Moylan, Elizabeth (Patricia), Nugent, Brigid (Teresa), O'Connor, Marian (St Ann), O'Dea, Mary Francis (Philomena), O'Donnell, Mary (Enda), O'Grady, Bernadette (Angela), O'Grady, Ethna (St John), O'Grady, Teresa (Agnes), O'Halloran, Anne (Albeus), O'Halloran, Barbara (Cecilia), O'Halloran, Eileen (Stanislaus), O'Malley, Teresa (Patrick), O'Shaughnessy, Kathleen (Dominic), Scollard, Katie (Raphael), Sheridan, Monica (Benedict), Shiels, Kathleen (Pius), Sunney, Anne (Brendan), Torsney, Margaret (Magdalen), Watson, Mary (Virgilius), Whelan, Nora (Baptist)

St John's Convent 1942   *Ballysadare*
Casey, Margaret, Casey, Mary Teresa (Teresita), Cassidy, Maureen (Veronica), Chambers, Ellen (Declan), Coen, Margaret (Emmanuel), Cuffe, Anne (de Porres), Cummins, Patricia, Cryan, Patricia (Rosarii), Duignan, Margaret (Imelda), Durkan, Kathleen (Immaculata), Durkan, Lilly (Agatha), Flannery, Freda (Ursula), Gallagher, Mary, Gallagher, Mary (Dolores), Glynn, Mary, Greally, Ursula, Horan, Margaret (Vincent), Keating, Delia (Francis), Kelly, Mary (Finian), Kerrins, Helen (Paul), Kilcoyne, Phyllis, Lowther, Nora Imelda (James), Lydon, Margaret (Regina), McDonnell, Evelyn (Alphonsus), McGinnity, Margaret (Aidan),

Ballysadare   McNicholas, Brigid (Elizabeth), Murray, Margaret (Mercedes), Noonan, Monica (Coleman), Nugent, Brigid (Teresa), Nugent, Helena (Clare), O'Donnell, Kathleen (Peter), O'Donnell, Mary (Enda), O'Grady, Bernadette (Angela), O'Grady, Mary (Ethnea), O'Shaughnessy, Kathleen (Dominic), Reidy, Margaret Mary (Celestine), Scanlon, Brigid (Christina), Sheils, Attracta (Michael), Sheridan, Monica (Benedict), Sherlock, Bridget (Philip),

Collooney   *Convent of Our Lady of Mount Carmel 1909 –*
Andrews, Brigid (Margaret), Brennan, Brigid (Fidelma), Casey, Mary (Evangelist), Casey, Mary Teresa (Teresita), Cassidy, Maureen (Veronica), Clancy, Philomena (Consilio), Coleman, Annie (Peter), Coleman, Cecilia (Nathy), Daly, Agnes (Margaret Mary), Donagh, Marian (Concepta), Dore, Margaret (Laurentia), Duignan, Margaret (Imelda), Dunleavy, Brigid (Bernardine), Flannery, Freda (Ursula), Gallagher, Mary, Hayes, Mary (Attracta), Houlihan, Anne (Columba), Kelly, Mary (Finian), Kennedy, Kate (Catherine), Kyle, Maggie (Anthony), Lafferty, Teresa (Rose), Lydon, Margaret (Regina), McCann, Margaret (de Lourdes), McCarrick, Bernadette (Nathy), McCarthy, Alice (Evangelist), McDonnell, Mary (Leo), Molloy, Sheila (Laboure), Murray, Margaret (Mercedes), Nugent, Brigid (Teresa), Nugent, Helena (Clare), O'Connor, Marian (St Ann), O'Dea, Mary Francis (Philomena), O'Donnell, Anne (Malachy), O'Grady, Mary (Ethnea), Oliver, Noreen (Monica), Scanlon, Brigid (Christina), Scollard, Katie (Raphael), Sheils, Attracta (Michael), Torsney, Margaret Mary (Magdalen)

Gurteen   *Convent of Our Lady of the Immaculate Conception 1954 –*
Cassidy, Maureen (Veronica), Cawley, Rosaleen (Patrick), Clancy, Philomena (Consilio), Coen, Margaret (Emmanuel), Cryan, Patricia (Rosarii), Duignan, Margaret (Imelda), Gallagher, Mary (Dolores), Keating, Delia (Francis), McGinnity, Margaret (Aidan), McNamee, Mary (Margaret Mary), Molloy, Sheila (Laboure), Mullen, Maureen (Vianney), Noonan, Monica (Coleman), O'Connor, Marian (St Ann), O'Grady, Mary Eithne (St John), O'Shaughnessy, Kathleen (Dominic), O'Shea, Augusta (Martha), Shiels, Josephine (Ambrose), Shiels, Kathleen (Pius), Torsney, Margaret Mary (Magdalen)
*   Philomena Clancy RSM, *A Journey of Mercy*

*APPENDIX 13: SISTERS OF CHARITY

Ballaghaderreen   Barry, Austin Peter, d. 1944
Coghlan, Joseph Bride, d. 1950
Connell, Mary Emerentia, d. 1932
Donnelly, Mary Maud, d. 1889
Duffy, Mary Uriel, d. 1954
Grady, Mary Thomas, d. 1960
Greene, Mary Monica, d. 1895
Grehan, Magdalen Oswald, d. 1921
Harris, Francis Columba, d. 1963
Hogan, Mary Gonzales, d. 1903
Kelly, Joseph Malachy, d. 1970
Kenny, Joseph de Lellis, d. 1911
Murphy, Mary Herman, d. 1922
O'Connor, Mary Consiglio, d. 1914
O'Connor, Mary Sabas, d. 1923
O'Halloran, Joseph Columbanus, d. 1927
Reilly, Joseph Cosmas, d. 1918
Rorke, Joseph Philomena, d. 1903

Seary, Mary Nazianzen, d. 1929   *Ballaghaderreen*
Other Sisters who served in Ballaghaderreen included Cajetan, Sr, Charles, Sr, Coffey,
Consilio, Dudley, Placidus, Ephrem, Sr, Eulalia, Sr, Francis Xavier, Sr, Hickey, Catherine,
Joseph, Sr, McLoughlin, Mary, Martin, Magdalen Rita, Sr, Mary Bernadette, Sr, Segrave,
Magdalen, Smollen, Theckla, Teresa, Sr, Wall, Berchmans (There were 17 Sisters there in 1890)

Barden, Aloysius Walburga, d. 1909   *Benada*
Bishop, Joseph Mel, d. 1976
Blake, Agnes Veronica, d. 1895
Carroll, Magdalen Rose, d. 1916
Connoly, Mary Athanasius, d. 1896
Dowling, Mary Caius, d. 1939
Harney, Mary Anthony, d. 1982
Kennedy, Mary Cecilia, d. 1969
Kinsella, Stanislaus Kotska, d. 1885
Kivil, Mary Cataldus, d. 1888
McVey, Mary Syra, d. 1920
Mahon. Mary Celsus, d. 1911
Mulligan, Mary Lasera, d. 1943
Phillips, Joseph Angela, d. 1914
Phillips, Mary James, d. 1976
Ryan, Mary Cecily, d. 1919
Walsh, Mary Dympna, d. 1939

Barrett, Joseph Dominic, d. 1933   *Foxford*
Birch, Aloysius Andrew, d. 1953
Bourke, Joseph Carmel, d. 1988
Butler, Mary Gualbert, d. 1914
Connington, Francis Aloysius, d. 1958
Cronin, Mary Stylites, d. 1942
Duffy, Mary Germanus, d. 1966
Feeney, Francis Columba, d. 1919
Fitzpatrick, Peter Alcantara, d. 1966
Gallagher, Mary Gregory, d. 1967
Gibbons, Mary Gonzaga, d. 1983
Harty, Mary Clare, d. 1914
Hasler, Mary Cordula, d. 1952
Herlihy, Joseph Felix, d. 1939
Hickey, Joseph Catherine, d. 1924
Hosey, Mary Mina, d. 1916
Kivlehan, Francis Attracta, d. 1984
McLoughlin, Teresa Francis, d. 1950
McNulty, Catherine de Ricci, d.1930
Morrogh-Bernard, Arsenius, d. 1932
Noonan, Mary Afra, d. 1942
Rush, Joseph Maura, d. 1925
Segrave, Mary Magdalen, d. 1925
Smullen, Mary Thecla, d. 1932
Wall, Stanislaus Kotska, d. 1898
Wall, Joseph Berchmans, d. 1912

Foxford   Walshe, Joseph Norbert, d. 1943
*   List, which only includes those who were buried in Ballaghaderreen, Benada and Foxford, was supplied by Marie Bernadette O'Leary RSC

Other Sisters who served in Foxford included, Delaney, Francis Xavier; Doran, Macrina; Meyler, Euphrasia; O'Leary, Marie Bernadette; O'Meara, Neri; Seaver, Gertrude; Walker, Mary Charles

APPENDIX 14: ST JOHN OF GOD SISTERS

Ballinamore   Anderson, Helen 'Ellie' (Martina), d. 13 Aug 1977
Bergin, Margaret (Cuthbert)
Biggins, Teresa (Teresa)
Bones, Elizabeth Anne (Elizabeth)
Brady, Sarah T. (Deirdre)
Brennan, Sarah Josephine (Francesca), d. 1 Mar 1989
Brennan, Mary Margaret (Mary Eugenia)
Burke, Mary (Mildred)
Burke, Annie Jane (Jane)
Butler, Philomena (Philomena)
Byrne, Bridget (Alcantara)
Byrne, Mary (Maria)
Cadogan, Margaret 'Peg' (Euphrasia)
Casey, Veronica 'Vera' (Baptiste)
Collins, Ann (Ann)
Collins, Catherine Philomena (Marie Louise), d. 15 June 1999
Conlon, Margaret Ita (Maris Stella)
Conneely, Siobhán Julia (Teresa)
Connolly, Ellen 'Helen' (Helen)
Connolly, Kathleen (Kathleen)
Connolly, Sarah Josephine (Marguerite)
Connolly, Mary Delia Christina 'Chrissie' (Teresina)
Connolly, Ellen (Columbiere), d. 6 Feb 1993
Conroy, Kathleen 'Kate' (Loreto)
Conway, Mary Kathleen (Alma)
Corbet, Sara 'Sadie' (Majella), d. 14 Aug 1995
Costello, Bridget (Fabian), d. 28 April 1976
Cox, Angela (Angela)
Cuddihy, Brigid Mary (Idus), d. 2 Aug 1994
Cullinane, Cecilia (Ann)
Dee, Hanorra Theresa 'Teresa' (Romanus)
Doyle, Patricia (Pat)
Doyle, Agnes (Emilian)
Duffy, Brigid (Eucharia)
Duffy, Margaret (Margaret)
Dunne, Mary Teresa 'Maura' (Cecily)
Enright, Elizabeth (Petrus)
Fallon, Bridget (Mary of the Cross)
Farrelly, Mary Ellen 'Nellie' (Concepta), d. 28 Nov 2000
Finn, Mary Angela (Therese)

Fitzsimmons, Bridget Antoinette 'Toni' (Raparata)   *Ballinamore*
Fleming, Paula (Paula)
Fleming, Mary 'May' (Natalie)
Flynn. Nora/Norah (Laurentia)
Fogarty, Margaret Mary/Kathleen (Ailbe)
Forde, Margaret Julia (Domitilla)
Forde, Margaret 'Maggie' (Edmund)
Forde, Cecilia Teresa (Frances)
Forde, Josephine Monica (Martha)
Furlong, Ellen 'Nellie' (Magdelena)
Gainford, Rose (Corona)
Gardiner, Bernadette (Brenda)
Garry, Teresa Ann (Teresa Ann)
Gildea, Winifred (Laboure), d. 7 Aug 2001
Haugh, Veronica 'Verna' (Verna)
Hayden, Mary (Cletus)
Hayes, Arabella Josephine (Edith)
Higgins, Kathleen Teresa (Christina) d. 2 Jan 1989
Hoare, Mary Ursula (Borromeo), d. 21 Mar 1941
Hoban, Margaret Rita (Martina)
Horkan, Mary Margaret (Nuala)
Hyland, Bridget Mary (Alicia)
Joyce, Annie May (Anna)
Joyce, Ellen 'Nellie' (Patrick)
Joyce, Teresa (Teresa)
Keane, Agnes Elizabeth (Agnes)
Kehoe, Elizabeth Mary 'Beth' (de Chantal), d. 15 Oct 1997
Kehoe, Mary Josephine 'Maura' (Inez), d. 21 Dec 1998
Kelly, Anna Mary 'Nancy' (Antoinette)
Kelly, Margaret 'Pearl' (Euphremia)
Kelly, Mary Teresa (Mary)
Kennedy, Mary Delia 'Baby' (Jude)
Kilroy, Mary Agnes (Vitalis)
Kissane, Mary Ellen 'Eileen' (Roch)
Kissane, Hannah Marie (Chrysostom), d. 19 July 1947
Lavelle, Margaret Mary Josephine (Helena)
Lawless, Elizabeth Mary (Chanel), d. 22 Sept 1972
Lovett, Eileen T. (Josepha)
Lovett, Mary (Maureen)
Lucey, Mary Agnes (Alban), d. 8 Dec 1999
Lynch, Margaret Mary 'Meg' (Oliver)
Maloney, Margaret Mary 'Rita' (Denise)
Masterson, Mary (Cecilia)
Masterson, Anne 'Annie' (Gemma)
McCormack, Bridie (Asicus), d. 28 Aug 1996
McDermott, Mary (Gabriel)
MacDermott, Marguerita 'Rita' (Rita)
McGrath, Bridie H. (Veronica)
McGuane, Catherine (Catherine)
McHale, Mary Teresa (Michelle)

Ballinamore	McHugh, Kathleen (Edwardine)
	McHugh, Penelope (Bernice)
	McMahon, Kathleen (Macartan), d. 18 Mar 1972
	Moran, Mary Bernadette (Isobel)
	Moran, Mary (Nathy), 6 Jan 1996
	Mordant, Margaret (Eymard), d. 3 Aug 1997
	Morris, Margaret P. (Eusibius)
	Morris, Kathleen 'Kate' (Kathleen)
	Morrissey, Mairéad Margaret Mary (Lorenzo)
	Muldowney, Bridget Teresa (Bridget)
	Mulkeen, Angela (Della), d. 17 Nov 1989
	Murphy, Elizabeth 'Lily' (Elizabeth)
	Murphy, Helena (Remedius), d. 5 Mar 1957
	Murray, Bridget (Declan)
	Neary, Anne Veronica 'Vera' (Assumption)
	Nolan, Mary (Aidan), d. 3 Aug 1974
	Noonan, Bridget Mary 'Bridie' (Jacinta)
	O'Brien, Kathleen/Catherine (Census), d. 6 Oct 1971
	O'Connell, Bridget 'Bridie' (Rufina)
	O'Connor, Margaret 'Peg' (Aquin), d. 15 April 1982
	O'Connor, Pauline (Pauline)
	O'Grady, Eileen (Eileen)
	O'Mara, Hannora 'Noreen' (Wilfred), d. 16 Oct 1999
	O'Regan, Mary Josephine (Mary/Carmella), d. 17 April 1989
	O'Reilly, Margaret (Domenica)
	O'Shaughnessy, Margaret Ann (Gratiae)
	O'Shea, Margaret Mary Carmel (Carmel)
	O'Sullivan, Patricia (Patricia)
	Phelan, Bridget 'Nellie' (Finian), d. 30 April 1992
	Prendergast, Mary Teresa 'Tess' (Ita)
	Prendiville, Nora Bernadette (Lucilla)
	Quinn, Margaret 'Maggie' (Irenaeus), d. 25 Mar 1997
	Quinn, Bridget Teresa (Bridie)
	Quinn, Mary 'Molly' (Carthage), d. 20 Sept 1999
	Raftice, Margaret Mary (Margaret)
	Regan, Helena Marcella 'Eileen' (Eileen Marcella)
	Rowley, Anne Lawrence (Rosalie)
	Ryan, Elizabeth Mary 'Bessie' (Tarcisius)
	Salmon, Bridget (Bridget)
	Salmon, Christina 'Noleen' (Maria)
	Salmon, Angela (Padraig), d.14 April 1987
	Salmon, Veronica 'Vey' (Sarto)
	Scully, Margaret Teresa 'Rita' (Boniface)
	Scully, Margaret Mary 'Mary' (Inviolata), d. 2 Dec 1988
	Slattery, Margaret Mary 'Rita' (Januarius)
	Smith, Winifred (Dionysius)
	Smith, Marie (Marie)
	Spelman, Mary (Mary)
	Stackpoole, Maura/Mary (Pauline), d. 15 June 1955
	Stafford, Mary (Kilian)

Sweeney, Emily Teresa (Emily)   *Ballinamore*
Taylor, Delia Agnes (Ethna), d. 10 April 1989
Tierney, Winifred Una (Alphonsus)
Tierney, Mary Kate 'Maureen' (Leonie)
Walsh, Francis (Geraldine)
Walsh, Mary (Mary), d. 23 Nov 1989
Walsh, Catherine Lauretta 'Kitty' (Michael)
Walsh, Margaret Mary 'Mog' (Augustine), d. 22 Feb 1998
Walsh, Mary (Ricardo)
Ward, Mary Julia (Julia)

Burke, Winifred 'Una' (Clement)   *Kiltimagh*
Conlon, Margaret Ita (Maris Stella)
Enright, Elizabeth (Petrus)
Higgins, Kathleen Teresa (Christina), d. 2 Jan 1989
Joyce, Annie May (Anna)
O'Regan, Mary Josephine (Mary/Carmella), d. 17 April 1989
Salmon, Angela (Pádraig), d. 14 April 1987

Anderson, Helen (Martina), d. 13 Aug 1977   *Ballymote*
Bannon, Ann
Brennan, (Cabrini)
Casey, Veronica (Baptiste)
Connolly, Helen
Connolly, (Marie Goretti)
Conway, Mary Kathleen (Alma)
Costello, Bridget (Fabian), d. 28 April 1976
Finn, Mary Angela (Therese)
Fogarty, Margaret Mary (Ailbe)
Gardiner, Bernadette (Brenda)
Hughes, Alberta
Kehoe, Mary Josephine (Inez), d. 21 Dec 1998
Kissane, Mary Ellen (Roch)
Lynch, Margaret Mary (Oliver)
McGrath, Bridie (Veronica)
Moran, Mary (Nathy), d. 6 Jan 1996
Mordant, Margaret (Eymard), d. 3 Aug 1997
Morris, Margaret P. (Eusibius)
Murray, Bridget (Declan)
O'Grady, Eileen
O'Mara, Hannora (Wilfred), d. 16 Oct 1999
O'Reilly, Margaret (Dominica)
Prendergast, Mary Teresa (Ita)
Quinn, Mary (Irenaeus), d. 25 Mar 1997
Rea, Louis
Rowley, Anne Laurence (Rosalie)
Ryan, Elizabeth Mary (Tarcisius)
Scully, Margaret Mary (Inviolata), d. 2 Dec 1988
Spelman, Mary
Sweeney, Emily

Ballymote   Taylor, Delia Agnes (Ethna), d. 10 April 1989
Walsh, Catherine Lauretta (Michael)
Ward, Julia

APPENDIX 15: BROTHERS

De La Salle Brothers: *St John's Monastery, Ballaghaderreen 1890 - 1985*
* *Information provided by Pius MacCarthy, Provincial Secretary.*
Aidan, Br (- 1915)
Brosnahan, Cornelius Lewis (1924 - 1926 and 1932 - 1936), d. 1962
Brosnahan, Imar Stanislaus (1931 - 1934), d. 1995
Buckley, Anthony (1977 - 1980), left 2002
Buckley, Malachy Foilan (1953 - 1961)
Carew, Gabriel Lewis (1904 - 1970), d. 1960
Daly, Dominic Stephen (1903 - 1913), d. 1971
Cross, Stephen (1968 - 1969), left 1971
Davis, Benignus (1913 - 1920 and 1926 - 1928), d. 1971
Dobbins, Sixtus Jerome, (1894 - 1895), left 1895
Donahue, Jarlath Nilus (1916)
Dowling, Andrew Cassian (1894), d. 1905
Doyle, Bernardine (1940 - 1940), d. 1997
Duggan, Vincent de Paul (1891 - 1893), d. 1894
Dunne, Christopher Luke (1946 - 1953), d. 1959
Egan, Philbert (1976 - 1980)
Fahey, Cyprian Benedict (1980 - 1984), d. 1984
Fitzpatrick, Baldwin Henry, (1890 - 1898), d. 1948
Griffin, Ambrose Francis (1890 - 1891), d. 1929
Hamill, Malachy of Jesus (1928 - 1934), d. 1982
Hannon, Damian Ulrick (1922 - 1925), d. 1933
Hanrahan, Philip James (1918 - 1924), d. 1959
Harrigan, Joseph Benedict (1914 - 1917), d. 1934
Healy, Cuthbert Alban (1975), d. 1989
Julian Aengus, Br (- 1931)
Kelly, Cassian Loman (1936 - 1946), d. 1961
Kelly, Mark Edmund (1890 - 1892), d. 1936
Kelly, Raphael (1975 - 1985), d. 1990
Lawless, Columba John (1903 - 1904), d. 1944
Lawrence, Br (1927 - 1927)
Leahy, Anselm Edward (1895 - 1900), d. 1941
Leavy, Damian Ulrick (1969 - 1972)
Lenihan, Polycarp Cyril (1894 - 1904)
Lynam, Segineus Aelred (1920 - 1921), left 1921
Lynch, Edward Gregory (1934 - 1937), d. 1971
Lynch, Ferdinand (1984)
Lynch, Gregory John (1937 - 1940), left 1940
Lyons, Sylvester (1971), left 1980
McBrien, Wilfrid Canice (1921)
McCormack, Anthony Jerome (1918 - 1918)
McGuinness, Columban Amedy (1957 - 1959), d. 1989
McLoughlin, Dermot Ultan (1947 - 1949 and 1949 - 1985), d. 1994

McSweeney, Hilarion of Jesus (1909 - 1910), d. 1949   *De La Salle Brothers:*
Meyler, Peter Ultan (1966 - 1968), left 1969
Molloy, Anthony Fabian (1912 - 1914), d. 1915
Moore, Finbar Michael (1890 - 1890), d. 1951
Moore, Gregory Paulian (1928 - 1932), d. 1969
Moynihan, Virgilius John (1950 - 1966)
Murphy, Edmund (1970 - 1972), d. 1972
Murphy, Francis Jerome (1909 - 1912), d. 1929
Neenan, Finian Michael (1959 - 1969), d. 1996
O'Brien, Basil (1983 - 1985)
O'Callaghan, Dominic Peter (1890)
O'Connor, Boniface Petrock (1917 - 1918), d. 1976
O'Connor, Henry Patrick (1893 - 1894)
O'Flaherty, John (1951 - 1957, 1965 - 1970 and 1976 - 1983), d. 1983
O'Rourke, Xavier Patrick, (1889-1900), d. 1947
O'Shea, Denis (1967 - 1969), left 1969
O'Sullivan, Fidelis (1972 - 1975), d. 1975
O'Sullivan, Martine (1940 - 1944), d. 1966
Ryan, Albeus (1917 - 1918), d. 1952
Shortall, Adrian (1982 - 1983)
Twomey, Ignatius of Jesus (1948 - 1949), d. 1984
Wallace, Josaphat Beanus (1934 - 1946), d. 1987
Walsh, Michael Rufus (1892 - 1894), left 1897

Foxford 1924-1932   *Franciscan Brothers,*
Superiors: Brendan Buckley, Conleth Mannion, Michael D'arcy

Swinford 1901-1918   *Marist Brothers,*
* *Swinford Echo 1959, p 92*
L.Briersack, Andrew Conway, A. Curran, Henry G. Currie, B. Gillan, James Goss, E. Horan, Leo Johnstone, A. Kelly, M.G. Long, William J. Long, Francis McCormack, Michael McNamara, James Maxwell, James W. Meehan, Benedict Myatt, John Mylius, Edward Turner, Joseph Whelan

APPENDIX 16: PASSIONISTS

St Joseph's Retreat, Cloonamahon, Collooney
Superiors: Austin Tierney (1944-47), Stephen Lafferty (1947-50), Placid McLoughlin (1950-53), Andrew Kennedy (1953-56), Peter Paul Boyle (1956-59), Salvian Maguire (1959-62), Anselm Keleghan (1962-71), Ephrem Blake (1971-74), Fabian Grogan (1974-1977), Marius Donnelly (1977-80), Hubert Hurley (1980-81), Anselm Keleghan (1981-85), Terence McGuckian (1986-91), Thomas Scanlon (1992-95), Evangelist McKiernan (1996-1999)
Community: Ephrem Blake, Angelo Boylan, Camillus Boyle, Peter Paul Boyle, Alexis Boyd, Fintan Bowen, Clement Bradley, John Baptist Byrne, Mel Byrne, Ronan Byrne, Pius Campbell, Michael Carroll, Damien Casey, Martin Claffey, Cyril Clarke, Hilarion Cleary, Basil Coleman, Donal Connolly, Neil Convery, John Corrigan, John Craven, Cornelius Crawley, Macartan Daly, Brian Darcy, Luke Delaney, Bede Devine, Thomas Devitt, Marius Donnelly, Victor Donnelly, Austin Dromey, Maurice Egan, Ambrose Fay, Shaun Michael Flanagan, Malachy Geoghegan, Fabian Grogan, Finian Harte, Finbar Haughey, William Hickey, Augustine Hourigan, James Bernard Hoyne, Hubert Hurley, Myles Kavanagh, Neil

Passionists   Kearney, Francis Keevins, Anselm Keleghan, Xavier Keleghan, Columba Kelly, Linus Kelly, Oliver Kelly, Andrew Kennedy, Walter Ketterer, Stephen Lafferty, Paul Mary Madden, Salvian Maguire, Reginald Mahon, Francis McAteer, Arthur McCann, Vincent McCaughey, Alphonsus McGlone, Terence McGuckian, James McIvor, Evangelist McKiernan, Paul McKeon, Placid McLoughlin, Norbert McPartlin, Leo Marren, Philip Moclair, John Francis Morris, Wilfrid O'Doherty, Bernard O'Donnell, Fergal O'Shaughnessy, Livinus Owens, Dermot Power, Thomas Scanlon, Austin Tierney, Damien Wilson

APPENDIX 17: PRIESTS AND RELIGIOUS FROM PARISHES IN ACHONRY WHO SERVED ELSEWHERE

b. born, c. approximately, prof. professed, d. died, ord. ordained, ent. entered
'pre-1911' refers to list compiled by Bishop Lyster who died in 1911.

Attymass   *Priests*
Cunney, Sean, Currower, b. 1929, ord. 1955, Paisley, Scotland
Gallagher, John F., Cullane, b. 1908, ord. 1935, Los Angeles & San Diego, d. 1990s
Gallagher, William, Derreen, b. 1883, ord. 1908, Perth, Australia, d. 1911
Melody, William, Currower, b. 1929, ord. 1959, Notre Dame, USA
Peyton, Patrick, Carracastle, b. 1909, ord. 1941, USA. (Rosary Crusade Priest), d. 1992
Peyton, Tom, Carracastle, b. 1906, ord. 1941, Indiana, USA
Quinn, John, Kildermot, b. 1906, ord. 1938, Nova Scotia, d. 1966

Sisters
Brogan, Mary, Currower, b. 1908, New York, d. 1952
Cunney OP, Rita, Currower, USA
Ferguson, Ann, Currower, b. 1914, prof. 1933, Hull, England
Ferguson, Margaret, Cullane, b. 1880, prof. 1903
Ferguson, Mary, Currower, b. 1920, prof. 1940, Hull, England
Ferguson, Mary, Carracastle, b. 1882, New York
Flannelly, Brigid A., Carracastle, b. 1930, prof. 1956, Pennsylvania & Florida, USA
Flannelly, Irene, Carracastle, b. 1938, USA
Flannelly, Mary, Ballycong, b. 1933, prof. 1952, Australia, USA, India, England, Malta & Scotland
Flannelly, Mary, Carracastle, Scranton, USA
Flannelly, Mary, Carracastle, b. 1928, prof. 1956, Pensylvania & Florida, USA
Gallagher, Ellen Kate, Derreen, prof. 1918, Ballina, d. 1960

Brothers
Reynolds, John, Kilgellia, b. 1892, Romsey, England

Ballaghaderreen   *Priests*
Carney, Charles, Ballaghaderreen, b. 1888, ord. 1913, Scotland, d. 1945
Carney, John, Ballaghaderreen, b. c.1886, Australia
Casey, Dominick, Lessine, b. 1888, ord. 1913, Scotland, d. 1969
Casey, John, Lessine, b. 1889, ord. 1914, Liverpool, d. 1939
Casey, Michael W., Lessine, b. 1902, ord. 1927, Nottingham, d. 1983
Caulfield, John, Culaherin, b. 1915, ord. 1940, New Zealand
Caulfield, Pádraig, Bockagh, b. 1916, ord. 1940, France, d. 1994
Coleman, Patrick, Banada, b. 1911, ord. 1936, Leeds, d. 1971
Corrigan, James (Killian), b. c.1890, Ballaghaderreen, Australia

Creaton, James, Ballaghaderreen, b. 1932, ord. 1958, Salford
Creaton, John, Ballaghaderreen, b. 1943, ord. 1967, Leeds
Cryan, Michael, Lung, b. 1924, ord. 1950, Fiji & Australia
Cullen, George, b. c.1899, Ballaghaderreen, Hobart
Cullen, John, b. c.1811, Ballaghaderreen, Sydney
Deignan, Luke, Hawksford, San Diego, USA, d. 1967
Deignan, Patrick, Drimalasson, b. 1908, ord. 1934, California
Doherty, Dominick, Crennane, b. 1931, ord. 1956, England
Dorrington, Edward, Ballaghaderreen, b. 1933, ord. 1958, Salford,
Durcan, Paddy, Derracruma, b. 1923, ord. 1947, Scotland, d. 1998
Flanagan, Sean, Ballaghaderreen, b. 1935, ord. 1959, Los Angeles
Flanagan CSSP, Thomas, Ballaghaderreen, b. 1920, ord. 1949, Nigeria, d. 1996
Freyne, Barry, Avondale, b. 1934, ord. 1960, Nigeria & USA
Hannify, Eamon, Ballaghadderreen, b. 1923, ord. 1948, Nigeria, d. 1984
Hanley, Andrew, Ballaghaderreen, b. 1915, ord. c.1940, San Diego, USA
Hanley OFM, Samuel, Ballaghaderreen, b. 1920, ord. 1946, South Africa, d. 1992
Hopkins, Michael, Boherbee, b. 1901, ord. 1926, London, d. c.1984
Kilcoyne, Patrick, Ballaghaderreen, b. 1949, ord. 1975, Nigeria & USA
Kilgarriff, Patrick, Ballaghaderreen, b. 1928, ord. 1953, England
Lavin, Thomas, Abbeyview, b. 1944, ord. 1974, Essex, England
McMahon, Seamus, Boherbee, b. 1939, ord. 1964, Fiji & Australia
McMahon, Desmond, Boherbee, b. 1936, ord. 1961, California
Macken, Joseph, Ballaghaderreen, b. 1930, ord. 1956, France
Madden, John, Ballaghaderreen, b. 1938, ord. 1963, Southwark
Morahan, Edward, Ballaghaderreen, b. 1885, ord. 1910, Africa & England, d. 1963
Morahan, Patrick, Banada, b. 1894, ord. 1918, West Virginia, d. 1945
Morahan, Thomas, Banada, b. 1908, ord. 1932, Fresno, USA, d. 1967
Naughton, John, Rooskey, b. 1941, ord. 1965, Southwark
O'Grady, Peter, Aiteenatagart, b. c.1912, ord. c.1937, USA
Regan, Patrick, Ballaghaderreen, b. 1904, ord. 1929, Australia, d. 1934
Reid, William, Icelawn, b. c.1922, ord. c.1947, Arizona, d. 1990
Sharkey, Michael J, Monasteraden, b. 1933, ord. 1958, Africa
Shryane, James, Ballaghaderreen, b. 1891, ord. 1914, Plymouth, d. 1960
Shryane, James, Ballaghaderreen, b. 1941, ord. 1965, Leeds & Hallam
Spelman, Gerry, Ballaghaderreen, b. 1930, ord. 1955, Leeds, d. 1990
Spelman, Joseph, Ballaghaderreen, b. 1932, ord. 1959, Los Angeles
Surlis, Paul, Shroofe, b. 1935, ord. 1961, Texas & New York
Towey, Edward, Barnaboy, b. c.1920, ord. c.1955, USA
Vesey, Patrick, Dernaslieve, b. 1894, ord. 1918, Los Angeles, d. 1925

Sisters
Caulfield, Kathleen, Bockagh, b. 1918, prof. 1941, Paignton, England
Caulfield, Nancy, Bockagh, b. 1917, prof. 1948, Paignton, England, d. 1948
Caron, Brigid, Aughalustia, b. 1905, prof. 1925, Australia, d. 1992
Carroll, Elizabeth, Ballaghaderreen, Kenya
Carty, Mary, Aughalustia, b. 1933, prof. 1959, Naples & W.Africa, d. c.1984
Cloran, Sr Louis, Ballaghaderreen, pre-1911, Auckland, New Zealand
Creevy, Mary, Ballaghaderreen, pre-1911, Tacoma, Washington
Coleman, Mary, Monasteraden, b. 1913, prof. 1936, England, d. 2001
Cunnane, Julianne, Ballaghaderreen, USA
Dillon, Mary, Ballaghaderreen, pre-1911, Holloway, London

Doherty, Maria, Crennane, pre-1911, Portland, Oregon
Duffy, Sr Euphremia, pre-1911, USA
Egan, Winifred, Aughalustia, b. 1903, prof. 1922, South Africa, d. 2000
Farrell, Sr, Ballaghaderreen, England
Flannery, Annie, Lissine, b. 1918, prof. 1938, South Africa
Freyne, Annie, Crennane, pre-1911, Portland, Oregon
Geever, Eleanor, Castlemore, b. 1938, prof. 1960, Texas, USA
Geever, Mai, Castlemore, b. 1942, prof. 1964, Texas, USA
Grady, Mary, Loomcloon, b. 1946, prof. 1966, Africa
Greevy, Agnes, Crennane, pre-1911, Providence, USA
Hagan, Lizzie, Ballaghaderreen, pre-1911, Chepstow Villas
Hagan, - ,Ballaghaderreen, pre-1911, Holloway, London
Jordan, Bridget, Crennane, pre-1911, Massachussets, USA
Jordan, Mary, Brooklawn, pre-1911, Massachussets, USA
Keegan, Pascal, Culaherin, Nigeria, d. 1986
Kilcoyne, Mary, Ballaghaderreen, b. 1943, prof. 1973, Australia, England & Scotland
Macken, Winifred, Ballaghaderreen, b. 1934, prof. 1956, Nigeria
Morrisroe, Mary, Crennane, pre-1911, Louisville, Kentucky
Regan, Delia, Crennane, pre-1911, Portland, Oregon
Roddy, Sr Winifrid, Derracarta, pre-1911
Rogers, Winifred, Monasteraden, b. 1909, prof. 1936, England, d. 2001
Shryane, Katie, Icelawn, pre-1911, Nottingham
Shryane, Mary, Icelawn, pre-1911
Towey, Anne, Culaherin, b. 1918, prof. 1937, England
Towey, Eleanor, Barnaboy, b. c.1932, Malta
Towey, Kathleen, Culaherin, b. 1924, prof. 1946, England

Brothers
Caulfield, Patrick,, Bockagh, b. 1867, South Africa, d. 1934
Corcoran, James Martin (Pascal of Jesus), De La Salle, Coolavin, Australia, d. 1979
Cunnane, Frank CSSR, b. c.1898
Donoghue, Br, De La Salle, b. c.1939
Egan, Thomas (Robert), De La Salle, Aughalustia, Australia & S. Africa, d. 1985
Feeney, Gerald CSSR,
Gara, Martin (Nathy Cyril), De La Salle, Ballaghaderreen, d. 1984
Jordan, Francis (Edward Joseph), De La Salle, Icelawn, Australia & England, d. 1968
Lavin, John, (Thomas), De La Salle, Abbeyview, b. 1943, prof. 1961, Nigeria & Hong Kong
Macken, James (Gerald), De La Salle, Ballaghaderreen, b. 1928, prof. 1953, Malaysia
Macken, Michael, (James), De La Salle, Ballaghaderreen, b. 1932, prof. 1957, Mauritius
McNicholas, Michael (Eliseus of Jesus), De La Salle, Ballaghaderreen, b. 1863, Baltimore,
    USA, d. 1892
Quinn, Br, St John of God, b. c.1932
Towey, John (Nathy Daniel), De La Salle, Doogara (Culaherin?), South Africa, d. 1997

Ballysadare   *Priests*
Harrison, James, Abbeytown, b. 1915, ord. 1942, Nigeria & USA
McGauran, Bernard, Ballysadare, b. 1821, ord. 1846, Quebec, Canada, d. 1882
McLoughlin, Michael, Streamstown, b. 1917, ord. 1942, Newcastle, England, d. 2000
Martin, William, Ballysadare, b. 1922, ord. 1947, Texas, USA, d. 1997

Sisters   *Ballysadare*
Harrison, Norah, Abbeytown, b. 1904, Pretoria, S.Africa
Lynch, Mary Rose, Abbeytown, b. 1899, prof. 1933, Texas, USA, d. 1993

Priests   *Ballymote*
Cassidy CP, Eustace, Ballymote, Scotland
Cassidy, Michael, Ballymote, b. 1937, ord. 1962, England
Cawley, Francis, Clooneen, b. 1916, ord. 1942, Peru & Jamaica, d. c.1991
Cryan, Michael, Ballymote, b. 1920, ord. 1945, England, d. c.2001
Cryan, Paul, Ballymote, b. 1915, ord. 1941, England, d. c.1988
Davey, Owen, Kilmorgan, b. 1844, ord. 1869, Australia, d. 1908
Dunleavy, Andrew, Ballymote, b. 1680, Paris, d. 1746
Hannan, Edward, Emlaghnaghten, b.1826, ord.1852, Toledo, USA, d.1902
Henry, James, Portinch, b. 1901, ord. 1926, Scotland, d. c.1978
Judge, Thomas E., Emlaghnaghten, b. 1864, ord. 1887, Chicago, USA, d. 1907
Kearns, Dominick, Knockadalteen, b. 1923, ord. 1948, Nigeria
McDermott, Liam, Ballymote, b. 1934, ord. 1959, South Africa
McDonagh, Peter, Derroon, b. 1936, ord. 1962, San Antonia, USA, d. c.1995
Mullen, Eamon, Carrigans, b. 1918, ord. 1942, USA, d. c.1992
O'Connor, Bernie, Ballymote, b. 1934, ord. 1958, Far East
O'Reilly, James, Ballymote, b. 1917, ord. 1942, California
Rogers, Patrick, Ballymote, b. 1943, Africa
Reid, Desmond, Ballymote, b. 1934, ord. 1964, Australia
Tighe, Denis, Mullacor, b. 1881, ord. 1906, Michigan, USA, d. 1954
Wims, Owen, Rathdooney, b. 1922, ord. 1948, Fresno, USA, d. c.1949

Sisters
Cassidy, Maureen, Ballymote, Jefferson City, USA
Cassidy, Rosie, Ballymote, Africa
Chambers, Bernadette, Ballymote, ent. 1961, Jefferson City, USA
Cryan, Patricia, Ballymote, Jefferson City, USA
Fox, Vera, Lisananny, Ghana & England
Kearns, Attracta, Carrigans,
Kearns, Delphina, Carrigans, Africa, d. c.1972
Keirns, Mary, Cartron, prof. 1880, England, d. 1964
Kelly OP, M., Ballymote, pre-1911, Natal, South Africa
Lavin, Catherine, Branchfield, b. 1883, Scotland
McGettrick, Katie, Cluid, California
McGettrick, Lily, Cluid, Texas
McGettrick, Mary, Rathdooney, Long Island
McGettrick, Winnie, Cluid, Beirut, d. c.1999
Mahon, Mary E., Carrowcushacly, prof. 1881, Jamaica
Nealon, Anne, Cloonlurg, b. 1921, prof. 1940, England, d. 2001
Quigley, Mary C., Corhober, England, d. 1982
Reynolds, Bridie, Cloonkeary, ent. 1961, Jefferson City, USA
Rogers, Josie, Emlaghfad, Texas, d. 1994
Rogers, Killian, Ballymote, Africa
Scanlon, Brigid, Upper Carrigans, Ballymote, ent. 1950, Jefferson City, USA, d. 1986
Shiels, Attracta, Corhubber, USA
Shiels, Kathleen, Corhubber, Jefferson City, USA

Ballymote

James Breheny

Walsh, Mary, Derroon, prof. 1906, South Africa & England
Wims, Mary, Rathdooney, England

Brothers
Breheny, James, Ardsallagh, b. 1946, ent. 1960, Dublin, Tuam, Drogheda & Westport
Hannon, John P., Keenaghan, b. 1940, prof. 1966, Bangalore, India & Perth
Kerins, Wilfred, Lecarrow, b. 1840, Glasgow
McGettrick, Nathy, Rathdooney, Mauritius
Quigley, Michael (Bernardine), De La Salle, d. 1990

Bohola

Priests
Coleman, John, Treenbontry, b. 1896, ord. 1922, USA, d. 1976
Doyle, Michael, Treenbontry, b. 1923, ord. 1948, Philippines, d. 1985
Doyle, T.J., Treenbontry, b. 1922, ord. 1948, USA, d. 2002
Clarke, Harry, Bohola, b. 1943, ord. 1967, Leeds
Dunleavy, Michael, Toughnane, Leeds, d.1969
Sheridan, Tom, Ardgullen, b. c.1920, ord. c.1945, England, d. 1970s

Sisters
McGeever, Ellen, Carragolda, b. 1912, Philadelphia, d. 1980s
Roche, Mary, Bohola, b. 1943, England & Africa
Roche, Mae, Tooromeen, England
Durkin, Mary, Carracastle, England, d. 2001
Ward Brigid, Treenfoughnane, b. 1900, USA, d. 1991
Deacy, Mary, Carragolda, b. 1930s, prof. 1950s, Africa, USA & England, d. 1996
Mulroy, Una, Laughtadurkin, b. 1919, prof. 1937, Belgium, France & UK, d. 1983

Bonniconlon

Priests
Jordan, Michael, Carralavin, b. 1958, ord. 1986, Nigeria
McLoughlin, Ambrose, Glenree, b. 1920, ord. 1944, Southwark
Mangan, Patrick, Rathreedane, b. 1935, ord. 1964, Albany, New York
O'Leary, Patrick, Bofield, b. 1907, ord. 1932, Scotland & England, d. 1972
Rea, Anthony, Cloontia, b. 1917, ord. 1942, Southwark, England

Sisters
Gallagher, Catherine, Bonniconlon, b. 1934, prof. 1960, USA
Howley, Assumpta, Cloontia, b. 1920, prof. 1947, London, Derby
Kelly, Brigid, Currigan, b. 1903, prof. 1928, Maryland, USA, d. 2000
McLoughlin, Agatha, Glenree, b. 1928, prof. 1955, India
Mullarkey, Mary, Rathreedane, b. 1919, prof. 1945, Birmingham, d. 1980
Murray, Mary Bernard, Kilgarvin, England

Bunninadden

Priests
Davey, M., Knocknagee, USA
Gallagher, Frank, Cloontiacunny, b. 1913, ord. 1938, Korea
Gildea, Hugh, Quarryfield, Liverpool, d. 1941
Gildea, John, Quarryfield, Liverpool, d. 1955
Hunt, James, Bunninadden, b. 1900, ord. 1925, Southwark, England, d. 1982
McGettrick, Bishop Thomas, Emlagh, b. 1905, ord. 1930, Nigeria, d. 1988
McGettrick, Eddie, Emlagh, b. 1949, ord. 1974, Brazil

Sisters   *Bunninadden*
Davey, Una, Coagh, USA
Doohan, Phelim, Quaryfield, b. 1915, Manchester
Doyle, Florine, Doocastle, London
Gildea, Leo, Quaryfield, Manchester
Keenan, Athanasius, Quaryfield, b. c.1912, Australia & Fiji
Keevens, Mary Ita, Killavil, USA
Hannon, Consolata, Moyrush, USA
Hannon, Maura, Moyrush, USA
McDermott, Mona, Bunninadden, Africa
McDonagh, Kathleen, Spurtown, b. 1935, Manchester
McManus, Bernadette, b. 1936, Fiji & Rome

Brothers
McGettrick, Martin (Victor Nathy), De La Salle, Rhinarogue, d. 1986 (see also Ballymote)

Priests   *Carracastle*
Caulfield, Sean, Lismulgee, b. 1924, ord. 1949, Utah, USA
Coleman, James, Castleduff, b. 1921, ord. 1946, USA
Gallagher, Daniel, Pulboy, USA
Gallagher, James, Pulboy, USA
Gallagher, Michael, Cashelcolane, b. 1939, ord. 1962, Leicester, England
Hunt, Desmond, Rooskey, b. 1928, ord. 1953, England
MacDonnell, Henry, Shragh, b. 1835, ord. 1885, Mauritius, d. 1895 (brother of Sir Anthony
    P. MacDonnell)
Owens, John, Fauleens, b. 1880, ord. 1905, California
Owens, Peter J., Gowel, b. 1956 [Clerical student] Sierra Leone, d. 1984
Vesey, Thomas, Baroe, b. 1915, ord. 1940, Menevia, Wales, d. 1962

Sisters
Cassidy, Mary, Bulkane, England, d. 1920s
Cawley, May, Shraigh, b. 1901, prof. 1936, Boston & New York
Coleman, Avellino, Cashelduff, b. 1900, New Jersey
Coleman, Noreen, Cashelduff, b. 1902, New Jersey
Davey, Eileen, Carracastle, b. 1921, Manchester
Doherty, Catherine, Bulkane, b. 1878, Tasmania, Melbourne, d. c.1954
Forkan, Evelyn, Tonnagh, b. 1930, Canada, USA & France
Frain, Margaret, Rooskey, USA
Horkan, Peg,, Barroe, b. 1912, prof. 1935, New York
Hunt, Catherine, Rooskey, b. 1902, prof. 1927, Florida
Hunt, Shelia, Rooskey, b. 1924, prof. 1952. Mexico & England
Keenan, Teresa, Brackloon, b. 1918, prof. 1936, London
Marren, Gertrude, Brackloon, b. 1926, Surrey, England
McDonagh, Annette, Shraigh, b. 1917, prof. 1939, Houston, Texas
McDonagh, Catherine, Shraigh, b. 1919, Manchester & Spain
*McDonnell, Shraigh
Morgan, Mamie, Gowel, b. 1912, prof. 1945, Australia
Parsons, Evelyn, Gowel, b. 1898, prof. 1924, Philadelphia, d. 1980
Parsons, Teresa, Gowel, b. c.1890, USA
Quinn, Annie, Rooskey, b. 1915, prof. 1937, Houston, Texas

Carracastle   Quinn, Teresa, Rooskey, b. 1917, prof. 1939, Houston, Texas
Quinn, Veronica, Rooskey, b. 1920, prof. 1941, Houston, Texas
Regan, Evelyn, Gowel, b. 1947, prof. 1970, Manchester & Scotland
Regan, Rose, Copplecurragh, b. 1918, prof. 1939, Leicester, England
Ryan, Moira, Gowlan, b. 1935, prof. 1955, Fiji & Scotland
Towey, Bea, Tonnagh, b. 1920, prof. 1940, London & Florida
Walsh, Katie, Gowlan, b. 1902, Florida & New York
*It was said that four sisters of Sir Anthony McDonnell of Shraigh became Sisters of Mercy and founded convents in USA. *Mayo Magazine* 1966, p. 95

Brothers
Callaghan, Thomas (Ireneus Martyr), De La Salle, d. 1872
Horkan, Jim, Barroe, b. 1921, Papua, New Guinea

Charlestown   *Priests*
Burke, Tommie, Charlestown, b. 1921, ord. 1945, Scotland, d. 1945
Casey CSSp, Sean
Cassidy, Joseph, Archbishop, Clonfert & Tuam
Cassidy CSSp, Louis, Charlestown, b. 1940, ord. 1966, Brazil
Cassidy, Patrick, Glann, b. 1891, ord. 1917, Birmingham, d. 1967
Cassidy, Patrick, Main St., ord. 1919, Birmingham
Cassidy SMA, Philip, Puntabeg, b. 1888, ord. 1920, Africa, d. 1926
Doherty CM, Pádraig, Charlestown, b. c.1922, ord. c.1947, England
Durcan SDB, William, Sonnagh, b. 1928, ord. 1956, Africa
Fitzpatrick, Eugene, Charlestown, b. c.1940, ord. 1986, Westminister
Halligan, John,
Hawkins, James Walter, Killaturley, b. 1942, ord. 1969, Barrow in Furness, England
Henry, Patrick, Bellaghy, b. 1943, ord. 1967, Leeds
Henry, Patrick, Tavneenagh
Howley, Thomas, The Square, b. 1907, ord. 1931, Southwark, d. 1993
Lynch, Patrick Christopher, b. 1921, ord. 1947
McGrath, Fr, Barrack St., England
Madden, Patrick, Ardra, b. 1924, ord. 1951, Florida
O'Connor, Frank, Bellaghy, b. 1889, ord. 1913, Liverpool, d. 1973
O'Doherty, Denis, Lurga, b. 1877, ord. 1902, Spain
O'Doherty, Archbishop Michael, Lurga, b. 1874, ord. 1897, Philippines, d. 1949
O'Donnell, Michael, Ballyglass, Killala
Philbin, M.P., Australia
Regan, Martin, Stripe, b. c.1920, ord. c.1945, England
Rush, Tom, Killalturley, USA
Stenson, Francis, Bracklagh, b. 1894, ord. 1919, Spain, d. 1968
Walsh, James B, Bellaghy, b. 1901, ord. 1925, Scotland, d. 1970

Sisters
Brennan, Bridget, Barnacuaige
Brennan, Brigid M., Church St.,Tottenham, London
Brennan, Mary, Barnacuaige
Brett SM, Laetitia, Bracklagh, England
Butler RSM, Eileen, Tavneenagh, San Francisco
Casey SM, Mary, Church St., b. 1945, prof. 1966, Ottery-St. Marys, England, d. 1978

Colleran SM, Joan, Dublin & Chicago *Charlestown*
Doherty, Brigid, Charlestown, ent. 1945, Jefferson City, USA
Doherty, Una, Tavneenagh, d. c.1960
Duffy, Helena, Tavneenagh, b. 1909, Philadelphia
Duffy, Maura, Killaturley, Sierra Leone
Flood SM, Adelaide, Dublin
Gallagher, Norah, Lurga, England
Gallagher SM, Teresita, Lurga, b. 1900, Ascot, d. 1982
Halligan, Annie, Sonnagh, Canada
Henry SL, Pearl, Taveenagh, Belfast
Horkan SM, Eva, Church St, b. 1939, prof. 1966, England
Jennings, Mai, Puntabeg, Dublin
Kearns, Mary, Barnacuaige, Poor Clare
McDonnell, RSC, Joseph Gonzaga, b. 1881
McGuire, Annie, Lowpark, England
Morris, Mary, Lurga, London
Mulligan, Andrena, Mexico & USA
Mulligan, Emerard, The Square, b. c.1905, Leeds & Bolton
Mulligan, Ethna, Church St., b. 1944, prof. 1967, England & USA
Mulligan SM, Margaret, Church St., b. 1946, prof. 1967, Australia & New Zealand
O'Doherty SL, Mary Bernadette, Tample
O'Donnell, Dervilla, The Square, b. 1958, prof. 1990, Nigeria & Kenya
Regan, Catherine, England
Regan, Eileen, Australia
Rogers OP, Lizzie, Charlestown, pre-1911, South Africa
Rogers, M. J., Charlestown, pre-1911, South Africa
Stenson SM, Mai, Bracklagh, England
Stenson, Mary, Bracklagh, England
Stenson, Nellie, Killeen
Tiernan MMM, Lurga, d. c.1960

Priests *Collooney*
Burke, Felix, Kinnegrelly, b. 1881, ord. 1906, British Army Chaplain 1914-18, d. 1951
Burke, Tom, Kinnegrelly, b. 1918, ord. 1934, Africa
Burke, Vincent, Kinnegrelly, b. 1926, ord. 1951, Southwark
Banks, Peter, Bella, b. 1945, ord. 1973, California
Cawley, Farrell, Ballinacarrow, b. 1935, ord. 1961, Nigeria
Cawley, John, Kilnamanagh, b. 1882, ord. 1906, Los Angeles
Collins, Fachna, Rathgran, b. 1925, ord. 1950, California
Flannery, Sean, Ardcotten, b. 1946, ord. 1971, England
Haran, Pádraig, Ardcotten, b. 1936, ord. 1960, Southwark
Haran, Michael, Lugnamacken, New York, d. 1914
Higgins, Jim, Collooney, b. 1924, ord. 1949, Africa
Jordan, Gerard, Ballinacarrow, b. 1918, ord. 1946, England
McGarry, John A., Collooney, b. 1910, ord. 1934, Scotland
McMorrow, Gerard, Collooney, b. 1964, ord. 1988, Brisbane, Australia
Mullen, Michael, Rathnarrow, b. 1891, ord. 1916, British Army & Los Angeles
Quigley, Michael, Doorla, b. 1921, ord. 1945, Oregan, USA
Quigley, Seamus, Rathnarrow, b. 1946, ord. 1971, Salford, England
White, Martin, Ballinabole, b. 1918, ord. 1943, Africa

Collooney   *Sisters*

Cawley, Patricia, Kilnamanagh, b. 1922, prof. 1943, Jefferson City, USA, d. 2001
Duffy, Kathleen, Camphill, b. 1955, prof. 1983, Rome & Ethopia
Gallagher, Mary E, Kinnegrelly, b. 1936, ent. 1955, Jefferson City, USA
Keogh, Kitty, Collooney, b. 1921, USA
Kerins,Dominick, Bella, b. 1913, prof. 1945, England
Lang, Frances J., Union, b. 1917, prof. 1940, Zambia
Niland, Carmel, Knockbeg, b. 1934, England & USA
Niland, Moyra, Knockbeg, b. 1941, Mexico
O'Harte, Bernadette, Lugnamacken, prof. c.1900, Wales
Quigley, Ursula, Rathnarrow, b. 1934, England
Torsney, Margaret Mary, Gadden, Collooney, ent. 1957, Jefferson City, USA
Wims, Catherine, ent.1974, Jeffferson City, USA

Brothers

Goulden, Thomas (Leontine), De La Salle, Collooney, b. 1850, New York, d. 1904
O'Grady, Gerard, Ballinacarrow, b. 1932, England

Coolaney   *Priests*

Carty, Michael, Coolaney, b. 1910, ord. 1934, Nottingham, d. 1991
Cawley, John, Coolaney, Los Angeles
Coleman, Peter, Lissalough, b. 1917, ord. 1945, Minnesota, USA, d. 1983
Downey, Michael, Coolaney, b. 1903, ord. 1928, England
Foley, Gerard, Ballinvalley, b. 1912, Wisconsin, USA, d. 1958
Gallagher, John, Meemlough, b. 1901, ord. 1926, Scotland, d. 1948
Gallagher, Joe, Carrowloghan, b. 1920, ord. 1947, California, d. c.1996
Gorman, Eamon, Carrowloughan, b. 1919, ord. 1948, Nigeria & USA, d. 1987
Henry, John, Carrow-na-Carrick, b. 1913, ord. 1939, South Africa, d. c.1965
Kivlehan, Patrick, Shancough, b. 1907, ord. 1934, Nigeria, d. c.1987
McHugh, Hugh, Carrowloughan, b. 1904, ord. 1929, Liverpool, d. c.1987
Morrin, Patrick J., Turin, Italy
Nerney, Michael, Coolaney, b. 1906, ord. 1931, England, d. 1963
Nerney, Patrick, Coolaney, b. 1894, ord. 1920, England, d. 1955

Sisters

Bowie, Maura, Carrownagaveen, b. 1935, California
Cunningham, Brigid Teresa, prof. 1904, Belgium
Foley, Mary, Ballinvalley, b. 1908, USA
Gorman, Mary, Killoran, b. 1917, prof. 1937, New Zealand
Lynch, Sr, Killoran P., pre-1911, Chepstow Villas
Lynch, Sr, Killoran P., pre-1911, Chepstow Villas
McDonagh, Annie, Coolaney, England
McGuiness, Phil, Coolaney, b. 1933, prof. 1953, Nigeria
Wims, Catherine, Carrownagleragh, b. 1956, prof. c.1974, USA & Peru

Curry   *Priests*

Colleary, Pádraig, Cully, b. 1949, ord. 1974, Phoenix, USA
Colleran, James, Curracunnane, b. 1898, ord. 1924, Scotland, d.1982
Collins, Martin E, Carrowilkeen, b. 1909, ord. 1929, New York, d. 1971
Collins, Patrick, Carrowilkeen, b. 1909, ord. 1934, Reading, England, d. 1970

Duffy, Tom, Sargura, b. 1897, Africa, d. 1979
Durcan, Sean, Cashel, b. 1941, ord. 1966, Leeds, England
Gallagher, Daniel Noel, Cashel South, b. 1940, ord. 1965, Mississippi, USA
Gallagher, Martin, Cloonrane, England, d. 1949
Gallagher, Patrick J., Cashel South, b. 1928, ord. 1954, Zimbabwe
Gilligan John, Curry East, b. 1940, ord. 1966, Leeds, England
Harte, Peter, Curry, b. 1897, ord. 1924, Scotland, d. 1973
Henry, Kevin, Curry, b. 1918, ord. 1944, USA, d. 1981
Jennings, John, Cully, b. 1914, ord. 1941, Liverpool
Jennings, John, Cully, b. 1884, ord. 1910, USA
Kennedy, Andrew, Broher, b. 1914, ord. 1939, Scotland
Kennedy, Denis, Broher, b. 1905, ord. 1931, Leeds, d. 1964
Kennedy, Edward, Broher, b. 1911, ord. 1935, Scotland, d. 1968
Kennedy, Martin, Curracunnane, b. 1895, ord. 1934, Wyoming
Leonard, John, Bunnacrannagh, b. 1870, Canada
McGuinn, Denis, Cashel, b. 1815, ord. 1848, Australia, d. 1887
McGuinn, Michael F., Curry East, b. 1919, ord. 1944, London, d. 2000
Marren, John, Curry, b. 1908, ord. 1933, Nigeria d. 1937
Marren, John, Rathmagurry, b. 1880, USA
Marren, John, Curry, b. 1952, ord. 1977, Kenya
Vesey, Edward, Ballincurry, b. 1936, ord. 1962, Ecuador, South America
Walsh, James, Cashel South, b. 1900, ord. 1925, California, d. 1958
Walsh, John, Powelsborogh, b. 1901, ord. 1926, Los Angeles, d. 1975
Walsh, Oliver, Cloonagh, b. 1933, ord. 1959, Chicago, d. 1969

Sisters
Brennan, Ann Jane, Ballincurry, b. 1914, Kent, England
Brennan, Bessie, Ballincurry, b. 1875, USA
Brennan, Brigid, Cloonagh, b. 1912, England, d. 1993
Brennan RSC, Bridget, Cloonagh, b. 1900, Cork, d. 1928
Brennan, Ellen, Leitrim South, b. 1907, New York, d. 1993
Brennan, Marjorie, Ballincurry, b. 1875, USA
Brennan, Patricia, Cloonraver, Africa
Brennan, Sadie, Rathmagurry, b. 1925, Australia
Brett, Mary E., Ballincurry, b. 1926, Africa
Browne, Anne, Powelsborogh, b. 1912, Africa
Burke, Bridie, Drimroe, b. 1910, prof. 1929, England, d. 1976
Burke, Helen, Drimroe, b. 1917, France
Cahill, Brigid (Theodora) b. 1876, Leeds
Cahill, Brigid, Carrarea, b. 1949, England
Coffey, Mary, Powelsborogh, b. 1945, prof. 1960, England
Collins, Mary, Carrowilkeen, b. 1923, Africa
Cooke, Belinda, Clooningan, b. 1924, India
Costello, Brigid, Powelsborogh, b. 1931, Philadelphia
Doherty, Brigid, Cully, b. 1920, USA
Duffy, Agnes, Curry East, b. 1913, England
Duffy, Bibanna, Sargura, b. 1875, Africa
Duffy, Brigid, Cloonaughill, b. 1902, Nigeria
Duffy, Germanus, Sargura, b. 1876, Africa
Durcan, Ann, Drimbane, b. 1904, England, d. 1986

Curry

Denis McGuinn

John Marren

Durcan, Mary Attracta, Ballincurry, b. 1899, Boston, d. 1990
Durcan, Mary James, Curracunnane, 1885, New Jersey, d. 1959
Feely, Brigid, Moylough, b. 1937, Detroit, USA
Flynn, Brigid, Tunnacullia, b. 1875, Philadelphia, d. 1948
Gallagher, Brigid, Cloonaughill, b. 1913, prof. 1934, Philadelphia
Gallagher, Mary, Ballincurry, b. 1886, USA
Gallagher, Sr Henry, Cashel, b. 1925, England, d. 1990
Gannon, Annie Kate, Sandyhill, b. 1923, prof. 1950, London
Gilligan, Eleanor, Curry East, b. 1945, prof. 1970, Birmingham
Gilligan, Kathleen, Montia, b. 1948, Surrey, England
Gilmartin, Elsie, Cloonraver, b. 1945, prof. 1966, Mexico
Gilmore, Catherine, Curry, b. 1928, England & USA
Hansberry, Emmanuel, Fule, Curry, Ottawa, Canada, d. c.1938
Haran, Mary, Cloonagh, b. 1914, prof. 1936, England
Henry, Catherine, Curry, b. 1879, prof. 1902, New York, d. 1960
Henry, Kathleen, Curry, b .1917, Kent, England
Henry, May, Curry, b. 1917, England, d. 1991
Jennings, Margaret, Cully, b. 1921, England, d. 1995
Jennings, Mary, Cully, b. 1919, Australia
Jennings, Mary, Cully, b. 1892, Cincinnati, USA
Johnson, Mary, Ballyglass, b. 1940, prof. 1959, Scotland
Kennedy, Anne Mary, Bunnacranna, b. 1925, prof. 1953, Kenya
Marren, Agnes, Curracunnane, b. 1928, prof. 1950, England
Maye, Annie, Moylough, b. 1929, England, d. 1988
Maye, Mary, Moylough, b. 1932, Leeds
Maye, Noreen, Moylough, b. 1933, England
McCormack, Julia, Sandyhill, b. 1920, London
McGoldrick, Kathleen, Drimbane, b. 1937, Australia
McGuinn, Agnes, Broher, b. 1905, USA
McGuinn, Marie, Cashel, b. 1920, England
McVann, Beatrice, Rathmagurry, b. 1941, Doncaster, England
Normally, Brigid, Ballincurry, b. 1907, Philadelphia, d. 1982
Peyton, Dominica, Cully, London
Reilly, Annie Kate, Cloonaughill, b. 1921, England
Walsh, Agnes, Cloonaughill, b .1910, Rome
Walsh Annie Kate, Cloonaughill, Rome
Walsh, Brigid, b. 1898, New York
Walsh Brigid Ann, Cashel South, b. 1904, Chicago
Walsh, Josie, Cashel South, b. 1913, England, 1986
Walsh, Sarah, Sargura, b. 1918, USA
Weaver, Margaret, Cully, b. 1910, England, d. 1996

Brothers
Burke, James, Curry, b. 1918, New Zealand, d. 1985
Coffey, Aidan, Powelsborogh, b. 1890, USA
Duffy, James, Sargura, b. 1865, prof. 1882, USA & Canada
Johnson, James, Ballyglass, b. 1926, USA
Walsh, Michael, Ballincurry, b. 1905, USA

Priests   *Foxford*
Michael, Cosgrave, Bealass, b. 1917, ord. 1942, Liverpool
Dorr, Donal, Foxford, b. 1935, ord. 1961, Nigeria
Dorr, Patrick, Foxford, b. 1905, ord. 1930, Nigeria, d. 1970
Eaton, T. J., Foxford, Mobile, USA, d. 1929
Fahy, Patrick, Foxford, b. 1935, ord. 1960, Philippines
Gallagher, John, Belgarriff, ord. 1933, Kansas, USA
Gallagher, Michael, Belgarriff, ord. 1921, Buffalo, USA
Hardy, Paschal, Foxford, b. 1932, ord. 1958. California
Hughes, Michael, Foxford, b. 1923, ord. 1948, California
Hunter, Seamus, Coolagagh, b. 1937, ord. 1968, Nigeria
Jones, Thomas, Foxford, b. 1899, ord. 1924, Florida, d. 1973
McNulty, Patrick, Cloonmung, b. 1925, ord. 1953, Los Angeles
Naughton, Peter, Bokeen, Australia
O'Hara, Denis, Irishtown, b. 1931, ord. 1956, Nigeria, d. 1995
O'Hara, Gerard, Irishtown, b. 1929, ord. 1954, South Africa, d. 1994
Ruddy, Andy, Foxford, b. 1912, Kent, England, d. 1978
Staunton, Patrick, Renbrack, b. 1935, ord. 1960, California

Sisters
Armstrong OP, Eliza, Backs, pre-1911, Tacoma, Washington
Conwell, Mai, Renbrack, b. 1916, prof. 1942, England & Wales, d. 2000
Cosgrave, Mary, Ballina Rd., Nigeria
Deasy, Teresa, Boherhallagh, Chicago & Rome
Doherty, Teresa, Belgarriff, prof. 1952, California
Hardy OP, Maggie, Foxford, pre-1911, Tacoma, Washington
Hardy OP, May, Foxford, pre-1911, Tacoma, Seattle
Healy, Honoria, Cloonmung, b. 1866, USA
Healy, Mary, Cloonmung, b. 1862, USA
Hughes, Nancy, Foxford, South Africa
Killeen, Mary, Station Rd., prof. 1951, Rome
McGuane, Ita, Foxford, Nigeria
McNulty, Sr, Boherhallagh, New York
McTigue, Mary, Irishtown, b. 1924, prof. 1955, South Korea & China
Molloy, Mary, Boherhallagh, b. 1938, England & Scotland
O'Hara, Brigid, Boherhallagh, b. 1939, Birmingham
O'Hara, Catherine, Boherhallagh, b. 1912, prof. 1934, New York, d. 1998
O'Hara, Mae, Boherhallagh, b. 1903, prof. 1928, USA, d. 1986
Sheerin, Mary, Boherhallagh, b. 1942, London & Bristol
Thornton, Kathleen, Station Rd, Africa
Thornton, Mary, Station Rd, USA

Priests   *Gurteen*
Callaghan, Peter, Drumlistna, b. 1883, ord. 1910, Liverpool, d. 1953
Casey, Columba, Moydoo, b. 1880, ord. 1909, London, d. 1947
Coleman, John Jerome, Doonrock, b. 1906, ord. 1934, Spokane, USA, d. 1992
Drury, Bishop Thomas, Moygara, b. 1902, ord. 1935, San Angelo, Corpus Christi, d. 1992
Finan Patrick, Killaraght, b. 1914, ord. 1941, Liverpool, d. 1988
Flanagan, Michael, Ardsoran, b. 1938, ord. 1965, Jefferson City, USA
Flanagan, Pádraig, Ardsoran, b. 1938, ord. 1963, Africa, England

Gurteen

Kilcoyne, Patrick, Gurteen, b. 1930, ord. 1955, Scotland, d. 1992
McDonagh, Roger, Gurteen, b. 1933, ord. 1959, Wales
McGovern, Pádraig, Gurteen, b. 1918, ord. 1944, London, d. 1995
Needham, Ciaran, Gurteen, b. 1924, ord. 1948, Brazil
McGrath, James, Stonepark, b. 1888, ord. 1914, New York, d. 1950
O'Grady, Frank, Rathmadder, b. 1945, ord. 1969, USA, Korea & Germany
Ryan, Michael, Rathmadder, b. 1934, ord. 1959, St. Brides, Scotland
Shannon, Fergal, Cloonanure, b. 1930, ord. 1964, Wales, d. 1995
Travers CM, Patrick, Killaraght, b. 1900, ord. 1931, France, d. 1987
Travers, Thomas, Killaraght, b. 1905, ord. 1930, England, d. 1965

Sisters

Armstrong, Juliana, Annaghmore, prof. 1940, New York
Cryan, Stanislaus, Derryknockeran, prof. 1906, Leeds, England, d. 1981
Dougal, Attracta, Cuppinagh, b. 1892, England, d. 1973
Duffy, Kathleen, Cloontycarn, b. 1938, prof. 1959, Los Angeles, d. 1996
Hunt, Gertrude, Rathmadder, b. 1938, prof. 1956, England & Madrid
McCormack, Brigid, Cloontycarn, b. 1902, New Jersey, USA, d. 1982
McDermott, Emma, Crosses, b. 1909, prof. 1928, Australia, d. 1979
McDonagh, Margaret, Gurtygara, b. 1920, prof. 1948, California
McDonagh, Mary, Crosses, b. 1901, prof. 1928, London, d. 1956
O'Beirne, Marguerite, Tavrane, prof. 1958, New Jersey
O'Beirne, Nathy, Tavrane, b. 1912, prof. 1930, China & England, d. 1981
Scanlon, Attracta, Clooneigh, b. 1919, prof. 1940, Africa & Italy
Shannon, Brigid, Cloonanure, b. 1934, prof. 1952, New Zealand
Shannon, Mary, Cloonanure, b. 1931, prof. 1951, South Wales

Brothers

McGovern, Francis, Mount Irwin, b. 1931, prof. 1948, Nigeria
O'Grady, Anthony, Doon Rock, b. 1910, prof. 1936, New York
Shannon SJG, Sean

Richard Devine SMA

Bernard Horan SMA

Keash

Priests

Breheny, John, Derrygola, b. 1932, ord. 1960, Liberia
Breheny, Kevin, Knockoconnor, b. 1934, ord. 1960, Kenya, d. 1985
Devine, Michael F., Cloonagh, b. 1880, ord. 1903, Elphin, d. 1951
Devine SMA, Richard, Cloonagh, b. 1931, ord. 1956, Nigeria
Hannon, Gerard, Cloonagh, b. 1900, ord. 1925, Southwark, England, d. 1987
Healy, John A., Cletta, b. 1862, ord. 1891, Chicago, d. 1924
Horan SMA, Bernard, Broher, b. 1935, ord. 1960, Nigeria
Rafferty, Nicholas, Derrynagrog, b. 1881, ord. 1905, Seattle, USA, d. 1957

John A. Healy

Sisters

Burns, Bridie, Knockalough, b. 1929, prof. 1947, Ascot, England
Burns, Colette, Knockalough, b. 1937, prof. 1956, England, d. 1995
Cosgrove, Mary, Broher, b. 1944, prof. 1968, Co Cavan
Cryan, Winifred, Broher, b. 1918, Scotland, d. 1966
Devine, Mary, Cloonagh, b. 1882, Denver, USA
Duffy, Mary, Carrowcrory, b. 1949, prof. 1967, Brazil
Gallagher, Mary, Drumrolla, b. 1947, prof. 1972, Zambia & Ghana
Henry, Molly, Greenan, b. 1910, Scotland, d. 1976

Bridie Burns

Higgins, Winnie, Derrygola, b. 1920, prof. 1937, France & England
Horan, Catherine, Broher, b. 1840, prof. 1868, Sligo, d. 1926
Lavin, Catherine, Derrygola, b. 1941, prof. 1959, Nigeria & Cameroon
Lavin, Margaret, Broher, b. 1920, prof. 1940, France & England
O'Connor, Kate, Toomour, b. 1873, Providence, USA
O'Connor, Pauline, Carrowreagh, b. 1950, prof. 1968, Australia & Scotland
O'Connor, Rosaleen, Carrowreagh, b. 1948, prof. 1966, Kenya & USA

Brothers
Redican, Brian, Townaghmore, b. 1939, prof. 1955, Zambia, Africa

Priests
Carrabine, Fr, Callow, Australia
Coleman, Edward, Listernan, b. c.1865, ord. 1890, Australia
Coleman SJ, Michael E, Listernan, b. 1858, ord. 1883, South Africa, China & Australia, d. 1920
Conlon, John T., Boleyboy, b. 1899, ord. 1923, Los Angeles, d. 1960
Dempsey, Mark, Carrowneden, b. c.1868, ord. 1893, Australia
Dunleavy, Brian, Carrowbeg, Dublin
Durkan, Fr, Dunmaynor, 19th century, USA
Filan, Dudley, Dunmaynor, b. 1830, ord. 1863, Philadelphia, d. 1900
Filan, Dudley, Dunmaynor, b. 1931, ord. 1957, Peru & England
Filan, Michael, Dunmaynor, b. 1819, ord. 1853, Philadelphia, d. 1819
Filan, Michael, Dunmaynor, b. 1852, ord. 1883, Mobile, Alabama d. 1923
Gallagher, Andrew, Tulleague,19th century, Los Angeles
Gallagher, Joseph, Ballinacurra, b. 1923, ord. 1947, Philippines
Gallagher, Peter, Tulleague, 19th century, Philadelphia
Holleran, Leo, Dromada Duke, New Jersey
Hurst, Patrick, Carramore Moy, b. c.1850, Scranton, Pennsylvania, d. 1910
Kirrane CSsR, Anthony, Carrownedin, Galway
Kirrane, Michael, Carrowneden, Australia
Judge, John, Parkroe, Killala
McDonnell, Michael, Callow, England
McManus, Martin, Creggaun, b. 1912, ord. 1938, Nigeria, d. 1998
McManus, Michael, Creggaun, b. 1922, ord. 1948, San Antonia
McNicholas, Martin, Graffy, early 20th century. Los Angeles
McNicholas, Thomas, Graffy, 20th century, Los Angeles
McNulty, John, Listernan, b. 1910, ord. 1935, Los Angeles, d. 1979
McNulty, Michael, Listernan, b. 1916, ord. 1940, Los Angeles, d. 1984
Marren, Vincent, Carrowliamore, ord. 1956, Clonfert
Naughton, Peter, Bokeen, Australia
O'Brien, Thomas, Boleyboy, California
O'Grady, James, Carroweena, b. 1933, ord. 1958, Los Angeles
O'Hara, Vincent, Attinaskolia, b. 1933, ord. 1958, Leeds
Philbin, Anthony, Carrowliambeg, b. 1879, ord. 1908, Egypt & USA, d. 1941
Philbin, James, Carrowliambeg, 19th century, Australia
Philbin, Michael J., Carrowliambeg, b. 1914, ord. 1942, Australia, d. 1984
Price, Francis, Dromada Gore, Canada
Ruane, Denis, Ballinaleck, b. 1907, ord. 1933, Adelaide, Australia, d. 1999
Stenson, Patrick, Carrowliam-more, b. 1939, ord. 1963, San Antonio, Texas
Tunney, Henry, Dromada Joyce, b. 1925, ord. 1950, Canada & England, d. 1988

Keash

Colette Burns

Killasser

Mary Gallagher

Pauline O'Connor

Rosaleen O'Connor

Patrick Stenson

James O'Grady

Sr Basil McNulty

John Conlon

Kilmovee

Sisters
Barry, Rita, Callow, Uganda
Burke OFM, Alexius, Carramore
Cogger, Julia, Carramore, b. 1897, England, d. 1983
Cogger, Norah, Carramore, b. 1895, Philadelphia d. 1918
Dempsey, Teresa, Cullen. b. 1935, prof. 1971, Uganda, Kenya, India & USA
Deacy, Ann, Cullin, Dublin
Doyle RSM, Bridget, Carramore, Limerick
Doyle SJG, Agnes, Carramore, b. 1950, Australia
Doyle SJG, Patricia, Carramore, prof. 1957, Australia
Dunleavy, Kathleen, Carrowbeg, b. 1920, prof. 1945, England & Wales
Dunleavy, Patricia, Carrowbeg, b. 1877, USA, d. 1957
Durcan, Sr Dominick, Killasser, pre-1911, USA
Gallagher RSM, Agnes, Tulleague, Nottingham, England
Gallagher, Gertrude, Tulleague, Jefferson City, USA
Hanly, Mary, Fross, Waterford
Heneghan, Sr.Solace, Ballincurra, Chicago
Holleran, Margaret, Dromada Duke, Columban Sister
Howley SJG, Norah, Carrowliambeg, b. 1921, prof. 1942, Australia, d. 1994
Igoe, Ann, Callow, Dublin
Maloney, Margaret, Tiranniny, b. 1935, prof. 1956, Australia
McAndrew, Francis, Coolagrane, Dublin
McDonnell, Ann, Cuillonaghton, England
McLoughlin, Bridie, Derreen, prof. 1958, Pennsylvania, USA
McManus, Gabriel, Creggaun, Drogheda
McManus, Honora, Carramore, b. 1878, prof. 1904, USA, d. 1975
McNulty, Sr Basil, Listernan, England
McNulty, Maryanne, Listernan, Africa, d. 1993
O'Grady SJG, Eileen, Dunmaynor, Perth, Australia
O'Grady RSM, Sr Ignatius, Carrowliambeg, Abbeyfeale
O'Grady, Mary Eithne, Killasser, b. 1957, Jefferson City, USA
Philbin, Catherine, Carrowliambeg, France & England, d. 1989
Price, Sr Xavier, Loobnamuck, Ireland
Reynolds, Mary Kate, Callow, b. 1913, prof. 1936, Surrey & Cambridge
Rowley, Annie Kate, Dromada Gore, b. 1921, prof. 1946, Dundee, Scotland
Rowley, Mary Ellen, Dromada Gore, b. 1905, prof. 1930, Dundee, Scotland, d. 1965
Ruane, Barbara, Ballinaleck, b. 1904, Adelaide, Australia, d. 1983
Stenson, Teresa, Carrowliam More, New Jersey, USA
Ward, Agnes, Doontas, b. 1936, prof. 1960, Nigeria

Brothers
Deacy, Patrick, Cartron, Dublin
Rochford, Michael, Cullin, Dublin

Priests
Bones, Anthony, Stonepark, Australia
Cribben, J.T., Carrowbeg, England
Duffy, Dominick, Ballyglass, Scotland
Duffy, John C, Clooncara, b. 1918, ord. 1943, Los Angeles, USA, d. c.1991
Duffy, Kevin, Kilkelly, Australia

Duffy, Michael, Clooncara, California
Dunleavy, Louis, Sinolane, b. 1931, ord. 1957, Florida, d. 1993
Flannery, James, Kilkelly, b. 1918, ord. 1943, England, d. c. 1991
Frain, Tom, Culcastle, ord. 1941, France
Griffin, John, Culclare, France
Henry, Joseph, Cloonamna, b. 1903, ord. 1928, Southwark, d. c.1956
Hunt, John, Shraheens, b. 1902, ord. 1929, USA
Kelly, John P., Kilkelly, Australia
Lafferty, James, Ballyglass, b. 1917, ord. 1943, London, d. c.1999
Lydon, Dominick, Shammer, USA
Mullen, Tim, Ballyglass, USA
O'Beirne, Fintan, Barcul, Australia
O'Beirne, Oliver, Barcul, Australia
O'Grady, Pádraig, Kilmovee, b. 1916, ord. 1941, Leicester, England
Shiel, Brendan, Kilkelly, Australia
Shiel, Joe, Kilkelly, Scotland
Shiel, Peter, Kilkelly, Australia
Snee, Patrick, Cloonturk, England
Tarpey SJ, James, Kilkelly, b. 1924, ord. 1957, Hong Kong, d. 2001
Towey, Dominick, Aughadefin, Scotland
Walsh, James, Kilkelly, b. 1898, ord. 1924, Scotland, d. 1965

Sisters
Bones, Elizabeth, Esker, Australia
Bones, Monica, Stonepark, England
Brett, Agatha, Liscosker, England
Cafferkey, Brigid, USA
Cafferkey, Gerard, Carrowbeg, USA
Cafferkey, Margaret, USA
Caulfield, Kate, Carralackey, USA
Duffy, Annie, Culclare, England
Duffy, Eucharia, Glann, Australia
Duffy, Margaret, Glann, Australia
Duffy, Winifred, Kilmovee, b. 1924, prof. 1955, England
Dunleavy, Brigid, Kilkelly, ent. 1941, Jefferson City, USA
Egan, Alphonsus, Tavrane, USA
Flannery, Freda, Kilkelly, ent. 1936, Jefferson City, USA
Foley, Bridie, Barcul, USA
Foley, Kathleen, Barcul, USA
Foley, Rose, Barcul, New Zealand
Frain, Catherine, Rusheens, Rhode Island, USA
Frain, Mary, Hong Kong
Harrington, Enda, Glann, USA
Harrington, Mary, Glann, USA
Higgins, Melanie, Culmore, England
Keirns, Lena, Derrylahan, USA
Mullen, Ellie, Ballinrumpa, USA
Mullen, Marie, Ballinrumpa, USA
Niland, Norah, Urlar, USA
O'Gara, Josephine, Culliagh, England

Kilmovee

John McNulty

Michael McNulty

Kilmovee

O'Grady, Rita, Culmore, England
Phillips, Magdelan, Urlar, England
Phillips, Mary, Glann, USA
Regan , Alphonsus, Tavrane, USA
Regan, Angela, Cloonamna, b. 1920, England, d. 1999
Regan, Annie, Egool, USA
Regan, Eileen, Egool, Australia
Regan, Ita, Shraheens, England
Regan, Mary Joseph, USA
Shiels, Sr Cormac, Kilkelly, France
Shiels, Marie Theresa, Kilkelly, France
Tarpey RSC, Cecil, Kilkelly, Africa
Tarpey OP, Kitty, Kilkelly, b. 1920, Dublin & Belfast, d. 1997
Towey, Ann, Aughadevin, Notre Dame, USA
Walsh, Stanislaus, Derrynalecka, USA

Brothers
Conway, Francis (Celestine Imar), De La Salle, d. 1996

Kiltimagh   *Priests*
Begley, Bernard, Kiltimagh, b. 1883, England, d. 1961
Brennan, Christopher, Kiltimagh, b. 1960, ord. 1985, Liberia
Burke, Tom, Craggagh, b. 1923, England
Cafferty, Tom, Kiltimagh, b. 1919, Nigeria
Cleary, Tom, Kiltimagh, b. 1928, Portugal, d. 1990
Corry, John, Garryroe, b. 1926, Rapid City, USA
Creighton OFM, Andrew, Ballinamore, ord. 1938, Rome (see following)
Creighton, John Joe, Ballinamore, b. 1912, Rome, d. 1985
Greally, Thomas, Ballyglass, b. 1922, Nigeria
Higgins, Dermot, Kiltimagh, b. 1913, ord. 1938, Nigeria, d. 1991
Higgins, Patrick, Kiltimagh, b. 1917, ord. 1941, Los Angeles, d. 1993

Timothy McNicholas

Hyland, James, Kiltimagh, b. 1888, ord. 1913, Australia, d. 1949
Lavin, Michael, Annaghill, b. 1904, USA, d. 1972
McNicholas, James, Treenagleragh, b. 1892, Liberia, d. 1939
McNicholas, Gerard, Derryvohey, b. 1941, Fiji Islands
McNicholas, Archbishop Timothy, Treenkeel, b. 1877, Cinncinati, USA, d. 1952
McTigue, John, Kiltimagh, b. 1890, ord. 1916, Brooklyn, USA, d. 1958
Madden, Louis, Kiltimagh, b. 1918, ord. 1944, England & Far East, d. 2001
Madden CP, Paul, James St, ord. 1945, Rome (see following)
Madden, Thomas, Kiltimagh, b. 1920, Rome
Morrin, Patrick, Kiltimagh, b. 1935, Ethiopia, d. 1977
O'Hora CP, Aidan, Treenagleragh, b. 1932, Paris

Louis Madden

Philbin, Bishop William, Kiltimagh, b. 1907, ord. 1931, Brighton, England, d. 1991
Roughneen, P.J., Kiltimagh, b. 1892, ord. 1916, Brighton, England, d. 1970
Ruane, Patrick, Annaghill, b. 1927, Brazil
Walsh, Joseph, Kiltimagh, b. 1958, ord. 1983, Australia
Walsh, Vincent, Main St, b. 1920, ord. 1944, China

Sisters
Begley, Katie, Kiltimagh, pre-1911, Manchester
Brennan, Ellen, Lisduff, b. 1894, England, d. 1948

Burke, Ann Marie, Gorthgarve, b. 1905, USA, d. 1991 *Kiltimagh*
Burke, Brigid, Gorthgarve, b. 1894, USA, d. 1981
Burke, Ellen, Gorthgarve, b. 1887, USA, d. 1962
Burke, Margaret, Gorthgarve, b. 1903, USA, d. 1987
Carney, Brigid, Treenagleragh, b. 1898, Egypt, d. 1980
Carney, Elizabeth, Thornhill, b. 1908, England, d. 2000
Carney, Margaret, Thornhill, b. 1896, England
Carney, Margaret, Treenagleragh, b. 1888, Rome & USA, d. 1963
Carroll OP, Rose, Kiltimagh, pre-1911, Natal, South Africa
Farrell, Ellie, Kiltimagh, pre-1911, Natal, South Africa
Connor, Katie, Kiltimagh, pre-1911, London
Costello, Sr Cuimin, Barnagarry, ent. St Louis Monaghan 1944
Forde OP, Sr Patrick, Main St, prof. 1937, Valance, France
Forde, Sarah, Cortoon, b. 1902, Belgium, d. 1983
Gallagher OP, Katie, Churchpark, b. 1887, Natal, South Africa, d. 1969
Gormally, Catherine, Carrandine, b. 1874, USA, d. 1956
Halligan, Delia, Devalash, b. 1893, USA
Jeffers, Ann, Thornhill, b. 1916, USA
Jeffers, Margaret, Thornhill, b. 1905, USA, d. 1986
Kane, Louis, Woods, b. 1900, South Africa, d. 1994
Keegan, Maureen, Ballyglass, b. 1914, Nigeria
King, Anna, Kiltimagh, b. 1890, USA
King, Mary A., Kiltimagh, pre-1911, Rome
King, Brigid, Kiltimagh, b. 1893, USA
King, Mary, Kiltimagh, b. 1882, USA
Lavan, Nora, Kiltimagh, pre-1911, San Antonio, USA
Lavin, Brigid, Churchpark, b. 1881, South Africa
Lavin, Brigid, Annaghill, b. 1911, USA
Lavin OP, Margaret, Churchpark, b. 1883, Natal, South Africa
McDonagh OP, Delia, Aidan St, prof. 1937, Valance, France
McHugh RSC, Mag., Kiltimagh, pre-1911, Kansas, USA
McNamara SM, Delia, Goulboy, prof. 1940, Trim, Co Meath
McNicholas, Brigid, Kiltimagh, b. 1911, Nigeria, d. 1991
McNicholas OP, Margaret, Treenagleragh, b. 1889, Natal, South Africa, d. 1958
McNicholas RSC, Sr, Kiltimagh, pre-1911, Kansas, USA
McNicholas, Sr Mochua, ent .St Louis, Monaghan, 1944
Mullaney, Catherine, Lisduff, b. 1909, USA
Mullaney, Ellen, Lisduff, b. 1881, USA, d. 1946
Mullaney, Mary, Lisduff, b. 1908, USA, d. 2000
O'Donnell, Mary, Thornhill, b. 1910, Africa
O'Hora, Katie, Treenagleragh, b. 1885, England, d. 1978
Philbin?, Sr Fantia, St Louis, Bury-St-Edmunds, England
Philbin, Margaret, Sacred Heart, Mount Anvil, Dublin
Regan, Maggie, Kiltimagh, pre-1911, Houston, USA
Reilly, Anne, Lisnamonaghy, b. 1889, South Africa, d. 1945
Reilly, Dympna, prof. c.1904, South Africa
Reilly OP, Katie, Lisnamonaghy, b. 1886, Natal, South Africa, d. 1958
Reilly, Rose, Lisnamonaghy, b. 1893, South Africa, d. 1971
Roughneen, Kate, Kiltimagh, pre-1911, San Antonio, USA
Roughneen, Mary, Kiltimagh, pre-1911, Kansas, USA

Kiltimagh	Sobelewski OFM, Mary, Kiltimagh, prof. 1966, Boston, USA
	Walshe, Annie, Kiltimagh, pre-1911, San Antonio, USA

Brothers
Casey, Patrick, Treenagleragh, b. 1848, Wales, d. 1934
Creighton, John, Cullilea, b. 1899, England, d. 1967
Daly, Joe, Kiltimagh, b. 1936, Canada

Lay Missionary
Costello, Mary, Creaggagh, Iceland

Mullinabreena   *Priests*
Doherty, Edward, Mullaghanarry, b. 1902, ord. 1928, England & USA, d. 1998
Finan, Joe, Carrowcurragh, b. 1932, ord. 1957, England
Gannon, Tom, Tubberdur, b. 1902, ord. 1926, England, d. 1955
Gilmartin, John James, Pullagh, b. 1905, Los Angeles, d. 1960s
Gilmartin, Michael, Rinbane, b. 1850s, Chicago
Ginty, Denis, Cashel North, b. 1903, ord. 1927, San José, USA, d. 1985
Henry, John, Carrowmore, b. 1901, ord. 1926, Washington DC, d. 1944
Henry, Patrick, Achonry, b. 1925, ord. 1949, Yorkshire, England

Sisters
Armstrong, Mary C., Carnavourane, b. 1902, prof. 1920, England & USA, d. 1987
Berreen, Maria, Rinbane, b. 1921, England
Gallagher, Stella, Ballinvalley, USA
Gilmartin, Brigid, Pullagh, b. 1904, prof. 1925, France, d. 1925
Gilmartin, Mary, Rinbane, b. 1899, prof. 1928, England, d. 1924
Gilmartin, Mary Ann, Pullagh, b. 1896, prof. 1923, France & England, d. 1961
Henry, Julia, Carrowmore, b. 1936, prof. 1960, England & Scotland, d. 1982
Johnston, Brigid, Carentavey, b. 1919, France
Johnston, Brigid, Carentavey, b. 1926, Wisconsin, USA
Johnston, Margaret, Carentavey, b. 1919, France
McCarrick, Agnes, Cloonbanif, b. 1919, prof. 1941, England & Scotland
McCarrick, Brigid, Cloonbanif, d. 1901
McCarrick, Norah, Cloonbanif, b. 1916, prof. 1939, England
McGowan, Mary Jane, Carrowmore, b. 1901, Africa
McGowan, Teresa, Carrowmore, b. 1894, prof. 1919, USA, d. 1967
Marren, Margaret, Streamstown, b. 1933, Devon, England
O'Donnell, Kathleen, Carrowrile, Lavagh, ent. 1939, Jefferson City
O'Hara, Brigid, Streamstown, b. 1902, Washington, USA, d. 1960s
O'Hara, Catherine, Streamstown, b. 1886
Roddy, Mary, Tullyhugh, b. 1933, prof. 1956, England, d. 1983
Sweeney, Peggy, Crimlin, b. 1886, Devon, England
Wims, Mary, Cloonbaniff, b. 1926, England

Straide   *Priests*
Clarke, Fr., Doogera, USA
Smith, John, Blanemore, b. 1938, ord. 1962, Korea
Smith, Malachy, Blanemore, b. 1941, ord. 1967, Korea
Smith, Patrick, Blanemore, b. 1936, ord. 1960, Korea

Sisters
Howley, Maria, Gurteens, prof. 1937, Birmingham
Walsh, Margaret, prof. 1972, Reading, England

Brothers
Moran, Robert, Aughaliska, b. 1875, prof. 1911, Liverpool

Priests
Brady, Pádraig, Cullane, ord. 1958, Peru
Burke, Bishop Thomas, b. Swinford 1846, son of Dr Ulic and Sarah Murphy who died in
   1847 and family emigrated to U.S. in 1850. Bishop of Albany, USA
Campbell, John F, Carrowbeg, b. 1891, ord. 1916, Philadelphia, d. 1940
Campbell CSSp, Pádraig, Swinford, b. 1920, ord. 1946, Nigeria & USA, d. 2002
Cassidy, Michael J., Brackloon, b. 1929, ord. 1954, Scotland
Cassidy, Martin J., Brackloon, b. 1932, ord. 1957, Scotland & Florida
Cassidy, Peadar, Brackloon, b. 1920, ord. 1945, Philippines, d. c.1980
Conlon, Anthony, Gortaraha, b. 1937, ord. 1962, West Virginia, USA
Durkan, James, Cloonaboy, b. 1947, ord. 1971, New Jersey, USA
Durkan, Thomas P., Cloonlumney, b. 1902, ord. 1927, Minnesota, USA, d. c.1965
Foy, Michael, Lisdurrane, b. 1904, ord. 1929, Minnesota, USA
Gallagher, Patrick, Tavanglass, ord. 1910, England
Grufferty, Thomas, Curryane, b. 1948, ord. 1973, England
Hurst, John, Swinford, b. c.1871, ord. 1896, Danvers, Minnesota, USA, d. 1926
Horkan, Martin T., Ballydrum, b. 1908, ord. 1932, England, d. c.1980
Kelly, Andrew, Swinford, b. 1915, ord. 1942, England, Asia & Peru, d. 1992   Jeremiah Lambe CSSp
Kelly CM, Patrick, Swinford, b. 1914, ord. 1940, England, d. c.1957
Kilgallon, John, Curryane, b. 1949, ord. 1974, England
Lambe CSSp, Jeremiah, Swinford, b. 1924, ord. 1952, Sierra Leone, W. Africa
Loftus, Charles, Swinford, b. 1911, ord. 1935, Los Angeles d. c.1959
Loftus, Thomas, Swinford, b. 1900, ord 1924, Scotland d. 1977
Loftus, John, Swinford, b. 1903, ord. 1925, China & USA, d. c.1988
McDonagh, Bishop Thomas, Midfield, b. 1911, ord. 1938, Florida, USA
McDonnell, Joseph, Rathscanlon, b. 1914, ord. 1939, Australia
McDonnell, Anthony, Rathscanlon, b. 1945, ord. 1970, Los Angeles
McGowan, John, Swinford, b. 1893, ord. 1918, Baltimore, USA, d. c.1947
McGowan, Anthony, Laughtadurkin, b. 1940s, Los Angeles
McHugh, Adrian, Swinford, b. 1939, ord. 1964, South Africa   Denis McManus CSSp
McHugh, Thomas, Knockavilla, b. 1944. ord. 1968, Southwark, England
McManus CSSp, Denis, Swinford, Africa & USA
McNicholas, John, Swinford, b. 1917, ord. 1941, England, d. 1986
Mulligan SJ, John, Swinford
Mulligan, Patrick, Swinford, b. 1882, ord. 1908, California, d. c.1938
Mulroy, James, Meelick, b. 1924, ord. 1947, Philippines, d. c.1965
Mulroy, Martin J., Ballintample, b. 1959, ord. 1984, Wales
Mulroy, Fr, Meelick, Wales
Mulroy, Timothy J., ord. 1995, Japan
O'Neill, Martin, Meelick, b. 1911, ord. 1936, Wisconsin, USA
Shaughnessy, Gerard, Laughtadurkin, b. 1956, ord. 1985, England
Sheridan, Thomas, Laughtadurkin, b. 1913, ord. 1939, England   Pádraig Campbell CSSp
Shiel, Joseph, Esker, b. 1891, ord. 1923, Calcutta, India, d. c.1969
Swords, Liam, Swinford, b. 1937, ord. 1962, Paris

Swinford   *Sisters*

Burke, Delia, Derryronane, prof. 1937, India & Pakistan

Burke, Mary, Derryronan, prof. 1939, Australia

Byrne, Molly, Derryronan, USA, d. c.1989

Campbell, Delia, Swinford, prof.pre-1911, Swansea, Wales, d. c.1960

Campbell, Margaret, Swinford, prof. pre-1911, Swansea, Wales, d. c1960

Campbell, Patricia, Swinford, Cork

Cassidy, Sadie, Brackloon, Hong Kong

*Clancy, Philomena, ent. 1949, Jefferson City, USA

Convey OP, Anne Theresa, Cullane, b. 1883, prof. 1912, San Rafael, California, d. 1969

Conwell, Brigid, Tullyroe, b. 1909, USA, d. 1989

*Coyle, Mary, ent. 1973, Jefferson City, USA

*Cuffe, Ann, ent. 1961, Jefferson City, USA

Cuffe, Marie, Culmore, prof. 1959, England, France & Italy

Curry, Eileen, Kinaffe, England

Curry, Baby, Kinaffe, New York, d. c.1955

Devaney, Brigid, Culmore, USA

Devaney, Babe, Culmore, USA

Doherty, M., Swinford P., pre-1911, Tasmania, Australia

Doherty, Elizabeth, Lisdurrane, b. 1896, ord. 1920, Tacoma & Oregan, USA, d. 1967

*Dooley, Alice, Swinford convent, ent. 1878, Sandhurst, Australia

*Dooley, Kate Mary, Swinford convent, ent. 1862, Sandhurst & Tasmania, Australia d. 1932

*Dooley, Nannie, Swinford convent, ent. 1871, Sandhurst, Australia

Doyle, Mary, Swinford, prof. 1949, USA

Durcan, Anne, Swinford P., pre-1911, France

Durkin, Delia, Cloonaboy, USA, d. c.1944

Durkin, Monica, Johnsfort, Chicago

Durkin, Mary, Swinford, USA

Durkin, Sr, Swinford, Canada

Fleming, Sr Ignatius, Swinford P., pre-1911, Castlebar

Gallagher, Teresa, Swinford, b. 1920, Scotland

Gallagher, Una, Swinford, prof. 1928, Wales

Gavigan, Anne, Derryronan, b. 1907, British Guiana & USA

Greally, Patsy, Swinford, Galway

Greally, Ursula, Swinford, Tuam

Groarke, Ann, Esker, b. 1865, prof. 1896, USA

Groarke, Mary, Esker, b. 1860, prof. 1894, USA

Groarke, Norah, Dublin Road, USA

Healy, Anne, Cloonlumney, b. 1907, New York

Healy, Brigid, Cloonlumney, b. 1909, New York

Healy, Sarah, Carnaculla, USA

Henry, Mary, Swinford, Scotland

Henry, Sr, Ballydrum, b. 1855, USA, d. c.1940

Horkan, Anna M., Liscottle, b. 1904, Philadelphia, d. 1990's

Hughes, Kate, Carrowbeg, pre-1911, Lisbon, Portugal

Hughes, Mary, Carrowbeg, pre-1911, Lisbon, Portugal

Jordan, Mary E., Meelick, b. 1926, prof. 1957, Tanzania

*Kearns, Helen, ent. 1964, Jefferson City, USA

Kelly, Mary, Midfield, prof. 1932, USA

Kelly, Mary T., Midfield, b. 1916, prof. 1934, USA

Kilgallon, Agnes, Carnaculla, prof. 1917, USA, d. 1978 *Swinford*
Kilgallon, Mary, Curryane, b. 1895, prof. 1920, USA, d. 1989
Kyle, Mary A., Swinford, prof. pre-1911, Rome
Kyle, Nora, Swinford, pre-1911, Kingston, Canada
Kyle, Teresa, Swinford, pre-1911, Rome
*Lally, Maureen, ent. 1958, Jefferson City, USA
Lavelle, Kathleen, Liscottle, prof. 1914, New York, d. c.1936
Lenehan RSC, Kate, Swinford, pre-1911, Mill Hill
Mahony, Mary A., Carnacross, b. 1917, prof. 1935, USA, d. c.1990
McCann, Margaret, Derryronan, b. 1929, prof. 1947, Jefferson City, USA
McGeever, Anne, Swinford P., pre-1911, Manchester
McGeever, Bea, Bothaul, USA
McGloin, Mary, Gortaraha, prof. 1957, Uganda, Kampala
McGloin, Nellie, Cloonfinane, prof. 1947, England
McHugh, Sr, Knockavilla, Australia
McManus OP, Ann (Enda), Derryronan, b. 1887, prof. 1933, San Rafael, California, d. 1969
McManus OP, Catherine (Veronica), Derryronan, b. 1882, prof. 1912, San Rafael,
    California, d. 1933
McManus, Sr, Derryronan, England (sister of above two)
McNicholas, Frances, Swinford, b. 1942, prof. 1966, Jefferson City, USA
*McNiffe, Kate, Swinford convent, ent. 1975, Sandhurst, Australia & New Zealand
McNulty RSC, Winifrid, Swinford P., pre-1911, Birmingham
*Martyn, Monica, Swinford convent, ent. 1855, Sandhurst & Tasmania, Australia, d. 1899
Mellet, Sr Ita, Swinford P., pre-1911, Southampton
Mellett, Margaret, Swinford, b. 1866, prof. 1889, British Guiana, d. c.1940
Moloney Sr, Swinford P., pre-1911, Mallow, Co Cork
Moore, Ellen, Carracannada, b. 1900, USA
Moore, Brigid, Cloonlara, Scotland, d. c.1989
Morris S.M., Colleen, Swinford, S.Leamington, Chicago, USA
Muldowney, Brigid, Tullinacarra. prof. 1949, Australia
Muldowney, Ellen, Carnaculla, Boston
Mulloy, Benignus, Carnaculla, USA
Mulroy, Florry, Laughtadurkin , prof. 1949, USA
Mulroy, Katie, Laughtadurkin, b. 1916, prof. 1950, England, d. c.1990
Mulroy, Maggie, Laughtadurkin, USA
Mulroy, Margaret, Laughtadurkin, England, d. c.1976
Mulroy, Maria, Laughtadurkin, England
Mulroy, Winnie, Laughtadurkin, b. 1919, prof. 1939, France, Belgium, England, d. c.1983
Munroe, Julia, Swinford, b. 1874, pre-1911, Philadelphia, USA, d. c.1957
Munroe, Mary Kate, Swinford, b. 1865, pre-1911, Hull, England.
Munroe OP, Norah, Swinford, b. 1876, pre-1911, Leicester
Murtagh, Sarah, Castleroyan, b. 1914, prof. 1941, England
Neary, Anne, Culmore, USA
Neary, Veronica, Tumgesh, Australia
Nestor, Ann, Derryronan, Africa
Nolan, Teresa, Lislackagh, USA
*Nugent, Brigid, ent. 1939, Jefferson City, USA
*Nugent, Helena, ent. 1927, Jefferson City, USA
O'Connell, Gertrude, Cloonaghboy, California
*O'Hara, Teresa, Swinford convent, ent. 1865, Sandhurst, Australia, d. 1916

Swinford   Oliver, Noreen, Tullinacurra, Peru
    *O'Shaughnessy, Kathleen, ent. 1937, Jefferson City, USA
    Philbin, Nellie, Meelick, prof. 1949, USA
    Prendergast, Mamie, Swinford, France & Belgium
    Quinn, Margaret, Midfield, prof. 1942, Australia
    Roache, Margaret, Midfield, USA
    Rowley, Anne, Cloonacanna, b. 1928, prof. 1950, Australia
    Salmon, Brigid, Derryronan, Texas
    Salmon, Delia, Carnaculla, prof. 1953, France
    Salmon, Mary, Swinford P., prof. pre-1911, Rome
    Salmon, Mary, Derryronan, Italy, d. c.1968
    Salmon, Mary, Derryronan, prof. 1961, Wales
    Scally OP, M., Swinford P., prof. pre-1911, Leicester
    *Sherlock, Brigid, ent. 1958, Jefferson City, USA
    Shiel, Nora, Carrarea, Fiji & USA,
    Spelman, Mary, Tullinacurra, Australia
    Stenson, Mary, Culmore, b. 1905, USA
    Sweeney, Mary, Ballyglass, USA, d. c.1964
    Sweeney, Mary, Ballyglass, b. 1921, prof. 1950s, USA
    Thornton, Breege, Swinford, b. 1936, Fiji, Australia & New Zealand
    Tunney, Mary, Culmore, b. 1901, Philadelphia, d. c.1964
    Walsh, Frances, Cloonlara, prof. 1952, Australia
    *Woods, Annie, Swinford convent, ent. 1875, Sandhurst, Australia

    * Swinford Sisters of Mercy born outside the diocese.

    Brothers
    Curry, Bernie, Kinaffe, b. 1931, England
    Fahy, Patrick, Brackloon, b. 1876, ord. 1933, Chicago, d. 1976
    Fitzpatrick, Joseph, Swinford, b. 1901, Montreal, England, d. 1985
    Forkin, William, Kinaffe, b. 1942, Korea
    McCarthy, Eugene, Swinford, b. 1892, ord. 1910, England, d. 1958
    Muldowney, Patrick, Tullinacarra, USA
    Mulloy, Michael, Swinford, b. 1949, ord. 1990, USA
    Rooney, Liam, Swinford, b. 1939, ord. 1963, England

Tourlestrane   *Priests*
    Battle, John C, Stonepark, b. 1901, ord. 1926, Scotland, d. 1978
    Brennan, Martin, Cloongoonagh, b. 1905, ord. 1933, USA
    Clarke, Thomas, Glenavoo, b. 1894, ord. 1919, New York, d. 1960
    Coghlan, Gerald P., Aclare, ord. c.1880. Philadelphia
    Connolly, Eugene, Kilbride, b. 1923, ord. 1947, England
    Conway, Brian, Aclare, b. 1940, ord. 1965, Africa
    Cunnane, Luke, Tullymoy, b. 1944, ord. 1968, California
    Cunnane, Jarlath, Tullymoy, b. 1953, ord. 1977, Los Angeles & South America
    Doherty, Charles, Caraloban, b. 1918, ord. 1943, Leeds, d. 1993
    Durkin, Edward, Cullen, b. 1903, ord. 1930, Scotland
    Durkin, Edward, Cullen, b. 1930, ord. 1956, Scotland
    Durkin, Bishop John, Glenavoo, South Africa
    Durkin, John, Cullen, b. 1895, ord. 1921

Durkin, Patrick, Dawros, b. 1941, ord. 1967, New Jersey

Feely, Patrick, Dawros, b. 1914, ord. 1939, Ipswich, England, d. 1980

Gallagher, Patrick, Ougaval, b. 1941, ord. 1966, California

Gavigan, Thomas, Aclare, b. 1920, ord. 1944, Sunderland, England, d. 1986

Goldie, Anthony, Kilmactigue, Dundee

Goldrick, William, Glenavoo, b. 1854, St Paul, Minesota

Goldrick, Henry, Glenavoo, b. 1880, St Paul, Minesota

Goldrick, Michael, Gurterslin, b. 1891, ord. 1921

Goldrick, James, Gurterslin, b. 1895, ord. 1931, California

Goldrick, John, Gurterslin, b. 1903, ord. 1931, California

Grady SJ, James, Stonepark, ord. pre-1889, Gardiner St, Dublin

Grady, Patrick J., Stonepark, ord. pre-1889, Buenos Aires, Argentina

Haran, Michael J., Glenavoo, b. 1920, ord. 1945, Los Angeles

Harte, Patrick, Cloongoonagh, b. c.1934, ord. c.1960, England

Henry, Gerard, Rhue, b. 1916, ord. 1942, Salford, England, d. 1994

Henry, James, Rhue, b. 1945, ord. 1971, California

Jones SJ, Daniel, Benada Abbey, ord. c.1850, Dublin

Jones SJ, James, Benada Abbey, b. 1828, ent. 1848, Barbados, Jamaica & England,
    d. Dec. 1892

Keavney, Patrick, Rhue, b. 1930, ord. 1965, Surrey, England

Kennedy, John, Cloonadiveen, b. 1941, ord. 1966, England

Kennedy, John Joseph, Cloonbarry, b. 1926, ord. 1950, USA

Leheny, Bernard, Aclare, b. 1941, ord. 1966, Los Angeles

Leheny, James, Aclare, b. 1905, ord. 1930, Los Angeles, d. 1955

Lundy, William, Culleen, b. 1914, California

McAlister, Leo, Aclare, b. 1929, ord. 1954, California

McGoldrick, Bishop, Tourlestrane P., ord. pre-1898, Duluth, USA

McGuinness, Stephen, Clooneen, ord. 1920

McGuinness, John T., Clooneen, California

Marren, Matthew, Dawros, b. 1885, ord. 1911, California, d. 1934

Marren, Matthew, Cloongoonagh, b. 1917, ord. 1943, Los Angeles

Marren, Martin, Dawros, b. 1842, ord. 1870, USA, d. 1905

Marren, James, Dawros, b. 1920, ord. 1944, California

Murphy, Daniel, Kilmactigue, b. 1858, Philadelphia, d. 1935

Murphy, Michael J., Knockbrack, b. 1930, ord. 1960, Nigeria & Ghana

Murphy CSSp, Vincent, (see above), d. 2002

Murtagh, Patrick, Tullinaglug, b. 1933, ord. 1958, London

Murtagh, Joseph, Tullinaglug, ord. c.1968, USA

Neary, Christopher, Claddagh, b. 1925, ord. 1950, California

Nealon, Michael, Coolrecuill, b. 1894, ord. 1922, Rome

Nealon, Patrick, Coolrecuill, b. 1892, ord. 1919, England

O'Hara, Bernard, Kilmactigue, b. 1894, ord. 1918, Liverpool, d. 1940

O'Hara, Eamon, Cloongoonagh, b. 1939, ord. 1963, England

O'Hara, James E., Cloongoonagh, b. 1908, ord. 1933, Los Angeles, d. 1972

O'Hara, John, Carrowreagh, b. 1894, ord. 1922, England

O'Hara, John F., Cloongoonagh, b. 1906, ord. 1931, Salamanca, d. 1989

O'Hara, Michael, ord. 1854, New Zealand

Quinn, Thomas, Glenavoo, b. 1936, ord. 1962, California

Walsh, John A., Carane, b. 1920, ord. 1947, California

Walsh, John E., Boycloonagh, b. 1929, ord. 1955, USA

Tourlestrane   Walsh, Michael, Tullinaglug, b. 1864
Walsh, Patrick, Rhue, b. 1916, ord. 1942, California
Walsh, Patrick J., Coolrecuill, b. 1951, ord. 1980
Walsh, Patsy, Coolrecuill, b. 1923, ord. 1949, Africa, d. 1955
Walsh, Robert, Rhue, b. 1917, ord. 1945, California

Brothers
Gilligan, Frank, Gurterslin, b. 1923, prof. 1955, Australia
Howley, Thomas (Edesius Michael), De La Salle, Kilmactigue, d. 1914
Marren, John, Dawros, b. 1885
Walsh, Michael J., Dawros, b. 1882, Missouri, USA

Sisters
Cawley, Belinda, Knockahoney, b. 1896, Philadelphia, USA, d. 1984
Doherty, Annie, Caraloban, b. 1920, Bexleyheath, England
Dunne, Maggie, Clooneen, b. 1886, England
Durkin, Rita, Culleen, b. 1934, Scotland
Gavigan, Cecelia, Claddagh, b. 1895, Belgium, d. 1956
Gavigan, Cecelia, Claddagh, b. 1922, France & Belgium
Howley, Mary, Caraloban, b. 1937, Brisbane
Jones SM, Elizabeth, Benada Abbey, ent. pre-1850, Elphin diocese.
Jones RSC, Georgina (Magdalen Attracta), ent. 1851, Galway, d. 1922
Jones RSC, Mary, (Laurence Justinian), Benada Abbey, ent. 1842, Dublin
McKeon, Mary, Coolrecuill, Scotland
Murtagh, Agnes, Tubberoddy, b. 1912, Melbourne, d. 2001
Murtagh, Bea, Tubberoddy, b. 1906, d. 1974
Murtagh, Kate, Tubberoddy, b. 1908, Melbourne, d. 1976
Murtagh, Nellie, Tubberoddy, b. 1915, Melbourne, d. 1988
Mullarkey, Mary, Mount Taffe, b. 1904, USA
Mulligan, Sr M Eugene, Gorterslin, b. 1921
O'Donnell OP, Mary Anne, Benada, prof. pre-1911, Washington, USA
O'Grady RSC, Anne (Bernardine), Stonepark, prof. pre-1889
O'Grady RSC, Bridget, Kilmacteigue, prof. pre-1911, Dublin
O'Grady RSC, Celia, Kilmactigue, prof. pre-1911
O'Hara, Thecla, Kilbride, b. 1892, New York, d. 1881
O'Hara, Vincent, Kilmactigue, b. 1907, Aukland, d. 1971

Tubbercurry   *Priests*
Bradley, Patrick, Cloonacool, b. 1881, ord. 1907, Baltimore, d. 1957
Brennan, Martin, Cloonacool, b. 1941, ord. 1970, South Africa
Brennan, Peadar, Cloonacool, b. 1935, ord. 1960, California
Conlon, Ambrose, Carntubber, b. 1905, Italy & England, d. 1979
Cryan, Martin, Tubbercurry, b. 1924, ord. 1959, Hong Kong
Cullen, Desmond, Tubbercurry, USA
Egan, Thomas, Cloonacool, b. 1925, ord. 1950, Africa
Flannery, Herbert A, Tubbercurry, b. 1891, England
Gallagher, John, Masshill, b. 1883, Los Angeles
Haran, Ignatius, Cloonacool, b. 1934, ord. 1959, USA
Henry, Denis, Cloonacool, b. 1942, ord. 1968, San Diego
Holohan, Thomas, Tubbercurry, b. 1921, ord. c.1947, Far East, d. 1999

Johnson, Kevin, Cloonacool, b. 1925, ord. 1959, Australia
Kelly, Patrick J., Doomore, b. 1942, ord. 1967, England, Kenya & Zimbabwe
Marren, Hugh, Carrowreagh Knox, b. 1945, ord. 1976, Atlanta, USA
Marren, Kieran, Tubbercurry, b. 1935, ord. 1959, USA
McCarrick, Martin, Doomore, b. 1884. ord. 1911, England. d. 1918
McCarrick, Roger, Cloonacool, b. 1935, ord. c.1961, France
McGuinness, J., Cloonacool, Australia
Morahan, Kieran, Tubbercurry, b. 1955, ord. 1980, Africa
Morahan, Seamus, Tubbercurry, b. 1924, ord. 1949, Japan
Neary, Thomas, Carrentubber, b. 1924, ord. 1948, USA
Nicholson, John, Ballyara, b. 1868, Galveston, USA
O'Connor, Denis, Masshill, b. 1894, Chicago, d. 1957
O'Grady, Thomas, Cloonacool, b. 1930, ord. 1956, Philippines & England, d. 2002
O'Rourke, P.A., Cloonacool, USA
Reynolds, Thomas, Cloonacool, b. 1915, ord. 1950, Africa & USA
Walker, Michael, Cloonacool, b. 1931, ord. 1957, Africa
Wynne, Roger, Cloonacool, b. 1911, ord. 1936, Australia, d. 1997

Sisters
Brennan, Mary, Tubbercurry, Mexico
Connolly, Norah, Carnaleck, b. 1910
Feehily, Mary Enda, Rathscanlon, Sunninghill, England, d. c.1990
Gallagher, Sr Henry, Rathscanlon, Sunninghill, England, d. 1992
Gallagher, Margaret Mary, Masshill, ent. 1965, Jefferson City, USA
Healy, Kathleen, Tubbercurry, prof. 1930, England
Johnston, Brigid, Carrentubber, b. 1925, prof. 1946, USA & Rome
McCarrick, Mary, Cloonacool, b. 1930, prof. 1952, New Zealand
McCarrick, Justine, Cloonacool, b. 1935, prof. 1956, Germany
McIntyre, Maureen, Cloonacool, b. c.1953, Australia
McVann, Sr, Cloonacool, England
Neary, Norah, Cloonacool, Scotland
Nicholson, Barbara, Tubbercurry, Birmingham, d. c.1980
Ross. Kathleen , Cloonacool, Australia
Sweeney, Norah, Doomore, b. 1921, prof. 1942, Fiji Islands

Brothers
Haran SJG, Eugene, Cloonacool, d. c. 1960

Achonry missionaries whose place of birth is unknown
Priests
Coen, Thomas, b. 1860, ord. pre-1895, Los Angeles
Devine, Denis, ord. c.1900, Elphin
Filan, Patrick, b. c.1855, Cistercian monastery, Leicester
Henry, Joseph, ord. c.1900, Chicago
Sweeney, Patrick, ord. pre-1800, USA
Wynne, Michael, ord. c.1900, Cincinnati, USA

APPENDIX 18: SCHOOLS IN 1825 AND 1835*

Schools & Teachers	Parish	Townland	1825 Teacher	Pupils	1835 Teacher	Pupils
	Achonry	Achonry	William Duggan	46	Martin Canovan	62
		Mullinabreena	John Kearns	60	Patrick Stenson	45
		Tubbercurry	John Hart	14	Patrick Coffy	53
		Tubbercurry	Pat Feheley	35	Patrick Disney	60
		Curry	James White	45	Bryan Kennedy	20
			John Wynne	18		
			Bryan Wynne	35		
			Patrick Griffith	130		
			Theopholis Golden	96		
			Peter Collins	42		
			Mr & Mrs Bartly	93		
			William Gardiner	64		
	Attymass	Mullahowney	Michael McDonnell	82	Margaret McDonnell	61
		Kilgella	Eneas McDonnell	86	Edward McNulty	80
		Currower	Patrick Diffely	13	Patrick McDonnell	112
	Ballymote	Ballymote	Pat O'Gara	100	Anthony Gallagher	100
		Ballymote	Jackson & Anne Hawkesley	115	Stewart & Catherine Woodland	128
		Diroone	John May	28	John May	74
		Knockadalteen	John McGettrick	34	John McGettrick	130
		Lissananny	Luke Feehily	22	John Hays	30
		Drumfin	John Kivlaghan	66	Catherine Ellis	40
		Branchfield	Thomas Brennan	60	John Rogers	130
					Sarah McGuinness	70
	Ballysadare	Ballysadare	Matthew Clifford	59	Bridget Tiernan	50
		Ballysadare	Hugh Gilmer	46	John McAlvee	123
					Hannah Palmer	60
					James Whiteside	70
		Killnamanagh	John Gallagher	50	John Gallagher	100
		Lugnadeffa	Luke Garry	–	John Jaiks	56
		Tubbercannon	Burke Brennan	40	Patrick Moore	20
		Luanuna	Charles Taafe	38	Peter McGauvran	35
		Lugawarry	Mary Anne Ellis	52	Thomas Carlow	80
		Knockbeg	Owen Gallagher	22		
		Lugnadeffa	Thomas Durkin	18		
	Ballaghaderreen					
		Ballaghaderreen	Edward Duffy	30	Edward Duffy	170
	(Kilcolman)					
		Ballaghaderreen	John Neilan	30	John Farrell	40
		Ballaghaderreen	Malachy Dowd	10	Patrick Murray	70
		Cragaghduff	Martin O'Hara	70	Martin O'Hara	79
		Derranacarta	John Duffy	60	Mary Matthews	71
		Monasteraden	John Casey	30	John Casey	131

*from Parliamentary Papers 1826-27, XII. I. & 1835, XXIV. I

Parish	Townland	1825 Teacher	Pupils	1835 Teacher	Pupils
(Castlemore)					
	Crunaun	Charles Shryane	28	Mary O'Donnell	105
	Cashelard	Michael Rush	62	Honor Giblin	101
	Rooskey	John Donohue	30		
Bohola	Bohola	Peter Walsh	60	James McManus	81
	Lismiraun	Mary Fitzgerald	34	Denis McDonnell	90
Bonniconlon	Bonniconlon	Michael Loftus	–	Anthony Tuffey	90
	Carrow	Patrick Langan	12	Patrick Langan	46
	Carrowlabane	Thomas Jordan	60		
Bunninadden	Tubberpatrick	Michael Irwin	49	Terence McHugh	76
(Kilturra)	Ballyfahey	Patrick Davey	42	Michael Rush	116
(Kilshalvey)	Trianvillan	Michael Gardine	40	James Anderson	314
	Clooncunny	Martin Higgins	50		
(Cloonoghill)	Moyrush	Luke McCoy	40	Thomas Carty	53
	Kilturagh	John Gorman	40	John Monaghan	106
	Bunninadden	Pat Callaghan	55		
Charlestown					
(Carracastle)	Carracastle	Patrick Gallagher	38	Michael Brennan	160
	Rooskey	Charles Shrihane	12	Michael Murray	50
	Lurga	Patrick Frain	22		
	Lavy	Laurence Duffy	25		
	Barroe	Michael Kelly	10		
	Kilbeha	Patrick Doherty	60		
Collooney	Collooney	John O'Brien	64	Hugh Brennan	136
(Kilvarnet)	Collooney	Mrs Frazier	33	Biddy McKim	109
	Collooney	John Bree	70	John Bree	45
	Ballinacarrow	Francis Harroghy	29		
	Carrowtearig	Robert Beattie	112	Michael Nulty	51
	Doragh	James O'Burne	48	Robert McAuley	88
	Templehouse	Jane Ellis	42	Jane Gunning	66
Coolaney	Coolaney	John Gibson	71		
	Coolaney	Elizabeth Davis	32	Elizabeth Davis	69
	Coolaney	Peter Ross	21	James O'Beirne	131
	Ballinvally	John Battle	50	Peter Redican	76
	Moymlough	Morgan Finn	34	Morgan Finn	35
	Carha	Peter Gilgan	–	Jane Mulherin	42
	Carrownacly	James Minane	19	James Minane	90
	Carrownacarrick	Andrew Lunney	52		
	Rathmacorick	Francis McDonough	48		
	Trimgrove	John Tanzy	34		
Foxford	Foxford	John Barden	50	John Barden	120
	Foxford	John Guthrie	50	Timothy O'Neill	74
	Boharshallagh	James Swift	51	Patrick Swift	135
	Cuilmore	Michael O'Brien	30		
	Toomore	Roger Sweeny	30		
Gurteen	Gurteen	Patrick Beirne	22	Peter Scanlon	88
	Moygara	Bartholomew Finn	22	James Brennan	61
	Kilfree	John Lea	24	Edward Mulrenan	57

Schools & Teachers

Parish	Townland	1825 Teacher	Pupils	1835 Teacher	Pupils
	Sraigh	John Nangle	20	James Scanlon	20
				Maria Gunning	49
				John Cunningham	45
				John Gildee	20
				John Hanner	66
				James Brett	49
				Terence McDermadroe	21
Keash	Keash	Patrick Rogers	30		
(Toomour)	Graniamore	John Moore	62	John Moore	70
(Drumatt)	Knockbrack	Manus McHugh	22	John Nangle	40
	Longwood	Francis Kenny	41	Francis Kelly	93
	Templevanny	Francis Soden	-	Francis Soden	136
Killasser	Lognahaha	Andrew Collins	70	John Loftus	130
	Boleyboy	James Durkan Sr	25	Michael Bryan	93
	Croghan	Edward Hart	65	John McNulty	84
	Kilduff	Arthur O'Neill	65	Edward Durkin	61
	Cartron	James Durkan Jr	57	Michael Durkin	85
	Killasser	Michael O'Donnell	34	Luke Heany	92
Kilmovee	Urlaur	Andrew Duffy	60	James Sheridan	77
	Glentavraun	James O'Brien	20	Owen Byrne	124
	Rodestown	Patrick O'Gara	54	Patrick Murphy	48
	Kilmorn	Patrick Carroll	49	Charles Carroll	74
	Corgarriff	Barth. Spelman	52		
	Raherolus	John O'Beirne	58		
Kiltimagh	Kiltimagh	Owen Reilly	70	Andrew & Mary Collins	114
	Kiltimagh	James Egan	30	Jane Robinson	69
				John Philbin	103
				John Sheeron	68
				Patrick Flaherty	178
Straide	Straide	Nicholas Hughes	76	Michael Hughes	35
	Deraneacha	Lewis Monaghan	45	John McNulty	50
				Peter Frane	45
				Anne Egan	111
Swinford	Swinford	John & Sarah Mullany	120	Eugene McGuire	104
		Ellen Gallagher	30	Mary Gallagher	24
	Tumgesh	J. G. Ormsby	26	James White	46
	Tullynahoe	Charles Taaffe	50	Thomas Enright	51
				Michael Stenson	50
				John Durkin	85
				Robert Jordan	51
(Meelick)	Meelick	Patrick Ryan	60	John Giblin	68
				Bridget Fleming	50
Tourlestrane	Kilmactigue	Thomas Leonard	60	Bridget Leyden	75
	Baratogher	John Jourdan	45	John Jourdan	134
	Drummartin	Thomas Henry	45	Thomas O'Gara	106
				Patrick Corcoran	60

APPENDIX 19:NATIONAL SCHOOLS AND TEACHERS 1832-1851

Achonry [1]

National Schools

Achonry Boys, 13 Nov 1844, application by Dean Hoare & James Gallagher PP for building grant on site given by John Armstrong, Chaffpool, 7 Aug 1845, grant given, teachers: Thomas Fenton (1846-48), John Dodd (1848), John Brennan, assistant (147-50)

Achonry Girls, as above, teachers: Hannah Fenton (1846), Jane Dodd (1848), workmistress, Ellen Brett (1850)

Carnegarragh, establ. April 1841, Jan 1842, application by Dean Hoare for teacher's salary, teacher, Patrick Griffith (1842-44), 1 Jan 1844 ceased to be NS

Carrowmore Boys, 22 July & 24 Aug 1833 applications for building grant and teacher's salary by Dean Theophilus Blakely & James Gallagher PP, teacher: John Dalton

Carrowmore Girls, as above, teachers: Mary Wynne (1837), Elenor McDonagh (1839), Penelope Dalton (1844), 15 April 1853, struck off the rolls 'as there is but one school room and the average attendance of both schools would not warrant a salary to two teachers'

Carrowrile, 1832, application by James Gallagher PP for teacher's salary and other requisites, teacher: Matilda Jennings

Attymass [2]

Treanlaur, 12 July 1839, applicant, Denis O'Kane PP (only one other school which is held in the parish chapel), 2 July 1840, grant given, 30 Dec 1841, grant cancelled as manager has determined to build another school.

Ballaghaderreen [3]

Aughalusta, establ. 1832, NS 4 Oct 1832; clerical applicants, B. Durcan & T. Mullaney, correspondant, D. Tighe. 1835, teacher: Martin McCormick

Backduff (Brusna), establ. 1831, NS 14 July 1832, as above, teacher: Patrick Murray

Ballaghaderreen, establ.1824, NS 28 Jan 1834, as above, teacher: Edward Duffy

Ballaghaderreen Girls, NS 10 Jan 1839, applicants, Rev. J. Seymour, Bishop McNicholas & Denis Tighe, teachers: Winny Giblin (1839), Honora Tully (1842), Jane McGawley (1846)

Monasteraden Boys, 14 Aug 1833, application by B. Durcan & T. Mullaney CC for building grant & teacher's salary, NS 29 Aug 1833, teacher: John Casey

Monasteraden Girls, as above, teachers: Mary McDonnell (1833), Mary Casey (1838), Honora Flaherty (1851)

Ballymote [4]

Ballymote, 17 Mar 1832, application by Patrick Durcan PP for building grant & teacher's salary. Terence Rodgers & Sarah McGuinness teach 120-150 boys & 90-100 girls in Ballymote chapel.

Ballymote Boys, NS 4 July 1833, applicants, Bernard O'Kane PP & Denis Tighe CC, teachers: Terence Rodgers (1833), Anthony Gallagher (1835), John May (1838), 17 Nov 1842, struck off the rolls, 24 May 1843 inspected, 17 July 1843, restored.

Ballymote Girls, 4 June 1840, application by B. O'Kane & J. Coghlan CC for teacher's salary which was granted 27 Aug 1840 to Sarah McGuinness.

Drumfin, NS 22 Aug 1833, applicant, B. O'Kane, teachers: John McGetrick (1833), John Ferrall (1835), Martin Battle (1842)

Emlanaughton (Littlebridge), 15 Nov 1832, application by B. O'Kane PP & D. Tighe CC, teachers: John May (1833), Andrew Neary and Michael Killoran (temporary), John Rodgers (1841)

1 ED 1/79, nos.10, 18, 55, 76, 99; ED 2/41, folios 20, 38, 64, 67, 108, 109, 157
2 ED 1/61, no.22; ; ED 2/32, folio 143
3 ED 2/32, folios 13, 19; ED 2/41, folios 15, 16, 70, 87; ED 1/61, nos.33, 70; ED 1/79, no. 14
4 ED 1/79, nos.3, 12, 39, 62, 112; ED 2/41, folios 13, 46, 47, 90

Kilmorgan, 17 Mar 1832, application by P. Durcan for a building grant & salary for John McGetrick who taught in Kilmorgan chapel for the last 8 years.
Knockmonagh, 4 April 1849, application for building grant by Denis Tighe PP

Ballysadare [5]

Ballysadare, 30 May 1850, application by Patrick Durcan PP for teacher's salary, teacher: Patrick McCarrick (McCormack?), workmistress, Alice Sheolan (1851)
Camphill Boys, 18 Oct 1834, application for building grant by P. Durcan & D. Tighe CC, NS 6 Nov 1834, teachers: Patrick McCormack (1836), Patrick Hurst (1839 temporary), Hugh Donohoe (1849), John Leonard (1851)
Camphill Girls, as above, teachers: Alice Sheolan (1836), Mary McDonnell (1838)
Liseneena Boys, 8 Feb 1835, application for building grant by P. Durcan, 4 June 1836, inspected, school 'perfectly finished', teachers: Hugh Donoghoe (1836), Francis McGovern (1849)
Liseneena Girls, as above, teachers: Judith Kilbride (1836), Eliza McDonnell (1838), Catherine Meredith (1846), Catherine Graham (1849)

Bohola [6]

Shanaghy, applicant, Peter Cooke PP, 17 Mar 1838, grant given, 22 Dec 1840, grant cancelled as manager, James Higgins, did not avail of it.
Tawnaghaknaff, 25 Nov 1839, applicant for building grant, James Higgins, 2 July 1840, grant given, 31 Mar 1840, grant cancelled as above.
Tounane, establ. 1834, NS 1 Oct 1839, applicant, James Higgins, teacher: James McManus.

Bonniconlon [7]

Bofield (Carrowcrom), NS 29 April 1845, Applicant, Bernard Egan PP, teacher: Michael Loftus
Bonniconlon (Kilgarvin), establ. 1818, NS 2 July 1840, applicant Thaddeus Mullaney, teacher: Anthony Touhy, workmistresses: Catherine Touhy (1845), Catherine Reilly (-1852), Jane Loftus (1852-)
Carha, NS 25 Aug 1842, applicant, Thaddeus Mullaney, teachers: Patrick Corcoran (1842-45), Myles Durcan (1845-1850), Michael Egan (1850)
Knockroe, NS 26 Oct 1848, applicant, Bernard Egan PP, teacher: Catherine Dockry

Bunninadden [8]

Doocastle, NS 3 Sept 1835, applicants, Thomas Healy & John Corley, teachers: John Fleming Lynch (1840), John Gallagher (1841), Terence McDermott (1842)
Doocastle Girls, N.S. 3 Sept 1835, applicants as above, teachers: Dorothea Lynch (1840-42), Mary Moffet (1842-45), Bridget Toolan (1846-48)
Killaville, 3 July 1832, application for teacher's salary by Bernard O'Kane & Thomas Healy, teacher: Michael Anderson (1832), workmistress: Eleanor Anderson (1851)

Carracastle [9]

Cloonfane, 20 Mar 1844, school being built on site given by Lord Dillon, teachers: Patrick Tarpey & Honor Boyle (1848)

Charlestown [10]

Bellaghy Boys, establ. 1839, NS 9 Dec 1841, applicant William McHugh PP, teacher: Michael

5   ED 1/79, nos. 28, 29, 116; ED 2/41, folios 28, 29, 32, 33, 80, 103, 129, 147
6   ED 2/32, folios 68, 114, 141; ED 1/61, no.23
7   ED 2/32, folios 70, 137, 190; ED 1/61, nos.2, 41, 105, 169
8   ED 2/32, folios 57, 58; ED 2/41, folios 4,73; ED 1/79, no.5
9   ED 1/61, nos.64, 164
10 ED 2/41, folios 59 & 60; ED 1/61, nos. 61,114,161; ED 1/79,no.65

Brennan. 17 May 1848 school transferred to Lowpark
Bellaghy Girls, as above, teacher: Margaret Brennan
Barnacogue, 20 Mar 1844, trustees, William McHugh PP, Francis O'Grady & Charles
Strickland, school built on site given by Lord Dillon

Collooney [11]
Ballinacarrow, 1851, application by Patrick Durcan PP for teacher's salary, teacher: Henry
Dwyer (1851), workmistress: Anne O'Connell (1855)

Coolaney [12]
Cabra, 28 Feb 1848, application for building grant by Patrick Hurst PP
Cappagh, 1852, application for teacher's salary for Hugh Healy
Coolaney, establ. 1830, 15 May 1845, application by Paul Henry PP for teacher's salary,
teacher: James Minane (-1847), 1847, school closed & used as meal depot, 2 Feb 1848, appli-
cation by Patrick Hurst PP for building grant
Dynode, July 1844, establ., 15 May 1845, application by P. Henry PP for teacher's salary for
Richard McCally, 1847 succeeded by J. Healy
Rockfield, 10 June 1850, application by Patrick Hurst for teacher's salary for Matthew Doyle,
workmistress, Rose Derrick (1853)

Curry [13]
Culla, 22 Feb 1841, application for building grant signed by John Flynn PP, Daniel Jones,
Benada Abbey and many others.
Curry, 1852, application by Michael Cawley CC & Luke Colleran, Bellaghy for teacher's
salary for Garrett Bourke, 1 Dec 1852, monitor, Luke Colleran, 1 Jan 1854, workmistress,
Mary Bourke

Foxford [14]
Foxford, establ. 1826, NS 24 Sept 1833, applicant, James Henry, teachers: Pat Swift (1833-
1837), Michael O'Brien (1837-1839), Andrew Collins (1839-41), John Cooke
Attimachugh, NS 25 Oct 1834, applicants, James Henry PP & Bernard Egan CC, teachers:
Michael O'Brien (-1837), Andrew Collins (1838), Peter McDonnell (1839), Margaret
McDonnell (1840), Michael Durcan (1847-49)

Gurteen[15]
Ardgallan, 1852, application by Peter Brennan PP for teacher's salary for Thomas Corcoran,
1852, workmistress, Anne Rourke, 8 May 1854, Corcoran resigned, 13 May, Rourke resigned
and school closed.
Ballynaclassa, 15 Aug 1844, application by P. Brennan for teacher's salary for Hugh Devine,
14 May 1845, application for same for workmistress, Anne Flanagan
Cloonenure, 15 Aug 1844, application by P. Brennan for teacher's salary, teachers: James
Brennan (1844-), Hugh O'Donnell, Patrick Carberry (-1854), workmistresses: Eleanor
McDonagh (1844), Anne Coleman (1845), Winifred Murray (1846)
Cloonloo, 12 June 1840, application by Constantine Cosgrave PP for teacher's salary, teacher:
Peter Scanlon (1840-)
Kilfree, 9 Feb and 11 May 1846, application by P .Brennan for salary for teacher, Michael
McGauran and for workmistress, Margaret Coen (Coyne?), who was Mrs McGauran by 1848

11 ED 2/41, folio 166
12 ED 1/79, nos.79, 80, 105, 106, 115; ED 2/41, folios 112, 113, 146, 169
13 ED 1/79, no.51; ED 2/41, folio 167
14 ED 2/32, folios 37, 146, 204; ED 1/61, no.52
15 ED1/79,nos.34, 40, 70, 71, 72, 91, 93, 94; ED2/41, folios 43, 100, 101, 117, 120, 142, 172

Killaraght, 7 Mar 1846, application by Constantine Cosgrave for salary for teacher, Laurence Corcoran

Lughome, establ. Aug 1845, application by Constantine Cosgrave for teacher's salary, teachers: George King (1846-47), Thomas Matthews (1847-51), 1 June 1851, school struck off the rolls as teacher was unfit and house unsuitable.

Mullaghroe, 15 Aug 1844 and 14 May 1845, applications by P. Brennan for teacher, John Tansey, and for workmistress, Jane Ward, Winifrid Finn (1845-51), Honor Tansey (1851-)

Ragwood, n.d. application by P. Brennan for building grant

Keash [16]

Drumaneel, 25 June 1840, application by James O'Hara PP for teacher's salary for Thomas O'Gara

Keash, as above for John Taaffe, 21 Nov 1840, application by same for building grant, 20 Dec 1845, application by same for salary for workmistresses: Catherine Taaffe (-1851), Anne Noon (1851-52), teachers: John Taaffe (-1847), Martin Carney (1847-52), Thomas Little (1852-)

Rathmullan, 1851, application by Constantine Cosgrave for teacher's salary for James O'Gara.

Templevanny, establ. 1824, July 1832, application by James O'Hara for teacher's salary for Francis Soden, NS 8 Nov 1832, 17 July 1845, Soden's salary withdrawn by the Board, 15 April 1847, school struck off the rolls.

Kilmovee [17]

Clooncarha, establ. in 1843, but held 'for many years previous in the chapel', 24 Mar 1844, school being built on site given by Lord Dillon, NS 10 Oct 1845, teacher: John Gallagher.

Kilmovee Girls, establ. Nov 1846, NS 1847, applicant, Charles Strickland, teacher: Margaret Dogherty

Tavrane Boys, NS 17 Dec 1840, applicant Patrick Sharkey OP, teacher: Matthew Cronin

Tavrane Girls, as above, teachers: Mary Woods (-1850), Honora Walsh (1850-)

Kiltimagh [18]

Bushfield, query, 23 April 1844, signed by B. Durcan PP & J. Brennan CC

Carrick, 4 May 1844, application for building grant signed by B. Durcan & J. Brennan

Canbrack, query, 22 April 1839, signed by B. Durcan PP & James Higgins CC

Greyfield, application for building grant by B. Durcan & J. Higgins, Jan 1840 grant given, Dec 1841 Durcan stated that he could not avail of the grant becaus he was unable to obtain a site.

Kiltimagh Boys, query 18 April 1839, signed as above. 2 July 1840, grant given by Board, 21 Nov 1840, Durcan stated that unless conditions of grants were changed he could not proceed. 23 Mar 1841 his request was denied and grant was cancelled.

Kiltimagh Girls, NS 17 Mar 1838, applicant, B.Durcan, teachers: Catherine Reilly (1840), Catherine Casey (1841)

Oxford, establ. 1839, NS 5 Sept 1839, teacher: Thomas Healy (1839-46)

Straide [19]

Straide, NS 20 Aug 1840, applicant John McHugh PP, teacher: James McNulty

Swinford [20]

Ballydrum, applicants, John Coleman PP & Constantine Cosgrave CC, 6 Nov 1334, building grant given by Board, 4 Nov 1836, inspected and building not yet commenced, 15 Dec 1836, grant cancelled.

16 ED 1/79 nos. 8, 43, 45, 46, 87; ED 2/41, folios 9, 44, 50, 93, 105, 135, 163
17 ED 1/61, nos.20, 68,136; ED 2/32, folios 127, 154, 156
18 ED 2/32, folios 61, 126139; ED 1/61, nos. 5,12, 72, 88
19 ED 2/32, folio 145; ED 1/61, nos.18, 19
20 ED 1/61, nos. 8, 126; ED 2/32, folios 49, 72, 115 & 116, 163 & 164

Faheens, applicants, John Coleman PP & James Higgins CC, 17 Mar 1838, grant given, 22 Dec 1840, grant cancelled

Meelick Boys, NS 31 Mar 1841, applicants, John Coleman PP & Michael Muldowney CC, teacher: Patrick Ryan (1842)

Meelick Girls, as above, teachers: Mary Fogarty / Haguerty? (1843), Mary Doyle nee Bolingbroke (1849)

Swinford Boys, NS 21 Nov 1939, applicants as above, teacher: Eugene Maguire (1841-45)

Swinford Girls, NS 25 Mar 1841, teachers: Mary Logan (1841-1847), Anne Duffy (1848), Winefrid Kearns, monitress (1850)

Swinford Workhouse, NS 24 Aug 1846, correspondent, Richard Kyle, clerk of the Union

Tourlestrane [21]

Benada Boys, application by Daniel Mullarkey PP, 29 Nov 1833, NS, teachers: John Jordan (1833-35), Pat Stenson (1835-)

Benada Girls, as above, teacher: Bridget Leydon, 17 July 1851, dismissed and school struck off the rolls

Castlerock (see also Mullany's Cross), 30 Sept 1844, application by D. Mullarkey for building grant, teacher: D.Mullarkey (1846), workmistress: Catherine Gilmartin (1856)

Kilmactigue, 26 Aug 1833, application by D. Mullarkey for building grant and teacher's grant, teachers: Michael O'Hara (1833-), Patrick Feely/ Feehily? (1841), workmistress, Bridget Feely (1845)

Largy, as for Kilmactigue, 1834, application for teacher's salary, teachers: Thomas O'Gara (1834), Pat Corcoran (1837), Stephen Hart (1841), Garrett Burke (1847), Stephen Donohoe (1852)

Mullany's Cross (see also Castlerock), 21 Oct 1842, application by D. Mullarkey for teacher's salary, teachers: John Jordan (1842), D. Mullarkey (1844). 25 Mar 1846, temporary school ceased and transferred to Castlerock

Tubbercurry [22]

Carrowntubber, 1833, application signed by James McHugh PP & Dean Blakely

Cloonacool Boys, 1833, application for building grant signed by James McHugh PP & Dean Blakely, 24 Oct 1834, grant of £50 'wholly inadequate', 11 Dec 1845, application signed by seven laymen (including Luke Brennan) for building grant, 18 June 1846 grant £100 made, teachers: John Balfe (1847), Bryan Kennedy (1848), Peter N. Burke (Jan. 1849), Martin Barrett (Sept. 1849)

Cloonacool Girls, as above, 13 Mar 1848, teacher's salary granted to Ellen Nenoe

Tubbercurry Boys, 1838?, application for building grant signed by James McHugh & Dean Blakely, teacher: Michael O'Brien (1841 – formerly Attimachugh & Foxford), monitors: Garrett Barry (1847), Patrick O'Brien (1853)

Tubbercurry Girls, as above, 23 Sept 1849 girls' school opened, teachers: Mary Anne Moffett (1840), Mathilda Nicholson (1842), workmistresses: Honor Healy (1852), M. A. Barry (1853), Eliza Connolly (1855)

21ED 1/79, nos.9,22,23,59,78,85; ED 2/41, folios 10, 11, 22, 23, 68, 74, 76, 88, 104, 111
22ED 1/79, nos. 26, 27, 35, 92, 104; ED 2/41, folios 35, 53, 118, 119, 126

APPENDIX 20: ST NATHY'S COLLEGE (-1995)[1]

St Nathy's College

Presidents: Edward Connington (1878-1881), Thomas Gilmartin (1881-1884), Michael E.Coleman (1884-1889), James Daly (1889-1911), Hugh O'Donnell (1911-1920), Ambrose Blaine (1920-1937), Eugene Foran (1937-1938), Thomas Curneen (1938-1949), James Colleran (1949-1955), John Walsh (1955-1960), Thomas Fleming (1960-1965), Charles Doherty (1965-1973), Thomas Lynch (1973-1973), Thomas Flynn(1973-1977), Robert Flynn (1977-1978), James Colleran (1978-1982), Andrew Johnston (1982-1996), Martin Convey (1996-)

Priests: Edward Connington (1878-1881), Thomas Gilmartin (1881-1884), Michael E. Coleman (1884-1889). Michael Doyle (1889-1893). James Daly (1889-1910), Patrick Morrisroe (1893-1895), James O'Connor (1893-1894), John Hurst (1895-1897), Thomas Quinn (1895-1899), J. Gallagher (1897), Charles Gildea (1899-1904), Thomas Gallagher (1900-1901), Dominick McGowan (1900-1901), Michael O'Doherty (1900-1904), Hugh O'Donnell (1904-1920), Ambrose Blaine (1906-1937), Patrick Bradley (1906-1907), John Cawley (1907-1908), Louis Henry (1908-1914), Eugene Foran (1911-1948), Roger McCarrick (1915-1930), Thomas H. Curneen (1920-1949), Patrick J. Vesey (1920-1924), John Kirwin (1923-1932), Francis Stenson (1923-1925), John Walsh (1926-1928) and (1931-1960), James Colleran (1929-1955), John F.O'Hara (1931-1935), John Wims (1932-1948), William Philbin (1934-1936), Thomas Foy (1935-1941), John O'Neill (1937-1941), Thomas Fleming (1937-1965), Joseph Higgins (1939-1956), James P. Walsh (1940-1947), Francis Cawley (1943-1963), Patrick Towey (1943-1946), Michael Keegan (1943-1964), John Tiernan, (1946-1968), James E. O'Hara (1947-1951), Charles Doherty (1948-1973), Thomas Vesey (1949-1955), Thomas Lynch (1949-1973), Padraig McGovern (1951-1957), Michael Duffy (1952-1969), Michael Giblin (1955-1977), Cornelius Gordon (1955-1964), Robert Flynn (1956-1978), James Gavigan (1957-1966), James A. Colleran (1960-1982), Louis Dunleavy (1962-1963), Gregory Hannon (1962-1982), Thomas Flynn (1964-1977), Michael Joyce (1966-1991), Andrew Johnston (1966-1995), Joseph Spelman (1967-1969), Patrick Lynch (1967-1981), James Finan (1968-1979), Michael Gallagher (1968-1969), Thomas Colleary (1972-1978), Joseph Caulfield (1978-1981), Martin Jennings (1979-1998), Thomas Towey (1980-1992), Andrew Finan (1980–), Francis Henry (1980-1983), Anthony Flannery (1983-1985), Peter Gallagher (1985-1995), Leo Henry (1986-), Martin Convey (1991–), James McDonagh (1995-2000)

Lay teachers: Mr O'Regan, Mr Barrett, Mr Carroll (1858-1878), Herr Thomas Litt (1898-1900), (Fr ?) Henry Fuller (1899-1900), B. Cullen (1903-1909), Thomas O'Donnell (1904-1906), George F. Cullen (1906-1934), Eugene O'Malley (1911-1912), Thomas O'Donnell (1916-1919), Charles Meade (1918-1919), William Carty, James J. Collier (1921-1934), Mr Gaughan (1928-1929), William O'Reilly (1928-1971), Richard Walsh (1934-1935), Capt Charles McDermott (1937), Larry McGettrick (1947-1950), Joseph (Michael?) Kirrane (1950-1952), Mrs Connolly (1962-1963), James Flanagan (1963-1998), Alex McDonnell, Pat Dooney, Thomas Fahy (1973-), Peadar O'Flaherty (1971- 1986), Patrick Mulligan (1974), Canice Clarke (1974-1986), Sean Kerins, Paul McGinly (-1977), John O'Mahony (1974-), Pat Curran (1977-), Patrick Henry (1978-), Oliver Feeley (1978-), Richard Barrett (1974- 1978), Thomas Sharkey, Patrick Hunt, Michael Hopkins (1977), Joe Keville (1978-), Declan Dunne (1982-3), Jacinta Shine (1983-4), Ann Farrell (1984-87), Gerard Carmody (1985-), Rena Burke (1987-), Teresa Egan (1988-), Mary Sheridan-Cunniffe (1987-), Edward Wray (1988-9), Oliver Lennon (1989-), Mary Finan (1989-), Cathal McGinn (1990-91),

1   From *St Nathy's College Journal* 1996

James Cunney (1990), James Tuohy (1990-), Brendan Foy (1990-), Thomas Ronayne (1990-), Seamus Curley (1990-), Michael Cormican (1992-), Kathleen Ryan (1992-93), Joe Kelly (1992-93), Helena Mulligan (1983-), Jacqueline Mullen (1989-), Oonagh Redmond (1993-), Kathrina Staunton (1993-), Rosemary Nee (1993-95)
Secretaries: Caitríona Cawley, Georgina Doohan, Ray Flynn, Geraldine Hanley, Mary O'Regan

APPENDIX 21: COLÁISTE PÁDRAIG, SWINFORD (1945-)

Priests: John O'Neill (1945-1969), Patrick Towey (1947-1960), Pádraig O'Grady (1947-1948), John McNicholas (1948-1970), Michael Duffy (1950-1951), Sean Leonard (1951-1980), Robert Flynn (1954-1954), Christopher Finan (1957-1984), Liam Cawley (1958-1964), Liam Swords (1964-1975), Michael Joyce (1967-1969), Martin Jennings (1975-1979), Joseph Caulfield (1980-1981), Barry Hogg (1981-1983), Leo Henry (1983-1986), Stephen O'Mahony (1984-2000), Adrian McHugh (2000-)   *Swinford*
Lay Teachers: P. Brennan, J. Broudet, Michael Campbell, Martin Carney, Philip Cawley, Fergus Coyle, Martin Crean, U. Dooney, Peter Fahy, N. Farry, Patrick Gallagher, Frank Gleeson, Gerry Kielty, John Kitching, Ambrose Lavin, Kevin McLoughlin, Máirtín McNicholas, John McNulty, Séamas Ua Mongáin, Ruairí Ó Núnáin, James B. Walsh, Patrick Walsh,

APPENDIX 22: MARIST CONVENT SECONDARY SCHOOL, TUBBERCURRY (1914-2002)

Sisters: Catherine Boland, Gertrude Byrne, Georgina Cawley, Marie Claire, Frances Cosgrove, Philippine Costello, Angela Cox, Teresa Cullen, Ciaran Earley, Cecilia Gavigan, Benen Henry, Mercedes Hunt, Mary Johnson, Eleanor Keaney, Raphael Keaney, Fanchea Kearns, Alvarez Kelly, Albert Kiernan, Maureen Layden, Maria Maye, Adrienne McCarrick, Ann McCormack, Marceline McCormack, Mary McDonagh, Brigid Mary McGuinness, Pacome McKevitt, Donal Moran, Margaret Mulligan, Calasanctius Murtagh, Ignatius O'Connor, Marie O'Reilly, Eunan O'Rourke, Peter O'Rourke, Gregory Quinn, Kathleen Regan, Moira Ryan, Dominic Rynne, Marie de Lourdes Towey, Geraldine Treacy, Marie Annunciata Varden, Venantius Walsh, Margaret Mary Wims.   *Tubbercurry*
Priests: Gerard Davey, Thomas Flynn, Francis Gallagher, John Geelan, Cornelius Gordon, Adrian McHugh
Lay-teachers: Rosemary Blaine, Mary Jane Brennan, Anna Brett, Linda Burke, Stan Burns, May Cahill, Ita Coleman, Carmel Collins, Mary Collins, Mary Conneely, Patrick J. Corry, Breege Corscadden, Doreen Craven, Mrs Cunnane, Pauline Cunnane, Ms Davis, Joyce Duffy, Edel Fagan, Celia Faul, Thomas Feeley, Geraldine Folan, Ursula Foran, Mary Fowley, Mary Gallagher, Veronica Gannon, Thomas Grogan, Patrick Hannon, Joseph Harney, Mary Hennessy, Mary Henry, Mary Hester, Margaret Houlihan, Bernadette Howley, John F. Kelly, Mary Kelly, Maureen Kerins, Oliver Lannon, Ann Lennon, Attracta Leonard, Seamus Loftus, Breege McCarrick, Edel McCool, Sinéad McGarvey, Kathleen McNulty, Patsy McVeigh, Eileen McEvilly, Mrs Meredith, Michael Middleton, Barbara Mitchell, Sean Mitchell, Ellen Moore, Marian O'Connor, Ms O'Hara, Richard O'Hara, Patricia O'Rourke, Nora Raftery, Rosanne Ravenscroft, Patricia Regan, Martina Roddy, Maura Selfe, Mrs Slevin, Pauline Stewart, Marian Wallace, Mary Walsh, Mary Watson, Claire Weber, Olive Wright, Angela Wrynn.

I am indebted to Brigid M. McGuinness SM for this list.

APPENDIX 23: ST JOSEPH'S SECONDARY SCHOOL, CHARLESTOWN 1942-2003

Charlestown   *Lay-teachers:* Phyllis Burke, Mary Casey, Darragh Coleman, Patricia Colleran, Kathleen Concannon, Martin Conlon, Gerry Conway, Austin Egan, Wilma Farrell, Bridie Fehily, Rita Griffin, Terry Griffin, Michael Hambley, Noel Kilkelly, Lorcan Leavy, Oliver Lennon, Mary McCarrick, Kay McIntyre, Marian Marren, John Meehan, Edel Nolan, Mary O'Connell, Philip O'Gorman, Gerardine O'Mahony, Cornelius O'Sullivan, Paddy Price, Harry Reilly, Sinéad Roache, Claire Robinson, Francis Ryan, Bernie Swords.

APPENDIX 24: BANADA ABBEY SECONDARY SCHOOL (1958- 2002)[1]

Principals: Paddy Tobin, Michael Collins
Priests: Jimmy Colleran, Seamus Collery, Liam Cawley, Louis Dunleavy
Sisters of Charity: Ann Dolores, Anne-Marie, Annunciata, Benen, Conleth, Dominica, Eileen, Elizabeth, Finbarr, Florence, Hilda, Joseph de Sales, Magdalene, Raphaelle, Rita, Thomas, Ursula
Lay-Teachers: Mary Brennan, Mrs Mary Brennan, Peadar Brennan, Brendan Burke, Breda Burns, Michelle Caden, Ciaran Cahill, Mai Cahill, Colette Carew, Derval Carolan, Andrea Carroll, Teresa Carroll (Keane), Joe Chestor, Kieran Christie, Miss Coffey, Jim Colleary, Luke Colleran, Catherine Collins, Michael Collins, Tom Coleman, Nuala Connolly, Bernardine Corcoran, Brid Corscadden, Claire Cowery, Mary Crowe, Jacqueline Dempsey, Marie Dolan, Angela Donaghue, Deirdre Donovan, Joe Duffy, Eugene Dunleavy, Frank Durkin, Sandrine Eirot, Maria Fahy, Anne Fallon, Maeve Flannery, Cathy Fleming, Ben Flynn, Nancy Flynn, Enda Forde, Marian Foy, Lawrence Frayne, Bernadette Frosberry, Catherine Gallagher, Mary Gallagher, Jacinta Gately, Patricia Gibbons, Tom Gilligan, Siobhán Gillespie, Pádraic Gilmore, Sheila Glavey, Mary Goldrick (Walsh), Mairéad Greene, Simon Griffin, Bernadette Groarke, Mary Halloran, Mary Hanley, Nuala Haran, Patrick Heffernan, Edel Hennigan, Eamonn Horkan, Yumiku Izumi, Christina Johnston, Tom Keane, Pat Kelly, Sharon Kelly, Stephen Kelly, Sylvan Kelly, Bríd Kenneally, Tom Kennelly, Jacqueline Kennedy, Teresa Kennedy, Maureen Kerins, Mary Jo Kilcoyne, Geraldine Kirrane, Noel Kissane, Martina Leahy, Mary Leavy, Maureen Leonard, Danny L'Homme, June Lynn, Martin McCarrick, Jean McConnell, Gary McConway, Siobhán McDonagh, Margaret McDonnell, Mary McDonnell, Yvonne McDonnell, Mrs McEvaddy, Harold McGovern, Ronan McGovern, Elaine McGowan, Bláithín McGrath, Tom McGuire, Margaret McHale, Caroline McHugh, Mr McIntire, Mary McKeon, Kathleen McLoughlin, Lorraine McLoughlin, Kevin McManamon, Aileen McPartland, Patsy McVeigh, Niamh Martin, Pádraic Maye, Ellen Moore, Maureen Moran, Lena Mullarkey, Helena Mulligan, Una Nealon, Liam Niland, Paul O'Brien, Marion O'Connor, Miss O'Connor, Mary O'Donaghue, Margaret O'Driscoll, Fergal O'Flaherty, Anne-Marie O'Hara, Patricia O'Hara, Con O'Meara, Ciara O'Shea, Mrs O'Toole, Margaret Phelan, John Quinn, Caitríona Rabbette, Patricia Regan, Joan Rennick, Murt Roache, Florence Rossignol, Mary Teresa Scanlon, Dermot Scully, Maura Selfe, Helen Shaughnessy, David Sheerin, Miss Smith, Swancha Stefan, John Swift, Sandra Tiernan, Anne Marie Tighe, Ita Tobin, Paddy Tobin, John Towey, Rhona Trench, Joe Varley, James Wade, Mary Walsh (Liston), Teresa Walsh, Mrs Watson, Mary Wilhare, Mary Wright, Brendan Wynne.
Secretary: Attracta Nealon. *Caretakers:* John James Cosgrave, John T. Durkin

---

[1] I am indebted to Michael Collins for the complete list of permanent and temporary staff. See David McVeigh, *For the Record: Banada Abbey Secondary School 1958-2002* for complete list of pupils

APPENDIX 25: ST JOSEPH'S SECONDARY SCHOOL, FOXFORD 1961-2003

Principals: Mary Alphonsus RSC, Conleth Cahill RSC, Margaret Ursula Doherty RSC, *Foxford*
Catherine Kieran Gorey RSC, Elizabeth Sanfey RSC, Bertie Towey, Sean McLoughlin,
Brendan Ford.

Lay-Teachers (present): Breege Blehein, Michael Brennan, Sean Butler, Mary Corcoran, Michael
Cosgrave, James Cunney, Seamus Durkan, Patricia Fielding, Deirdre Foy, Pádraig Gallagher,
Nora Giblin, John Halligan, Patricia Healy-Ruane, Marie Joyce, Catherine Kelly, Seamus
Kelly, Mary Lavin, Sharon McHale, Maria McHugh, Marian McNamara, Joe McNamara,
Emma Mannion, Mary O'Connell, Geraldine O'Haire, Breege O'Hara, Maeve O'Reilly,
William Thornton

APPENDIX 26: ST MARY'S SECONDARY SCHOOL, SWINFORD [1]

Lay-Teachers: Mrs Allen, Vincent Armstrong, M. Bilbow, Garry Carey, Sarah Carpenter, Mary *Swinford*
Casey, Edel Casserly, Lynn Coffey, James Concannon, Helen Conneely, Gus Conry, Declan
Costello, Teresa Costello, Barbara Daly, Laura Doherty, Mary Doherty, Moira Dolan, Fiona
Duddy, Mary Dumphy, Eilish Durkan, Mary Howley, Bridie Fitzpatrick, Colette Frain, Teresa
Gallagher, Ann Gannon, Catherine Gavaghan, Angela Gill, Ruth Glennon, Joanne Goggin,
John Golden, Mairéad Golden, Tonya Golding, Michael Gordon, Sinéad Groarke, Mary
Hanley, Maureen Hefferan, Delia Hegarty, Fiona Hegarty, Olivia Hegarty, Mary Hennigan,
Mary Hester, Simon Hierle, Eamon Horkan, Mr Horkan, Mary Howley, Catherine Hughes,
Marian Hughes, Maura Hurst, Monica Keane, Mary Kelly, Mary Kelly, Joe Kennedy, Eugene
Kenny, Siobhán Kenny, Marie Kenny, T. J. Kilgallon, Marjorie Killalea, Mary Larkin, Mary
Lavin, Colette Lee, George Lee, Darragh Leonard, Deirdre Linnane, Paul Lundy, Máire
McCallion, Sheila McDonagh, Margaret McDonnell, Lynette McGarry, Ceola McGowan,
Bríd McGrath, Damien McGrath, Deirdre McGuinness, Miss McGuinness, Ultan Macken,
Maureen McNeela, James Maloney, Sean Mitchell, Susan Moran, Tomas Morley, Jacqueline
Mullen, Michael Mulligan, Christina Murphy, Maria Needham, Donal O'Beara, Rody
O'Brien, Bobby O'Connell, Cora O'Connell, B. O'Connor, Kathleen O'Connor, Joe O'Dea,
Angela O'Doherty, Marie O'Neill, Gaelle Ordeig, Maureen Owens, Margaret Phelan, John
Prenty, Mairéad Quinn, Maureen Reddington, Christine Regan, Noleen Smyth, Mary Soden,
Margaret Stack, Olive Swords, Paul Toal, Joan Walsh, John Walsh, Miss J.Walsh, Seamus Walsh
Auxiliary Staff: Tom Brennan, Mary Conboy, Cathy Conlon, Johnny Duffy, Mary Horkan,
Pat Moore, Gerry Moran, Michael O'Neill

APPENDIX 27: ST LOUIS SECONDARY SCHOOL, KILTIMAGH

Regina Anderson, Gerry Boyle, Maura Brennan, Ronan Brett, Aiden Burke, Sally Anne Byrne, *Kiltimagh*
Shane Byrne, Nora Cafferky, Tom Caulfield, Bríd Clancy, Catherine Collins, Karen Convey,
Patricia Creighton, Madeleine Cunnane, Linda Davey, Don Dillon, Ann Dingerkus, Cahil
Doherty, Carmel Dooley, Tony Duffy, Murt Dunleavy, Teresa Durkan, Áine Egan, Philomena
Farragher, Pádraig Filan, Andrew Finn, Richard Finn, Deirdre Fitzsimon, Marie Flanagan,
Terence Flanagan, Mary Freely, Evelyn Giblin, Angela Gill, Maureen Gilrane, John Glavey,
Christine Gormally, Ann Groark-Murphy, Renee Harkin, Rosario Heaney, Sally Higgins,
Fionnuala Jordan, Bernie Keane, Anna Kenelly, Netta Kennedy, Chris Kennelly, Carmel
Kiernan, Paddy Lavelle (Deputy Principal and Principal), Rita Lynch, Finola Lyons (Deputy
Principal), Mary McDonnell, Michael McFaddan (Principal), Mai McGreavy, Muriel
McNicholas, Catherine McNulty, Mary McNulty, Hugh McTigue (Deputy Principal and
Principal), Andrea Maloney, Angela Maloney, Carmel Mangan, Mary Mannion, Kevin Meers,
Geraldine Molloy, Áine Moran, Mai Morrisey, Michael Mulvihil, Denise Nagle, Peigín Ní

---

1   Information compiled by Mairéad Golden

Kiltimagh   Fhlaithearta, Máire Ní Mhaoilmhichíl, Máire Ní Scolaí, Sinéad Noon, Róisín O'Boyle, Nora O'Connor, Simone O'Neill, Brenda Ormsby, Fr Michael Quinn, Michelle Rabbete, Oonah Redmond, Gerry Riordan, Mary Smyth, Annie M. Thompson, Rhona Tiernan, Mary Tierney, Rhona Trench, Adele Tuffy, Aideen Ueno, Bríd Uí Néill, Joe Waldron, Michael Walsh, Nuala Whelan

APPENDIX 28: VOCATIONAL SCHOOLS

Ballaghaderreen   *Ballaghaderreen Vocational School:*[1]
Principals: Michael Joseph Tiernan, Bob O'Connor, Peader Noone, Oliver Hynes, Patrick Hunt, Niall Sharkey, Edward Reilly & Alex McDonnell.
Teachers: Denis Boyce, Mary Callaghan, Thomas Callaghan, Vincent Carroll, Bernardine Caron, Liam Caron, Kitty Chapman, Patsy Chapman, Thomas Colleran, Mr Coppinger, Una Cox, K. Curley, Marie Delaney, Patrick Dooney, Una Dooney, Michael Duignan, Miss Duke, Michael Edgeworth, Salome Egan, Kathleen Fitzmaurice, Mr Foley, Maureen Glynn, Carmel Harrison, Bernadette Jordan, Miss Keyes, Eugene McCarthy, Gerry McGarry, Anne McGivney, Muriel McKeown, Joe McNicholas, Pauline Martin, Geraldine Moran, Liam Morris, John Murray, Anne Naughton, Martin Naughton, Sean O'Flanagan, Mr O'Mahoney, Mrs Phillips, Nancy Reidy, Mr Rooney, Michael Scally, Mary Sharkey, Thomas Sharkey, Evelyn Sweeney, Pat Taffe, Fintan Temple, Renie Webb, William Webb

Gurteen   *Gurteen Vocational School*
Staff members since the school opened in 1954: Judith Bailey, Maura Brett, Mary Brody, Linda Burke, Liam Caron, Kieran Christie, Paddy Conheady, Joe Connaghton, Aine Costello, Michael Costello, Michael Cummins, Sr Dominick, Teresa Durkin, Sr Emmanuel, Tom Finan, Michael Finneran, Norah Fitzpatrick, Martin Flynn, Felix Gaffney, Christy Gallagher, Fred Gallagher, Mary Gallagher, Carmel Gavigan, Eimear Harte, Gene Harte, Denis Johnson, Ted Kelleher, Eamon Kilgannon, Terry Leyden, Fergal Lyons, Clare Maloney, Colm Mullarkey, Sean Mulvey, Don Murray, Maura Noone, Una O'Gara, Patricia O'Hara, Teresa O'Malley, Eoin O'Slattera, John Reid, Diane Roemer, Nicholas Ryan, Ben Strong

Swinford   *Swinford Vocational School*
Colm Carter, J. Casserly, Miss K. Cunningham, Renée McManus, Michael Mulligan, Martin O'Kelly, Louis O'Malley, Owen Roe O'Neill, Marie O'Neill, Sean O'Regan, Miss A. Ryan, Edward Thornton

APPENDIX 29: RECIPIENTS OF QUAKER GRANTS DURING THE GREAT FAMINE

Quaker Grants   *Parish Priests:* James Henry Bunninadden, Daniel Mullarkey, Kiltimagh, John Coghlan, Kilmovee, James Higgins, Charlestown, Denis Tighe, Ballaghaderreen, Denis O'Kane, Carracastle and Roger Brennan, Adm., Tourlestrane.
Curates: Michael Muldowney, Achonry, P. J. O'Connor, Bohola and Patrick Groarke, Kilkelly.
Ministers: Dean Hoare, Achonry, Archdeacon Verschoyle, Coolaney, John Garrett, Ballymote, William Tyndall, Kilmactigue, B. W. Eames, Swinford, John Hamilton, Tubbercurry, Henry Perceval, Templehouse, E. A. Lucas, Collooney, Geoffrey Mostyn, Foxford and Brownslow Lynch, Kiltimagh.
Laymen: G. V. Jackson, Carramore, Ballina, Charles Strickland, Loughglynn, J. A. Holmes, Clogher, Ballaghaderreen, Dr Ulic Burke, Swinford, Henry Joseph McCarrick, Aclare, Joseph

---

1   Alex McDonnell, *St Nathy's College Journal* 1996, p 45

McDonnell, Doocastle, Edward P. McDonnell, Kilkelly, John Bolingbroke, Meelick and William Fetherstone, Tourlestrane.

Women: Mrs Jones, Benada Abbey, Miss Perceval, Templehouse, Arabella MacDermot, Coolavin, Elisabeth Holmes, Clogher, Ballaghaderreen, Frances Kelly, Ballaghaderreen, Abby Fleming, Keash, Catherine Rice, Achonry and Kate P. Thompson, Knockadoo House, Coolaney.

Quaker Grants

APPENDIX 30: DR MACCORMACK'S RELIEF FUND 1879-80[1]

Date		Donor and Address	Amount
Dec	23 1879	Per P. Egan, Dublin from Messrs Boutellan & Co, Cognac, France	£10
	24	T. D. Sullivan, part of a sum collected by	
		Miss Fanny Parnell, New Jersey	£4
		J. T. Payne, Natchez, Miss.	£5
	28	Most Rev. Dr Croke, Archbishop of Cashel	£50
		Joseph McManus, 2 Upper Gardiner St, Dublin	£1
		Timothy Byrne, Athy	£1
	29	Rev J. Petit, St Patrick's Training School	£5
	30	Rev John Behan, St Nicholas, Francis St, Dublin	£50
		Miss O'Byrne, Ulverton Cottage, Dalkey	£1
	31	Rev William Cullen, Liscarton Castle, Navan	£5
Jan	3 1880	Edward Magee, Lombard Chambers, Liverpool	£20
		'Lover of the Irish Poor' per Rev Matt Doyle, Kilmeade, Fonstown	£20
		Thos. Strickland, 39 Dame St, Dublin	£5
		Thos Farrell, 21 Fitzwilliam Place, Dublin	£1
	7	Right Rev. Dr O'Reilly, Bishop of Liverpool	£50
		John Lynch, solr., Liverpool	£1
	8	Dublin Diocesan Collection	£150
		Edward Hogan, 2 Abercorn Terrace, North Circular Road, Dublin	£5
	9	From an American per Sr M. Francis Clare, Kenmare	£10
	10	Paul Cullen, Prospect, Victoria Park, - , Liverpool	£10
	11	Bishop of Down & Connor	£5
	13	Primate of All Ireland	£10
	14	Dublin Diocesan Collection Committee	£200
		Miss E.A. Surtees, Balnagown Castle, Parkhill, R.shire,	£10-2-0
		Two French Ladies by M. Louis Marest, Amiens	£10
	15	John Lynch, solr., Bootle, Liverpool	£1
	16	Hugh Cullen, Oak Hill Park, Old Swan, Liverpool	£50
	24	National Land League per M. Davitt	£100
		M. Louis Marest, Amiens	£4
	26	Dr Gilmour, Bishop of Cleveland	£200
		Dr O'Connell, Bishop of Marysville,	£37-18-0
	29	St Vincent's College, Castleknock	£10
		Archbishop of Dublin	£200
	30	John Lynch, Bootle, Liverpool	£2
Feb	2	Rev E.F. Prendergast, St Malachy's, Philadelphia, USA	£57-4-11
		V. Rev. J.W. Bewick (portion of the Hexham & Newcastle collection)	£100
	3	Rev Michael O'Brien, Lowell, Mass. USA	£40
	4	Wm. J. Power, 225 North Eighteenth St, Philadelphia	£10-4-11

MacCormack's Fund

1 ADA

MacCormack's Fund	Date	Donor and Address	Amount
		Rev Francis P. O'Neill, St James' Church, 3722 Chestnut St, Philadelphia	£61-12-0
		J. Plunkett, 250 West 19 St, New York	?
	7	Rev Thomas Kieran, St Anne's Church, 31 Ward, Philadelphia	£40
		Belfast Collection per Bishop of Down & Connor	£50
		Fr. Barry, America, per Bishop of Elphin	£50
	9	Archbishop of Philadelphia	£100
	10	Bishop of Liverpool	£50
	11	A priest of San Francisco, California	£6
		Bishop of Rochester, USA	£70
		Archbishop of Dublin	£300
	14	John Lynch, solr., Bootle, Liverpool, (4th sub.)	£2
	17	Achonry portion of Holy Father's & Propaganda's donations	£17-15-10
		Rev H. Dudley Filan, Philadelphia	£20
		Rev Michael Filan, Philadelphia	£40
		Bishop of Providence, USA	£100
	19	Diocese of Chicago	£205-15-3
		Diocese of Hartford	£200
		Diocese of Fort Wayne	£50
	23	Archbishop of Philadelphia (2nd remittance)	£50
		Relief Committee, Sterling, USA per Rev C. J. O'Callaghan	£5
	24	Rev H.P. Fleming, St John's Church, Orange, New Jersey	£20-12-0
		Augusta, Ga., per Mr Austen Mullarkey, of which Ballymote received £20 per Dean Moore	£100
		L'Univers per M. L. Veuillot	£39-11-3
	25	V. Rev G. Carter, Hendon, N.W. London	£1-15-0
		Mons. Freppel, Bishop of Angers, France (2,000 fr)	£78-19-10
	27	Bishop of Ferns	£8
		Coadjutor Bishop of St Paul's, Minnesota	£40
Mar	1	Bishop of St John, New Brunswick, per Bishop of Elphin	£50
		Bishop of St Joseph, Missouri, per Bishop of Limerick	£20
		Portland (U.S.) Relief Committee per Rev D. M. Beadley	£33
		Bishop of Rochester USA (2nd remittance)	£20
		Baltimore USA Irish Relief Committee per Mr Foley	£400
	2	Rev A. J. Gallagher, St Patrick's Church, Pottsville, Pa. USA	£50
		Right Rev Dr Hennesy, Bishop of Dubuque	£100
	3	Archbishop of Philadelphia (3rd remittance)	£200
	4	Bishop of Alton, USA per Archbishop of Tuam	£150
	7	Monsieur L. Veuillot	1,000 frs
	9	Eveque d'Autun, France	500 frs
		Bishop of Covington, Ky., USA	£100
		Mr P .J. Enright, Decorah, Iowa, USA	£6
		V.Rev Dr Mullen, Adm.of the Diocese of Chicago	£308-9-2
		Bishop of Albany, N.Y.	£308-0-2
		Diocese of Burlington per V. Rev. T. Lynch V.G.	£50
		Rev P. Fitzsimmons, Rector, Church of the Immaculate Conception, Camden, New Jersey, USA	£30
	11	Philadelphia Irish Relief Committee per Wm. Thompson	£100
		Rev P. F. Connolly, St Mary's Church, Bodenstown?, New Jersey, USA	£41-0-6

Date		Donor and Address	Amount	MacCormack's Fund
		Right Rev Dr Mullen, Bishop of Eric, USA	£100	
	12	Archbishop of Dublin	£400	
		Pottsville USA grant for Kilmovee & Lisacull	£21	
		Bishop of Springfield, USA	£200	
		Bishop of Fort Wayne, Indianapolis, USA	£50	
		Rev R. F. Byrne SJ, Trinity Church, Georgetown, USA	£20-8-2	
Mar	18	Rev D. M. Bradley, Bishop's House,Portland,USA	£22-15-0	
		Bishop of Los Angeles	£30	
	19	Bishop of Salford per V. Rev Canon Sheehan VG	£150	
		Mrs Ellen Ewing Sherman, 817 15th St, Washington	£162-17-7	
	22	Bishop of Grass Valley, per Rev G. Montgomery, San Francisco	£11	
		Rev D. J. Casey, Campbellford, Ontario, Canada	£41	
		Cardinal McCloskey, Archbishop of New York	£250	
	23	Right Rev Dr O'Hara, Bishop of Scranton, USA	£150	
	25	Rev. T. Keates, St Mary's, Bermingham, (from one of his flock)	£5	
		Rev. John O'Brien, St Augustines, Port Elizabeth, South Africa	£100	
	27	Irish Relief Association, St Louis, USA	£20	
		Bishop of Rochester, USA	£20	
	30	Mrs Ellen Ewing Sherman, Washington	£41-12-9	
		Bishop of St Paul, USA	£51-0-5	
		Bishop of La Crosse, USA	£42-13-0	
		Bishop of Buffalo, USA	£150	
		Archbishop of Philadelphia	£100	
		Nun of Kenmare	£50	
April	8	Bishop of Brooklyn, USA	£212-4-7	
		Rector of the Seminary of St Francis de Sales, Milwaukee for Lixnaw & Ballaghaderreen convents	£24	
		Archbishop of Toronto, Canada	£61-11-1	
	13	Rev G. P. Coghlan, St Aloysius' Church, Pottstown, Pa., (to be equally divided between Foxford & Swinford)	£20	
		Bishop of Erick, USA	£50	
		Bishop of La Crosse, Wisconsin, USA	£13-11-1	
	19	Mrs General Sherman, Washington	£32-5-2	
		Mayor of Charleston, USA	£50	
		Rev T. H. Wallace, St Joseph's, Lewiston, Maine	£12-2-0	
		Rev P. E. Smyth, St Bridget's Church, Jersey City	£10	
	20	Archbishop of Dublin	£400	
	22	Bishop of Alton, USA per Archbishop of Tuam	£50	
		James O'Brien, 1106 S. Broad St, Philadelphia	£10	
		Very Rev Aug. Benomes, VG, Indianapolis	£14-12-6	
May	1	Bishop of Cleveland, USA	£105	
		Rev J. J. Hynes, Chico, California per Rev G. Montgomery	£10	
		Cornelius Horgan, Pittsburg, USA	£40	
		Bishop of Dubuque, USA	£100	
	12	Rev Thaddeus Hogan, Trenton, New Jersey	£10	
	14	Rev J.A. Kendall, Bellefontaine, USA	£25-3-0	
	28	Thos. Hopkins, Pottsville, USA	£5	
		Irish Philadelphia Committee per Wm. Thompson, chairman	£23-10-4	
		Archbishop of San Francisco per Archbishop of Tuam	£50	

MacCormack's Fund

Date	Donor and Address	Amount
June 3	Archbishop of Dublin	£400
	M. Louis Veiullot, editor of *L'Univers*	£39-8-0
	St Louis Irish American Relief Association per Peter L. Foy, president	£50
16	Rev John O'Brien, St Augustine's, Port Elizabeth, South Africa	£100
June 19	From Chicago per Land League	£44-14-4
27	Archbishop of Cashel	£200
July 1	M. Louis Veiullot, *L'Univers*, Paris	1000 frs
	Mrs Waters, Edenballymore, Derry	£4
3	Rev D.J. Reardon, Chicago	£40-13-0
11	Rev D.J. Casey, Campbellford	£12-5-5
July 18	Rev H. Beerhorst, Pastor of Elen Grove	£26-6-2
	Sr M. F. Clare (Kenmare) for the fever-stricken	£100
	Fr O'Connor, Enniscorthy	£25
	Mr O'Brien (General Post Office, Dublin)	£2
27	Bishop of Dubuque	£200
29	Very Rev R.A. Coffin, Clapham, London	£5
	Rev W. Timothy, Shipston on Stour, per Bishop of Clonfert	£25
Aug 13	Archbishop of Dublin	£417-14-7
	Rev H. Farrelly per Mrs Healy, Haristown	£20
Sept 6	Bishop of Liverpool (for Sisters of Charity)	£9-7-!0
	Bishop of Kildare	£20
Total		£10,419 1s 5d

APPENDIX 31: RELIEF COMMITTEES 1880

Relief Committees

Achonry: Chairman, Capt. J.W. Armstrong, vice-chairman, P. Lowry PP, treasurers, Canon Heather, rector, Achonry and P. Lowry PP, secretary, Michael Keveney CC, members, Dr Flannery, dispensary, Tubbercurry, Dr Roe, dispensary, Coolaney, P. J. McKim PLG, farmer, Branchfield, Edward Martin, farmer, Abbeyview, Ballinacarrow, William Crosbie, farmer, Carrowcorragh, Tubbercurry, William Doherty, farmer, Mullaghanarry, do, John Allen, farmer, Tubbertelly, do, James Healy PLG, Carniard, do, Dominick O'Donnell, farmer, Carrowrile, Ballinacarrow

Attymass: Chairman & treasurer, Rev John O'Grady, secretary, Daniel J. Henry, members, E. H. Perry, Protestant, James Scott, Protestant, Thomas Scott MD, Protestant, Rev Mr Chapman, Protestant curate, Roger Irwin, William Irwin, P. Woods, P. Dillon, merchant, Ballina, J. J. Kenny, merchant, Ballina

Ballaghaderreen: Chairman, Bishop Francis Joseph MacCormack, secretary, Patrick C. Peyton, merchant, treasurers, John Flannery, landed proprietor and merchant, James Gordon, merchant, members, O. Stenson, Adm, Denis O'Hara CC, Andrew Dillon MD, Stephen McDermott MD, Henry Stewart, Protestant and large land-holder, John Cawley, foreman, Monica Duff's

Ballymote: Chairman, Capt. Richard Gethin JP, vice-chairman, Matthew Finn PP, secretary, Jackson Hawksby, treasurer, Dean Moore, members, R. Morrison, merchant, M. Flannery, do, J.G. Reynolds, solicitor, M. Davy, shopkeeper, Patrick Berren, do, Henry Rogers, do, R. L. Morrison, do, J. D O'Brien, do, John Dockry, do, James B. O'Brien, do, B. Coghlan, do, J. A. O'Brien, do, Patrick Coghlan, do, Patrick Dawson, do, Michael Keenan, do, Michael Judge, do, Patrick Flanagan, do, A. McMunn, medical officer, Robert A. Duke JP, R & R. Gorman, merchants, J. M. L. Tew, manager, Ulster Bank, C. W. Gillmor, farmer, John Tighe, farmer, John Cogan, farmer, James Gormley, farmer

Bohola: Chairman, Thomas Judge PP, vice-chairman, D. H. Mellet, treasurer, John Aitken, secretaries, P. Clarke Jr, Thomas King & Martin Sheridan, members, P. Clarke PLG, Dominick Jordan, P. Naughton, Jacob White, Samuel Higgins

Bonniconlon: Chairman, Peter Harte PP, vice-chairman, Charles Downing JP, treasurer, John Beatty PLG, secretaries, Patrick Walsh, national teacher, Carnaglough Lodge and Michael Loftus, national teacher, members, J. S. Darling, Thomas H. Scott MD, Rev W. Skipton, rector, Ballina, Thompson M. Connell, Presbyterian farmer

Bunninadden: Chairman, Canon James McDermott PP, vice-chairman, Canon Heather, rector, treasurer, Joseph McDonnell D'Arcy, secretary, John Ormsby Cooke, members, Dominick O'Connor PLG, Dr Flannery, Dr Phillips, Dr Roe, Dr Walsh, Martin D'Arcy, C. Phibbs JP, M. Burke CC, R. McDermott, John O'Dowd, Charles Grahame, Pat Murray, Bart. Roddy

Carracastle: Chairman, Patrick Durcan PP, vice-chairman, P. C. Philllips MD, secretaries, Thomas Davey and Michael Casey, members, P. Mannion CC, Thomas Richardson, Patrick Boland, Michael Phillips, Thomas McCaffrey, John Brennan, Michael Vesey, John Peyton, John Regan, Patrick Griffin, Henry O'Hara, Martin Hunt, Patrick Doherty, Patrick Tonra, Patrick Cosgrave

Charlestown: Chairman, Thomas Loftus PP, secretaries, Michael J. O'Doherty and J. Doherty, treasurer, Hibernian Bank, Tubbercurry, members, James Fitzgerald, merchant, J. W. Mulligan, do, P. W. Mulligan, do, J. M. Henry, do, Patrick Mulroony, do, John Doherty, do, Patrick Doherty, do, Patrick J. Doherty, do, James Gallagher, do, John Cassidy, do, Thomas Murphy, do, P. A. Mulligan, do, John Morrisroe, do, John McDermott, do, Bushfield, Michael McDonnell, do, Michael Moffatt, do, Lowpark, Henry Campbell, do, Patrick Harrington, do, James C. Brady PLG, Hagfield House, Michael J. Doherty, national teacher, John Doherty, do, Tample, Luke Lavin, do, Tarrigna, Patrick J. Cassidy, do, Glann, Michael Cassidy, do, Barnacuige, John Marren, do, Corthoon, Patrick E. Henry, farmer, William Kelly, do, Cashel, John Costelloe, do, Hagfield, James Higgins, do, Bracklough, John O'Donnell, do, John Gallagher, do, Phillip Mulligan, do, Glann, Hugh Cassidy, do
N.B. No Protestant clergyman in this district.

Collooney, Ballysadare, Ballinacarrow: Chairman, Colonel Cooper, treasurer, George Allen, secretaries, William Heron and Dr Moloney MD, members, Rev Mr Hewson, rector, Collooney, Venerable Archdeacon O'Rorke PP, Rev Mr Jamieson, rector, Ballysadare, Rev P. Mulligan CC, Alexander Sim, merchant, Collooney

Coolaney: Chairman, Archdeacon Hamilton Townsend, Rathbarron, secretary, P. J. McDonald PP, treasurer and assistant-secretary, Charles McKensie, sub-agent, Annaghmore, members, Rev Mr Little, Coolaney, John McManus, farmer, Coolaney, John Battelle, shopkeeper and farmer, do, R. Phibbs PLG, farmer, do, John McHugh PLG, farmer, Carrowloughan, Thomas Henry, farmer, Killoran, Dr St George Roe, dispensary district, Coolaney, Martin McCarrick, John Tahoney

Curry: Chairman, Canon Peter O'Donoghue PP, vice-chairman, Luke Colleran, secretary, John Gunning CC, treasurer, manager, Hibernian Bank, Tubbercurry, members, James Colleran, James Johnstone, Peter Colleran, John Brennan, Dominick Murphy, James Kennedy, Hugh Gallagher

Foxford: Chairman, Michael O'Donnell PP, vice-chairman, Rev R. J. Eames, Clk, Foxford, secretary, Major D. R. Fair JP, treasurer, S O'G McDermott JP, Cloongee House, members, L. N. McDermott MD, Belgariff House, John McGloin, landed proprietor, Matthew Sheils, farmer

Gurteen: Chairman, Abraham Powell, Tinnacara, vice-chairman, Roger Brennan PP, secretary & deputy vice-chairman, Rev W. J. Haire, treasurer, R. Powell, Cuilmore, members, James P. Costello, Kilfree, James McKeon PLG, Thomas Leonard PLG,, James Hunt, P. Hunt CC, Dr Walsh

Relief Committees   *Keash:* Chairman, Matthew Finn PP, Ballymote, vice-chairman, Mark Cooke PP, Keash, secretaries, Joseph Gorman and James Murphy CC, Keash, treasurer, Richard Gorman PLG, Templevanny, members, John Finn PLG & farmer, Keash, Abraham Heron, deputy Co Surveyor, Abbeyfield, Timothy Kielty, farmer, Rooskey, Rev John Dewart, the Manse, Ballymote, Richard Knott, gentleman, Battlefield

Killasser: Chairman, Roger O'Hara PP, secretary, Thomas Bowler CC, treasurer, manager, Hibernian Bank, Swinford, members, Dr O Grady MD, Swinford, Dr McDermott MD, Foxford, S O'G McDermott JP, Foxford, Rev J. Eames, rector, Foxford, Francis Keane, landed proprietor, Killasser, Michael McNulty, landed proprietor, Cullen, Foxford, Patrick Keane PLG, Blackpatch, Swinford, Martin Peyton PLG, Clooneanra, do, George Cuffe, farmer, Carramore, do, Peter Gallagher, farmer, Parkroe, Killasser, Michael J. Harte, national teacher, Knocks, Killasser, Patrick O'Keane, national teacher, Killasser, Edward Cunningham, national teacher, Callow, Foxford, Martin Casey, national teacher, Carramore, Swinford, Patrick Dunne, national teacher, Tumgesh, do

Kilmactigue: Chairman, Patrick Scully Adm, secretary, Patrick Mullarkey, Drummartin, treasurers, Patrick Nelan, Gurtermone and Patrick Durkan, do, members, Rev M. Costello, rector, J. Cullen CC, John McCarrick, H. McGloin PLG, James Mullarkey PLG, Mark Derbin PLG, William Evans, Edward Limson, Michael Howley, William Mullarkey, James Stack, Daniel Mullarkey, Pat Stenson.

Kilmovee: (1) Chairman, James Little, vicar, secretary, Peter O'Grady, members, John McDermott PP, Capt. George O'Grady JP
(2) Chairman, John McDermott PP, vice-chairman, Capt. O'Grady JP, members, Thomas Doyle CC, Hugh Craig, shopkeeper, John Irwin, gentleman farmer, Michael Shiel, farmer

Kiltimagh: Chairman, Mathias Leonard PP, vice-chairman, Leonard McManus, Killedan Hse, treasurer, John Armstrong, secretary, William Philbin, members, M. J. Burke MD, Patrick Moran PLG, John Cawley, Thomas Murphy, Henry F. O'Donoghue, Dominick Murtagh, John McNicholas, Patrick J.Hughes, James Leonard, Peter Dunne, Thos. P. Lavan[1]

Straide: Chairman, James O'Donnell PP, vice-chairman, John Maley PLG, secretary, George A. Hally, gentleman farmer, Straide Hill, members, Andrew Walsh PLG, Longfield House, Thomas Moloney, farmer, Cloonconra, John Trayney, farmer, Derrinea, Michael Coghlan, farmer, Gurteen, Edward Hughes, farmer, Ballylahen, James Higgins, farmer, do, John Corban, farmer, Longfield, Laurence Sheridan, farmer, Ashbrook
N.B. No Protestant rector in the district.

Swinford: Chairman, Bernard Durcan PP, secretary, Thomas Conlan CC, treasurer, Hibernian Bank, Swinford, members, Rev J. N. Constable, rector, Swinford, P. Staunton CC, Patrick Mannion, merchant, William Horkan, merchant, Michael J. Corley, merchant, John P. O'Connor, merchant, Patrick J. Mellet, merchant, Timothy Corley, merchant, Edward Dolphin, merchant, J. P. O'Donnell, merchant, James Henry, merchant, Thomas Meehan, merchant, E. F. Gallagher, merchant, Michael J. Mellet, merchant, C. P. Devitt, butcher, John R. Meade, pawnbroker, Andrew J. Durkan PLG, Peter Horkan, farmer, John A. Henry, farmer, William J. O'Connor, farmer

Tubbercurry: Chairman, Michael Staunton PP, secretary, Nicholas H. Devine, merchant, treasurer, William P. Reynolds, manager, Hibernian Bank, Tubbercurry, members, Rev R. A. Geddes, rector, Glebe, Tubbbercurry, P. Lohan CC, Cloonacool, James G. Flannery MD, Joseph McDonnell MD, Francis Cooke PLG, merchant, Thomas Hanley PLG, merchant, John Mullarkey, merchant, Mark Brennan, merchant, Patrick Benson, merchant, Patrick Burke, merchant, Michael Anderson, merchant, James Donohoe, Ballyard, Edmund Gray, gentleman, Camaleck House, Walter Henry, gentleman, Donnore House

---

1   *C.T.* 19 July 1879 & 24 January 1880

APPENDIX 32: TUBBERCURRY RELIEF LIST FOR WEEK ENDING 24 JANUARY 1880, giving for each recipient the name, age, occupation, number in family, number of acres, town-land, the amount and value of the relief given.

Tubbercurry

1. Biddy Doherty, 70, Lodgings, 1,Tubbercurry, 2 stones, 1/10
2. Martin McDonnell, 50, Labourer, 6, do, 4, 3/9
3. Mary Heally, 65, Householder, 4, do, 4, 3/9
4. William Henry, 62, Labourer, 2, do, 2, 1/10
5. Martin Mahon, 36, do, 7, 4, 3/9
6. Patrick Durcan, 40, do, 8, do, 4, 3/9
7. John Irwin, 63, Tailor, 3, do, 2, 1/10
8. Patt Colleary , 40, Labourer, 5, do, 4, 3/9,
9. Edward Fawl, 42, do, 10, do, 4, 3/9
10. Michael Coleman, 40, Shoemaker, 6, do, 4, 3/9
11 Luke Walshe, 60, do, 3, 3, 2/9
12 Widow Casey, 55, Lodgings, 3, 2, 1/10
13 Sam Ginn, 62, Carpenter, 3, 2, 1/10
14 Mary Scanlon, 36, Servant, 1, 2, 1/10
15 Hughy Owens, 38, Labourer, 8, 2, 1/10
16 Mary Derrig, 60, 1, 2, 1/10
17 Patt Smith, 50, Blacksmith, 7, 4, 3/9
18 Mrs Killoran, 54, Householder, 20, 4, 3/9
19 Mrs Byrne, 65, do, 1, 2, 1/10
20 Mrs Walshe, 64, do, 2, 4, 3/9
21 Mary Carroll, 40, do, 5, 4, 3/9
22 James Donohoe, 60, do, 3, 3, 2/9
23 James Phillips, 70, do, 1, 2, 1/10
24 James McGlone, 48, do, 7, 4, 3/9
25 Widow Redican, 66, do, 1, 2, 1/10
26 Nelly Keavensy, 72, do, 1, 2, 1/10
27 Widow Durcan, 65, do, 2, 2, 1/10
28 Biddy Reid, 56, Milkvendor, 5, 4, 3/9
29 Cath. Gibbons, 32, Householder, 3, 2, 1/10
30 John Hughes, 38, Labourer, 4, 4, 1/10
31 Richd. Howley, 44, do, 6, 4, 3/9
32 Honor Howley, 65, do, 1, 2, 1/10
33 Martin O'Brien, 48, Weaver, 6, 4, 3/9
34 Cath. Murran, 40, Householder, 4, 4, 3/9
35 Thomas McGenane, 30, Labourer, 2, 2, 1/10
36 Honor Moran, 56, Milkvendor, 2, 2, 1/10
37 James Marren, 42, Labourer, 3, 2, 1/10
38 Mrs McManus, 55, 2, 2, 1/10
39 Michl. Cawley, 56, Smith, 6, 4, 3/9
40 William Feeny, 48, Nailor, 5, 4, 3/9
41 Atty Durcan, 65, 1, 2, 1/10
42 Honor Carroll, 70, Milkvendor, 4, 4, 3/9
43 James Lyons, 19, - 10, 4, 3/9
44 Biddy Shiels, 48, Householder, 3, 4, 3/9
45 Mrs Nicholson, 72, Householder, 1, 2, 1/10
46 Michl. Coleman, 43, Shoemaker, 6, 4, 3/9

Relief List 1880

47 Charles Moffet, 38, Carpenter, 8, 4, 3/9
48 Mrs A. Brennan, 63, - , 1, 2, 1/10
49 Mrs Clarke, 45, Lodgings, 4, 4, 3/9
50 Ketty Vesey, 56, Householder, 3, 3, 2/9
51 Thos. Callaghan, 63, Smith, 4, 4, 3/9
52 Martin Durcan, 38, Labourer, 2, 4, 3/9
53 John Higgins, 53, Labourer, 5, 4, 3/9
54 Arthur Merdith, 51, Labourer, 4, 4, 3/9
55 Cathe. Smith, 33, Servant, 2, 2, 1/10
56 Bryan Sweeny, 66, Labourer, 2, 2, 1/10
57 James Gallagher, 52, Labourer, 4, 4, 3/9
58 John McGetrick, 60, Carpenter, 7, 4, 3/9
59 Paddy McGuinn, 56, Labourer, 6, 4, 3/9
60 Biddy Murtagh, 64, Householder, 3, 4, 3/9
61 Anthony Murray, 32, Labourer, 3, 2, 1/10
62 Nancy Kirrane, 70, - , 1, 2, 1/10
63 Charles Cuffe, 63, Labourer, 2, 4, 3/9
64 Cathe. Brennan, 30, - , 1, 2, 1/10
65 Pat Donohoe, 39, Shoemaker, 3, 2, 1/10
66 John Mullarkey, 50, Shoemaker, 8, 4, 3/9
67 James Sweeny, 60, Labourer, 4, 4, 3/9
68 Mary Gaffney, 28, Servant, 1, 2, 1/10
69 Jas. Gaffney, 36, Painter, 5, 4, 3/9
70 Bryan Sweeny, 34, Labourer, 1, 2, 1/10
71 Nelly, Sweeny, 38, - , 1, 2, 1/10
72 Mrs Morrisroe, 62, Householder, 1, 2, 1/10
73 Mrs Maye, 54, Cottier, 5, 4, 3/9
74 Mrs Scanlon, 66, - , 2, 2, 1/10
75 Owen Gorman, 38, Farmer, 5, 5 acres, 4, 3/9
76 Patt Murran, 65, Labourer, 1, 2, 1/10
77 Anthony Connell, 48, Farmer, 6, 6 acres, 4, 3/9
78 Paddy Hunt, 46, Cottier, 3, 4, 3/9
79 Mrs Jordan, 66, - , 1, 2, 1/10
80 Michl. Phillips, 54, Farmer, 4, 2 acres, 4, 3/9
81 Mrs Gurry, 36, Farmer's widow, 5, 4 acres, 2, 1/10
82 Luke Connell, 42, Farmer, 7, 4 acres, 2, 1/10
83 John McGowan, 60, Labourer, 6, 4, 3/9
84 Paddy Duffy, 65, Labourer, 1, 4, 3/9
85 Charles Heally, 38, Labourer, 6, 4, 4/9
86 Paddy Banks, 54, Labourer, 1, 2, 1/10
87 Paddy Dyer, 58, Labourer, 2, 2, 1/10
88 Bartly Noone, 40, Tinner, 9, 4, 3/9
89 Jack Brennan, 37, Labourer, 7, 4, 3/9
90 Jack Brett, 42, Labourer, 8, 4, 3/9
91 Tom Brennan, 68, Labourer, 1, 2, 1/10
92 Paddy Derrig, 70, Labourer, 1, 2, 1/10
93 Widow Gibbons, 66, - , 1, 2, 1/10
94 John Holmes, 62, Labourer, 3, 3, 2/9
95 Patt Gaffney, 39, Labourer, 1, 2, 1/10
96 Mary Spelman, 40, Servant, 1, 2, 1/10

97 Jack Gildea, 54, Labourer, 2, 4, 3/9

98 Michl. Murray, 54, Farmer, 5, 4 acres, 4, 3/9
99 Tom Durcan, 56, Labourer, 7, 5 acres, 4, 3/9
100 Mary Walshe, 65, - , 20, 3, 2/9
101 John Walshe, 40, Farmer, 5, 4 acres, 4, 3/9
102 Susan Brennan, 75, - , 1, 2, 1/10
Rathscanlon
103 Mrs Patt Hunt, 40, Farmer, 5, 5 acres, 4, 3/9
104 Mrs Michl. O'Connor, 45, Farmer, 4, 6 acres, 4, 3/9
105 James Golden, 50, Farmer, 6, 5 acres, 4, 3/9
106 Miss Golden, 30, - , 1, 4, 3/9
Tullacusheen,
107 Lawrence Killoran, 48, Farmer, 10, 7 acres, 4, 3/9
108 Pat. Killoran, 45, Farmer, 7, 8 acres, 4, 3/9
109 Patt Dowd, 35, Farmer, 10, 7 acres, 4, 3/9
110 James Phillips, 60, Farmer, 3, 4 acres, 3, 2/9
111 Patt Wynne, 30, Farmer, 2, 5 acres, 4, 3/9
112 Michl. Callaghan, 40, Farmer, 2, - , 4, 3/9
113 Paddy Harraghy, 65, Farmer, 2, - , 2, 1/10
114 Mrs Dowd, 40, Farmer, 7, 6 acres, 4, 3/9
115 Pat Henry, 50, Farmer, 6, 5 acres, 4, 3/9
Cursola
116 Mrs Marren, 50, Farmer, 6, 4 acres, 4, 3/9
117 Rose Mullarkey, 50, Farmer, 4, 5 acres, 4, 3/9
118 Patt. Marren, 45, Farmer, 7, 4 acres, 4, 3/9
119 Jack Browne, 70, Farmer, 6, - , 4, 3/9
120 Patt Gildea, 40, Farmer, 8, 7 acres, 4, 3/9
121 Jas. Gallagher, 35, Farmer, 4, 5 acres, 4, 3/9
122 Mary O'Hara, 40, Farmer, 4, 4 acres, 2, 1/10
Cloonacool
123 Bridget Maye, 30, - , 1, 2, 1/10
124 James Quinn, 40, Farmer, 6, 10 acres, 4, 3/9
125 Denis Sweeny, 60, Farmer, 2, 5 acres, 2, 1/10
126 James Henry, 45, Farmer, 6, 10 acres, 4, 3/9
127 Patt McGloin, 40, Mason, 5, 2, 1/10
128 Mary Henry, 40, - , 5, 8 acres, 2, 1/10
129 Mary Henry, 30, - , 1, 2, 1/10
130 John Dyer, 70, Smith, 1, 2, 1/10
Doomore
131 Mary Connell, 40, 3, 3, 2/9
132 Mary Finegan, 50, 2, 2, 1/10
133 James Haran, 56, Farmer, 4, 4 acres, 2, 1/10
134 Tom Connolly, 65, 5, 3, 2/9
Carane
135 Mary Haran, 50, 3, 3, 2/9
136 Michl. Gildea, 36, Farmer, 7, 5 acres, 2, 1/10
137 Frank Knox, 40, 5, 2, 1/10
138 John Walker, 60, Farmer, 6, 8 acres, 3, 2/9
Carrentubber
139 Tom Brennan, 60, Farmer, 2, 8 acres, 3, 2/9

Relief List 1880

140 Patt Durcan, 45, Farmer, 6, 8 acres, 4, 3/9
Carrowrregh Knox
141 Mary Brennan, 30, Farmer, 3, 5 acres, 4, 3/9
142 John Callely, 50, Farmer, 9, 5 acres, 4, 3/9
143 Frank Gettins, 40, 1, 2, 1/10
144 John Walshe, 56, Farmer, 4, 12 acres, 4, 3/9
Carnaleck
145 Charles Finan, 60, Farmer, 6, 6 acres, 3, 2/9
146 Michl. Finan, 55, Farmer, 7, 8 acres, 3, 2/9
Ballyara
147 John Cunane, 60, 6, 4, 3/9
148 Richd. Morrison, 55, Farmer, 7, 8 acres, 4, 3/9
149 Jack Heally, 60, 2, 8 acres, 4, 3/9
150 Michl. Quinn, 45, Farmer, 6, 4 acres, 4, 3/9
151 Mary Derrig, 70, 2, Kilkimmen, 2, 1/10
152 Frank Quinn, 35, 8, 5 acres, Ballinagrass, 3, 2/9
153 Patt Snee, 45, Labourer, - 3, Tubbercurry, 3, 2/9
154 Hugh Feely, 45, Farmer, 8, 10 acres, Kilkimmin, 4, 3/9
155 Mary McLoughlin, 35, 1, Carnaleck, 2, 1/10
156 Mary Murphy, 40, 2, Carnaleck, 4, 3/9
157 Peter McEntire, 45, Farmer, 9, 2 acres, Leitrim, 4, 3/9
158 Owen Durcan, 40, Farmer, 5, 5 acres, Leitrim, 3, 2/9
159 Jas. McCarrick, 70, 1, Cloonacool, 2, 1/10
160 Mary Nary, 30, 1, Cloonroosk, 2, 1/10
161 Michl. McEntire, 30, Farmer, 4, 8 acres, Leitrim, 4, 3/9
162 Domk. Woods, 45, Farmer, 8, 7 acres, Leitrim, 4, 3/9
163 Cathe. Henry, 56, 1, Loughil, 3, 2/9
164 Michael Battle, 45, Farmer, 8, 7 acres. Cloonacool, 4, 3/9
165 Bridget Furey, 60, 3, Tubbercurry, 2, 1/10
166 John McGoldrick, 60, Farmer, 5, 8 acres, Corsola, 2, 1/10
167 Widow O'Connor, 63, 1, Corsola, 2, 1/10
168 Widow Wynne, 50, 1, Clooneen, 2, 1/10
169 Mary Hunt, 35, 1, Tullacusheen, 2, 1/10
170 John Durcan, 40, 4, Tubbercurry, 3, 2/9
171 Michl. Gildea, 40, Farmer, 6, 8 acres, Tullacusheen, 4, 3/9
172 James Gildea, 45, Farmer, 4, 5 acres, Tullacusheen, 3, 2/9
173 James Gildea, 47, Farmer, 6, 3 acres, Tullacusheen, 4, 3/9
174 James Cryan, 40, Farmer, 7, 6 acres, Tullacusheen, 3, 2/9
175 Patt Hillas, 45, Farmer, 5, 10 acres, Carrentubber, 4, 3/9
176 Mary Kelly, 30, Servant, 1, Tubbercurry, 2, 1/10
177 Pat Mullarky, 45, farmer, 6, 10 acres, Cursola, 2, 1/10
178 Michl. Mullarky, 50, Farmer, 6, 8 acres, Cursola, 2, 1/10
179 Michl. Durcan, 42, Farmer, 2, 5 acres, Carrentubber, 2, 1/10

APPENDIX 33: NUMBERS OF SINGLE FEMALE EMIGRANTS AIDED BY VERE FOSTER

Vere Foster Female Emigrants

Mr Vere Foster's Irish female emigration fund (private circulation, Oct 1884) in NLI, MS 13552. (Numbers are of successful applicants. The numbers of applications are attached to the names of the priests who signed them but their parishes are not listed. As there were a certain number of clerical changes for the period 1880-1884, the figures given above for certain parishes are not definitive.)

Swinford: B. Durcan, PP, 46, Thomas Conlan, CC, 75, John N. Constable, rector, Killconduff and Killedan, 452
Carracastle: P. Durcan PP, 131, P. Mannion CC, 29
Foxford: J. Eames, rector, 17, M. O'Donnell, PP, 126, J.McNicholas CC, 82
Killasser: Thomas Judge PP, 100, Thomas Bowler CC, 24
Kiltimagh: M. Leonard, 228, Arthur Devine CC, 49
Charlestown: Thomas Loftus PP, 161
Kilmovee: John MacDermott PP, 7, Roger O'Hara PP, 179, Thomas Doyle CC, 93
Bohola: J. O'Grady PP, 121
Bonniconlon: Peter Harte PP, 39
Ballaghaderreen: O. Stenson ADM, 151, D. O'Hara ADM, 613
Straide: James O'Donnell PP, 32
Gurteen: Roger Brennan PP, Peter O'Donohue PP, 133, W. F. Haire, Vicar of Killaraght, 13
Curry: Thomas Conlan PP, 112, E. W. Connington CC, 7
Keash: M. Cooke PP, ? John Dewart, Presbyterian minister, 1
Ballymote: M. Finn PP, 41, Edward Meehan CC, 8
Achonry: P. Lowrey PP, 84, M. Keveney CC, 14
Collooney: T. O'Rorke PP, 48, P. Mulligan CC, 7, Mr Hewson rector, Collooney, 2
Bunninadden: James MacDermott PP, 41, Owen Stenson PP, 58, Mathew Burke CC, 16
Coolaney: P. McDonald PP, 19, Archdeacon Hamilton Townsend, 1
Kilmactigue: P. Scully adm, 127, James Cullen CC, 25, J.W. Costello, rector, ?
Tubbercurry: M.D. Staunton PP, 120, P. Lohan CC, 1

Vere Foster Female Emigrants

APPENDIX 34: LAND LEAGUE BRANCHES

Ballaghaderreen: Chairman, Owen Stenson Adm., treasurers, Edward Connington and Denis O'Hara, secretaries, Hubert Judge and Patrick C. Peyton, executive committee, John Flannery, James Grogan, Thomas Spelman and Martin Bligh.[1]
Carracastle: President, Patrick Durcan PP, vice-president, Michael Phillips, vice-president, Denis Boland, deputy vice-president, Patrick Mannion CC, secretary, Thomas Gallagher, assistant secretaries, Thomas Richardson and Patrick O'Donnell.[2]
Foxford: President, P. J. Coghlan, treasurer, Michael Higgins, secretary, Anthony McAvady, executive committee, Thomas Clynes, Pat Doherty, John O'Donel, James Vaughan, James Walsh, Michael Gallagher, Thomas Barrett, Martin Langan, William Fox and Michael Murphy.[3]
Kilkelly: President, Thomas Dunleavy, Sinolane, vice-president, James Duffy, Glan, treasurer, Mathias Lydon, Kilkelly, secretary, Michael Hurley, Tavrane, committee: Thomas Lydon, Kilkelly, Michael Duffy, Knockbrack, Thomas Forkan, Carrabeg, James Grennan, Urlaur & James Duffy, Sinolane[4]
Kilmovee: President, Thomas Fleming, members, M. O'Gara, P.J. Craig, J. Walsh, P. Duffy, Mr McKensie, M. O'Grady, M. Shiel.[5]
Kiltimagh: Chairman, Mathias Leonard PP, vice-chairman and treasurer, P. Moran PLG, secretaries, John McGloin, Thomas Murphy and Thomas P. Lavan, members, Luke Carney, John Armstrong, Michael McNicholas, John McTigue and Anthony Carney.[6]
Straide: President, Patrick White, treasurer, M.J. Hughes, secretaries, J. Coghlan and W. F. Hughes, executive committee, Patrick McNicholas, Patrick Roach, John Kielty and Edward Hughes.

Land League Branches

1   *C.T.* 2 Mar 1880
2   *C.T.* 21 Feb 1880
3   *C.T.* 11 Mar 1880
4   *C.T.* 12 June 1880
5   *C.T.* 19 June 1880
6   *C.T.* 27 Mar 1880

Land League
Branches

Swinford: Chairman, Edward Dolphin, treasurer, Timothy Corley, members, P. R. Staunton CC, Patrick Mannion, E. F. Gallagher, J. P. O'Connor, A. P. Dolphin, James A. Henry, W .J. O'Connor, Hugh Heaney, John Feeny, Thomas Frain, E. Lenahan, James Horkan, Rathscanlan, Michael Munro, Peter Horkan, James Bourke, P. Moloney, Thomas F. Devitt[7]

APPENDIX 35: EVICTIONS 1880

Evictions 1880

Aclare, 6 Aug 1880, (landlord, Jane C. Lambert): Michael Cunney, 10 in family, William Durkan, 11 in family, Peter McDermott, 5 in family, Matthew Narey, 11 in family, Nicholas Gilligan, 11 in family, John Dyer, 9 in family, James Howley, 8 in family[8]

Ballysadare, K illoslasly, 10 May 1880, (landlord, Charles Phibbs, Ballymote): Denis Burns, 6 in family [9]

Curry, 25 May 1880, (landlord, Col. Richard Phibbs, Hydepark, London): John Walsh, 10 in family, Widow Mary McGuinn, 9 in family, Thomas Henry, 6 in family

Gurteen, Ardsorran, 25 Mar 1880, (landlord, James Ward, Boyle): Henry Crummy, 7 in family

Keash, Derrygoola, 21 Mar 1880, (landlord, E. R. King-Harmon, Rockingham, Boyle): Matthew and Owen Brehony, 19 in family

Killasser, (landlord, Roger McCarrick, Cloonbarry, Co Sligo): Patt Ford, Dromada Duke, 5 in family, Thady Higgins, Thomas McNulty, Henry Clarke and Michael Mulligan[10]

Kiltimagh, 15 June 1880, (landlord, Mrs O'Connor, Elphin): Widow Mary Walsh, Poolavaddy, Patt Hennigan, Ardbooley, 7 in family, Tom Long, Ardbooley, 5 in family, Michael Henehan, Poolavaddy, 6 in family[11]

26 Aug 1880, landlord, (George E. Browne, Brownespark): Michael Clark, Kiltimagh, 4 in family, Honor Prendergast, Kiltimagh, 5 in family, Hugh Kelly, Kiltimagh, 9 in family, Widow Julia Walsh, Kiltimagh, 4 in family, Pat Higgins Jr, Derrykinlough, 5 in family, James Higgins, Derrykinlough, 4 in family, Pat Prendergast, Kiltimagh, 3 in family, James Clarke, Kiltimagh, 5 in family, Michael Brennan, Cordorragh, 7 in family, Mary Conlon, Kiltimagh, 5 in family[12]

Meelick, 8 April 1880, (landlord, George A. Moore): James McEvaddy, 9 in family, Ballymiles, Nappy McNicholas, widow, Tullyroe, 6 in family, William McNicholas, 7 in family, Tullyroe

Tubbercurry, Seven families, comprising 60 persons, evicted 4 August 1880 from Carane by William Alexander and a police party. Eccles Gilligan, 10 in family, John Dwyer, 10 in family, James Howley, 8 in family, Peter McDermott, 3 (orphans), William Durkan, 12 in family, Michael Cunny, 12 in family, Pat Howley, 5 in family[13]

APPENDIX 36: IRISH NATIONAL LEAGUE DELEGATES AT MAYO CONVENTION IN CASTLEBAR NOV 1885

Mayo Convention
1885

Charlestown: John McDermott, James Leonard, J. P. Mulligan, P. A. Mulligan.
Ballaghaderreen: James Coleman, Thomas Spelman, James Gordon.
Bohola: P. O'Hara, P. Clarke.
Carracastle: P. O'Donnell, P. Cosgrove, M. Phillips., Anthony Joyce.
Kiltmagh: D. Murtagh, T. Conlon, M. Laven.
Kilmovee: Michael Walsh, John Sheridan, P. J. Craig, John Irwin.[14]

7   *C.T.* 9 Oct and 6 Nov 1880
8   CSORP (1881) 10680
9   NLI Ms. 17709
10   NLI Ms. 17,709
11   NLI Ms.17,714
12   NLI Ms. 17,714
13   NLI Ms. 17,709, *C.T.* 14 and 21 Aug and *S.C.* 14 Aug 1880
14   *C.T.* 7 November 1885

APPENDIX 37: INL & GAA DELEGATIONS AT BALLYMOTE CONVENTION 4 JANUARY 1891[1]

Collooney INL: Denis Moran, Dominick Bree, Hugh Conlan
Highwood INL: R. Hart, N. S. Flynn, Thomas Ballantine
— *GAA:* Thomas MacDermott
Keash INL: Michael Gray, John Boylan, Owen Hanna
— *GAA:* John McDonagh, John McGowan, Michael Henry
Culfadda INL: P. Nerney, Richard Alcock, Thomas Walsh
— *GAA:* Michael Shannon, Owen Brehan, Patrick McGlynn
Cloonloo INL: Thomas Wynne, John MacDonagh, P. Boylan
Bunninadden INL: John O'Dowd, John O'Beirne, Hugh Preston.
Killavil GAA: Michael Scully, R. Brennan, John Sheridan, R. Taylor PLG
Kilcreevan INL: James Kane, Roger McGowan, Patrick Cowley
Gurteen INL: James Hyland, John Higgins, Mathew Boland, John Hunt
Ballymote INL: M. Flannery, Thomas Cregan, John Kilmartin, John Flanagan PLG,
    James Harman
Coolaney ? GAA: P. W. McLoughlin, Martin Horan
Monasteraden INL: M. Flannery, Joseph Rogers, James Garhan
Killorey INL: Peter Foley
Sooey INL: John Forsney, John Kelly, James Flanagan
Achonry INL: William Henry, Peter Fry PLG, William Marren, Denis Gallagher, Peter
    Marren, W. Warner

Ballymote Convention 1891

APPENDIX 38: DELEGATES OF TENANTS' DEFENCE ASSOCIATIONS AT MAYO CONVENTION 15 JAN 1890

Attymass: P. Smith, Thomas Gaughan, J. Hennigan
Ballaghaderreen: J. Jordan, P. Skyane, J. McDermott, E. Geever, D. McCoy, M. Morrisroe
Bohola: J. P. O'Connor, P. O'Hara, P. McNicholas, D. B. Jordan, James Lyons, T. O'Carroll,
    J. McNicholas
Charlestown: P. Murphy, M. Doherty, P. Gallagher, J. Brady
Killasser: J. Doyle, P. Gallagher, M. J. Brett, P. Hughes, J. Naughton
Kilmovee: J. Walsh, J. Sheridan, J. Irwin, J. Reid, J. Regan, P. Higgins
Kiltimagh: C. Burke, D. Murtagh, T. McNicholas, E. Lavin, M. Reilly, J. Forde
Swinford: D. J. O'Connor, F. Davitt, E. Dolphin, P. E. Henry, M. O'Neill, J. McNicholas
Straide: P. McNicholas, J. Morrin, P. Coban, J. Lavelle
Midfield: P. Doyle, M. Turner, P. Cuniff, T. McGeever
Kilkelly: Thomas Higgins, D. Phillips, M. Duffy, W. Duffy, John Towey, Tom Towey, James
    Lydon, P. Nee?

Mayo Convention 1890

APPENDIX 39: PARNELL LEADERSHIP COMMITTEES

Ballaghaderreen subscribers:to the national Parnell Leadership Committee:
P. Beirne, Dr Coen, Edward Kelly, Neary Bros., M. Raftery & Co., James Howley, W. H.
Stuart, Michael Solan, Jas. Cunniffe, Thos. Rogers, John Gallagher, James Gordon Jr, John
Callaghan, Jas. Gordon Sr, Wm Grennan, P. Brennan, D. Gara

Swinford subscribers to the national Parnell Leadership Committee:
John O'Connor, P. J. Campbell (treasurer), J. Mellet (secretary), Thos. Fitzgerald (president),
James Horkan, Martin McNicholas, Michael Munroe, William Walsh, Joseph Cox, Patrick

Parnell Leadership Committees

Feeney, James McNicholas, James Henry, Anthony Gallagher, Peter Gallagher, J. Kearns, Patrick Bourke, John McNulty

Swinford Parnell Leadership Committee:
Thos. Fitzgerald, president, P. J. Campbell, treasurer, M. J. Mellet, secretary. Committee: John P. O'Connor, T. Corley, C. W. Armstrong, M. Monroe, M. McNicholas, James McNicholas, John McNicholas, P. W. Shanley, Jas. Horkan, Jas. Henry, P. J. Durkan PLG, P. J. Clarke PLG, P. Jennings PLG, J. Kearns, E. Comer, W. Walsh, J. Cox, J. Mellet

Bonniconlon Parnell Leadership Committee arranged by townlands:
President: M.F. Loftus, vice-President: Jas. Moran, treasurer and secretary: Michael Ruane. Committee: *Carra:* Ml Melvin, B. Mulrooney, Ned McCarrick. *Sandfield & Saltfield:* Jas. Ruane, John Ruane, Ned Ruane, Anthony Culkin. *Kilbride:* John Jordan, John Durcan, Joe Mullarkey. *Carranaglough:* W. McLaughlin, Jas. Durcan, Ml Durcan. *Wood & Currigane:* M. Moran, Thos. Moran, John Fleming. *Cloonta:* Michael Kelly, John Kelly, Anthony Loftus. *Knockroe:* Ml. McKenzie, John Ruane, Ml Ruane. *Carralabin:* Ml Durcan, Jas. Ruane, Tom Ruane (Ned). *Rathredane:* John Gilliard, Tom Gilliard, Jas. Howley. *Bonniconlon:* Pat Kelly, John McAndrew. *Drumsheen & Newton:* Pat Mullen Sr, Pat Mullen Jr. Kilgarvin, *Chaffhill & Templetigan:* Anthony Gilmartin, Ml Gallagher, Ml Harrison. *Carrareagh:* Wm Clarke, Jas. Clarke. *Carracrum & Bofield:* Jas. Crean, Thos. Crean. *Ella & Sallymount:* Ml Higgins, Peter Sweeney, Pat Morgan

Bonniconlon GAA (and Band) who presented an address to Parnell in Ballina:
Ml. Melvin, captain, Michael Ruane, secretary, J. Mullarkey, president, Edward Ruane, John Lawrence, John McCarrick, John Melvin, James Moran, James Durcan, John Durcan (1), Michael Kelly, James Durcan (2), John Dempsey, Michael Rape, John Rape, Pat Culkin, Ml Jordan, Jas. Crean, Michael Clarke, Pat Lavelle, Andy Lavelle, Pat Mullin, Martin Igoe, Wm Clarke, Tom Lavelle, Henry Richards, Thomas Richards, Anthony Gilmartin, John Lavelle, T. Lavelle, J. Moran, J. McAndrew

Foxford Parnell Leadership Committee
John J. Boland, chairman, T. P. O'Donnell PLG, vice-chairman, Patrick J. Jones, secretary, P. J. Coghlan, treasurer. Committee: P. J. Shiel, John O'Donnell, M. Gaughan, John M. Shiel, Jas. Gaughan, John Eaton, M. Howley, E. Hardy, J. E. Boland, John Gethins, Thos. Henahan, Jas. Walsh, John Boyle, John Morrison, M. A. Shiel, P. J. Hardy, Wm McAndrew

Attymass signatories to an address presented to Parnell in Ballina.
B. J. Woods, Anthony Durkan, Pat Gallagher, Pat McDermott, M. Mullin, John Ruane, Martin Commons, J. Flannery, Pat Mullin, James Melody, Chas. Strudgeon, John Loftus, Michael Smith, James Smith, Michael Commons, Pat Ferguson, M. Mullin, Michael Mullin, M. J. Henry, F. X. O'Neill, J. Durkan. Thos. J. Flynn, M. McNulty, F. Morrison, M. Hennigan, F. Doherty, J. Barrett, T. Gallagher, J. Mullin, M. Culken, A. Gallagher, J. Neary, M. Melody, T. McGuinness, T. Hennigan, J. Durkan, W. Ferguson, T. Flannelly, M. Hughes, G. Hughes, N. Melody, P. Mullin, R. Melody, D. Smith, D. O'Connell, J. Vinar, T. Walsh, Wm McNulty, J. Walsh, D. Doherty

APPENDIX 40: LAY DELEGATIONS FROM ACHONRY WHO ATTENDED THE CO MAYO CONVENTION IN CASTLEBAR ON 27 JUNE 1892

Swinford: P. M. Henry, C. P. Davitt, M. McNicholas, J. Gallagher, C. Pade, W. Gallagher
Swinford Board of Guardians: C. P. Davitt, J. Irwin, M. Sheridan, T. Carney, J. McNicholl, P. Moran, C. Gallagher, T. Dunlevy

Straide: Pat McGeever, Hugh Kielty, Patrick Roche, M. Ronayne, J. Marron, Thos. Lavelle, P. O'Donnell

Killasser: M. Rogers, M. Kerrane, W. Felan, R. Davis, D. Naughton, P. Naughton, J. Sherin

Bohola: John Kilcullen, J. P. O'Connor, Martin Sheridan, James Foy, J. Walsh, Thomas Lyons, Thomas Colgan

Kiltimagh: M. McDonagh, M. Walsh, Myles O'Donnell, Dominick Murtagh, Thos. Carney, A. Walsh, Charles Burke, J. Regan, T. P. Lavan, P. Mellin, T. Conlon, C. Jordan, M. Murphy, T. Gallagher

Carracastle: Henry O'Hara, J. Kelly, John Finn, P. Sweeny

Glan and Kilkelly: Thos. Harrison, John Mulligan, Dominick Phillips

Ballaghaderreen: Martin Towey, Martin Peyton, Thos. O'Grady, James P. Jordan, Richard Morrisee

Kilmovee: P. Cox, J. Sheridan, Bernard Flannery

APPENDIX 41: DISTRESSED PETITIONERS IN SWINFORD UNION 1895

Drumshinnagh, Culmore, Swinford: The inhabitants of the village of Drumshinnagh, Culmore in Swinford parish asked the office of Public Works to undertake the construction of a road from the public road right through the village across the railway line. James Doyle, Michael Doyle, Michael Devaney, Bridget Devaney, Martin Devaney, Michael Nery, Mary Sheerin, James Gallagher, Martin Horkan, Michael Niland, Ellen Higgins, Mary Sheerin, widow, Mary Niland, Michael Lynsky, Pat McNulty, John Higgins, John Niland, Michael O'Neal, Anthony Doyle, Mary Henry, Patrick M. Henry, Bridget McNulty, Mary McNulty, Patrick Price, Andrew Price, Pat Laven, James Johnston, Peter Niland, Thomas Niland, Edward Gavahan, Willman Sloyan. Petition was certified by Francis Davitt PLG and M. J. Burke CC Swinford 25 Feb 1895.[1]

Rabaun: A petition from Rabaun, where about eighty families there and in the adjoining townlands were 'suffering much from starvation', asked for the construction of a relief road through Rabaun and Castlesheenaghan signed by Michael Muldowny, James Tolan, Thomas Cunningham and Thomas O'Malley, 26 Feb 1895.[2]

Killasser

Carramore: petition endorsed by Thomas Judge, and his curate, James McKeon, among others and signed by the inhabitants of Carramore to the Under-Secretary asking for the construction of a relief road, 5 Mar 1895.[3] endorsed by Leonard O'G. McDermott, medical officer, Foxford, T. Conlon CC, Foxford, Peter Gallagher, Attymachugh, Thomas Higgins PLG, Martin Casey, Carramore national school. Signatures witnessed by J. McNicholas, secretary, Carramore: John x Durkan, Catherine x Hannon, Anne x Kennedy, Patrick x McNulty, Pat x Connor, Martin x Durkan, Michael x Melvin, Anthony x Fox, Anthony x Ruane, Anthony x Kelly, Honor x Tunny n.d. Feb 1895.[4]

The inhabitants of Tulleague, Knocks, Drumagh, Carrowliamore, Carrowliambeg and Carroweeny asked to have relief provided by the drainage of three tributaries of the Moy river. They had very small holdings, seldom exceeding 5-10 acres and were in extremely distressed circumstances, 'many on the verge of starvation'.

Tulleague: Patrick Gallagher, Andrew Gallagher, John Gildea, Pat Gallagher (Joe)

Knocks: James Gildea, Thomas Gallagher, Andrew Stenson, John Stenson

Carrowliamore: John Moran, Michael Carty, William Marren, Michael Marren, John Cunney, Michael Cunney, James Ginty

1 Dil. P. 6803
2 Dil. P. 6803
3 Dil. P. 6803
4 Dil. P. 6803

Petitioners 1895

Drumagh: Thomas Brett, Pat Brett, Pat Cregan, James Donegan, John Calvy

Carroweeny: Pat Kelly, Edward Kelly, Mathew Cosgrove, John Tully

Dromadaduke: A petition from Dromadaduke to Swinford Guardians sought road work for twenty-three families 'who are starving for want of food and work'. Michael Holleran, John Brennan, Thomas Brennan, John McLoughlin, Michael Heaney, Anthony Kenny

Carrowmoremoy, Carrow Beg, Blackpatch and Cloongleevragh: Daniel Hiland, Michael Hurst, John Hanly, James Davitt, Anthony Convey, John Heneghan, Pat Keehan, James Kenny, Edward O'Donnell, James x Durkan, Pat Durkan, Michael Clarke, Thomas Durkan, Pat Moloney, Anthony Haran, Michael Hurst, Martin x McGowan, James x Hennigan, Patrick x McGowan, Ned x Hennigan

Brackloon

Carnaculla: Thomas Durkan, John Muldowney, John Campbell, Mark Durkan, James Kilgallen, Owen Lavin, Martin Gallagher, Michael Durkan, Margaret Healy, Michael L. Durkan, James Durkan, Edward Colman, Martin Mulloy, Pat Salmon, Martin T. Durkan, Widow McNicholas, Pat McNicholas, William Kilgallen, Michael Muldowney, James O'Hara, Martin Durkan, James McNicholas, Michael McNicholas, Thomas Convey, Michael Doyle, Anthony Kelly, Michael Doherty, Pat Doherty, Martin Mulligan, Martin Doherty, Michael P. Doherty, Martin Conlon, Michael Mulligan, James McDonagh, Pat Lyden, Thomas Smyth, Michael Smyth, Martin Lavin

Tullinacurra: Thomas Devany, Robert Hoote?, Richard Durkan, Martin Durkan, Andrew Durkan, Michael Oliver, John Devany, Michael Muldowny, Daniel Brennan, John Spelman, John McManus, Martin Mulloy, Bryan Mulloy, Pat Muldowny, John Gallagher, Michael Gallagher, Pat Brennan, John Durcan, Thomas O'Brien, Thomas Foley

Tonroe: Andrew Muldowny, Martin O'Malley, John Devany, Michael Gavaghan, Owen O'Malley

Argullen: Patt Egan, Widow Salmon, John Sheridan, Dominick Sheridan, Thomas McNicholas, John McNicholas, Martin Lavin, Mark Lavin, Thady Lavin, James Learman?, Patt Higans, Patt McDonough, Andrew Brennan

Ardhoom: Thomas Gallagher, Anthony Durkan, Michael Durkan, Pat Doyle, Anthony Gallagher, Honor Murphy, William Murphy, Catherine Quinn, Thomas O'Hora, Anne Doyle, Pat McDonnell, James McNicholas

Cragagh: Dominick Regan, James Kelly, John Conner, John Kelly Jr, John Kelly Sr, Pat Kelly, Dominick Cosgrave, Thomas Regan, Thomas Mulligan, Bridget Regan, John Quinn, Mary Mulligan, Mary Kelly

Curragoola: John Clossick, John Duffy, Pat Clossick, Anthony Towey, Pat O'Donnell, John Gilgarriff, Pat Caufield, Andrew Towey, Michael Kelly, Dominick Higgins, Andrew Towey Sr, Pat Reid, John Reid, Michael Reid, Thomas Gallagher, John Gallagher, Thomas Duffy

APPENDIX 42: JORDAN TENANTS OF TOOROMIN

Tooromin Tenants

Patrick Conlon, Pat Redington, John Clarke Jr., J. T. McNicholas, J. McNicholas, M. McNicholas, Andrew Clarke, J. Redington, Thomas Byrne, Thomas Elliott, Michael Roache, Honor Conlon, J. McDonagh, Thomas & Catherine Conlon, Michael T. Conlon, John Byrne, Richard McNicholas, M. M. Conlon, Michael & Henry King, Martin Higgins, James King, Owen Morris, John Clarke Sr, Henry & Honor King, James & Timothy Moran, Michael Moran, James and Mrs Jeffers[1]

1 *Mayo News,* Mar 1916

APPENDIX 43: PARISH MISSIONS 1858-1910[1]

1858, (16-30 May), Swinford, Jesuits   *Missions*
1861, (12 May-2 June), Ballaghaderreen, Jesuits
1866, (30 Sept-14 Oct), Swinford, Jesuits
1867, (19 May-2 June), Tourlestrane, Jesuits (Healy, Fortescue, Corcoran, McEnroe)
1869, (2-23 May), Ballaghaderreen, Passionists (Pius Devine, Sebastian Keens, Gregory
    Callaghan, Dominic O'Neill)
1873, (1-23 May), Swinford, Jesuits
1873, (May), Benada, 'little mission', Jesuit (Corcoran)
1874, (3-24 May), Charlestown, Passionists (Arthur Devine, Alphonsus O'Neill, Sylvester
    McManus, Malachy Graham)
1876, (Sept), Ballymote, Redemptorists (4)
1877, (Mar), Swinford, Jesuits
1880, (Oct), Foxford, Redemptorists (John Harbison and three others)
1881, (May), Ballaghaderreen, Redemptorists
1881, (11 Sept-), Kiltimagh, Redemptorists (Condon, McCormack, O'Farrell)
1882, (Sept, 3 weeks), Tourlestrane, Redemptorists (Palliola, Frohn, Power)
1886, (Sept), Tubbercurry, Oblates
1889, (3-24 Feb), Ballaghaderreen, Redemptorists (Geoghegan, Graham, O'Brien); (winter),
    Coolaney, Franciscans (3); (winter), Mullinabreena, Franciscans (3); (15 Dec-), Straide,
    Franciscans (3)
1890, (Jan), Kiltimagh, Oblates; (Jan), Foxford, Franciscans
1891, (May), Bunninadden, Oblates (Nicholl, O'Dwyer, Furlong)
1892, (Oct, 2 weeks), Foxford, Oblates (Nicholl, O'Dwyer, Furlong, Brady)
1894, (6-20 Mar), Curry, Redemptorists (Hall, McNamara, Peters); Ballaghaderreen, retreat,
    Oblates; (16 Sept-7 Oct), Swinford, Redemptorists (Geoghegan, McNamara, Bannon)
1895, Tourlestrane, Dominicans
1898, (Feb, 3 weeks), Ballaghaderreen, Redemptorists (O'Laverty, Routledge, Murray)
1903, (25 Jan-1 Feb), Kiltimagh, Vincentians (James O'Donnell); (1-15 Feb), Foxford,
    Vincentians (Robert Jones, James O'Donnell); (31 Jan-7 Feb), Mullinabreena,
    Vincentians (Thomas Hardy, Thomas McCarthy)
1904, (24-31 Jan), Foxford, Vincentians (Jones, O'Sullivan); (24-31 Jan), Carracastle,
    Capuchins (Matthew, Angelus); Killasser, Vincentians (Farrell, Flynn); Bohola,
    Vincentians (Farrell, Flynn); (31 Jan-7 Feb), Attymass, Vincentians (Jones,
    O'Sullivan); (31 Jan-15 Feb), Mullinabreena, Vincentians (Hardy, McCarthy);
    (13-20 Nov), Charlestown, Redemptorists (Coyle, Hargedon); (20-28 Nov),
    Curry, Capuchins (Peter, Mark, Benignus); (5-8 Dec), Ballaghaderreen, Redemptorist
    (Somers)
1905, (12-18 Mar), Ballaghaderreen, Capuchins (Fiacre, Leonard, Camillus); Carracastle,
    Capuchins; Curry, Capuchins; Foxford, Vincentians; Attymass, Vincentians; Killasser,
    Vincentians; Bohola, Vincentians; Mullinabreena, Vincentians; Charlestown, Redemptorists
1906, (13 May-3 June), Collooney, Redemptorists (Burke, Hartigan, Sutton); (Nov),
    Gurteen, Capuchins (Leonard, Camillus)
1907, (10-24 Feb), Ballaghaderreen, Redemptorists (Somers, Sampson, Hartigan); (April),
    Tourlestrane, Vincentians (Walsh, Flynn, McDonnell); Kiltimagh, Vincentians; (20 Jan-
    3 Feb), Foxford, Vincentians (Michael O'Farrell, Daniel McCarthy, Stanislaus Power);

---

1 List compiled from information supplied by Thomas Davitt CM, Dan Bray CSSR, Kevin Laheen SJ, Michael
   Hughes OMI, Inchicore, Dublin, Andrew O'Loughlin, archivist, Mount Argus, Dublin, and culled from local news-
   papers. The list is by no means complete with the exception of 1904-1909 which was taken from that compiled by
   Bishop Lyster and now in the diocesan archives.

Missions   (May), Collooney, Redemptorists (Somers, Brighan?); (12 Oct-3 Nov), Swinford, Jesuits (Phelan, Kelly, Benett); (3-17 Nov), Keash, Capuchins (Sylvester, Clement, Bernardine);

1908, (9-23 Feb), Attymass, Vincentians (Flynn, Gorman); (1-8 Nov), Keash, Capuchin (Stanislaus); (8-22 Nov), Gurteen, Capuchins (Benedict, Angelus)

1909, (31 Jan-7 Feb), Foxford, Vincentians (O'Farrell, Henry); (Feb.), Bohola, Dominicans (Ryan,Kieley); (31 Oct-14 Nov), Charlestown, Redemptorists (Carthy, Cussen, Sutton); (31 Oct-24 Nov), Bonniconlon, Vincentians (O'Farrell, Henry, Lavery, O'Regan); (14-21 Nov), Attymass, Vincentians (O'Farrell, Henry, Lavery) (12 Oct-31 Oct), Temperance Crusade by Redemptorists (Tierney, Carthy, Cussen) in all parishes except Charlestown, Bonniconlon and Attymass

1910, (1-15 May), Curry, Redemptorists; (6-13 Nov), Foxford, Vincentians (2); (13-27 Nov) Killasser, Vincentians (2)

APPENDIX 44: WORLD WAR I DEATHS[1]

Achonry (see Mullinabreena)

Attymass   Private Patrick Barrett, Regimental No. 7557, Connaught Rangers, killed in action, France, 8 Oct 1918

Private Michael Daly, Mullahowney, Reg. No. 9985, Royal Irish Regiment, died 14 Feb 1815, age 22

Private Patrick Gilboy, Reg. No. 12042, The East Lancashire Regiment, 6th Batt., died, Gallipoli, 25 Aug 1915, age 24 (Bonnifinglass)

Private Patrick Henry, Reg. No. 10161, Connaught Rangers, 1st. Batt., killed in action, France, 23 Nov 1914, age 22

Private Thomas Mullen, Reg. No. 7845, Connaught Rangers, 2nd Batt., killed in action, France, 21 Oct 1914

Ballaghaderreen   Lance-Corporal Michael Casey, Reg. No. 349, Royal Munster Fusiliers, killed in action, Gallipoli, 9 Aug 1915

Private John Cassidy, Reg. No. 18350, King's Liverpool Regiment, died of wounds, France, 23 Sept 1916

Private John Cawley, Church St, Reg. No. 43298, Royal Inniskilling Fusiliers, killed in action, France, 9 Sept 1916, age 34

Private Robert Connolly, Reg. No. 11155, Connaught Rangers, killed in action, France, 20 Nov 1917 (Buckhill)

Gunner Dominick Corrigan, Reg. No. 124225, Royal Garrison Artillery, died of wounds, home, 15 June 1918

Corporal Timothy Francis Cronin, Reg. No. 9010, Manchester Regiment, 2nd Batt., killed in action, France, 26 Aug 1914

Private William Crosbie, Clogher, (son of Sgt Crosbie, RIC), Reg. No. 3442, 7th Leinster Regiment, killed in action, France, 20 April 1916, age 19

Private John Cryan, Reg. No. 2652, Royal Irish Lancers, killed in action, France, 21 June 1917

Private P. J. Doherty, Reg. No. 8647, Royal Irish Rifles. killed in action France & Flanders, 7 July 1916

Private Patrick Doohan, Reg. No. 13466, South Lancashire Regiment, 2nd Batt., killed in action, France, 29 June 1915

Private Edward Duffy, Reg. No. 23098, Royal Dublin Fusiliers, killed in action France & Flanders, 12 Aug 1916

---

1   Names taken from *Ireland's Memorial Records 1914-1918*, Dublin, 1923, *Soldiers Died in the Great War*, CD Rom, Naval and Military Press Ltd, Michael Feeney & P. J. Clarke, *Mayo Soldiers Died in the Great War*, unpublished type-script, James McGuinn, *Sligo Men in the Great War 1914-1918* (1994), *Connaught Telegraph, Sligo Champion, Western People*

Private Patrick Duffy, Reg. No. 29833, Manchester Regiment, 23rd Batt., killed in action, France, 22 Oct 1917 *Ballaghaderreen*

Private Thomas Egan, Reg. No. 5477, King's Liverpool Regiment, 8th Batt., killed in action, France, 12 Sept 1916

Private William Farrell, Reg. No. 9045, The South Staffordshire Regiment, 2nd Batt., killed in action, France, 10 Mar 1915

Private John Finn, Dernabruch, Cloontia, Reg. No. 13090, York & Lancaster Regiment, 8th Batt., died of wounds received at Friecourt Wood, France, 9 Aug 1916, age 29

Private Thomas Frain, Reg. No. 8040, 2nd Leinster Regiment, killed in action, France, 20 Oct 1914

Private Thomas Gara, Reg. No. 5106, Connaught Rangers, 5th Batt., killed in action, Salonica, 7 Dec 1915

Sergeant Martin Grady, Reg. No. 16317, The East Lancashire Regiment, 8th Batt. (formerly Manchester Regiment), killed in action, France, 31 May 1917

Private Martin Grennan, Reg. No. 37945, Manchester Regiment, killed in action, France, 28 Mar 1917 (Castlemore)

Private Peter Henry, Reg. No. 49621, Cheshire Regiment, killed in action, France, 24 Mar 1918

Corporal Martin Higgins, Clooncara, Ballaghaderreen, killed in Dardanelles, Jan 1916

*Corporal Patrick Higgins, Reg. No. 4354, Connaught Rangers, 5th Batt., killed in action Salonika, 7 Dec 1915 (Boyle)

*Private James Albert Judge, Reg. No. 8395, Connaught Rangers, 1st Batt., killed in action, France, 5 Nov 1914 (Aconry)

Lance-Corporal Michael Keane, Reg. No. 5407, Connaught Rangers, 1st Batt., died, Mesopotamia, 2 July 1916

Private Patrick Kelly, Cloonmeen, Cloontia, Reg. No. 23146, Royal Dublin Fusiliers, 8th Batt., killed in action, France, 9 Sept 1916, age 31

Private Patrick Kilgariff, Reg. No. 27871, King's Liverpool Regiment, 4th Batt., killed in action, France, 18 Aug 1916

2nd Lieutenant Hugh Maurice MacDermot, Royal Irish Fusiliers, 6th Batt., killed in action, Dardanelles, 7 Aug 1915 (son of Prince of Coolavin)

Private Edward Meehan, Reg. No. 18985, The Border Regiment, 1st Batt., killed in action. Gallipoli, 21 Aug 1915

Private Thomas Moffatt, Reg. No. 5185, Irish Guards, 1st Batt., killed in action, France, 11 Sept 1916

*Private Thomas Mulrenan, Reg. No. 18989, Royal Munster Fusiliers, 2nd Batt., killed in action, 4 Oct 1918; decoration M. M. (Ballinameen?, Co Roscommon)

Private Thomas O'Gara, Reg.No.5106, Connaught Rangers, killed in action Salonika, 7 Dec 1915

Private John Regan, Reg. No. 104, Connaught Rangers, 5th Batt., died, Gallipoli, 26 Jan 1917

Private John Rodgers, Reg. No. 13074, South Lancashire Regiment, 7th Batt., died of wounds, France, 12 Dec 1915

Private John Snee, Reg. No. 14978, Royal Scots, 12th Batt., killed in action, France, 20 Oct 1916

Gunner Edward Towey, Reg. No. 43121, Royal Garrison Artillery, killed in action, France, 29 Nov 1917

Private James Towey (Cloonlumney), Reg. No. 18000, The Sherwood Foresters, 9th Batt., died, Gallipoli, 14 Aug 1915

Private Martin Towey, Reg. No. 8973, Irish Guards, 2nd Batt., killed in action, France, 31 July 1917

* There is a doubt whether this person is a native of the parish as his address is misspelt or otherwise not clear.

Ballaghaderreen	Private Patrick Towey, Reg. No. 29479, Royal Warwickshire Regiment, 2/7th Batt., killed in action, France, 3 Dec 1917, (Ardcull, Co. Mayo)
	*Private Patrick Towey, Reg. No. 2164, Royal Munster Fusiliers, 7th Batt., killed in action, Gallipoli, 16 Aug 1915 (Sligo)
Ballymote	Private Mark Cawley, Reg. No. 4 / 8367, Argyll & Sutherland Highlanders, died of wounds, France, 5 Oct 1916

Private Michael Joseph Cawley, Reg. No. 18382, Machine Gun Corps, killed in action, France, 2 Sept 1918

Private Patrick Cawley, Reg. No. 9709, 2nd Leinster Regiment, killed in action, France, 18 Oct 1914

Private John Chambers, Reg. No. 4853, Connaught Rangers, enlisted, Galway, killed in action, France, 26 April 1915

Private Michael Clarke, Reg. No. 8473, Royal Irish Regiment, killed in action, Gallipoli, 17 Aug 1915

Private Patrick Connolly, Reg. No. 106862, 43rd Garrison Batt., Royal Fusiliers, died, typhoid fever, Sligo Infirmary, 10 Jan 1919, age 44,: decoration, King's Long Service Medal

Rifleman William Conroy, enlisted Rotherham, killed in action, France, 30 Nov 1917

Private John Downey, Reg. No. 22366, Royal Dublin Fusiliers, 9th Batt., died of wounds, France, 5 Sept 1916

Private John Duffy, Reg. No. 22324, Inniskilling Fusiliers, 1st Batt., killed in action, France, 1 July 1916

Private J. Feeney, killed in action, Flanders, 1914

Rifleman John Ferguson, Reg. No. 5296, 8/9th Royal Irish Rifles, killed in action, France, 15 Dec 1916

Private Peter Flanagan, Reg. No. S2 SR/01830, Royal Army Service Corps, died, France, 21 Feb 1917

Private Thomas Flanagan, Reg. No. 6851, Royal Irish Regiment, 7th Batt., killed in action, France, 31 Oct 1918

Private Timothy Forbes, Irish Guards, enlisted, Boyle, killed in action, France & Flanders, 15 Nov 1916

Private Thomas Gallagher, Reg. No. 2860, Irish Guards, 1st Batt., killed in action, France, 14 Sept 1914

Lance-Corporal Michael Gilmartin, Reg. No. 9914, 2nd Leinster Regiment, killed in action, France, 27 Sept 1914

Private Arthur V. Gorman, Reg. No. 25325, Royal Irish Regiment, 7th Batt., killed in action, France, 21 Mar 1918

Private Michael Healy, Reg. No. 5550, Irish Guards, 1st Batt., killed in action, France, 15 Sept 1916

Private Michael J. Healy, Reg. No. 7970, Irish Guards, 2nd Batt., killed in action, France, 13 Sept 1916

Private Michael John Judge, Reg. No. 33075, Norfolk Regiment, 1/5th Batt., (Territorial Force), died, Egypt, 28 Oct 1918

Private Michael Keene, Reg. No. 44086, 2nd Royal Inniskilling Fusiliers, died of wounds, France, 15 Oct 1918

Private Charles Kilpatrick, Reg. No. 3/3667, Seaforth Highlanders, 1st Batt., died of wounds, Persian Gulf, 6 Nov 1917

Private Michael McGuinn, Reg. No. 6967, Connaught Rangers, died of wounds, France, 25 Sept 1914

Private Terence McGuire, Reg. No. 7886, Connaught Rangers, 2nd Batt., killed in action, France, 28 Oct 1914

Private James McLoughlin, Reg. No. 14910, 9th Royal Inniskilling Fusiliers, killed in action, *Ballymote*
France, 24 Mar 1918

Acting Corporal John McNicholas, Reg. No. 190634, Royal Engineers (formerly Highland
Light Infantry), killed in action, France, 28 June 1917

Private Martin Meehan, Reg. No. 17522, 1st Royal Dublin Fusiliers, died, France, 23 Jan
1917

Sergeant John Muldoon, Reg. No. 4466, Connaught Rangers, 6th Batt., killed in action,
France, 3 Sept 1916

Private Patrick Mulligan, Reg. No. 6390, Royal Irish Regiment, 2nd Batt., killed in action,
France, 21 Aug 1918

Lance-Corporal Thomas Mulligan, Connaught Rangers, 2nd Batt., killed in action, France,
21 Oct 1914

Private Michael Quigley, (Carnaree), Reg. No. 10777, Connaught Rangers, 1st Batt., died of
wounds, France, 19 Mar 1915

Private Michael Regan, Reg. No. 11139, Connaught Rangers, 6th Batt., killed in action,
France, 5 Feb 1916

Private James Reynolds, Reg. No. 8451, Connaught Rangers, 1st Batt., killed in action,
France, 23 Nov 1914

Private Michael Reynolds, Reg. No. 9256, Connaught Rangers, 1st Batt., killed in action,
Mesopotamia, 18 April 1916

Private Edward Sharkey, Reg. No. 7283, Irish Guards, 2nd Batt., died of wounds, France, 20
Sept 1916

Private John Welsh, Reg. No. 26742, Royal Dublin Fusiliers, 8/9th Batt., killed in action,
France, 30 Mar 1918

Private William Browne, Reg. No. 8863, Connaught Rangers, enlisted, Sligo, died, *Ballysadare*
Mesopotamia, 4 Aug 1916

Gunner James Dooney, Reg. No. 23432, Royal Garrison Artillery, died of wounds, France, 1
Aug 1916

Private Joseph Gallacher, Reg. No. 310318, Gordon Highlanders, 7th Batt., killed in action,
France, 16 April 1917

Private Henry Howley, Reg. No. 16654, Royal Irish Fusiliers, 7/8th Batt., killed in action,
France, 22 Feb 1917

Private John McCann, Reg. No. 7577, Irish Guards, 2nd Batt., died of wounds, France, 29
Mar 1918

Private Edward Mullen, Reg. No. 5236, Connaught Rangers, 5th Batt., killed in action,
Salonica, 7 Dec 1915

Private Herbert Mullen, Reg. No. 14274, 5th Royal Inniskilling Fusiliers, killed in action,
France, 12 Oct 1918

Private Joseph Murphy, Reg. No. 14146, Royal Munster Fusiliers, 2nd Batt., killed in action,
France, 10 Nov 1917

Private Terence Murphy, Reg. No. 8713, Connaught Rangers, 2nd Batt., killed in action,
France, 25 Feb 1915

Michael O'Gara, killed in action, France, 1914

Corporal Thomas Carroll, Reg. No. 4214, Connaught Rangers, died of wounds, France, 12 *Bohola*
June 1917, age 32

Private Michael Deacy, Reg. No. 18651, Northumberland Fusiliers, 13 Batt., died, France, 26
Sept 1915

Private J.Kilgallon, Carrownleva, Reg. No. 11365, South Lancashire Regiment, died 16 Aug
1915

Bohola   Private Martin Kilgallon, Reg. No. 6693, Connaught Rangers, 1st Batt., died of wounds, India, 5 May 1916

*Private Patrick Moran, Reg. No. R.S. 4/236231, Royal Army Service Corps, died, Balkans, 17 Sept 1917 (Bohal, Co Mayo)

Bonniconlon   Private Patrick Cabry, Reg. No. 6689, Connaught Rangers, killed in action, Mesopotamia, 17 April 1916

Private John Boland, Reg. No. 9775, Irish Guards, killed in action, France, 9 Oct 1917

Private John Cowley, Newtown, Reg. No. 18983, Royal Lancaster Regiment, died 9 April 1916

1st Class Stoker, Patrick Jordan, Reg. No. 38523, HMS Cumberland, 24 Sept 1918, age 42

Private P. Kelly, Chaffhill, Reg. No. 28803, Lancashire Fusiliers, died 21 Oct 1916

Private Martin McKenzie, Carrowcrom, Reg. No. 40617, 2nd Royal Inniskilling Fusiliers, killed in action, France, 18 Sept 1917, age 24

Sergeant James Mullen, Drumsheen, Reg. No. 29337, Royal Inniskilling Fusiliers, 1st Batt., died from meningitis, France 18 June 1917, age 29

Private John Murray, Glenree, Reg. No. 621, Coldstream Guards, died, France, 22 Dec 1914, age 38

Private M. Murray, Glenree, Reg. No. 22228, Welsh Regiment, died of wounds, 9 Jan 1917, age 44

Private Michael Murray, Reg. No. 9181, Connaught Rangers, 1st Batt., killed in action, France, 19 Dec 1914

Lance Corporal Thomas Murray, Glenree, Reg. No. 27/1494, Northumberland Fusiliers, (Tyneside Irish), 1 July 1916, age 29

Private Anthony Neary, Reg. No. 17610, 1st Royal Dublin Fusiliers, killed in action, Gallipoli, 29 June 1915 (Coulkarney, Coolcarney?, Co Mayo)

*Private Thomas Tunney, Reg. No. 471, 6th Leinster regiment, killed in action, Gallipoli, 17 Aug 1915 (Drumneen?, Co Mayo)

Bunninadden   Private John Boland, Reg. No. 9775, Irish Guards, killed in action, France, 9 Oct 1917

Private Richard Cawley, Reg. No. 5396, Connaught Rangers, died, Mesopotamia, 8 June 1916

Private James Coleman, Reg. No.19750, Royal Lancashire Regiment, killed in action, Mesopotamia, 9 April 1916

Private Tom Coleman (Killavil), killed in action, Gallipoli, 1915

Private Joseph O'Dowd, Reg. No. 4442, Connaught Rangers, 6th Batt., killed in action, France, 17 May 1916

Carracastle   Private John Carney, Reg. No. 6480, Royal Welsh Fusiliers, died, home, 15 July 1916

Private John Cawley, Reg. No. 13987, Lancashire Regiment, killed in action, France, 9 May 1916

Private Patrick Cuddy, Reg. No. 26249, Royal Dublin Fusiliers, died of wounds, France, 11 Nov 1916

Private Patrick Egan, Reg. No. 7706, Royal Irish Regiment, 2nd Batt., killed in action, France, 15 Oct 1914

*Private Michael Finn, Reg. No. 18897, The Border Regiment, 1st Batt., killed in action, France, 1 July 1916

*Lance-Corporal James Finn, Reg. No. 3346, 4th Leinster Regiment, killed in action, France, 17 May 1918

Private Michael Marren, Brackloon North, Reg. No. 68329, Machine Gun Corps (Infantry), 1st Batt., (formerly Connaught Rangers), killed in action, France, 5 Dec 1917, age 31

Private John Tansey, Reg. No. 41982, Royal Inniskilling Fusiliers, 8th Batt., killed in action, France, 5 Aug 1917

Private Thomas Cain, Reg. No. 32128, 1st Garrison Battalion (formerly Lancashire Fusiliers), died, home, 12 June 1916

Private Patrick Colleran, Reg. No. ?, Yorkshire Light Infantry, killed in action, France, 27 Sept 1915

Private Denis Collins, Reg. No. 2667, Durham Light Infantry, killed in action, France, 5 Nov 1916

Private Timothy Corley, Reg. No. 3797, Connaught Rangers, killed in action, France, 22 Jan 1915

Private William Daly, Reg. No. 8879, The East Surrey Regiment, 3rd Batt., died, home, 18 Nov 1918

Private Michael Downey, enlisted, Castlerea, Reg. No. 8988, Connaught Rangers, died of wounds, Mesopotamia, 25 April 1916

Lance-Corporal Patrick Duffy, Reg. No. 13948, The East Lancashire Regiment, 7th Batt., died of wounds, France, 23 Nov 1916 (Tonroe)

Private Patrick Egan, Lavy More, Reg. No. 7706, Royal Irish Regiment, died 15 Oct 1914, age 34

Private Thomas Flatley, Reg. No. 30/242, Northumberland Fusiliers (Tyneside Irish), killed in action, France, 28 April 1917

Bombardier Thomas Fleming, Gowel, Reg. No. 69359, Royal Field Artillery, died of wounds 2 Oct 1917, age 23

Private James Frain, Bellaghy, Reg. No. 3851, Connaught Rangers, 1st Batt., enlisted, Swinford, killed in action, France, 26 April 1915, age 22

Private William Frain, Reg. No. 16355, 1st Royal Dublin Fusiliers, died of wounds, France, 14 May 1918

Private James Gallagher, Reg. No. 1357, Royal Munster Fusiliers, 1st Batt., died, France, 19 Feb 1917

Private John Gavaghan, Reg. No. 2066, 37th Battalion, Australian Infantry, died 8 June 1917, age 32

Lt. Col. James Halligan, 2nd Leinster, killed in action, France & Flanders, 18 Aug 1916

Lance Corporal Patrick Henry, Lavinagh, enlisted St Helens, Lancs., Reg. No. 13487, Royal Dublin Fusiliers, died of wounds, 17 Oct 1918, age 32

Private James Horan, Brogher, Reg. No. 202268, King's Own Yorkshire Light Infantry, died 4 Oct 1917

Private James Leonard, Sargura, Reg. No. 5874, Connaught Rangers, 20 Nov 1917, age 28

Private Thomas Vincent McAuliffe, Lowpark, Reg. No. 10917, Connaught Rangers, 1st Batt., killed in action, Mesopotamia, 21 Jan 1916 (Lowpark, Co Mayo)

Private Patrick McDonagh, Corthoon, Reg. No. 22262, West Yorkshire Regiment, 2nd Batt., died of wounds, France, 16 Aug 1916, age 30

*Private Anthony McHale, Reg. No. 15494, Yorkshire Light Infantry, 10th Batt., killed in action, France, 1 July 1916 (Tavnajh, Tawnyinah? Co Mayo)

Private Thomas McNamara, Reg. No. 3/3131, Yorkshire Light Infantry, 7th Batt., killed in action, France, 20 Sept 1916

Private Thomas M. McVann, Reg. No. 8081, Royal Irish Regiment, enlisted, Ballina, killed in action, France & Flanders, 5 April 1918

Lance-Corporal D. Mulholland, Charlestown, Royal Irish Rifles, killed, Feb 1911?

Private D. O'Connor, Glasgow, born, Charlestown, Reg. No. 266287, Seaforth Highlanders, died, 6 Sept 1917, age 18

Private James Phillips, Reg. No. 250681, Durham Light Infantry, 1/6th Batt., (formerly Yorkshire Regiment) killed in action, France, 14 April 1917

*Private John Phillips, Reg. No. 17567, Norfolk Regiment, 1st Batt., killed in action, France, 4 June 1916

Charlestown	Sapper Michael Regan, Ballyglass, Reg. No. 82680, Royal Engineers (formerly Yorkshire Regiment), killed in action, France, 1 Nov 1915, age 38
	Private Michael Richardson, Ranaranny, Reg.No.1833, South Lancashire Regiment, died 13 July 1916, age 28
	Captain James P. Roche, Leinster Regiment, killed in action at Messines, 7 June 1917; age 20 (born in Kildare), decoration, M. C. June 1916
	Private Patrick Joseph Tarpey, Reg. No. 7338, Yorkshire Light Infantry, 2nd Batt., died of wounds, France, 10 June 1915, age 33
	Private Martin Welsh, (Killeen), Reg. No. S/10008, Seaforth Highlanders, 1st Batt., (formerly Royal Field Artillery), killed in action, Persian Gulf, 7 Jan 1916
Collooney	Gunner John Cooney, Royal Field Artillery, killed in action, France, 18 Sept 1917
	Lance-Corporal John (Jack) Feeney, enlisted Sligo, Reg. No. 27371, 2nd Royal Dublin Fusiliers, killed in action, France, 3 May 1917, age 26
	Private Thomas Feeney, Reg. No. 4619, Connaught Rangers, 6th Batt., killed in action, France, 21 Mar 1918
	Corporal Robert Fordham, Royal Dublin Fusiliers, killed in action France & Flanders 20 April 1917
	Private Frank Leydon, Reg. No. 9765, Irish Guards, 1st Batt., killed in action, France, 17 Sept 1916
	Private, Joseph Leydon, Irish Guards, killed in action, France, 22 Aug 1914
	*Lance-Corporal James Murray, Reg. No. 40989, West Yorkshire Regiment, 2nd Batt., (formerly Northumberland Fusiliers), killed in action, France, 16 Aug 1917 (Clooney?, Co Sligo)
	Lance-Sergeant Patrick O'Connor, (Cloughfin), Reg. No. 4936, Irish Guards, 2nd Batt., killed in action, France, 17 Oct 1915, age, 25
	Private Patrick Joseph Rock, Reg. No. 3703, The Royal Scots, 1st Batt., killed in action, France, 4 May 1915
	Rifleman James Scanlon, 7th Royal Irish Rifles, killed in action, France, 7 Aug 1916
	Corporal Charles Whelan, Reg. No. 25480, Royal Dublin Fusiliers, 10th Batt., killed in action, 13 Nov 1916
Coolaney	Private Hugh Conlon, Killoran, Reg. No. 15866, 2nd Royal Dublin Fusiliers, killed in action, France, 12 April 1915
	Private James Murphy, Reg. No. 7860, Royal Munster Fusiliers, 1st Batt., killed in action, Gallipoli, 1 May 1915
	*Private Thomas Nicholson, Reg. No. 20765, Northumberland Fusiliers, 12th Batt., killed in action, France, 3 July 1916 (Cillolen?, Co Sligo)
Curry	John P. Durkin, Munster Fusiliers, killed in action France & Flanders 14 Sept 1916
	Private Patrick Kennedy, Reg. No. 11964, The Border Regiment, 1st Batt., killed in action, France, 15 Oct 1918
	Private Thomas Kennedy, Connaught Rangers, killed in action, Salonica, 7 Dec 1915
	Bombardier Patrick Kerins, Reg. No. 294619, Royal Garrison Artillery, killed in action, France, 21 April 1917
	Private Michael Leonard, Reg. No. 18175, 2nd Leinster Regiment, killed in action, France, 30 May 1918
	John Normonly (Montiagh), American Forces, killed in action, France, 1918
	Martin Normonly (Montiagh), Coldstream Guards, killed in action, Mons, 1914
	Private Thomas Parsons, Botuny, Reg. No. 27038, Welsh Regiment, died 8 Aug 1915, age 35
	Private Peter Stenson, Reg. No. 7607, Coldstream Guards, killed in action, France, 8 Sept 1914

Private Thomas Curley, Reg. No. 18619, 2nd Royal Dublin Fusiliers, killed in action, France, 1 July 1916

Doocastle

Private John Gallagher, Reg. No. 5434, Connaught Rangers, 1st Batt., killed in action, Mesopotamia, 17 April 1916

Gunner Michael Hunt, Goulaun, Doocastle, Reg. No. 28244, Royal Field Artillery, died of wound, home, 30 Oct 1914, age 39

Private Thomas Kennedy, Reg. No. 19865, 1st Royal Dublin Fusiliers, killed in action, Gallipoli, 7 Aug 1915

Private Patrick May, Reg. No. 5119, Connaught Rangers, 2nd Batt., killed in action, France, 15 Sept 1914

Private Patrick McDonnell, Reg. No. 22462, 1st Royal Dublin Fusiliers, died of wounds, France, 31 May 1918

Private Patrick Murray, Machine Gun Battalion, died 11 Nov 1918

Private Joseph O'Dowd, (Principal, Doocastle NS), Connaught Rangers, killed in a trench by a grenade, 16 June 1916

Private James Beavens, Convent St, Reg. No. 21695, Royal Irish Fusiliers, died of wounds 7 May 1916, age 18

Foxford

Private Michael Boyle, Reg. No. 4327, The Lancashire Fusiliers, killed in action, France, 12 May 1917

Sergeant Michael Boyle, Reg. No. 10913, Royal Irish Rifles, enlisted, Chesterfield, Derby, died of wounds, France, 19 Nov 1917

Private Patrick Clarke, Reg. No. 5267, Irish Guards, died of wounds, France, 19 May 1915

2nt Lt. Thomas Reginald Coghlan, Pontoon, Royal Irish Fusiliers, died of wounds, 24 Oct 1918, age 26

Private Martin Doherty, Curranara, Reg. No. 21331, Royal Irish Fusiliers, 7/8th Batt., killed in action, France, 10 Aug 1917, age 29

Sapper Michael Flynn, enlisted Edinburgh, Reg. No. 79904, Corps of Royal Engineers, killed in action, France & Flanders, 16 April 1916

Private James Gallagher, Lancashire, Reg. No. 72746, Machine Gun Corps (Infantry), 1st Batt., (formerly East Lancashire Regiment), killed in action, France, 17 Sept 1917, age 27

Private Michael Gallagher, Reg. No. 3790, Connaught Rangers, 2nd Batt., killed in action, France, 8 Nov 1914

Private William Hanley, Reg. No. 16646, Royal Irish Fusiliers, 1st Batt., killed in action, France, 1 Jan 1918

Rifleman James Higgins, Reg. No. 6601, Royal Irish Rifles, killed in action, France & Flanders, 15 Sept 1914

Private Larry Higgins, Belgarrow, Reg. No. 5798, Connaught Rangers, 5th Batt., killed in action, France, 9 Oct 1918, age 28

Private Patrick Higgins, Reg. No. 17347, Royal Dublin Fusiliers, 9th Batt., killed in action, France, 9 Sept 1916

Private Austin Hopkins, Reg. No. 212056, 41st Agra Labour Corp, died 1 June 1919 (buried in Ballyhaunis Abbey)

Gunner Patrick J. Horkan, Reg. No. 70733, Royal Field Artillery, died, Mesopotamia, 9 May 1917, age 23

Private Patrick Kelly, Reg. No. 556, Royal Munster Fusiliers, 2nd Batt., killed in action, France, 4 Oct 1918

Private Francis Langley, Ballinisland, Reg. No. 6494, Connaught Rangers, 6th Batt., died, France, 14 June 1918, age 20

Corporal John Lyons, Reg.No.280, Connaught Rangers, died at home, 2 April 1915

Foxford   Private Patrick Murray, enlisted Ballina, Reg. No. 5974, Connaught Rangers, killed in action, France & Flanders, 21 Mar 1918, age 28

Sergeant Thomas Price, Reg. No. 8569, 2nd Leinster Regiment, killed in action, France, 20 Aug 1915

Private Thomas Quinn, Reg. No. G/3073, The Middlesex Regiment, 18th Batt., killed in action, France, 20 July 1916

Lance Corporal J. Roach, Liverpool, Reg. No. 41656, Royal Welsh Fusiliers, died 18 Sept 1918, age 22

Private Martin Roach, Whitnorth, Co Mayo, enlisted Birmingham, Reg. No. 7652, Royal Irish Regiment, 2nd Batt., killed in action, France, 1 May 1915

Gunner Thomas Roache, Pullagh, Reg. No. 89619, Canadian Field Artillery, died 5 July 1917, age 32

Private Garrett Ruane, Rinaney, Reg. No. 3561, Irish Guards, 1st Batt., killed in action, France, 18 May 1915, age 27

Guardsman Michael Screeney, Reg. No. 8479, Scots Guards, killed in action, France, 21 Oct 1914

*Private Patrick Screeney, Reg. No. 10491, West Riding Regiment, 2nd Batt., killed in action, France, 5 May 1915 (Mayo)

Private Thomas Sheerin, Borhallagh, Reg. No. 9483, Irish Guards, died 9 Oct 1917, age 30 (spent 10 years in RIC and resigned to enlist)

Private Thomas Walsh, Askilaun, Killasser, Reg. No. 15749, York & Lancaster Regiment, killed in action, 24 Oct 1918, age 29

Private Thomas Welsh, enlisted Edinburgh, Reg. No. 43095, Royal Inniskilling Fusiliers, killed in action, 9 Sept 1916

Gurteen   Acting Lance-Corporal James Clancy, Reg. No. 91965, Royal Army Medical Corps, died, home, 3 Nov 1918

Rifleman Thomas Hannon, Reg. No. 54007, King's Royal Rifle Corps, 13th Batt., (formerly Royal Irish Rifles), killed in action, France, 12 Sept 1918

*Private John Hegarty (Kilfree), Reg. No. 2128, Manchester Regiment, 1st Batt., killed in action, France, 21 Dec 1914

Private Laurence Mullaney, Reg. No. 11546, Irish Guards, 2nd Batt., died of wounds, France, 3 Aug 1917

Private Thomas Mulligan, Reg. No. 5720, Connaught Rangers, killed in action, France, 3 Sept 1916

Private Patrick Murphy, Reg. No. 9488, Irish Guards, 2nd Batt., killed in action, France, 15 Sept 1916

Private Dominick Oates, Reg. No. 5435, Connaught Rangers, 1st Batt., killed in action, France, 2 Sept 1915

Private Hugh O'Connor, Reg. No. 6999, Irish Guards, 2nd Batt., killed in action, France, 21 Oct 1915

*Private James Phillips, Reg. No. 28762, Sherwood Foresters, 10th Batt., killed in action, France, 14 Feb 1916. (Girthaum? Co Sligo)

Lance-Corporal Patrick Phillips, Reg. No. 156111, Royal Engineers, 10th Tunnel Co., killed in action, France, 16 Nov 1917

Private Hugh Toolan, Reg. No. 37222, King's Liverpool Regiment, 1st Batt., killed in action, France, 28 April 1917

Sapper John Wade, (Kilfree), Royal Engineers, killed in action, France, 12 April 1916

Keash   Private James Brehony, Reg. No. 6807, Royal Scots Fusiliers, died, France, 26 Feb 1915

Private Peter Casey, Reg. No. 5524, Connaught Rangers, died of wounds, France, 23 June 1917

Private John Kelly, Reg. No. 7767, Royal Irish Regiment, 1st Batt., died of wounds, *Keash*
Mesopotamia, 7 Aug 1915

Quarter-master Veterinary Sergeant Edgar S. Robinson, Battlefield, Culfadda, Connaught
Rangers

Edgar A. K. Robinson (son of above), Connaught Rangers

Private Edward Boyle, enlisted Swinford, Reg. No. 3889, Connaught Rangers, killed in action *Kilkelly*
France & Flanders, 26 April 1915

Private Patrick Cuddy, Reg. No. 26249, Royal Dublin Fusiliers, died of wounds, France, 11
Nov 1916

*Private John Duffy, Reg. No. 29943, Royal Scots, 13th Batt., killed in action, France, 21 Aug
1916 (Killvally?, Co Mayo)

Lance Sergeant B.Dunleavy, Gowlane, Reg. No. 14841, Coldstream Guards, killed in action
25 Sept 1918, age 25

Private Thomas Duffy, Liscosker, Reg. No. 8875, Yorkshire Regiment, killed in action 11 July
1916, age 38

Private Timothy Feely, Cloontirk, Reg. No. 5262, Connaught Rangers, killed in action, 7 Dec
1915, age 42

Private John Harrington, Reg. No. 17867, The Loyal North Lancashire Regiment, 7th Batt.,
killed in action, France, 23 July 1916

Private Peter Horan, Urlaur, Reg. No. 32176, East Lancashire Regiment, killed in action 22
Sept 1917, age 26

Private Bernard Hynes, Reg. No. 29630, Royal Dublin Fusiliers, died of wounds, France &
Flanders, 7 July 1916

Private Thomas Kerins, Lurgan, enlisted Liverpool, Reg. No. 10153, The East Lancashire
Regiment, 8th Batt., killed in action, France, 3 June 1916, age 24

Private James Kennewaly, enlisted Lancashire, Reg. No. 18264, Prince of Wales Volunteers
(South Lancashire Regiment), died at home 30 Dec 1915

Gunner Thomas Moran, Tullaganny, Urlaur, Reg. No. 285292, Royal Garrison Artillery, died
of wounds 15 June 1918, age 33

Private Peter Murphy, Salmonford, Reg. No. 36533, Northumberland Fusiliers, killed in
action 11 April 1918, age 32

Private Patrick Neafsy, Clougholly, Reg. No. 6534, Irish Guards, killed in action 27 Sept
1915, age 23

Private Edward Convay, Reg. No. 1395, Irish Guards, killed in action, France, 10 June 1915 *Killasser*

Private Corr, killed in action, Aug? 1915

Lieutenant Richard Thomas Cuffe, Killasser Hse, Royal Air Force, 54th Squadron, killed in
action near Chateau Thierry, 21 July 1918, age 22

Sergeant Edward Duffy, Tiraninny, Reg.No.8569, 2nd Battalion Leinster Regiment, killed in
action, 20 Aug 1915, age 36

Bombardier Edward Harte (Knocks) Reg. No. 54631, Royal Garrison Artillery, killed in
action, France, 5 Feb 1917; decoration, M. M. (awarded Military Cross posthumously)

Lance-Sergeant Patrick Higgins, Reg. No. 16859, The East Lancashire Regiment, 11th Batt.,
killed in action, France, 28 June 1918

Private Michael Hurst (Carrowmoremoy), killed in action

Private – Loftus, Lancashire Regiment, killed in action, Aug? 1915

Private Sweeney, Killasser, killed in action, Aug? 1915

Private James Doherty, Reg. No. 19439, The East Lancashire Regiment, 1st Batt., (formerly *Kilmovee*
Lancashire Fusiliers), died of wounds, France, 13 May 1915

Private Patrick Duffy, Reg. No. 8849, Irish Guards, 2nd Batt., killed in action, France, 24 Mar
1918

Kilmovee Private Richard Forkin, Reg. No. 12591, King's Liverpool Regiment, 1st Batt., died of wounds, France, 10 Mar 1915

Private Edward Higgins, Reg. No. 12705, 1st Royal Dublin Fusiliers, killed in action, Gallipoli, 29 June 1915

Private Martin Higgins, Reg. No. 555, The Lancashire Fusiliers, 1st Batt., killed in action, Gallipoli, 4 June 1915

*Sergeant Dominick Dan Jordan, Killamoree?, Co Mayo, 50th Batt. Canadian Infantry, (Alberta Regiment), killed in action, 25 April 1918, age 38

Private James Judge, Reg. No. 307437, West Yorkshire Regiment, 1/8th Batt., died, France, 25 July 1917

Private John Mannion, Reg. No. 12674, Manchester Regiment, 19th Batt., killed in action, France, 23 July 1916

Private M. Mullen, Culclave, Reg.No.41775, Lancashire Fusiliers, died of wounds 4 June 1917, age 37

Private J. Mulligan, Reg. No. 9587, The Sherwood Foresters, 2nd Batt., killed in action, France, 20 Oct 1914

Private James Mulligan, Cloonierin, Kilmore, Reg. No. 3030279, 116th battalion, Canadian Infantry, died of wounds 28 Aug 1918, age 24

Private P. O'Donnell, Uggool, Reg. No. 3/5043, Connaught Rangers, killed in action, 21 Aug 1917, age 30

Private Michael Walsh, Reg. No. 2904, Connaught Rangers, 5th Batt., killed in action, Gallipoli, 28 Aug. 1915

Kiltimagh Corporal Michael Ansboro, Conderry (native of Bohola), Reg. No. 791, The Lancashire Fusiliers, killed in action, France, 26 Aug 1914, age 32

Private Michael Brennan, Reg. No. 7816, Royal Munster Fusiliers, killed in action, France, 17 July 1916

Gunner John Brown, Main St, Reg. No. 38105, Royal Field Artillery, killed in action, France, 25 April 1917, age 31

Private Michael Carroll, Cloonkedagh, Reg. No. 26171, South Lancashire Regiment, killed in action, France, 15 June 1917, age 3?

Private Thomas Casey, Reg. No. 22375, Royal Dublin Fusiliers, killed in action, France, 16 Aug 1917

Private Thomas Conway, Carrownteeaun, Reg. No. 10660, Irish Guards, killed in action 14 Nov 1916, age 32

Private Michael Deacey, Killedan, Reg. No. 18651, Northumberland Fusiliers, killed in action 26 Sept 1915, age 25

Rifleman Martin Fitzpatrick, Reg. No. 1838, 1st Royal Irish Rifles, killed in action, France, 9 May 1915

Private James Forkan, died of wounds France & Flanders, (buried in Kiltimagh)

Private Patrick Forkan, killed in action France & Flanders (from family report)

Gunner James (John?) King, Reg. No. 21316, Royal Garrison Artillery, died, 18th Casualty Clearing Station, France, 25 Sept 1918 (Killedan?)

Private J. Lyden, Main St, Reg. No. 7566, South Lancashire Regiment, died of wounds 21 July 1916, age 29

Private Patrick McNicholas, Treenagleragh, Reg. No. 14125, Royal Munster Fusiliers, 1st Batt., died of wounds, France, 9 Aug 1918, age 32

Private William McNicholas, Reg. No. 1574, Connaught Rangers, killed in action, France, 21 Mar 1918

Rifleman Michael Murtagh, Canbrack, Reg. No. 40027, Royal Irish Rifles, killed in action 16 Aug 1917, age 28

Private John Regan, Ballyglass, Reg. No. 11808, Irish Guards, killed in action 20 Jan 1918, age 40

Kiltimagh

Private Patrick Roughneen, Reg. No. 11015, West Riding Regiment, 8th Batt., killed in action, Mediterranean, 21 Dec 1917

Private Michael Solan, Reg. No. 2302, Royal Warwickshire Regiment, 19th Batt., killed in action, France, 23 Mar 1918

Gunner James Staunton, Reg. No. 106414, Royal Garrison Artillery, died of wounds, France, 17 May 1917

Private John Francis Tuohy, Aidan St, enlisted, Bury, Lancs.,Reg. No. 27451, Royal Dublin Fusiliers, killed in action 27 May 1917

Private Michael Walshe, Reg. No. 66014, 24th Battalion, Canadian Infantry (Quebec regiment), killed in action 17 Sept 1916, age 55

Private Michael Walsh, Lisduff, Reg. No. 5813, Connaught Rangers, 6th Batt., killed in action, France, 20 Nov 1917, age 35

*Lance-Sergeant Patrick Walsh, Reg. No. 18947, The Loyal North Lancashire Regiment, 7th Batt., killed in action, France, 23 July 1916 (Killinagh? Ireland)

Private Michael Connell, Reg. No. 662, Irish Guards, killed in action, France, 25 Oct 1915

Mullinabreena

Private John Devaney, Achonry, killed in action France & Flanders, 1917

Private Philip Goulden, Achonry, Reg. No. 26141, Royal Dublin Fusiliers, 10th Batt., died of wounds, France, 14 Nov 1916 (Achonry)

Private – Henry (Achonry), American Forces, killed in action, France, 1918

Private James Albert Judge, Achonry, Connaught Rangers, killed in action, France & Flanders 5 Nov 1914

Private Michael Dunleavey, Oughtagh, Ummoon, Reg. No. 3830, Irish Guards, died 1 Sept 1914, age 24

Straide

Private John Roache, Reg. No. 6921, Royal Munster Fusiliers. died 26 July 1917, age 27

Private James Patrick Rowan, Reg. No. 2629, Connaught Rangers, 6th Batt., killed in action, France, 31 Jan 1917

Private John Smyth, Reg. No. 4231, Irish Guards, 1st Batt., killed in action, France, 6 Nov 1914, age 20

Private Matthew Calvey, Cloonlumney, Reg. No. 38450, Cheshire Regiment Labour Corps (formerly Shropshire Light Infantry), killed in action, France, 9-10 Aug 1918, age 19

Swinford

Private Michael Campbell, Reg. No. 12496, York & Lancaster Regiment, killed in action, France, 25 April 1917

Private Martin Clarke, Collaugh, Meelick, Reg. No. 13687, Durham Light Infantry, killed in action, France, 19 Dec 1915, age 40

Private Thomas Colgan, enlisted Darlington, Reg. No. 2595, Royal Irish Regiment, killlled in action, France, 13 Aug 1917

Private Timothy Corley, enlisted Swinford, Reg.No.3797, 2nd Connaught Rangers, killed in action, France & Flanders 22 Dec 1914

Patrick Convey, Midfield, killed in action, France & Flanders

Private Michael Doherty, Currabawn, Reg. No. 21331?, 7th-8th Battalion, Royal Irish Fusiliers, killed in action, 6 July 1916, age 25

Private James Duffy, Reg. No. 24188, Northumberland Fusiliers, 9th Batt., died, France, 8 Feb 1917 (Killaturley, Co Mayo)

*Private John Joseph Duffy, Reg. No. 9650, Connaught Rangers, 5th Batt., killed in action, France, 9 Oct 1918 (Rahbane, Co Mayo, Rabaun?)

Private John Durkan, Reg.No.6221, 5th Connaught Rangers, killed in action, France & Flanders, 9 Sept 1918

Private Thomas Durkin, Reg. No. 17921, Royal Inniskilling Fusiliers, 1st Batt., killed in action, Gallipoli, 15 Dec 1915

Swinford Private William Durkin, Reg. No. 27/1436, Northumberland Fusiliers (Tyneside Irish), killed in action, France, 1 July 1916

Private Michael Forkin, Reg. No. G/52236, The Middlesex Regiment, 23rd Batt., (formerly Yorkshire Regiment), killed in action, France, 24 Mar 1918, age 38

Private James Gallagher, Cullaun, Reg. No. 16426, King's Own Scottish Borders, killed in action, 25 Sept 1915, age 30

Private James Gallagher, Connaught Rangers, killed in action, Sept? 1915

Private James Gallagher, Reg. No. 9595, Irish Guards, 1st Batt., killed in action, France, 1 Dec 1917 (Cloongullane)

*Private Martin Gallagher, Reg. No. 1581, Irish Guards, 1st Batt., killed in action, France, 26 Oct 1914 (Gallon, Co Mayo)

Private Michael Gallagher, Cullaun, Reg. No. 16648, The Border Regiment, 1st Batt., died at sea, 19 Sept 1915, age 33

Private Patrick James Gallagher, Essex, Reg. No. 16053, Bedfordshire Regiment, 8th Batt., killed in action, France, 16 Oct 1916, age 22

Private Thomas Gallagher, Reg. No. 25/982, Northumberland Fusiliers (Tyneside Irish), died, France, 1 July 1916

Private Thomas Gavaghan, Reg. No. 43159, 7th Royal Irish Fusiliers, killed in action, France, 5 Sept 1916

Acting Sergeant Hubert Ginty, Reg. No. 29915, The Sherwood Foresters, 1st Garrison Batt., (formerly South Staffordshire Regiment), died, Egypt, 9 Nov 1918

Private Martin Groarke, enlisted Manchester,Reg. No. 26883, Royal Dublin Fusiliers, killed in action, France & Flanders, 21 Mar.1918

Corporal Hugh Heaney, Reg. No. 166405, Labour Corps (formerly Notts & Derby Regiment), died, home, 3 Nov 1917

Private John Henry, Culmore, Reg. No. 4906, Irish Guards, 2nd Batt., died of wounds, France, 27 Nov 1917; decoration, D.C.M.

Private Michael Henry, Reg. No. 2609, Connaught Rangers, 6th Batt., killed in action, France, 5 Feb 1916

Private John Higgins, Ballydrum, Reg. No. 34553, King's Own Yorkshire Light Infantry, 6th Batt., (formerly Durham Light Infantry), killed in action, France, 12 Mar 1917

Private Patrick Horkan, Reg. No. 43283, 7th Royal Inniskilling Fusiliers, died of wounds, France, 15 Sept 1916, age 24 (special memorial at North end of plot 2, row c)

Driver Thomas Keane, Reg. No. 26626, Royal Field Artillery, killed in action, France, 22 Oct 1918

Private John Lavin, Reg. No. 202918, The Yorkshire Regiment, 4th Batt., killed in action, France, 23 April 1917

Private Michael Lavin, Reg. No. 18507, North Staffordshire Regiment, 3rd Batt., died, home, 9 Mar 1916

Corporal Francis Leonard, Reg. No. 5762, Connaught Rangers, 6th Batt., killed in action, France, 20 Nov 1917

*Private James Leonard, Reg. No. 5874, Connaught Rangers, 6th Batt., killed in action, France, 20 Nov 1917 (Co Mayo)

*Private Thomas Leonard, Reg. No. 5182, Connaught Rangers, 5th Batt., killed in action, Salonika, 7 Dec 1915 (Co Mayo)

Private Thomas McConville, Reg.No.14123, 1st Royal Munsters, died of wounds, the Somme, 13 Sept 1916

Private Patrick McDonnell, Reg. No. 6550, Connaught Rangers, 1st Batt., killed in action, Mesopotamia, 11 Mar 1916

Private John McHugh, Kilbride Cottages, Reg. No. 5579, Connaught Rangers, 5th Batt., *Swinford*
killed in action, Salonica, 8 Dec 1915, age 32

Private John McHugh, Reg. No. 13797, The Lancashire Fusiliers, 2/5th Batt., died of wounds,
France, 20 Nov 1917

Martin McManus, Cullane, Reg. No. 19990, 3rd Batallion Grenadier Guards, killed in action
27 Nov 1917, age 35

Acting Corporal Edward James McMenamin, Reg. No. 9613, 2nd Royal Inniskilling Fusiliers,
killed in action, France, 21 Mar 1918

Private R. McNicholas, Loughcurragh, Reg. No. 56224, The King's (Liverpool Regiment),
killed in action 30 Oct 1917

Lieutenant Michael John McNulty, Royal Dublin Fusiliers, 5th Batt., (attached 9th Batt.),
killed in action, France & Flanders, 4 Sept 1915

Private Thomas Monelly, Reg. No. 300161, West Riding Regiment, 2/5th Batt., killed in
action, France, 26 May 1918

Private Michael Muldowney, Rabawn, Reg. No. 16262, King's Own Yorkshire Light Infantry,
10th Batt., killed in action, France, 19 Aug 1916, age 26

Private Thomas Mulroy, Lisbrogan, Reg. No. 26959, King's Liverpool Regiment, 11 Batt.,
died of wounds, France, 28 Mar 1918, age 44

Private Andrew Neary, Reg. No. 41346, Royal Inniskilling Fusiliers, 8th Batt., killed in action,
France, 6 Sept 1916 (Cullane?, Co Mayo)

Private William Joseph O'Connor, Reg. No. 1078829 Princess Patria's Canadian Light
Infantry (Eastern Ontario Regiment), killed in action, 14 Aug 1918, age 38

Lance-Corporal Thomas O'Grady, enlisted Lancashire, Reg. No. 26677, Royal Inniskilling
Fusiliers, 7/8th Batt., killed in action, France, 21 Mar 1918

Private Michael O'Hagan, Lislackagh, Reg. No. 34760, King's Own Yorkshire Light Infantry,
9th Batt. (formerly Yorkshire Regiment), killed in action, France, 26 Aug 1918, age 33

Sergeant Michael O'Hara, Kilbride Cottages, Reg. No. 3780, Connaught Rangers, 2nd Batt.,
killed in action, France, 1 Nov 1914, age 23

Sapper Michael O'Reilly, Reg. No. 14049, Royal Engineers, 11th Field Co., killed in action,
France, 23 Oct 1914

Private John Philbin, Reg. No. 23504, Royal Inniskilling Fusiliers, 1st Batt., killed in action,
France, 1 July 1916

Private William Philbin, Reg. No. 24/849, Northumberland Fusiliers (Tyneside Irish), killed
in action, France, 1 July 1916

Private John Phillips, Reg. No. 702517, The London Regiment, 23rd Batt., (formerly
Oxfordshire & Buckinghamshire Light Infantry), killed in action, France, 9 Dec 1917

Private Patrick Price, Reg. No. 3222, The Lancashire Fusiliers, 2nd Batt., killed in action,
France, 12 Oct 1916

Private Michael Clarke, Aclare, Reg. No. G/998, Royal Irish Fusiliers, died, Egypt, 2 June 1916   *Tourlestrane*

Private Michael Cunnie (Carrane), killed in action, France.

Private John Flemming, enlisted Galway, Reg. No. 6464, Connaught Rangers, 6th Batt., killed
in action France & Flanders, 16 Aug 1917

Private Henry Lundy, Aclare, American Forces, died in action, France, 1918

*Private Matthew Mullen, Acalre, Reg. No. 41775, The Lancashire Fusiliers, 1st Batt. (for-
merly Border Regiment), died of wounds, home, 4 June 1917 (Culclare?, Co Mayo)

Private Bernard Neary, Kilmactigue, Reg. No. 28046, 1st Royal Dublin Fusiliers, killed in
action, France, 29 Mar 1918

Joseph Walsh, drowned when *The Leinster* steamer was sunk by German submarine, 1918

Tubbercurry   Driver John Alexander Allen, Reg. No. 4/092021, Royal Army Service Corps, died of enteric fever, Salonica, Balkans, 14 July 1916

Private John Boland, Reg. No. 12037, Loyal North Lancashire Regiment, killed in action, Gallipoli, 10 Aug 1915

Private Patrick Brennan, King's Liverpool Regiment, killed in action France & Flanders, 15 Sept 1916

Private James Cunnane (Tullamoy), American Forces, killed clearing mines, France, 12 Nov 1918

Private Henry Elliott, Reg. No. 20542, South Lancashire Regiment, 11th Batt., killed in action, France, 23 Mar 1918

Private Thomas Grady, Reg. No. 916, Connaught Rangers, 5th Batt., killed in action Gallipoli, 22 Aug 1915

Lance-Sergeant James Haran, Cloonacool, Reg. No. 4655, Irish Guards, 1st Batt., killed in action, France, 1 Feb 1915

Patrick J. Kilcoyne (Ougham), age 24, died at sea when ship was torpedoed in Bay of Biscay,17 April 1917

Private Thomas Killoran, Reg. No. 20491, Royal Irish Fusiliers, 7/8th Batt., killed in action, France, 16 Aug 1917

Private Charles Lundy, Cashel, Reg. No. 5501, Connaught Rangers, 5th Batt., died of wounds, Salonika, 6 Oct 1916

Private Michael Lundy, Cashel, American Forces, killed in action, Dardanelles, 1916

Sergeant John F. McGuinn, Cashel, Reg. No. 5097, Irish Guards, 2nd Batt., died of wounds, France, 27 Mar 1916

Private Patrick McGuinn, Ougham, Reg. No. 4509, Connaught Rangers, 2nd Batt., killed in action, France, 8 Nov 1914 (Ougham)

Sergeant-Major Michael Mannion, died in military hospital, France, Oct 1917

Private John Moran, Reg. No. 17017, The Loyal North Lancashire Regiment, 6th Batt., killed in action, Mesopotamia, 5 April 1916

Corporal Joseph Neary, Reg. No. 280508, Royal Garrison Artillery, killed in action, France, 21 April 1917; decoration, M.M.

Private John Noone, American Forces, killed in action, France, Nov 1918

Sapper Charles Quinn, Cloonacool, Reg. No. 146950, Royal Engineers, Tunnel Co., killed in action, France, 16 Oct 1918

John P. Quinlan, Cloonacool, 165th American Infantry, killed in action, France & Flanders, 18 Oct 1918

Private John Stokes, Cloonacool, Reg. No. 1778, Irish Guards, 1st Batt., died of wounds, France, 19 May 1915

Private Frank Sweeney, Reg. No. 421297, Labour Corps (formerly Connaught Rangers), died of wounds, France, 16 Oct 1917

Private Christopher Walker, Reg. No. 10307, Irish Guards, 2nd Batt., died of wounds, France, 24 April 1918

Private Francis Walsh, American Forces, killed in action, Flanders, Nov 1917

Private James Walsh, Reg. No. 39516, ?Highland Light Infantry, 17th (Service) Batt., killed in action, France, 2 Dec 1917

*Private Patrick Walsh, Reg. No. 4491, Connaught Rangers, 5th Batt., killed in action, France, 10 Oct 1918 (Co Sligo)

*   There is a doubt whether this person is a native of the parish as his address is misspelt or otherwise not clear.

APPENDIX 45: SOME WORLD WAR I PARTICIPANTS

'McNulty (secretary Swinford Board of Guardians) got a return of those who joined the army from most of the parishes in your constituency.'[1]

Private Thomas Brady, Kilvanloon, joined Aug 1914, awarded D.C.M. Oct 1916   *Ballaghaderreen*
Constable Cantwell RIC Ballaghaderreen, volunteered for the front, July 1915
Private T. Forkan, Ballaghaderreen, wounded Nov 1917
Lieutenant Frank MacDermot, Coolavin, Army Service Corps
Private J. Merrigan, Connaught Rangers, wounded Sept 1917
Constable J. Regan RIC, joined Irish Guards, Feb 1915, wounded Sept 1917
Private T. Reid, wounded Nov 1917.

Private – Clarke (brother of Michael Clarke, killed at Gallipoli)   *Ballymote*
Private Gussie Dowling (son of P. J. Dowling PO), joined the army Mar 1918
Private – Dowling (brother of above)
F. W. Gorman, senior clerk Ballymote PO, joined the army April 1917
Captain William Knox, Connaught Rangers
Private J. McGettrick, Connaught Rangers, wounded, Sept 1917
Private E. Shannon, Connaught Rangers, wounded, Sept 1917

Lance-Corporal P. Howley, wounded Nov 1917   *Ballysadare*
Private Fred Scott (son of J. W. Scott, Fisheries, Ballysadare)
Private Jim Scott (brother of above)
Private – Scott (brother of above)
Private – Scott (brother of above)

Private Michael Ansboro (Carroward), POW in Germany, Nov 1917   *Bohola*
Private William Bourke (Carroward)
Private Ignatius Morley (Carroward)
Private James Morley (Carroward)
Private Martin Morley (Carroward), invalided out before Nov 1917

Lt. Dr. J. M. Ahern (son-in-law of John O'Dowd MP) volunteered June 1916   *Bunninadden*
Sergeant-Major P. J. Benson, Royal Engineers (photo, *S.C.* 15 April 1916)
Private Michael Friel, RIC, joined Irish Guards June 1916
Private Joe King, Connaught Rangers, POW at Limburg, 8 Mar 1915

Private Michael Joseph Duffy, Charlestown?   *Charlestown*
Private Henry Durcan, emigrated to US and joined US army
Michael Louis Henry, Killavil, chaplain, Mar 1916
Private James Leonard, Connaught Rangers
Private T. McGowan, Tawnyinah, Irish Guards, military medal for gallantry Aug 1918
Lieutenant J. P. Marren, Cortoon, Royal Irish Regiment, Military Cross for gallantry
Lieutenant T. J. Marren, Cortoon
Private Timmons, POW at Limburg and Gissen, 17 Sept 1915

Major William Bruen, Connaught Rangers, awarded the MC.   *Collooney*
Felix Burke, Kinegrelly, chaplain, 16th Irish Division
Nurse Ginnie Burke SRN, Kinnagrelly
Brigadier-General Bryan Cooper, Markrea Castle, Connaught Rangers, wounded, Aug 1915
Sergeant W. Martin, Royal Irish Rifles, wounded April 1917.

1   Denis O'Hara to John Dillon, 26 Sept. 1917, Dil. P. 6769 (not found)

Collooney	Rev M. J. Mullins, son of Patrick Mullins, ordained in Maynooth Dec.1916, joined army as chaplain, in convalaescent home in England, Oct 1917, after long illness in France (photo in uniform, *S.C.* 27 Oct 1917))
Doocastle	Sergeant A. Rogers, Connaught Rangers
Foxford	Private Willie Fox, Foxford National Volunteer, joined Irish Brigade, Feb 1915 Lieutenant Dick Shiel (son of Isaac Shiel)
Kilkelly	Private J. Horan, Glentavraun, POW at Limburg, 17 Sept 1915
Killasser	Private Daniel Barry (Corlee) Private James Barry (Corlee) Private Patrick Brady (Lismoran) Private Thomas McAndrew (Corlee) Private Martin Neary (Lismoran)
Kilmovee	Sergeant Duffy, Kilmovee, Royal Irish, POW in Limburg, 17 Sept 1915 Private James McCann, Uggool, POW at Limburg, 17 Sept 1915
Kiltimagh	Private Charles Brown, Main St, 3rd Batt. Connaught Rangers Private – Brown, Main St, (brother of above) Private Thomas Brown, Main St, King's Irish Liverpool Rifles, wounded at Neuve Chapelle, Oct 1916 Private – Canavan, Dublin Fusiliers Private – Canavan, Dublin Fusiliers (brother of above) Private – Canavan, Dublin Fusiliers (brother of above) Corporal Patrick Carroll, Attavally, Royal Engineers Private James Gallagher, Trenagleragh, Connaught Rangers. Private John Goulding (Golden?), Aidan St, lost a leg Private Edward Jordan, James St, wounded at Battle of the Somme 1916 Private M. Kelly, Kiltimagh, Connaught Rangers Private John Lydon, 2nd South Lancashires Lieutenant Dermot A. M. MacManus, Killedan House, wounded at Gallipoli, 31 July 1915 Private J. McNicholas, Connaught Rangers Private Thomas Malley, D Company, 2nd Batt. Connaught Rangers. Patrick Moloney, Royal Navy Private James O'Brien, Dublin Fusiliers Private M. M. Regan, 3rd Batt. West Riding Regiment, York Patrick Reilly, Cartron, Ambulance Corps, US Army in France
Mullinabreena	Private Andy Derhams, Carrowcorragh Private Mick Derhams, Carrowcorragh, (brother of above) Private Willie Derhams, Carrowcorrag, (brother of above)
Swinford	Private James P. Callaghan, 3rd Batt. Irish Guards, left for the front, July 1915, home on leave, Aug 1916 Captain John Francis Campbell, chaplain, US army Private J. S. Clarke, awarded DCM July 1915 and promoted to Sergeant Private M. Clarke, Connaught Rangers, wounded, Sept 1917 Private James Gallagher, Irish Guards, 3rd Batt. Private Michael Gavigan, Swinford, Connaught Rangers, wounded at La Bassee, Feb 1915 Private Halligan, Swinford, POW Limburg, July 1915 Corporal Thomas Kneafsey, joined Irish Guards Oct? 1915

Private – Kneafsey, Irish Guards (brother of above)   *Swinford*
J. F. McNicholas, 10th Commercial Battalion, RDE, wounded at Arras, April 1917
Mr. Marks, Provincial Bank, Swinford, volunteered for the front, Feb 1916
James. B. O'Connor, 10th Commercial Battalion, wounded at Arras, April 1917
Private Joseph O'Connor, left for the front, July 1915
Frank Whiston, Swinford, left for the front, July 1915

Private John Cunnane, Tullamoy   *Tourlestrane*
Private James Keaveny, Gorteslin, American Forces

Private Peter Brennan   *Tubbercurry*
Private Tom Gibbons
Private Jim Gorman
Private Patrick Henry, Connaught Rangers
Private Kavanagh, Connaught Rangers, wounded at Ypres, Jan 1915
Private James Keaveny, Gorteslin, American Forces
Private Patrick Lundy, Cashel
Private John Mannion
Driver Philip Mannion (brother of above), wounded, Mar 1917
Private Thomas Mannion (brother of above)
Private Edward Quinn, Cloonacool
Private Denis Wynne

APPENDIX 46: SINN FÉIN CLUBS

Achonry: Michael Gallagher, president, Pat O'Neill DC, vice-president, Luke Brennan, treasurer, James Judge and Hugh Kerins, secretaries. Members: A. Healy, Peter Brennan, Thomas Rogers, H. O'Neill, John Scanlon, Thomas Hunt, W. Donagh, John Brennan, John Brehony, John Smith, John O'Connell and M. Gannon.[1]
A hundred members were enrolled in the Moylough club in August.
Moylough: Luke Snee, president, C. J. Gildea and J. J. Hunt, secretaries.[2]
Sinn Féin East-Mayo Executive (24 Feb. 1918) [3]
Officers: Representative to Ard Comhairle: J. F. Shouldice. President: J. F. Campbell. Vice-president: – Doyle and J. Doherty. Treasurers: P. O'Hara and T. Jordan. Secretaries: T. Ruane and S. Corcoran
Delegates: Ballaghaderreen: J. Flannery and T. O'Hara. *Bohola:* J. Walsh. *Bohertee:* Patrick Towey and T. Cunnane. *Brusna:* P. Freyne and M. Regan. *Carracastle:* P. Cassidy and E. Regan. *Edmondstown:* P. Finan and P. Higgins. *Foxford:* P. Grennan. *Hagfield:* M. Brennan. *Kiltimagh:* T. Ruane and M. De Burca. *Kilkelly:* T. Sharkey and P. Tarpey. *Lecarrow:* Joseph Doherty and P. Carney. *Lavey:* Thomas and James Egan. *Rooskey:* William Tonry and B. McGarry. *Swinford:* P. Durkan, P. Henry, and J. Comer, secretary. *Tullinacurra:* J. Sweeney and A. McDowney. *Sonnagh:* J. McEntyre and T. Foley.

APPENDIX 47: CIVIL WAR FATALITIES IN ACHONRY

Harry Brehony, Collooney, republican, 16 February 1923
Capt. Brennan, army, December 1922
Matt Brennan, Cloonagh, Curry, army, November, 1922

1 *S.C.* 21 July 1917
2 *S.C.* 18 Aug 1917
3 *W.P.* 2 Mar 1918

Volunteer Thomas Browne, Kiltimagh, army, January 1923
Volunteer Clarke, army, December 1922
Adjutant John Durcan, Curry, republican, 13 September 1922
Christopher Farrell, Dublin, civilian, 17 January 1923
Commandant Thomas Flannery, Ballaghaderreen, republican
Capt. Tom Healy, Pontoon, Foxford, army, September 1922
Volunteer Sean Higgins, Foxford, army, September 1922
Matt Hunt. Powelboro, Tubbercurry, army?, 5 November 1922
Capt. Eugene Kelly, Lisacul, Ballaghaderreen, republican, June 1922
Quarter-Master Ned Kilroy, Curry, republican, 22 December 1922
– McCaffrey, Co Cavan, army, November 1922
Martin McGuinn, Curry, republican, February 1923
Peter McNicholas, Swinford, army, 25 April 1923
– McPartland, Sligo, civilian, 6 November 1922
– Moran, Bohola, republican
Michael Mullen, Carralabin, Bonniconlon, republican, 14 July 1922
Commandant Jim Mulrenan, Lisacul, Ballaghaderreen, republican, October 1922
Volunteer Patrick Mulrenan, Lisacul, Ballaghaderreen, republican, December 1922
James Joseph O'Connor, Powelboro, Tubbercurry, army?, 5 November 1922
Commandant Thomas Ruane, Kiltimagh, army, July 1922
Commandant Michael Scally, Ballymahon, Co Longford, army, August, 1922
Frank Scanlon, Cloonacool, republican?, 6 November 1922
Volunteer Harry Spelman, Kiltimagh, army, March 1923
Patrick Stenson, Curry, republican, March 1923
Volunteer J. Traynor, Fermanagh, army, August 1922
4 National soldiers shot dead at Rockwood Ambush, 13 July 1922
National soldier killed at Carnagopal between Benada and Curry August 1922
National soldier shot dead in Tubbercurry, 25 January 1923
Republican (unnamed) killed at Gurteen, 9 July 1922

Bibliography

ARCHIVES

Ballaghadereen

Achonry Diocesan Archives:

Dr Lyster's Book E: clerical changes and appointments 1903-12; parish missions 1904-10; average school attendance for *relatio status;* Maynooth prizes 1904-07; notes on 23 priests including Ambrose Blaine and Michael Louis Henry; Benada girls' lace class 1905-08; Foxford Woollen Mills 1907; students in Maynooth, Salamanca, Rome and Paris; girls who entered foreign convents (n. d.); list of 66 students including bishops, Thomas McGettrick and William Philbin; students in Irish College, Paris 1935; dates of ordinations of curates 1887-1910; average school attendance 1906; convent visitations, Kiltimagh 1911-18, Swinford convent 1913-34, Ballymote convent 1935-38, Collooney convent 1914-41

Dr Lyster's Book G: De Clero Dioecesano – notes on 82 priests, including Denis O'Hara, Michael Keveney, Dominick O'Grady, Edward Connington, the Staunton brothers etc; clerical changes and appointments 1888-1903; curates with dates of ordinations 1888-1908

Dr Lyster's Book H (continued by Morrisroe), Confirmations by MacCormack 14 May 1872-14 May 1877; obituaries 1832-88 and 1887-1942; Confirmations 1888-1942; Swinford Convent of Mercy 1888-1910; dedication of churches; priests' ordinations 1888-1940; Foxford convent 1891-1911, St Louis Kiltimagh 1897-1910; prebends of Achonry; nuns' obituaries 1888-1912; 1 Jan.1901, list of old Achonry chalices; Marist convent Tubbercurry 1901-1908; Marist Brothers, Swinford 1901-1919; succession of parish priest since the beginning of 19th century (which Canon Judge gave to Bishop MacCormack); Ballymote convent 1902-1908; notes on eight priests; succession of deans and archdeacons; Achonry Chapter 1888-1930

Book (no designation): number of marriages each year from 14 April 1868-1 April 1874 in each parish; number of marriages in each parish for each year from 1875-1941; number of schools in Tubbercurry, Bunninadden, Ballymote, Keash, Carracastle, Ballaghaderreen, Kilmovee and Swinford in 1884; Relief Fund of Dr MacCormack 1879-80

Book (Bishop Durcan): Induction fees paid to Bishop McNicholas 1840-50 and paid to Bishop Durcan 1853-70 giving the names of the priests and the year of induction; number of marriages in parishes in 1834, in some in 1853 and in others in 1856-66

Baptismal & Marriage Registers (on microfilm – originals in each parish): Attymass, baptisms from 1875, marriages from 1894; Ballaghaderreen, baptisms from 1855, marriages from 1830, Ballymote, baptisms from 1856, marriages from 1824; Ballysadare (see Collooney); Bohola, baptisms & marriages from 1857; Bonniconlon, baptisms from 1870, marriages from 1897; Bunninadden, baptisms from 1850, marriages from 1841; Carracastle, baptisms from 1853, marriages from 1847; Charlestown, baptisms from 1847, marriages from 1844; Collooney, baptisms from 1842, marriages from 1858; Coolaney, baptisms from 1878, marriages from 1846; Curry, baptisms and marriages from 1867; Foxford, baptisms from 1873, marriages from 1870; Gurteen, baptisms from 1845, marriages from 1873; Keash, baptisms from 1843, marriages from 1842; Kilmovee, baptisms from 1854, marriages from 1824; Killasser, baptisms & marriages from 1847; Kiltimagh, baptisms from 1861, marriages from 1834; Mullinabreena, baptisms from 1884, marriages from 1865; Straide, baptisms from 1888, marriages from 1886; Swinford, baptisms from 1808, marriages from 1826; Tourlestrane, baptisms from 1845, marriages from 1848; Tubbercurry, baptisms & marriages from 1859

Dublin
Byrne & Son, W. H., Suffolk St, Dublin, architectural drawings.

Dublin City Archives
CH 1/39/1 (Tubbercurry), 24 (Ballymote), 25 (Bunninaddem), 37 (Swinford), 42 (Carracastle), 59 (Collooney), 63 (Bonniconlon), 130 (Charlestown), 190 (Foxford), 199 (Keash), 219 (Ballaghaderreen), 266 (Bohola), 267 (Kilmovee), 296 (Kilmactigue), 303 (Attymass), 319 (Killasser), 364 (Gurteen), 416 (Curry), 421 (Killoran), 426 (Achonry), 519 (Straide)

Dublin Diocesan Archives
346/1

Irish Architectural Archives, 73 Merrion Square

Irish Jesuit Archives

National Archives
Chief Secretary's Office Registered Papers (CSORP)
Constabulary Reports
Distress Papers (DP)
ED 1/61 (Mayo), nos. 2, 5, 8, 12, 18, 19, 20, 22, 23, 33, 41, 49, 52, 61, 64, 68, 70, 72, 88, 105, 114, 126, 136, 161, 169
ED 1/79 (Sligo), nos. 3, 5, 8, 9, 10, 12, 13, 14, 22, 23, 26, 27, 28, 29, 18, 34, 35, 39, 40, 43, 45, 46, 51, 52, 55, 59, 62, 65, 70, 71, 72, 76, 78, 79, 80, 85, 87, 91, 92, 93, 94, 99, 104, 105, 106, 112
ED. 2/32 (Mayo), folios 13, 19, 37, 49, 57, 58, 68, 61, 70, 72, 114, 115, 116, 126, 127, 137, 139, 141, 143, 145, 146, 154, 156, 163, 164, 190, 204,
ED 2/41 (Sligo), folios 4, 9, 10, 11, 13, 15, 16, 22, 23, 28, 29, 32, 33, 35, 43, 44, 46, 47, 49, 50, 53, 59, 60, 68, 70, 72, 73, 74, 76, 80, 87, 88, 90, 93, 100, 101, 103, 104, 105, 111, 112, 113, 115, 116, 117, 118, 119, 120, 126, 129, 135, 142, 146, 147, 163, 166,167, 169, 172
Fenians Arrests and Discharges 1866-69
Fenian Briefs
Fenian Files
Habeas Corpus Suspension Act (HCSA), lists and statistics of persons arrested and discharged under the habeas corpus suspension act or convicted for their part in the Fenian conspiracy.
Relief Commission Papers (RLFC)
Outrage Papers (OP), Mayo 1834, 1836, Sligo 1834, 1835, 1836, 1837
Society of Friends' Famine Papers (SFFP)
State of Country Papers, 2362/18

National Library
O'Hara Papers,
Mss.13, 552, 17, 709, 20, 280
Amy Mander Papers, Ms. 24,526
Plunkett Papers, Ms. 11,408

Oblates of Mary Immaculate Archives, Inchicore, Dublin

Passionist Order Archives, Mount Argus, Dublin

Religious Sisters of Charity Generalate Archives, Sandymount, Dublin
RSCG/H 13/91, 'Annals of Benada',
H 26, 'Annals of Foxford', vol. 1 (1891-1905), vol. 2 (1905-1915), vol. 3 (1915-1923)
H 26 / 75, Frank Sherry's eyewitness account of the Easter Rising 1916
H 26 / 1, 2, 6, 48, 87, 98, 105, 110, 111, 170, 171, 174, 178,
H 26 / 449 Memoirs of Agnes Morrogh Bernard
H ?, 'Annals of Ballaghaderreen'

Trinity College Archives
Dillon Papers, nos. 6455-7 (Adelaide & John Blake Dillon), 6457 (Christina Dillon), 6759
(John O'Dowd), 6728 (Michael Davitt), 6759, 6766 (John Lyster), 6769, (Denis O'Hara),
6770 (Martin Henry 47-70, Michael Keveney 124-139, John O'Grady 172-187), 6771,
6803, 6806, 6808, (Swinford Board of Guardians), 6819, 6822, 6885 (Anne Deane), 6886,
6887, 6888, 6889 (Agnes Morrogh Bernard), 6892 (F. J. MacCormack 94-103)

Trinity College Library
TCD OL microfilm 395

University College Dublin Archives Department
Mulcahy Papers
P 7 / A / 33, 38, 40, 52, 53
P 17a / 119, 121, 132
P 7a / 15, 17
P 7 / B / 22, 23, 25, 73, 74, 75, 91, 98, 109, 110, 114, 197, 198, 199, 203, 214, 215
Moss Twomey Papers
P 69 / 30 (Report of Enemy Round-up on Ox Mountains, 1923)
P 69 / 33 ('Diary of Activities of 4th Brigade, 3rd Western division from beginning of hostil-
ities to 30 Nov. 1922')
P 69 / 34 Report of 4th Western Division
P 69 / 107, 127
O'Malley Notebooks/P17b/109 (Tom Carney), 113 (Johnny Greely), 133 (Maurteen
Brennan, Jim Hunt,Tom Scanlon), 137 (Jack Brennan)
P7/A/38, 40, 52, 53

Vincentian Archives, Dublin, St Paul's, Sybil Hill, Raheny

Dundalk
Redemptorist Archives, St Joseph's Monastery
Apostolici Labores, vol.1 (1876-98)
Chronica Domestica, vol.1

Paris
Irish College Archives

Rome
Irish College Archives
Kirby Papers

Propaganda Fide
Acta, vols. 214, 237, 257, 258
Lettere, vols. 302, 303, 304, 307, 308, 312, 313, 314, 316, 341, 342, 343, 346, 356, 363, 365, 366, 369, 370
N.S., vol. 69, 189, 259, 323
Scritture originali riferite nelle Congregazioni Generali, vols. 975, 998, 1026, 1028
Scritture riferite nei Congressi, Irlanda, vols. 23, 24, 25, 29, 31, 32, 35, 36, 37, 38, 39, 42, 43, 45
Udiense, vols.56, 59, 60, 61, 67, 79, 81, 84, 87, 91, 101, 114, 115, 117, 120, 126, 130, 141, 144, 149, 150, 164, 170, 174, 175, 179, 180, 181,183, 187, 198, 212, 216, 226, 227, 232, 241, 245

Vatican Archives
Congregazio Consistoriale, Relationes Diocesium, 5

PRINTED MATERIAL

Abbott, Richard, *Police Casualties in Ireland 1919-1922* (2000)
Achonry/Mulinabreena Developing the West Group, *From Plain to Hill. A short History of the Parish of Achonry.* (1995)
Atkinson, Sarah, *Mary, Aikenhead: Her Life, her Work and her Friends* (1879)
Barrow, John. *A Tour round Ireland* (1835)
Blunt, William Scawen, *The Land War in Ireland*
Bohola. Its History and its People
Bohola Post
Boylan, Henry, *Dictionary of National Biography*
Bowen, Desmond, *Souperism, Myth or Reality? A Study in Souperism* (1970)
Butler, Katherine, *The Story of Benada*
Canning, Bernard T., *Bishops of Ireland 1870-1978*
Carroll, Denis, *They Have Fooled You Again. Michael O'Flanagan (1876-1942), Priest, Republican, Social Critic* (1993)
Catholic Registry
Church of the Immaculate Conception, Killavil 1861-1991
Cill Mobhi 1886-1996
Clancy, Phyl, *A Journey of Mercy. From Birth to Re-Birth* (1984)
Coleman, Vincent, *Carracastle Then and Now* (1982)
'The MacDonnells of Palmfield House' in *Carracastle Then and Now*, pp. 37-8
Comer, Michael & Murphy, Micheal, *The Burma Road, Claremorris to Collooney Railway* (1996)
Concise Dictionary of National Biography
Congested Districts Board Reports, First, 3 Dec 1892 - Twenty-Seventh, 31 Mar. 1919

Connolly, S.J., *Priests and People in Pre-Famine Ireland 1780-1845* (1982)

Cooke, Coleman, *Mary Charles Walker, The Nun of Calabar* (1980)

Coolahan, John, *Irish Education, History and Structure*

Corfe, Tom, *Phoenix Park Murders*

Corish Patrick J., *Maynooth College 1795-1995* (1995)

Corran Herald, nos. 1-36, 1985-2003 (ed. James Flanagan)

Culmore National School 1869-1999. Down Memory Lane

Cunningham, John, *St Jarlath's College, Tuam, 1800-2000*

Curry: 100 years of Gaelic Games 1889-1989 (1989)

Curry-Moylough 2000 (1999)

Curry Parish Magazine (1993)

Davitt, Michael, *The Fall of Feudalism in Ireland* (1904)

D'Arcy, W., *The Fenian Movement*

de Brún, Pádraig, *The Irish Society's Teachers* (forthcoming publication)

De Latocnaye, *Promenade d'un Francais dans l'Irlande* (1797), translated as *Rambles through Ireland* (1798)

Denieffe, Joseph, *A Personal Narrative of the Irish Revolutionary Brotherhood*

Devon Commission: Evidence taken before the Commissioners appointed to inquire into the occupation of Land in Ireland, 1844

Devoy, John, *Recollections of an Irish Rebel ... a personal narrative* (1929)

Dictionary of National Biography

Doherty, John, *Achonry Priests in the Twentieth Century,* (unpublished typescript)

Dublin Opinion, Dec. 1936

Duffy, Eugene, 'Mother Arsenius and the Eye of Providence in *Survival or Salvation? A Second Mayo Book of Theology,* pp. 81-98

Duffy, P. J., *Killavile and its People* (1985)

Farry, Michael, *Killoran and Coolaney: A Local History* (1985)

Sligo 1914-1921: a chronicle of conflict (1992)

The Aftermath of Revolution, Sligo 1921-23 (2000)

Feeney, Michael & Clarke, P. J., *Mayo Soldiers Died in the Great War* , (unpublished typescript)

Finlay SJ, T. A., *Foxford and the Providence Woollen Mills*

Finn, J., *Gurteen, Co Sligo: Its history, traditions and antiquities* (1981)

Flanigan, Patricia, 'Secondary Education in Ballymote' in *Corran Herald,* no. 14 (1988)

Flynn, Robert, *Church of the Immaculate Conception, Ballymote* (1983)

Foy, T., *The Parish of Bunninadden* (1949)

Fryer, C. E. J., *The Waterford and Limerick Railway* (2000)

Gildea, Denis, *Mother Mary Arsenius of Foxford* (1936)

Work is Worship. Foxford 1892-1942 (sermon preached in Foxford 26 April 1842)

Gilmartin, Thomas, *A Manual of Church History*

Goodbody, Rob, *A Suitable Channel. Quaker Relief in the Great Famine* (1995)

Gurteen: Its People and its Past (1993)

Hackett, J. D., *Bishops of the United States of Irish Birth or Descent* (1936)

Hall, Rev James, *Tour through Ireland,* 2 vols. (1813)

Hall, Mr and Mrs S. C., *Ireland: Its scenery, character, etc.,* (1841)

Hierarchia Catholica

Healy, John, *Death of an Irish Town* (1968)

Healy, John, *Maynooth College Centenary History* (1895)

Higgins, John, Timoney, Mary B., Connolly, Br Thomas, Kielty, John (eds.), *Keash and Culfadda A Local History* (2001)

History of Attymass (2000)

Ireland's Memorial Records 1914-1918 (Dublin 1923)

Irish Builder

Irish Catholic Directory

Jeffery, Keith, *Ireland and the Great War* (2000)

Jennings, Martin, (ed.), *Swinford Re-Echo. Parish Inscapes* (1981)

'St Nathy's College: Historical Background' in *St Nathy's College Journal* (1996) pp. 9-18

Joyce, Bernie, *Agnes Morrogh-Bernard 1842-1932, Foundress of Foxford Woollen Mills*

Kerr, Donal A., *'A nation of Beggars'? Priests, People and Politics in Famine Ireland 1846-1852* (1994)

— *The Catholic Church and the Famine* (1996)

Kilgannon, T., *Sligo and its Surroundings: A descriptive and pictorial guide to the history, antiquties, scenery and places of interest in and around Sligo* (1926)

Kilcoyne, John, 'A History of Tubbercurry' appended to Killoran, Anne, *Saga of the Killoran Clan* (1990)

Killaraght: A History (2002)

Kiltimagh Church Centenary (1988)

Laheen, Kevin A., *Jesuits in Killaloe*

— (ed.) 'Jesuit Parish Mission Memoirs 1863-76' in *Collectanea Hibernica*, nos, 39 and 40 (1997-8) pp. 272-311, no. 41 (1999) pp. 153-225, no. 42 (2000) pp. 120-180

Larkin, Emmet, 'The Devotional Revolution in Ireland, 1850-75' in *American Historical Review*, vol. 77, no. 3 (June 1972), pp. 625-652

Leslie, J. B., *Biographical Succession List of the Clergy of Achonry and Killala,* (typescript in the Representative Church Body Library, Braemor Road, Dublin).

Lewis, Samuel, *Topographical Dictionary of Ireland*

London Builder

Lyons, F. S. L., *John Dillon, A Biography* (1968)

— 'The Irish unionist party and the devolution crisis of 1904-5' in *Irish Historical Studies*, vol. vi, no. 21 (Mar. 1948)

McCarrick, Frank, *Father Denis O'Hara, a short biography* (unpublished thesis)

McDonagh, J. C., *History of Ballymote and the Parish of Emlaghfad,* (1936)

McDonnell-Garvey, Maire, *Mid-Connacht. The Ancient Territory of Sliabh Lugha* (1995)

McGettrick, Thomas, *Memoirs of Bishop T. McGettrick* (1988)

McGrath, Declan, 'The building of Ballymote Church' in *Corran Herald*, no.15 (1988)

McGuinn, James, *Curry* (1984)

— *Sligo Men in the Great War 1914-1918* (1994)

MacManus, L., *White Light and Flame*

McNally, Patricia, 'Alec McCabe 1866-1872' in *Corran Herald*, no. 6 (1986)

— 'Father P.J. O'Grady' in *Corran Herald*, no. 5 (1986)

McNeill, Mary, *Vere Foster 1819-1900. An Irish Benefactor* (1971)

McTiernan, John C., *Sligo: Sources of Local History* (1994)

— *Olde Sligoe. Aspects of Town and County over 750 Years* (1995)

— *In Sligo Long Ago* (1998)

McVeigh, David, *For the Record: Banada Abbey Secondary School 1958-2002* (2002)

Marist Convent, Tubbercurry, Co Sligo Centenary Magazine (2001)

Messenger

Micks W.L., *History of the Congested Districts Board*

Moody, T. W., *Davitt and Irish Revolution 1846-82* (1981)

Morris, Morgan, *Charlestown and its Surroundings* (1988)

Morrissey, James, *On the Verge of Want* (2001)

Murphy, J. A., 'The Support of the Catholic Clergy in Ireland, 1750-1850' in *Historical Studies*, V (1965), pp. 103-121

Murray, Patrick, *Oracles of God. The Roman Catholic Church and Irish Politics 1922-37*, (2000)

National Education Report 1856

National Education Report 1866

Neligan, James, 'Parish of Kilmactige', in W. S. Mason, *A Statistical Account or Parochial Survey of Ireland,* vol.2, pp. 349-98

Noone, M. J., *Michael O'Doherty, Archbishop of Manila, His Life and Times*

Oblate Missionary Record (1891, 1892)

Ó Cathaoir, Brendan (ed.), *John Blake Dillon* (1993)

The Diary of Charles Hart (2003)

O'Connor, John, *The Workhouses of Ireland. The Fate of Ireland's Poor* (1995)

O'Donovan Rossa, Jeremiah, *Irish Rebels in English Prisons*

— *My Years in English Jails*

O'Gallagher, Marianna, and Dompierre, Rose Masson, *Eyewitness Grosse Isle, 1847* (1995)

O'Hara, Bernard, (ed.), *Killasser, a history* (1981)

— (ed.), *Mayo: Aspects of its Heritage,* (1982)

— *The Archaeological Heritage of Killasser, Co Mayo* (1991)

Ó Laighin, Pádraig G., *Eadbhard Ó Dufaigh, 1840-1868* (1994)

O'Leary, John, *Fenians and Fenianism*

O'Malley, Ernie, *The Singing Flame*

On the Record (Cloonloo Parish Community)

O'Regan, J., *Articles Worldwide and Local*

O'Rorke, Terence, *History, antiquities and present state of the Parishes of Ballysadare and Kilvarnet in the County of Sligo with notices of the O'Haras, the Coopers, the Percevals and other local families*

— *The History of Sligo: Town and County,* 2 vols.

Parliamentary Papers (1825), vol. 12

Parliamentary Papers 1835), vol. 35

Pauline, Sr M., *God Wills It*

Pender, S., 'Survey of Rossa's Papers' in *Journal of Cork Archaeological and Historical Society*, LXXVIII (May-Meitheamh) 1973, pp. 14-26

Proceedings of the Mansion House Committee

Reports and papers relating to the proceedings of the committee of 'Mr Tuke's fund' for assisting emigration from Ireland (private circulation, 1885)

Reports on the condition of the peasantry of County Mayo to the Mansion House Committee

Richardson, Douglas Scott, *Gothic Revival Architecture in Ireland,* doctoral dissertation, Yale University (1970)

Second Report of the Commissioners on Public Instruction

Seymour, A.J., *Reminiscences of Charles Seymour of Connaught* (1895)

Seymour, Rev. Charles, *Twenty-Six Sermons by the Rev. Charles Seymour with an introductory preface containing a brief memoir of the author's life by Charlotte Elizabeth* (1835)

Sharp, John, *Reapers of the Harvest: The Redemptorists in Great Britain and Ireland* (1989)

Shean, Francis, 'Lord McDonnell of Swinford' in *Swinford Echo* (1966) pp.95-6

Slator's National Commercial Dictionary of Irish, English and Scottish Towns

Sobolewski, Peter and Solon, Betty, (eds.) *Kiltimagh Our Life & Times*

Soldiers Died in the Great War, CD Rom, Naval and Military Press Ltd

Souvenir programme, official opening of Fr O'Hara Memorial Park, Charlestown, 3 June 1951

Spelman, Joseph, *Church of the Assumption, Collooney* (1993)

St Nathy's College Journal (1996)

St Patrick's Church, Gurteen 1866-1997

Sullivan, A. M., *Speeches from the Dock*

Swinford Echo 1959, 1960, 1961, 1962, 1963,1964, 1965, 1966, 1967

*Swinford Echoes,*1993

Swinford GAA Club Commemorative Programme 1979

Swinford Historical Society, *An Gorta Mór. Famine in the Swinford Union.*

Swinford Parish Church Centenary (1991)

Swords, Liam, *A Hidden Church: The diocese of Achonry 1689-1818* (1997)

— *In their own Words. The Famine in North-Connacht 1845-1849* (1999)

The Dublin Builder & Architectural, Engineering, Mechanics and Sanitary Journal, vol. 11 (1 Sept. 1860)

Thom's Directory

Tierney, Mark, 'Calendar of Croke Papers', *Collectanea Hibernica,* vol.13, pp.116-17

Tracey, J. J., Master of Architecture thesis, Queen's University, Belfast

Tubbercurry Macra na Tuaithe, *Tubbercurry and its Surroundings* (1982)

Tuke, J. H., *Narrative of Visits to Distressed Districts in Ireland, Nov.-Dec. 1847: A Visit to Connaught in Autumn 1847*

Voices – Ballaghaderreen (2003)

Yeats, W .B., *Come gather round me Parnellites*

Young, Arthur, *A tour in Ireland: with general observations on the present state of the kingdom: made in the years 1776, 1777 and 1778, and brought down to 1779,* 2 vols. (1780)

NEWSPAPERS

An Claidheamh Solais

An Phoblacht, 5 Nov. 1827 (lengthy obituary of Philip Mulligan PP Carracastle)

Commercial Gazette, Cincinnati

Connaught Ranger

Connaught Telegraph

Cork Examiner

Daily Despatch of Richmond

Daily News
Dublin Evening Post
Dublin Herald
Enniscorthy Echo
Freeman's Journal
Galway Vindicator
Irish American
Irish Catholic
Irish Independent
Irish Times
Irish World
Labour World
Manchester Guardian
Mayo Constitution
Mayo Examiner
Methodist Times
Nation
National Press
New York Herald
Pall Mall Gazette
Sligo Journal
Sligo Champion
Sligo Independent
Sunday Independent
Sunday World
The Irishman
The Irish People
The Times
Tyrawley Herald
United Ireland
United Irishman
L'Univers
Western Journal
Western People
Westminister Gazette

Index